P9-CQW-721

THE ROUTLEDGE HANDBOOK OF ETHNIC CONFLICT

A definitive global survey of the interaction of ethnicity, nationalism and politics, this handbook blends rigorous theoretically grounded analysis with empirically rich illustrations to provide a state-of-the-art overview of the contemporary debates on one of the most pervasive international security challenges today. Fully updated for the second edition, the book includes a new section which offers detailed analyses of contemporary cases of conflict such as in Ukraine, Kosovo, the African Great Lakes region and in the Kurdish areas across the Middle East, thus providing accessible examples that bridge the gap between theory and practice.

The contributors offer a 360-degree perspective on ethnic conflict: from the theoretical foundations of nationalism and ethnicity to the causes and consequences of ethnic conflict, and to the various strategies adopted in response to it. Without privileging any specific explanation of why ethnic conflict happens at a particular place and time or why attempts at preventing or settling it might fail or succeed, the *Routledge Handbook of Ethnic Conflict* enables readers to gain a better insight into such defining moments in post-Cold War international history as the disintegration of the Soviet Union and Yugoslavia, and their respective consequences, the genocide in Rwanda, and the relative success of conflict settlement efforts in Northern Ireland.

By contributing to understanding the varied and multiple causes of ethnic conflicts and to learning from the successes and failures of their prevention and settlement, the *Handbook* makes a powerful case that ethnic conflicts are neither unavoidable nor unresolvable, but rather that they require careful analysis and thoughtful and measured responses.

Karl Cordell is Professor of Politics at Plymouth University. He co-edits the journals *Ethnopolitics* and *Civil Wars* and has an extensive publication record in the fields of ethnopolitics, German politics and the politics of ethnicity in Central Europe.

Stefan Wolff is Professor of International Security at the University of Birmingham. Frequently advising governments and international organisations, he specialises in the management of international security challenges, especially in relation to conflict settlement and post-conflict state building. Among his publications are more than 20 books and special issues of journals, as well as over 80 journal articles and book chapters. He is co-editor of *Ethnopolitics*.

THE ROUTLEDGE HANDBOOK OF ETHNIC CONFLICT

Second edition

Edited by Karl Cordell and Stefan Wolff

Routledge
Taylor & Francis Group

LONDON AND NEW YORK

Second edition published 2016
by Routledge
2 Park Square, Milton Park, Abingdon, Oxon OX14 4RN

and by Routledge
711 Third Avenue, New York, NY 10017

Routledge is an imprint of the Taylor & Francis Group, an informa business

© 2016 selection and editorial material, Karl Cordell and Stefan Wolff, individual chapters, the contributors

The right of Karl Cordell and Stefan Wolff to be identified as authors of the editorial material, and of the individual authors as authors of their contributions, has been asserted by them in accordance with sections 77 and 78 of the Copyright, Designs and Patents Act 1988.

All rights reserved. No part of this book may be reprinted or reproduced or utilised in any form or by any electronic, mechanical, or other means, now known or hereafter invented, including photocopying and recording, or in any information storage or retrieval system, without permission in writing from the publishers. Printed in Canada.

Trademark notice: Product or corporate names may be trademarks or registered trademarks, and are used only for identification and explanation without intent to infringe.

First edition published by Routledge 2011

British Library Cataloguing in Publication Data
A catalogue record for this book is available from the British Library

Library of Congress Cataloging in Publication Data
The Routledge handbook of ethnic conflict / [Edited by] Karl Cordell and
Stefan Wolff. -- 2nd edition.
pages cm
Handbook of ethnic conflict
1. Ethnic conflict--Handbooks, manuals, etc. 2. Culture conflict--Handbooks, manuals, etc.
3. Social conflict--Handbooks, manuals, etc. I. Cordell, Karl, 1956- II. Wolff, Stefan.
III. Title: Handbook of ethnic conflict.
HM1121.R68 2016
305.8--dc23
2015028346

ISBN: 978-1-138-28173-8 (pbk)

Typeset in Bembo
by Taylor & Francis Books

For our grandparents

CONTENTS

Contents

Contents

ILLUSTRATIONS

Tables

Boxes

CONTRIBUTORS

Sandra Barkhof is Lecturer in History at the Faculty of Arts, University of Plymouth. She teaches Modern European and East Asian History. Her research interests include: European integration and European identity, Chinese and Japanese History, and German History with particular focus on imperial German colonialism in China and the Pacific. She is currently working on a study of German POWs in Japan during the First World War.

David Carment is a full Professor of International Affairs at the Norman Paterson School of International Affairs, Carleton University and Fellow of the Canadian Defence and Foreign Affairs Institute (CDFAI). He is also a NATO Fellow and listed in *Who's Who in International Affairs*. In addition he serves as the principal investigator for the Country Indicators for Foreign Policy project (CIFP). David Carment is a Senior Fellow at The Centre for Global Cooperation Research, Germany (2014–2015).

Stéphanie Chouinard is a Ph.D. candidate at the School of Political Studies, University of Ottawa, Canada. She is a research fellow at the Francophonie and Public Policy research chair. Her research focuses on judicial activism, minority rights, and language rights and policies, in Canada and in Europe.

Colin Clark is currently Professor of Sociology and Social Policy at the University of the West of Scotland. His research interests are mainly within the field of ethnic and racial studies, including issues of migration, integration, citizenship and identity. Colin's long-term ethnographic work with various Roma, Gypsy and Traveller communities in the UK and central Eastern Europe has resulted in a variety of published outputs. He is a Trustee of Romano Lav (Roma Voice) and a Board member of the Coalition for Racial Equality and Rights, both based in Glasgow. In his rather limited spare time he tweets: @profcolinclark.

Daniele Conversi is Research Professor with the Ikerbasque Foundation and the *Euskal Herriko Unibertsitatea* (EHU/UPV)/Universidad del País Vasco, Bilbao, Euskadi (Spain). He has worked in various international institutions, including Cornell University and the Central European University, Budapest. His key interest is theories of nationalism. He has also published on globalization and genocide. His first book, *The Basques, the Catalans and Spain*, is widely used across disciplines. Daniele is currently covering the cases of Italy, ex-Yugoslavia and Spain.

Karl Cordell is Professor of Politics at Plymouth University. He co-edits the journals *Ethnopolitics* and *Civil Wars* and has an extensive publication record in the fields of ethnopolitics, German politics and the politics of ethnicity in Central Europe.

Jenny Engström–Baron is an independent researcher on Balkan politics, women and violence, peace and conflict studies. She is the author of numerous papers and journal articles, and *Democratisation and the Prevention of Violent Conflict: Lessons Learned from Bulgaria and Macedonia* (Ashgate, 2009).

Martin Fischer is a doctoral candidate at the Norman Paterson School of International Affairs, Carleton University, Ottawa. He is the co-author (with David Carment) of 'R2P and the Role of Regional Organizations in Ethnic Conflict Management, Prevention and Resolution: The Unfinished Agenda', *Global Responsibility to Protect*, and 'Three's Company? Toward an Understanding of Third-Party Effectiveness', in Chris Coyne and Rachael Mathers (eds), *Handbook of the Political Economy of War* (Edward Elgar Publishing, 2011).

Chris Gilligan is a Senior Lecturer in Sociology at the University of the West of Scotland. He previously held lecturing posts at Aston University and the University of Ulster. He is Reviews Editor for the journal *Ethnopolitics*. He has edited (or co-edited) five collections; three on the peace process in Northern Ireland and two on migration and social division. His work has been published in a range of academic journals, including: the *Journal of Peace Research, Nations and Nationalism, Policy and Politics* and *Translocations*.

Monika Heupel is a Junior Professor for International and European Politics at the University of Bamberg, Germany. Before, she was a Research Associate at the WZB Berlin Social Science Center. Her research interests include security studies, global human rights policy, and international organizations. Her work has been published, among others, in *International Studies Quarterly, European Journal of International Relations, Security Dialogue, Cooperation and Conflict* and *Politische Vierteljahresschrift*.

Donald L. Horowitz is the James B. Duke Professor of Law and Political Science at Duke University and co-author of, among other works, *Ethnic Groups in Conflict* (University of California Press, 2000) and *The Deadly Ethnic Riot* (University of California Press, 2001). In 2009, he received the Distinguished Scholar Award of the Ethnicity, Nationalism, and Migration Section of the International Studies Association.

James Hughes is Professor of Comparative Politics at the London School of Economics and director of its Conflict Research Group. His research is concerned with the causes, motivations for, and dynamics of political violence. His recent books include: *EU Conflict Management* (Routledge, 2010); and *Chechnya from Nationalism to Jihad* (University of Pennsylvania Press, 2007).

Jennifer Jackson Preece is currently Senior Lecturer in Nationalism at the London School of Economics. She is the author of *Minority Rights: Between Diversity and Community* (Polity, 2005) and *National Minorities and the European Nation-States System* (OUP, 1998) as well as various articles and edited book chapters in the general area of ethnic conflict and minority protection.

Erin K. Jenne received her Ph.D. from Stanford University. She is a Professor at the International Relations and European Studies Department at Central European University in Budapest. She has received numerous grants and fellowships, and is currently part of a MINERVA grant with the US Defense Department investigating the effects of Chinese soft power using computer-aided content analysis (CATA). Her first book, *Ethnic Bargaining: The Paradox of Minority Empowerment* (Cornell University Press, 2007) is the winner of Mershon Center's Edgar S. Furniss Book Award in 2007 and was also named a Choice Outstanding Academic Title by Choice Magazine. She has published numerous book chapters and articles in *International Studies Quarterly*, *Security Studies*, *Regional and Federal Studies*, *Journal of Peace Research*, *Civil Wars*, *Political Science & Politics*, and *Ethnopolitics*. She is an associate editor for *Foreign Policy Analysis*. Her latest book, *Nested Security: Lessons in Conflict Management from the League of Nations and the European Union* was published by Cornell University Press in 2015.

Argyro Kartsonaki is a Doctoral Researcher in the Department of Political Science and International Studies at the University of Birmingham, UK. Her current research focuses on contemporary self-determination conflicts. Kartsonaki holds an MA in European Public Policy from the University of Crete and a BA in International Economic and Political Studies from the University of Macedonia.

Stuart J. Kaufman is Professor of Political Science and International Relations at the University of Delaware. He is author of *Modern Hatreds: The Symbolic Politics of Ethnic War* (Cornell University Press, 2001) and co-editor of *The Balance of Power in World History* (Palgrave, 2007).

David E. Kiwuwa is Associate Professor of International Studies and Research Director at the School of International Studies, University of Nottingham at the Ningbo China Campus. He specializes in democracy and democratic transition, ethnic politics, peace building and conflict analysis and the politics of China and Africa. He is an award winner of the PSA (UK) Lord Bryce Prize and recently a visiting Fung Global Fellow at Princeton University. He has published a number of works among which is *Ethnic Politics and Democratic Transition in Rwanda* (Routledge, 2012). Currently he is engaged in research on the Politics of Language in Rwanda and the China Silk Road project/One Belt, One Road.

Joe Landry is a Ph.D. Candidate and SSHRC Joseph-Armand Bombardier Canada Graduate Scholar at the Norman Paterson School of International Affairs at Carleton University. His research interests include fragile states, civil-war, forced migration, the security-development nexus and terrorism. He is currently working as managing editor of the *Canadian Foreign Policy Journal*, and as a research assistant with the SSHRC funded 'Country Indicators for Foreign Policy' project.

Tetyana Malyarenko is Professor of Public Policy at the Donetsk State University of Management, Ukraine. Her main research areas of interest include societal and economic aspects of security in transition states, human security and good governance, social conflicts and civil wars. Professor Malyarenko has held visiting professorships at, among others, the

Wilson Center for International Scholars, Washington DC and the University of California Berkeley. To date her publications include five books and over fifty refereed journal articles and book chapters.

Joseph Marko is professor at the Institute for Austrian, European, and Comparative Public Law, Political Science, and Administration of the Karl-Franzens University of Graz and director of the University Centre for South-East European Studies. He served previously as one of the three international judges at the Constitutional Court of Bosnia and Herzegovina, and as member of the Council of Europe's advisory committee, established under the Framework Convention for the Protection of National Minorities. He also served as political advisor to the High Representative in Bosnia and Herzegovina. He is the author or co-author of six books, and has edited or co-edited a further twenty.

John McGarry is Professor of Political Studies, and Canada Research Chair in Nationalism and Democracy at Queen's University, Kingston, Ontario, Canada. He is the co-author (with Brendan O'Leary) of *Explaining Northern Ireland* (Blackwell, 1995) and *The Northern Ireland Conflict: Consociational Engagements* (OUP, 2004). In 2008–09, he served as Senior Advisor on Power-Sharing to the United Nations (Mediation Support Unit).

Ian O'Flynn is a Senior Lecturer in Political Theory at Newcastle University, UK. His main research interest is in exploring the implication of deliberative democracy for multicultural and multinational societies. He is the author of *Deliberative Democracy and Divided Societies* (Edinburgh University Press, 2006) and his articles have appeared in journals such as *British Journal of Political Science* and *Political Studies*. He was a postdoctoral research fellow at the University of Essex and has also held visiting positions at Harvard University, the University of Pennsylvania and the Australian National University.

Brendan O'Leary is Lauder Professor of Political Science and Director of the Penn Program in Ethnic Conflict at the University of Pennsylvania. In 2009–10 he was the Senior Advisor on Power Sharing for the Standby Team of the Mediation Support at the United Nations. Recent books include *How to Get Out of Iraq with Integrity* (University of Pennsylvania Press, 2009), *Terror, Insurgency and the State* (University of Pennsylvania Press, 2007), *The Future of Kurdistan in Iraq* (University of Pennsylvania Press, 2005), and *The Northern Ireland Conflict: Consociational Engagements* (OUP, 2004).

Bill Park is Senior Lecturer in the Defence Studies Department, King's College. He is the author of monographs, articles, and the like on a range of Turkish domestic and foreign policy issues, including *Turkey-KRG Relations after the US Withdrawal from Iraq: Putting the Kurds on the Map* (Strategic Studies Institute, US Army War College, 2014), and *Modern Turkey: People, State and Foreign Policy in a Globalized World* (Routledge, 2011). He is currently writing a book on Turkey's regional Kurdish predicaments. He is on the editorial board of the journal *Mediterranean Politics*.

Benjamin Reilly is Dean of the Sir Walter Murdoch School of Public Policy and International Affairs at Murdoch University, Western Australia. He is a political scientist specializing in democratization, comparative politics and political development. Formerly Professor of Political Science, head of the Policy and Governance program and Director of the Centre for Democratic Institutions in the Crawford School of Public Policy at the Australian National

University (ANU), Professor Reilly has also worked with the Australian government, the United Nations and other international organizations, and held visiting appointments at Harvard, Oxford, and Johns Hopkins universities. He has authored or edited seven books and over 100 scholarly papers, and received financial support from the Carnegie Corporation of New York, the United States Institute of Peace, the East-West Centre, the National Endowment for Democracy and the Australian Research Council. He holds a Ph.D. in Political Science from the ANU.

Joseph Ruane is Associate Professor of Sociology at University College Cork, Ireland. His main research interests are in the area of the sociology of state- and nation-building, and comparative colonial, ethnic, religious and centre–periphery relationships; as well as the sociology of Ireland (north and south). Among his many publications are *After the Good Friday Agreement: Analysing Social and Political Change in Northern Ireland* (with Jennifer Todd, University College Dublin, 2000) and *Europe's Old States in the New World Order: The Politics of Transition in Britain, France and Spain* (with Jennifer Todd and Anne Mandeville-Briot, University College Dublin, 2003).

David Russell is the Deputy Director of the Northern Ireland Human Rights Commission and a non-executive director of the Northern Ireland Community Relations Council. He has published widely including, 'The Devolution of Human Rights and the Northern Ireland Assembly', in M. Hunt, H.J. Hooper and P. Yowell, *Parliaments and Human Rights* (Hart, 2015), with I. O'Flynn (eds) *Power Sharing: New Challenges for Divided Societies* (Pluto Press, 2005) and articles in *Political Studies, Ethnopolitics, European Human Rights Law Review, International Relations*, and other journals.

Frans Schrijver is a teaching fellow in Political Geography at the University of Sheffield. He is the author of *Regionalism after Regionalisation* (Amsterdam University Press, 2006). His teaching and research interests include the geographies of nationalism, citizenship, and the politics of territorial identities.

Asaf Siniver is Associate Professor (Reader) in International Security in the Department of Political Science and International Studies at the University of Birmingham. He works on conflict resolution and third-party mediation, the Arab–Israeli conflict and the international relations of the Middle East, contemporary US foreign policy, foreign policy analysis and international security. He has published books, journal articles, reports and policy briefs on these issues, and has advised governmental and non-governmental actors working in these areas. He is co-editor of the journal *Civil Wars* and a Leverhulme Trust Research Fellow.

David J. Smith is Professor of Baltic History and Politics at the University of Glasgow. His work has focused on issues of statehood, nationality and minority rights in Central and Eastern Europe, with particular regard to the Baltic States. He is currently completing a monograph on the theory and practice of non-territorial cultural autonomy in the region, based on AHRC-funded research. Previous publications include: *Estonia. Independence and European Integration* (Routledge, 2001) and *Cultural Autonomy in Contemporary Europe* (co-edited with Karl Cordell) (Routledge, 2008).

Eva Sobotka works at the European Union Agency for Fundamental Rights (FRA). She holds a Ph.D. in Politics and International Relations from Lancaster University in the United

Kingdom. She has served as elected Scientific Committee Member of the European Academic Network for Romani Studies and has published on human rights, Holocaust and Human Rights Education, Roma and conflict resolution.

Jennifer Todd is Director of the Institute for British Irish Studies, School of Politics and International Relations, University College Dublin and has published extensively on the Northern Ireland conflict and settlement, and on issues of ethnicity, identity and identity change. She is presently researching comparative patterns of conflict resolution.

Sean Winchester is a Ph.D. student at the Norman Paterson School of International Affairs, Carleton University. His research focuses on understanding the causes of wartime violence against civilians and evaluating the effectiveness of United Nations peacekeeping operations.

Stefan Wolff is Professor of International Security at the University of Birmingham. Frequently advising governments and international organisations, he specialises in the management of international security challenges, especially in relation to conflict settlement and post-conflict state building. Among his publications are more than 20 books and special issues of journals, as well as over 80 journal articles and book chapters. He is co-editor of *Ethnopolitics*.

ACKNOWLEDGMENTS

The editors would like to thank Nicola Parkin, Craig Fowlie, Olivia Hatt, and Lydia de Cruz at Routledge for their faith in us and for their patience. Thanks are also extended to the contributors to this new and expanded edition of the *Handbook*. Special praise is due to Kris Wischenkamper for her diligence as copy editor to this revised second edition. As ever we take full responsibility for any inadvertent errors that may have crept into the text.

1

THE STUDY OF ETHNIC CONFLICT

An introduction

Karl Cordell and Stefan Wolff

In the first edition of this volume our opening sentence stated that: 'Ethnic conflict remains one of the prevailing challenges to international security in our time'. Sadly, not much has changed since we wrote these words. Conflicts that in some way involve an ethnic dimension can be found across each of the world's continents. What drives such conflict is at base, rarely, if ever, some kind of genetically or culturally determined marker that results in two different peoples being unable to co-exist alongside one another. Rather, conflicts are caused by competition for (increasingly) scarce resources, the agendas of political activists and more especially political elites and through the manipulation and essentialisation of identity markers of which ethnicity is but one. Left unchecked, or managed poorly, such conflict threatens the very fabric of the societies in which it occurs, endangers the territorial integrity of existing states, wreaks havoc on their economic development, destabilises entire regions as conflict spills over from one country into another, creates the conditions in which transnational organised crime can flourish, and offers safe havens to terrorist organisations with an agenda far beyond, and often unconnected to, the conflict in question. To be sure, not every conflict has all of these consequences and not all of them occur in equal scale everywhere. Yet, one feature that most ethnic conflicts above all share is the sheer human misery that they create: people get killed, tortured, maimed, raped; they suffer from displacement, starvation, and disease. If for no other reason, social scientists need to study ethnic conflict in order to understand better what its causes are, how it can be prevented, managed, and resolved. While we may never be able to stop ethnic conflicts from happening, understanding them better will improve our abilities to respond more quickly and more effectively, thus reducing the scale of human suffering.

Ethnic conflicts have been a subject of social scientific inquiry for a long time now, and the subject has become firmly established as a field of study across a range of disciplines from political science and international relations to sociology, anthropology, and psychology. It is taught widely at universities across the world, at undergraduate and postgraduate levels, and numerous doctoral dissertations are written every year on a wide range of aspects of ethnic conflict. As with the original edition of the *Handbook* we do not propose a new theory of ethnic conflict or conflict resolution, but rather a comprehensive introduction to the study of this subject, reflecting the state of the art in this field. Motivated to explore a wide range

1

of different dimensions of ethnic conflict, we have been very fortunate to be able to assemble a team of scholars, all of whom are expert in their area and can shed light on specific aspects of ethnic conflict, offering well-argued insights, and complementing each other's views so that what emerges is an overview of the way in which ethnic conflict is being studied today.

The purpose of this introductory chapter is three-fold. First, we offer some empirical backing to our assertion that ethnic conflict is today one of the prevailing challenges to international security. Second, proceeding from this background, we discuss what the questions are that need to be asked about ethnic conflict, how we and our contributors go about answering them with the help of concepts, theories, and methods, and how this has translated into the structure of our *Handbook*. Third, we explore whether we can draw any more general conclusions about ethnic conflict from the contributions to this *Handbook* – not in the sense of a new theory of ethnic conflict, but rather in the sense of what we know and understand today of this particular phenomenon and where this knowledge and under-standing might lead us in the future, both in terms of research agendas and in terms of practically dealing with ethnic conflicts and their aftermath.

Ethnic conflict as an international security challenge

In the original volume of the *Handbook* we paid attention to the international ramifications of conflicts that at first sight are not overtly international in their dimensions and are not necessarily ethnic in terms of their drivers and content. One such conflict was and remains that which blights Yemen. The various strands of the Yemeni conflict are somewhat difficult to disentangle, but they involve Al Qaeda in the Arabian Peninsula (AQAP): partisans of former President Ali Abdullah Saleh; supporters of rival current president Abd Rabbuh Mansur Hadi, Shia Houthi rebels led by Mohammed Ali al-Houthi and the separatist Southern Movement. Conflicts such as those occurring in Yemen are highly complex in their causes and consequences, and it would be simplistic to explain them purely in terms of ethnic difference, even if conceived of as predominantly tribal or religious. Yet, neither can we ignore that such differences have mattered greatly and fuelled today's conflicts over time, hardening divisions between combatant factions and increasing mistrust and grievances as both sides committed atrocities against civilian populations, be it by killing civilians in suicide attacks or by razing entire villages to the ground. This is further complicated by external 'meddling' in these conflicts – Saudi Arabia, a one-time supporter of tribal uprisings in the 1990s, aimed at weakening the Yemeni government during its border dispute with Riyadh, has subsequently sided with Sana'a when the threat from al-Qaeda extended to the Saudi monarchy, while Iran has allegedly indirectly supported the Houthi rebels, who hail from the north of Yemen, but whose area of operation now encompasses much of the centre of the country. In sum what we have here is a local conflict that also reflects the regional power struggle between Iran and Saudi Arabia. Ongoing domestic conflicts, some with clear ethnic dimensions, thus have very obvious implications beyond the locality in which they occur, shaping and being shaped by broader regional and international developments. Indeed, the Yemeni conflict can be seen as but one element of a series of interlinked conflicts that is currently convulsing the Middle East and North Africa, which although pitting partisans of Islam against one another, with regards to the Kurds has an obvious ethnic dimension, and as such has facilitated a growing sense of cross-border intra-Kurdish solidarity that has been increasingly evident ever since they first came into conflict with Islamic State in 2013.

Switching between continents, another conflict that is currently in the international limelight is that between Ukraine and Russian-backed rebels in the Donbas region of south-eastern

Ukraine. In March 2014 Russia annexed Crimea ostensibly to protect this 'historically Russian' territory from attacks by the partisans of 'Ukrainian fascism', who in February 2014 had overthrown the regime of President Viktor Yanukovych. At one level, whether or not the apparent concern that 'fascists' had come to power in Kiev is genuine is irrelevant. In justifying his government's annexation of the territory, President Putin referred to the (primordial) Russian nature of Crimea thereby implying that it was not and never had been the sovereign territory of others whether they be Ukrainians or Tatars. Moreover, since then Putin has unleashed a torrent of hyper-nationalist propaganda in Russia which seeks to justify support of separatists in the Donbas by reference not only to the threat posed by 'Ukrainian fascists', but also the close cultural ties between the people of the Donbas and the Russian Motherland. The potential international ramifications of this conflict are obvious, given the substantial Russian minorities in Latvia and Estonia and the pro-Russian stance of the political leadership in the diplomatically and geographically isolated breakaway state of Transnistria, which is in part at least dependent upon Moscow for its very survival. These aforementioned conflicts add to a series of other conflicts that we identified as being significant in the first edition of the *Handbook*. In 2010, we noted how during the 1990s in southeast Asia, another local al-Qaeda offshoot – Jemaah Islamiyah – grafted itself onto pre-existing ethnic conflicts in southern Thailand, the Aceh province of Indonesia, and Mindanao in the Philippines. Whereas the conflict in Aceh has been peacefully resolved, the conflict in southern Thailand rumbles on and despite the signing of multiple peace agreements, the latest being in March 2014, the best that can be said of Mindanao is that fighting has subsided. Such conflicts persist not only because of the inability of the warring parties either to achieve a decisive military victory, as in Sri Lanka in May 2009, or to reach any political accommodation, as in Northern Ireland in 1998, but also because for some of the combatants, wars are extremely profitable and a return to peace may injure the economic interests of those who profit from conflict. As is evident from among others the conflicts in Liberia, eastern Democratic Republic of Congo (DRC) and Sierra Leone, one of the ways in which various rebel groups have gained notoriety in recent years, is less than for their struggle on behalf of aggrieved victims of oppression but more for criminal activities such as kidnappings, resource exploitation and extraction and extortion rackets that have, over time, turned rebel movements into organised crime operations, whatever the notional political goals of the perpetrators. In addition to the aforementioned examples, similar links, differing in scale and intensity, between ethnic conflict, organised crime, and/or international terrorism can be observed in Iraq and Afghanistan, Somalia and Nigeria, in Myanmar, Bangladesh and northeast India, and in the separatist regions of Chechnya, Ingushetia, South Ossetia, Abkhazia, and Transnistria. The important point here is this: ethnic conflicts, if left to fester, over time have the potential to transmorph into an even more deadly mix of overlapping and converging agendas of different interest groups that are difficult to disentangle and even more difficult to resolve. Understanding these dynamics is important: it should motivate the international community to preventive rather than reactive action, and it should foster a comprehensive approach to conflict analysis and a context-sensitive approach to conflict settlements.

Not every ethnic conflict, of course, has similar regional and global ramifications. Neither are there, in fact, that many conflicts generated solely on the grounds of ethnic difference. According to data compiled by the Peace Research Institute Oslo (PRIO 2009; Harbom and Wallensteen 2009), between 1946 and 2008 there were 174 internal and internationalised internal conflicts. Of these, in line with the definition we develop below, 90 would fall into the category of ethnic conflicts, of which 65 were struggles specifically over territorial control. Likewise, Quinn's analysis of violent self-determination conflicts – the 'quest of national and indigenous peoples for self-governance' (Quinn 2008: 33) – has found that, since the 1950s, '79 territorially concentrated ethnic groups have waged armed conflicts for autonomy or independence' (ibid.). While this figure excludes ethnic conflicts in which the overall aim of the combatants is to retain, or attain, control of the state as a whole (i.e., in PRIO terms, conflicts in which the incompatibility is government), the same general trend also applies: since the peak of such conflicts in the early 1990s, there have been fewer outbreaks of new conflicts (or re-escalations of previously settled or contained ones) than settlements, so that the total number of violent self-determination conflicts has declined (see also Hewitt 2010) significantly. Yet, what is also clear from these and other analyses is that it is unlikely that we will see a complete disappearance of ethnic conflicts in the near future.

Conceptualising the study of ethnic conflict

The fact that ethnic conflicts will remain with us as a significant international humanitarian and security challenge in itself justifies their in-depth study, because we cannot deal with them effectively unless we understand them. This means that we have to clarify the relevant concepts and theories which provide the foundation for any study of ethnic conflict and allow us to situate this subject within and across disciplinary boundaries, engage with key methodological issues, and identify the terms of the debate and the main underlying assumptions. Even more fundamentally, we need to clarify the actual subject of our inquiry. Ethnic conflict is a term loaded with often legitimate negative associations and entirely unnecessary confusions. The most important confusion is that ethnic conflicts are about ethnicity – it often forms an important part of the explanation, but rarely offers a comprehensive explanation on its own. Generally speaking, the term conflict describes a situation in which two or more actors pursue incompatible, yet from their individual perspectives entirely just goals. Ethnic conflicts are one particular form of such conflict: that in which the goals of at least one conflict party are defined in (exclusively) ethnic terms, and in which the primary fault line of confrontation is one of ethnic distinctions. Whatever the concrete issues over which conflict erupts, at least one of the conflict parties will explain its dissatisfaction in ethnic terms. That is, one party to the conflict will claim that its distinct ethnic identity is the reason why its members cannot realise their interests, why they do not have the same rights, or why their claims are not satisfied. Thus, ethnic conflicts are a form of group conflict in which at least one of the parties involved interprets the conflict, its causes, and potential remedies along an actually existing or perceived discriminating ethnic divide. In other words, the term ethnic conflict itself is a misnomer – or to put it differently, an ethnic conflict involves at least one conflict party that is organised around the ethnic identity of its members. Hence, few would dispute that conflicts that have occurred, or are occurring in Northern Ireland, Kosovo, Cyprus, Rwanda, the DRC, Kashmir, and Sri Lanka, to name but a few, are ethnic conflicts. That is so because in each of these cases organised ethnic groups confront each other and/or the institutions of the states in which they live. All of these conflicts have been violent, yet violence in each of them was of different degrees of intensity and duration. In contrast, relationships between Estonians and Russians in Estonia and the complex dynamics of interaction between the different linguistic groups in Canada, Belgium, and France are also predominantly based on distinct ethnic identities and (incompatible) interest structures, yet their manifestations are less violent and are better described in terms of tensions than conflict. Thus, the way in which we use the term 'ethnic conflict' in this *Handbook* is to describe situations in which combatants take recourse to the systematic use of violence for strategic purposes and in which at least one combatant defines itself primarily in relation to a distinctive ethnic identity.[1]

Regardless of the extent to which contributors to the first edition of the *Handbook* have revised their original contribution, they and the new contributors to this volume share one fundamental assumption, which is that although ethnic conflicts may well be complex political phenomena, they can be understood. From this conviction of our ability to understand the dynamics of ethnic conflict also flows our relative optimism that we can do something about ethnic conflicts in a broad sense: ideally prevent or settle them, but if this proves impossible at a certain period of time, at the very least manage them in a way that contains their consequences. In other words, studying ethnic conflicts means to study their causes and consequences, and the ways in which third parties respond to them. As we have demonstrated in greater detail elsewhere (Cordell and Wolff 2009; Wolff 2006), this involves engagement with theories of ethnic conflict and conflict resolution. These are obviously related to each other and inform each other, not least because they are built on a range of overlapping concepts and more general theories, including theories of ethnicity, of inter-ethnic relations, and of political science, especially comparative politics, and international relations. In order to give the *Handbook* a coherent structure that reflects this approach, the part immediately following this intro-ductory chapter deals with the 'Theoretical foundations for the study of ethnic conflict' and deals with the conceptual and theoretical tools of the subject matter, thus establishing the parameters of the dimensions and nature of the debate in this regard. Thus, the *Handbook* commences with an analysis by Jennifer Jackson Preece of the nature and origin of that much contested term: the nation. Jackson Preece takes as her point of departure the fact that any discussion of this term is bound to be controversial, precisely because there is still no consensus, either within or without academia, as to how to define the nation. Nor is there any wider societal consensus of the relationship between modern nations and entities from which members of modern nations claim linear descent. Such claims, more often than not, shape not only people's views of themselves, but also give rise to demands vis-à-vis people perceived to be non-members of a particular nation. This is the connection between Jackson Preece's conceptual analysis of the *nation* and Daniele Conversi's discussion of *nationalism*. As he points out, since 1789, nationalism has been a motivational force for millions of people and as such, and despite its allegedly inchoate structure, is an ideology, and that the key to our under-standing of nationalism is appreciating how it operates as an ideology. Another connection between *nation* and *nationalism* is established by the question of who actually constitutes the nation, and this issue is considered by Colin Clark. He examines the traditional 'civic' versus 'ethnic' dichotomy and demonstrates the relationship between intellectual output, historical location and political process. Examining the work of such noted scholars as Hans Kohn, Liah Greenfield, and Michael Ignatieff, Clark pays particular attention to notions of choice and context, and illustrates the complexities of the situation through the judicious employ-ment of case studies. In so doing, he brings home the point that what at first sight appears to be clear-cut, in fact is opaque. The very fact that there is this distinction, however debatable, between ethnic and civic nations, points to another paradox that students of ethnic conflict frequently encounter: the nation-state is in a sense a misnomer, in few if any states people equally identify (themselves and others) as members of the same nation and citizens of the same state. Rather, there are far more nations than states, even if not all self-declared nations necessarily make explicit claims to independent statehood. And thus, we confront the issue of 'Stateless nations in a world (and a discipline) governed by nation-states'. Stéphanie Chouinard considers the question how in principle we reconcile the demands of stateless nations with a state system that effectively excludes the bulk of nations from ever achieving statehood, and introduces some key aspects of the examination of the causes and consequences of ethnic conflict and the responses to it that follow in Parts II and III of the *Handbook*.

Having thus conceptually framed the *nation* and its 'derivatives', we are left with the challenge of elaborating in more detail another core dimension in the study of ethnic conflict: the notion of 'ethnicity'. Two contributions address this issue by exploring the relationship between ethnicity and religion and between ethnicity and race. First, Joseph Ruane and Jennifer Todd explore a variety of conceptual, analytical, and theoretical issues that embrace the relationship that sometimes exists between the desire for national self-determination and the longing for an end to the repression of religion. Ruane and Todd start from the premise that many apparently ethnically based conflicts involve a religious element, and argue that we cannot, however, conclude in reverse that commitment to a given religious belief system will automatically lead to adherence either to a particular ideology or to a given mode of political action. In other words, much in the same way in which the mere presence in the same state of different ethnic groups does not automatically lead to conflict between them, neither is it inevitable that religious groups are inherently conflictual with one another. Part I of the *Handbook* closes with a second exploration of ethnicity. Chris Gilligan deals with fundamental conceptual and terminological issues of distinguishing this term (ethnicity) from that of *race*, which is a more complicated task than disentangling the relationship between ethnicity and religion because of the intellectual discomfort and obfuscation sometimes arising in the context of scholarly discussions of this link. Yet, as Gilligan points out, there may be only one human race, but racism exists, and as such the debate over the relationship between ethnicity and race cannot be ignored, if only because discrimination based on ethnic difference is more often than not labelled as 'racist'.

Part II of the *Handbook* examines the causes and consequences of ethnic conflict. Linking the discussion here to that of Part I, the first contribution is Stuart Kaufman's analysis of ethnicity as a generator of conflict. As he points out, ethnic identities are not new phenomena, but can be traced back through history. Importantly, analysis of the historical record demonstrates that ethnic difference does not in itself generate conflict. Rather, it only becomes a mobilisational badge toward the instigation of violence under certain circumstances. Outlining, among others, 'instrumentalist' and 'psycho-cultural' theories that seek to explain why and how a shared ethnic identity provides not only the basis for socio-cultural commonalities, but also a refuge from which collective violent action can be launched and rationalised, Kaufman prepares the ground for the contributions that follow.

Stuart Kaufman's insights are of particular value because of the fact that we are still living with the consequences of a series of extraordinary events that took place in the closing years of the twentieth century. The period was, among other things, marked by a third wave of democratisation. Authoritarian regimes fell in Latin America, South-East Asia, throughout the Eurasian land mass, and most poignantly of all, following the fall of the Berlin Wall in Central and Eastern Europe. Yet, the downfall of 'really existing socialism' did not mark either the end of history nor indeed the arrival of perpetual peace. As new states emerged from the ruins of the old, submerged conflicts came up for air and drew breath, or indeed emerged seemingly out of nowhere. Many of these conflicts incorporated an ethnic dimension, and regardless of whether they did or not, the emergence of such conflicts indicated that whatever democratisation is, it is most definitely more akin to a process than it is a symbolic declarative act. The correlation, especially in Central and Eastern Europe and the former Soviet Union, between the beginning of democratisation and the onset of many an ethnic conflict – the early 1990s mark, according to most datasets on civil and ethnic wars, an all-time high in these conflicts – warrants more detailed analytical treatment. Hence, Jenny Engström-Baron investigates the relationship between democracy and democratisation, our understanding of these terms, and most importantly the appropriateness of Western strategies of democratisation in societies that are fragile, vulnerable, and prone to instability. As she points out, democracy is a word that most of us can readily identify with and applaud; yet, simply transposing liberal democratic blueprints to societies that are radically different from the consolidated Western democracies that serve as their model can have unforeseen and incalculable consequences. In other words, in a fragile situation, democratisation strategies can in fact incur more costs than they bring benefits. While they may not cause ethnic conflict per se, they are among the factors that facilitate it by creating circumstances, as Kaufman notes, in which ethnic identity can easily be used to radicalise people and mobilise them to use violence.

The consequences of ethnic violence are always negative, affecting above all the civilian population in, and beyond, the areas in which conflict occurs. The most extreme, in terms of their humanitarian consequences are ethnic cleansing and genocide, which sometimes prepare the ground for, and on occasion are the result of, two other phenomena closely associated with negative consequences of – and not solutions to – ethnic conflicts, namely partitions and secessions and irredentas. The examination of these phenomena concludes Part II of the *Handbook*. Erin Jenne analyses *ethnic cleansing*, demonstrating that mass expulsions of population are nothing new and that history is littered with numerous examples of the practice. To this end she pays attention to definitions of the term and the debate that exists in both international law and the wider court of public opinion. She also points out that despite history being littered with numerous examples of human displacement on a mass scale, when the practice re-emerged in Europe (and elsewhere) in the 1990s, a collective reaction of stunned horror pervaded the political landscape, creating a situation in which it was easy, if not politically correct, to conflate *ethnic cleansing* with *genocide*. Jenne clearly draws the necessary distinction between the two, leaving the conceptual space for Jim Hughes to investigate attempts to eradicate entire population groups. Hughes, like Jenne, starts out by showing that genocide is not a new phenomenon and was practised long before the Holocaust was visited upon the European Jews. In terms of its contemporary definition, it is a phenomenon that entered the public consciousness, scholarship, and the realms of international law with the Holocaust. He also points out that the term 'genocide' is open to interpretation and that there is considerable debate as to whether genocide is epiphenomenal or in some way the by-product of the age of nationalism and the advent of the modern nation-state.

Moving on from policies designed to 'solve' problems by means of mass murder, in his contribution, Brendan O'Leary considers the merits of partition as a solution to ethnic conflict. He distinguishes partition from 'adjacent phenomena' such as secession or border adjustment, and draws on a number of case studies in order to highlight the complexities involved in the modalities of partition. In order to provide for a clearer understanding of the subject matter, O'Leary outlines and discusses the arguments put forward by various partitionist schools and explains their modalities. His overall assessment is that partition rarely solves anything, and is just as likely to result in the creation of a situation in which the pre-existing problems are simply re-cast. Ultimately, he argues that, in situations where two or more groups are putting forward mutually irreconcilable claims for territorial exclusivity or dominance, the parties should be encouraged to consider various power-sharing strategies that result in the gradual erosion of the conviction that politics is a zero-sum game. Donald L. Horowitz's exploration of irredentas and secessions also considers 'adjacent phenomena' which to separate is no easy task. Secession is defined as the attempt by one ethnic group claiming a homeland to withdraw its territory from a larger state of which said territory forms a part. Irredentism, on the other hand, may be defined as the endeavour of members of an ethnic group, state-sponsored or otherwise, to retrieve ethnic kin by means of the annexation of the territory inhabited by their kinfolk. As with partition, neither secessions nor irredentas offer any genuine resolution to the underlying problems in most of the conflicts in which they have been applied.

What then of the related question of responses to ethnic conflict? The ideal solution to ethnic conflict, of course, would be its prevention. Even though, and perhaps even especially because, it is unlikely that full-scale prevention will ever be possible, it is necessary to engage with the theory and practice of conflict prevention. Hence, the objective of the contribution by David Carment *et al.* is, through an evaluation of relevant theory and policy, to enable a better understanding of why achieving conflict prevention remains such a tricky task, and how it might be performed better in the future. With prevention still too often failing, managing and (hopefully) settling ethnic conflicts remain the predominant, if second-best, responses. In turn, Asaf Siniver considers different management and settlement practices, including negotiation, mediation, arbitration, and adjudication, as well as, on occasion, the application of armed force, while carefully distinguishing between conflict management and conflict settlement, and assessing the efficacy of strategies employed for either purpose. Importantly, and complementing the contributions by Carment and his co-contributors, and Siniver, Eva Sobotka argues in her chapter on the variety of international actors and their various strategies of responding to ethnic conflict that their involvement needs to be seen in historical perspective. The historical track record of international conflict prevention, management, and settlement is illuminating: it has been very much an iterative learning process that began to take shape after 1945 and gained from successes and failures alike.

One of the important insights scholars and practitioners have gained from their examination of responses to ethnic conflict is that peace settlements, whatever their concrete content and circumstances, are not the end point but rather a milestone, albeit a tremendously important one, in dealing with ethnic conflict. Studying the subject in as comprehensive a manner as possible, therefore, requires an analysis of post-conflict reconstruction. Monika Heupel's contribution offers a discussion of both the state of the art scholarship and practice, as well as how knowledge and understanding of what works, and how and why, has evolved. One of the insights derived from the analysis and practice of post-conflict reconstruction is that it is a multifaceted process and that in order to succeed, its political-institutional, economic, and social dimensions need to be integrated into a comprehensive strategy and involve more than just the 'elites'. This last point is crucial, because without the involvement of people, post-conflict reconstruction will inevitably fail. This is nowhere more obvious than when it comes to building democratic states and societies after conflict, because, as Ian O'Flynn and David Russell argue in Part III, democracy consists of more than representative institutions and the ability of citizens to vote for candidates to such institutions. Rather, in order for a society to become truly democratic there must be an opportunity structure and culture that allow citizens to organise autonomously so that they may enter into constructive dialogue with the state and be able to influence the political process outside of the confines of conventional liberal democratic structures. To this end they engage in a thoroughgoing debate on how (liberal) democratic structures need to be embedded within ethnically divided societies in order that they move away from the politics of polarisation.

Clearly, the success of building democratic states and societies after ethnic conflict (or in an effort to prevent it) is crucially dependent on the support that citizens give to the project. This support, however, depends to a significant degree on whether they see their interests properly reflected in the core institutions of such a democracy, and this brings us to the next set of contributions, all of which deal with the issue of institutional design. Joseph Marko emphasises the significance of an effective system of human rights standards and enforcement mechanisms. Picking up on the earlier examination by Colin Clark of the traditional dichotomy that exists between civic and ethnic understandings of the nation-state, Marko examines human rights conceptually and practically by focusing on the relationship of the individual to the nation, and the rights of the individual as citizen, as it is these two dimensions that enable a more precise definition of human rights and how they are best applied and understood in situations of ethnic conflict and its aftermath. While human rights are a fundamental component of democratic structures, they are but one part of the overall set of institutions. In the context of ethnic conflict, in particular, the impact of institutional design on the quality and sustainability of democracy also extends to the issues of representation and participation in decision making. These essentially political arrangements are hotly contested not only between the conflict parties, but also within the academic community. Here they have given rise to a range of theories of 'conflict resolution' which all share a degree of optimism about the possibility of settling ethnic conflict qua the creation of institutions that accommodate as widely as possible otherwise incompatible claims of the parties to the conflict. However, this is where the consensus ends, and the prescriptions various scholars make about how to settle ethnic conflicts vary widely (but are perhaps not always as mutually exclusive as their proponents claim).

The contributions that follow Marko's (none of which rejects the importance of human rights in their own analysis and recommendations) examine specific aspects: territorial pluralism, the accommodation of ethnic diversity in unitary states, non-territorial autonomy, and power sharing. In their contribution, John McGarry and Brendan O'Leary investigate territorially based solutions to ethnically driven conflicts: pluralist federation, decentralisation, federacy, and cross-border territorial arrangements. This delineation is as important as it is precise, whilst also making it clear that it is not always feasible, or indeed viable, to seek the accommodation of ethnic diversity qua different forms of territorial self-governance. Ethnically diverse unitary states exist and are, as Frans Schrijver explores, able to accommodate diversity. However, this is not unproblematic as accommodation strategies are often rejected by ethnic majorities because they contradict foundational claims that the state is either ethnically homogenous or that minority nations contained within a given nation-state are either too small or widely dispersed for territorial solutions to be of any real value. The fact of territorial dispersion is one that has long been recognised in political science. One of the most imaginative responses to it is the Austro-Marxist idea of cultural (or non-territorial) autonomy. David Smith elaborates this notion of national cultural autonomy by exploring its origins and highlighting the originality of its solutions, precisely because it seeks to de-couple the demand for autonomy from that of territorially based self-determination. Ideally suited to states where minorities are territorially dispersed, he assesses its contemporary application in theory and in the political-institutional practice of countries as diverse as Hungary, Latvia, and Russia.

Territorial, non-territorial, and unitary strategies of conflict settlement often, but not inevitably, go hand-in-hand with the practice of power sharing. Two chapters examine two distinct approaches – centripetalism is the topic Benjamin Reilly elaborates; consociational power sharing that examined by Stefan Wolff and Karl Cordell. Reilly begins his contribution by pointing out that the 'third wave' of democracy witnessed during the closing years of the twentieth century generated a substantial increase in the number of states claiming adherence to liberal democratic principles. He also observes that this wave of democratisation coincided with an increased incidence of internal violence, in which ethnicity seemed to be a key component. Reilly's recommendation to deal with such ethnic conflicts is through centripetalism, an approach designed to pull political actors toward compromise and thereby to re-enforce the political centre, and thus enabling ethnically divided societies to move beyond the entrenchment and institutionalisation of ethnic difference. This is in some contrast to Wolff and Cordell's contribution on consociational power sharing, which takes as its starting point John Stuart Mill's observation on the difficulty of establishing democracy in countries composed of many different nationalities, and seeks to counter Mill's pessimism. Exploring the origins, nature and dynamics of consociational power sharing, they outline its major features and illustrate why it is an appropriate model to be considered by those who wish to heal societal divisions that have led to the outbreak of conflict, or indeed apply consociational mechanisms before rifts have led to a breakdown in inter-group relations. Wolff and Cordell are not blind to the limitations of consociational solutions, and therefore pay attention to the way in which cleavages operate in such societies. They also demonstrate how consociationalism is not limited to one continent or geopolitical area and can operate in either unitary or federal states and therefore can operate as a useful adjunct to either system of state-wide government.

Part III of our *Handbook* has so far concentrated on conflict resolution strategies implemented within an over-arching (liberal) democratic framework. We are only too well aware that such frameworks are by no means ubiquitous, and that authoritarian states, too, have to face up to the challenges of ethnic conflict. While some contributors in Part II have already examined the consequences of some classically authoritarian 'solutions' to ethnic differences – ethnic cleansing and genocide – not every authoritarian state is equally ruthless. As Sandra Barkhof shows in the closing contribution to this section, authoritarian regimes have a wider range of policy options at their disposal, which they employ in their efforts to achieve homogeneity and dampen down or extinguish ethnic conflict, and often do so with lasting success, albeit at a considerable cost to those at the receiving end of such policies. She does so by highlighting the means at the disposal of authoritarian regimes through comparative analysis with liberal democratic states and practices, and elaborates analysis of the role that ethnic movements have played in recent years in effecting the transition from authoritarian to liberal democratic modes of governance.

One failing of the original edition of the *Handbook* is that although rich in conceptual material and references to empiric data, it lacked detailed case studies. In order to rectify this omission, this new edition of the *Handbook* contains a closing section containing individual contributions that assess in detail the nature of recent and current conflicts in which ethnicity is in some way held to have been a factor. To that end, Bill Park assesses the nature of the conflict between Kurds and Arabs in Iraq. In turn, David Kiwuwa seeks to disentangle the causes, nature, and consequences for the multiplicity of conflicts that have blighted the lives of so many in the Great Lakes Region of Africa. For her part, Tatyana Malyarenko examines the nature and causes of the conflict that currently bedevils Ukraine. Finally, Argyro Kartsonaki considers elements of the conflict between Kosovo and Serbia, with a particular focus upon the attempted secession of the early 1990s. This representative cross-section of conflicts not only complements the material included in earlier sections of the *Handbook*, but should hopefully inform and aid the reader in his or her understanding of the nature of such conflicts, and the circumstances by which ethnic difference is turned from being a constructed and malleable set of characteristics to one that is solidified and becomes a marker of definition in opposition to the ubiquitous (and feared) 'other'.

Ethnic conflict: what we know (and can do) about it

As with its predecessor, the new edition of the *Handbook* does not claim to provide any definitive answers on its subject. Being, as it is, a highly dynamic phenomenon, subject to a variety of factors, none of which is static either, the nature and impact of ethnic conflict have changed over time and will most likely continue to do so in the foreseeable future. As our contributors have demonstrated, some of the factors that cause people to engage in violence rather than to seek peaceful accommodation of their disputes might be more enduring, but the scale, frequency, intensity, and consequences of such violence have been subject to great variation, as have the timeliness and effectiveness of responses to it. While it may not be definitive in its scope, the *Handbook* does offer, however, a fairly comprehensive account of its subject, incorporating essays on its theoretical foundations and a range of different view-points on what its causes and consequences are and how we can best respond to it and the broader security threats that emanate from it. Even though there are no definitive answers here, and even though we, as editors, do not take sides in some of the lasting debates that the study of ethnic conflict has given rise to, the *Handbook* as a whole does help our under-standing of the subject matter in a number of respects where there is implicit and explicit consensus among editors and contributors.

The first of these is that ethnic conflict is not a natural or inevitable phenomenon. Its origins lie in human choices and action predicated upon individually and collectively sub-jective perceptions of reality, the (presumed) mismatch between this perceived and a desired reality, and the course of action adopted to bring the two into congruence. Regardless of the precise nature of individual motivations (greed or grievance, inequality or insecurity), it also takes means and opportunities to embark on a strategy of violence in attempts to resolve such incompatibilities.

Second, this approach to the causes of ethnic conflict enables a clearer perspective on its consequences, too. There is always a human and humanitarian side to this as violence is more often than not directed against people. Yet the consequences of ethnic conflict have a wider impact beyond the locale in which it takes place. Through various actors and through the formal and informal structures of their interaction, ethnic conflicts are no longer, if they ever were, merely unhappy local affairs. Insecurity and instability are contagious and they have a tendency to spread across borders and affect people and places far beyond their physical origin. With the sole exception of Tunisia, this phenomenon has in recent years been most apparent in the aftermath of the 'Arab Spring' and its failure to engender democratic change, no matter how defined.

Third, herein lies an obvious threat to international security, but also an opportunity for the effective prevention, management, and settlement of ethnic conflicts. The nature of some of these threats is clear from the preceding paragraph. An additional challenge is that the persisting international significance of ethnic conflicts makes them, and the people affected by them, pawns in regional and global power plays. Yet, being aware of the potentially significant international consequences of ethnic conflicts can equally also spur international action, give it more weight and resources, and increase its effectiveness. This does not mean that every attempt at preventing, managing, or settling ethnic conflict will succeed, but there is clearly a track record that demonstrates that such conflicts are not immune to constructive responses. The trick is how to replicate for example, the (relative) successes of Sierra Leone and East Timor as opposed to the death-traps of, say, Somalia and Libya.

A final point worth making concerns the (academic) study of ethnic conflict. Without a doubt, ethnic conflict is a complex and dynamic phenomenon. However, as this new edition of the *Handbook* has demonstrated, over time scholars have developed the con-ceptual and analytical tools and appropriate methods for its study so that we can gain significant and relevant insights into its causes and consequences, which in turn can inform and shape context-sensitive policy responses to individual, real-world cases of ethnic conflict.

Note

1 This also means that violent riots or protest demonstrations in themselves do not 'qualify' as ethnic conflicts. They may be part of an ongoing ethnic conflict, but they can also occur in situations of ethnic tensions or disputes, i.e., where a situation may occasionally escalate into violence, but where its use is not part of the normal repertoire of interaction among ethnic groups and/or between them and state institutions.

References

Cordell, K. and Wolff, S. 2009. *Ethnic Conflict: Causes – Consequences – Responses.* Cambridge: Polity Press.

Harbom, L. and Wallensteen, P. 2009. 'Armed Conflicts, 1946–2008', *Journal of Peace Research*, 46 (4): 577–587.

Hewitt, J. J. 2010. 'Trends in Global Conflict', in *Peace and Conflict 2010*, ed. J. J. Hewitt, J. Wilkenfeld and T. R. Gurr. Boulder CO and London: Paradigm Publishers, 27–32.

PRIO (Peace Research Institute Oslo). 2009. *UCDP/PRIO Armed Conflict Dataset v. 4–2009.* Available online at: http://www.prio.no/CSCW/Datasets/Armed-Conflict/UCDP-PRIO/ (Accessed 14 January 2010).

Quinn, D. 2008. 'Self-determination Movements and their Outcomes', in *Peace and Conflict 2008*, ed. J. J. Hewitt, J. Wilkenfeld and T. R. Gurr. Boulder CO and London: Paradigm Publishers, 33–38.

Wolff, S. 2006. *Ethnic Conflict: A Global Perspective.* Oxford: Oxford University Press.

PART I

2

ORIGINS OF 'NATIONS'

Contested beginnings, contested futures

Jennifer Jackson Preece

Introduction

Any discussion of 'nations' and nationalism is immediately confronted by the continued controversy that surrounds the main terms of the debate. The 'nation' is a fundamentally contested concept. Although academics, policy-makers, and nationalist leaders make recourse to the language of nationalism on a daily basis, the precise meaning of the term defies an easy explanation. Is the 'nation' simply a by word for political communities that have acquired recognition as independent sovereign states? Or should it also extend to sub-state cultural communities variously described in the literature as 'stateless nations' or 'national minorities'? A universally agreed definition of the concept 'nation' does not exist in large part because the politics of nationalism is one of inclusion and exclusion. Thus, whosoever sets the terms of the debate also sets the criteria for national membership and belonging – a power few nationalists are prepared to relinquish. And while the various academic definitions of 'nation' on offer may share certain key characteristics having to do with a shared identity, territory, and history, the precise emphasis given to these core 'national' ingredients shifts, often considerably, from one commentator to another. Indeed, the Organization for Security and Cooperation in Europe's first High Commissioner for National Minorities, Max van der Stoel, when asked to define the communities falling under his remit, famously resorted to the expedient view that 'I know one when I see one!' (Stoel 1993).

Underscoring this semantic confusion is a further and in many respects even more significant debate on the origins of 'nations'. Not only are we not sure precisely what a 'nation' is, we are equally unsure of where and when it came from. Are 'nations' an invention of modernity? Or are they primordial communities that extend deep into the pre-modern period? And what, if any, bearing does this debate on origin have on current political controversies surrounding 'nations' and nationalism? It is precisely these issues that this chapter seeks to explore.

'Nations' and modernity

Theorists such as Ernest Gellner, Benedict Anderson and Elie Kedourie who espouse a modernist position on the origins of 'nations', irrespective of their many other disagreements, view the 'nation' as a relatively recent invention intended to answer that most vexing of modern political conundrums 'where does sovereignty lie?' (Hinsley 1966: 157). For modernists, the emergence of 'nations' is fundamentally linked to the transformation of social, economic and especially political life that first began in Europe during the eighteenth and especially the nineteenth centuries and eventually spread around the globe through European overseas empire and subsequent decolonisation. What is often referred to as the 'great transformation' (Polanyi 1957 [1944]) ultimately gave rise to consolidated territories with capitalist economies, a linguistically unified public, and a popularly sovereign government. It is at this point in the history of political ideas that the concept of the 'nation' achieves political salience. Who are the people in whom sovereignty ultimately resides? The people are the nation and the state exists as the expression of the national will. As article 3 of the 1789 *Declaration of the Rights of Man and of the Citizen* so eloquently put it:

> The principle of all sovereignty rests essentially in the nation. No body and no individual may exercise authority which does not emanate from the nation expressly.

From this point onwards, the discourse of modernity was infused with a national rhetoric: 'national economies', the 'national interest', 'national self-determination' and, above all, the 'nation-state' thus became the ultimate expressions of modern political life, so much so in fact that even one of the most highly regarded critics of the modernist position, Anthony Smith, conceded that 'the basic features of the modern world require nations and nationalism' (Smith 1995).

The pervasiveness of 'nations' and 'nationalism' in the modern world is nowhere more readily apparent than in the modern political map. Whereas the pre-modern map of Europe was a complicated and confusing intermingling and overlapping of many juridical territories – empires, dynasties, principalities, ecclesiastical feudatories, etc. – the modern map discloses a clearly defined juridical patchwork of equally sovereign nation-states (Jackson 2000: 157). But this juridical uniformity and territorial neatness did not come without a price; the modern world of nation-states was also accompanied by an unprecedented attempt to limit the number of claimants for independent statehood (Mayall 1990: 35). The initial redistribution of territory from empires to nation-states was viewed as a 'one-off affair' despite the fact that many putative nation-states were anything but homogeneous national communities, and numerous territorially 'trapped' sub-state national communities continued to aspire towards sovereignty (Jackson Preece 1998). Out of this fundamental discrepancy in the modern landscape emerges the problem of ethnonational conflict.

Obviously, the 'great transformation' was a complex historical process involving a wide array of interrelated changes in society, economy and polity. For this reason, it is only to be expected that the causal interpretation of these factors varies significantly from one 'modernist' nationalism theorist to another. A brief comparison of the explanations put forward by three of the most widely cited modernist thinkers on nationalism illustrates both the commonalities and differences which characterise modernist perspectives on the origin of 'nations'.

Elie Kedourie saw the 'great transformation' as a fundamentally top-down intellectual revolution. In his account, it was a new way of thinking about political life as disclosed in German idealist philosophy and the European Romantic Movement that is ultimately responsible for this transformation. Thus, Kedourie famously characterised nationalism as a 'doctrine invented in Europe at the beginning of the nineteenth century' which purports to supply a criterion for the determination of the unit of population proper to enjoy a government exclusively its own, for the legitimate exercise of power in the state, and for the right organisation of a society of states (Kedourie 1960: 9).

Few nationalism thinkers would dispute the content of Kedourie's definition of nationalism, although many would reject his prioritising of ideas.

In contrast to Kedourie, Ernest Gellner adopted a materialist view of the origin of 'nations' (Gellner 1983). For Gellner, the transition from agrarian to industrial society was the key to explaining the emergence of 'nations' and its concomitant ideology of nationalism. Industrial society is crucially dependent upon the effective organisation of the mass population which in turn creates a mass, literate society. As people left their traditional rural communities for work in the big industrial cities, they increasingly needed to speak and ultimately also to read and to write in a common language. In Gellner's view, this bottom-up transformation was reinforced by a top-down imperative: employers, generals and ultimately the political rulers needed to be able to communicate with the newly industrialised masses in order to effectively control them. According to Gellner, these material changes set the crucial historical context for the political salience of 'nations' and the ideology of nationalism.

Finally, Benedict Anderson in his constructivist account offers a middle way between the materialist Gellner and the idealist Kedourie. Anderson credits the rise of a mass vernacular print media and its effect on the emergence of a unified 'national' identity as the key component of the 'great transformation' (Anderson 1983). According to Anderson, the role of a vernacular media was crucial to the rise of nations because it created the context through which individuals imagined themselves members of mass, national communities beyond their immediate locale. The 'great transformation' was often a painful process of dislocation for the individuals caught up in it. Those peasants who became industrial workers lost their traditional way of life with its close association to village, church, extended family, and inherited custom. Relocated to the more anonymous landscape of the large industrial city they became expendable 'cogs in the wheel' of the industrial machine. A new sentimental attachment to the 'nation' provided a communal association to replace the familiar agrarian life left behind. Hence where once the seasons and the divine were glorified in song and celebrated in communal festival now the 'nation' became the focal point of music, artistic representation and public commemoration. Without this public re-imagining, the 'nation' could not have achieved its role as the basic organising idea of modernity.

'Nations' before modernity

Those nationalism theorists such as Adrian Hastings, Walker Connor and Anthony Smith who are sympathetic to what is often referred to as the 'primordial position' see the 'nation' as a social category of a much longer duration. They reject the core modernist assumption that nations emerge from the 'great transformation'. As Anthony Smith made clear in his famous 'Warwick Debate' with Ernest Gellner:

> Modern political nationalisms cannot be understood without reference to these earlier ethnic ties and memories, and, in some cases, to pre-modern ethnic identities and communities. I do not wish to assert that every modern nation must be founded on some antecedent ethnic ties, let alone a definite ethnic community; but many such nations have been and are based on these ties, including the first nations in the West – France, England, Castile, Holland, Sweden – and they acted as models and Pioneers of the idea of the 'nation' for others. And when we dig deeper, we shall find an ethnic component in many national communities since – whether the

17

nation was formed slowly or was the outcome of a more concerted project of 'nation-building'.

(Smith 1995)

The 'primordialist position' on the origin of 'nations' may be traced back to those same German Romantic philosophers such as Fichte and Herder that Elie Kedourie cited as 'inventors' of the modern discourse on nationalism. In their writings, the emphasis is not on modernity as the necessary precursor for an 'invented' national community, but instead on ancient and inherited social practices, above all language, as the source of authentic 'national' community.

These primordialist arguments give a whole new dimension to the modern ideology of nationalism. If the only genuine communities were associations of original language speakers, then linguistic affinity and vernacular speech were not simply a means to an end (the proper functioning of industrial economy, society, and politics), but an end in itself (the basis of popular sovereignty). Similarly, whereas modernists' theories of nationalism postulate a decisive break between the pre-modern agrarian past and the modern, industrial present, primordialist theories emphasise the importance of continuity over change. Indeed, the political project of nationalism becomes as much a rejuvenation of past customs and practices as a creation of new motifs and usages. As Kedourie explains in his analysis of German Romantic thought:

> it is incumbent on a nation worthy of the name to revive, develop and extend what is taken to be its original speech, even though it might be found only in remote villages, or had not been used for centuries, even though its resources are inadequate and its literature poor – for only such an original language will allow a nation to realise itself and attain its freedom.
>
> *(Kedourie 1960: 67)*

In this way, the nationalist discourse is said to emerge from the pre-modern past – primordialists thus subscribe to variations of what James Mayall refers to as a 'Sleeping Beauty thesis' according to which 'nations' have always existed but need to be reawakened into modern political consciousness (Mayall 1996: 10). Contemporary scholars who are sympathetic to the primordialist position accept that the ideology of nationalism as an adjutant to the doctrine of popular sovereignty is a modern development, but they challenge the modernist claim that the emergence of the ideology precedes the formation of the 'nation' qua identity and community.

For example, Adrian Hastings (1997) disputes the common modernist assumption that the social category of the 'nation' may be traced back only so far as the American and French Revolutions of the late eighteenth century. 'If nationalism became theoretically central to western political thinking in the nineteenth century, it existed as a powerful reality in some places long before that' (Hastings 1997: 2).

Indeed, Hastings claims that England, which he identifies as a prototype of both the 'nation' and the 'nation-state', clearly manifests itself long before the 'great transformation':

> an English nation-state survived [the Norman Conquest of] 1066, grew fairly steadily in the strength of its national consciousness through the later twelfth and thirteenth centuries, but emerged still more vociferously with its vernacular literary renaissance and the pressures of the Hundred Years War [1337–1453] by the end of the fourteenth.
>
> *(Hastings 1997: 5)*

What, then, in Hastings' view gives rise to a 'nation' if not modernisation? He believes a 'nation' arises where a particular ethnic group perceives itself existentially threatened either by an external attack or by the state system of which it has hitherto formed a part (Hastings 1997).

Perhaps even more intriguingly, Walker Connor rejects the whole idea of dating 'nations' and the origins debate which follows on from it.

> Failure to appreciate that national identity is predicated upon sentient history undergirds a current vogue in the literature on national identity to bifurcate contributors in terms of (1) 'primordialists' and (2) 'social constructivists'/'instrumentalists'/ 'modernists'.
>
> *(Connor 2004: 11)*

Connor claims that *when* a 'nation' came into being is irrelevant because it fails to appreciate the emotive essence of the idea itself. While he accepts that in strictly factual or chronological terms a 'nation' may indeed be a 'modernist' invention, he believes that in the minds of its members the 'nation' nevertheless remains 'eternal', 'beyond time', and 'timeless' and, ultimately, 'it is not facts but perceptions of facts that shape attitudes and behavior' (Connor 2004: 11).

But even if we accept the primordialist contention that 'nations' do indeed have a much longer duration than modernist accounts suggest, we are still left with the need to explain the much more recent advent of national ideologies. The ethnosymbolism approach favoured by Anthony Smith (Smith 1991, 1998, 2004) purports to offer a solution to this intriguing puzzle. According to Smith, the enduring features of national identities are myths and memories. Writers and artists are the bridge between the 'primordial' and 'modern' 'nations' precisely because they are able to refashion these ancient and inherited ethnic traditions into a contemporary national identity. This explains why national politics and policies often have symbolic goals such as access to education and broadcasting in the national language, the preservation of ancient and sacred sites such as the (Serbian Orthodox) Decani Monastery in (majority Muslim) Kosovo, the right to wear religious symbols like headscarves and turbans in public places and so on. According to Smith, 'materialist, rationalist and modernist theories tend to have little to say about these issues, especially the vital component of collective memories' (Smith 1995).

Contested beginnings, contested futures

The debate on origins may at first glance appear to be of only theoretical interest – a subject for academic debate perhaps, but one lacking in contemporary political significance. Such an impression is deeply misleading, for the way in which one defines a 'nation', be it modernist or primordialist, has a direct consequence on political controversies surrounding the basis for independent political community and membership within it – which communities may claim sovereignty, how territories and peoples may be transferred or acquired, how succession is regulated when larger communities break up into smaller communities or when several communities combine into one (Wight 1977: 153).

If the 'nation' is an invented social category linked to the process of modernisation, then nationalism is fundamentally concerned with economic transition and democratisation. Which group of people become incorporated into an emergent 'nation' is determined by contemporary economic and political circumstances and not by cultural or linguistic ties emanating from the distant past. Accordingly, modernising nationalists are not so much concerned with redrawing the political map as with infusing new meaning into existing juridical territories.

Alternatively, however, if the 'nation' is a primordial community defined by ancient and inherited cultural traits, then nationalism is fundamentally concerned with a cultural politics of authenticity. Only bona fide members of the same pre-existing cultural community are capable of forming a genuine, primordial 'nation'. Primordial nationalists are thus intent upon identifying 'historic nations' and bringing about congruence between the organic cultural landscape and the contemporary political map.

The fundamental programmatic difference between modernising and primordial nationalists is clearly revealed in their divergent responses to linguistic and ethnic diversity. For modernising nationalists, both language and ethnicity is a means to an end (the modern nation-state); for primordialists language and ethnicity are ends in themselves because they disclose intrinsic organic national community.

Modernising nationalists view vernacular language policy as a key component of the creation and consolidation of capitalist economies and democratic institutions. From this perspective, language policy is utilitarian – which vernacular language becomes the national language of economy and politics is determined by expediency, usually because it has the largest number of speakers or is the already established language of law and commerce.

The central importance of a common, public language as a precondition for democratic government is a recurring theme in modernist thought from the late eighteenth century onwards. The best known proponent of this view is John Stuart Mill whose oft quoted essay *On Representative Government* contends that 'among a people without fellow feeling, especially if they read and speak different languages, the united public opinion necessary to the working of representative government cannot exist' (Mill 1861).

Political stability in a democratic system of governance is thus often equated – indeed considered dependent upon – linguistic homogeneity. The obvious implication of this perspective is that linguistic minorities ought properly to be assimilated into the official, public language to ensure equal and effective political participation and the proper working of representative institutions. Linguistic diversity may, at best, be confined to the home, but it should have no place in the public life of a democracy.

A similar emphasis on linguistic assimilation as a key component of the creation and consolidation of civic institutions is a recurring theme in the state-building discourse from the mid-nineteenth century onwards (Jackson Preece 2005: 107–110). We see evidence of this rationale in the administration of mandated and trust territories, in the new or enlarged states of Central and Eastern Europe between the two world wars, in the decolonised states of Asia and Africa after 1945, and in the post-communist states of Central and Eastern Europe after 1989. In all of these cases, the logic underscoring policies of linguistic assimilation directed at minorities is strikingly similar to that outlined by Mill and Durham. The 1995 State Language Law of Slovakia is a typical example. It identifies the Slovak language as the

> expression of sovereignty of the Slovak Republic and the general means of communication for its citizens, which guarantees them freedom and equality in dignity and rights in the territory of the Slovak Republic.
>
> *(Daftary and Gal 2003: 47)*

In sum, according to the modernists perspective, the 'nation' is presumed to be one, and the public language of the state and its civic representative institutions are intended to embody this unity of political purpose.

Primordial nationalists look upon language as a marker of intrinsic national community. Here the stress is not on the utility of a common language for the proper functioning of economic and political institutions as in Mill, but rather on the cultural significance of language as the natural and indeed essential medium through which each individual and, by extension, each community understands the world and their place in it. From this perspective, every language is a particular way of thinking. What is understood in one language can never be perceived in exactly the same way in another language; the essence of genuine, culturally specific meaning simply cannot be translated. Following on from this, true community is only possible amongst native speakers of the same original language since it is only in such linguistic circumstances that complete understanding and mutual sympathy can exist.

These linguistic arguments – which like Kedourie we can trace back to German romantic writers such as Herder and Fichte – gave a new dimension to the idea of popular sovereignty (Jackson Preece 2005: 110–112). If the only genuine communities were associations of original language speakers, then linguistic affinity was not simply a means to an end (the proper functioning of representative government), but an end in itself (the basis of popular sovereignty). Instead of being an expression of representative government, language was the basis of statehood. The nineteenth-century quest for statehood thus became as much a philological as a political endeavour. Throughout the Hapsburg and Ottoman Empires in Central and Eastern Europe, a nascent nationalism was expressed and developed through literary efforts: Adamantios Korais (1748–1833) helped invent modern Greek through his translation of the classics; Josef Jungmann (1773–1847) wrote a Czech grammar and history of Czech literature; Stephen Katona (1732–1811) wrote a history of Hungary; Dositej Obradovic (1740–1811) published in contemporary Serbian as distinct from old Slavonic; to name only a few examples (Kohn 1960: 527–576).

Consequently, linguistic diversity is problematic, not in terms of institutional accountability or stability (as in the discourse of civic language), but because it confuses and potentially corrupts original language communities. Foreign accretions and borrowings obscure original meanings and in so doing threaten to weaken the mutual understanding and sympathy which is the special preserve of genuine community; accordingly such foreign intrusions must be 'cleansed' to preserve the purity of thought and concomitant identity. By the same token, in circumstances where one original speech community is assimilated into another, the former can have no experience of genuine individuality or community. In Fichte's words, such an assimilated language community is merely the 'echo of a voice already silent ... they are, considered as a people, outside the original people, and to the latter they are strangers and foreigners' (Kedourie 1960: 68).

From this perspective, the only appropriate response to linguistic diversity is the creation of separate and indeed homogenous political communities on the basis of linguistic affinity. Secession or irredentism thus become the obvious political objective of linguistic minorities. Meanwhile, the majority language community can tolerate or assimilate such minorities only at their own peril since either programme could potentially dilute the purity of their own linguistic usage. Such a conclusion, of course, unavoidably leaves those minorities who are incapable of forming their own, independent language communities vulnerable to policies of assimilation or segregation or expulsion or worse.

A similarly contrasting approach may be discerned in modernist and primordialist approaches to ethnicity (Jackson Preece 2005: 149–157). For modernising nationalists, national identity is primarily defined through a shared political and economic experience. Thus cultural programmes are generally understood in terms of civic virtues and not the defence of ethnic purity per se. Modernising nationalists tend to relegate ethnicity to the private sphere. Minority ethnic identities may be tolerated within the home where distinct languages, traditions, myths and memories may be preserved, provided these do not conflict with nor in any way undermine the prevailing civic culture. Obviously, such private identities do not receive public recognition from the civic nation-state. Instead, public institutions actively support the civic national culture and language within public life to the exclusion of all others. And where necessary in defence of this civic culture, assimilationist or paternal policies may be directed towards nonconformist ethnic groups.

In contrast, primordial nationalists are much more overtly concerned with ethnic politics. In this perspective, you will recall that national membership is determined by purportedly 'natural' and thus innate characteristics which by definition cannot be changed by assimilation or tutelage. The individual no longer determines his or her nation: instead, the nation determines the individual. Thus although the freedom of minorities to express and develop their distinct ethnic identities may be limited in either civic or ethnic nation-states, the latter are arguably far more hostile towards ethnic minorities and thus potentially more destructive not only of ethnic minority identities but in extreme circumstances even their physical survival.

Once the ethnic bond is accepted as the raison d'être of the state, ethnic diversity becomes a threat to popular sovereignty. When the right to rule is justified on the basis of an ethnic affinity between the population of a state and its government then the existence of ethnic minorities challenges the authority of those in power. In order to preserve its territorial integrity and domestic stability, the ethnic nation-state tends to act as if it is a homogenous ethnic community. If (as is often the case) such a state is not in fact ethnically homogeneous, than it must 'endeavour to make the facts correspond to the ideal', regardless of the rights and liberties of those among its citizens who do not belong to the majority ethnic group (Cobban 1970: 109). At the same time, the reverse is also true: every ethnic nation or fraction thereof which is not an independent state must strive to become one. National survival is thus dependent upon the survival of the *ethnie* within its historic homeland.

Already in the 1848 movement for German unification, one can discern the various dilemmas which arise in the context of building states on the basis of ethnic criteria. German unification was meaningless without a clear understanding as to which territories ought to be included in it. The answer adopted at the Frankfurt Assembly revealed an ethnic imperative: territories with predominantly German populations or German rulers would be included. This might at first glance seem a perfectly reasonable basis for admission – until, that is, one begins to ponder the anomalies. Switzerland had a significant German speaking population and historic ties to the German ruled Holy Roman Empire, but was nevertheless excluded from the list. Schleswig and Holstein had a significant Danish population and war over these provinces was only averted in 1848 by British and Russian intervention; such a war did eventually occur in 1864 and resulted in the loss of Danish territory to Prussia. Alsace could not be included without a war with France in 1870–1. Bohemia was a part of the German ruled Hapsburg Empire, but the majority of its population spoke Czech, and a Czech nationalism as distinct from the German was already developing there (indeed, the Czech intellectuals led by the historian Palacky famously turned down an invitation to send a representative to the Frankfurt Assembly) (Seton-Watson 1977: 95). Ultimately, of course, the status of the German speaking minority in the Sudetenland was used to justify the transfer of Czechoslovakian territory to Germany in 1938, and in 1939 Bohemia and Moravia were occupied by the Nazis and an independent, pro-Axis Slovak puppet state was created.

The assumption underlying all of these responses is that political stability in an ethnic nation-state cannot tolerate ethnic diversity, as such divisions will undermine the integrity of the overarching political order by calling into question the myth of common descent upon which it rests. In other words, this perspective views ethnicity in zero sum terms, such that coexistence between ethnic groups within the same jurisdiction is not an option. Although bleak, such an outlook nevertheless reflects a normative position: the well-being of individuals and their respective political communities is herein understood as dependent upon the fulfilment of ethnicity, which in turn is seen to embody the 'natural order' in its purest form.

Those who were unsuccessful in the great race to capture their own nation-state in which their culture and language would reign supreme were then confronted with the unenviable choice of either assimilation into the majority (assuming this choice existed, which was not always the case) or acceptance of a permanent position as minority with the attendant risk of discrimination and persecution. Barring these alternatives, the only other option available was to engage in a politics of secession or irredentism intended to overcome, once and for all, the unpalatable minority position. But such revolutionary nationalists must then overcome the opposition of the international society which remains fundamentally biased in favour of the sovereignty and territorial integrity of existing states.

Conclusion

The national discourse is a core component of contemporary political life, so much so in fact that ours is a world of 'nation-states', 'national sovereignty' and 'national identities'. Yet despite the clearly defined lines on the modern political map, ours is also a world of ethno-cultural diversity, within as well as between states. 'National' identities are malleable rather than fixed and they can and do conflict. Thus, perhaps, it is only to be expected that the 'nation' is a fundamentally contested concept that defies easy definition or explanation. We may think we 'know one when we see one' but others are likely to disagree with our perceptions not only for academic but crucially also for political reasons.

This chapter has sought to demonstrate that academic controversies on the origin of 'nations' are intricately entangled in current political controversies on the future of 'nations'. To ask the question 'What is a nation?' unavoidably also requires reflection on the underlying issue 'When is a nation?'; and when we locate and define a 'nation's origins' we are, in effect, also mapping, often literally, its current political claims and aspirations. What is the 'Serbian Nation'? Was it born at the Battle of Kosovo Polje in 1389 or in Slobodan Milošević's speech at Kosovo Polje in 1989? A primordialist origin potentially presages a political claim for a 'Greater Serbia' including all or part of the territory of a now ambiguously independent Kosovo. A modernist origin links the rise of Serbian nationalism to the end of Yugoslav communism and may be more compatible with existing international norms on sovereignty, self-determination and the recognition of states. Either way, however, past and present controversies become inextricably intertwined. If Milan Kundera is right, and the 'struggle of man against power is the struggle of memory against forgetting' (Kundera 1996: 4), then what nationalist leaders are fighting for is 'access to the laboratories where photographs are retouched, and biographies and histories rewritten' (Kundera 1996: 21–22).

Further reading

Gellner, E. 1995. 'Do Nations Have Navels?' Warwick Debate on Nationalism. Available online at: http://gellnerpage.tripod.com/Warwick2.html (Accessed 3 September 2015).
Smith, A. D. and Hutchinson, J. (eds) 1994. *Oxford Readers: Nationalism*. Oxford: Oxford University Press.

References

Anderson, B. 1983. *Imagined Communities: Reflections on the Origins and Spread of Nationalism*. London: Verso.
Cobban, A. 1970. *The Nation State and National Self-Determination*. New York: Crowell.
Connor, W. 2004. 'The Timelessness of Nations', *Nations and Nationalism*, 10 (1/2): 35–47.
Daftary, F. and Gal, K. 2003. 'The 1999 Slovak Minority Language Law: Internal or External Politics?' In F. Daftary and F. Grin (eds), *Nation-Building, Ethnicity and Language Politics in Transition Countries*. Budapest: Open Society Institute.
Gellner, E. 1983. *Nations and Nationalism*. Oxford: Blackwell.
Hastings, A. 1997. *The Construction of Nationhood: Ethnicity, Religion and Nationalism*. Cambridge: Cambridge University Press.
Hinsley, F. 1966. *Sovereignty*. London: Watts and Co.
Jackson, R. 2000. *The Global Covenant: Human Conduct in a World of States*. Oxford: Oxford University Press.
Jackson Preece, J. 1998. *National Minorities and the European Nation-States System*. Oxford: Oxford University Press.
Jackson Preece, J. 2005. *Minority Rights: Between Diversity and Community*. Cambridge: Polity Press.
Kedourie, E. 1960. *Nationalism*. London: Hutchinson University Library.
Kohn, H. 1960. *The Idea of Nationalism*. New York: Macmillan.
Kundera, M. 1996. *Book of Laughter and Forgetting*. New York: Harper.
Mayall, J. 1990. *Nationalism and International Society*. Cambridge: Cambridge University Press.
Mayall, J. 1996. *Nationalism and International Relations*. London: University of London External Programmes.
Mill, J. S. 1861. 'On Representative Government'. Available online at: https://ebooks.adelaide.edu.au/m/mill/john_stuart/m645r/chapter16.html (Accessed 3 September 2015).
Polanyi, K. 1957 [1944]. *The Great Transformation: The Political and Economic Origins of Our Times*. Boston: Beacon Press.
Seton-Watson, H. 1977. *Nations and States: An Inquiry into the Origins of Nations and the Politics of Nationalism*. London: Methuen.
Smith, A. D. 1991. *National Identity*. Harmondsworth: Penguin.
Smith, A. D. 1995. 'Nations and their Pasts', Warwick Debate on Nationalism. Available online at: http://gellnerpage.tripod.com/Warwick.html (Accessed 3 September 2015).
Smith, A. D. 1998. *Nationalism and Modernism*. London: Routledge.
Smith, A. D. 2004. *Antiquity of Nations*. Cambridge: Polity.
Stoel, M. 1993. 'Keynote Address at the Opening of the Organization for Security and Cooperation in Europe Minorities Seminar in Warsaw'. Available online at: http://www.osce.org/hcnm/38038 (Accessed 3 September 2015).
Wight, M. 1977. *Systems of States*. Leicester: Leicester University Press.

3

MODERNITY, NATIONALISM AND IDEOLOGY

Daniele Conversi

Introduction

As with other socio-political terms, there is no universally agreed definition of ideology in social theory and political science and the concept remains a broadly contested one. In contrast, nationalism can be more easily defined as a modern ideological movement constructed around a self-defined nation and aiming at controlling the state and its ancillary political institutions within a bounded territorial space. In Anthony D. Smith's classical definition, nationalism is 'an ideological movement to attain and maintain autonomy, unity and identity on behalf of a population, some of whose members conceive it to constitute an actual or potential "nation". It is an active movement inspired by an ideology and symbolism of the nation' (Smith 1999: 256; 2009: 61; 2010: 9). Elsewhere, Smith reiterates that ideology is a key element in the success of nationalism as 'it serves to unify and focus the many grievances and aspirations of different social groups within a particular community or state, and to explain to and activate "the people"' (Smith 1998: 116).

However, its main constituent, the term 'nation', is probably so slippery and self-referential as to defy any attempt at an 'objective' definition. For Smith, a nation is 'a named human population sharing an historic territory, common myths and historical memories, a mass, public culture, a common economy and common legal rights and duties for all members' (Smith 1991: 14). However, this attempt at a definition encounters renowned operational problems. Elsewhere, I have stressed how stateless nations may lack the public, let alone mass, culture, necessary to be included in the above definition, neither can they enjoy a 'common economy' or 'legal rights and duties' for all, or most, of their members (Conversi 2006). These attributes are most often attached to the 'nation-state', a term which in itself derives from the previous affirmation of nationalism and its capture of the state (Connor 1994). Moreover the very term 'nation' lends itself to multiple interpretations in various European languages (Hroch and Malecková 2000). Given the vacuity and fruitlessness of attempting to pin down the nation as a unified concept, it is worth concentrating our efforts on the study of nationalism instead.

In this chapter, we shall see that nationalism can be primarily identified as an ideological movement and that ideology plays a central role in its initial formation and further diffusion. Interestingly, the origins of ideology and nationalism can be both traced back to the French Revolution: while the genesis of the term 'nationalism' is an issue of relative contention, the initial use of the term 'ideology' can be historically ascribed to the Lockean liberal aristocrat philosopher Antoine Destutt de Tracy: His *Eléments d'idéologie* (Destutt de Tracy 1970 [1805]) attempted to identify a positivist 'science of ideas' founded on the centrality of human sensations in the development of knowledge (Head 1985; Kennedy 1978). However, Napoleon transformed it into a pejorative term of abuse parodying de Tracy's followers as 'the ideologues'. Napoleon condemned ideology as an ambiguous doctrine that would undermine the rule of law, seeing 'in the thought of de Tracy a threat to his authority' (Eccleshall 1994: 4). Napoleon's usage subsequently eclipsed the original meaning of the term ideology to the point that even Karl Marx, who identified de Tracy as a reactionary bourgeois, used the term in a purely disparaging way, a use continuing up to Foucault and Deleuze (Malešević and Mackenzie 2002).

The *Oxford English Dictionary* gives several definitions of ideology, beginning with 'a system of ideas or ideals, especially one that forms the basis of economic or political theory or policy' (*OED* 1997: 908). Therefore, a relationship between ideology and political action needs to be established. This chapter describes generally ideology as a set of ideas articulated around a socio-political programme devised by specific individuals, which we may recognize occasionally as 'the ideologues' and, until recently, could be identified as 'intellectuals'. Today, they appear to us most often as media pundits.

What is ideology and what is it not? The reply mostly depends on the replier. Protean concepts like modernity, progress, development and, the latest arrival, globalization are imbued with ideology, yet not all scholars and social commentators promptly recognize this status. Although the way these terms are used implies adherence to ideological constructs and platforms, chrono-centrism prevents identifying them as ideologies. From the promontory of the present time, we can look backward and discern ideology where our forefathers simply saw the natural order of things, but in our day it may be more difficult to see the wood for the trees.

The term ideology can be used in two possible ways: one *neutral*, the other *critical* or *pejorative* (Thompson 1990: 56). While the critical use is implicit in any analytical study of ideology, is a neutral approach at all possible? Indeed, it may be difficult to 'stand by' and see ideology in purely objective terms, since scholarly endeavours are also informed by ideology. Most often, ideology is enriched by passion. As knowingly synthesized by the poet, film director and social analyst Pier Paolo Pasolini (1922–1975), it stems directly from passion: 'Passion, analytical in itself, gives way to ideology, synthetic in its nature' (*La passione, per sua natura analitica, lascia il posto all'ideologia, per sua natura sintetica*) (Pasolini 1994: 493).

Most scholars of nationalism agree that ideology is paramount to the creation and reproduction of nationalism, although they accord different degrees to its centrality. An illustrious exception was Ernest Gellner, who disagreed with the importance of ideology. Gellner (2006) argued that nationalism needs neither intellectuals nor an ideology, since nationalism was a semi-spontaneous response generated *ex-machina* by a fragmented social system disrupted by the uneven impact of industrialization – although he recognized that nationalism developed first in the West. More commonly, Elie Kedourie (1993) regarded nationalism as a fully fledged ideology spreading across the world via aping and imitation. Kedourie, Gellner and Smith are representative of various 'schools' of thought concerned with the origins of nations and the nature of nationalism. Kedourie's explanation is entirely centred on ideology; Gellner radically excludes its importance, whereas Smith adopts a more nuanced position seeing the role of nationalist ideology as shaped by pre-existing myths and symbols.

Before considering the relationship between nationalism and ideology, we should understand what is broadly meant by ideology, what is not, and why not. Beside liberalism and conservatism, communism, socialism and fascism have been named as emblematic twentieth-century ideologies. Capitalism is more often seen as a socio-political system founded on the adoption of market economy principles. It is less generally accepted as an ideology and is thus often subsumed as a practice of liberalism – jointly with its ideological sub-varieties: laissez-faire capitalism, radical capitalism, and corporate capitalism. Yet, the very belief in capitalism as the ideal, standard socio-political system, as well as the panacea for all sorts of social problems, rests on firm ideological grounds. Many have idealized capitalism as the most perfect and unmatchable socio-economic model, indeed as the only possible one. Susan Sontag acutely observed that 'the ideology of capitalism makes us all into connoisseurs of liberty – of the indefinite expansion of possibility' (Sontag 1989: 77; 2013).

Other unsuspected candidates to the category of ideology proliferate: The US-led 'war on terror', justifying ends and means, was shaped as an ideology of a good and virtuous (American) society fighting against 'evil' (Conversi 2010b). In the USA, the very notion of Manifest Destiny can be read as an overarching ideology consistently and systematically utilized as a 'cover story' for the establishment and continuance of the 'colonial triad of settlers, Indigenous peoples, and slaves' (McCoy 2014).

In fact, these visions were formulated within, and as responses to, the crises brought about in different stages and periods by the end of an era. However termed: agricultural society, the *Ancien Régime*, the Dark Ages, or by some other name: by opposition to the latter, the term *modernism* encompasses all those world visions which fully embraced modernity and its consequences. It seeks to conceive new scenarios of 'togetherness' and competing political projects based on the full acceptance and endorsement of modernity. *Modernism* has thus been articulated through a set of often-incompatible ideas whose socio-political programme was predicated on a (Western-centred) vision of modernity as the supreme good, and hence on the rejection of elements which, according to its competing ideological foundations, could be perceived as 'anti-modern'. The cult of modernity, progress and development became the *idée fixe* of the industrial and post-industrial age. In short, modernism has permeated not only all other ideologies, including nationalism, liberalism, fascism and communism, but also every major aspect of modern social life. In a nutshell, modernists predicate that all that is modern is positive, while all that is 'anti-modern' needs to be rejected. Given that both Nazism and Stalinism viewed themselves as modernizing ideologies, we can figure out what could it mean then to find oneself at the wrong side of the 'modern/anti-modern' spectrum.

Modernist ideology is often encapsulated in the popular myth of the 'mad scientist', who, blinded by an absolute faith in progress, crafts Frankenstein-like monsters in his secluded laboratory. The 'mad scientist' paradigm operates within a set of beliefs which are often a radical and gross interpretation of prevailing visions of modernity, while it is often erroneously interpreted as a personal ambition verging on pathology and emanating from individual attitudes. But similar attitudes did not emerge casually in a post-religious, particularly post-Christian, world. They were part and parcel of the prevailing *Zeitgeist* unleashed by the advent of Western-style modernity. Here I intend to stress the link between the notions of modernity, progress and nationalism. In fact, modernism as the ideology of progress is deeply related to nationalism. For Liah Greenfeld (1992) it is impossible to conceive modernity outside nationalism, since the latter provided the ideological forge and mould to shape the former. Modernity is simply unthinkable outside a non-nationalist world, so that nationalism 'represents the cultural foundation of modern social structure, economics, politics, international relations, education, art, science, family relation, and so on and so forth' (Greenfeld 2006a: 162; 2013). However, the opposite can also be said in that modernism is seen as the structural foundation of all of the above. The totalizing nature of nationalism overlaps hence with the doubly totalizing nature of modernity. For this reason, one can legitimately suspect that Greenfeld is speaking about the ideology of modernity, rather than the ideology of nationalism – even though she seems to reject a clear-cut distinction between the two.

Modernity, nationalism and ideology

The term 'modernism' has different meanings in various fields: so, among art historians, it is notably used to describe an artistic movement that emerged in late nineteenth- and early twentieth-century Europe. In this chapter, 'modernism' refers to a wider ideological category, which sees modernity as the founding parameter of a new era implicitly defined by the belief in unlimited progress. This has remained the dominant ideology and paradigm at least till the beginning of the twenty-first century and it is probably the most popular ideology across the world. Modernism thoroughly accompanied the growth of nationalism and, in most cases, preceded it – although Greenfeld asserts that nationalism preceded modernity and indeed it acted as its midwife.

For most scholars of nationalism and modernity, the *incipit* of both remains the French Revolution, which is also when the term ideology was first coined. The doctrine of nationalism was officially formulated in the *Declaration of the Rights of Man*, its public display of symbols touched off with the *Fête de la Fédération* in the Summer of 1790 and its definitive test occurred in the battlefield at Valmy (1792). Before the French Revolution, the propaganda apparatus of absolute monarchs was largely confined to the upper elites and exercised via the Courts, as loci of aggregation and public display of Royal paraphernalia aiming to 'seduce' or coopt provincial elites. Absolute sovereigns increasingly appropriated religious symbolism to prop up their legitimacy via appeals to their subjects, particularly under Louis XIV, the *roi soleil*. At those times, ideology was still largely overlapping with religion. Although the primary movers and motives have not been clearly identified, the St Bartholomew's Eve massacres against Huguenots (Protestants) in Paris (1572) indicated an obsession by ruling elites with the power of socio-religious ideas. The targets were not cultural or religious differences *per se* but 'ideological' opposition and dissent, as heterodox communities were considered dangerous by ruling elites (Conversi 2012b).

With modernity, secular ideology seized the state in 'absolute' terms. The targets were no longer framed in purely religious terms, but in terms of their entropy or counter-entropy (Gellner 2006), that is, their cultural compatibility or incompatibility with an increasingly centralized, expanding and control-freak state. To the most radical of Jacobins, cultural difference became anathema. Under the French revolution, the physical extermination of ideological-cultural opponents was pursued within a new 'national' framework, which slowly evolved into a broader drive to 'nationalize' the masses (Conversi 2007; 2012b) Nihilism itself originated in French revolutionary discourse and, since then, the conviction that modernity is essentially nihilistic informs some of the most influential strands of philosophical, political, and aesthetic modernism (Weller 2011). Since the French Revolutionary wars, in particular after the French victory at Valmy, ideology became essential in the way wars were to be fought over the next two centuries (Conversi 2015). After years of ideological emphasis on the sacrality of *La Patrie* (the Fatherland), French citizens began slowly to identify with the soldier as the supreme expression of collective will, viewing war as the finest of national virtues (Lynn 1996: 121). Even before the *levée en masse*, volunteers were drafted in through an array of visual effects and media grandeur, often surrounded by a festival atmosphere punctuated by martial music (Ozouf 1988).

The systematic mass killing by government troops also led some historians to identify the *Vendée* massacres (1793–6) as the first modern genocide (Conversi 2012b; Levene 2008;

2014). Most historians recognize the use of ideology and nationalism as mass propellers since the French Revolution. The destructive nature of European state-building was palpable to many citizens, yet patriotic-nationalist intoxication made opposition impossible. Thus, few intellectuals found the courage to denounce it, let alone oppose it. The 'thinner' ideology of anarchism developed largely in contrast to the practice of *étatisme*, whose ideological glue was provided by nationalism (see Ostergaard 1981; 1983). Intensively mobilized during periods of inter-state conflict, patriotism allowed the state to gain a foothold in society and penetrate areas from which it was initially excluded. Opposing the nation-state as an institution and patriotism as its legitimating belief, Leo Tolstoy linked both to organized violence (Christoyannopoulos 2008; Tolstoy 1926). If we look through the lenses of long-term historical processes, we can discern 'the relative modernity of both nationalism and organized violence as both were generated by coercive bureaucratization and centrifugal ideologization', thanks to the nation-state's unprecedented capacity to penetrate embedded networks of 'micro-solidarity' (Malešević 2013a; 2013b: 197).

Dominant nations, dominant ideologies and cultural hegemony

The rapid demise of Marxism after 1989 has involved the abandonment of some important concepts, which can still be useful to socio-political analysis. In Marx's analysis, ideology is part of the *superstructure*, nearly an accessory of the economic structure made of class relations. Yet, beyond this apparent blunder, Marxist scholars have refined the concept through the years, while still holding that ideology is forged by the bourgeoisie as a tool to convince members of other classes that the bourgeoisie's interests are the interests of all. For Antonio Gramsci, the dominant classes establish *cultural hegemony* through patterns of consumptions, values, norms, habits, and so on (Gramsci 2011: 20 and 207). Cultural hegemony explains why the bourgeoisie can so easily enforce its models of 'false consciousness' amongst the working-class, whose interests should be rationally at odds with those of the bourgeoisie, but are side-lined in the name of inter-class allegiances, notably through consumerism and nationalism. In fact, nationalism shares the status of 'false consciousness' with other non-class related ideologies and practices, *in primis* the 'fetishism of commodities', so vital to maintaining the system of 'class supremacy' (Marx 2007: 81–96).

More recently, ideology has been defined as the way 'in which meaning serves to sustain relations of domination' (Thompson 1990: 58), specifically the domination of some classes over others. This 'meaning' needs to be synthesized and diffused through the articulation of ideas into a cohesive and viable ideology. In fact, once firmly established and enshrined in power relations, ideology is spread by means of mass manipulation. If seized by the state and the mainstream media, nationalism/patriotism can certainly become an ideology most suitable for the concentration of power into the hands of a few.

Most ideologies are embedded into political power, and the crucible of power in the modern era is the nation-state. The more controlling and authoritative the state is, the more pervasive its founding ideology, and vice versa. Althusser identifies a plurality of Ideological State Apparatuses, those 'realities' which 'present themselves to the immediate observer in the form of distinct and specialised institutions' and which function both via violence and ideology (Althusser 1971: 143). These are distinct from the unique (Repressive) State Apparatus holding sway alone over the public domain, yet the distinction between public and private 'is a distinction internal to bourgeois law', while 'the State [controlled by the ruling class] ... is "above the law" ... [it] is neither public nor private; on the contrary, it is the precondition for any distinction between public and private' (Althusser 1971: 144).[1] The essential distinction is in fact that 'the Repressive State Apparatus functions "by violence", whereas the Ideological State Apparatuses *function "by ideology"*' (145, italics in the original). In accordance with what we have described so far, violence is opposed to ideology, yet there is an obvious complementarity between them.[2] An ideal model of supremely repressive State functioning purely by repressive measures is clearly impossible, so that violence and repression always need to be supplemented by ideology. Althusser brings forward the example of the Army and the Police which 'also function by ideology both to ensure their own cohesion and reproduction, and in the "values" they propound externally' (Althusser 1971: 145). On the other hand, a 'pure' Ideological State Apparatus cannot exist, as ideology also needs to be supplied by violence, even though this may be 'very attenuated and concealed, even symbolic'. As various forms of nationalism always underpin the functioning of the modern state, its performance has been historically rooted in both violence and ideology. However, before seizing the state, nationalism is also expressed in a plurality of 'Ideological State Apparatuses', including trade unions, lawyers, physicians, lower and higher education, and the very family, where notions of common descent are actuated since early childhood. For Althusser, these apparatuses serve their purpose of reproducing the power of the bourgeoisie and reinforcing the capitalist system. He then explicitly relates nationalism to the communications apparatus ruled by the mass media, together with chauvinism, liberalism, moralism and economism (Althusser 1971: 154–155).

In terms much cruder than Gramsci, the Orwellian word 'brainwashing' as a strategy of mind control was coined to define a method of coercive persuasion widely used under Communism. The original Chinese term made it into English during the Korean War and its popularization is credited to the anti-communist intelligence agent Edward Hunter (1902–1978) (Seed 2004: 27–31; Taylor 2004: 3–6). Beyond its obsession with the spectre of 'communist world domination', Hunter's *Brain-washing in Red China* (1951) became a classical crude description of how ideology-driven manipulation can radically alter the very identity of the individual and destroy her/his sense of the past.[3] Such form of all pervasive control has been absorbed into daily routine and assumed as *habitus* by most citizens. To resume, China's Ideological State Apparatus was used in full strength to instill the official ideology into the minds of citizens to the point of terminating previously existing sentiments, attitudes and world visions. Although during the Cold War only communist brainwashing became 'worth' considering, both Mao and Stalin operated through patriotic/nationalist mobilization, speaking in the name of the very subjects they oppressed, which can be even harder to oppose.

Is nationalism an ideology?

In the modern era, ideologies have become mass phenomena that moved millions of people: as such they have permeated most forms of thought, including scholarly thought. They have been often embraced with such an ardour and naive enthusiasm as to become avenues of fanaticism, self-immolation and mass suicide. After the end of the Second World War, the word 'ideology' was unsurprisingly discredited. Many observers at the time considered that competing ideologies had led to some of the worst human excesses in human history. Nationalism came in for particularly heavy criticism as it was claimed by some to be the direct ancestor of fascism in its various guises.

After the Second World War (later on, outside Europe), political ideologies were thus seen as mass propellers unleashing major human dislocations. Amongst them, it is customary to consider nationalism as a particularly powerful ideology destined to mobilize massive crowds. Unlike other ideologies, nationalism was rarely formulated through a coherent system of thought and a precise programme. It lacked recognized foundational thinkers and its protean nature meant that it remained often parasitic of other ideologies, by simply adapting to them, while, of course, shaping them. Therefore, there are authors who consider nationalism as a dependent, weak form of ideology (see San Martin 2002). Postulating a distinction between fully fledged and 'thin' ideologies, Michael Freeden argues that nationalism 'severs itself' from a broader ideological agenda, while being incorporated into various 'host' ideologies. Like green thought and feminism, nationalism deliberately replaces and removes central concepts, thus being structurally unable 'to offer complex ranges of argument, because many chains of ideas one would normally expect to find … are simply absent' (Freeden 1998: 750). As its operational incapacity leads to a shrinking of the political dimension, nationalism is defined as a 'thin-centered ideology'. Yet, it is still recognized as an ideology.

If nationalism is an ideology, either 'thin' or 'fat', is it plausible to see it, not merely as an ideology among others, but as *the* dominant ideology of the modern age? Indeed there is strong scope/reason for arguing so and for affirming that nationalism is 'the dominant operative ideology of modernity' since 'nearly all contemporary socio-political orders … tend to legitimize their existence in nationalist terms' (Malešević 2006: 317). This is in line with Smith's assertion that in every continent 'nationalism has become the main legitimating belief system' (Smith 1998: 116) and Connor's recognition of the centrality of nationalist ideology in legitimating power (Connor 2004). If nationalism is the ideology that underpins the nation-states' system, then nationalism can be described as 'the most successful ideology in human history' (Billig 1995: 22). It is a convincing argument, but this chapter reformulates it by incorporating the wider ideological context within which nationalism first emerged and then thrived: This is the all-pervasive context of molecularly expanding modernity and the ideology of technocratic materialism and corporatism which accompanied it.

Inescapable asymmetries: nationalism, modernism and developmentalism

Modernity is founded on all-pervasive asymmetric concepts: on the one hand, the 'modern', the insider; on the other hand its antagonists, the 'anti-modern', the outsider. Modernist discourses are founded on self-concepts, antonyms and binary couples, like civilized vs. barbarians, modern vs. anti-modern, advanced vs. backward, developed vs. under-developed, progressive vs. reactionary, people vs. plebs, majorities vs. minorities, North vs. South, superior vs. inferior, and so on. Opposition constitutes the hub around which all modernist concepts emerge, coalesce and expand in multiple directions. In virtue of its unique capacity to articulate oppositional concepts into asymmetric incompatibilities, and as the key facilitator of modernity, nationalism becomes inherently homogenizing. The process of nationalizing spaces requires the othering of those who resist homogenization (Conversi 2008). At the same time, this process can lead to the extreme of constructing state ideologies focusing on one or more target groups as 'anti-nation' to the point of annihilation (Murray 2014).

From a discursive standpoint, asymmetrical concepts, self-concepts, and counter-concepts play a crucial part in the development of power-ridden political asymmetries – as identified by Reinhart Koselleck's (1923–2006) and his historical semantics approach (Junge and Post-outenko 2011). They lie at the core of new attempts to understand the interaction between modernity and nationalism as homogenizing forces.

Asymmetric concepts are central to the building of the modernizing nation-state. In the past, the state's developmental ambitions were envisioned as instrumental to nation-building. Because nation-building was conflated, and confused, with state-making, the formation of common institutions was predicated on otherness and imbued with nationalist ideology. This often led to a fall of state legitimacy and hence a loss of control by the state (Guyot-Réchard 2013).

Modernism, like nationalism, is founded on the reiteration of asymmetrical concepts and it is thus an intrinsically exclusionary ideology. For modernists, *modernity* is largely defined against *anti-modernity* (reaction, obscurantism, etc.), rather than on its own. Prevailing notions of modernity are largely based on a (Western-centred) common-sense understanding of what is qualitatively and quantitatively modern. This is in turn based on a (Western-centred) common-sense understanding of what is *not* modern. Modernist notions like 'progress', 'growth', 'advancement' and 'development' were all-pervasive in the years leading to the First World War and totalitarianism. They were a central component of the predominant mindset let loose by the diffusion of Westernizing modernity (La Branche 2005; Latouche 1996). In the process, non-Western ideologies and world visions were discarded and destroyed, in short labelled as 'anti-modern'. 'Development' itself became an ideology or, even more, a 'global faith' imposed by the West on an often recalcitrant world (Rist 2002). For Christopher Lasch (1991), with its belief in a linear, steady, indefinite rise in living standards as the inevitable destiny of mankind, the 'faith in progress' assumes the eschatological trappings of established religions.

Modernism assumed various forms: as a 'right' to which all citizens are entitled, or as a 'must' for state leaders to impose upon often reluctant populations. In its extreme forms, it became the ideology of development for development's sake at whatever the costs. At such extremes, modernism can be re-defined as *'developmentalism'*. Far from being a secondary ideology, the latter has indeed accompanied nationalism and socialism well into the twentieth century, moving centre-stage with the advent of totalitarianism and its obsession with mass industrialization and the development of tightly controlled communication networks. This can be exemplified by Fritz Todt's (1891–1942) ideology of road building as key to German economic strength and Gottfried Feder's (1883–1941) Taylorist vision of technocracy as the 'perfect' society ruled by engineers. Turning citizens and peasants into pliable 'masses' through overwhelming state machines, totalitarian and post-totalitarian regimes justified destruction in the name of 'progress' and economic development. Extreme developmentalism, or the obsession with 'catching up' with the core countries of the wealthy West, irrespective of its human costs, was already visible in the 'desperately modernizing' drive of the Russian military before the Bolshevik revolution (Mann 2005: 99) or in the obsessive Westernizing trends emerging within the Ottoman Empire just before its collapse (Mann 2005: 114–119). More recently, the ideology of development allied with security concerns has been central in carrying out most contemporary genocides, notably in Rwanda (Uvin 1998; Verwimp 2000).

Later on in the twentieth century, Taylorism became an influential method of maximizing industrial efficiency and serializing mass production. The Soviet Union's NEP (*New Economic Policy*) before 1928 belonged to a broader developmentalist crusade and Lenin's embrace of Taylorism's 'scientific' method was more than

> a means of discipline that could remould the worker and society along more controllable and regularized lines … Lenin encouraged the cult of Taylor and of another great American industrialist, Henry Ford, inventor of the egalitarian Model 'T', which flourished throughout Russia at this time: even remote villagers knew the name of Henry Ford (some of them believed he was a sort of god who organized the work of Lenin and Trotsky).

> *(Figes 2002: 463)*

From a scientific method, Taylorism had become an ideology, indeed a faith, which was host of a broader ideology of progress. The 'natural' unit of reference for the ideology of progress was the nation, indeed the nation-state, remarkably so in the Soviet Union, where Wilsonian–Leninist principles of self-determination and popular sovereignty became the norm (Connor 2004: 34–37). The cult for discipline and work became part of a wider militarization of society which reached its peak later on under Stalin, as totalitarianism reinforced its global clench. Some radical Taylorists envisaged indeed 'the mechanization of virtually every aspect of life … from methods of production to the thinking patterns of the common man' (Figes 2002: 463).

Taylorism's weight upon Hitler's plans was even more substantial. By 1938, the over 2,000 km of German *Autobahn* network began to surpass in its extent the US highway system. The ideology of a highly inter-connected and powerful nation, envisioned as a unified living body, aimed at seducing every single citizen. Hitler's idea of a *Volkswagen* (car of the people) dated back as early as 1933, owing much to Ford's 'Model T'. This is well beyond what elsewhere has been narrowly defined as 'the paradox of reactionary modernist reconciliation' (Herf 1986).[4] In Italy, the avant-garde ideology of Futurism (1909–1945), with its idolatry for the machine, its cult of mass violence and its contempt for ordinary lives, produced the first artistic synthesis of all these trends (Conversi 2009a; Higueras 2011). In Turkey, the anti-traditionalist Westernizing drive of Mustafa Kemal Atatürk provided a unique model of modern *völkisch* state for European Nazi-Fascism: defying Western powers after Turkey's defeat in the First World War, Atatürk's rebellion in Ankara became a major Weimar media event in the early 1920s, the 'star in the darkness' which inspired the *Hitlerputsch*, while Hitler's unconditional admiration for Atatürk led him to emulate his radical construction of a new nation (Ihrig 2014). Mussolini's equally immense admiration for Atatürk was only nuanced by their mutual rivalry over the Dodecanese islands, which had been occupied by Italy after the Libyan war (1912–1945). In general, as I have argued, the stress on mass emotions and irrationality (including the rejection of Enlightenment rationalism) and the full embrace of modern technology were coeval and belong to the same world vision. They date back to the battle of Valmy and the birth of state-making nationalism with its radical, exclusive and unrivalled appropriation of '*Vive la Nation!*' cries and easily stirred cheering crowds (Conversi 2015).

In his classic *Seeing Like a State*, James Scott uses the term '*high modernism*' to question the success of the homogenizing, standardizing state founded on a hyper-modernist engineering ethos spread gradually outward to non-state spaces (Scott 1998). In contrast with interwar Europe, post-colonial elites appealed to rationality while focusing on the supposed welfare of the recipient populations: they designed it in order to 'improve the human condition' through dynamics of standardization, homogenization, and grid-making. Beyond the *dirigisme* of a centrally planned economy, the bureaucratic optics of high-modernism 'occludes the social and cultural worlds both of marginalized citizenries and of the bureaucrats themselves' through reductionism and a self-proclaimed 'cult of efficiency' (Herzfeld 2005). This applies not only to developmentalist states as repositories of power, but also to neo-liberal economies and unhindered global corporations. Scott discusses this as a failure, perhaps overemphasizing the capacity of popular resistance to state-planned improvement schemes (Scott 1985). But the historical record shows that authoritarian regimes met with scant resistance and rarely with vocal opposition.

The concept of *developmental state* or *developmental dictatorship* can be useful in this respect and it has been systematically applied to the cases of Italy's Fascism (Gregor 1979) Spain's Francoism (Saz Campos 2004), and Japanese-occupied Manchuria in 1931–1945 (Murakami

2012). A national-developmentalist ideology underpins nearly all totalitarian systems, whose regimes attempted to shape a *new man* as the ideal citizen ready to inhabit the promised land of a new industrialist utopia. Soviet and Maoist propaganda posters depicted the advent of mass industrialization in superbly idealized terms, as the gateway to a new millennium. Nazi-Fascist regimes shared with Socialist-Communist ones variants of a Western-centred ideology of development while paying lip service to 'tradition' and honouring the 'fathers' of the nation. Totalitarian systems marred nationalism and ideologies of progress in quasi-religious, mythopoietic terms (Griffin 2007). An extreme, rather than moderate, modernist ideology was the main common denominator amongst all these regimes and surpassed by a long way the already commanding prominence of nationalism and patriotism.

Progress, modernization and development are social concepts associated with power and thus conceal the traits of ideological dominance. Indeed, being more pervasive and 'material' than other ideologies, modernism can be described as the dominant ideology of the modern times. As progress and related concepts became intrinsic attributes of the nation, they were fully appropriated by nationalism. A step further, Greenfeld (1992) suggests that they cannot even be conceived in a world without nations and outside nationalism.

I have defended the general view that nationalism cannot be conceived outside modernity, but only to identify modernity itself as embedded in its own ideology, modernism. Let us now relate the above to what nationalism studies have so far produced on this relationship. Although for most scholars nationalism is indistinguishable from modernity, others argue that modernity provided only a catalyst for pre-existing groups to seize power or negotiate power-sharing arrangements through representative leaders. For some authors, nationalism was no mere chaperon of modernity, but it provided a congenial tool to impose modernization and spread the ideology of progress among the masses: in the footsteps of Hans Kohn, Liah Greenfeld (1992; 2006b; 2013) argues that ideas were central to the birth and spread of nationalism. This is a view shared by political philosophers, like Kenneth Minogue, and historians of ideas, like Elie Kedourie. Greenfeld also argues that nationalism was essential to the propagation of the 'spirit of capitalism' (Greenfeld 2001).

Intellectuals and the media: from ideology to *imagology*

Intellectuals play a different role at different times and in different countries. A clue of their importance can be found in the way their freedom of speech is restrained by incumbent regimes. How do governments react to the activity and writing of intellectuals able to articulate some form of uncomfortable political opposition? The murder of Anna Politkovskaia (2006), Sergei Protazanov (2009), Natalia Estemirova (2009) and other Russian activists points to the central role of the writer in articulating ideas about freedom in Russian politics and society. It also underlines the government's fear of losing control of the official discourse and the ruthless way the citizen is supervised by exercising absolute jurisdiction over the public sphere. Similarly in Tajikistan 50 to 80 journalists were killed from 1990 to 2000, in a period in which glasnost and perestroika were just beginning to create a liberal press (Allison 2006; see also Atkin 1995).

Situated in between the media pundit and the fully fledged intellectual, the figure of the journalist has a specific impact in early stages of democratization, when the written word may still enjoy a greater influence than the unmediated image. The stance articulated by the murdered Russian writers was powerful enough to warrant their elimination, also because it was framed in highly non-nationalist terms and advocated universal human rights transcending nationhood. Quite the opposite can be said of the nationalist *raison d'Etat* of the murderers, since Putin's exploit of state patriotism has affected minorities; non-nationalists, universalists, human rights activists and rival Russian nationalists as well.

The intellectuals have often played a central role in nationalism studies, beginning with the work of Carlton Hayes and, to a lesser extent, Hans Kohn. As we have seen, Elie Kedourie places intellectuals at the core of his explanation of the spread of nationalism. From an original emphasis on the role of intellectuals, Anthony D. Smith has subsequently nuanced their centrality, because nationalist ideologies are

> not simply the product of intellectuals, nor are most intellectuals … free-floating and disoriented, nor are most of them able to exercise the kind of influence that Kedourie attributes to them. The same is true of their ideas, which are effective in society to the extent that they mesh with pre-existing popular notions and collective memoirs. Only then can they mobilize large numbers of people.
>
> *(Smith 1998: 116)*

However, ethnosymbolism dismisses elites' manipulation outright, so that the dynamics of power are not laid bare or critically discussed. On the other hand, intellectuals played a key role in the passage from *ethnie* to nation (Conversi 2006).

Yet what does the word 'intellectual' mean? Which are its contours? How sophisticated does a nationalist intellectual need to be? How refined and deep the ideas to be propagated? The founder of Basque nationalism, Sabino Arana y Goiri (1865–1903), was not a champion of finesse and could scarcely articulate his thoughts in a coherent, let alone pleasant, way. Reading his *Obras Completas* (Complete Works) is a daunting task, as the collection is replete with vehement interjections, caustic tirades and ranting sermons interspersed with slang and xenophobic epithets. Yet, Arana's work was central to the success of Basque nationalism, with long-term repercussions on its subsequent evolution (Conversi 1997). What matters is the founding intellectual(s)' organizational capacity. In spite of his limited vocabulary and incapacity to enunciate in-depth observations, Arana was certainly an excellent agit-prop, an orator and haranguer perfectly capable of perorating the Basque cause amongst a small coterie in which he emerged as the charismatic catalyst. Such managerial ability also derived from his ability to communicate in the language of the people and from his ability to mobilize the founding myths of Basque nationalism (Douglass 2004). Basque nationalism owed most of its visual symbols and values to Arana. Considering that he died at the young age of 33, Arana's achievement was immense: he single-handedly formulated the first Basque nationalist programme, coined the country's name (Euskadi), defined its geographical extension, founded its first political organization, wrote its anthem and designed its flag (Conversi 1997: 53). All these required impeccable organizational skills and a total dedication to the cause. Thus, in spite of his hidebound and paltry educational qualifications, Arana could be described as an 'intellectual' because he was able to articulate and marshal the national aspirations of his followers. This can be visualized as a boundary-building enterprise: Arana's goal was to create, re-create, and reinforce the boundary between Basques and non-Basques, that is, to define a modern Basque identity. Frenetic, compulsive boundary-building was indeed one of the core elements of the epochal changes brought about by modernization and modernism (Conversi 2014).

Nowadays, the surrogate 'intelligentsia' is centred around media operatives – those who need more appearance than brain, and those whose subliminal passages have direct impact on human thought and actions. Does this mean that nationalism can today subsist without intellectuals? Is ideology possible or even thinkable without intellectuals? A passage from Milan Kundera's novel, *Immortality*, can shed light on this question:

we can rightfully talk of a gradual, general, planetary transformation of ideology into imagology ... All ideologies have been defeated: in the end their dogmas were unmasked as illusions and people stopped taking them seriously ... Reality was stronger than ideology. And it is in this sense that *imagology* surpassed it: imagology is stronger than reality, which has anyway long ceased to be what it was for my grandmother, who lived in a Moravian village and still knew everything through her own experience: how bread is baked, how a house is built, how a pig is slaughtered and the meat smoked, what quilts are made of, what the priest and the schoolteacher think about the world; ... she had, so to speak, personal control over reality.

(Kundera 1992: 126–127, my italics)

In their triumphant path towards the conquest of hearts and minds, dominant ideas have regularly been accompanied by powerful images. Images serve to convey rational, irrational and non-rational messages by using emotional styles and instinctive methods. In an era dominated by one-way, or unidirectional, media, most notably the radio and television, these images have become increasingly simple (the internet is not necessarily unidirectional, allowing the user a margin of self-determination and sometimes the possibility to interact and respond). In the passage from ideology to *imagology*, forms of banal nationalism have rapidly spread without the mediation of intellectuals and without the need for soliciting critical thought. This led to a global impoverishment of politics and the rise of 'banal' forms of mass mobilization though artificial simulation (Simons 2000). In practice, the reign of image belongs to a 'hyper-reality' which merges reality with fantasy (Baudrillard 1994: 1–42), as well as an all-encompassing ideology no longer mediated by intellectuals. Thus, the answer to the opening question is that in technologically advanced postmodern societies intellectuals may indeed become redundant, despite the fact that ideology permeates society at all levels. In various ways, the totalitarian nightmare of a homogeneous world order deprived of critical thought, yet firmly grounded on ideology, risks becoming a reality in the wake of neo-liberal globalization. Where the iron fist of totalitarianism failed, the velvet glove of globalization seems on the verge of succeeding. Yet, nationalism and ethnic conflict seem to expand with global homogenization, either as a reaction to it or as its 'natural' companion.

Why have intellectuals become redundant in a media-dominated, 'post-critical' world? Part of the answer lies in the rise of banal nationalism. As we have seen, a purely mentalist definition of ideology is no longer commonly accepted. Ideology is rather seen as encompassing a variety of current pre-reflexive manifestations, including behaviour, attitudes and patterns of consumption. For Michael Billig (1995), even the pettiest manifestations of nationhood are based on nationalist ideology: We are deeply steeped in a nationalized world vision, thus becoming unconscious carriers and replicators of nationalist ideology, whether we accept or reject nationalism in principle. Typical examples are those who 'restrict the term "nationalism" to the ideology of "others"' (Billig 1995: 16). By sin of omission, the very fact of nationalizing (i.e., attributing blame of nationalism to) others, particularly stateless nations, implies a certain degree of nationalist performance. As with other ideologies, its proponents can easily detect its shadow elsewhere, but not at home. 'Subconscious' nationalism is also common in mainstream academia: when scholars quote approvingly Ernest Renan's famous defence of the '*nation de volonté*' (nation of will) smuggling it as an example of 'civic', or even 'civilized', nationalism, they are not simply espousing an ideological stand, but also tacitly endorsing a nationalist-inspired vision, which is ultimately goaled towards exclusion.

Whereas Billig focuses on the daily ideology of banal nationalism, Althusser focuses on the untold, which he calls *lacunar discourse*; things are merely suggested rather than openly enounced. Indeed, ideology-supporting discourse does often work by changing the meanings of terms: The revolutionary triad *Liberté, Egalité, Fraternité* also served to underpin its opposite: unfreedom, inequality, and conflict. The most nationalist of the triad, *fraternité*, was the last one to be added, with its emotional and communitarian stress on kin-related moral obligations (Ozouf 1997: 4353–4389). Nationalism seems to advocate strong egalitarian values proclaiming the equality of all citizens or, rather, all the members of the nation. However, this 'equality' is largely fictitious and, once seized by the state, the concept is usually usurped to promote more demanding forms of surreptitious inequality (Conversi 2008). In times of war and under mass conscription, 'equality' is to be paid by ordinary citizens with their own lives: war demands that ultimate sacrifice is made on the basis of citizens' equality, although informed citizens may know well that the rich usually bribe their way out of war.

Finally, a whole set of irreflexive habits can be thought as expression of ideology. As externally induced behaviour, consumerism may not be perceived as an ideology in itself, but as part of a collective inclination to equate personal satisfaction with the incessant pursuit of material possessions. Already in 1899, the US sociologist Thorstein Veblen (1857–1929) identified patterns of 'conspicuous consumption', that is, the act of spending money for the sake of appearance and for attaining or maintaining social status – even though the phenomenon was quantitatively less pronounced before the era of mass consumerism. With the expansion of homogeneous global consumption patterns since at least the 1970s, the ideological aspects of the process seem to have passed unnoticed. Yet, systematic attempts to oppose consumerism and other behavioural '-isms' are likely to be perceived in terms of ideology. For instance, *enoughism*, a set of recently proposed practices and lifestyles based on ideas for a better world, is clearly dedicated to defeating consumerism in both ideology and practice (Naish 2008).[5]

Globalism, nationalism and ideology

In the 1960s, the 'end of ideology' was prematurely announced anticipating a new era liberated from the dogmas of socialism, liberalism and conservatism (Bell 1960). Over half a century on, some of these conjectures have seemingly materialized, finding a suitable symbolism in the fall of the Berlin Wall. But, whether or not an end of all ideologies really took place during the age of 'reflux', those vast socio-political changes are still firmly set within a greater ideological narrative: modernity. Moreover, nationalism remained with us and, as we all know, its appeal continues to develop.

The ostensibly 'paradoxical' relationship between globalization and nationalism has been stated and restated countless times. Likewise, various reasons have been indicated as the main culprits for this 'unexpected' outcome. One of them is the demise of cultural certainties and traditions ensuing from the process of global homogenization. It is still highly debatable whether globalization has actually bolstered cultural exchanges and *métissage*, or whether, rather, it has limited inter-ethnic relations to superficial domains by filtering inter-cultural contacts through the lenses of Westernization – or indeed Americanization (Conversi 2009b; 2010a; 2012a).

The copious and repetitive literature on globalization has so far failed to produce any ground-breaking text, even in the form of a journal article. The very term 'globalization' appears increasingly undefined, hard to grasp and shrouded in conceptual ambiguity, with some authors pushing its meaning back to Portugal's imperial expansion or even to the times of the Roman Empire, thus making it scholarly inoperative. Historically, the concept's current usage emerged in the wake of the global imposition of neo-liberalism as 'the ideology of the Washington consensus' (Callinicos 2003: 149).

There is an ongoing debate as to whether globalization is part of an ideology, an ideology in itself, or rather a mere economic/cultural fact. For William Greider, globalization is not ideology, but naked power: 'The great, unreported story in globalization is about power, not ideology. It's about how finance and business regularly continuously insert their own self-interested deals and exceptions into rules and agreements that are then announced to the public as "free trade"' (Greider 2000). For others, globalization is a new phase of particularly harmful and penetrating imperialism and some see it as deeply related to war (Barkawi 2006). Finally, others see its hidden agenda as implying a total restructuring of power relations throughout the world with the dramatic potential of unleashing 'a tide of global resentment' (Smith 2006).

However, in line with what we have said, globalization was also accompanied by the all-pervasive ideology of *globalism*. In other words, globalization, the actual practice, should be distinguished from *globalism*, its accompanying ideology – which is tacitly assumed by many scholars working in the area of globalization. For Manfred B. Steger *globalism* not only is 'a new ideology, but also constitutes the dominant ideology of our time against which all of its challengers must define themselves' (Steger 2002: 11). This is reflected in the all-pervasive hyper-productivism framing all sorts of economic relations, including the global food system (Rosin 2014). Ideological articulations of the 'public good' and appeals to industrial development provided the legitimating ground for various forms of exclusion and dispossessions under both state-led developmentalism and neo-liberalism. Yet, the globalist 'land broker states' have proven 'unable to achieve the ideological legitimacy of their predecessor', leading to more widespread conflicts over land (Levien 2013). The rhetoric is unmistakably pragmatic, acting in the name of promoting 'social justice', now kindly provided by the market as the new elected means to development. Yet, resistance to nationalist developmentalism has emerged as part of a broader cross-class and international series of movements expressed in a host of local variants, like resistance movement against coal power plants, dam construction and depletion of groundwater sources in Turkey (Arsel, Bengi and Adaman 2015; Kadir-beyoglu 2010), protest against mining corporations' attempts to develop open-cast cyanide leach gold mine in Transylvania (Velicu 2012), projects of urban gentrification and 'mega-gentrification' (Lees 2012), repressive forms of militaristic developmentalism in India's north-eastern regions (Ningthoujam 2013), and so on. In all these cases the downsized state that emerged from neo-liberal globalization has played a nationalist-development card similar to its high modernist predecessor, although it has allowed for the articulation of a certain level of dissent.

If globalism is an ideology, is it a variant, indeed a deepening, of the ideology of modernism? Given the latter's relationship with nationalism, we should not be surprised to see patriotic and ethnic conflict accompanying both. Ultimately, the answer depends on whether we chose to consider globalization as a new, and more radical, phase of modernization, or as an entirely new departure from it, as argued by post-modernists.

Some scholars, who years before had anticipated and celebrated the end of ideology, found nothing to rejoice in in the new era as they discovered that corruption had largely replaced ideology on a global scale (Bell 1993). After the Cold War, unconstrained American rule over world politics, economy, law and culture became the norm and its consequences upon daily practices, attitudes and lifestyles will permeate contemporary ideology for generations to an extent which still needs to be fully weighed up.

Conclusions

Although ideologies are central to the study of nationalism, there has been disagreement about whether or not nationalism is truly an ideology. However, it is an undeniable fact that nationalism is associated with modernity and, as I have argued, modernity in itself is based on the ideology of modernism. We have seen how nationalism can be either described as the dominant ideology of modernity, or as one among many modern ideologies. If nationalism is freeloading on other ideologies, which is then the core ideology around which it gravitates? Whereas most scholars agree that nationalism developed in tandem with modernity, few have considered modernity as conveyed by its own specific ideology. None of the major nationalism scholars identifies the possibility that nationalism can indeed be host to the wider ideology of modernism, since the latter is rarely identified as such.

By articulating specific projects for action, ideologies can become modern tools for mass domination, particularly when seized by incumbent regimes. They are distinguished from other forms of manipulation by their reliance on political thought and action, obedience to a set of principles, and the embodiment of related ideas in symbols, myths and rituals. As we have seen, this implies that our daily lives are unconsciously permeated by ideological content, including many routine habits that we may perceive as 'facts'.

This chapter has asserted the following points: a definition of ideology cannot be conceived in purely mentalist terms and needs to incorporate more general dispositions, particularly the dimension of *habitus* and unreflective behaviour. At any rate, nationalism is an ideology, either 'thin' or 'banal'. Indeed, it is the most powerful ideology of the modern age and it may even be its defining ideology. But modernity itself needs to be reconceived and redefined as an ideology and, in order for this to be achieved, the term *modernism* has been used and explored here.

Notes

1 As for the ideological state apparatuses, 'it is unimportant whether the institutions in which they are realized are "public" or "private". What matters is how they function' (Althusser 1971: 144).
2 'No class can hold State power over a long period of time without at the same time exercising its [cultural] hegemony over, and in, the State Ideological Apparatuses' (Althusser 1971: 146, original in italics).
3 Recently the brain-washing metaphor has been extended to 'deep capitalism' and cultural Americanization. Conveyed through films and fictions, brain-washing has slowly mutated 'from an external threat to American values to an internal threat against individual American liberties by the U.S. government' (Seed 2004: 1).
4 Indeed, its roots go back to Weimar and earlier: Germany's 'three mandarin thinkers', Heidegger, Schmitt and Freyer, all devoted numberless pages to the issue of technological supremacy. Before handing in his resignation as rector of the University of Freiburg (1934), Martin Heidegger had advocated Nazi ideology and Germany's urgent need to combine *Technik* and *Kultur* (Herf 1986: 109).
5 Enoughism, not inevitably a branch of green thought, is a quintessential cosmopolitan ideology, where the concern for the nation is wholly subordinated to that for the ecumene. In this sense, it belongs to a large group of universalist ideologies which aim to provide an alternative to nationalism, as well as to consumerism.

Further reading

Baudrillard, J. 1994. *Simulacra and Simulation*. Ann Arbor: University of Michigan Press.
Billig, M. 1991. *Ideology and Opinions: Studies in Rhetorical Psychology*. London: Sage Publications.
Brown, D. 1998. *Contemporary Nationalism*. London: Routledge.
La Branche, S. 2005. 'Abuse and Westernization: Reflections on Strategies of Power', *Journal of Peace Research*, 42(2): 219–235.

Leoussi, A. S. and Grosby, S. (eds) 2006. *Nationalism and Ethnosymbolism: History, Culture and Ethnicity in the Formation of Nations.* Edinburgh: Edinburgh University Press.

Scott, J. C. 1998. *Seeing Like a State: How Certain Schemes to Improve the Human Condition Have Failed.* New Haven: Yale University Press.

Smith, A. D. 1996. *Nations and Nationalism in a Global Era.* Cambridge: Polity Press.

References

Allison, O. (2006) 'Selective Enforcement and Irresponsibility: Central Asia's Shrinking Space for Independent Media', *Central Asian Survey*, 25(1): 93–114.

Althusser, L. (1971) 'Ideology and Ideological State Apparatuses', *Lenin and Philosophy and Other Essays.* New York: Monthly Review Press/London: New Left Books, pp. 121–176.

Arsel, M., Bengi, A. and Adaman, F. (2015) 'Environmentalism of the Malcontent: Anatomy of an Anti-coal Power Plant Struggle in Turkey', *The Journal of Peasant Studies*, 42(2): 1–25.

Atkin, M. (1995) 'Islam as Faith, Politics, and Bogeyman in Tajikistan', in M. Bourdeaux (ed.) *The Politics of Religion in Russia and the New States of Eurasia.* Armonk, NY: M.E. Sharpe, pp. 257–259.

Barkawi, T. (2006) *Globalization and War.* Lanham, MD: Rowman & Littlefield.

Baudrillard, J. (1994) *Simulacra and Simulation.* Ann Arbor: University of Michigan Press.

Bell, D. (1960) *The End of Ideology: On the Exhaustion of Political Ideas in the Fifties.* Glencoe, IL: The Free Press.

Bell, D. (1993) 'The Old War. After Ideology, Corruption', *The New Republic*, 209(8/9): 18–22.

Billig, M. (1995) *Banal Nationalism.* London/Thousand Oaks, CA: Sage.

Callinicos, A. (2003) *An Anti-Capitalist Manifesto.* Cambridge: Polity Press.

Christoyannopoulos, A. (2008) 'Leo Tolstoy's Anarchist Denunciation of State Violence and Deception', in E. Kofmel (ed.) *Anti-Democratic Thought.* Exeter/Charlottesville, VA: Imprint Academic, pp. 20–47.

Connor, W. (1994) *Ethnonationalism: The Quest for Understanding.* Princeton, NJ: Princeton University Press.

Connor, W. (2004) 'Nationalism and Political Illegitimacy', in D. Conversi (ed.) *Ethnonationalism in the Contemporary World: Walker Connor and the Study of Nationalism.* 2nd edn. London/New York: Routledge, pp. 24–49.

Conversi, D. (1997) *The Basques, the Catalans and Spain: Alternative Routes to Nationalist Mobilization.* Reno: University of Nevada Press/London: Hurst & Co.

Conversi, D. (2006) 'Mapping the Field: Theories of Nationalism and the Ethnosymbolic Approach', in A. S. Leoussi and S. Grosby (eds) *Nationalism and Ethnosymbolism: History, Culture and Ethnicity in the Formation of Nations.* Edinburgh: Edinburgh University Press, pp. 15–30.

Conversi, D. (2007) 'Homogenisation, Nationalism and War: Should We Still Read Ernest Gellner?', *Nations and Nationalism*, 13(3): 371–394.

Conversi, D. (2008) '"We Are All Equals!" Militarism, Homogenization and "Egalitarianism" in Nationalist State-building (1789–1945)', *Ethnic and Racial Studies*, 31(7): 1286–1314.

Conversi, D. (2009a) 'Art, Nationalism and War: Political Futurism in Italy (1909–1944)', *Sociology Compass*, 3(1): 92–117.

Conversi, D. (2009b) 'Globalization, Ethnic Conflict and Nationalism', in B. Turner (ed.) *The Routledge International Handbook of Globalization Studies.* London: Routledge/Taylor & Francis, pp. 346–366.

Conversi, D. (2010a) 'The Limits of Cultural Globalisation?', *Journal of Critical Globalisation Studies*, 1(3): 36–59.

Conversi, D. (2010b) 'Post-September 11th Conflicts', in N. Young (ed.) *Oxford International Encyclopedia of Peace.* Oxford: Oxford University Press, pp. 550–555.

Conversi, D. (2012a) 'Comparing European and American Nationalisms: A Response to Alberto Martinelli's Nationalism in the 21st Century', *Quaderni di Scienza Politica*, 19(3): 469–488.

Conversi, D. (2012b) 'Nación, estado y cultura. Para una historia política y social de la homogeneización cultural (1789–1945)', *Historia Contemporánea*, 45(3): 429–473.

Conversi, D. (2014) 'Modernity, Globalization and Nationalism: The Age of Frenzied Boundary-building', in J. Jackson and L. Molokotos-Liederman (eds) *Nationalism, Ethnicity and Boundaries: Conceptualising and Understanding Identity Through Boundary Approaches.* Abingdon: Routledge, pp. 57–82.

Conversi, D. (2015) 'War and Nationalism', in J. D. Wright (ed.) *International Encyclopedia of the Social & Behavioral Sciences.* 2nd edn. Oxford: Elsevier, pp. 363–370.

Destutt de Tracy, A. L. C. (1970 [1805]) *Éléments d'idéologie. I, Idéologie proprement dite.* Paris: Courcier.

Douglass, W. (2004) 'Sabino's Sin: Racism and the Founding of Basque Nationalism', in D. Conversi (ed.) *Ethnonationalism in the Contemporary World: Walker Connor and the Study of Nationalism*. 2nd edn. London/New York: Routledge, pp. 95–112.

Eccleshall, R. (1994) *Political Ideologies: An Introduction*. London: Routledge.

Figes, O. (2002) *Natasha's Dance: A Cultural History of Russia*. London: Allen Lane.

Freeden, M. (1998) 'Is Nationalism a Distinct Ideology?', *Political Studies*, 46(4): 748–765.

Gellner, E. (2006) *Nations and Nationalism*. 2nd edn. Oxford: Blackwell/Ithaca: Cornell University Press [1st edn 1983].

Gramsci, A. (2011) *Prison Notebooks*. New York: Columbia University Press.

Greenfeld, L. (1992) *Nationalism: Five Roads to Modernity*. Cambridge: Harvard University Press.

Greenfeld, L. (2001) *The Spirit of Capitalism: Nationalism and Economic Growth*. Cambridge, MA: Harvard University Press.

Greenfeld, L. (2006a) 'Modernity and Nationalism', in G. Delanty and K. Kumar (eds) *The SAGE Handbook of Nations and Nationalism*. London/Thousand Oaks, CA: Sage Publications, pp. 157–168.

Greenfeld, L. (2006b) *Nationalism and the Mind: Essays on Modern Culture*. Oxford: Oneworld.

Greenfeld, L. (2013) *Mind, Modernity, Madness. The Impact of Culture on Human Experience*. Cambridge: Harvard University Press.

Gregor, A. J. (1979) *Italian Fascism and Developmental Dictatorship*. Princeton, NJ: Princeton University Press.

Greider, W. (2000) 'Media and Trade: A Love Story – The "Best and Brightest" Rushed, post-Seattle, to Embrace the Corporate Line', *The Nation*, 271(4): 18.

Griffin, R. (2007) *Modernism and Fascism: The Sense of a Beginning under Mussolini and Hitler*. Basingstoke: Palgrave Macmillan.

Guyot-Réchard, B. (2013) 'Nation-building or State-making? India's North-East Frontier and the Ambiguities of Nehruvian Developmentalism, 1950–1959', *Contemporary South Asia*, 21(1): 22–37.

Head, B. (1985) *Ideology and Social Science: Destutt de Tracy and French Liberalism*. Dordrecht: M. Nijhoff.

Herf, J. (1986) *Reactionary Modernism: Technology, Culture, and Politics in Weimar and the Third Reich*. Cambridge: Cambridge University Press.

Herzfeld, M. (2005) 'Political Optics and the Occlusion of Intimate Knowledge', *American Anthropologist*, 107(3): 369–376.

Higueras, A. (2011) 'Contestation from the Top: Fascism in the Realm of Culture and Italy's Conception of the Past', in H. Silverman (ed.) *Contested Cultural Heritage*. New York: Springer, pp. 193–204.

Hroch, M. and Malecková, J. (2000) 'Nation: A Survey of the Term in European Languages', in A. S. Leoussi (ed.) *Encyclopaedia of Nationalism*. New Brunswick, NJ: Transaction, pp. 203–208.

Hunter, E. (1951) *Brain-washing in Red China*. Galway: MW Books.

Ihrig, S. (2014) *Atatürk in the Nazi Imagination*. Cambridge, MA: The Belknap Press of Harvard University Press.

Junge, K. and Postoutenko, K. (eds) (2011) *Asymmetrical Concepts After Reinhart Koselleck. Historical Semantics and Beyond*. New Brunswick: Transcript Verlag.

Kadirbeyoglu, Z. (2010) 'In the Land of Ostriches: Developmentalism, Environmental Degradation and Forced Migration in Turkey', in T. Afifi and J. Jäger (eds) *Environment, Forced Migration and Social Vulnerability*. Berlin: Springer, pp. 223-.

Kedourie, E. (1993) *Nationalism*. 4th edn. Oxford: Blackwell.

Kennedy, E. (1978) *A Philosophe in the Age of Revolution: Destutt de Tracy and the Origins of 'Ideology'*. Philadelphia: American Philosophical Society.

Kundera, M. (1992) *Immortality (Nesmrtelnost)*. 2nd edn. New York: HarperCollins.

La Branche, S. (2005) 'Abuse and Westernization: Reflections on Strategies of Power', *Journal of Peace Research*, 42(2): 219–235.

Lasch, C. (1991) *The True and Only Heaven. Progress and Its Critics*. New York: W.W. Norton & Co.

Latouche, S. (1996) *The Westernization of the World: The Significance, Scope and Limits of the Drive Towards Global Uniformity*. Cambridge: Polity Press.

Lees, L. (2012) 'The Geography of Gentrification: Thinking through Comparative Urbanism', *Progress in Human Geography*, 36(2): 155–171.

Levene, M. (2008) 'The Vendée: A Paradigm Shift?', in A. Jones (ed.) *Genocide*. London: Sage, pp. 38–55.

Levene, M. (2014) *Devastation. The European Rimlands 1912–1938*. Oxford: Oxford University Press.

Levien, M. (2013) 'Regimes of Dispossession: From Steel Towns to Special Economic Zones', *Development and Change*, 44(2): 381–407.

Lynn, J. A. (1996) *The Bayonets of the Republic: Motivation and Tactics in the Army of Revolutionary France, 1791–94.* Boulder, CO: Westview.

Malešević, S. (2006) 'Nationalism and the Power of Ideology', in G. Delanty and K. Kumar (eds) *The SAGE Handbook of Nations and Nationalism.* London/Thousand Oaks, CA: Sage Publications, pp. 307–319.

Malešević, S. (2013a) 'Is Nationalism Intrinsically Violent?', *Nationalism and Ethnic Politics*, 19(1): 12–37.

Malešević, S. (2013b) *Nation-States and Nationalisms: Organization, Ideology and Solidarity.* Cambridge: Polity Press.

Malešević, S. and Mackenzie, I. M. (eds) (2002) *Ideology after Poststructuralism.* London: Pluto Press in association with SSRC.

Mann, M. (2005) *The Dark Side of Democracy. Explaining Ethnic Cleansing.* Cambridge: Cambridge University Press.

Marx, K. (2007) *Capital: A Critique of Political Economy – The Process of Capitalist Production (vol. 1-Part 1).* New York: Cosimo (edited by Friedrich Engels, 1867).

McCoy, K. (2014) 'Manifesting Destiny: A Land Education Analysis of Settler Colonialism in Jamestown, Virginia, USA', *Environmental Education Research*, 20(1): 82–97.

Murakami, H. (2012) 'Emergence of the Japanese Developmental State: Japanese Management of "Manchukuo" through Special Corporations', *Asian Journal of Political Science*, 20(2): 129–153.

Murray, E. H. (2014) 'Re-evaluating Otherness in Genocidal Ideology', *Nations and Nationalism*, 20(1): 37–55.

Naish, J. (2008) *Enough: Breaking Free from the World of More.* London: Hodder & Stoughton.

Ningthoujam, R. (2013) 'Disturbed Valley: A Case of Protracted Armed Conflict Situation in Northeast India', *Anuario de acción humanitaria y derechos humanos (Yearbook of Humanitarian Action and Human Rights)*, 11, pp. 185–205.

OED (1997) Oxford: Oxford University Press.

Ostergaard, G. (1981) 'Resisting the Nation-state', in L. J. Tivey (ed.) *The Nation-State; The Formation of Modern Politics.* Oxford: Martin Robertson, pp. 171–196.

Ostergaard, G. (1983) *Resisting the Nation State: The Pacifist and Anarchist Tradition.* 2nd edn. London: Peace Pledge Union.

Ozouf, M. (1988) *Festivals and the French Revolution.* Cambridge, MA: Harvard University Press.

Ozouf, M. (1997) 'Liberté, égalité, fraternité', in P. Nora (ed.) *Les Lieux de Mémoire.* 2nd edn. Paris: Editions Gallimard, pp. 4353–4389.

Pasolini, P. P. (1994) *Passione e ideologia.* 5th edn. Milan: Garzanti. [1st edn 1960].

Rist, G. (2002) *The History of Development: From Western Origins to Global Faith.* New rev. and expanded edn. London: Zed Books.

Rosin, C. (2014) 'Engaging the Productivist Ideology through Utopian Politics', *Dialogues in Human Geography*, 4(2): 221–224.

San Martin, P. (2002) 'A Discursive Reading of the Emergence of Asturian Nationalist Ideology', *Journal of Political Ideologies*, 7(1): 97–116.

Saz Campos, I. (2004) 'Fascism, Fascistization and Developmentalism in Franco's Dictatorship', *Social History*, 29(3): 342–357.

Scott, J. C. (1985) *Weapons of the Weak: Everyday Forms of Peasant Resistance.* New Haven: Yale University Press.

Scott, J. C. (1998) *Seeing Like a State: How Certain Schemes to Improve the Human Condition Have Failed.* New Haven: Yale University Press.

Seed, D. (2004) *Brainwashing: The Fictions of Mind Control – A Study of Novels and Films since World War II.* Kent, OH: Kent State University Press.

Simons, J. (2000) 'Ideology, Imagology, and Critical Thought: The Impoverishment of Politics', *Journal of Political Ideologies*, 5(1): 81–103.

Smith, A. D. (1991) *National Identity.* Harmondsworth: Penguin/Reno: University of Nevada Press.

Smith, A. D. (1998) *Nationalism and Modernism: A Critical Survey of Recent Theories of Nations and Nationalism.* London: Routledge.

Smith, A. D. (1999) *Myths and Memories of the Nation.* Oxford: Oxford University Press.

Smith, A. D. (2009) *Ethno-symbolism and Nationalism: A Cultural Approach.* London: Routledge.

Smith, A. D. (2010) *Nationalism: Theory, Ideology, History.* 2nd edn. London: Wiley-Blackwell.

Smith, D. (2006) *Globalization: The Hidden Agenda.* Cambridge: Polity.

Sontag, S. (1989) *AIDS and its Metaphors.* New York: Farrar, Straus and Giroux.

Sontag, S. (2013) *Illness as Metaphor and AIDS and Its Metaphors.* Harmondsworth: Penguin Books.

Steger, M. B. (2002) *Globalism: The New Market Ideology*. Lanham, MD: Rowman & Littlefield.

Taylor, K. (2004) *Brainwashing: The Science of Thought Control*. Oxford: Oxford University Press.

Thompson, J. B. (1990) *Ideology and Modern Culture: Critical Social Theory in the Era of Mass Communication*. Stanford, CA: Stanford University Press.

Tolstoy, L. (1926) *War – Patriotism – Peace*. New York: Vanguard Press/University Press of the Pacific (edited with introduction by Scott Nearing).

Uvin, P. (1998) *Aiding Violence: The Development Enterprise in Rwanda*. West Hartford, CT: Kumarian Press.

Velicu, I. (2012) 'To Sell or Not to Sell: Landscapes of Resistance to Neoliberal Globalization in Transylvania', *Globalizations*, 9(2): 307–321.

Verwimp, P. (2000) 'Development Ideology, the Peasantry and Genocide: Rwanda Represented in Habyarimana's Speeches', *Journal of Genocide Research*, 2(3): 325–361.

Weller, S. (2011) *Modernism and Nihilism*. New York: Palgrave Macmillan.

4

THE NATION-STATE

Civic and ethnic dimensions[1]

Colin Clark

Introduction

Nationalism is not a single beast. There are different varieties of nationalism. It can be well argued that some of the speeches by Conservative members – particularly those who regard themselves as Eurosceptic – are nationalistic. It seems that British nationalism is fine, but any other nationalism – Scottish, Welsh or Irish – is bad. That is not an acceptable distinction. If I were to draw such a distinction, it would be between ethnic nationalism, which is bad and should be rejected wherever it raises its ugly head, and civic nationalism, which is a good and progressive force that can be found all over the world spreading democracy and increasing the rights of ordinary people whatever their ethnic background. It is civic nationalism which is wound up in the Bill – a nationalism that gives the people who live in Scotland, no matter who they are, the same democratic rights as can be expected by people living in any other democratic society.

(*Mr John McAllion, Hansard, 23 Feb. 1998: Column 134*)

On 23 February 1998, during a debate in the House of Commons on the intricacies of the Scotland Bill, the Labour MP for Dundee East, Mr John McAllion, offered the above contribution in response to a suggestion by the Conservative MP for Woodspring, Dr Liam Fox, that certain devolutionary aspects within the Bill could trigger negative forms of 'residual English nationalism' and damage the nature of the Union holding Great Britain together. Of course, Fox's undue concerns were placed to the side and the Scotland Bill soon became an Act. In May 1999 the Scottish Parliament, located in Edinburgh, started up again for business having last met in March 1707. The Scotland Act (1998) devolved all powers to the Edinburgh Parliament except those issues referred to as 'reserved matters' – and, indeed, it was a lengthy list, including constitutional affairs, foreign policy, immigration, and as such the Union was not about to crumble anytime soon. In relation to this chapter on the civic and ethnic dimensions to the nation-state, McAllion's statement at Westminster gives us some indication of the lively, dichotomous debates that can occur when examining the many philosophical, geographical and political territories that nationalism can cover. It is also emblematic of the rather broad and sweeping statements that have been made in the respective names of both civic and ethnic forms of nationalism. We shall see that the reality of this apparent distinction to which McAllion refers – 'good' civic nationalism and 'bad' ethnic nationalism – is much more contested and complex than would first appear. The dichotomy itself needs to be explained and problematized as well as asking questions about whether or not different forms of civic nationalism can in fact be reactionary and, similarly, whether some forms of ethnic nationalism can actually be progressive. In this chapter we will examine this apparent divide and offer some thoughts, analysis and examples to illustrate that the ethnic–civic distinction is indeed less stable and more fragile than appears from a brief examination of the literature within nationalism studies, as well as looking at different views from civil society and other agencies. To begin with we need to set out the parameters of the debate and look closely at what the civic and ethnic dimensions to the nation-state are.

Ethnic and civic nationalisms

> Civic nationalism maintains that the nation should be composed of all those – regardless of race, colour, creed, gender, language or ethnicity – who subscribe to the nation's political creed. This nationalism is called civic because it envisages the nation as a community of equal, rights bearing citizens, united in patriotic attachment to a shared set of political practices and values.
>
> *(Ignatieff 1994: 3–4)*

> There is considerable evidence that modern nations are connected with earlier ethnic categories and communities and are created out of pre-existing origin myths, ethnic cultures and shared memories; and that those nations with a vivid, widespread sense of an ethnic past, are likely to be more unified and distinctive than those which lack that sense.
>
> *(Smith 1996: 385)*

Debates rage on the topic of the 'ethnic' and the 'civic' in nationalist discourses. For Ignatieff (1994) the appeal of civic nationalism is obvious, rejecting as it does any appeal to the 'who and what' of the citizens found within its territory – more important is a common belief in agreed political practices and values. For Smith (1996) this is somewhat illusionary because you cannot escape the fact that the 'ethnic past' is a vital element for even the most 'modern' of nations and indeed those without, or denying, this past will ultimately become undone in denial. But where do these discussions begin? A common starting point for discussing the ethnic-linguistic and civic-political distinction is the work of historians such as Friedrich Meinecke (1970 [1907]) and Hans Kohn (1944). In his influential work, Meinecke made an important distinction between what he termed 'cultural nations' and 'political nations' – the former having common 'cultural heritage' and the latter having a shared 'political history and constitution'. For Kohn (1944), a useful distinction was to be drawn between 'Eastern' and 'Western' nationalisms with the dividing line being the River Rhine. To the West of this river was a kind of nationalism that displayed qualities of being both rationalistic and voluntaristic in nature, whilst to the East was a nationalism that was much more deterministic and organic. Such early work set the tone for more recent debates, many of which still tend to offer generalized caricatures rather than substance and specifics: it is regularly, and lazily, asserted that ethnic nationalism is associated with xenophobic attitudes and exclusionary policies, as well as violence when required, and civic nationalism is associated with highly liberal states who actively encourage the integration of new members with appeals to humanistic and universal values. Is it really this simple?

The distinction is clearly not as straightforward as convention dictates. Whilst accepting this, it is still useful to spend time looking at Kohn's 1944 book *The Idea of Nationalism*. This text has attracted much attention, largely because some of its content still resonates today. Kohn, writing in the context of Nazism and the war, was focused on looking at the origins of national identities and he clearly regards nations as modern entities that emerged around the mid to late eighteenth century. However, in arguing this, he acknowledges that modern nations are a 'product' of historical forces and do come from 'somewhere' and that this past needs to be recognized and paid attention to. In many ways, the work of Kohn has been pivotal in shaping the thinking and direction of many scholars in the field of nationalism studies offering a variety of perspectives, such as Anthony Smith, Ernest Gellner and Benedict Anderson. For example, the place and role of history and the past is important in Smith's 'ethno-symbolist' work, whilst Kohn's ideas of nationalism being ingrained within populations via 'high culture' and mass education systems is familiar to Gellner's body of work. Similarly, Kohn also notes the role of print capitalism in such 'nationalizing' campaigns and also speaks of nationalism being a 'state of mind'; this is somewhat akin to Anderson's later claims to the 'imagined communities' that we all, by necessity, inhabit. In Kohn's framework, nations are something different from the other group identities we all share, such as those governed by family, community, town or religion. Kohn appreciates the ever-changing, non-static nature of nations and the political and socio-economic forces that can often drive such changes and re-drawing of maps, borders and boundaries. However, despite this ebb and flow, Kohn offers some foundations that are usually required to assist in the development of nations, including language, traditions, descent and religion.

In considering the place and direction of German nationalism, Prague-born Kohn established the dichotomy between what could be termed 'Eastern' and 'Western' nationalisms. He looked around Europe at the time of writing and concluded that rather more progressive and favourable forms of nationalism could be identified in the West, when compared to the more reactionary and hostile types witnessed in the East. Drawing on contemporary examples, Kohn suggested that those nationalisms evident in the West were forms that were influenced by ideas of the nation as a grouping or 'association of citizens' who were governed by common laws within a shared, bordered territory. Within its borders, and on its own soil, the civic nation promotes the principle of *jus soli* ('law of the soil') and membership is theoretically open to all, or at least not closed off in any definitive and absolute way. Across in the East, Kohn argued, it appeared that different examples of nationalisms were formed and established on a foundation that much preferred a strong belief in similar ethnic origins and common culture. On this basis, members of the nation were part of something larger than themselves and were part of the nation for life, even if moving across shores and residing in other territories. In the case of the East then, it was argued that citizenship was given by birth, through descent and blood, and fixed via the principle of *jus sanguinis* ('right of blood') rather than *jus soli*. It has been argued by Smith (2001), that the source of this contrast is largely concerned with class dynamics – that is, in the East, due to the rule of autocrats and landowners, organic and authoritarian forms of nationalism developed whilst in the West, due to an assertive (some would say ruthless) bourgeoisie class, civic enterprise and mass citizen-nations were promoted.

It goes without saying that, like much work in the social sciences, Kohn's framework is rather static and one-dimensional in character. The rigid dichotomy between East and West does present somewhat essentialized and reified ideas of nationalism, identity and culture and as such has been subject to criticism, especially when considering the nature and extent of any such distinction between East and West as well as specific examples that challenge the divide (such as the Czech lands and Ireland, to name but two cases in point). Indeed, Smith (1991: 11) informs us that it is 'historic territory, legal-political community, legal-political equality of members, and common civic culture and ideology' that give us the building blocks of the 'Western' *model* of the nation; but are such aspects, to some degree, not also evident in certain 'Eastern' *realities*? If nothing else, we can see here the issue in comparing and contrasting 'models' with 'real life': clear boundaries and borders tend to collapse when shifting between the two worlds, depending on the examples being drawn upon and the time period being consulted. Indeed, with the time/place context very much placed in the foreground, Shulman (2002) sought to show the inherent weaknesses in those common arguments that suggest that civic nationalism is dominant in Western Europe and North America, whilst ethnic nationalism is somehow the preserve of Central and Eastern Europe. Shulman argues that state policies, in practice, tend to flow from a combination of civic, ethnic and cultural conceptions of national identity and he gives us various explanations for finding strong cultural national identities in the West as well as strong civic national identities in the East. To support his contention, Shulman analyses a range of survey data from some 15 countries to get a sense of what such measurements can tell us about 'common' thinking and practices with regards to national identity. This is done by assessing attitudes on issues such as state policies towards assimilation and immigration as well as the various criteria adopted for granting national membership. Shulman, in presenting and analysing the survey data, argues that on the basis of this data the 'civic-as-West' and 'ethnic-as-East' dichotomy on many measures is false and on other measures is only 'weakly true'.

However, before consigning Kohn's classic work to a dusty shelf we should note that some (normative) elements of Kohn hold good and are worthy of retaining, not least the notion (at least in theory) of 'choice' – that is, within the civic engagement, we can *choose*, to some degree, where we belong, whereas in the ethnic model we are born into a nation and even though we may decide to leave (to begin a new life on another continent) we are forever attached to our place of birth. And Kohn is not alone, obviously, in attempting to draw up such typologies, and one can find in other work notions of what might be termed 'continuous' (Seton-Watson 1965) and 'created' (Tilly 1995) nations as well as broader separations between nationalisms based on ethnicity and those based on territory. However, what is important to bear in mind here is that these typologies and models are exactly that – typologies and models. The truth of the (practical, geographical) matter is that nationalisms change shape and identity over time and place and, indeed, in most cases, will incorporate aspects of *both* the civic and ethnic. So the question remains: is the distinction between the two types of nationalism worth anything more than a theoretical exercise on paper or can it have analytical purchase as Kohn hoped it would?

This is a question that hangs and has many answers. It is unfortunate that crude distinctions still abound, where civic nationalism – especially when combined with hearty doses of liberalism – is regarded as being (almost) a step in the right direction and deserving of space, whilst varieties of ethnic nationalism – especially in the context of events in the Balkans and other territories in the 1990s and 2000s – are widely regarded as being outside mainstream democratic discourse and consideration. Indeed, if we look to the work of political philosopher David Miller (1995) we can see that his concept of the nation revolves around a set of preferences that specifically and intentionally avoid mention of genealogies and ethno-linguistic heritage and practices. Instead, public culture, residence and history come to the foreground, excluding any 'dangerous' aspects that rely on 'blood and belonging' – ideas of descent. Even so, as Orwell (1953 [1945]) powerfully argued, it does seem that nationalism, whatever its key ingredients, must *always* have the potential to produce exclusionary policies that are driven by latent xenophobic sentiments and tendencies. One of the most obvious examples of this has been the plight of minority groups such as Jews and Roma, whose treatment over many years, across different areas of Europe and beyond, has shown in explicit detail that even those nations with strongly developed civic nationalist states – such as France or England – can spectacularly fail to support minority group rights and offer appropriate protection (Smith 1994). It is evident then that although ethnic nationalism is characterized as exclusionary, reactionary, 'bad', it is also the case that examples of civic nationalism can also struggle and fail when it comes to hearing the claims of different cultures within its borders. A genuine and meaningful multiculturalism, if nothing else, demands for a 'plural nation' that is not content to stop at merely 'celebrating diversity', but goes further than this to specifically include the many cultures that are represented within its borders: to weave and embed myriad cultures into the fabric of the nation state and the governing bodies and institutions that claim to speak in its name (Parekh 2005). As an example of this, but not without its controversy, is the United States of America. Built up via historical processes of conquest, slavery, civil war, migration and immigration, America has become, when compared to other nations, a relatively plural and polyethnic nation and yet it is also a nation that is bound together by common laws, languages and allegiances, not to mention the everyday celebrations of flag and constitution. This does not change the fact, however, that the (very relative) unity we see today is the product of earlier brutality and oppression – a point made famous by Renan in his essay *Qu'est-ce qu'une nation?* back in 1882 (Renan 1994 [1882]: 17–18). Indeed, America is often upheld in the literature as something of an 'ideal' civic nation and yet like many other countries, such as France and England, it consciously, for many years, withheld civic status to various groups of people, not least women, Native Americans and Black slaves.

A key idea then is that civic nationalism offers the possibility to all people that they can be citizens of the nation. If we look at the examples of France and England at different time periods this idea seems problematic. For example, at the time of the French Revolution – often viewed as the dramatic and bloody beginnings of civic nationalism – we can see that conditions were attached to who could, or might, be a citizen, especially when gender entered the equation. Certainly, it is noteworthy that women only gained the right to vote in France in 1945 so it took a long time to reformulate the notion of 'universal citizenship' to ensure this wasn't just about male citizens. Similarly, if we turn to England, and draw on the work of Liah Greenfeld (1992), we can see that for Greenfeld the civic–ethnic contrast or dichotomy is fundamentally related to the differences between individualism and collectivism and she goes on to argue that during the fifteenth and sixteenth centuries, due to major socio-economic structural changes, the word 'nation' in England adopted new meanings. However, despite the promises and possibilities within the civic–individualist framework for all to be members of the nation, the reality in England meant that many sections of the population, for historical and contemporary reasons, were routinely ignored from the benefits and rights of civic membership, such as women, Catholics and the poor. The issue here, in a sense, is to illustrate the fact that the 'rules' of the civic conception of nationhood have been 'broken' from almost the very beginning and the exception soon becomes the norm. We need to acknowledge, of course, the dangers of applying present day standards to the past, but the concern is that such exclusions are not just confined to the vaults of history: we continue to witness the operation of exclusionary politics in both East and West that seeks to deny citizenship to those considered to be on the 'outside' (of the civic nation) looking in. You only need to think of the problems faced by refugees, migrants and asylum-seekers in trying to gain entry to many different nations to get a perspective on the seriousness of this issue. Indeed, the recent work of Vicki Squire confirms this point by critically examining the debates over asylum in recent years and she shows us how far asylum has been characterized as a matter of asylum-seekers ('them') being a socio-economic and political 'problem' and a 'threat' to 'host' states ('us'). Looking across the UK and the European Union in particular, Squire argues that various neo-liberal responses to the asylum process has been chiefly driven by concerns over securitization, criminalization and economics rather than any adherence to international conventions or laws. When examined in their historical and political context, this is not a surprise and asylum-seekers are routinely rendered as scapegoats for the dislocations that are produced as a result of broader shifts in globalized thinking on the nation state. To escape this manner of exclusionary politics, Squire argues for a radical change of direction in how states conceive and respond to asylum as well as identity and citizenship more broadly (Squire 2009).

In all of this, it does seem to be the case that despite the apparent contrasts and differences between the ethnic-linguistic and civic-political nationalisms on display, there is a particular 'closeness' between the actual *policies* that emerge out of such manifestations. In a sense, for analytical precision and depth, it is perhaps better to think of nationalism as a whole rather than trying to create 'civic/ethnic', 'political/cultural' or 'good/bad' distinctions that might be helpful at a general hypothetical level, but are rendered problematic when applied to 'real-world' examples and situations. Indeed, it is important to remember that this distinction is merely a normative and analytical one: it cannot account for specific nationalisms and it cannot account for potential trajectories of any 'nationalism-at-large'. It seems clear, whether reading the work of Anthony Smith (1998) or Eric Hobsbawm (1992), that even those nationalisms claiming to be 'the most' civic and political ('Western') are, in reality, very often guided, forged and influenced in their development via the ethnic and linguistic. The example of France alone illustrates this point, both during and after the Revolution. The same is true for those nationalisms that seem, at first glance, to be virulent strains of the 'ethnic': for example, John Breuilly (1993) has shown that in the case of German nationalism around the 1850s, many speeches and debates in Parliament illustrated both civic and territorial aspects in addition to the 'ethnic' ones on display (and Germany is often presented in the literature as an atypical model of the 'ethnic'). You can see today, all around Europe, examples of the relatively harmonious fusion and merging of the ethnic and civic, whether in Scotland, Switzerland or the Czech and Slovak lands. Of course, we can also witness the opposite, especially if we cast our gaze to Israel or India. In essence, tracing a clear pattern of historical development using such dichotomous concepts is inherently problematic.

It is worth looking at the critiques of the ethnic/civic distinction a little more to fully understand these discourses. Indeed, as has been noted by Spencer and Wollman (2002), the distinction between ethnic and civic forms of nationalism is problematic in many ways. At a 'deep' philosophical level, the actual separation of the two is not without concern. Is it not the case, for example, that all nations are, at a fundamental level, 'ethnic' nations? Each nation will claim their uniqueness and their borders and boundaries and in so doing will be excluding of those who are not considered members of that particular nation ('aliens' or 'others'). If we follow the work of Brubaker (1998), for example, we can see how it often depends on how narrow or broad we stitch 'culture' onto the distinction that is suggested operates between the ethnic and the civic. Ethnic nationalism can place emphasis on the importance on descent and heritage, and by doing so, can be restrictive. This narrowness of interpretation can mean that there are few examples of ethnic nationalism in existence as such a framework means that any emphasis on 'common culture' has to be defined as an example of civic nationalism. From the other side, if ethnic nationalism is classified in a broader ethnocultural sense, and conversely civic nationalism is interpreted narrowly as displaying acultural notions of citizenship, then the problem is reversed – all nationalisms would be defined as ethnic/cultural and the civic conception would be rendered almost meaningless. You can see here the power of questioning the intellectual distinction between ethnic-linguistic and civic-political and, further, Kohn's (1944) Western and Eastern division is challenged. In this kind of framework, even the prime examples of civic nationalism – America, England, France etc. – would be reclassified, as they obviously contain cultural aspects to their nationalisms (Özkirimli 2005).

Is the civic 'model' the one to aspire to then? If we look to the work of Gans (2003) it can be observed that the idea of civic nationalism, as a political entity that is voluntary and is ethnically 'colour-blind' (both literally and metaphorically), is in fact a fallacy that does not hold true. Gans argues that adherence to shared ideas cannot be seen as any kind of nationalism, unless drawing upon vague and abstract notions of 'common culture'. That is, civic nationalism in any kind of 'pure' form does not actually exist, given historical developments and philosophical definitions of what constitutes nations. Similarly, Brown (2000) argues that the ethnic/civic question is, for most people, a mute one – given that the majority of the population in so-called civic nations have no choice in their national identity as they acquire citizenship by birth. Further, gaining entry to other 'civic' nations may be as limited as in the case of 'ethnic' nations (for example, witness the visa/legal problems faced by someone trying to permanently move from France to America, especially for reasons *other* than work or marriage). So, civic nations, like ethnic nations, can be equally demanding in terms of allegiances to 'blood and soil', and can also take measures to resist voluntary renunciations of national identity and citizenship. This point is made very well by Muro and Quiroga (2005) who look at the example of Spanish nationalism, a geography that provides fertile ground for examining the interplay between the ethnic and civic. They argue that when considered historically, Spanish nationalism has had at least two recognizable 'versions' – a 'liberal' incarnation and a 'conservative-traditionalist' project. This was especially the case during the nineteenth century. However, in turning to the twentieth century, Muro and Quiroga suggest that although these two ideological projects cemented themselves into party-politics, the Basque and Catalan nationalist movements caused a shift in thinking and helped, to an extent, unify Spanish nationalists to defend '*Reino de España*' ('the Kingdom of Spain') against these new regional sources of separatist identity politics. In the present context, they suggest, Spanish nationalism is a struggle between centre and periphery with appeals to 'civic' status and nationhood used to compete with regionalist forces.

Another criticism of the ethnic and civic distinction is the 'normative project' (Smith 1996) that can shadow and follow the debate, leading to the airing of moral favouritism, prejudice and bias. For example, McCrone (1998: 7) discusses the 'great fault-lines' of Eastern and Western thinking on nationalism and notes that even going back to Kohn's work, we can recognize the thinly disguised idea that Western (political) forms of nationalism – the kinds that produced 'citizens' – are somehow superior or 'better' than Eastern (ethnic and cultural) forms of nationalism which simply produce 'the folk'. McCrone (1998: 9) concedes that whilst commentators such as Gellner (1994), in his work on the time-zones of Europe, and Brubaker (1992), in his work on French and German models of nationalism, have put the civic/ethnic distinction to good academic use, he still suggests that ultimately the distinction 'does lend itself to Eurocentric caricature – why can't *they* be more like *us*?'. This is certainly a theme that is apparent in some of the literature on the ethnic/civic distinction, and moral judgements do not seem to be too far from the surface. Consider the work of Plamenatz (1976) who as recently as the mid-1970s spoke of an Eastern kind of (ethnic) nationalism as being 'backward', 'imitative' and 'illiberal' whilst the Western (civic) variety is upheld as one that is 'culturally better equipped' for ensuring 'success and excellence'. Challenging such static and reified ideas is the more recent work of Stefan Auer (2004). In an interview for Radio Prague (Vaughan 2005) about his book *Liberal Nationalism in Central Europe*, Auer captures this theme vividly and his last sentence is especially important I would suggest:

> the book is partly a response to a number of scholarly studies that were written immediately after the collapse of communism, that argued or suggested that the process of post-communist transition will be hampered or undermined by the forces of nationalism. So what happened in Yugoslavia was seen as epitomizing the problems of Eastern Europe. It was argued that the nations of Eastern Europe were more inclined to adopt this kind of xenophobic form of nationalism … There is a vast body of literature that differentiates between 'civic nationalism' and 'ethnic nationalism'. Civic nationalism is seen as a kind of progressive force that fits into the project of liberal democracy and is characteristic of Western nations like Britain and France. Opposed to it is usually a concept of ethnic nationalism that, so it was argued, was characteristic of Eastern Europe. I thought that that sort of schematic division of Europe was unhelpful in understanding what was going on in Central and Eastern Europe. In fact, it's quite unhelpful in understanding what's going on in Western Europe.
>
> *(Vaughan 2005)*

So what are we left with here? Has the ethnic/civic distinction – such a 'keeper' within the field of nationalism studies – lost all of its contemporary analytical purchase? In an increasingly global world is it now somehow less important, given that nation-states have, it is argued, given way to cosmopolitan cities and new transnational realities? As has been suggested above, there is perhaps some scope for continuing to employ the distinction as a Weberian 'ideal-type' model and focus more on the advantages this approach can give us and focus less on using the dichotomy when it comes to 'real world' scenarios. Or, perhaps, a better approach is to recognize that the distinction between civic and ethnic is now redundant and actually creates more problems than it could ever solve – and in its place alternatives should be fostered and employed. This is where we can return to Brubaker (1998) who has helpfully suggested a 'state-formed' and 'counter-state' dichotomy for (better?) understanding different types of nationalism. In using the term 'state-formed', Brubaker is arguing that the terms 'nation' and 'state' are in accordance, both in terms of territory and institutions. By 'counter-state', he is talking about the exact opposite – where 'nation' is *opposed* to the territorial and institutional framing of the currently positioned state. As Brubaker argues (1998: 300–301) in explaining each new distinction, there is nothing necessarily 'civic' about state-formed nationalism and likewise counter-state nationalism need not be 'ethnic'. What is important here is that the *state* is the frame of reference, not the *nation*. These conceptions of nationalism can incorporate ethnic and cultural aspects of nationhood as well as paying heed to the importance of territory and individual political histories. So, counter-state nationalisms can have 'civic' qualities whilst 'state-formed' nationalisms can have 'ethnic' components and roots. However, is this distinction any more relevant and useful than the 'Eastern' and 'Western' options presented by Kohn back in 1944?

Conclusion

It is worth noting, in closing this brief chapter, that even though the distinction between civic and ethnic nationalisms has been largely agreed as problematic, and of limited value beyond a kind of 'ideal type' model-making, it continues to be a source of much scholarly angst and debate. Indeed, if commentators are not arguing about the origins and/or endings of nationalism, then it is usually the civic/ethnic distinction – and other such dichotomies – that spill forth and hold attention. An example of this was the 18th Annual meeting of the Association for the Study of Ethnicity and Nationalism (ASEN) at the London School of Economics, London, during April 2008. Including speakers such as Oliver Zimmer, Paul Gilroy and Bhikhu Parekh, the conference was concerned with the topic of ethnic and civic conceptions of nationhood and the conference promotional material suggested that:

> It has long been standard in the field of nationalism studies to classify nations according to which principle serves to unify the nation. The distinction between the Western, political type of nationalism, and Eastern, genealogical nationalism as systematized by Hans Kohn in 1945 has been used, extended and adjusted by scholars of nationalism to conceptualise a framework of 'inclusive' nationalism based on citizenship and territory and 'exclusive' nationalism based on common ethnic ties and descent. This conference seeks to assess the continuing relevance of this dichotomy in its various forms: its contribution to theoretical work on nationalism, its usefulness for historical interpretation and its value for contemporary policy-making.
>
> *(ASEN 2008)*

Although clearly written to attract papers and general interest, the framing of the conference is nonetheless interesting and reflects the continued 'hardness' and rigidity of thinking on this dichotomy. It has been shown in this chapter, by drawing on some of the thinking of key scholars in the field, that the civic/ethnic distinction is an extension or a new way of thinking about the political/cultural distinction, and in the field of nationalism studies such dichotomies are going to be around, just like nation-states, for a long time yet.

Note

1 This chapter could not have been written without the assistance of Elizabeth R. Lambert who has taught me all I know about the fluidity of transatlantic borders and the enduring nature of nation-states.

Further reading

Brubaker, R. (2004) *Ethnicity without Groups*, Cambridge, MA: Harvard University Press.
Greenfeld, L. (2002) *Nationalism: Five Roads to Modernity*, Cambridge: Cambridge University Press.
Kohn, H. (1944) *The Idea of Nationalism: A Study of its Origins and Background*, New York: Macmillan.
Miller, D. (1995) *On Nationality*, Oxford: Oxford University Press.
Smith, A. (1998) *Nationalism and Modernism*, London: Routledge.

References

ASEN (2008) *Nationalism, East and West: Civic and Ethnic Conceptions of Nationhood*, Annual Conference announcement and call for papers, London School of Economics, London. Available online at: http://www.lse.ac.uk/collections/ASEN/conference_08.html (Accessed 18 June 2009).
Auer, S. (2004) *Liberal Nationalism in Central Europe*, London: Routledge.
Breuilly, J. (1993) *Nationalism and the State*, Manchester: Manchester University Press, 2nd edn.
Brown, D. (2000) *Contemporary Nationalism: Civic, Ethnocultural and Multicultural Politics*, London: Routledge.

Brubaker, R. (1992) *Citizenship and Nationhood in France and Germany*, Cambridge, MA: Harvard University Press.

Brubaker, R. (1998) 'Myths and Misconceptions in the Study of Nationalism', in J. Hall (ed.) *The State of the Nation: Ernest Gellner and the Theory of Nationalism*, Cambridge: Cambridge University Press.

Gans, C. (2003) *The Limits of Nationalism*, Cambridge: Cambridge University Press.

Gellner, E. (1994) *Encounters with Nationalism*, Oxford: Blackwell.

Greenfeld, L. (1992) *Nationalism: Five Roads to Modernity*, Cambridge: Cambridge University Press.

Hobsbawm, E. (1992) *Nations and Nationalism since 1780: Programme, Myth, Reality*, Cambridge: Cambridge University Press, 2nd edn.

Ignatieff, M. (1994) *Blood and Belonging: Journeys into the New Nationalism*, London: Vintage.

Kohn, H. (1944) *The Idea of Nationalism: A Study of its Origins and Background*, New York: Macmillan.

McAllion, J. (1998) Speech in the House of Commons on the Scotland Bill (1998), 23 February 1998, Column 134. Hansard. Available online at: http://www.publications.parliament.uk/pa/cm199798/cm hansrd/vo980223/debtext/80223-39.htm#80223-39_spnew2 (Accessed 11 July 2009).

McCrone, D. (1998) *The Sociology of Nationalism*, London: Routledge.

Meinecke, F. (1970) [1907] *Cosmopolitanism and the National State*, Princeton: Princeton University Press.

Miller, D. (1995) *On Nationality*, Oxford: Oxford University Press.

Muro, D. and Quiroga, A. (2005) 'Spanish Nationalism: Ethnic or Civic?', *Ethnicities*, 5(1): 9–29.

Orwell, G. (1953) [1945] 'Notes on Nationalism', *England, your England and other Essays*, London: Secker and Warburg.

Özkirimli, U. (2005) *Contemporary Debates on Nationalism: A Critical Engagement*, Basingstoke: Palgrave Macmillan.

Parekh, B. (2005) *Rethinking Multiculturalism: Cultural Diversity and Political Theory*, Basingstoke: Palgrave Macmillan, 2nd edn.

Plamenatz, J. (1976) 'Two Types of Nationalism', in E. Kamenka (ed.) *Nationalism: The Nature and Evolution of an Idea*, Canberra: Australian National University Press.

Renan, E. (1994) [1882] 'Qu'est-ce qu'une nation?' in J. Hutchinson and A. D. Smith (eds) *Nationalism*, Oxford: Oxford University Press.

Seton-Watson, H. (1965) *Nationalism Old and New*, London: Methuen.

Shulman, S. (2002) 'Challenging the Civic/Ethnic and West/East Dichotomies in the Study of Nationalism', *Comparative and Political Studies*, 35(5): 554–585.

Smith, A. D. (1991) *National Identity*, London: Penguin.

Smith, A. D. (1994) 'Ethnic Nationalism and the Plight of Minorities', *Journal of Refugee Studies*, 7(2/3): 186–198.

Smith, A. D. (1996) 'Opening Statement: Nations and their Past', *Nations and Nationalism*, 2(3): 358–365.

Smith, A. D. (1998) *Nationalism and Modernism*, London: Routledge.

Smith, A. D. (2001) *Nationalism*, Cambridge: Polity Press.

Spencer, P. and Wollman, H. (2002) *Nationalism: A Critical Introduction*, London: Sage.

Squire, V. (2009) *The Exclusionary Politics of Asylum*, Basingstoke: Palgrave Macmillan.

Tilly, C. (1995) *European Revolutions, 1492–1992*, Oxford: Wiley-Blackwell.

Vaughan, D. (2005) 'Can Nationalism in Central Europe Be a Force for Good? – An Interview with Dr Stefan Auer', *Radio Prague*, 23 October 2005. Available online at: http://www.radio.cz/en/print/article/71970 (Accessed 12 August 2009).

5

STATELESS NATIONS

Stéphanie Chouinard

Introduction: stateless nations in a world (and a discipline) governed by nation-states

The world population is composed of a yet-to-be-known number of groups sharing historical, religious, linguistic, and/or cultural affiliations. Some of these groups have won the historical lottery of the Westphalian system, in a sense, by inheriting the power to govern their own nation-state, which means that one national group has succeeded in consolidating its state on a given territory. This nation-state model, a creation of early modern Europe, postulates that the nation is the sovereign of the state. It has become the ideal-type through which Western academics look at the world political order. The very fact that our international organization is called the United *Nations* (as opposed to the United *States*) is a strong tribute to what has now become a tradition of conflating the notions of 'nation' and 'state'. This tradition is present in modern classics of state-building theory, such as the works of Gellner (1989) and Anderson (1983). It also became the prism through which the level of modernity of a certain region of the world has been evaluated. A state that suffered from nationalist conflict was considered to be a state that had not yet gone through the entire process of modernization – an incomplete evolution of sorts. In the 1990s, Eric Hobsbawm wrote that the nation 'is a social entity only insofar as it relates to a certain kind of modern territorial state, the nation-state, and it is pointless to discuss nation and state except insofar as both relate to it' (1992, cited in Keating and McGarry 2001: 1).

Some other nations, however, have not been so lucky as to inherit a sovereign political entity. Stateless nations, also known as national minorities, are as their name suggests nations that lack their own state. They pose one of the greatest challenges to contemporary political science, as they refute the ideal-type that is the nation-state upon which our entire international system relies. Even the very place where the equation of nation and state was said to have first taken form in European history, France, is home to a handful of national minorities who have made various claims for self-determination, such as the Basque, the Corsican, and the Breton.

Governments have taken various positions towards stateless nations throughout history, often aiming to rid their territory of those minorities, using different coercive, and sometimes violent, measures.

Some minorities were physically eliminated, either by mass expulsion [...] or by genocide. Other minorities were coercively assimilated, forced to adopt the language, religion, and customs of the majority. In yet other cases, minorities were treated as resident aliens, subjected to physical segregation and economic discrimination, and denied political rights.

(Kymlicka 1996: 2)

However, despite these efforts to create culturally homogeneous states, there remain many more nations or national minorities in the world today than there are states. The United Nations now represents 193 states, with South Sudan being the latest admitted member in 2011 following its successful secession from Sudan that same year, while the number of nations in the world is estimated to be between 3,000 and 6,000 (Nimni 2011: 55). Moreover, very few of those UN member states (fewer than 20) are considered to be ethnically homogeneous. Stateless nations appear, in this light, to be more the norm than the exception in a world that insists on using the nation–state model as an ideal-type to be achieved. As Alfred Cobban writes, in his book on the nation–state and national self-determination, 'one of the difficulties of the history of ideas is that names are more permanent than things. Institutions change, but the terms used to describe them remain the same' (1969: 23).

Stateless nations may take different shapes or forms, which is reflected in the fact that, still to this day, there is no decisive definition of a stateless nation, or even of a national minority. For each criterion regarding shared culture, language, religion, or territory that could be brought forward as part of a definition, an exception may be found. This makes for a very fuzzy set of qualities to look for in order to determine whether a group belongs to this category. Moreover, these criteria are not fixed in time and may change over the course of history, as well as the claims a group may make about them.

Stateless nations may also be found in different territorial patterns. When their population is contained on a defined territory within a single nation-state where they constitute a minority, such as the Québécois within Canada (Gagnon, Guibernau and Rocher 2003), or the Welsh within the United Kingdom, they are qualified as 'internal' nations. What we call 'dispersed' nations, on the other hand, are nations whose population is scattered across a number of states, such as the Kurds, who are found in a number of countries including Turkey (where they constitute the largest minority), Iran, Iraq, and Syria (Updegraff 2012). Finally, there are national minorities that we call 'border' minorities, whose population is found on the border of the country adjacent to their homeland. An example of this would be the German minority in Denmark and the Danish minority of Germany, respectively in the North and South Schleswig regions (Schaefer-Rolffs and Schnapp 2014).

But what truly distinguishes stateless nations from other types of minorities, such as ethnic minorities, is their claim for self-determination. One of the traditional claims of stateless nations takes 'the form of increased autonomy for the nation, most often expressed as a desire for constitutional change' (Thomsen 2010: 3). At the extreme end of the spectrum of claims for autonomy, we find claims for independence or secession from the broader nation-state in which they partake. Indeed, the term 'stateless' itself seems to imply that these nations *should* also have a state of their own. According to Gallagher Cunningham, 'there are currently over one hundred stateless nations pressing for greater self-determination around the globe. The vast majority of these groups are unlikely to achieve independence' (2014: 2). One exception to this is the Roma, who are a quintessential 'dispersed' minority. They have no claim to a certain territory or homeland as they are traditionally nomadic, a custom for which they have been targeted during the Holocaust and have been persecuted in various countries for decades. Their lack of permanent abode has also caused them to be left mostly legally unprotected and particularly prone to discrimination (Gilbert 2014).

The nation-state model has also been challenged significantly in the last decades. A number of world events have participated to this, such as the 'authoritarian interlude from the 1920s to the end of World War II' (Safran 2000a: 1) in Europe, which shed a dark light on majoritarian nationalism, and the resurgence of ethnic nationalism in the Balkans following the collapse of the Soviet Union. The last decades have also witnessed an increase in the migration of individuals between countries. This migration is sometimes voluntary, as individuals are seeking better economic opportunities than the ones they can find in their homeland. This is a symptom of what we commonly call 'globalization', which is marked by 'a process of global economic integration, with increased mobility in capital, goods, and services, and to a lesser extent, labour' (Keating and McGarry 2001: 3). The relatively newly established Turkish community in Germany is a good example of that kind of population movement. However, some of this migration is the result of political conflict, as individuals sometimes have to flee in order to avoid persecution. They then become refugees. Another side of globalization further participates in the weakening of the nation-state model, through the creation of numerous supra-state (international or regional) organizations that undermine the power of the nation-states, most oftentimes, ironically, with their own consent. One example of this would be the European Union. These populations do not typically create new stateless nations nor make demands similar to stateless nations. Their increased presence in states where they do not partake in the majority culture, however, contributes to unveil the fact that today, most countries in the world do not correspond to the model of a mono-national state, and that the idea of an ideal-typical nation-state is fallacious. Yet, the biggest challenge to the nation-state model, and the international order more largely, is still considered to be stateless nations and their demands for greater recognition and self-determination, as they question the very integrity of the existing nation-states and the legitimacy of their respective governments.

Some stateless nations do indeed succeed in gaining full self-determination, sometimes after episodes of violence; such was the case of South Sudan in 2011. Others fail, sometimes repeatedly, as we were reminded by Scotland's referendum seeking complete sovereignty from the United Kingdom in October 2014, or Québec's 1980 and 1995 referendums. The international community also has an interest in protecting the territorial integrity of the existing states; they have so seldom recognized the peoples' right to self-determination that legal theorists are wondering whether this right is but a 'legal fiction' (Lapidoth 1997: 22). The creation of new states also tends to repeat the majority/minority pattern, as the newly created state is often home to a minority. Such is the case of the Albanian minority in Montenegro, which claimed its independence from Serbia in 2006 (Milacic 2012: 365). Moreover, some nuance regarding the claims of stateless nations to self-determination is necessary. It was traditionally assumed that these claims *always* involved seeking a separate state, a posture that provoked both confrontation on behalf of nationalist movements and repression. This assumption has however been revisited, and 'it is now recognized that statehood is only one possible outcome of the national claim and that there are many other constitutional formulas that can accommodate it' (Keating 2012: 10). As Keating (2012: 15) observes, 'a doctrine of self-determination as the right to negotiate one's position within the state and international order rather than as limited to secession' may altogether be more helpful and more readily accepted by the international community and its member states.

Legal protections for stateless nations: a step in the right direction, but often insufficient

In order to resolve the challenge of stateless nations, and minorities more generally, a number of options have been considered. Mechanisms of legal recognition and protection have been implemented, especially at the supra-national and international levels. In 1991, the Conference on Security and Co-operation in Europe adopted a *Declaration on the Rights of National Minorities*. In 1992, the United Nations (UN) adopted unanimously the *Declaration on the Rights of Persons Belonging to National or Ethnic, Religious and Linguistic Minorities*, which states that member states of the UN must protect their minorities, protect and promote their cultures, languages, and religions, and ensure the minorities' participation in the political and economic life of the state. The Declaration also protects the minorities' basic human rights as well as rights of association. In 1994, the Council of Europe adopted the *European Framework Convention for the Protection of National Minorities*. In 2001, the *UNESCO Universal Declaration on Cultural Diversity* reinforced the nation-states' duty to protect minorities. However, these declarations on behalf of the international community have often proven to fall short of the protection needed by national minorities. Some member states of these supranational or international organizations have refused to sign or ratify those treaties. The treaties' wording is also notoriously vague; the *Declaration on the Rights of National Minorities*, for example, does not offer a definition of 'national minority', which means it is up to each ratifying state to apply the treaty as it sees fit. Some nation-states, despite ratifying these declarations, have continued to answer inadequately to their duties (Roy 2006: 9). Lack of proper state action has sometimes resulted in political violence and revived demands for secession on behalf of the national minorities, creating a 'cycle' entailing 'both attempts at accommodation' and 'repression' of groups demanding self-determination (Gallagher Cunningham 2014: 3). This challenge has become a fascinating puzzle for political theorists eager to find methods to properly accommodate the demands of groups without undermining state integrity. A number of types of accommodations and state policies have been created and implemented in order to manage nationalist conflicts, whether violent or peaceful. These mechanisms usually involve the granting of different levels of recognition. Yet, as Gagnon *et al.* remark, 'few methods are adequate to the task of accommodating [stateless nations'] demands for both recognition and autonomy' (Gagnon, Guibernau and Rocher 2003: vi).

Accommodating stateless nations: recognition and autonomy

One of the formulas for accommodating cultural diversity brought forward by political scientists is multiculturalism. Multiculturalism, as its name suggests, allows for the recognition of a multitude of cultures within a state, sometimes supported by state policies to maintain diversity. However, multiculturalism has proven to fall short of fulfilling the demands of stateless nations. 'However generous the impulses that animate it, multiculturalism cannot respond to [stateless nations, such as] internal nations. Indeed, it is quite inimical to them' (Gagnon, Guibernau and Rocher 2003: vii). One of the reasons is that multiculturalism brings all cultures on an equal footing, therefore undermining the claims of stateless nations. This caveat has become evident in Canada shortly following the adoption by the federal government of such a policy in 1970. As Kymlicka explains, 'French Canadians have opposed the "multiculturalism" policy because they think it reduces their claims of nationhood to the level of immigrant ethnicity' (1996: 17), a sentiment that appears to be shared by other stateless nations.

Another common mechanism of accommodation of diversity is consociationalism, which is a form of power sharing used in 'fragmented but stable democracies'; it was first discussed in academic literature by Arend Lijphart (1969: 211). Consociationalist democracies function on the premise that the elites of each subculture present within a single state will work towards achieving stability through bargaining, oftentimes through the use of a 'grand coalition' cabinet where all subcultures are represented. However, this option also falls short of the self-determination usually requested by stateless nations.

Finally, decentralization of certain state powers or structures, in which the jurisdiction of a state on a field of intervention is delegated, is another option aimed at recognizing the internal diversity of a state, so that those structures can adapt to the cultural, linguistic, and/or religious particularities of stateless nations. However, those powers are not delegated directly to the minorities.

Not only have these first three types of accommodations (multiculturalism, consociationalism, decentralization) proven to be insufficient to respond adequately to stateless nations' demands but they have also failed to address the plea of stateless minorities that happen to spread over more than one state. This is why we will now turn to mechanisms of accommodation for stateless nations, which can all fall under the philosophical underpinning called 'post-sovereignty'. 'Like other post- concepts, this does not suggest that sovereignty has disappeared, rather that it has been transformed and is no longer the dominant mode of political organization' (Keating 2012: 11). Unlike the classical view of state sovereignty, which is seen as indivisible, post-sovereignty allows for competing conceptions of sovereignty to coexist through 'constitutional pluralism'. Constitutional pluralism, according to Keating, does not require that the different parties agree on the ontological foundations of the constitution or on a specific endpoint to negotiations, but that they agree on the procedures of these negotiations and on the division of powers within the constitution. Moreover, '[i]t also requires a shared commitment to constitutionalism, that is to working within institutions, proceeding according to democratic principles and not unilaterally changing the rules' (Keating 2012: 14).

From this normative view of a state's constitution flow procedures or mechanisms that offer different degrees of autonomy for different national groups, while preserving the integrity of the statehood.

Autonomy: theory and practice

Taken in the etymological sense, autonomy refers to the Latin words '*auto*' and '*nomos*', or the power to adopt one's 'own' 'norms' or 'rules' (Lapidoth 1997: 29). It is quite a 'slippery' concept within the realm of social sciences, which is its strength as much as its weakness. This is discussed by Ruth Lapidoth (1997: 29): 'While there is general agreement on the basic concept of autonomy, there are many conceptions of the concept, that is, different views on its interpretation'. William Safran (2000b: 11) goes in the same direction: 'self-government and autonomy are often used interchangeably, and autonomy has undergone incessant conceptual stretching'.

Historically, autonomy has been closely tied to the concept of self-determination. In the 1920s, Georg Jellinek had defined an autonomous entity as 'one based solely on its own laws, and with all the material and functional attributes of statehood: the authority to govern, to administer, and to judge' (Lapidoth 1997: 30). For this author, autonomy is therefore congruent with sovereignty. This interpretation is however not unanimous. Paul Baland, for his part, differentiated autonomy from sovereignty by stating that the limits of autonomy were established by the sovereign (Lapidoth 1997: 30). Rudolf Bernhardt proposed a nuanced position, demonstrating the existence of wide and narrow variations of the concept. In the wide sense, it would signify 'the limits of State interference, on the one hand, and the autonomous determination and regulation of certain affairs by specific institutions on the other hand' (cited in Lapidoth 1997: 32). In the more narrow sense, it would mean protection and self-determination measures for minorities. This second interpretation is the most popular in the literature, according to this author. Some authors define autonomy in a territorial fashion, such as Léon Duguit, who defines it in terms of a region holding a certain level of legislative independence from the central state, whereas others, such as Henry Barthélémy, rather define it in terms of power devolution (Lapidoth 1997: 30). Pierre Foucher attempts to conciliate those two last points of view, by stating that '[a]utonomy confers a margin of appreciation, a sphere of liberty within which a political power may be exerted'[1] (Foucher 2012: 93). Conceived as such, autonomy may mean, for example, 'the right to make decisions without governmental oversight regarding their content, in matters regarding which the state relinquished its right to an entity put in charge to exert this right' (Foucher 2012: 93).

Regardless of the challenge brought by the elasticity of the notion of autonomy in the literature, it has become a precious concept for minorities, because it supports the claims for a certain level of political power, without ever going as far as complete self-determination. It therefore offers an interesting alternative to claims for secession, which, in fact, are often poorly received and very seldom recognized, both by the individual nation-states and by the international community (Keating 2012: 14).

Goals and results flowing from the granting of a certain level of autonomy to minorities are also up for debate in the literature. As Safran (2000b: 12) explains, there is widespread disagreement among authors regarding 'which kind of autonomy is more likely to prevent, or lead to, secession and which is to be avoided'; 'which kind is more likely to satisfy the cultural claims of minorities' and finally, 'which minority is entitled to what kind of autonomy, and for what reason'. While there is a widespread consensus that stateless nations are entitled to a greater autonomy than most other kinds of minorities, such as ethnic minorities (Kymlicka 1996), there are two broad categories of autonomy found in the literature on stateless minorities, which sometimes overlap, and sometimes complete each other, but mostly flow from different ways to apprehend how political powers should be granted to minorities: territorial and non-territorial autonomy.

Territorial autonomy

Territorial autonomy is a category within which are found mechanisms of power devolution upon part of the territory belonging to a state. In other words, it echoes the idea that a certain authority is granted upon a circumscribed territory within the state. It is a kind of autonomy most often claimed by minorities which are territorially concentrated (international minorities) or that have claims to a historic homeland. National minorities prefer it to other options of power devolution 'because it creates an additional level of government, which may provide more regular, and better funded, ethnocultural services' (Safran 2000b: 14). This allows not only for a certain political power, but also for the expression of identity through public and social policies (Béland and Lecours 2008). Most states are not keen, however, to grant territorial autonomy, as they sometimes see it as a threat to their territorial integrity and a slippery slope towards secessionism.

Federalism is one of the most common forms of territorial autonomy. Some authors consider federalism and autonomy to fall in two different categories of state organization (Ackrén

2009; Olausson 2007). According to Thomas Benedikter, autonomy 'is a specific territorial organization having its own constituent features. It should not be confused with a sub-category of federalism … [It] is a political and constitutional organization sui generis that deserves distinct attention and analysis in theory and in practice' (cited in Lluch 2011: 135). However, territorial autonomy and federalism also share deep normative ties, as autonomy 'is the search for gradually expanding spheres of self-government within existing state structures and thus autonomists adopt elements of the federal idea, given that they are proponents of a peculiar form of multilevel government combining elements of shared-rule and partial territorial self-rule' (Lluch 2011: 135). I believe this is worth discussing.

Federalism is a form of state political organization where sovereignty is divided and powers are shared between two levels of government, the central government and the federated entities. It is organized according to what Daniel Elazar called the 'self-rule/shared-rule' or 'autonomy-participation' dichotomy (McGarry and O'Leary 2007: 180). On one hand, the principle of autonomy signifies in this instance that 'each member state of the federation, including the central state, may act freely within its own sphere of jurisdiction and may make decisions that will not be revised by another level of government'[2] (Pelletier 2013: 47). On the other hand, the principle of participation indicates that the constitutive elements of the federation also take part in the central decision-making process, where decisions concerning the entire polity are made. This relationship between the constituent entities of the federation is explained as a 'limited but permanent union […] seeking to conciliate unity and diversity within a given political or social space'[3] (Rocher 2006: 96–97). The result is that federal states are in constant tension, 'inherent to the very structure of federations, between the imposition of common values by a central government and the federated entities' protection of their own powers'[4] (Karmis 2006: 63).

Power sharing arrangements within federations vary widely from one country to the other, along a continuum from very little to very much power devolution from the centre to the federated units. As a general rule, jurisdiction over defence, monetary policy and foreign affairs is dealt with by the central government, while jurisdiction over cultural and social affairs is kept at the lower level. However, 'the distinction between foreign and domestic policy is increasingly hard to make, as international regimes penetrate almost all policy spheres' (Keating 2012: 19), especially for member states of the European Union.

The federation may also be symmetrical in its power sharing, which means that all of the federated units have the same powers, or asymmetrical ones, where one or more units get a different set of powers than the other units of the federation. However, many states demonstrate resistance to asymmetrical arrangements, as devolution of more power to one of the federated units may trigger demands for the same powers by all the other ones. This has been the case in Canada for Québec, and in Spain for Catalonia and the Basque country (Keating 2012: 25).

This precarious balance between the two levels of powers is at the very base of the federal system. It is also seen as the base for the management of nations within the state: 'to each nation let a province be given' (McGarry and O'Leary 2007: 190). Some further conditions of accommodation must also be met. Among them, Pinder (2007: 8–9) lists expectations of security, economic and environmental benefits, democratic institutions at both the central and constituent levels, absence of a hegemonic federated state within the federation, and flexibility for the social institution's adaptation to national cultures and customs. Democratic power-sharing arrangements of consociational or consensus-based nature, such as vetoes for national minorities on constitutional or sensitive questions, offer an added protection to majority rule and are deemed to be a stabilizing element of a multinational federation

(McGarry and O'Leary 2007: 204). Finally, there must be a desire for effective shared rule by committed politicians and citizens acting in good faith for a federation to function, as some of those power-sharing arrangements may give groups the power to stalemate political decisions. The reunion of these conditions within the same federation is not impossible, but proves to be a difficult task, as the fluctuating but ever-present nationalist tensions in federations such as Spain, Canada, and Belgium can attest. Moreover, it appears that federalism may incite, rather than discourage, stateless nations to organize towards secession, as it 'provides the minority with political and bureaucratic resources that it can use to launch a bid for independence' (McGarry and O'Leary 2007: 192). Finally, federalism fails to accommodate minorities too small in number or who are dispersed across the territory. Such is the case, for example, of the Francophone population living outside of the province of Québec.

Non-territorial autonomy

Other autonomy arrangements for national minorities do not rely on territory, but rather on cultural claims and especially the protection of the minority's culture, although these two dimensions (territorial and cultural) are not exclusive and are actually conjoined in most stateless nations. Non-territorial forms of autonomy then seek to foster arrangements regarding 'matters which affect the maintenance and reproduction of a group's culture' (Roach 2005: 13).

This type of autonomy is less extensive in scope but more fitting to dispersed minorities or minorities lacking a historical homeland (Lapidoth 1993). It entails, for example, the right to the management of educational and cultural institutions for the minority. It offers the minority a political conscience and bolsters its values, and above all, offers a legal protection against majority interference in those domains (Safran 2000b: 28; Nimni 2005; Nimni 2007). This kind of autonomy is not new: already, at the time of the Ottoman Empire, the Millet system protected non-Islamic religious communities. Following the First World Ward, some countries, such as Estonia and Lithuania, went beyond their obligations and allowed their minorities to create institutions to protect and promote their religion, language and culture.

This kind of autonomy is more readily accepted by states, as it does not question their territorial integrity (Safran 2000b: 11). However, it cannot do away completely with the question of territory, as services or institutions that are at the base of this type of autonomy have to exist in a given space. According to Safran, '[t]he idea of territoriality is suggested by the existence of networks of institutions – cultural, educational, social, commercial, and/or religious – that serve the particular needs of ethnic communities' (2000b: 12).

We have found three versions of non-territorial autonomy in the literature, which we will briefly explore here: personal autonomy, institutional completeness, and cultural autonomy. Also named national-cultural autonomy, *personal autonomy* appeared at the end of the nineteenth century in the writings of Karl Renner and Otto Bauer. Renner and Bauer were both members of the Social-Democrat Party of Austria-Hungary and were aiming, at the time, to find a solution to the problem of secessionist movements threatening to tear apart the Empire. Renner's oeuvre, *State and Nation*, published for the first time in 1899, attempted to demonstrate the possibility to conceptualize a new model of management of cultural (and national) diversity (Nimni 2007: 345–346). Bauer, for his part, published in 1907 *The Question of Nationalities and Social Democracy* in which he was seeking 'to remedy class divisions through a platform of equal rights for all national minority groups' (Roach 2004: 92).

As its name suggests, this kind of autonomy relies on the 'personalist' premise, or in other words the premise that '[t]otalities of persons can be divided only according to personal, and not territorial, characteristics' (Renner 2005 [1899]: 32). Individuals, and not territory, are the right-bearers, and thus those rights follow the individuals wherever they may be within the state. Renner therefore thought of the nation as 'a public law corporation, in a position comparable to that of the Church. Just as the latter embraced communities based on shared belief, so the nation should be thought of as an association of equal individuals, bound by a common culture' (Smith and Hiden 2012: 12).

Another central premise to Renner and Bauer's theory is democracy; the internal organization of each community or nation in the polity must rely on individuals' consent to be a member of one or another autonomous community (Nimni 2005: 10). This model also allows for each community to decide for themselves the level of autonomy they wish to take in charge and opens the door to partial autonomy in sectors deemed of primordial importance. According to Ephraim Nimni, national-cultural autonomy also enforces cross-cultural dialogue, as it relies on the premise that

> the most controversial issues in the relationship between ethnic and national groups are issues concerning language, education and the recognition of cultural rights in the public domain. Here, networks of communication across cultural boundaries are crucial because the model recognizes both communities and individuals as legitimate interlocutors.
>
> *(Nimni 2007: 347)*

The (Austrian) Social-Democratic Party never adopted Renner and Bauer's model as official policy, nor was it implanted in the Austro-Hungarian Empire. However, national-cultural autonomy has been going through a revival of sorts in the last decade, as political theorists have attempted to rehabilitate it in order to formulate a criticism of the liberal nation–state model, or to mitigate some of the challenges met by multicultural and multinational theories (Nimni 2005, 2007; Roach 2004, 2005; Smith and Hiden 2012). It could also be used to meet some of the challenges flowing from globalization, such as growing individual mobility, discussed earlier (Rethmann, Szeman and Coleman 2010). It is also a good fit for national minorities seeking a strong kind of autonomy, but for whom secession is not a viable option (Nimni 2005: 11).

Institutional completeness is a model of non-territorial autonomy first discussed in Raymond Breton's 1964 publication 'Institutional Completeness of Ethnic Communities and Personal Relations of Immigrants'. This paper presented the results of his study of immigrants' patterns of integration – as they integrated either into the majority, into a community of different ethnic background than theirs, or their own ethnic community. He showed that the more an ethnic community was institutionally organized, the more likely it was to attract and retain members. A community's 'institutional completeness', then, varied on a spectrum going from informal ties between individuals, to an ethnic community performing 'all the services required by its members. Members would never have to make use of native institutions for the satisfaction of any of their needs, such as education, work, food and clothing, medical care, or social assistance' (Breton 1964: 194). A couple of decades later, Breton steered his model in the direction of political economy, taking a more individualistic stance. He then explained how the demographic stability of a minority depended on its members' choices to partake in the institutions of the minority (Breton 1985: 77). The minority, in order to survive, could not only make use of internal constraints, but also make use of 'selective motivations' towards its members in order to retain them. He explains those motivations as 'advantages accessible only to those who participate in the production and the maintenance of communal cultural goods' (Breton 1985: 84). The community will then have to ensure it can offer certain services and activities to attract and retain individuals within its sphere. Economic motivations, in particular, are of primordial importance, as they would be the most attractive reason for individuals to integrate to a certain group. This is why Breton sees the job market as an important institution within his model (Breton 1985: 89).

Cultural autonomy

Cultural autonomy bears no ties to national-cultural autonomy described above, except in its application to minorities. The concept has been developed and extrapolated from the postulates of Joshua Fishman's linguistic revitalisation. It is a model that has been conceived with linguistic minorities in mind, but which can be applied to any minority group concerned with its cultural sustainability. According to Fishman, 'cultural autonomy applies to minorities that want to ensure the reproduction of their group within a state. He distinguishes this kind of autonomy to *political* autonomy, a notion he reserves for groups aiming at protecting their language by getting their own state'[5] (Landry, Forgues and Traisnel 2010: 93). The admitted goal of these academics is to reinject politics into Fishman's concept and for the minority to take in charge its 'linguistic arrangement integrated to a project of political self-determination'[6] (Landry 2009: 19). Despite the cultural starting point of this process of self-determination, they argue that it is an endeavour of a definitely political nature: 'the group makes claims for resources, self-management powers, and governance which, depending on the geopolitical context, may or may not be territorial in nature and more or less confront the power of the state'[7] (Landry, Forgues and Traisnel 2010: 93).

Three elements sustaining the collective identity of the group are mobilized in cultural autonomy: ideological legitimacy, institutional completeness, and socializing proximity. Ideological legitimacy relates to the way the state and majority citizens perceive and treat the minority, giving it its legitimacy and status. It therefore appeals to the level of recognition that is granted to the minority. Institutional completeness, as it is understood here, is closely related to Breton's definition: it represents 'the taking in charge of social and cultural institutions [...] which reveals the group's capacity to manage its "boundaries of identity"'[8] (Landry, Forgues and Traisnel 2010: 99). Finally, the socializing proximity brings back the question of geographic space into non-territorial autonomy, which echoes Safran's (2000b) warning, as discussed earlier. This notion relates to the family–neighbourhood–community ties through which a minority ensures intergenerational transmission of language and culture. As it turns out, the necessity of a critical mass within a given territory in order for a minority to be able to practise any form of autonomy ultimately seems to be non-territorial autonomy's Achilles heel.

Conclusion: accommodating stateless minorities within a nation-state framework

The issue of successfully accommodating stateless minorities within nation-states, that is, on the one hand, providing these stateless nations with enough recognition and autonomy for them to thrive within the larger states, and on the other hand, preventing secession or secessionist claims from arising, has been puzzling political scientists for decades. There is still much research to be done to fully grasp the variables that make one case successful and another a failure. Moreover, as we have discussed, nationalisms are here to stay: globalization, far from weakening sub-state nations as was first predicted, has actually participated in their revival. In this chapter, we have shed light on a variety of possible arrangements, whether or not relying on the principle of territoriality, that offer both recognition and autonomy to stateless minorities, on one hand, while preserving the integrity of the multinational state in which they partake, on the other hand. We have also aimed to highlight each model's strengths and shortcomings.

As we made clear, there is no cookie-cutter solution to the challenge of stateless minorities. Every stateless nation is different from the others in terms of demographics, economics, geographic situation, history with the state(s) where they are found and the other groups, majoritarian or not, with whom they share those states, claims for recognition, and the kind and depth of autonomy to which they aspire. The key to the puzzle may lie, as Keating (2012: 26) argues, in everyone working in good faith towards 'getting the widest agreement on governing arrangements in conditions where there is not an existing consensus, which necessarily entails compromise'. The relationship between state governments and stateless minorities has evolved in positive ways in the last decades, in part due to pressure from the international community. One may be optimistic that genuine effort to accommodate stateless minorities will become the international norm and that assimilation and persecution of minorities will eventually be a thing of the past. These wishes are still a long way from being fulfilled, but continuing research on multiculturalism, nationalism, multinationalism, and autonomy arrangements are as many steps toward the organization of better relationships between minorities and majorities in the world.

Notes

1 Personal translation.
2 Personal translation.
3 Personal translation.
4 Personal translation.
5 Personal translation; in italics in original text.
6 Personal translation.
7 Personal translation.
8 Personal translation.

References

Ackrén, M. 2009. *Conditions for Different Autonomy Regimes in the World: A Fuzzy Set Application*, Abo: Abo Akademi University Press.
Anderson, B. 1983. *Imagined Communities. Reflections on the Origin and Spread of Nationalism*, London: Verso.
Béland, D. and A. Lecours. 2008. *Nationalism and Social Policy. The Politics of Territorial Solidarity*, Oxford: Oxford University Press.
Breton, R. 1964. 'Institutional Completeness of Ethnic Communities and the Personal Relations of Immigrants', *American Journal of Sociology* 70(2), 193–205.
Breton, R. 1985. 'L'intégration des francophones hors Québec dans des communautés de langue française', *Revue de l'Université d'Ottawa* 55(2), 357–376.
Cobban, A. 1969. *The Nation State and National Self-Determination*, London: Fontana.
Foucher, P. 2012. 'Autonomie des communautés francophones minoritaires au Canada: le point de vue du droit', *Linguistic Minorities and Society* 1, 90–114.
Gagnon, A. G., M. Guibernau and F. Rocher. 2003. *The Conditions of Diversity in Multinational Democracies*, Montréal: Institute of Research on Public Policy.
Gallagher Cunningham, K. 2014. *Inside the Politics of Self-Determination*, Oxford: Oxford University Press.
Gellner, E. 1989. *Nations et Nationalisme*, Paris: Payot.
Gilbert, J. 2014. *Nomadic Peoples and Human Rights*, London: Routledge.

Hobsbawm, E. 1992. *Nations and Nationalism Since 1870: Programme, Myth, Reality*, Cambridge: Cambridge University Press.

Karmis, D. 2006. '"Togetherness" in Multinational Federal Democracies: Tocqueville, Proudhon and the Theoretical Gap in Modern Federal Tradition', in M. Burgess and A. Gagnon (eds), *Federal Democracies*, London: Routledge, 46–63.

Keating, M. 2012. 'Rethinking Sovereignty. Independence-Lite, Devolution-Max and National Accommodation', *Revista d'Estudis Autonòmics i Federals* 16, 9–29.

Keating, M. and J. McGarry. 2001. *Minority Nationalism and the Changing International Order*, New York: Oxford University Press.

Kymlicka, W. 1996. *Multicultural Citizenship*, Oxford: Oxford University Press.

Landry, R. 2009. 'Autonomie culturelle et vitalité des communautés de langue officielle en situation minoritaire', *Revue de la Common law en français* 11, 19–43.

Landry, R., É. Forgues and C. Traisnel. 2010. 'Autonomie culturelle, gouvernance et communautés francophones en situation minoritaire au Canada', *Politique et sociétés* 29(1), 91–114.

Lapidoth, R. 1993. 'Autonomy: Potential and Limitations', *International Journal of Group Rights* 1, 269–290.

Lapidoth, R. 1997. *Autonomy. Flexible Solutions to Ethnic Conflicts*, Washington: United States Institute of Peace Press.

Lijphart, A. 1969. 'Consociational Democracy', *World Politics* 21(2), 207–225.

Lluch, J. 2011. 'Autonomism and Federalism', *Publius: The Journal of Federalism* 42(1), 134–161.

McGarry, J. and B. O'Leary. 2007. 'Federation and Managing Nations', in M. Burgess and J. Pinder (eds), *Multinational Federations*, Abingdon: Routledge.

Milacic, S. 2012. 'La fragmentation au nom de quoi?', in S. Pierré-Caps and J. D. Mouton (eds), *États fragmentés*, Nancy: Éditions universitaires de Lorraine, 357–377.

Nimni, E. 2005. *National Cultural Autonomy and Its Contemporary Critics*, Abingdon: Routledge.

Nimni, E. 2007. 'National-Cultural Autonomy as an Alternative to Minority Territorial Nationalism', *Ethnopolitics* 6(3), 345–364.

Nimni, E. 2011. 'Stateless Nations in a World of Nation-states', in K. Cordell and S. Wolff (eds), *Routledge Handbook of Ethnic Conflict*, Abingdon: Routledge, 55–66.

Olausson, P. M. 2007. *Autonomy and Islands: A Global Study of the Factors that Determine Island Autonomy*, Abo: Abo Akademi University Press.

Pelletier, R. 2013. 'Constitution et fédéralisme', in R. Pelletier and M. Tremblay (eds), *Le parlementarisme canadien*, 5th edn, Québec: Presses de l'Université Laval.

Pinder, J. 2007. 'Multinational Federations', in M. Burgess and J. Pinder (eds), *Multinational Federations*, Abingdon: Routledge.

Renner, K. 2005 [1899]. 'State and Nation', in E. Nimni (ed.), *National Cultural Autonomy and its Contemporary Critics*, Abingdon: Routledge, 15–47.

Rethmann, P., I. Szeman and W. D. Coleman. 2010. *Cultural Autonomy. Fictions and Connections*, Vancouver: UBC Press.

Roach, S. C. 2004. 'Minority Rights and the Dialectics of the Nation: Otto Bauer's Theory of the Nation and Its Contributions to Multicultural Theory and Globalization', *Human Rights Review* (October–December), 91–105.

Roach, S. C. 2005. *Cultural Autonomy, Minority Rights and Globalization*, Aldershot: Ashgate.

Rocher, F. 2006. 'La dynamique Québec-Canada ou le refus de l'idéal fédéral', in A. G. Gagnon (ed.), *Le fédéralisme canadien contemporain*, Montréal: Presses de l'Université de Montréal, 93–146.

Roy, I. 2006. *Vers un droit de participation des minorités à la vie de l'État?*, Montréal: Wilson & Lafleur.

Safran, W. 2000a. 'Introduction', in W. Safran and R. Maiz, *Identity and Territorial Autonomy in Plural Societies*, 1–7. London: Frank Cass.

Safran, W. 2000b. 'Spatial and Functional Dimensions of Autonomy: Cross-national and Theoretical Perspectives', in W. Safran and R. Maiz, *Identity and Territorial Autonomy in Plural Societies*, London: Frank Cass, 11–34.

Schaefer-Rolffs, A. and K.-U. Schnapp. 2014. 'Special Politics for Minority Political Participation in the Danish-German Border Region', *International Journal on Minority and Group Rights* 21(1), 48–71.

Smith, D. J. and J. Hiden. 2012. *Ethnic Diversity and the Nation State. National Cultural Autonomy Revisited*, Abingdon: Routledge.

Thomsen, R. C. 2010. *Nationalism in Stateless Nations: Selves and Others in Scotland and Newfoundland*, Edinburgh: Birlinn.

Updegraff, R. 2012. 'The Kurdish Question', *Journal of Democracy* 23(1), 119–128.

Legislation

Conference on Security and Co-operation in Europe. 1991. *Declaration on the Rights of National Minorities.*

United Nations. 1992. *Declaration on the Rights of Persons Belonging to National or Ethnic, Religious and Linguistic Minorities,* available online at http://www.un.org/documents/ga/res/47/a47r135.htm.

Council of Europe. 1994. *European Framework Convention for the Protection of National Minorities,* available online at http://conventions.coe.int/Treaty/en/Treaties/Html/157.htm.

UN Educational, Scientific and Cultural Organization (UNESCO). 2001. *Universal Declaration on Cultural Diversity,* available online at http://www.refworld.org/docid/435cbcd64.html.

6

ETHNICITY AND RELIGION

Joseph Ruane and Jennifer Todd

Introduction

Religiously informed conflicts have become increasingly prominent throughout the world – conflicts surrounding immigration in Europe, conflict at religious interfaces, the Islamicisation of ethno-national movements from Palestine to Malaysia, the emergence of jihadist movements from Al Qaeda to ISIL (Islamic State in the Levant). In 2003, Steve Bruce estimated that three quarters of the conflicts since 1960 had a religious component, in the sense that many of those involved 'explain or justify their causes by reference to their religion' (Bruce 2003). Twelve years later this remains the case. Most also have an ethnic component: for example, jihadist movements take advantage of ongoing ethno-religious conflicts in Syria and Iraq. This raises an important set of questions about the interrelation of religion and ethnicity in identity formation, group mobilisation and conflict. How do religiously defined, ethnically defined and ethno-religiously defined groups-in-conflict differ in their behaviour and aims? Is religiously informed ethnic conflict distinctive in its form and dynamics? What specific resources are associated with ethnic and with religious solidarity? How far does the historic sequencing of state-building, nation-building and religious-formation affect the ways ethnicity and religion intersect?

Religions provide important resources for ethnic groups in conflict: already developed ideologies, ready-made organisational structures and international linkages, habits of authority and rule-following, sacred legitimacy (Fox 2002; Smith 2003; Stewart 2009). They may also do much more, partially changing the character of conflict, the values, aims and boundaries of populations, the identities of individuals, the dynamics of intra-group rivalries, the organisation of parties, the commitment of leaders, the relation to the state.

Much recent research focuses directly on religion and conflict with little reference to ethnicity (see Juergensmeyer 2008; Toft 2007). Much of the recent 'terrorism' literature details the ways in which religious belief is used to legitimate terrorist activity and suicide bombing (for a critical analysis, see Stewart 2009). This does not, however, show that there is a new phase of 'religious' or 'civilisational' conflict where religion plays a central role in constituting the groups-in-conflict and their aims. Huntington's (2002) claim to this effect ignores the differences in political culture within each world religion and the many overlaps between them (Norris and Inglehart 2004: 133–155). Moreover it is far from clear that religious groups in conflict behave differently from non-religious ones. Despite frequent arguments that religious conflicts are more violent than others, an overview of large-scale conflicts since 1956 shows that the nominally religious ones are somewhat less frequent and less deadly than the nominally secular (Stewart 2009). The role of specifically religious identities, divisions and motivations in conflict needs to be analysed in comparison to ethnic and ethno-religious identities, divisions and motivations.

This task is hindered by the relative isolation of scholarship on ethnicity from scholarship on religion. The sociology of religion is potentially a rich mine of analyses and models relevant to the study of ethnicity: models of culture-change (secularisation), identity change (conversion), the emergence of new religious movements, the impact of religious groups and ideas on political culture and political organisation, and of the interrelation of society-wide, group, organisational, and individual level change (Davie 2007; Demerath 2001; Gorski and Altinordu 2008; Snow and Machelek 1984). There is also a historical–sociological tradition that traces interlinkages between religious practices, elites and values, on the one hand, and socio-political development on the other, showing how religious movements – early Calvinism and its impact on the values and *habitus* of the elite – came to inform European capitalist development (Weber 1930) and early-modern state formation (Gorski 2003); others have traced the role of religions in nation formation (Greenfeld 1992; Hastings 1997; Ihalainen 2005; Marx 2003; Van der Leer and Lehmann 1999). A further important strand of recent research focuses on popular attitudes, tracing periods when political elites use religious values to mobilise or control populations, to broker new ethno-political alliances, to frame concepts of nationhood, or to compensate groups for their increasing distantiation from the state (see variously Brown 2010; Bruce 1994: 22–31; Gal 2007; Kinnvall 2002; Shenhav 2006: 46–76).

While the classic studies of ethnicity, ethno-nationalism and ethnic conflict did not pay particular attention to religion, there was one exception: the ethno-symbolist perspective associated with the work of Anthony D. Smith. Smith (2003) emphasises the self-conceptions of some ethnic groups as 'chosen peoples'. He distinguishes the expansive 'missionary peoples' with a sacred mission of proselytism or exemplary profession of faith, and the bounded 'covenantal peoples', whose religiously informed obligations and expectations intensify their will to ethnic solidarity and survival (see also Cauthen 2004). Correlatively, as D. H. Akenson (1992) has shown in his comparative study of three 'covenantal' settler peoples, Ulster Protestants, Afrikaaners, and Israelis, the political context and the interests it generates also affect the forms of religion that become dominant.

Contemporary scholarly interest in 'everyday life' and the everyday manifestations of ethnicity (Brubaker 2006; Jenkins 2008) opens a wide field for research into the intertwining of ethnicity and religion at the everyday level. Some studies show the complexities of the intersection in peaceful, multi-ethnic societies (for example Levitt's (2008) study of religion as a source of everyday activism among immigrants in the USA). There are also many studies of the interrelation of ethnicity and religion in conflict situations (for example Kakar's (1996) study of Hindu and Muslim rioters in Hyderabad). Such research raises important theoretical and explanatory questions. Where ethnicity and religion are intertwined, is religion simply a legitimatory resource for other interests? Or do religious beliefs themselves inform the framing of interests and assumptions about the world to a point where, in Walter Benjamin's terms, religion is the puppet-master pulling the strings of seemingly secular groups (Benjamin 1969: 253–255)? And how are religious and ethnic ideas and aims put to use in processes of mobilisation and intra-group contest? As we show below, attempts to answer these questions have required some reframing of concepts of ethnicity.

Concepts of religion and ethnicity

Classical scholarship on ethnicity and ethno-nationalism carefully distinguished religion from ethnicity. Anthony D. Smith defined ethnicity as involving each of the following six features: a common name; a myth of common ancestry; shared historical memories; elements of common culture; a link to a homeland; a sense of solidarity (Smith 1986: 21–31). Definitions are contested in the wider literature, but there is some consensus that central to ethnicity is perceived territorially based descent, which in turn tends to generate quasi-kin feelings of solidarity (Conversi 2002). Religion may be defined substantively as beliefs and practices concerned with the sacred, with particular religions identified in terms of institutionally based and bounded sets of such beliefs and practices, and the religious (confessional) groups who participate in them. On Smith's definition of ethnicity, religion may form the common culture that partially constitutes the ethnie, but ethnicity requires also a territorial and descent-related emphasis. On other accounts, ethnic solidarity is a function of (perceived) descent (Connor 1994), or even simply of group boundaries, rather than of any particular cultural or religious content.

While the conceptual distinctions are clear, many groups fall into both categories. Smith (2003) has shown how religion informs and on occasion defines particular ethnic groups. Jews, Copts and Sikhs are, for example, at one and the same time ethnic and religious groupings, and religions like Hinduism, Judaism and Shintoism are sometimes categorised as 'ethnic religions' (Coakley 2002). In other cases, the coincidence of religion and ethnicity is historically contingent and specific to particular territorial areas. So, for example, in Northern Ireland conflict is rooted in the emergence of groups that were simultaneously distinct in ethnic origin (seventeenth-century incomers from Scotland and England vs Gaelic Irish and 'old English' twelfth-century incomers), in religion (Protestant vs Catholic), in nationality (British vs Irish) and in state loyalty (unionist vs nationalist). While the religious distinction did not and does not totally coincide with the ethnic, national or political distinctions, the overlaps remain extremely significant (Whyte 1991: 65–93). Religiously derived concepts inform political views, even while there is very wide variation both in religious beliefs and in the prioritisation of these beliefs (Mitchell 2006: 91–132; Wolffe 2014).

Similar overlaps of religion and ethnicity are present in many conflict regions: from Macedonia to Sri Lanka; from Cyprus to Israel and Palestine; from the Côte d'Ivoire to the Lebanon; from Sudan to ex-Yugoslavia (see Bruce 2003: 43–57). In other cases, religious resonances are implicit rather than overt. In Canada, the Catholicism of Francophones, as distinct from the Protestantism of the traditional Anglophone community, was an important element in the historical construction of a French Canadian identity (Bouchard 2004). Basque conflict with the Spanish centre took its most acute form in the mid twentieth century when it was a conflict between (anti-clerical) Basque socialists and clericalist Francoists, and this memory persists in the one-time Francoist stronghold of Navarre.

Conflicts based on ethnic divisions devoid of religious resonance exist (for example, most of the internal French ethno-national conflicts and some residual Northern European ones, and ethnic conflicts in Rwanda, Burundi, the Democratic Republic of Congo, Angola and Mozambique), although it is less common to find religious groups in conflict devoid of ethnic resonance. But the mix of religion and ethnicity is very common, and where it occurs it is difficult to assess the relative strength of each. Stewart (2009), based on a wide-ranging preliminary review, shows that it is much easier to assess the relative importance of religious and ethnic motives and aims for political leaders than for the mass of their supporters. Where a population is at once ethnically and religiously distinctive, it is difficult to assess which identity is dominant because self-definitions tend to fluctuate over time. Competing ethnic parties' definitions of the identity of their constituents vary situationally and for competitive advantage, and often (as Pragnere (2013) shows with respect to Northern Ireland) have very little effect on the wider population. Sometimes the distinctions are asymmetric, with one population defining themselves primarily in religious terms and the other in ethnic terms – for example pre-war rural Bosnian Muslims, identifying primarily as a cultural-religious community, contrasted themselves with Serbs and Croats, with a stronger consciousness of ethnic descent (Bringa 1995). Nor are there easy ways to define groups structurally: while sometimes discrimination may take place primarily on religious or primarily on ethno-political grounds, this too may vary between sites of discrimination and over time.

One could distinguish a continuum where religion acts as a mere 'marker' for ethnicity at one end (Bruce 2003: 47–50) and is formative of the ethnic identity in question at the other (for example, Shenhav 2006: 77–109). Few cases consistently fit either end of the continuum. In cases of substantive overlap between religion and ethnicity, it is best to see the distinctions as inherently composite, allowing for slides of meaning, degrees of situational choice and competition over definition, and often a division of labour between religious and political organisations and leaders. While composite divisions allow considerable leeway for everyday interaction (in pre-war Bosnia, or in Northern Ireland), they also allow for fusion to make for a totalising and polarising division – what Bar-Tal (2013) calls an institutionalised 'conflict ethos' that is at once socially and individually embedded.

Much of the recent literature on ethnicity, conflict and violence bypasses the religion/ethnicity interrelationship by definitional fiat, including in the category of ethnic group those groups defined by religion.[1] If the benefit of this approach is to extend the range of comparative quantitative analysis, the cost is to preclude comparison of religion and ethnicity as contrasting sources of identity, community and conflict. The 'inclusive conception of ethnicity' implicitly allows our understanding of ethnicity (with its strongly territorialised and descent-based resonances) to impose an ethnicising vision on highly complex social realities. By including all ways of constructing 'peoplehood' (populations with a sense of historic community and solidarity (see Lie 2004)) under the heading of 'ethnic', we lose the conceptual capacity to see the variety of meanings and solidarities that religion may bring to the sense of peoplehood.

An alternative strategy is to investigate empirically the different ways that 'peoples' construct themselves, exploring how religious beliefs, practices and memories, and ethnic histories, myths and associated values, affect group formation. Are the effects of religion and ethnicity additive, with ethnic and religious distinctions each reinforcing the other, socially and culturally? Are they complementary, with each contributing a distinct set of attributes and functions to group belonging? Do they coexist in tension, the focus of intra-group competition, and if so are there any general patterns to be found across cases in terms of the relative strength of each factor? Or are there interactive effects with dynamic and emergent properties producing a much more complex field of relationships where the ethnic and the religious cannot easily be separated out? When are the effects additive, when complementary, when conflicting, when interactive?

In exploring these issues, we focus on three areas of current research on ethnicity and religion.

i *Geopolitical and geohistorical research.* This maps the formation of different types of historic communities through processes of ethnogenesis/nation-building, confessionalisation, state formation and territorial formation. It explores how the sequencing of these processes affects the ways peoplehood is defined by different populations and how this affects socio-cultural divisions and repertoires – the inherited social grammar of division.

ii *Ethnographic, sociological and economic analysis of group solidarities and resources.* What specific resources (institutional, ideological, personal, political) are produced by ethnic and by religious solidarity and how do these vary in combination? Who benefits from shifting from a primarily ethnic to a primarily religious focus or vice versa?

iii *Cultural and symbolic research into everyday meanings, motives and identities.* How do individuals merge or distinguish ethnic and religious categories in their everyday lives, and how do they use these resources to change themselves and their society?

The roots of many of today's 'ethno-religious' conflicts lie in large-scale historical processes: the formation and collapse of states, empires and civilisations, the growth of world religions and their diffusions and internal splinterings, the voluntary and involuntary movement of populations, the intersection of culture and religion with class and caste, and in the more recent period the emergence of modern concepts of state, nationhood and ethnicity. One possible outcome of these processes is a nation-state in which religion and national identity are fused (Bruce 2003: 43). Much more common are state- and territorially based conjunctures of conflicting ethnic and religious identities.

The process has been mapped for Europe by Stein Rokkan (Flora 1999). Successive waves of conquest and occupation, penetration and retrenchment produced a complex distribution of ethnic-linguistic groupings across Western Europe. On this were superimposed the divisions of the reformation, setting the scene for more than a century of religious war and for a still longer period of religious persecution. Three major zones of confessional relations emerged: a majority Catholic/minority Protestant crescent, from Poland through Southern Europe to Ireland; a majority Protestant/minority Catholic region, largely in Northern Europe; and mixed interface regions between these (Martin 1978). Religious understandings were embedded in state institutions and practices, became part of elite and everyday understandings of how the state functioned (Gorski 2003) and were imposed, to the extent possible, on the wider population. In the first two zones, nation (in the pre-modern sense) and confession became tightly intertwined, leaving religious minorities such as the Huguenots of France, the Protestants of Bohemia, the Catholics of England, struggling to affirm their claim on full membership of the nation (for the Huguenots, see Benedict, Daussy and Lechot 2014). The third zone was one of confessional rivalry that later extended to the definition of the nation and the form and boundaries of the state (see Wolff 2003). In all three zones, minority religions could take on some of the attributes of ethnicity, including a sense of grievance/superiority, a particular world view, and a sense of solidarity (Smith 2003).

English and British state-building exemplifies many of these processes. It was greatly eased by the success of Protestantism throughout Great Britain. This allowed political–territorial and religious–constitutional compromises to be put in place in the late seventeenth century (Pocock 1989) and led to the centrality of Protestantism to British national identity in the eighteenth and nineteenth centuries (Colley 1992; Hastings 1997). Correlatively, English Catholics were marginalised in Great Britain well into the nineteenth century (Duffy 1982) and Irish Catholics politically marginalised in Ireland under the Union and in Northern Ireland until the end of the twentieth century. Religiously informed ethno-national tensions characterised the British–Irish relationship until the latter part of the twentieth century.

The settlement colonies of North America and the southern hemisphere that all but destroyed the pre-existing social order tended to reproduce European intersections between ethnicity and religion: they did so with a different dynamic determined by an immigration-based state and society. Much more complex patterns emerged where imperial rule formed an overlay on an older social and cultural world that it profoundly modified, but did not replace. There the ethnic and religious mix was re-shaped in successive phases of colonial settlement, missionary activity and free or directed population movement. Coloni- alism introduced new groups that were religiously as well as ethnically distinct, who came as settlers (South Africa, Zimbabwe) or as workers or slaves brought in by the colonial power (Malaysia, Kenya and the Caribbean countries). Missionary activity went hand in hand with the process of colonisation, though with limited success in the areas of the old world religions. Ethnicity and religion provided colonial states with alternative or complementary resources for strategic management. In parts of sub-Saharan Africa, the colonial state emphasis was on ethnic rather than religious distinction. Still today, religious distinction continues to be personally salient, often more so than ethnic; but it is ethnic distinction that is seen as crucial in public life, in party politics and in the distribution of public offices (Langer 2010; Stewart 2009). A different historical and contemporary distribution of resources in South Asia led states to give higher public salience to religion and religio-caste distinction (Kaviraj 2007; Van der Leer and Lehmann 1999; for internal variation in India, see Varshney 2003).

These historical developments often entwined religion, state-hood and legitimating political cultures – permeated by religious assumptions – and made likely composite identities and ideologies where a group's relation to the state was at once religio-cultural and ethno-territorial. Asymmetric conflicts developed as religious minorities 'trapped' in one empire or nation-state came into conflict with dominant ethnies, or ethnic minorities came into conflict with dominant religio-national states. The resulting conflicts – whether in Bosnia, Northern Ireland or Israel – are not adequately characterised as either ethnic or religious: the populations, in relation to each other and to the state, are compositely and asymmetrically defined and self-defining.

While theorists of conflict tend to focus on failures of minority integration, the successes are also instructive. Contrasting the successful integration of historic (ethno)-religious mino- rities in some states (France and Czechoslovakia) and the relative failure of integration in others (Ireland) shows the importance of minority participation in constitution-building from a religious just as much as from an ethnic perspective (Ruane and Todd 2009).

Religion and ethnicity as sources of group solidarity and as political resources

Religion and ethnicity are each an important source of group identity and solidarity. The scholarly literature contrasts the symbolic resources associated with each domain: a messianic religious notion of time, where radical shifts are possible, and an unbounded notion of space is often contrasted with a nation-state notion of clock time and tightly bounded space (Anderson 1991: 6). Tensions may arise between the universalistic, trans-territorial and sacred aspect of many world religions and the particularist, bounded character of ethnicity (Coakley 2002: 212–213), but there can also be a borrowing of tropes one from the other. Smith (1986: 34–7; 2003: 166–217) has noted that nations often take on some of the sacred character and temporality usually associated with religions. Equally, at times religious minorities take on the sense of history, of origin myth, territorial base and cultural distinction usually identified as ethnic (Bringa 1995; Ruane 2010). The result changes the form of religion and ethnicity: Gerber (2007) and Lybarger (2007) show how Islam is used and transformed by (ethno- nationalist) believers to make it consistent with national aims, thereby in turn changing the dominant conception of the ethnie and the nation.

There are often major differences in religious and ethnic organisational resources. Pre-politicised ethnicity tends to be inchoate and immediate, associated with neighbourhoods and family ties, open to radically diverse modes of articulation (see for example Chong 2007). It may coexist with a highly organised and institutionalised religion, with a highly elaborated and universalistic ideological (theological) perspective, developed conceptions and practices of authority, and established repertoires of mobilisation and contestation. Religions often have international organisational structures, whereas ethnies are locally situated, dependent on diasporas for transnational support. Whether this gives rise to a comfortable division of labour within a composite population, or to intra-group competition is situational. Historically, Protestantism and Britishness were mutually reinforcing (Colley 1992) and created a wider (and largely Protestant) British world, from North America to Australia and New Zealand. This comfortable cohabitation has been challenged by newer minorities, whose self-definition (as primarily ethnic, ethno-religious, or religious) is itself shaped by state policies and sponsorship of different ethno-cultural or trans-ethnic religious organisations (Joly 2012).

In cases of overlap, a simple 2x2 diagram (see Table 6.1 below) distinguishing the possible variations in strength of identity, degree of group solidarity and extent of institutionalisation of ethnicity and religion allows an initial mapping of the data. This allows us to show different trajectories of group-development, so that a group (for example, Palestinians) may move from segment 4 to segment 2 in the initial process of nationalist politicisation with later movement towards segment 1, as they invest their nationality with religious meaning. The diagram of course is overly simple: actual analysis has to distinguish the unevenness in degree and type of identity, solidarity and institutionalisation. Very strong identifications may also be thin (relatively empty of content and narrative) with solidarity limited to small groups and with limited institutionalisation, as contemporary secular working class loyalism in Northern Ireland illustrates. Meanwhile, highly institutionalised religions and nationalisms may also be shallow in terms of public identification and may quickly change once the opportunity arises.

In short, the ways ordinary people construct and understand their sense of peoplehood are at once subtle, powerful and complex. Contemporary analysis has begun to deconstruct the sharp distinction between ethnicity and religion, but it remains to reconstruct more adequate and nuanced typologies and theories of the role of religious and ethnic distinction in group formation. We have here distinguished populations that conceive of their 'peoplehood' in a composite way from those that adopt simple religious or ethnic self-conceptions. We suggest – but cannot argue here – that composite groups follow a distinctive logic of conflict, prone to sway from permeable to polarised relations, and open to complex internal political alliances with divisions of labour between religious-oriented and ethnic-oriented organisations. There may also be asymmetries in conflicting populations, where the groups-in-conflict differentially prioritise religion and ethnicity. Contemporary jihadist organisations are distinctive in working at once from a composite ethno-religious population in an immediate zone of conflict, and also from a much wider set of international religious allies willing to spread the violence internationally.

Table 6.1 Religion and ethnicity: identity, solidarity and institutionalisation

		Religion (identity, solidarity, institutionalisation)	
		High	*Low*
Ethnicity (identity, solidarity, institutionalisation)	High	1	2
	Low	3	4

Everyday ethnicity and religion: individual choice and change

The cultural content of identity – whether and which religious values or ethnic origins are emphasised in everyday distinction-making – is important in orienting action, framing felt-grievances, limiting the forms of likely mobilisation, and acknowledging and accepting settlement opportunities. A whole range of qualitative studies has explored how the high-lighting of religious or ethnic distinction and particular interpretations of that distinction may have major social consequences in drawing boundaries and making them more or less permeable, in brokering new alliances, and in opening the way for actors to grasp new opportunities (McAdam, Tarrow and Tilly 2001: 124–159). Research on the increasing politicisation of religious cleavages in Nigeria and Palestine, for example, shows how populations disappointed with 'national' leadership use religious resources to further their aims (Igwarra 2007; Lybarger 2007; Stewart 2009). Indeed subgroups – gender and generational – may escape from the constraints of their 'ethnic' elders by emphasising their religious commonalities (Joly 2012).

Here too, the study of religion provides interesting comparisons and models for the study of everyday ethnic and ethno-religious identification. The extensive research on different dimensions of secularisation and sacralisation (for discussion, see Davie 2007: 46–66; Gorski and Altinordu 2008) shows a thinning out of religious identity, movement away from traditional 'set packages' of belief, and a 'vicarious' identification, whereby non-believers support believers in their belief and practice (Davie 2007: 126–128, 140–143). The parallels with processes noted in the field of ethnicity are striking: the lack of salience of 'everyday ethnicity' together with a (vicarious) unwillingness to give up on 'nationalist' politicians and move-ments, a 'pluralisation' of concepts of national identity, and related processes of boundary blurring and ethnic change (Brubaker, Fox and Grancea 2006; Keating 2001).

Conclusion

Some recent research, finally, suggests that religious commitment can aid conflict resolution precisely because it gives individuals resources and legitimations for radical change (for the Northern Ireland case, see Brewer, Higgins and Teeney 2011; Ganiel 2008). Reverend Dr Ian Paisley – First Minister of the re-constituted 2007 Northern Ireland Executive in partnership with Deputy First Minister Martin McGuinness of Sinn Féin – may be taken as an example. A long-time critic of all political compromise, he commented on their respective political about-turns: 'We were turned towards the darkness, now we are turned towards the light.' For him, as for at least some ordinary people in Northern Ireland, religious beliefs and values allowed a reorientation of values and identities in a new political order.

Note

1 For example, Horowitz (2000: 17–18) includes in his category of ethnic groups those groups 'defined by ascriptive differences, whether the indicium of group identity is color, appearance, language, religion, some other indicator of common origin, or some combination thereof'. He refers to this as the 'inclusive conception of ethnicity'.

Further reading

Bruce, S. (2003) *Politics and Religion* (Cambridge: Polity Press).
Demerath, N. J. III (2001) *Crossing the Gods: World Religions and Worldly Politics* (New Brunswick: Rutgers University Press).

Hastings, A. (1997) *The Construction of Nationhood: Ethnicity, Religion and Nationalism* (Cambridge: Cambridge University Press).
Smith, A. D. (2003) *Chosen Peoples: Sacred Sources of National Identity* (Oxford: Oxford University Press).

References

Akenson, D. H. (1992) *God's Peoples. Covenant and Land in South Africa, Israel and Ulster* (Ithaca, NY: Cornell University Press).
Anderson, B. (1991) *Imagined Communities*, revised edition (London: Verso).
Bar-Tal, D. (2013) *Intractable Conflicts: Socio-Psychological Foundations and Dynamics* (Cambridge: Cambridge University Press).
Benedict, P., H. Daussy and P. O. Lechot (eds) (2014) *Histoire, mémoire et identités en mutation: Les huguenots en France et en diaspora (XVIe–XXe siècles)* (Paris: Droz).
Benjamin, W. (1969) 'Theses on the Philosophy of History', pp. 253–264 in *Illuminations* (edited and with introduction by H. Arendt) (New York: Schocken).
Bouchard, G. (2004) *La pensée impuissante: Échecs et mythes nationaux canadiens-français (1850–1960)* (Montréal: Boréal).
Brewer, J., G. Higgins and F. Teeney (2011) *Religion, Civil Society and Peace in Northern Ireland* (Oxford: Oxford University Press).
Bringa, T. (1995) *Being Muslim the Bosnian Way. Identity and Community in a Central Bosnian Village* (Princeton: Princeton University Press).
Brown, G. (2010) 'Legible Pluralism. The Politics of Ethnic and Religious Identification in Malaysia', *Ethnopolitics* 9(1), 31–52.
Brubaker, R. (2006) *Ethnicity without Groups* (Cambridge, MA: Harvard University Press).
Brubaker, R., J. Fox and L. Grancea (2006) *Nationalist Politics and Everyday Ethnicity in a Transylvanian Town* (Oxford: Princeton University Press).
Bruce, S. (1994) *The Edge of the Union: The Ulster Loyalist Political Vision* (Oxford: Oxford University Press).
Bruce, S. (2003) *Politics and Religion* (Cambridge: Polity Press).
Cauthen, B. (2004) 'Covenant and Continuity: Ethno-symbolism and the Myth of Divine Election', *Nations and Nationalism* 10(1/2), 19–33
Chong, N. G. (2007) 'Ethnic Origins and Indigenous Peoples: An Approach from Latin America', pp. 312–324 in A. S. Leoussi and S. Grosby (eds), *Nationalism and Ethnosymbolism: History, Culture and Ethnicity in the Formation of Nations* (Edinburgh: Edinburgh University Press).
Coakley, J. (2002) 'Religion and Nationalism in the First World', pp. 206–225 in D. Conversi (ed.), *Ethnonationalism in the Contemporary World: Walker Connor and the Study of Nationalism* (London: Routledge).
Colley, L. (1992) *Britons: Forging the Nation 1707–1837* (New Haven: Yale University Press).
Connor, W. (1994) *Ethno-nationalism: The Quest for Understanding* (Princeton: Princeton University Press).
Conversi, D. (ed.) (2002) *Ethnonationalism in the Contemporary World: Walker Connor and the Study of Nationalism* (London: Routledge).
Davie, G. (2007) *The Sociology of Religion* (London: Sage).
Demerath, N. J. III (2001) *Crossing the Gods: World Religions and Worldly Politics* (New Brunswick: Rutgers University Press).
Duffy, E. (1982) '"Englishmen in Vaine": Roman Catholic Allegiance to George I', pp. 345–365 in S. Mews (ed.), *Religion and National Identity* (Oxford: Basil Blackwell).
Flora, P. (ed.) (1999) *State Formation, Nation-Building and Mass Politics in Europe. The Theory of Stein Rokkan* (Oxford: Oxford University Press).
Fox, J. (2002) *Ethnoreligious Conflict in the Late Twentieth Century: A General Theory* (Lanham, MD: Lexington Books).
Gal, A. (2007) 'Historical Ethno-symbols in the Emergence of the State of Israel', pp. 221–230 in A. S. Leoussi and S. Grosby (eds), *Nationalism and Ethnosymbolism: History, Culture and Ethnicity in the Formation of Nations* (Edinburgh: Edinburgh University Press).
Ganiel, G. (2008) *Evangelicalism and Conflict in Northern Ireland* (London, New York: Palgrave Macmillan).
Gerber, H. (2007) 'The Muslim Umma and the Formation of Middle Eastern Nationalisms', pp. 209–220 in A. S. Leoussi and S. Grosby (eds), *Nationalism and Ethnosymbolism: History, Culture and Ethnicity in the Formation of Nations* (Edinburgh: Edinburgh University Press).
Gorski, P. S. (2003) *The Disciplinary Revolution: Calvinism and the Rise of the State in Early Modern Europe* (Chicago: University of Chicago Press).

Gorski, P. S. and A. Altinordu (2008), 'After Secularization?', *Annual Review of Sociology* 34, 55–85.

Greenfeld, L. (1992) *Nationalism: Five Roads to Modernity* (Cambridge MA: Harvard University Press).

Hastings, A. (1997) *The Construction of Nationhood: Ethnicity, Religion and Nationalism* (Cambridge: Cambridge University Press).

Horowitz, D. L. (2000) *Ethnic Groups in Conflict*, 2nd edition (Berkeley: University of California Press).

Huntington, S. P. (2002) *The Clash of Civilizations and the Remaking of World Order* (New York: Free Press).

Igwarra, O. (2007) 'Holy Nigerian Nationalisms', pp. 267–280 in A. S. Leoussi and S. Grosby (eds), *Nationalism and Ethnosymbolism: History, Culture and Ethnicity in the Formation of Nations* (Edinburgh: Edinburgh University Press).

Ihalainen, P. (2005) *Protestant Nations Redefined: Changing Perceptions of National Identity in the Rhetoric of the English, Dutch and Swedish Public Churches, 1685–1772* (Leiden: Brill).

Jenkins, R. (2008) *Rethinking Ethnicity*, 2nd edition (London: Sage).

Joly, D. (2012) 'Race, Ethnicity and Religion: Social Actors and Policies', HAL Archives-ouvertes.fr. Available online at: https://halshs.archives-ouvertes.fr/halshs-00754959/document (Accessed 20 April 2015).

Juergensmeyer, M. (2008) *Global Rebellion: Religious Challenges to the Secular State* (Berkeley: University of California Press).

Kakar, S. (1996) *The Colors of Violence, Cultural Identities, Religion and Conflict* (Chicago: Chicago University Press).

Kaviraj, S. (2007) 'The Making of a Language of Patriotism in Modern Bengali', pp. 248–264 in A. S. Leoussi and S. Grosby (eds), *Nationalism and Ethnosymbolism: History, Culture and Ethnicity in the Formation of Nations* (Edinburgh: Edinburgh University Press).

Keating, M. (2001) *Plurinational Democracy* (Oxford: Oxford University Press).

Kinnvall, C. (2002) 'Nationalism, Religion and the Search for Chosen Traumas: Comparing Sikh and Hindu Identity Construction', *Ethnicities* 2(1), 79–106

Langer, A. (2010) 'The Situational Importance of Ethnicity and Religion in Ghana', *Ethnopolitics* 9(1), 9–29.

Levitt, P. (2008) 'Religion as a Path to Civic Engagement', *Ethnic and Racial Studies* 31(4), 766–791

Lie, J. (2004) *Modern Peoplehood* (Cambridge, MA: Harvard University Press).

Lybarger, L. D. (2007) *Identity and Religion in Palestine: The Struggle between Islamism and Secularism in the Occupied Territories* (Princeton: Princeton University Press).

McAdam, D., Tarrow, S. and Tilly, C. (2001) *Dynamics of Contention. Cambridge Studies in Contentious Politics* (Cambridge: Cambridge University Press).

Martin, D. (1978) *A General History of Secularisation* (Oxford: Basil Blackwell).

Marx, A. F. (2003) *Faith in Nation: Exclusionary Origins of Nationalism* (Oxford: Oxford University Press).

Mitchell, C. (2006) *Religion, Identity and Politics in Northern Ireland* (Aldershot: Ashgate).

Norris, P. and R. Inglehart (2004) *Sacred and Secular: Religion and Politics Worldwide* (Cambridge: Cambridge University Press).

Pocock, J. G. A. (1989) 'Conservative Enlightenment and Democratic Revolutions: the American and French Cases in British Perspective', *Government and Opposition* 24(1), 81–105.

Pragnere, P. (2013) *National Group Boundaries in Conflict Situations: Northern Ireland and the Basque Country. Definitions, Evolutions, Instrumentalisations and Effects*, unpublished Ph.D. thesis, University College Dublin and EHESS Paris.

Ruane, J. (2010) 'Ethnicity, Religion and Peoplehood: Protestants in France and in Ireland', *Ethnopolitics* 9(1), 121–135.

Ruane, J. and Todd, J. (2009) 'Protestant Minorities in European States and Nations', *National Identities* 11(1), 1–8.

Shenhav, Y. (2006) *The Arab Jews* (Stanford: Stanford University Press).

Smith, A. D. (1986) *The Ethnic Origins of Nations* (Oxford: Basil Blackwell).

Smith, A. D. (2003) *Chosen Peoples: Sacred Sources of National Identity* (Oxford: Oxford University Press).

Snow, D. A. and Machelek, R. (1984) 'The Sociology of Conversion', *Annual Review of Sociology* 10, 167–190.

Stewart, F. (2009) 'Religion vs Ethnicity as a Source of Mobilisation. Are there Differences?', *MICRO-CON Working Paper no. 18*. Available online at: http://www.microconflict.eu/publications/RWP18_FS.pdf (Accessed 22 April 2015).

Toft, M. D. (2007) 'Getting Religion? The Puzzling Case of Islam and Civil War', *International Security* 31(4), 97–131.

Van der Leer, P. and H. Lehmann (eds) (1999) *Nation and Religion: Perspectives on Europe and Asia* (Princeton: Princeton University Press).

Varshney, A. (2003) *Ethnic Conflict and Civic Life: Hindus and Muslims in India* (London: Yale University Press).

Weber, M. (1930) *The Protestant Ethic and the Spirit of Capitalism* (London: George Allen and Unwin).

Whyte, J. (1991) *Interpreting Northern Ireland* (Oxford: Clarendon).

Wolff, S. (2003) *Disputed Territories: The Transnational Dynamics of Ethnic Conflict Settlement* (Oxford: Berghahn).

Wolffe, J. (ed.) (2014) *Catholics, Protestants and Muslims: Irish Religious Conflict in Comparative Perspective* (London: Palgrave Macmillan).

7

RACE AND ETHNICITY

Chris Gilligan

Introduction

The distinction, or commonality, between race and ethnicity is a recurring problem in ethnic and racial studies. Attempts to try and separate the two and treat them as distinct categories continually run into theoretical and practical difficulties, but using the terms interchangeably is also unsatisfactory. Confusion over the use of the terms is compounded by the different, sometimes inconsistent, meanings given to them. The term race is also a morally and politically charged one. Given these difficulties it is perhaps understandable that scholars who study ethnic conflict, for the most part, avoid using the term race at all. There is, however, something lost when this approach is taken. In terms of intellectual resources, for example, there is a rich and extensive literature on race and racism which scholars of ethnic conflict rarely, or only superficially, engage with. Using the term ethnic instead of race might appear to be more enlightened, but it can easily be used to evade the difficult moral and political issues associated with the use of the term race or, worse, to pretend that they have no relevance to the study of ethnic conflict. In this chapter I aim to help students of ethnic conflict to engage with the broader literature on race and ethnicity, by providing some guidance to help grapple with the slippery concepts of race and ethnicity.

Pinning down slippery concepts

In the social sciences, in political discourse and in everyday conversation the English language meaning of the term ethnicity is closely related to the terms race, nation, a people, clan and tribe (Connor 1978; Eriksen 2002; Fenton 2003; Hughey 1998; Jenkins 2008). The terms are sometimes used as synonyms for each other, but there is also slippage between the uses of the terms. Krishnamurthy, commenting on the alternating use of the terms 'ethnic' and 'tribal' in a newspaper article, asks: 'If the two terms are genuinely synonymous, is "tribe" ever used of the people of former Yugoslavia? ... Is "ethnic" the superordinate term, with "tribal" available only for subsets of the human population such as Africans?' (Krishnamurthy 1996: 132). Krishnamurthy's rhetorical questions point to an inconsistency in use of the terms. The use of the term tribal in the African context, but not the former Yugoslavia, indicates that there are underlying assumptions which inform the use of the terms. Tribal, he suggests, is being used pejoratively to convey primitiveness and lack of industrial development as explanations for ethnic conflict in African countries. This kind of usage is intimately bound up with a deeply ingrained worldview which assumes that people in the West are white, modern, civilised, industrialised and affluent and people in Africa are black, traditional, primitive and impoverished (a view which also assumes that blackness is non-Western).

One approach which social scientists take to avoid this kind of slippage in use, and to try to make their assumptions evident, is to attempt to specify the meanings of the key terms which they employ. Fenton, for example, explains that the terms ethnic group, race and nation share 'a single centre – or "core" … Common to all three is an idea of descent or ancestry and very closely implicated in all three we find ideas about culture … [which] typically include myths about the past, beliefs about the "kind of people we are", and the idea that "culture" defines a group' (2003: 13). He also points out some of the divergences between the three terms. Nation, unlike the other two, is assumed to be 'associated with a state or state-like political form' (Fenton 2003: 23). Race contains two ideas that make it distinctive: 'that "local" groups are instances of abstractly conceived divisions of humankind, and … that race makes explicit reference to physical or "visible" difference as the primary marker of difference and inequality' (Ibid.). And there are three specific features of the term ethnic group: '1. that the group is a kind of sub-set within a nation-state, 2. that the point of reference of difference is typically culture rather than physical appearance, and 3. often that the group referred to is "other" (foreign, exotic, minority) to some majority who are presumed not to be "ethnic"' (Ibid.). Fenton's distinction between a common core and distinctive ideas provides a way of understanding why the terms race and ethnicity sometimes appear to be synonyms for each other (due to their common core) and sometimes appear to be distinct terms (due to the distinctive ideas encapsulated in them). Part of the reason for the slippage is that in some contexts the terms *are* synonyms for each other, while in other contexts they are not. Fenton provides orientation points for our reading of his text. This is useful, but only up to a point.

These orientation points help us to follow many of the contemporary academic texts on race and ethnicity, but they will not help us navigate them all. If we assume that there are correct and precise definitions of the terms, and Fenton has provided these, we will soon become confused again. We can illustrate this through looking at the idea that race refers to the use of physical features as markers of difference while ethnicity refers to cultural ones. This idea is disputed by a number of authors who, since the 1980s in Europe and more recently in the United States of America (USA), have pointed to the development of a 'new racism' (or 'cultural racism') which tries to promote negative measures against non-whites on the grounds that they are culturally incompatible with 'white' society (Barker 1981; Gilroy 1990; Giroux 1993; Lentin 2004: 85–96). Some authors even argue against the distinction between culture and physical features as markers. Sociobiologists challenge the distinction from a very different direction. The leading proponent of this perspective in the study of race and ethnicity, van den Berghe, argues that: 'All organisms are programmed to be nepotistic, i.e. to behave favourably (or "altruistically") to others in proportion to their real or perceived degree of common ancestry' (1995: 360). He argues that biology and culture are interrelated, rather than being distinct domains. That, for example, 'human culture is necessarily "carried" by biological organisms who reproduce … culture itself is non-genetically transmitted, but it cannot be transmitted except through flesh and blood individuals who, if they fail to reproduce, generally stop passing on their culture' (van den Berghe 1988: 255). This approach suggests that people procreate with others who share the same cultural background and consequently, in practice, there is a major overlap between biological and cultural reproduction, and physical and cultural markers of difference. This approach elides the distinction between race and ethnicity made by Fenton. The examples of sociobiology and analyses of 'new racism' indicate that the way in which the terms race and ethnicity are defined can vary significantly according to the theoretical perspective employed by the author.[1]

Pinning down concepts, through defining them, helps us to get a clearer picture of the phenomena we are studying. In the case of race and ethnicity, however, slipperiness is not a distraction which prevents us from understanding the phenomena. Slipperiness is inherent to phenomena which are categorised as ethnic and racial. Attempts to pin down the terms run the risk of turning historically and socially fluid, contingent and highly contextual phenomena into eternal, fixed, static and universal ones. To understand the phenomena we study in ethnic and racial studies we also need to understand why the terms are slippery. Defining them does not help us to do that.

Race and ethnicity in context

One problem with attempting to define the terms race and ethnicity is that in order to do so we are forced to generalise. Generalisation requires us to remove the terms race and ethnicity from any *particular* social or historical context, and consequently it can appear as though the definitions are universal and eternal. Fenton, however, is well aware that the terms race and ethnicity do not have fixed meanings, and that 'how ethnicity is discussed is very much contextual' (2003: 25). The terms race and ethnicity only come to life and have meaning in particular social and historical contexts. Take, for example, the categories Malay, Black, Irish, Jewish and Ethiopian. Each of these has, at one time or another, been referred to as a racial group, or as an ethnic group, or as a nation. The terms themselves do not help us to determine whether the people being referred to are considered to be a nation, a race or an ethnic group. To determine this we need to look at the geographical context in which people are being categorised; the social milieux in which the categories are being employed, and the historical period in which the process of categorisation takes place.

Different milieux

One of the reasons for the slippage in usage, which Krishnamurthy identifies, is that the terms race and ethnicity (nation, tribe, clan …) are being employed in newspaper articles. In newspapers there is not usually the same requirement for precision that is demanded from academic texts. Journalists generally make fewer demands on their audience. Journalists usually attempt to address their readers in terms that are immediately explicable. They tend to draw on widely held tacit understandings to convey the stories they want to tell. In many instances the difference between academic and journalistic writing is not a particular problem, they serve different purposes and address different, but overlapping, audiences. The difference is also often unproblematic because different milieux not only have their own way of talking, their own idiom, but they also have their own technical language. Terms such as acculturation, ethnie, primordialism, and racialisation, for example, are rarely found outside of academic texts on race and ethnicity. The terms race and ethnicity – and subcategories such as Malaysian, Black, Irish, Jewish or Ethiopian – are, however, categories employed in both academic analyses and everyday discourse.

Banton draws our attention to this problem when he says that in everyday talk about race and ethnicity a person 'rarely employs any concept of ethnicity. He or she uses a practical language embodying proper names, such as Malay, Chinese, and Indian' (Banton 1994: 6). These terms are employed within what he calls an actor's model of the social structure, and they are used 'to navigate a course through daily life, helping to identify the shallow water, the best channels, and the likely reactions of other vessels' (Ibid.). These categories help people to orientate themselves in the real world which they inhabit. In this context, Banton suggests, a certain looseness is useful. In real world contexts people often recognise that there are different degrees of ethnicity. As Banton puts it: '[a]nyone who speaks this [practical] language knows that persons assigned to these categories vary in their cultural distinctiveness. In the languages they use, the costumes they wear ... some are more culturally distinctive, and in this sense, more "ethnic"' (Ibid.). Put simply, one Chinese neighbour might be more Chinese than another and all Chinese neighbours might be more Chinese at particular times of the year. This actor's model differs from what he calls an observer's model, which looks 'for regularities of which the actors are unaware or about which actors have insufficient information' (Ibid.). An observer's model seeks to penetrate surface appearances and understand the social processes which give rise to phenomena such as ethnic identification, or racial discrimination. Actor's models rely on tacit everyday understandings which come from being embedded in that particular social context. The observer attempts to generalise from these particular embedded contexts. They attempt to discern patterns, to infer underlying dynamics or to make explicit the tacit understandings which people hold.

Brubaker (2004) makes a similar distinction between 'categories of practice' and 'categories of analysis'. Categories of practice are '"native" or "folk" or "lay" categories ... of everyday social experience, developed and deployed by ordinary social actors' (Ibid.: 31). They are used by lay actors in 'everyday settings to make sense of themselves, of their activity, of what they share with, and how they differ from, others' (Ibid.). But they are also used 'by political entrepreneurs to persuade people to understand themselves and their predicaments' in ways that serve the interests, or objectives, of those political actors (Ibid.: 32). Social analysis, he points out, 'requires relatively unambiguous analytical categories' (Ibid.: 29). At first sight the use of categories by administrators – ethnic categories used in censuses, ethnic monitoring forms and racial and ethnic terms in legislation are good examples – might appear to be relatively unambiguous, and certainly less slippery than everyday use. The terms are fixed in ink by the people who draw up the forms, or the legislation. Fixing the terms in ink, however, does not fix their meaning. This meaning is, at least in part, given by the person filling out the form, or the judge interpreting the law. When you fill in the form you decide if you are 'black' or 'white', 'Asian-American' or 'Chinese'. The person who inserted the terms into the form cannot be certain that the person who filled it in has the same idea in mind when they do so (although that does not usually stop administrators from acting as if they can be certain of the intended meaning). The purpose of these forms is not to understand the meaning of the categories but to allocate people to categories for some purpose, or to enable the judiciary to adjudicate on disputes which are brought before them. In this sense they are what Brubaker calls categories of practice.

There are several different ways of talking race and ethnicity, and these vary by setting. The way that terms are used depends on the ideas that are being conveyed, and ideas are in part shaped in relation to the audience they are being conveyed to and the purpose they are being conveyed for. The fact that the actual terms used in these milieux are often the same should not blind us to the fact that they are sometimes being used with different meanings.

Spatial contexts

Discourses of race and ethnicity are also different in different countries, and often differ in different parts of the same country. They are, for example, different in the USA compared to the UK. This is partly due to the different histories of the countries. Fenton draws attention to the significance of the different contexts when he says that in the USA a discourse of race dominates and 'ethnic groups and ethnic differences often have a "white" connotation. By contrast in Britain, where the public discourse focuses more on ethnicity, the term "ethnic groups" retains its meaning of minority status and foreign origins; ethnic groups in the UK are not white' (Fenton 2003: 39). (The term 'white' is also relational, contextual and conflates myriad differences: see Garner 2007.) Discourses of race and ethnicity also differ in different regions within a country, between the southern and northern states of the USA, for example. Even within a particular city discourses around race and ethnicity can vary. One study of London in the 1980s, for example, found that in one district the 'decline in the housing and economic circumstances of these residents was "explained" by correlating these changes with the presence of variously defined "problem families", black people and Vietnamese refugees' (Back 1996: 239). The other district, by contrast, was viewed by its inhabitants 'as a place where harmonious [race or ethnic] relations existed' (Ibid.).

The way that different national contexts shape discourse can be seen by looking at an example of one particular category. If we take the category Irish, for example, we find different discourses around Irishness in Ireland than in other national contexts. In recent years significant immigration into the Republic of Ireland has led to significant debate about who can be considered Irish. In 2004 the Constitution was changed to racialise, or ethnicise, citizenship by making descent rather than residence the principle criterion by which citizenship was determined (Mulally 2007). In the context of Northern Ireland Irishness is usually a reference to the section of the population who identify themselves politically and culturally as Irish nationalists, in contrast to those who identify themselves politically and culturally as British or Ulster unionists (Gilligan 2007). To make matters more confusing Irishness and Britishness are often conflated with the religious categories Catholic and Protestant (see Ruane and Todd, this volume). In the rest of the UK Irishness is usually employed in discussions of immigration from Ireland, and the second and third generation descendants of immigrants from Ireland. In the USA the discourse around Irishness is also usually focused on immigrants from Ireland, and their descendants (Garner 2003).

Historical context

At the beginning of the twentieth century the superiority of the White race was an important component of the worldview of political elites on both sides of the North Atlantic. The idea of White superiority was used to justify the colonial domination of large parts of the 'non-white' world by European powers, and a range of racially discriminatory measures in the USA. A wide range of factors have been identified as playing a role in the discrediting of racial thinking since then. Prominent amongst these have been: the growing influence of egalitarian ideas; political agitation for civil rights for black people; horror at the consequences of the racial exterminationist policies of the Nazis; the rise of Japan as a non-White international power; the rise of anti-colonial movements; the discrediting of the science behind ideas of biological superiority; and ambivalences about the promotion of White solidarity (Barkan 1993; Bonnett 2003; Furedi 1998; Grant 1968: 175–214; Lauren 1988; Malik 1996; Wolton 2000). The marginalisation of assertions of racial superiority is indicated by the inclusion of clauses on 'respect for the principle of equal rights and self-determination of peoples' and 'promoting and encouraging respect for human rights and for fundamental freedoms for all without distinction as to race, sex, language or religion' in the Charter of the United Nations (UN), ratified in 1945 (UN 1945: Chapter 1).

The discrediting of the idea of racial superiority did not, however, mean that practices based on this idea ceased. Policies of racial segregation continued in the USA, and Britain actually expanded its Empire after 1945. After the Second World War, however, ideas of racial superiority could not be used as justification, and instead there was a shift to a welfarist discourse of development and a race relations discourse of the protection of minority peoples. This new language helped provide 'justification enough for the European powers to re-establish their empires' (Wolton 2000: 154). After 1945 racial language became increasingly coded, as it became increasingly politically and socially unacceptable to speak openly about race. As Furedi puts it: 'in the new egalitarian climate the assumptions of racial superiority did not disappear, they merely became less explicit' (1994: 55). This can present difficulties for social scientists because it is more difficult to assess the extent to which racial thinking has an influence on the phenomena that we investigate in the post-war period. The end of the Cold War has shifted the discourse again. Furedi suggests that a

> new moral equation between a superior North and an inferior South helps legitimise a two-tiered international system ... Race no longer has a formal role to play since the new global hierarchy is represented through a two-tier moral system. Gradually the old silent race war has been replaced by moral crusades and by 'clashes of civilisations'.
>
> *(Furedi 1998: 240)*

The development of ethnic conflict studies, as a clearly identifiable sub-discipline, dates from the post-Cold War period. And the rationale for Western intervention in situations of ethnic conflict is often motivated in moral terms. This raises a range of uncomfortable questions for scholars of ethnic conflict, one of these being the extent to which the use of the term ethnic may involve an implicit reworking of older racial thinking.

The historically changing nature of discourses around race and ethnicity can be seen in the shift away from the term race and the coining and subsequent rise in use of the term ethnicity. The story of how the term ethnicity came to eclipse race is still a major gap in the literature on ethnic and racial studies.[2] If the shift is mentioned at all it is usually treated as a pragmatic choice on the part of social scientists. As one introductory textbook puts it, because 'of its confusing usage and its questionable scientific validity, many sociologists and anthropologists have dispensed with the term *race* and instead use *ethnic group* to describe those groups commonly defined as racial' (Marger 2000: 25: italics in the original). Changing the terms, however, does not end the confusion. At best it allows the researcher to investigate the social dynamics involved, without getting too hung-up on tortuous discussions of terminology. At worst it is used to evade the history of race as something which is no longer relevant.

In this section I have suggested that race and ethnicity are slippery concepts for good reason, and that attempts to ignore, avoid or downplay the slipperiness of the terms can lead the student of ethnic politics to misunderstand, or only gain a partial understanding of, the phenomena which they are studying.

Race and ethnicity as constructs

In this final section I will explore the idea that the terms race and ethnicity are elusive terms because the phenomena which they refer to – races and ethnic groups – do not actually exist. This might seem like an odd point. How, you might be asking yourself, can anyone study ethnic politics or ethnic conflict if ethnic groups do not exist? Indeed, how can there be ethnic conflict if ethnic groups do not exist? Hopefully I can explain, but before I do let us have a look at race. Banton warns that in attempting to make generalisations 'the observer often comes to mistaken conclusions which take a long time to clear up. One such confusion was that of race' (1994: 6). The mistake was to take the observation that people from different parts of the world look physically different in some ways and conclude that humanity must therefore be divided up into different, biologically distinct, races. The consensus view in modern science rejects that conclusion. Scientists point out that there is greater genetic variation within any given human population than between two different populations, they argue that the lines drawn to demarcate different races are arbitrary and the fact that skin colour has acted as an identifier of different races is a result of historical processes, not something which is determined by nature (Malik 2008).

So races do not exist in any biological sense, they are social constructs. Races are created and reproduced in human minds, not through biological processes. The idea of race is sustained by people who hold racist views, but the word race also provides 'part of the rationale for all the legislation, international and national, which has been designed to combat discrimination based on ideas of race' (Banton 1994: 7). Here we can see another reason why the term race is slippery, because it is simultaneously rejected and upheld in contemporary public policy, often by the same people. Social scientists who take a social constructionist perspective on the world suggest that we can deal with the slipperiness of race as a term by focusing on 'the construction and reproduction of the idea of "race"' (Miles and Brown 2003: 91). Miles and Brown criticise those who set out to explain race relations, saying that in taking 'race relations' as one of their analytical categories they are participating in the process of reproducing the idea of race. Rather than examine interactions between entities that do not exist (races), they suggest, the task for social scientists is the 'generation of concepts with which one can grasp and portray the historical processes by which notions of "race" become accepted and/or used in a plurality of discourses' (Ibid.: 92). They employ the analytical concept of racialisation to examine the *processes* through which group boundaries marked by biological differences are generated, and people are allocated to those groups (Ibid.: 99–103).

Miles and Brown extend their argument when they say 'ethnic groups are no more objective or real than "races"' (2003: 96). This claim is more contentious than the claim that races do not exist. Miles and Brown, however, are not the only proponents of this idea. Students of ethnic politics may be familiar with the idea from the work of Brubaker, who suggests that one of the most problematic conceptual errors in the study of ethnicity, race and nationhood is '"groupism" … the tendency to take discrete, bounded groups as basic constituents of social life, chief protagonists of social conflicts, and fundamental units of social analysis' (2004: 8). Participants in ethnic politics, he observes, do present ethnic groups as bounded entities, in fact it is crucial to their practice as ethnopolitical entrepreneurs. Social scientists, however, should avoid adopting '*categories of ethnopolitical practice* as our *categories of social analysis*' (Ibid.: 10; italics in the original). This does not mean that we should avoid or ignore phenomena which are described as ethnic. We should, in fact, acknowledge that the process of ethnicisation can generate 'phases of extraordinary cohesion and moments of intensely felt collective solidarity', but we should also remind ourselves that groupness is 'variable and contingent rather than fixed and given' (Ibid.: 12). Phases of extraordinary cohesion rarely endure for very long, and 'high levels of groupness may be more the result of conflict (especially violent conflict) than its underlying cause' (Ibid.: 19: see also Kaufman in this volume) One straightforward way in which we can stay sensitive to the fact that ethnic conflict is not conflict between ethnic groups is to remind ourselves that 'the chief protagonists of most ethnic conflict … are not ethnic groups as such but various kinds of organizations …

[including] states ... terrorist groups ... political parties, ethnic associations ... churches ... television stations, and so on' (Ibid.: 14–15). These organisations may claim to represent ethnic groups, but we should not accept these claims at face value.

A useful strategy to avoid slipping into groupism, Brubaker suggests, is to distinguish 'consistently between categories and groups ... rather than presume – the relation between them' (2004: 12). Ethnopolitical actors work to collapse the distinction between the category ethnic and the group. Social scientists should not assist them in this endeavour, but instead should step back and draw attention to the attempts to do so. Continually keeping in mind the distinction between categories of practice (e.g. ethnic, ethnicity) and categories of analysis (e.g. ethnicisation) should help us to maintain the critical distance necessary for analysis. We should be careful, for example, not to talk about ethnic violence because in doing so we 'do not simply *interpret* the violence ... [we] *constitute* it *as ethnic*' (Ibid.: 16; italics in the original). In situations of 'ethnic conflict', he suggests, violence 'may have as much or more to do with thuggery, warlordship, opportunistic looting, and black-market profiteering than with ethnicity' (Ibid.: 19). If we are attentive to the social construction of ethnicity we can better discern the range of dynamics and processes which are at play in situations which are characterised as ethnic.

In this section I have suggested that race and ethnicity are slippery concepts because the things which they refer to – races and ethnic groups – do not exist, but in practice many political actors and domestic and international institutions act as if they do exist (whether because they assume that ethnic groups exist, or because they want to make ethnicity an important dimension of political identification). A key way to handle this slippage is to keep in mind the distinction between categories and groups, to remember that groupness is variable and contingent and to focus on processes which construct phenomena as ethnic or racial. In short, to think in terms of ethnicisation and racialisation.

Conclusion

At this point you might think the concepts race and ethnicity are just as slippery as they always seemed, or they may seem even slipperier. If so you have grasped at least part of what I was trying to do. Race and ethnicity are slippery terms for several reasons. In everyday situations and in social analysis the two terms are often collapsed into each other by the people who use the terms. At the same time there are persistent attempts to distinguish between the terms. They are also slippery because they are employed as categories of practice as well as categories of analysis, but as categories of analysis they do not usually succeed in escaping the embrace of practice. And they are slippery because ethnopolitical actors attempt to collapse the distinction between groups and categories, while many social scientists strive to maintain the distinction. The point of this chapter was not to reassure you that the terms can be pinned down or tamed. The slipperiness is symptomatic of the lack of clarity which the concepts express. If we keep these points in mind when we carry out our research then we will be better equipped to get behind the surface appearances and the commonsense understandings of the phenomena which we seek to analyse.

Acknowledgements

Thanks to Carol Marley, Steve Fenton, Karl Cordell and Stefan Wolff for useful comments on an earlier draft of this article.

Notes

1 There is insufficient space in this short chapter to outline or analyse the range of perspectives. For useful texts which do analyse a range of perspectives see: Malešević (2004); Rex and Mason (1988). All analyses, including this one, inevitably involve some kind of theoretical underpinnings. This article is written from a constructivist perspective.

2 Some of the elements are known. These include the discrediting of race as a concept, the shift from biological to cultural conceptions of group difference and inequality, the coining of the term ethnicity to explain the persistence of group identification amongst third and fourth generation descendants of immigrants in the USA, the application of the term ethnic to inter-group conflict in post-colonial societies and to secessionist movements in Europe in the 1970s. For some useful texts which provide some of the pieces of the picture see: Banks (1996); Barkan (1993); Glazer and Moynihan (1970); Malik (1996).

Further reading

Many introductory student texts which cover the topics of race and ethnicity fumble over, or evade, the conceptual problems outlined in this chapter. Fenton (2003) is a notable exception, and I would recommend it to the beginner. My favourite texts which grapple with the issues in this chapter are: Malik (1996), which takes a long historical sweep from the Atlantic slave trade to postmodernism, and Brubaker (2004), which contains a collection of some of his most thoughtful articles on methodological issues relevant to the study of racialisation and ethnicisation. As a collection it lacks the narrative cohesion of Malik's study, but the contents of its chapters will seem more immediately relevant to students of ethnic politics. For excellent historical accounts of the discrediting of racial thinking, a major gap in the study of ethnic politics, read Barkan (1993), Furedi (1998), Lauren (1988) and Wolton (2000).

Barkan, Elazar, (1993), *The Retreat of Scientific Racism*, Cambridge, Cambridge University Press.
Brubaker, Roger, (2004), *Ethnicity Without Groups*, Cambridge, Harvard University Press.
Fenton, Steve, (2003), *Ethnicity*, Cambridge, Polity Press.
Furedi, Frank, (1998), *The Silent War*, London, Pluto.
Lauren, Paul Gordon, (1988), *Power and Prejudice*, Boulder, Westview Press.
Malik, Kenan, (1996), *The Meaning of Race*, Houndmills, Macmillan.
Wolton, Suke, (2000), *Lord Hailey, the Colonial Office and the Politics of Race and Empire in the Second World War*, Houndmills, Macmillan.

References

Back, Les, (1996), *New Ethnicities and Urban Culture*, Abingdon, Routledge.
Banks, Marcus, (1996), *Ethnicity*, London, Routledge.
Banton, Michael, (1994), 'Modelling ethnic and national relations', *Ethnic and Racial Studies*, 17(1), 1–18.
Barkan, Elazar, (1993), *The Retreat of Scientific Racism*, Cambridge, Cambridge University Press.
Barker, Martin, (1981), *The New Racism*, London, Junction Books.
Bonnett, Alastair, (2003), 'From White to Western: "racial decline" and the idea of the West in Britain, 1890–1930', *Journal of Historical Sociology*, 16(3), 320–348.
Brubaker, Rogers, (2004), *Ethnicity Without Groups*, Cambridge, Harvard University Press.
Connor, Walker, (1978), 'A nation is a Nation, is a State, is an Ethnic Group, is a...', *Ethnic and Racial Studies*, 1(4): 379–388.
Eriksen, Thomas Hylland, (2002), *Ethnicity and Nationalism* (second edition), London, Pluto Press.
Fenton, Steve, (2003), *Ethnicity*, Cambridge, Polity Press.
Furedi, Frank, (1994), *The New Ideology of Imperialism*, London, Pluto.
Furedi, Frank, (1998), *The Silent War*, London, Pluto.
Garner, Steve, (2003), *Racism in the Irish Experience*, London, Pluto.
Garner, Steve, (2007), *Whiteness: An Introduction*, London, Routledge.
Gilligan, Chris, (2007), 'The Irish Question and the Concept "Identity" in the 1980s', *Nations and Nationalism*, 13(4), 599–617.
Gilroy, Paul, (1990), 'The end of anti-racism', *Journal of Ethnic and Racial Studies*, 17(1), 71–83.

Giroux, Henry A., (1993), 'Living dangerously: identity politics and the new cultural racism', *Cultural Studies*, 7(1), 1–27.

Glazer, Nathan and Moynihan, Daniel P. (1970), *Beyond the Melting Pot* (second edition, original published in 1963), Cambridge (Mass.), MIT Press.

Grant, Joanne, (1968), *Black Protest: History, Documents and Analysis*, New York, Fawcett Premier.

Hughey, Michael W. (ed.), (1998), *New Tribalisms: The Resurgence of Race and Ethnicity*, New York, NYU Press.

Jenkins, Richard, (2008), *Rethinking Ethnicity* (second edition), London, Sage.

Krishnamurthy, Ramesh, (1996), 'Ethnic, racial and tribal: The language of racism?', in Carmen Rosa Caldas-Coulthard and Malcolm Coulthard (eds), *Texts and Practices: Readings in Critical Discourse Analysis*, London, Routledge.

Lauren, Paul Gordon, (1988), *Power and Prejudice*, Boulder, Westview Press.

Lentin, Allana, (2004), *Racism and Anti-Racism in Europe*, London, Pluto Press.

Malešević, Siniša, (2004), *The Sociology of Ethnicity*, London, Sage.

Malik, Kenan, (1996), *The Meaning of Race*, Houndmills, Macmillan.

Malik, Kenan, (2008), *Strange Fruit*, London, Oxford, Oneworld.

Marger, Martin N., (2000), *Race and Ethnic Relations* (fifth edition), Stamford, Wadsworth.

Miles, Robert and Brown, Malcolm, (2003), *Racism* (second edition), London, Routledge.

Mulally, Siobhan, (2007), 'Children, citizenship and constitutional change', in Bryan Fanning (ed.), *Immigration and Social Change in the Republic of Ireland*, Manchester, Manchester University Press.

Rex, John and Mason, David (eds), (1988), *Theories of Race and Ethnic Relations*, Cambridge, Cambridge University Press.

UN [United Nations], (1945), *Charter of the United Nations*, available online at: http://www.un.org/en/documents/charter/ (accessed 3 September 2015).

van den Berghe, Pierre L., (1988), 'Ethnicity and the sociobiology debate', in John Rex and David Mason (eds), (1988), *Theories of Race and Ethnic Relations*, Cambridge, Cambridge University Press, 246–263.

van den Berghe, Pierre L., (1995), 'Does race matter?', *Nations and Nationalism*, 1(3), 357–368.

Wolton, Suke, (2000), *Lord Hailey, the Colonial Office and the Politics of Race and Empire in the Second World War*, Houndmills, Macmillan.

PART II

8

ETHNICITY AS A GENERATOR OF CONFLICT

Stuart J. Kaufman

Introduction

Ethnic identities have existed throughout recorded history. Even in ancient times, ethnic groups such as the Hebrews, Babylonians and Egyptians were important political actors (Smith 1986), just as contemporary Serbs and Kurds are. These different groups typically have interests or goals that are competing in some way, and these differences often lead to political or social conflict. Most of these conflicts involve little or no violence, instead being expressed through religious expression, economic competition, social segregation, competition among ethnically based political parties, or other peaceful means. Still, especially when the issue at stake is the political dominance of one group over another, violent ethnic clashes do some-times occur, leading sometimes to riots and in the worst cases to civil wars, mass expulsions of populations, and even genocide.

Experts disagree about the extent to which ethnicity causes or generates conflict. One group, the "instrumentalist" school of thought, sees ethnic identity as little more than a tool used by elites to pursue competition over tangible goods such as economic opportunity. From this perspective, there is no such thing as "ethnic conflict" at all, and ethnicity does not cause or generate conflict; it merely provides a framework or a label in which other sorts of competition occur. Other scholars, in the "psycho-cultural" school of thought (Ross 2007), argue that ethnic conflict is very real, and that conflicts – over the status of the holy sites in Jerusalem, for example – often stem directly from the way people define their ethnic iden-tities, and are not primarily about the participants' desire for material goods. Thus ethnicity can be – though it does not necessarily have to be – a generator of conflict.

What is ethnic conflict?

Discussions of ethnicity and ethnic conflict are notoriously imprecise, because people disagree about what counts as an ethnic conflict. Are race relations between blacks and whites in the United States an example of low-violence ethnic conflict, or is racial conflict a different category altogether? If race is different, does the distinction extend to Rwanda, where Hutus and Tutsis – both black – referred to their difference as one of race? Are relations between Muslims and Hindus in India, or between Sunni and Shi'a Arabs in Iraq, cases of ethnic conflict, or do they belong in different categories as "religious", "communal", or "sectarian" conflicts?

For an anthropologist, what these cases all have in common is that the groups involved are primarily ascriptive – that is, membership in the groups is typically assigned at birth and is difficult to change. In theory, Indian Muslims can convert and become Hindu, and Iraqi Sunnis can become Shi'a, but in practice few do, and the conversion of those few is not always accepted by their new co-ethnics. Identities of this kind, then, are "sticky", hard to change even if they are not marked by the kind of obvious physical differences that distinguish African-Americans from white Americans. Based on this commonality, I will use the broader definition of ethnicity that encompasses all of these kinds of ascriptive groups. According to Anthony Smith (1986), a group is an ethnic group if its members share the following traits: a common name, a believed common descent, elements of a shared culture (most often language or religion), common historical memories, and attachment to a particular territory.

In the past, experts disagreed widely about where ethnicity comes from. Some, focusing on the evidence that many ethnic identities seem to go back hundreds or thousands of years, asserted that ethnicity was a "primordial" identity, and implied that it was essentially unchangeable. They emphasized that groups often worked hard to make their identity unchangeable, sometimes carving that identity onto their bodies through tattoos or circumcision (Isaacs 1975). Even when they do not go that far, however, people tend to stick to the identities – especially the language and religion – they learn first from their parents. This view of ethnicity implies that ethnic conflict is based on "ancient hatreds" that are impossible to eradicate and nearly impossible to manage.

There is another, more complicated side to ethnic identity, however. Most people have multiple identities that are either "nested" (as subgroups within larger groups) or overlapping. The average Cuban-American is at the same time also an American Hispanic or Latino, an American Catholic, an American, and a member of the worldwide Catholic Church. Which identity is more important to her is likely to depend on the situation: when listening to the Pope, she is likely to respond as a Catholic; when watching the US president, as an American; and when thinking about US policy toward Cuba, as a Cuban-American.

Furthermore, identities do sometimes change, with new ones emerging and old ones disappearing, especially in times of crisis. For example, when the Soviet Union was breaking apart in the early 1990s, Ukrainians and Russians in the Transnistria region of Moldova came together as "Russophones" – people who preferred to speak Russian rather than Moldovan – to resist the assertiveness of the ethnic Moldovans (Kaufman 2001). On the other hand, the "Yugoslav" identity disappeared when the country of Yugoslavia did in 1991, so people who formerly called themselves Yugoslavs had to shift to another identity as Serbs, Croats, or members of some other group.

Noticing that people shift their identity – or at least the identity they use politically – based on the situation, a second group of scholars emerged to argue that ethnic identity is not "primordial" at all, but merely "instrumental" (Hardin 1995). From this perspective, people follow "ethnic" leaders when it is in their interests to do so, and leaders try to create ethnic solidarity when it works for them. This view of ethnic identity implies that ethnic conflict can be blamed primarily on selfish leaders who mislead their followers in pursuit of their own power. The conflicts themselves, these scholars argue, are typically not really "ethnic" at all – in many cases, clashes are motivated by economic or criminal disputes, but are later reinterpreted as having been ethnically motivated for political purposes (Brass 1997).

A third point of view about ethnic identity mixes the other two views by emphasizing the degree to which people create their identities. Expressed in book titles such as *The Invention of*

Tradition (Hobsbawm and Ranger 1992), this view points out that ethnic identities are "socially constructed". They are not "natural" in the sense that a simple primordialist view would assume; even racial distinctions are just a matter of custom. For example, most African-Americans accept the label "black", but in South Africa, most of them would be classified as "coloured" – of mixed race – rather than as the darker, purely African "blacks". Most Americans would not notice the difference, but in Apartheid-era South Africa, the difference would have shaped every aspect of people's lives.

Furthermore, constructivists pointed out, the source of these customs was "invented traditions": writers or scholars who created what Anthony Smith calls a "myth-symbol complex". This myth-symbol complex establishes the "accepted" history of the group and the criteria for distinguishing who is a member; identifies heroes and enemies; and glorifies symbols of the group's identity. In most cases, these mythologies "mythicize" real history, taking real events but redefining them as the morally defining experiences of their people. In many cases, these events are what Vamik Volkan (1997) has called "chosen traumas", such as the Holocaust for Jews or the 1389 Battle of Kosovo Field for Serbs. In some cases, however, histories and myths are invented out of whole cloth to create new identities.

These constructivist insights can be viewed as a way to settle the argument between primordialists and instrumentalists, because constructivist ideas explain both the insights and the problems of the other two views. For example, most Serbs honestly believe that their identity is primordial, forged in the fires of battle against the Turks at Kosovo in 1389, so their perception is that their conflicts with Muslims are the result of primordial "ancient hatreds". In fact, though, that view of history was the result of late nineteenth-century Serbian politics and educational policy (Snyder 2000); before then, most Serbs did not think of themselves as Serbs at all. Similarly, Serbian politicians like Slobodan Milošević did indeed use Serbian ethnic identity instrumentally to pursue their own power in the 1990s, but that identity only "worked" politically because it had been socially constructed before. Any old identity will not do.

Another question is how to tell whether a particular conflict is an ethnic conflict. Most African countries are multi-ethnic, for example, but African civil wars often involve warlords competing for control over resources such as diamond mines, so ethnicity has little to do with who is on which side. A conflict is ethnic only if the sides involved are distinguished primarily on the basis of ethnicity. Often one or both sides in an ethnic conflict will be a coalition of ethnic groups, rather than a single one, but the conflict is still ethnic because the people involved choose sides on the basis of their ethnic group membership, rather than other considerations such as economic interests.

An overview of ethnic conflicts

Ethnic groups and ethnic conflicts are everywhere. One comprehensive survey found a total of 275 ethnic or communal groups in 116 countries around the world that were socially disadvantaged in some way – "minorities at risk". Put together, the groups included more than one billion people, or about 17.4% of the world's population (Gurr 2000: 9–10). Of the 50 biggest countries in the world by population, only four – Poland, Tanzania, Nepal, and North Korea – did not have at least one "minority at risk" (and Tanzania has many ethnic groups: they were merely judged not to be "at risk"). Some of these groups are very small, in mostly homogeneous countries: Australia's lone "minority at risk", the Aborigines, are only about 1% of the country's population; while Japan's only minority, the Koreans, are only one-half of one percent. Some of the groups are very large and important, however:

Malaysia's Chinese minority is 27% of the population, and India's oft-mistreated Muslims are 11% of India's population. Overall, it is accurate to say that most countries in the world are ethnically diverse, and ethnic relations yield some degree of conflict in most of them.

Most of the time, the existence of minority groups does not lead to violence or even to serious conflict. In 1995, most of the "minorities at risk" (58%) were either politically inactive or mobilized only for routine politics. Another 15% were a bit more volatile, engaging in demonstrations, rioting, or both. Still, violent ethnic conflicts were unfortunately plentiful: 49 (18%) ethnic groups were engaged in "small-scale rebellion" in 1995, and another 22 (8%) were fighting a "large-scale rebellion" (Gurr 2000: 28). These numbers, however, were just about the worst ever: the long-term trend is that the number of violent ethnic conflicts increased fairly steadily from the end of World War II until the mid-1990s, but then it started to drop. A separate survey for 2003 lists only ten "intermediate armed conflicts" or "wars" that were more or less ethnic conflicts. Those conflicts were: the Karen insurgency in Burma, Hutu–Tutsi conflict in Burundi, the Kashmir insurgency in India, Palestinian resistance against Israel, the Muslim rebellion in the southern Philippines, the Chechnya conflict in Russia, the Tamil separatist conflict in Sri Lanka, two separate wars in Sudan (one against southern Christians, another in Darfur), and the Kurdish insurgency in Turkey (Wallensteen 2002).

What are these violent conflicts about? The simplest answer is political power in a disputed territory. Most of the conflicts involve a regional minority that wants to separate and form its own state, or at least its own autonomous region. The conflicts in Burma (Karens), India (Kashmir), Palestine (vs. Israel), Philippines (Muslims), Russia (Chechnya), Sri Lanka (Tamils), and Turkey (Kurds) are more or less of this type. In other cases, the insurgent ethnic group wants to take over government of the whole country: thus Burundi's majority Hutus wish to take power from the minority Tutsi government. Often the goals and stakes are unclear, as rebels may disagree with each other. For example, some Palestinians want to establish their own state alongside Israel, but others are fighting to replace Israel with a Palestinian state. The role of ethnicity itself in generating these conflicts – both the violent and the non-violent ones – remains the subject of dispute. The remainder of this chapter explores these issues.

Ethnicity as generator of non-violent conflict

It is misleading to say that ethnicity itself is cause of any conflict, violent or not. It is never true that two individuals or groups come into conflict merely because A has one ethnic identity and B has another. Ethnically defined street gangs, for example, may claim that they attack individuals of other groups merely because of ethnic difference, but this is not true. Most often, gang members attack because they are "defending their turf" – because they are gang members fighting turf wars, not merely because they are members of different ethnic groups.

That said, ethnic identities can generate conflict by associating different groups with different interests. Thus many ethnic groups are distinguished from each other because their native languages are different, so they tend to disagree over language policy. If one group's mother tongue is the official language of their country, members of that group will probably find it easier than non-native speakers to get certain benefits – for example, they are more likely to do well on university entrance exam or civil service tests. In one longstanding example of such a dispute, members of Sri Lanka's Sinhalese majority have long championed a "Sinhala Only" language policy that disadvantages the Tamil-speaking minority. Similarly, a group that includes substantial numbers of relatively recent immigrants (such as American Latinos) is likely to benefit from liberal immigration policies, while native groups may feel disadvantaged by such policies. One way of thinking about this process (Hale 2008) suggests that the role of ethnic identity is to reduce people's uncertainty by clarifying who is the "us" whose interests (in this case, language interests) will be pursued.

When ethnic groups are distinguished by religion or sect, several other types of problems can occur. Those who deeply believe that theirs is the one true faith are likely to desire laws that restrict the practice or spread of rival faiths, discriminating against the adherents of those rival faiths. They may restrict the availability of ritually banned foods, offending those who wish to eat those foods. They may give their faith official government status, devaluing the status of believers in other religions. They may also push for religiously motivated laws offensive to practitioners of other faiths. Finally, there may be conflict on all of these issues within religious groups between hard-liners who wish to entrench their faith in law and moderates who are more concerned with accommodating minority groups and their own less pious co-religionists. Such issues are especially common in Muslim-majority countries, many of which designate Islam as the official religion (Fox 2007), but there are exceptions. In Muslim-majority Uzbekistan, the government discriminates *against* the Muslim faithful, associating religious piety with support for the terrorist Islamic Movement of Uzbekistan. Russia under Putin, on the other hand, sparked disputes by banning certain religious organizations and restricting the growth of others while supporting the Russian Orthodox Church.

Most common of all is probably conflict between ethnic groups over economic goods. Sometimes these conflicts are interpreted as being "merely" economic disputes and not ethnic at all, but this view is misleading. In ethnically diverse societies, economic issues are almost always at the same time ethnic issues. People tend to have more contacts with people within their ethnic group than outside it, and people tend to use the resulting intra-ethnic networks of personal ties when making economic decisions – whom to buy goods from, whom to hire, where to go to look for work, and so on. In the USA, the resulting dynamics may create "institutional racism" – the tendency for white employers to favour white job applicants not because of animosity toward minority groups, but merely because their personal contacts are mostly white. Another way economic and ethnic interests may align is when particular ethnic groups come to specialize in particular lines of work, resulting in the emergence of "middleman minorities" who are prominent in retail trade in some areas (Horowitz 1985). Finally, when ethnic groups are concentrated in particular regions, economic competition between regions comes to be defined in ethnic terms.

When the group cleavage involves racial difference, it almost always also involves a history of racial discrimination, inevitably yielding tensions and a wide range of approaches to dealing with them. Rwanda, after the 1994 genocide, has tried to ban any official consideration or even mention of the formerly central Hutu–Tutsi divide as a way of managing that dispute – and of obscuring the fact that most government leaders after the 1990–94 civil war have been members of the Tutsi minority. South Africa focused on a transition to political democracy as the group that had been most discriminated against, the blacks, formed the majority of the population. The United States, to overcome the legacy of its centuries of racial discrimination, created a policy of "affirmative action" giving special benefits to members of previously repressed groups, especially African-Americans – and sparking continuing controversy and resistance by some who are disadvantaged by those policies.

What makes these different kinds of groups – and group conflicts – similar is that the ethnicity comes to define people's identity, generating conflict over issues that go beyond the specific cleavages that separate the groups. In Northern Ireland, for example, the main line of cleavage is between Catholics and Protestants, but the issues are not religious per se. Rather, the issue is one of national loyalty – Catholics ("nationalists") wish Northern Ireland to become part of the Republic of Ireland, while Protestants ("unionists") wish to maintain its union with Great Britain. Even after the 1998 Good Friday agreement settled the violent conflict between these groups, tensions continue over issues like the right of Protestant "Orange Order" groups to conduct marches through Catholic neighborhoods (see Ross 2007).

The example of Orange Order parades illustrates another key fact about ethnic conflict: sometimes the issues at stake are not tangible interests at all, but purely symbolic ones. In 1950s Warri, Nigeria, ethnic Itsekiri and Urhobo clashed violently over the issue of whether the traditional Itsekiri ruler should be given a title implying he "was paramount ruler over the entire Province" (Horowitz 1985). Other symbolic ethnic disputes involve the rules governing the wearing of Islamic head scarves in France and Turkey, and rules governing archeological digs in Jerusalem (Ross 2007). In Bendery, Moldova in 1990, clashes were sparked by ethnic Moldovan efforts to raise their flag in that ethnically Russian, and soon to be separatist, city (Kaufman 2001: 141).

Why are symbolic issues like these often contested so fiercely? Psycho-cultural theorists point out that in psychological experiments, people randomly assigned to groups tend to evaluate their own group more highly than other groups, even when they are told they are not competing; and they tend to prefer to maximize the difference between their group's profits and those of another group even if there is an alternative that would give their group a bigger profit. Donald Horowitz (1985) – in explaining the riot over the Itsekiri chief's title and other similar events – argues that these findings explain ethnic conflict well: what is at stake is not just absolute benefits but group self-esteem, or, in his terms, group worth and legitimacy.

Symbolic politics theory (Kaufman 2001) provides a similar explanation of such events. Symbolic politics theory begins with the fact, noted above, that an ethnic identity is defined by a "myth-symbol complex" that sets out not only who is in the group, but also who the group's heroes and villains are, what its history is, and what it means to be a group member. From this perspective, Orange Order parades are so contentious in Northern Ireland because they are meant to commemorate William of Orange's Protestant victory at the 1690 Battle of the Boyne – which is, of course, seen as a great defeat in the Catholic myth-symbol complex, and so its commemoration in Catholic neighborhoods is seen as an insult. The insult, of course, is part of the point of the exercise, as again the issues are group worth and legitimacy: the right to march through Catholic neighborhoods was for many decades symbolic of Protestant political dominance, and higher social status, in Northern Ireland.

The tendency of political conflicts to line up with ethnic divisions often causes political parties in ethnically diverse countries to become associated with particular ethnic groups. Belgium, for example, began with the typical European range of ideologically based parties such as Christian Democrats and social democrats, but all of these parties later split on linguistic lines between French-speakers and Flemish-speakers. The same process occurred in many ethnically diverse Caribbean countries as well (Horowitz 1985). Malaysia exemplifies a different model, in which the parties were from the beginning ethnically oriented, with the United National Malay Organization and the Malaysian Chinese Association being for many years two of the leading parties. Nigeria at its birth followed the Malaysian pattern, but later changes in Nigerian election law required presidential candidates to gain political support across ethnic and regional lines, leading to the rise of more ethnically diverse parties.

Ethnicity as a generator of violent conflict

As noted above, ethnic conflicts are usually managed peacefully. Sometimes, however, ethnic diversity does lead to ethnic violence. In the statistics about ethnic conflicts quoted above, the violent conflicts fell into two broad categories: riots, and armed conflicts or civil wars.

Ethnic riots

Deadly ethnic riots have occurred all over the world, but how and why they occur seems puzzling. Particularly puzzling is why rioters tend to be very careful in attacking only members of the target ethnic group, while at the same time making no distinction between men, women and children of that group, and indulging in unspeakable brutality in how they are killed, with rape, torture and mutilation not uncommon. After the killing is done, there is usually no remorse on the part of the killers: "they had it coming" is the attitude typically expressed by rioting communities all over the globe (Horowitz 2000).

One comprehensive survey, which takes a social psychological approach, finds three main factors that lead to deadly ethnic riots (Horowitz 2000). First, there needs to be a hostile ongoing relationship between the groups – tensions of long standing to motivate the killing. Second, there needs to be authoritative social support: potential rioters need to be assured by public statements from community leaders in their group that the leaders agree killing members of the other group is justified. At the same time, this support usually extends to the security forces: riots usually become large only if the police are sympathetic, or at least do not make determined efforts to stop the killing.

Finally, there needs to be a stimulus, some event – usually implying some sort of threat – that provokes fear, rage, or hatred in the rioting group. For example, a report (true or not) of a violent attack by one of "them" against one of "us" might spark a widespread cry to "teach them a lesson". Alternatively, a political change – even a potential one – might provoke a similar outburst. In 1958, for example, Sri Lankan Prime Minister S.W.R.D. Bandaranaike, a Sinhalese, signed a power-sharing deal with the leader of his country's Tamil minority, but quickly backed away under political pressure. *After* the deal was abrogated, ordinary Sinhalese vented their wrath at the very idea of such power-sharing by attacking innocent Tamils in a large-scale riot.

Another approach to explaining ethnic riots focuses not on psychology but on social organization. In India, for example, hostile relations between the Hindu and Muslim communities are common, but most of the riot violence is concentrated in just a few cities. Why is that? The riot-prone cities, in turns out, have "institutionalized riot systems": community activists and extremist organizations that benefit from keeping tensions high, politicians who benefit from occasional violence, and criminals and thugs who can profit from it (Brass 1997). On the other hand, Indian cities with little or no riot violence have community organizations (business groups, labour unions, etc.) that cross communal lines, bringing Hindus and Muslims together instead of driving them apart (Varshney 2002).

Ethnic civil wars

Explanations of ethnic civil wars divide along similar lines: social psychology approaches, social mobilization approaches, and instrumentalist approaches. Instrumentalist approaches start with what creates the opportunity for rebels to act: weak governments, large populations and inaccessible terrain create the opening extremists need to act (Fearon and Laitin 2003).

Also important in most instrumentalist arguments are extremist leaders seeking to grab or hold onto power, who stir up ethnic disagreements and provoke violence to create a "rally around the flag" effect uniting their group around their own leadership (Gagnon 1995). Extremist media also plays a key role in this view, as these extreme outlets seek popularity by appealing to group loyalties, presenting the news in terms of "us" against "them" (Snyder 2000). These two factors work together: extremist leaders provide heroes for the extremist media to promote, while one-sided media portrayals seem to validate the extremist leaders' claims that their group must unite against the "enemy". In most of these accounts, security fears play a crucial role: the argument by extremist politicians and media outlets that one's own group is in danger is what makes their appeals seem credible.

Some instrumentalists go a step further and claim that civil wars involving these issues are not ethnic at all, but merely about political power or economic benefits. These scholars argue that the statistical link between ethnic diversity and civil war is weak, and that the main causes of civil war are poverty, weak governments, and other factors that make it easy to start a guerrilla campaign (e.g., Fearon and Laitin 2003). It is also true, however, that while economic grievances are always present, in ethnic conflicts they are expressed in ethnic terms. In Mindanao in the southern Philippines, for example, the poor – Christians as well as Muslims – are all disadvantaged by inadequate government spending on education and infrastructure. But the Communist New People's Army, which tries to exploit such rich/poor distinctions to gain support, has had little luck in Muslim areas. Rather, Muslims there respond to specifically Muslim rebel groups who emphasize the differences between Muslims and Christians, not between rich and poor (McKenna 1998). In other cases, it is not the poor ethnic group but the rich one that rebels: in Yugoslavia, for example, it was the relatively prosperous Slovenes and Croats who first tried to secede, because they felt they were being held back by the more "backward" ethnic groups in the rest of the country. In these cases, the contest for power and wealth takes a peculiarly ethnic form.

Like instrumentalist approaches, social mobilization approaches consider the roles of leaders, but they are also interested in how ethnic groups mobilize – that is, how do members of the group get together the people and resources needed for collective action? The answer, these theorists point out, is that people use social organizations and networks that already exist, like political parties and labour unions. Successful mobilization efforts find "brokers", people who can link different groups and networks together to help them cooperate in a single movement (McAdam, Tarrow and Tilly 2001). This provides one answer to the question: Why do people mobilize as *ethnic* groups instead, for example, of organizing as economic interest groups? It is because people's social networks tend to be mostly within their ethnic group; barriers of language or religion typically separate them from members of other groups.

Social psychological approaches focus on a different puzzle: Why do followers follow these extremist leaders? Even if people mobilize as ethnic groups to look out for their interests, why do they follow extremist leaders who want violence, instead of following moderate leaders who will work for peace? Symbolic politics theory suggests that when the group's myth-symbol complex points to the other group as an enemy, its members will be predisposed to be hostile to the other group. Politicians will then be able to appeal to symbols of past hostility – such as Slobodan Milošević referring to the Battle of Kosovo Field – to rouse people's emotions against the enemy that symbol brings to mind (Muslims, in the case of Kosovo). If the group is at the same time convinced that they are in danger of extinction – of being wiped out as a group – they can be persuaded to back extreme measures that are justified as "self-defense" (Kaufman 2001).

One point on which the different approaches agree is that even when groups are differentiated by religion, violent conflicts are rarely religious in the sense of one group trying to impose its religion on another. For example, even though Sri Lanka's Tamils are Hindu while the majority Sinhalese are Buddhist, neither group wants the other to convert. Rather, the rebel Liberation Tigers of Tamil Eelam want to establish their own state (Tamil Eelam) in northern and eastern Sri Lanka, while the Sinhalese-dominated government wants to prevent that outcome. The Kashmir, Chechen, Palestinian, and Philippine-Muslim conflicts have a similar flavor. The biggest exception is Sudan, where the main grievance of the Christian and animist southerners was the attempt by the Sudanese government to impose Islamic law on the whole country, including them.

To see how these complex processes play out in practice, let us consider in more detail the example of one prominent case of ethnic warfare, the 1990s fighting in the former Yugoslavia. Yugoslavia, formed in the aftermath of World War I, was a multi-ethnic state with no majority group. The three largest groups all spoke the same language, Serbo-Croatian, but differed in their religion tradition among Serbs (Orthodox Christians), Croats (Catholics) and Bosnian Muslims. The fourth-largest group, the Slovenes, are Catholics but speak a different (though related) language; the next-largest, the Albanians, are Muslims who speak a wholly unrelated language. Before World War II, Yugoslavia was ruled by a Serbian king and dominated by Serbian politicians. During World War II, the Germans conquered the country and placed Croatian fascists, the Ustashe, in power in the regions of Croatia and Bosnia, where they engaged in genocidal violence against the Serbs. As the war ended, Communist partisan leader Josip Broz Tito took power in Yugoslavia, massacring the Ustashe and re-creating Yugoslavia as a nominal federation of six Republics: Serbia, Croatia, Bosnia-Hercegovina, Slovenia, Macedonia and Montenegro (Kaufman 2001).

When Tito died in 1980, the loss of his charismatic authority severely weakened Yugoslavia's government. The increasingly powerful Republic governments more and more allowed the kind of mutually hostile mythmaking Tito had tried to stamp out. For example, nationalist Serbs began talking about the menace of the Albanian minority in the symbolically important Kosovo region, while labelling any Croatian disagreement as evidence of resurgent Ustashe fascism. As symbolists would note, ethnic myths and fears were growing. The leader of Serbia's League of Communists, Slobodan Milošević, noticed the power of this nationalist sentiment and in the late 1980s became its spokesman, repressing the Albanians and attempting to impose Serbian control on the whole of Yugoslavia (Gagnon 1995). In response to this Serbian threat, voters in Slovenia, Croatia and Bosnia turned to supporting their own nationalist leaders – with the Croatian nationalists reviving the national symbols last used by the Ustashe fascists, raising alarm among Serbs and making Milošević's appeals ever more plausible.

Yugoslavia was dying. Slovenia moved first, declaring independence on June 25, 1991. The Croats quickly followed, sparking a months-long war in which the Yugoslav army conquered areas in Croatia inhabited by Croatia's Serbian minority. The agony of Bosnia-Hercegovina was to last longer. Home to a mixture of Bosnian Muslims, Serbs and Croats, Bosnia was torn three ways. Serbs wanted to remain in Yugoslavia; fearing Serbian domination, the Muslims wanted to secede and form an independent Bosnian state, while Croats wanted their areas (especially western Hercegovina) to join Croatia. In 1992 a coalition of Muslims and Croats therefore declared Bosnian independence, sparking a three-sided civil war in which Serbia and Croatia – trying to take over chunks of Bosnian territory – provided military assistance to their co-ethnics in Bosnia, while the Muslims were the principal victims. Under the slogan, "Only Unity Saves the Serbs", Serbs exaggerated the disadvantages of separation from Serbia into a threat to their national existence, and used this invented threat to justify – and invent the term – "ethnic cleansing": the Serbs' program of massacring enough of their ethnic enemies to force the rest to flee any territory they claimed. Finally, in 1995, a Croatian military counteroffensive backed by NATO air power prompted the Serb side to agree to stop the fighting.

Conclusion

Ethnicity generates conflict in a number of different ways. When ethnic groups are differentiated by language, then disputes about the use of language, especially in government and education, tend to line up across ethnic divides. When ethnic groups are differentiated by religion, disputes over the role of religion and the influence of religious values on public policy tend to arise. Regardless of what differentiates groups, economic interests – and disputes – tend to pit ethnic groups against each other due to the importance of social networks in causing members of ethnic groups to favor their own economically. In addition to disputes over tangible interests, ethnic politics also often turns into contests for status or group worth, so groups may seek political dominance as a way of expressing their desire for high social status. When this sort of seeking for group dominance becomes especially pronounced, and especially when groups' myth-symbol complex encourages hostility toward other groups, peaceful ethnic disputes can escalate into violent conflict.

Further reading

Brass, P. R. (1997) *Theft of an Idol: Text and Context in the Representation of Collective Violence* (Princeton: Princeton University Press).
Horowitz, D. L. (1985) *Ethnic Groups in Conflict* (Berkeley: University of California Press).
Kaufman, S. J. (2001) *Modern Hatreds: The Symbolic Politics of Ethnic War* (Ithaca: Cornell University Press).
Laitin, D. D. (2007) *Nations, States and Violence* (Oxford: Oxford University Press).
Ross, M. H. (2007) *Cultural Contestation in Ethnic Conflict* (Cambridge: Cambridge University Press).

References

Brass, P. R. (1997) *Theft of an Idol: Text and Context in the Representation of Collective Violence* (Princeton: Princeton University Press).
Fearon, J. D., and Laitin, D. (2003) "Ethnicity, Insurgency, and Civil War", *American Political Science Review* 97, no. 1 (February), pp. 75–90.
Fox, A. (2007) "Islam and Modern Education", *The Muslim World* 23, no. 1, pp. 29–37.
Gagnon, V. P. (1995) "Ethnic Nationalism and International Conflict: The Case of Serbia", *International Security* 19, no. 3 (Winter).
Gurr, T. R. (2000) *Peoples Versus States* (Washington, DC: United States Institute of Peace).
Hale, C. R. (2008) *Engaging Contradictions* (Oakland: University of California Press).
Hardin, R. (1995) *One for All: The Logic of Group Conflict* (Princeton: Princeton University Press).
Hobsbawm, E., and Ranger, T. eds., (1992) *The Invention of Tradition* (Cambridge: Cambridge University Press).
Horowitz, D. L. (1985) *Ethnic Groups in Conflict* (Berkeley: University of California Press).
Horowitz, D. L. (2000) *The Deadly Ethnic Riot* (Berkeley: University of California Press).
Isaacs, H. R. (1975) *The Idols of the Tribe: Group Identity and Political Change* (New York: Harper and Row).
Kaufman, S. J. (2001) *Modern Hatreds: The Symbolic Politics of Ethnic War* (Ithaca: Cornell University Press).
McAdam, D., Tarrow, S., and Tilly, C. (2001) *Dynamics of Contention* (Cambridge: Cambridge University Press).
McKenna, T. M. (1998) *Muslim Rulers and Rebels: Everyday Politics and Armed Separatism in the Southern Philippines* (Berkeley: University of California Press).
Ross, M. H. (2007) *Cultural Contestation in Ethnic Conflict* (Cambridge: Cambridge University Press).

Smith, A. D. (1986) *The Ethnic Origins of Nations* (New York: Blackwell).
Snyder, J. (2000) *From Voting to Violence: Democratization and Nationalist Conflict* (New York: W. W. Norton).
Varshney, A. (2002) *Ethnic Conflict and Civic Life: Hindus and Muslims in India* (New Haven: Yale University Press).
Volkan, V. (1997) *Bloodlines: From Ethnic Pride to Ethnic Terrorism* (New York: Farrar, Straus & Giroux).
Wallensteen, P. (2002) *Understanding Conflict Resolution: War, Peace and the Global System* (London: Sage).

9

DEMOCRACY AND DEMOCRATISATION

Jenny Engström-Baron

Introduction

Since the end of the Cold War and the collapse of communism in Eastern Europe, democracy has become widely touted as the political system best poised to deliver peace, both between states and within them. The emergence of complex United Nations (UN) peace operations also saw an increased focus on elections and democratisation as components of post-conflict reconstruction (see, for example, Namibia, Cambodia and Mozambique). Democracy today is widely accepted as a universal value, and the holding of elections is generally perceived as minimum requirement for legitimate government. Yet, as this chapter will show, importing liberal democracy to a society riven by inter-group competition, deep-seated grievances, and strong identity-based politics, does not necessarily produce peace and equality.

Democratisation as peace-building in ethnically divided societies?

Yet whereas Western policy-makers continue to insist on promoting democracy as a means toward more peaceful communities around the world, scholars remain in disagreement over the actual relationship between democracy, ethnic diversity and peace/violence. Snyder (2000) and Horowitz (1985; 1993), among others, argue that the introduction of democracy in societies divided along ethnic and/or religious lines, can be not only ineffective but also inappropriate, because majority rule, competitive party politics, and an open political system can exacerbate, rather than mitigate, inter-ethnic tensions (Horowitz 1985: 291). The initiation of democracy, they warn, may generate violent conflict, as democratisation allows populist politicians to manipulate ethnic divisions for their own gain, thus increasing the risk of ethnic groups acting in their own narrow interests, as opposed to the general interest of the political community as a whole, i.e. the state. The phenomenon of ethnic politics – the formation of political parties along ethnic lines, and the pursuit of political agendas limited to the protection of the interests of one's own identity group – with its emphasis on collectivist principles sits uneasily with Western liberal democratic principles of individualism. A strong element of ethnic politics in incipient democracies is seen as a stepping-stone towards an accelerating spiral of conflicting inter-ethnic interests that eventually may culminate in violence between ethnic groups occupying the same territorial space. In such instances, the democratisation process is bound to undermine the unity of the state, provoke conflicts over the allocation of political, economic and social resources, and make fair, just and efficient government more difficult (Rothstein 1993: 27). It is believed that, when introduced in ethnically heterogeneous societies, democratic processes feed conflict and potential violence, which may eventually result in such a rise in the level of inter-communal conflict that 'any belief in democracy as a peaceful lever of change is extinguished in the competition which it encourages' (Austin and Gupta 1994: 267).

Others hold a less pessimistic view of democratisation in plural societies. De Nevers, for example, suggests that democratisation can serve either to mitigate inter-ethnic conflict or to exacerbate it, depending on a host of factors including how speedily ethnic issues are recognised; the extent to which inter-ethnic tension was already present at the start of the democratisation process; relative size and power of ethnic communities; the ethnic distribution of power in the previous regime; the political stance of major ethnic leaders; the presence of ethnic kin in neighbouring countries; and the ethnic composition of the army (De Nevers 1993: 61).

De Nevers points out that national unity is a necessary precondition for successful democratisation (Ibid.). Political moderation, too, must be present if democratisation is to have a conflict mitigating impact in ethnically divided states. Moderation can be promoted via an electoral structure that is inclusive and encourages power-sharing among different ethnic groups (Ibid.: 62–63). By allowing for the establishment of an inclusive means of government that takes into account the diversity of interests and needs of all ethnic groups, democratisation has the potential to help mitigate inter-ethnic tension and prevent the eruption of ethno-political violence (Ibid.: 75). De Nevers further notes that '[b]ecause in most cases democratization includes a negotiating phase, there is an inherent opportunity in the process to address issues raised by ethnic tensions', and that '[f]or democratization to reduce ethnic tension, the inclusion of all relevant groups in the negotiating process is required; in addition, there must be a willingness by all parties to work for, and then accept, a mutually beneficial agreement' (Ibid.: 65).

In *Wars, Guns and Votes*, Collier posits that the peace promoting benefits of democracy/ democratisation depend in large part on the level of economic development in a country. Whereas democracy tends to promote peace and stability in more economically advanced societies, it has the opposite effect on poor countries, or what Collier calls 'the bottom billion' (Collier 2009). The reason for this, Collier argues is that 'in these societies, democracy does not deliver either accountability or legitimacy' (Ibid.: 24).

It follows that we cannot be satisfied simply with assuming that since democracy is purportedly a system designed to mediate competing interests in society, it will suffice as a tool for intercommunal conflict. Any conflict rooted in basic human needs such as security, recognition, identity and autonomy, cannot be resolved through competitive bargaining, as the ontological quality of human needs means that they are in essence non-negotiable. To the extent possible, according to Burton's theory, individuals will seek to meet their needs within socially and legally established norms in society. But, if societal norms hinder rather than enable their pursuit of needs, then, 'subject to values he attaches to social relationships, he will employ methods outside the norms, outside the codes he would in other circumstances wish to apply to his behaviour' (Burton 1988: 52–53).

The democratic system of governance is peculiar in that it contains within it characteristics of cooperation as well as competition and inclusion and also exclusion. As a system for mediating conflicting interests in society it appears to have fared well overall. But is it a system capable of mediating needs-based conflict? The answer must be – it depends. It appears, however, that the liberal definition of democracy, with its emphasis on the individual rather than the collective, and on the equality of opportunity rather than equality of outcome, is sometimes inadequate as a mechanism for protecting the needs of citizens, especially in societies where – despite an official adherence to civic ideals – the ethnic majority dominates. For by taking a neutral stance to the conception of the common good, it is in reality perpetuating the majority culture's values, culture and preferences. Whilst liberal democracy may justifiably be regarded as a fair system for negotiating competing interests, it therefore falls short in terms of protecting people's needs in a society where political and economic power is unevenly distributed.

In multi-ethnic countries in general, the limits of democratisation as a conflict-mitigating tool depend very much on the nature of the conflict at hand. If the conflict is largely one of competing interests, implementation of democratic rules and principles may serve to promote peaceful cohabitation, but if the conflict is rooted in needs, the advancement of democracy is unlikely to facilitate the resolution of the conflict.

Elections alone don't make a democracy

Since the early 1990s, Western powers, notably the United States of America and the European Union, but also international institutions like the United Nations and the Organisation for Security and Cooperation in Europe (OSCE), have sought to promote elections as a key feature of democracy. Consequently, countries ravaged by war and lacking in the infrastructure necessary for conducting free and fair elections, have often been pushed, prematurely, into electing a new government. The result, however, has not always been an increase in democracy and democratisation, as witnessed in Iraq, Bosnia, Afghanistan, etc.

As Collier points out, American and European pressure on the bottom billion has indeed resulted in a rise in elections held, but what is problematic is how democracy has come to be seen largely as synonymous with elections. However, elections alone do not make a democracy. For elections to be meaningful, there needs to be in place the necessary political infrastructure to ensure that elections are free and fair (Collier 2009: 15). Diamond, in turn, points out that democracy is impossible without freedom of speech and association and the rule of law (Diamond 2008: 21).

According to the International Institute for Democracy and Electoral Assistance (IIDEA), a political system is deemed democratic only if it allows for meaningful competition for political power; inclusive participation, expressed through free and fair elections; and civil and political rights that safeguard the integrity of political competition and participation (Harris and Reilly 1998: 19). Civil and political rights are absolutely essential to democratic governance given that democracy is fundamentally about the equal right of every citizen to participate in public affairs and to exercise control over government (Beetham 1998: 73). A democratic regime with the proper institutions (a legislative, executive and judicial branch) that holds multiparty elections on a regular basis, cannot be considered genuinely democratic unless its citizens enjoy full civil and political rights which permit them to choose their political representatives in a society that allows for a free media, access to alternative sources of information, and freedom of thought, expression and association. As Diamond notes, if a country holds regular, multiparty elections and has an established national assembly, a court system, constitution, etc., 'but the people are not able to vote their leaders out of power because the system is, in effect, rigged, then the country has … [a] pseudodemocracy' (Diamond 2008: 23).

Challenges to successful democratisation

Liberalism, with its focus on the individual rather than the community, has come to represent the premise and foundation of modern democracy in the West (Parekh 1993: 157). The Western concept of liberal democracy imposes a restriction on the state's authority over its citizens, by virtue of its focus on individual rights. Civil and political rights are not only intrinsic to a particular form of democracy but also are inherent in any modern democratic system, since without them the democratic principle would effectively be non-functional.

In ethnically divided states, however, the issue of human rights becomes complicated by the demand from some ethnic minorities for group rights. This begs the question whether individual rights – a concept intimately linked with liberal democracy – are sufficient in societies where a minority perceives its freedom and survival to be threatened. Where the asymmetry of power structures favours the majority ethnic group, the principle of individualism/liberalism often fails to deliver its promise of a just society, and instead perpetuates the status quo, that is, the asymmetrical power structures, thus allowing the majority ethnic group to retain a position of cultural hegemony vis-à-vis the minority groups.

Zakaria warns of the emergence of what he calls 'illiberal democracies': regimes that habitually disregard any constitutional limits on their power and violate the human rights of citizens (Zakaria 1997: 22). He distinguishes between democracy and constitutional liberalism, where the latter is characterised by the rule of law, separation of powers and the protection of basic liberties, including freedom of speech, assembly, religion and the right to own property. Democracy, on the other hand, is characterised by free and fair multiparty elections (Ibid.).

Another challenge to democratisation is the problem of weak states. Sørensen notes that it is exceedingly difficult to construct stable democracies out of weak states that lack the institutions necessary for democracy, and where trust and mutual acceptance among competing groups are in short supply (Sørensen 2008: 142). The premature introduction of democratic rule in the form of elections in weak states can even lead to an increase in violent conflict (Ibid.: 143). State building is therefore a necessary precondition to democracy in weak states. At the same time, Collier argues that one of the main mistakes in the West's approach to state building 'has been to forget that well-functioning states are built not just on shared interests but on shared identity. Shared identity does not grow out of the soil; it is politically constructed' (Collier 2009: 9).

Democracy is generally associated with majority rule, a principle which is not without controversy, especially in societies divided along ethnic and religious lines. Defenders of majority rule, however, maintain that the principle of political equality, which is fundamental to democracy, is secured over time since majorities and minorities are bound to trade places in the long term. This means that today's winners will become tomorrow's losers, and vice-versa. As Beetham points out, this argumentation presumes a functional principle of reciprocity, so that 'I agree to be bound by a decision which goes against me in return for your being bound when it goes in my favour and against you' (Beetham 1999: 20). Such an arrangement may work sufficiently well in a culturally homogenous society, but when the majority rule is applied to states with deep ethnic divisions, and where politics is ethnically aligned, there is a considerable risk that the electoral majority and minority become identical to the ethnic alignments in society. Consequently, majorities and minorities become frozen, thus violating the principle of political equality since the minority is permanently on the losing side of the political game. As Touraine points out, the idea of democracy is intrinsically connected to the idea of rights, and democracy cannot, therefore, be reduced to majority government (Touraine 1998: 23).

A challenge to democratic development in ethnically plural societies is the tendency for the emerging party system to form along ethnic lines, thus undermining the liberal democratic principle of citizenship based on civic ideals. Western observers, therefore, tend to view ethnic politics as fundamentally contrary to democratic norms of inclusion and equal rights. Horowitz, for example, states that, in societies divided along ethnic lines, inclusion in the government tends to correlate with inclusion in the community, just as exclusion from government means exclusion from the community (Horowitz 1993: 18). Consequently, party politics only serve to reinforce ethnic divisions, thus rendering democracy harmful to inter-ethnic peace and stability. Yet prohibiting ethnically based parties does not necessarily promote peace and democracy. In fact, a constitutional ban on political organisation along ethnic lines may itself be a manifestation of ethnic politics, as its tendency is to privilege the majority ethnic group.

The security of one's group (ethnic, linguistic, etc.) identity, both of the majority and the minority ethnic groups, as well as socio-economic security, play a significant part in shaping the political agenda of ethnic parties, insofar as a high level of security experienced by an ethnic community will weaken the perceived need to pursue a narrowly defined, ethnocentric political platform. Whether or not – or to what extent – an ethnically based party limits itself to a narrow, ethnic chauvinist political agenda is likely to be influenced by its sense of security and recognition within the larger society it inhabits.

How democracy comes about

The arcane notion of democratisation being an organic process that happens naturally when the time is ripe, has given way to the realisation that democracy is highly agency driven. In Di Palma's words, democracy is 'crafted'. It follows that democratisation is always a conscious, and often strategic, undertaking. But does a state need democrats in order to democratise? Not according to Ágh, who suggests that democrats are the results, not the precondition of democratisation (Ágh 1998: 19). Typically, democratisation is seen as more probable if two conditions are present:

1   'when there are clear splits among existing autocratic leaders, in which some urge reform in order to accommodate popular demands for change, while others in the ruling group seek to preserve the current order at all costs';
2   'when power has been strongly centralized in the person of a charismatic leader who has ruled for many years, sometimes for decades. When such leaders centralize power in their own person, usually with a cadre of loyalists around them, the end of a leader's tenure – often from natural causes – can induce a political vacuum in which there is rapid political change'.

(Large and Sisk 2006: 71–72)

'Diffusion' is sometimes cited as an important factor in the democratisation processes. Di Palma, for example, suggests that '[n]ew democracies are ... less the result of cumulative, necessary, predictable, and systematic developments than of historical busts and booms, global opinion climates, shifting opportunities, and contingent preferences' (Di Palma 1990: 15). However, that is not to say that global circumstances are always decisive in determining whether or not democratisation takes place. Whereas it might determine the fall of a non-democratic regime, it does not necessarily lead to democratisation, which as stated, is a deliberate process. More specifically, Di Palma's 'crafting' describes four main aspects of democratisation:

- 'the quality of the finished product', i.e. the choice of democratic institutions and rules;
- the structure of the decision making that determines those institutions and rules;
- the nature of the 'craftsmen' involved in the process (coalitions, alliances, etc.);
- the timing of each step taken during the transition.

(Di Palma 1990: 8–9)

A much debated issue within democratisation theory has been whether democratisation necessitates certain preconditions in order to be successful. In the past it was said that a requisite for democratisation was a strong middle class, a theory that has since been refuted by cases where democratisation was successful despite the absence of a powerful middle class. Market economy has also been said to be a necessary condition for democracy to be successful. Whilst the debate continues, it seems there are at least two indisputable preconditions necessary for democratisation to succeed.

First, before democratisation can be initiated, an issue that must be resolved is, who are the people? That is, who are the nations that are going to democratise? A certain degree of national unity is a necessary precondition for democratisation to be effectively implemented. Why? Because, as Beetham points out, in conditions that allow for freedom of expression and association, democratic government is thus dependent upon popular consent. This implies that, if people are unwilling to agree on a framework for cohabitation, the imposition of authoritarian rule is the only alternative to war or secession (Beetham 1999: 82). Moreover, national unity is absolutely essential precisely because of the divisive nature of electoral competition.

The expression 'national unity' is highly problematic though, as it seems to presume the existence of single-nation-states, rather than multi-ethnic, multi-national states. Few states, however, can be said to be authentic nation-states, and those that might qualify often had to resort to force in order to attain the status of nation-state. According to Dankwart Rustow, national unity is present when 'the vast majority of citizens in a democracy-to-be … have no doubt or mental reservations as to which political community they belong to' (cited in Sørensen 2008: 47). In regards to ethnically divided societies, Rustow's definition might be slightly amended to reflect the need for sufficient consensus across ethnic groups making up the citizens of the state. Hence, national unity can be said to exist when 'the vast majority of citizens in a democracy-to-be [including a majority of members of all ethnic groups] … have no doubt or mental reservations as to which political community they belong to'. Without a unified political community, i.e., without a general consensus about what constitutes the nation, efforts to develop democracy are likely to be severely undermined by conflicting perceptions of the identity and character of the political community. Hence, a common framework to which all communal divisions in society can pledge their allegiance is absolutely essential for democracy to work. We might therefore say that what matters is not only that democracy is introduced, but also that it is done so based on broad societal consensus. In fact, unless the process of determining the shape of the new democratic system is itself subject to an inclusive participatory process that goes some way towards honouring the democratic principle of 'rule by the people', the outcome may indeed be unstable.

A second precondition for any democratic system, one which is often neglected in discussions of democracy, is the existence of a popular will to democracy; that is, the various subgroups of the population must agree that democracy is desirable, and commit themselves to the democratic process, and to the rules inherent in it. Contrary to authoritarian systems of governance, democracy cannot function effectively unless there is an overall consensus that democracy is the preferred choice, and any attempt at democratisation in an unwilling domestic environment is bound to fail. Thus, the legitimacy and viability of a democratic regime rests on such a will to democracy.

Democratisation and marginalised groups

Whilst democracy is intimately bound up with human rights protection, democratisation has not always resulted in greater inclusion of marginalised groups. In Apartheid South Africa, democracy was limited to the white population and it was only after a prolonged violent campaign by the ANC followed by negotiations at a time when the regime was beginning to face up to its own demise, that the majority of South Africa's population was included in the political process. In Rwanda, colonial rule that had favoured the Tutsi minority eventually gave way to Hutu majority rule, with Tutsis suffering repeated attacks that culminated in the 1994 genocide. And whilst some ethnic minorities – notably the Turkish minority in Bulgaria – have benefitted from the democratisation process in Eastern Europe following the collapse of communism, the Roma remain on the fringes of political life. In societies where the democratic process has successfully integrated previously marginalised groups, negotiations have typically been preceded by some measure of civil strife. In Macedonia, a former Yugoslav republic, a brief armed conflict in 2001 was followed by an elaborate peace agreement between the ethnic Macedonian majority and the Albanian minority that effectively revised the Macedonian constitution to strengthen the political power of the country's largest minority. In Kenya, ethnic divisions were highlighted in a wave of widespread violence, mainly between the Kikuyu and Luo ethnic groups, following the country's controversial presidential elections in 2007. Civil strife eventually came to an end with the help of outside mediation which brought about a power-sharing agreement whereby Mwai Kibaki, the incumbent president and a Kikuyu remained in his post whilst Raila Odinga, a Luo, assumed the post of prime minister. In Bulgaria, the transition from communism to democracy was carried out mainly through negotiations between the old communists and the democratic opposition. Excluded from the negotiations, however, were the country's Turkish minority, who went on to form their own political party, the Movement for Rights and Freedoms (MRF). Despite a constitutional ban on ethnic parties, the MRF was allowed to participate in national elections and won enough votes to become an influential force in Bulgarian politics. Its political inclusion was made possible largely as a result of a national effort to overcome inter-communal tensions that were a legacy of communist-era oppression of the Turkish minority. Yet another example of a democracy where inter-group conflict still persists is Turkey, where the government continues to pursue a strategy of assimilation by proscribing the use of Kurdish in public affairs. Examples of democracies that continue to deny minority rights to some of its citizens can be found in Western Europe too, notably in Greece, where the government refuses to acknowledge the presence of any ethnic minorities, including a Macedonian one.

Conclusion

Although few would dispute that democracy is currently the political system best suited for managing plural identities and conflicting interests, the road towards democracy – democratisation – is more often than not a bumpy one, especially in societies fraught by inter-communal tension. Neither democracy nor democratisation is a panacea for ethnic (or religious) minorities, as witnessed by the experience of Eastern Europe's Roma population, and there is no guarantee that all segments of society will be included in the political life of the state. Ideally, however, democratisation offers a chance for dissenting voices to be heard and for minorities (and disgruntled majorities) to challenge policies they perceive as unjust and discriminatory. Flaws aside, democracy continues to stand out as a political system that offers the best chance for mediating conflicts non-violently. The fact that calls for democracy around the world are growing stronger also points to the fact that people on all continents, regardless of ethnicity or religion, are increasingly recognising its value.

Further reading

Collier, P. (2009) *Wars, Guns and Votes: Democracy in Dangerous Places* (London: The Bodley Head).

Diamond, L. (2008) *The Spirit of Democracy: The Struggle to Build Free Societies Throughout the World* (New York: Times Books).

Gurr, T.R. (2000) *People versus States: Minorities at Risk in the New Century* (Washington, DC: United States Institute of Peace Press).

Harris, P. and Reilly, B. (1998) *Democracy and Deep-Rooted Conflict: Options for Negotiators* (Stockholm: International Institute for Democracy and Electoral Assistance).

Sørensen, G. (2008) *Democracy and Democratization: Processes and Prospects in a Changing World* (3rd edn) (Boulder, CO: Westview Press).

References

Ágh, A. (1998) *Emerging Democracies in East Central Europe and in the Balkans* (Cheltenham: Edward Elgar Publishing Ltd).

Austin, D. and Gupta, A. (1994) 'The Politics of Violence in India and South Asia', in P. Janke (ed.), *Ethnic and Religious Conflicts: Europe and Asia* (Brookfield, VT: Research Institute for the Study of Conflict and Terrorism).

Beetham, D. (1998) 'Democracy and Human Rights: Civil, Political, Economic, Social and Cultural', in J. Symonides (ed.), *Human Rights: New Dimensions and Challenges* (Brookfield, VT: UNESCO and Dartmouth Publishing Company).

Beetham, D. (1999) *Democracy and Human Rights* (Cambridge: Polity Press).

Burton, J. (1988) 'Human Needs versus Societal Needs', in R. Coate and J. Rosati (eds), *The Power of Human Needs in World Society* (Boulder, CO: Lynne Rienner).

Collier, P. (2009) *Wars, Guns and Votes: Democracy in Dangerous Places* (London: The Bodley Head).

De Nevers, R. (1993) 'Democratization and Ethnic Conflict', in M. Brown (ed.), *Ethnic Conflict and International Security* (Princeton, NJ: Princeton University Press).

Di Palma, G. (1990) *To Craft Democracies: An Essay on Democratic Transitions* (Berkeley, CA: University of California Press).

Diamond, L. (2008) *The Spirit of Democracy: The Struggle to Build Free Societies Throughout the World* (New York: Times Books).

Harris, P. and Reilly, B. (1998) 'The Changing Nature of Conflict and Conflict Management', pp. 9–31 in P. Harris and B. Reilly (eds), *Democracy and Deep-Rooted Conflicts: Options for Negotiators* (Stockholm: International IDEA).

Horowitz, D. (1985) *Ethnic Groups in Conflict* (Berkeley, CA: University of California Press).

Horowitz, D. (1993) 'Democracy in Divided Societies', *Journal of Democracy*, vol. 4, no. 4, October, 18–38.

Large, J. and Sisk, T. (2006) *Democracy, Conflict and Human Security: Pursuing Peace in the 21st Century* (Stockholm: International IDEA).

Parekh, B. (1993) 'The Cultural Particularity of Liberal Democracy', in D. Held (ed.), *Prospects for Democracy: North, South, East, West* (Cambridge: Polity Press).

Rothstein, R. (1993) 'Democracy and Conflict', in E. Kaufman and S. Abed (eds), *Democracy, Peace, and the Israeli-Palestinian Conflict* (Boulder, CO: Lynne Rienner Publishers).

Snyder, J. (2000) *From Voting to Violence: Democratization and Nationalist Conflict* (New York, NY: W.W. Norton).

Sørensen, G. (2008) *Democracy and Democratization: Processes and Prospects in a Changing World* (3rd edn) (Boulder, CO: Westview Press).

Touraine, A. (1998) *What is Democracy?* (Boulder, CO: Westview Press).

Zakaria, F. (1997) 'The Rise of Illiberal Democracy', *Foreign Affairs*, vol. 76, no. 6, November/December, 22–43.

10

THE CAUSES AND CONSEQUENCES OF ETHNIC CLEANSING

Erin K. Jenne

Introduction

Ethnic cleansing refers to "the expulsion of an 'undesirable' population from a given territory due to religious or ethnic discrimination, political, strategic or ideological considerations, or a combination of these" (Bell-Fialkoff 1993: 110). On the most basic level, it is the deliberate policy of homogenizing the ethnic makeup of a territory. As this definition suggests, ethnic cleansing comprises not only ethnic expulsions and extermination during war, but also policies of ethnic homogenization undertaken during times of relative peace. In strategic terms, it involves the removal of targeted minorities from a given territory and the subsequent reset-tlement of members of the dominant group in the minorities' abandoned homes and property. In sum, ethnic cleansing consists of policies of ethnic expulsion and resettlement, which may be implemented either violently or non-violently. These policies are all undertaken with the purpose of achieving ethno-territorial homogenization.

The expression "ethnic cleansing" did not enter the modern lexicon until the 1980s, when Kosovar Serbs publicly accused the Albanian majority of ethnically cleansing the province. The term was later applied retroactively to the Serb campaign against the Muslims during the Bosnian war as well as Belgrade's attempts to empty Kosovo of ethnic Albanians in the late 1990s. Although the concept itself is relatively new, the phenomenon to which it refers is as old as human civilization itself. The ancient Assyrians used collective deportations to manage internal unrest and rebellions as early as the thirteenth century BCE; both the Assyrians and the Babylonians exiled Jewish populations in the seventh and fifth centuries BCE. During and after the Crusades, Jews were massacred and expelled from Germany, England and France. In Southeast Asia, meanwhile, over 100,000 Cham people were driven out of their homes by the Vietnamese in the late fifteenth century. At the same time, the Roma and Jews were being expelled from Spain. During the religious wars, the Huguenots were driven out of France; and hundreds of thousands of Spanish Muslims or Moriscos were exiled from Spain in the early seventeenth century. In nineteenth-century America, many Native American tribes in the territories were corralled onto reservations under the policy of "Indian removal." In Haiti, too, tens of thousands of French settlers were expelled from St. Dominique by Haiti's new leaders, who declared the country an "all-black" nation. Following World War

II, as many as 11 million ethnic Germans were driven out of East European countries on charges of collaboration with Nazi Germany.

After World War II, around half a million Ukrainians and Belorussians were exiled from Poland to the territories of the Soviet Union, while two million Poles were transferred from the Soviet Union to Poland (Wolff 2004: 17). Over 12 million people were displaced in the 1947 partition of India, including as many as a million dead. The 1974 division of Cyprus into Greek and Turkish regions led to the internal displacement of as many as 200,000 people.

Ethnic cleansing is still practiced in the contemporary period. Aside from the Balkans, hundreds of thousands of ethnic Georgians were expelled from Abkhazia in the early 1990s. In the meantime, hundreds of thousands of Azeris and Armenians were exiled from their homes during the Nagorno-Karabakh war. After Kurdish guerrillas were crushed by Saddam Hussein's government in the First Gulf War, millions of Iraqi Kurds fled to Iran and Turkey to escape collective retaliation. In 1994, 500,000 Tutsis and Hutu political moderates were murdered and expelled from Rwanda in a coordinated effort by Hutu extremists to eliminate their political opponents. Indeed, it would appear that violent ethnic cleansing has accompanied most every deadly conflict. In peacetime as well, countless programs of "silent ethnic cleansing" have been undertaken by political elites to consolidate their hold over a given territory. Such policies are difficult for the international community to monitor, much less prevent or resolve.

Definitions: ethnic cleansing, genocide and population transfers

Ethnic cleansing, genocide and population transfers are often used interchangeably, so it is worth parsing their meanings. Naimark (2001: 3–4) and Bell-Fialkoff (1993: 110) believe that the principal distinctions between these concepts lie in the *type and extremity of ethnic removal*. In their view, genocide and population transfers are both subsets of ethnic cleansing, with population transfers the most moderate form and genocide the most extreme. Their implied *targets* are another distinguishing feature. According to the Prevention and Punishment of the Crime of Genocide adopted by the UN General Assembly in 1948, genocide refers to "acts committed with intent to destroy, in whole or in part, a national, ethnical, racial or religious group" (Art. 2). In contrast, ethnic cleansing and population transfers are designed to move or remove ethnic groups from a given territory. Because of its focus on human destruction, genocide is viewed as the most sinister and deadly of the three.

The underlying *goals* of the three policies constitute a third important difference. Genocide and ethnic cleansing are undertaken by one side of the conflict to rid the territory of one or more ethnic groups, while population transfers aim to resolve conflict through ethnic separation with the implied consent of the conflict parties as well as the international community (Wolff 2004: 13). A final distinction is their *ethical and legal standing*. Genocide is a crime under international law, whereas ethnic cleansing and population transfers are not – although the acts that comprise ethnic cleansing, such as deportations, *are* war crimes and crimes against humanity (Waters 2006: 4, fn 4). Nonetheless, it must be said that genocide, ethnic cleansing and population transfers shade into one another in terms of impact, severity, targets and methods. As Hayden (1996: 736) notes, "[p]hysical slaughter enters the picture as an element of ethnic cleansing, since, after all, it usually takes a great deal of pressure to persuade people to leave their homes for 'homelands' that they might, in fact, never have seen."

These differences aside, choosing from among these terms is a politically loaded act with clear policy implications. Establishing that a campaign of ethnic removal constitutes genocide (as opposed to ethnic conflict or population transfers) implies a responsibility by the international community to halt the violence (Power 2002). The politics of naming is particularly evident in the distinction between ethnic cleansing versus population transfers. Hayden (1996: 734) observes that *our enemies* engage in "ethnic cleansing" to further their private interests, while *we* undertake "population transfers" to save lives and rebuild peace. The former is used to vilify expulsions by hostile governments, while the latter is used to legitimize similar policies by friendly governments. Indeed, a cursory examination of the record shows that the same event can be termed either ethnic cleansing or population transfers depending on one's perspectives.

Ethnic cleansing in international law and public opinion

Beginning in the interwar period, states began experimenting with the exchange of minority groups as a means of solving deeply interwoven ethnic problems within the context of changing patterns of political conflict in eastern Europe. The centuries-long intermingling of ethnic populations in Europe came to be seen as a problem in light of the turn-of-the-century ideal of national self-determination under which territorialized national minorities had a right to self-government. This principle informed the 1919 Allied reconfiguration of Central and East European borders in the wake of collapsed multi-national empires. In some cases, large minorities were stranded outside the borders of their putative national homelands, and the Allies dealt with these mismatches by concluding minority treaties with the new multiethnic states. In other cases, however, states were permitted to approximate a one-to-one nation-state fit through population transfers. The League-supervised Greco-Turkish and Greco-Bulgarian population exchanges are widely viewed as a success since these countries have not engaged in war since the early 1920s. However, it may be argued that the exchanges merely legitimatized Turkey's expulsions of ethnic Greeks from the Anatolian Peninsula after Greece's failed invasion. In fact, the vast majority of the 1.2 million Greek refugees involved in the transfers were expelled *before* the League-supervised exchanges got underway. Did these transfers constitute an externally mediated program of conflict management or did they simply provide cover for policies of national homogenization by the Turkish state?

Large-scale programs of ethnic cleansing re-emerged after World War II when millions of Germans and Hungarians were deported from East European countries. The interwar population exchanges served as a blueprint for these transfers, most notably in the case of German minorities. As many as 3 million ethnic Germans were deported from Czechoslovakia, leading to tens of thousands of deaths and summary executions in 1945. These actions were retroactively legalized under the 1946 Beneš Decrees, which sanctioned the forcible exile and expropriation of Germans from the Sudetenland. Following the mass expulsions, international public opinion began to turn against population transfers as an acceptable means of conflict resolution. Beginning with the Nuremberg judgment that Nazi population transfers constituted a war crime, the policy of involuntary resettlement gradually came to be seen as an anathema to the international community.

During the 1990s Yugoslav wars, these expulsions were given the moniker of ethnic cleansing in the international press. The 1993 UN Sub-Commission on Prevention of Discrimination and Protection of Minorities came out against the practice, and the subsequent Rome Statute of the International Criminal Court (Art. 7) designated population transfers a "crime against humanity." Despite the taboo nature of population exchanges today, a small group of security studies scholars began to re-examine population transfers in the 1990s, arguing that it is an unfortunate but possibly indispensable method of post-war peacebuilding (Posen 1993; Mearsheimer and Van Evera 1995; Kaufmann 1996, 1998; Downes 2004, 2006). These (mostly) hard-nosed realists have argued that, albeit costly and morally repugnant, partition and population exchanges may be the only means of resolving an intransigent conflict in which two or more groups are locked in mortal combat. On the heels of internecine warfare, neither side can trust that the other will not take the opportunity to vanquish them if they disarm – thus, post-war reintegration of warring groups is a hopeless and potentially dangerous endeavor. To the argument that population transfers violate human rights, partition advocates argue that far worse atrocities would result from failing to partition the groups into separate territorial enclaves. Kaufmann urged policy makers to "endorse separation" in conflicts with significant sectarian violence, "otherwise, the processes of war will separate the groups anyway, at much higher human cost" (Kaufmann 1998: 123). The argument for internationally supervised population transfers clearly turns on whether such atrocities are the inevitable by-product of group fears in the wake of sectarian violence or a deliberate policy of ethnic cleansing by self-interested ethnic elites.

The logic of ethnic cleansing

Ethnic cleansing consists of two broad tactics that can be executed simultaneously or sequentially. The perpetrators first use force, the threat of force, or other methods of intimidation to induce members of the targeted group(s) to flee. They then resettle the newly abandoned homes with displaced members of the dominant group. In this way, ethnic cleansers create permanent facts on the ground, helping them to consolidate their territorial claims.

The first step, ethnic removal, involves not only exiling "enemy" groups from the territory (through induced flight, forced expulsions or mass murder), but also destroying or purposely defiling their sites of national significance, including graveyards, churches, monuments and other landmarks that tie the group to the land. In this way, ethnic cleansers sever both the corporal and symbolic links between the targeted group and the desired territory. It was not by accident that Serb paramilitaries destroyed Muslim mosques and burned libraries, manuscript collections and archives that served as the repositories of Bosnian Muslim national history. This ensured "the destruction of communal memory by the ethnic cleansers" (Riedlmayer 2007: 117). The centuries-old Ottoman bridge in Mostar, an important Muslim landmark, was destroyed for similar reasons. A Croatian militiaman explained the incident to a British reporter: "It is not enough to clean Mostar of the Muslims – the relics must also be removed." These policies of "cultural genocide" are designed to complete the process of ethnic cleansing by wiping out the group's national history and erasing all signs of its ties to the territory (Carmichael 2002; Cigar 1995; Gallagher 2003). Mass rape and forced impregnation serve as additional methods of ethno-territorial conquest. According to MacKinnon (2006: 145), "ethnic rape" is "an instrument of forced exile, to make you leave your home and never come back ... It is rape to shatter a people, to drive a wedge through a particular community ... It is rape as genocide."

The second step in the ethnic cleansing process is to resettle members of the dominant group in the homes of the displaced minorities and to replace or repurpose sites of national significance belonging to the undesired groups. This two-step process can be observed in most cases of ethnic cleansing, particularly during ethnic civil war. Ethnic segregation is the predictable result. In the Bosnian war, for example, many Serbs driven out of the Federation were resettled in the homes of Bosniaks or Croats in Republika Srpska (RS). Many Bosniaks and Croats expelled from RS were in turn resettled in the homes of ethnic Serbs who had fled the Federation. Similarly, the Shi'as of Iraq were driven out of Sunni strongholds and Sunnis from Shi'a neighborhoods. Both Sunnis and Shi'as were likewise expelled from Kurdish territory in the north. Displaced minorities tend not to return to their homes, but resettle in territories where they can become part of the local majority. With each step, it becomes increasingly difficult for the expelled groups to reclaim their homes, livelihoods and national homelands. The territory has become effectively rebranded for the dominant group in whose name the campaign was waged.

The difficulty of returning minority refugees or internally displaced persons (IDPs) to their homes indicates that ethnic cleansing campaigns continue well beyond the formal peace settlement. Koser and Black (1999: 8) note that after war "returnees are often actively directed to certain areas, either to strengthen the position of one party against another, or, as in several recent conflicts such as that in the former Yugoslavia, as a continuation of 'ethnic cleansing.'" The Ottomans, for example, moved Muslims into newly conquered Balkan territories while simultaneously transferring Christian communities to Thrace and Anatolia in order to consolidate control over lands they had already won in battle.

It should also be noted that while ethnic cleansing is usually associated with violence, it may also be conducted during periods of relative peace – through campaigns of intimidation, threats of force, or various forms of discrimination. As a general rule, ethnic war nearly always involves ethnic cleansing, but ethnic cleansing need not involve ethnic war. Territorial gains are territorial gains, whether begotten under conditions of peace or war. A key difference is that war can provide cover for extensive ethnic purges that would be difficult to justify during times of peace. For instance, during the 1999 NATO war, Slobodan Milošević was able to accelerate a decade-long campaign of "quiet ethnic cleansing" in Kosovo to a rapid violent expulsion of Kosovar Albanians under the cover of NATO bombing.

The drivers of ethnic cleansing

Some have argued that contemporary ethnic cleansing is the unique by-product of system-level variables such as modernity, state formation or national self-determination. According to Bartov (1996: 3–4), the "mechanized, rational, impersonal, and sustained mass destruction of human beings, organized and administered by states, legitimized and set into motion by scientists and jurists, sanctioned and popularized by academics and intellectuals, has become a staple of our civilization." Mann (2005) makes the controversial claim that ethnic cleansing is the outgrowth of democratic norms under which the demos is equated with ethnos, thus laying the groundwork for the exclusion of rival ethnic groups, sometimes through violence. Still others contend that the age of nationalism and the doctrine of national self-determination both invites and justifies policies of ethnic cleansing (Hobsbawm 1995; Naimark 2001).

A second stream of scholarship identifies grass roots factors that facilitate ethnic cleansing. An essentialist line holds that the explosive force of nationalism and pernicious stereotypes about "the other" fuel popular support for such campaigns. In this view, grievances from past experiences of victimization and collective desires for revenge may lead victims of ethnic cleansing to become perpetrators in later periods (Lieberman 2006). In a now largely discredited thesis, Goldhagen (1996) argues that the German people favored expulsions and extermination of Jews during the 1930s and 1940s due to "eliminationist anti-Semitism" rooted deep in the German culture. Interestingly, Goldhagen's culturalist narrative was written to rebut a social-psychological explanation of mass participation in the Holocaust. In this account, Browning (1992) draws explicitly on the work of Stanley Milgram to deconstruct the motives of individual members of German police reserve units tasked with sending

Jews to concentration camps in Poland. They were ordered to shoot any excess persons who did not fit on the train cars destined for the camps. Although allowed to opt out of this task by their superiors, these individuals declined to do so – not out of animus toward the Jews, but rather out of a desire for social approval and deference to authority.

Alternative grass roots explanations focus on ecological drivers of conflict, such as economic competition or social divides between groups. One argument follows that deeply divided societies – where social, class and ethnic cleavages coincide – are at greater risk of mass violence than more cohesive societies (Kuper 1981; Horowitz 1985; Fein 1993). In an account based on the logic of opportunism and inter-group competition, Götz (2007) contends that the Reich procured support for the Holocaust from working-class Germans by redistributing Jewish wealth among ordinary Germans – parcelling out Jewish furniture to those who had suffered from Allied bombing and transferring Ukrainian food and French luxury goods acquired by the Wehrmacht through its foreign wars. In this view, the complicity of ordinary Germans was borne of common greed or opportunism. Similarly, Gross (2006) describes cases in which Jews who returned to their homes in Poland *after* the Holocaust were killed in pogroms organized by their Polish neighbors. He demonstrates that the Poles were largely motivated out of a fear of losing their newfound status and wealth that they had appropriated from their Jewish neighbors. As a general rule, there is a strong tendency of the dominant group to acquiesce to, if not actively participate in, elite-organized campaigns that target ethnic minorities.

Still other grass roots arguments focus on mutual enmities stoked by national symbolism (Kaufman 2001), mutual fears of victimization during state transition (Posen 1993), and state institutions that can be used to mobilize people to engage in violence. Drawing on extensive field work in Rwanda, Strauss (2006) concludes that the genocide in 1994 could not have taken place in the absence of these conditions on the ground. Others dispute the very notion that ethnic violence is the result of grass roots fears or "all-against-all" Hobbesian war – a dynamic strongly suggested by the label "ethnic war." In one such critique, Mueller (2000: 62) contends that the violence and ethnic cleansing in Bosnia, Croatia and Rwanda "came about not because people generally gave into murderous enmity, but because they came under arbitrary control of armed thugs." Ethnicity, in this view, served as "an ordering device or principle [upon which politicians organized their campaigns], not as a crucial motivating force." Although politicians and other leaders routinely recruit paramilitary groups to achieve their war aims, they quickly and easily lose control of the situation. It follows from this that "a mass of essentially mild, ordinary people can unwillingly and in considerable bewilderment come under the vicious and arbitrary control of small groups of armed thugs" (Mueller 2000: 42).

In this view, ethnic cleansing is an *elite-driven* project rooted in perceived political or economic imperatives, ideologies of racial purity, or private interests of individual leaders, special interests or governments. Such arguments stand in marked contrast to those that focus on inter-group competition, mutual hatreds and fears as the basic impetus for ethnic cleansing. Rather than viewing ethnic cleansing and other mass violence as a product of inter-group dynamics, where groups are assumed to be monolithic actors whose interests inform elite preferences, elite-based arguments draw a clear distinction between the responsibilities that ordinary people have in perpetrating the violence and those of the architects of such campaigns. In this formulation, programs of ethnic cleansing are designed by elites – sometimes to benefit the dominant group, sometimes to stabilize the state, and sometimes to serve their narrow self-interests. For their part, ordinary people are forced or manipulated into cooperating with such policies – either through active participation or passive support.

Ethnic cleansing is sometimes undertaken by elites in the interest of state- or nation-building. Pappe (2006) argues, for example, that the destruction of hundreds of Palestinian villages by Israel in 1947–49 was a deliberate policy of state-building by Israeli elites and not, as sometimes argued, a defensive response to an earlier wave of Arab–Israeli violence or fears of Palestinian rebellion. Similarly, Martin (1998: 858) explores the origins of Stalin's programs of ethnic cleansing in which approximately 800,000 members of mostly diasporic nationalities were arrested, deported or executed between 1935 and 1938. These operations were undertaken partly to consolidate new national territories and partly out of suspicions by the Soviet leadership that diasporic nationalities in the borderlands were disloyal subjects vulnerable to manipulation by outside actors seeking to undermine the Soviet state.

As a rule, programs of ethnic cleansing are designed and executed by a handful of elites based on perceived strategic or economic imperatives, ideological convictions or personal self-interest. Browning and Jurgen (2004) demonstrate, for instance, that the commitment of Hitler's inner circle to "racial imperialism," the aim of ridding Central and Eastern Europe of its inferior races, led the Reich to abandon a relatively mild program of ethnic cleansing the Jews from the region to one of exterminating the Jews as the fortunes of Germany changed during the course of the war. Valentino (2004: 234), too, writes that mass killing "is usually conceived of and organized by a relatively small number of powerful political or military leaders acting in the service of their own interests, ideas, hatreds, fears and misperceptions – not reacting to the attitudes or desires of the societies over which they preside." He adds that "[p]erpetrators do not need widespread social support to carry out mass killing," negative popular support or compliance is more critical to the success of such campaigns than active support by the wider population. Although Valentino focuses specifically on mass killing, his theory applies equally well to ethnic cleansing. In this view, ethnic cleansing campaigns are executed to achieve a specific end, including radical political reforms, seizing and settling territory, and suppressing insurgency. Consistent with this line of argumentation, Downes (2008) puts forward a strategic theory of mass violence to explain civilian targeting during war. He contends that the decision to target civilians during war derives from a desperate desire to win the conflict while minimizing the costs of lives and resources on one's side and, second, the desire for territorial conquest. Strauss (2006), too, argues that the ethnic cleansing in Rwanda was at least partly due to the hardline leadership's attempt to use mass violence to hold onto power in the face of growing international pressures to liberalize and democratize.

Naturally, elite and mass-level explanations of ethnic cleansing are not incompatible, and many authors advance one theory to account for elite policies of ethnic cleansing and another to explain public willingness to participate in them or permit their execution. However, most scholars tend to locate the impetus for ethnic cleansing primarily at the elite or at the grass roots level.

Conclusion

Distinguishing ethnic cleansing from genocide is critical to attaining a fuller understanding of the logic underlying such campaigns. Since ethnic cleansing is principally aimed at securing and consolidating control over territory, rather than the destruction of an ethnic group, this implies a greater range of solutions to such conflicts. The most effective of these would contain a regime of land- or resource-sharing and would target implicated elites rather than focus on ameliorating inter-group animosities through truth commissions and the like.

Second, our understanding of ethnic cleansing should be broadened to encompass both violent expulsions and policies of quiet ethnic cleansing undertaken during periods of peace.

It should also include not only the exile of unwanted groups, but also the resettlement of homes and property with members of the dominant group. This broadened perspective suggests the need for interventions with a broader mandate than simply ending violent conflict and keeping the peace. Third parties should instead monitor and sanction policies of territorial aggrandizement – not only during times of violence, but prior to the outbreak of conflict and following the cessation of hostilities.

Finally, since ethnic cleansing is the key driver of wartime (and peacetime) segregation, effective conflict mediation requires an assessment of the extent to which ethnic cleansing is driven by inter-group fears or competition rather than a deliberate policy of state-building or rent-seeking by a small circle of elites. If the former, then ethnic cleansing is an extremely unfortunate but inevitable by-product of ecological pressures, and the international community should use population transfers to complete the separation of groups to prevent additional mass murder and violent expulsions driven by conditions on the ground. If the latter, then the international community should identify and target the architects of ethnic cleansing using a mix of legal and economic (and possibly even military) sanctions.

If societal cleavages or political or economic factors on the ground are *not* the main impetus of ethnic cleansing, and such policies are instead driven by the agendas of small groups of elites, then the most effective means of deterring or halting ethnic cleansing is changing elite behavior rather than trying to affect large-scale political or economic changes such as democratization and economic development (Valentino 2004). Prevention is, of course, easier than the cure, and the first step in preventing ethnic cleansing campaigns is monitoring elite behavior, which might involve examining the statements and beliefs of influential political elites and powerful groups in society. An effective early warning system for ethnic cleansing before it comes to fruition is clearly the most desirable policy response.

Further reading

Bell-Fialkoff, A. (2005) *Ethnic Cleansing*, New York, St. Martin's Press.
Browning, C. R. (1992) *Ordinary Men: Reserve Police Battalion 101 and the Final Solution in Poland*, New York, HarperCollins.
Naimark, N. M. (2001) *Fires of Hatred: Ethnic Cleansing in 20th Century Europe*, Cambridge, Harvard University Press.
Pappe, I. (2006) *The Ethnic Cleansing of Palestine*, Oxford, Oneworld Publications.
Power, S. (2002) *"A Problem from Hell": America and the Age of Genocide*, New York, Basic Books.
Valentino, B. A. (2004) *Final Solutions: Mass Killing and Genocide in the 20th Century*, Ithaca, Cornell University Press.

References

Bartov, O. (1996) *Murder in our Midst: The Holocaust, Industrial Killing, and Representation*, Ithaca, Cornell University Press.
Bell-Fialkoff, A. (1993) "A Brief History of Ethnic Cleansing," *Foreign Affairs*, vol. 72, no. 3, pp. 110–121.
Browning, C. R. (1992) *Ordinary Men: Reserve Police Battalion 101 and the Final Solution in Poland*, New York, HarperCollins.
Browning, C. R. and Jurgen, M. (2004) *The Origins of the Final Solution: The Evolution of Nazi Jewish Policy, September 1939–March 1942*, Nebraska, University of Nebraska Press/Yad Vashem.
Carmichael, C. (2002) *Ethnic Cleansing in the Balkans: Nationalism and the Destruction of Tradition*, London, Routledge.
Cigar, N. L. (1995) *Genocide in Bosnia: The Policy of "Ethnic Cleansing,"* College Station, A&M University Press.
Downes, A. B. (2004) "The Problem with Negotiated Settlements to Ethnic Civil Wars," *Security Studies*, vol. 13, no. 4, pp. 230–279.

Downes, A. B. (2006) "More Borders, Less Conflict? Partition as a Solution to Ethnic Civil Wars," *SAIS Review*, vol. 26, no. 1, pp. 49–61.

Downes, A. B. (2008) *Targeting Civilians in War*, Ithaca, Cornell University Press.

Fein, H. (1993) *Genocide: A Sociological Perspective*, London, Sage Publications.

Gallagher, T. (2003) *The Balkans After the Cold War: From Tyranny to Tragedy*, London and New York, Routledge.

Goldhagen, D. (1996) *Hitler's Willing Executioners*, London, Vintage Books.

Götz, A. (2007) *Hitler's Beneficiaries: Plunder, Racial War and the Nazi Welfare State*, New York, Holt.

Gross, J. (2006) *Fear: Anti-Semitism in Poland After Auschwitz*, London, Random House.

Hayden, R. M. (1996) "Schindler's Fate: Genocide, Ethnic Cleansing, and Population Transfers," *Slavic Review*, vol. 55, no. 4, pp. 727–749.

Hobsbawm, E. J. (1995) *The Age of Extremes*, London, Abacus.

Horowitz, D. (1985) *Ethnic Groups in Conflict*, Berkeley, University of California Press.

Kaufman, S. J. (2001) *Modern Hatreds: The Symbolic Politics of Ethnic War*, Ithaca, Cornell University Press.

Kaufmann, C. D. (1996) "Possible and Impossible Solutions to Ethnic Civil Wars," *International Security*, vol. 36, no. 4, pp. 136–175.

Kaufmann, C. D. (1998) "When All Else Fails: Ethnic Population Transfers and Partitions in the Twentieth Century," *International Security*, vol. 23, no. 2, pp. 120–156.

Koser, R. and K. Black (1999) *The End of the Refugee Cycle*, Oxford, Berghahn Books.

Kuper, L. (1981) *Genocide*, New Haven, Yale University Press.

Lieberman, B. (2006) *Terrible Fate: Ethnic Cleansing in the Making of the Modern World*, Chicago, Ivan R. Dee.

MacKinnon, C. (2006) *Are Women Human? And Other International Dialogues*, Cambridge, Harvard University Press.

Mann, M. (2005) *The Dark Side of Democracy: Explaining Ethnic Cleansing*, Cambridge, Cambridge University Press.

Martin, T. (1998) "The Origins of Soviet Ethnic Cleansing," *The Journal of Modern History*, vol. 70, no. 4, pp. 813–861.

Mearsheimer, J. J. and S. Van Evera (1995) "When Peace Means War," *New Realism and International Security*, Cambridge, MA, MIT Press.

Mueller, J. (2000) "The Banality of 'Ethnic War,'" *International Security*, vol. 25, no. 1, pp. 42–70.

Naimark, N. M. (2001) *Fires of Hatred: Ethnic Cleansing in 20th Century Europe*, Cambridge, Harvard University Press.

Pappe, I. (2006) *The Ethnic Cleansing of Palestine*, Oxford, Oneworld Publications.

Posen, B. R. (1993) "The Security Dilemma and Ethnic Conflict," *Survival*, vol. 35, no. 1, pp. 27–47.

Power, S. (2002) *"A Problem from Hell": America and the Age of Genocide*, New York, Basic Books.

Riedlmayer, A. (2007) "Crimes of War, Crimes of Peace: Destruction of Libraries During and After the Balkan Wars of the 1990s," *Library Trends*, vol. 56, no. 1, pp. 107–132.

Strauss, S. (2006) *The Order of Genocide: Race, Power, and War in Rwanda*, Ithaca, Cornell University Press.

Valentino, B. A. (2004) *Final Solutions: Mass Killing and Genocide in the 20th Century*, Ithaca, Cornell University Press.

Waters, T. (2006) "On the Legal Construction of Ethnic Cleansing," The Berkeley Electronic Press (bepress) Legal series, University of Mississippi Law School. Available online at: http://law.bepress.com/expresso/eps/951 (Accessed 3 September 2015).

Wolff, S. (2004) "Can Forced Population Transfers Resolve Self-Determination Conflicts? A European Perspective," *Journal of Contemporary European Studies*, vol. 21, no. 1, pp. 11–29.

11

GENOCIDE

James Hughes

Introduction

The greatest challenge for understanding genocide is that, while there is almost universal revulsion today at what the term is presumed to encapsulate – mass killing and group-annihilation – there is in fact no consensus over the definition of what acts are covered, which groups are protected, nor of what causes it. While there are theoretically informed studies of particular genocides, or certain patterns of genocide, a comprehensive theory, which applies to all genocides in all periods of history and across all regimes and cultures in which they have occurred, remains elusive. In the absence of a coherent theory of genocide, the possibility of plausible prediction is wanting. According to some analysts there has been an average of almost one case of genocide per year since 1945 (Harff and Gurr 1988, 1996: though it should be noted that their dataset also includes what they term 'politicides'). Academic scholarship on genocide has grown immensely in response to the Holocaust, post-colonial conflicts, and civil wars in developing countries. Yet, until the Yugoslavian civil wars of the early 1990s the international community was reluctant to even attribute the word genocide to any particular conflict, and generally prefers to use, as in the case of Rwanda, the more diluted term 'acts of genocide'.

There are, broadly, two main areas of contention in the question of genocide. Firstly, there is a lack of agreement over the very definition of the term, and even whether this matters for how perpetrators should be dealt with. Secondly, scholars are divided over the extent to which genocide is strictly a phenomenon of the modern era and linked to modern state-building, or is a recurrent feature of human history. Clearly, the capacity of the modern-state to engage in genocide has grown exponentially, yet how one interprets the modernity of genocide itself will shape the identification of the principal causes of genocide. This is perhaps the most vigorously disputed arena – between those who seek to find the drivers of genocide in historical events, ancestral hatreds, racism and other extremist ideologies, radical leaders and crisis contingencies; and those who stress the role of social structural determinants such as plural societies, uneven power relations, group competition and materialist grievances.

Definitions

The term 'genocide' was coined by Polish legal scholar Raphael Lemkin in 1943 (Lemkin 1944), but as early as 1933 he had formulated the concept, proposing that a new crime of 'barbarity' under international law be created to cover acts that included, among others, 'acts of extermination' directed against 'ethnic, religious or social collectivities whatever the motive (political, religious, etc.)'. Lemkin's conceptualization developed prior to the Holocaust. The most important sources of inspiration for his thinking were historical genocides, from the more recent – the genocide and deportation of Armenians by Turks from the Ottoman Empire in 1915 and after – to earlier patterns of European colonization and colonial genocides. Lemkin's concern with genocide was intellectually grounded in his study of international law and the concept of universal human rights, both of which developed largely from philosophical and legal debates that began in the sixteenth century over the legitimacy and conduct of European colonization. By the time he wrote *Axis Rule* in 1944 the European present, in the form of Nazi extermination policies, had caught up with its genocidal past. Nevertheless, there was a lack of clarity in Lemkin's original conceptualization of genocide, for he did not distinguish it sufficiently from other forms of mass violence but rather understood it as incorporating 'massacres, pogroms, actions undertaken to ruin the economic existence of the members of a collectivity'. He was the first, nevertheless, to stress the 'existential' threat posed to a 'collectivity' by genocide as opposed to other kinds of mass atrocities (Lemkin 1933). Today, genocide is most frequently associated with the extermination of the Jews by the Nazis during the Second World War – a genocide that is by far the most studied and commemorialized, including a 'Holocaust Remembrance Day' held annually on 27 January (the date of liberation of Auschwitz-Birkenau extermination camp by Soviet troops) – a date first commemorated in Germany from 1995, but established as an international commemoration by the UN in 2005.

Despite the Holocaust, embedding the concept of 'genocide' in international law after the Second World War was problematical due to a lack of consensus on its meaning and application. The Convention on the Prevention and Punishment of Genocide was passed by the UN General Assembly in December 1948 and became international law in 1951. The term was not employed in the Charter of the International Military Tribunal established by the Allies under the London Agreement of 8 August 1945. There were several references to acts of 'extermination' including 'on political, racial or religious grounds', mostly but not solely in reference to persecution of Jews, and they were subsumed within the category of 'crimes against humanity' (Nuremburg Trial Proceedings 1945a). However, somewhat confusingly, the term 'genocide' was mentioned once in the Indictment at the Nuremberg Trials, and that was actually under count three – 'War Crimes', rather than count four 'Crimes against Humanity'. The Indictment against leading Nazi officials charged that they

> conducted deliberate and systematic genocide, viz., the extermination of racial and national groups, against the civilian populations of certain occupied territories in order to destroy particular races and classes of people and national, racial, or religious groups, particularly Jews, Poles, and Gypsies and others.
>
> *(Nuremburg Trial Proceedings 1945b)*

The Nuremburg trials therefore employed the concept before it was actually specified as a crime under international law, but also narrowly framed it as a crime perpetrated by states and their agents in time of war.

Lemkin aimed for a more expansive conceptualization of genocide that did not limit it to a crime of inter-state war, and made it a crime of international concern. His ideas were more fully, though not comprehensively, embodied in the process leading to the Convention in 1946–8. Trygve Lie, the Secretary-General of the UN, invited Lemkin along with two other highly reputed jurists – Donnedieu de Vabres of France and Vespasin Pella of Romania – to prepare a draft convention. Lemkin's core ideas that genocide posed an 'existential' threat to a group, and generally assumed three main forms (physical, biological, and cultural destruction) were retained in the Convention. However, one of the most contentious issues in the framing of the Convention was the nature of the groups to be covered by it. Resolution 96 (1) of the United Nations General Assembly of 11 December 1946 on 'The Crime of Genocide' referred to 'racial, religious, political and other groups' (United Nations 1946). The last category was too unrefined and was dropped in subsequent discussions and drafts. The draft prepared by Lemkin et al. for the Secretary-General in 1947 limited the range of groups protected to 'racial, national, linguistic, religious or political groups of human beings' (United Nations 1947). This limitation was even further diluted in the final convention. Article II of the Convention defined 'genocide' as 'acts committed with intent to destroy, in whole or in part, a national, ethnical, racial or religious group as such'. Acts covered included:

> a) Killing members of the group; b) Causing serious bodily or mental harm to members of the group; c) Deliberately inflicting on the group conditions of life calculated to bring about its physical destruction in whole or in part; d) Imposing measures intended to prevent births within the group; e) Forcibly transferring children of the group to another group.
>
> *(United Nations 1948)*

Lemkin's notion that genocide included the extermination of 'social collectivities' was dropped, for this was seen as a euphemism for 'class war' by the USSR. The Nuremburg Trials' inclusion of 'political' groups in the crime of 'extermination' was also abandoned. The Stalinist regime of the Soviet Union had conducted in the early 1930s one of the worst (in numerical terms) genocides in history by its extermination of 'kulaks' (nominally 'wealthy peasants'), which included the *Holodomor* famine genocide in Ukraine (Conquest 1987). Due to the USSR's opposition to the inclusion of 'political' groups as a protected category, and to secure the passing of the Convention at the General Assembly, its framers settled on a narrow definition of the groups covered and thereby intentionally excluded not only political, but also cultural linguistic and socio-economic groups (Whitaker Report 1985). It also excluded other groups that had been subjects of genocide by the Nazis such as the disabled (the first social category to be actually captured by a Nazi state programme of extermination), and homosexuals. The Holodomor genocide is an example of the paradoxical politicization of genocide that has been shaped by the narrow framing of the definition in the Convention. The Ukrainian peasantry was not specifically or disproportionally targeted by Stalinist dekulakization, which ravaged the Soviet peasantry in general, but the exclusion of political and social groups from the definition reinforced Ukrainian claimants' construction of these historical events as a genocide in national and ethnic terms, rather than within the frame of social class.

Because the crime of genocide was not part of international law prior to 1945, trials of former Nazi officials and collaborators post-Nuremburg have usually involved charges of 'crimes against humanity' with no mention of 'genocide'. This was the case, for example, in the most prominent of the post-Nuremburg trials of Nazis, the case of Adolf Eichmann in

Israel in 1961. Eichmann's 15 count indictment cited 'physical extermination of the Jews' among other 'crimes against humanity' (Trial of Adolf Eichmann 1961). The Genocide Convention envisaged prosecution by the national courts of the territory where the crime took place, and by an international criminal court, not universal jurisdiction. For some law scholars the Eichmann trial was part of the positive process of creating an international legal architecture based on 'Cosmopolitan' (aka Western Liberal) norms – a process that was accelerated by judicial activism on crimes against humanity, war crimes and genocide during the 1990s (Benhabib 2005). Such interpretations are based on a poor historical understanding of the post-Second World War era and ignore the seminal work on genocide provided by scholars such as Leo Kuper. It was Kuper's series of studies in the 1980s that drew attention to the failure of the international community to prevent and punish genocide (Kuper 1981, 1984, 1985). Kuper highlighted the perverse ironies inherent in the international treatment of genocide: the Convention stipulated that genocidal states were expected to prosecute themselves, and no international tribunal or court had been set up as a guardian to the Convention; and the United Nations system itself protected perpetrators because, as he put it: 'the sovereign territorial state claims, as an integral part of its sovereignty, the right to commit genocide, or engage in genocidal massacres, against peoples under its rule, and that the United Nations, for all practical purposes, defends this right' (Kuper 1984: 161).

Recommendations made by Kuper and others for strengthening international jurisdiction, the Convention, and preventing genocide made little progress during the Cold War. Even internal UN reports were largely ignored. In 1985 the report of the United Nations' Special Rapporteur on genocide – the so-called 'Whitaker Report' – suggested that 'considerations of both of proportionate scale and of total numbers are relevant' in determining acts of genocide, and recommended that 'political' and 'sexual' groups be included among those specifically protected by the Convention. Given the weakness of international and domestic action many, like Kuper, turned their energies to developing nongovernmental organizations (NGOs) which could monitor conflict, raise media and public awareness, act as an early warning system, and pressure states and international organizations such as the UN to act. (There are by now a number of such advocacy organizations; most notably in the case of genocide is Genocide Watch http://www.genocidewatch.org.) The idea of forceful international action to constrain genocide within states informed the development of the concept of 'humanitarian intervention' by the UN or states in concert or alone, but as we shall discuss later, this idea only became salient in international politics after the Cold War had ended.

Cold War politics heavily militated against not only a wider definition of the crime but also its prosecution through universal jurisdiction. Acts of genocide, including several involving hundreds of thousands of victims, such as those against political opponents (the murder of some half million 'communists' by the Indonesian military in 1966–5), against declared 'class enemies' (the deaths of some 1.7 million Cambodians by starvation, overwork, untreated illness, or execution during the Khmer Rouge regime in 1975–9); against ethnic groups (the Tutsi genocide of hundreds of thousands of Hutus in Burundi in 1972; the Guatemalan military campaigns of extermination of at least 200,000 indigenous Maya in 1982) went unpunished. Cold War politics meant that the superpowers and great powers that dominated the international system, whatever the political orientation of their regime, often connived in the mass atrocities of proxy wars. After the Second World War, for example, the ideology of 'counter-communism' led the USA to attempt to forcibly resist the spread of hostile 'communist' regimes, first in North Korea in the early 1950s, and then in Vietnam in the 1960s and early 1970s. In his later years Robert McNamara, US Defense Secretary during the Vietnam War, recoiled at the 3.2 million Vietnam dead (excluding South Vietnamese military) and the near genocidal policies of the USA: 'we were trying to do something that was militarily impossible—we were trying to break the will; I don't think we can break the will by bombing short of genocide' (McNamara cited in Scheer 1995). US paranoia about a 'domino-effect' in the spread of communism in South East Asia led it to support a number of genocidal regimes in the region, notably Indonesia's military rulers, who, having exterminated their communist opposition in the mid-1960s, massacred some 300,000 East Timorese seeking an independent state after Portuguese decolonization in 1975. With the backing of the USA and China the followers of Pol Pot's genocidal Khmer Rouge regime continued to hold the Cambodian seat at the United Nations long after they had been ousted from power by a Vietnamese military intervention in 1979 (much criticized in the West). The USA, Australia and all other Western nations refused aid, trade and diplomatic relations with the new anti-genocidal Vietnamese-supported Cambodian regime, and the UN even imposed sanctions on it. The international community did not act when Saddam Hussein's regime in Iraq perpetrated genocide against the Kurds in the 'Anfal' campaigns culminating in 1988, which included the use of chemical weapons against civilian areas (Human Rights Watch 1993), but only intervened when he attacked oil-rich Kuwait. The many examples of hypocrisy in the international community highlighted by Kuper and other genocide scholars were despite the duty imposed by Article I of the Convention on its contracting states 'to prevent and to punish' the crime.

As these cases and others demonstrate, during the Cold War the USA, USSR, China and their allies tended to be indifferent to genocidal acts perpetrated by regimes and governments that were considered to be allies, partners or of strategic importance. After the Cold War, however, some of these genocides were more widely recognized, notably that in Cambodia. Here lies a contradiction, for having refused to prevent or prosecute the genocide in Cambodia during the Cold War, the USA was at the forefront of attempts to institute international criminal proceedings against Pol Pot when he was ousted from the Khmer Rouge leadership in 1997. Yet, the domestic parties in Cambodia had reached a peace agreement to end civil war in 1991 that specifically excluded war crimes trials of Khmer Rouge leaders, and former Khmer Rouge foreign minister Ieng Sary was even pardoned in 1996. An agreement in 1997 between the government of Cambodia and the UN led to the establishment of a special court in Cambodia (mostly funded by the UN, and with some international representation among the judges) to try those former Khmer Rouge leaders guilty of crimes against humanity, genocide and other crimes. Almost ten years later, in 2007, under pressure from the UN, Cambodia began the prosecution of a small group of five senior Khmer Rouge leaders, including Ieng Sary, but the indictments gave prominence to various crimes against humanity, and downplayed genocide (Cambodia 2007). These trials were concluded by 2014, with only three convicted and sentenced to life terms of imprisonment. (Ieng Sary died, and his wife was found mentally unfit to stand trial.) A legitimate question is whether the prosecution of these five individuals served any positive purpose. Advocates believe that such trials are an important step against impunity – a salient factor in the new international norm of 'transitional justice' that emerged in the 1990s – as well as being a forum for disseminating knowledge about Khmer Rouge crimes. But the trials arguably have also done more political harm than good by destabilizing some of the fundamental political compromises undertaken internally to end the Cambodian civil war, and demonstrating the messy interface between domestic and international jurisdiction in the pursuit of genocidists.

After the fall of communism, despite the new openness for action in the international system, states remained unwilling to fulfil their duties under Article I as evidenced by the failure to intervene in a timely manner to prevent genocides in Rwanda (1994) and former

Yugoslavia (1992–6). The changed international climate did, nevertheless, create opportunities for a new international judicial activism against perpetrators of war crimes, crimes against humanity and genocide. Since the early 1990s, national courts, whether of the territory where genocide was committed or elsewhere, and the ad hoc international tribunals created by the Security Council, such as the International Criminal Tribunal for Rwanda (ICTR) and the International Criminal Tribunal for the Former Yugoslavia (ICTY), have proactively interpreted Article VI of the Convention as permissive of universal jurisdiction despite the article's explicit wording. The conceptualization of the crime of genocide, however, became confused with other forms of mass intimidation and violence in the expulsion and transfer of populations during warfare, whether inter-state or intra-state. This may be illustrated by the term 'ethnic cleansing'. This term first came into wide currency as a result of the conduct of civil war in Bosnia-Herzegovina from 1992–6. The term, a translation from the Serbo-Croat term '*etničko čišćenje*' is derived from the communist party's sense of 'purge', and in practice covered a spectrum of actions from non-violent administrative intimidation, discrimination and punishment, to violent expulsion and mass murder, and thus is of doubtful value in assessing genocide (Bell-Fialkoff 1993; Petrovic 1994). Nevertheless, the powerful rhetorical critique resonating from this vague term led to its wide employment by diplomats, politicians and especially journalists to indicate policies aimed at the 'ethnic' purification of territory. UN General Assembly Resolution 47/121 of 18 December 1992 is very explicit in its paragraph 9 of the Preamble, declaring that: 'the abhorrent policy of "ethnic cleansing" ... is a form of genocide'.

According to the convention, genocide must involve the 'physical' destruction of a group 'in whole or in part'. Forced transfer and expulsion of populations, however brutal, generally falls short of a true definition of genocide, as do massacres and other mass atrocities. The key question is whether there is a specific intent, what in legal jargon is termed *dolus specialis*, present. Is there intention to destroy a group 'as such', and what does this mean? 'Death marches' of expelled populations have been a key feature of many historical cases of genocide, such as the Armenians, the Jews, and Cambodians. Generally, however, ethnic cleansing and mass atrocities lack the intention of physical destruction of the group. From an analytical, as opposed to legal, perspective the question in each context must be whether ethnic cleansing is on a spectrum where it may be a precursor to, signal of, or precipitant of genocide. Great episodes of ethnic cleansing in the twentieth century illustrate how the definition of what is 'ethnic' cleansing becomes blurred, and the linkage between ethnic cleansing and genocide is far from clear-cut. Some transfers were state administered cooperatively, or were conducted by Great Power agreement with the support of the international community of the day. The Greek-Turkish transfers of population agreed in the convention of Lausanne (1923) involved over two million persons, and fused religious with national identity. The target groups for ethnic cleansing in this case were nominally religious groups ('Muslims' and 'Greek Orthodox'), not ethnic. The Potsdam Agreement between the USSR, USA, and Great Britain in August 1945 to manage postwar Germany and Eastern Europe, determined that 'the transfer to Germany of German populations, or elements thereof, remaining in Poland, Czechoslovakia and Hungary, will have to be undertaken' (Potsdam Agreement 1945). Over 12 million persons were affected and, according to German government figures, between two and two and a half million persons died in what was declared by the Allies to be an 'orderly and humane' process. Some forced transfers and expulsions of populations resonate with genocidal intent even if large scale physical destruction of the target group is absent in practice, as in the cases of the *Nakhba*, the forced expulsion and flight of some 700,000 Palestinians under the Jewish armed forces' 'Dalet Plan' during the 1948 war (Morris 2003); and in the Bosnian civil war, over two million persons were displaced, the bulk of whom were Bosnian Muslims and Bosnian Croats forcibly displaced by Serb armed violence. A recent International Court of Justice judgment in relation to the war between Croatia and Serbia in 1991–5, rejected a claim and counter claim of genocide by these states, because of the absence of proofs of specific intent, but did find that both states had committed 'acts of genocide' under article II of the Convention (International Court of Justice 2015).

Since the early 1990s, tension has arisen between the judicial activism of United Nations' courts and national courts, with the former attempting to provide rigorous and substantive judgments against perpetrators of genocide and other crimes against international humanitarian law, while the latter tend to make superficial and lightweight claims to 'customary international law' (Schabas 2003). Universal jurisdiction has in fact involved few genocide prosecutions. Obstacles to prosecution are not just political, but include not least the problem of proving intent to destroy a group 'as such'. Outside of the United Nations' courts, such as the ad hoc tribunals on Former Yugoslavia and Rwanda, the special court on Sierra Leone and the special tribunal on Cambodia, the small number of prosecutions by states suggests that such trials are more symbolic and political in intent rather than serious efforts to prosecute perpetrators and thus deter the crime. National courts in Rwanda, Bosnia and Herzegovina, Croatia and Kosovo have also held trials based on the provisions of the Convention. Several European states have prosecuted the government ministers, military officers and individuals of other states for genocides (notably, Germany in cases relating to Bosnia and Herzegovina, and Belgium in cases relating to Rwanda).

The Rwanda case illustrates many of the problems inherent in prosecuting the crime of genocide. This genocide arose when a long running civil war in an ethnically divided society, with a majority Hutu and minority Tutsi population in conflict, escalated in 1994 and triggered a Hutu elite mobilization for the annihilation of the minority group. When the Tutsi dominated Rwanda Patriotic Front came to power in the aftermath of the genocide, the mass punishment of perpetrators was made possible. A retrospective genocide law was passed in 1996, but with some 120,000 accused in detention, the legal system in what was already a weak state simply could not cope. The sheer scale of potential cases in Rwanda meant that to prosecute the suspects by normal legal measures would have taken more than 100 years. The ICTR was established by the UN in 1994, and by 2015 just a small number (93) of the highest level suspects were arrested, detained and tried, of whom 61 were convicted and 14 acquitted (for the cases see http://www.ictr.org). To deal with the case backlog in Rwanda itself a radical approach was taken. A special law of 2002 established a grassroots community justice system (the *gacaca* 'courts') with minimal legal process (or protections) for judging the ordinary *genocidaires*. Some 12,000 such courts, involving hundreds of thousands of local participants, have judged and speedily convicted the low-level suspects, although the process has raised concerns about lack of due process and the role of revenge and score-settling. Rwanda is an illustrative case of how a new regime uses genocide, and key mechanisms of transitional justice (trials and truth narratives), for the goal of regime consolidation and social control.

Important developments in the prosecution and of the legal concept of genocide emerged from the ad hoc International Criminal Tribunals established to deal with the cases of Rwanda and Yugoslavia. Technically, the first head of government to be convicted of genocide was Pol Pot in 1979 (by a 'revolutionary tribunal' of the Vietnam-backed Cambodian regime), though this was in absentia and he died before being brought to justice. The first head of government to be convicted and imprisoned for genocide is former Rwandan prime minister Jean Kambanda (1998), who pleaded guilty. In the case of Bosnia-Herzegovina high level Serbian officials were indicted by the ICTY for genocide or complicity to commit genocide, including the first sitting head of state, FRY president Slobodan Milošević (2001). Bosnian Serb leader Radovan Karadžić was originally indicted for genocide in 1995, but was only arrested and put on trial in 2008, and his verdict is awaited after the trial concluded in 2014.

One of the brutal characteristics of the civil wars in Yugoslavia was the systematic use of rape against women. By the mid-1990s this type of rape was increasingly being analysed by legal scholarship and in UN reports on conflict within the lens of international legal instruments such as the Genocide Convention (Chinkin 1994). The Akayezu decision by the ICTR in September 1998 illustrates some of the forwards–backwards contradictory legal development. This case established the precedent that in a context of mass violence systematic rape is an act of genocide when it is designed to 'prevent births within a group' (ICTR 1998). Equally, the ICTR compounded existing confusion over the definition of a protected group under the Convention by reaffirming a Soviet-influenced definition of 'group'. Based on its reading of the *travaux préparatoires* of the Genocide Convention, it pronounced that protection only extended to 'stable' groups that are

> constituted in a permanent fashion and membership of which is determined by birth, with the exclusion of the more 'mobile' groups which one joins through individual voluntary commitment, such as political and economic groups. Therefore, a common criterion in the four types of groups protected by the Genocide Convention is that membership in such groups would seem to be normally not challengeable by its members, who belong to it automatically, by birth, in a continuous and often irremediable manner.
>
> *(ICTR 1998)*

The court reaffirmed not only a politicized reading of 'group', but also a meaning that is archaic, and oblivious to the role of social construction in group identity.

The Krstic decision of the International Criminal Tribunal for the Former Yugoslavia in August 2001, concerning events in the UN designated 'safe haven' of Srebenica in August 1995, established a link between ethnic cleansing, rape as a tool of war, and genocide. Bosnian Serb forces under General Ratko Mladić pressured the outnumbered UN and Bosnian Muslim forces to surrender. Many tens of thousands of Bosnian Muslim civilians and soldiers were taken prisoner under guarantees of safety, many were abused and raped, and at least 7,000 Bosnia Muslim males approximating to fighting age were separated out and subsequently murdered. By judging Srebenica to be an act of genocide the ICTY took up the recommendation of the Whitaker Report and established the precedent that the reference in the Genocide Convention to 'in whole or in part' essentially meant instances when 'the alleged perpetrator intended to destroy at least a substantial part of the protected group' (ICTY 2001).

Arguably, the international adjudication on the genocidal aspects of the international and internal armed conflicts of the 1990s has been more backward looking than directional. On the one hand, the tribunals significantly expanded the definition of genocide by widening the interpretation of acts considered to fall under the intention to destroy the 'group as such'. On the other hand, they reaffirmed a politicized and restrictive understanding of 'group' in evaluating who is protected by the Convention. The contemporary conceptualization of the act of genocide has also been strongly influenced by the much looser formulations of Lemkin of the 1930s, thus confusing the existential threat to a group with other forms of 'barbarity' in warfare and armed conflict such as massacre and mass rape. The Rome Statute establishing the International Criminal Court (ICC) in 1998 did not develop the concept any further, and merely incorporated the definitional part of the genocide convention verbatim in its Article 6. Illustrating some progress in international law since Nuremburg, the Statute did, however, establish genocide as the most serious of the crimes of concern to the international community under its jurisdiction (Rome Statute 1998).

The politicization inherent in action to prevent genocide became more salient in the international community in the wake of the Yugoslav civil wars. There was a brief interlude of flirtation in some Western states with the doctrine of 'humanitarian intervention', the tenets of which were most succinctly stated by UK prime minister Tony Blair during the Kosovo crisis: 'the principle of non-interference must be qualified in important respects. Acts of genocide can never be a purely internal matter' (Blair 1999). Two recent cases involving claims of genocide illustrate many of the dilemmas of intervention and the problem of politicization and state interests: Kosovo and Darfur. President Clinton's framing of NATO's unilateral military intervention in Kosovo in 1999, subsequently approved by the UN, as an effort that 'stopped deliberate, systematic efforts at ethnic cleansing and genocide' was made after the war ended, not before, and came in response to media pressure about the motives for the war (Clinton 1999). Much controversy surrounds the motives for this intervention and whether the claim of genocide was employed by NATO states to legitimize a war pursued against Serbia's Milošević regime for other political and strategic reasons. There have been no indictments at the ICTY for genocide in Kosovo. NATO's intervention may have been intended to stop a potential genocide against Kosovar Albanians, but it also allowed Albanian violent ethnic cleansing of the vast bulk of the Kosovar Serb population (some 200,000 people).

In the case of Sudan's Darfur region, the divisions in the international community over how to respond were even more starkly apparent. This was the first major test case for the efficacy of the newly appointed (in 2004) UN Special Adviser on the Prevention of Genocide. The first Special Adviser (2004–07), Juan E. Mendez, an internationally distinguished human rights and transitional justice advocate, struggled to have Darfur classified as genocide. The United Nations estimates that 300,000 people died in a six-year internal armed conflict starting in 2003, the bulk through hunger and disease, and more than two million more have been displaced. A UN report on Darfur of 2005 found that the Sudanese government was not pursuing a policy of genocide, though war crimes were rampant in the conflict, and it recommended ICC prosecutions in this vein (United Nations 2005). Several Sudanese leaders have been indicted by the ICC, including the first sitting head of state President Omar al-Bashir. Al-Bashir was, in fact, charged in July 2008 with genocide and crimes against humanity, with the indictment alleging he orchestrated systematic killings, rape and deportation by Janjaweed militia groups against ethnic minorities. The ICC prosecutor, Luis Moreno-Ocampo, who was formerly an experienced prosecutor of military human rights abuses and war crimes in Argentina, declared that the main genocidal weapons in Sudan were 'rape, hunger, fear' and 'Al Bashir does not need gas chambers, bullets or machetes. This is Genocide by attrition' (Moreno-Ocampo 2008). The credibility of the ICC has been challenged, however, by the fact that presently only Africans have been indicted. In the case of Darfur many powerful states, including the USA and China, have been reluctant to classify it as a case of genocide – for such a classification would require international intervention under the Convention. In addressing the 'genocidal attrition' question, academic studies of Darfur are more nuanced. Prunier described the complex civil war and counterinsurgency in Darfur as an 'ambiguous' or 'quasi-genocide' (Prunier 2005). In August 2009 the main regional organization, the

African Union, rejected the genocide claims and declared that its member states would not enforce the ICC indictment and claims to jurisdiction.

Causes

A formidable problem in the study of genocide is to account for its very occurrence. For decades scholars have debated the causes and the motivations of the perpetrators. Today, most scholars reject as unsatisfactory accounts of genocide that attribute its cause to any single process or event trigger. Factors such as historic, racial, ethnic, and religious enmity between groups in a particular territory may provide a context where objective, structural conditions such as redistributions of power, a deteriorating economic situation, rising social inequalities, and sudden demographic changes may contribute to tensions between groups. But such group tensions have been historically and are today fairly ubiquitous and they do not deterministically lead to genocide. Given the ubiquity of group tensions across time, space and cultures, one might say that what is surprising is that the occurrence of genocide is relatively rare. This makes the predictive power of genocide scholarship poor, while claims of genocide and 'genocide risk' tables and maps are highly politicized. The study of genocide stresses the role of catalysts and additional fomenting drivers in contexts of increased tensions and raised anxieties. Studies give prominence to the presence of charismatic leaders or 'conflict entrepreneurs' who mobilize groups around exclusivist, racist ideologies, and who communicate a discourse and programmatic direction for mass inter-group violence. However, there is little agreement on why certain contexts or triggers turn mass violence into genocide in some cases and not others.

The two major perspectives in the study of genocide are the structural or functional approach, and the 'intentionalist'. The connection of genocide with modernity is, to be more precise, an association with the origins and development of the modern state. In this sense, modernity provides a structural explanation of its cause. For Baumann, there is an 'elective affinity' between genocide and 'modern civilization', which hinges on the organizational capacities of the modern bureaucratic state for social engineering (Baumann 1989). The association of genocide with the state builds on the seminal work of Franz Neumann, and later Hannah Arendt, on the nature of the totalitarian state as a twentieth-century phenomenon, with its capacity to draw on modern technology and communications for mass mobilization of society, and of the role of genocide and terror as part of its ideological logic (Neumann 1942; Arendt 1951). Twentieth-century genocide, noted Fein, 'is virtually always a state crime – not a collective outburst, a riot or communal violence' (Fein 2001). The state-of-the-art techniques and organizational mode of genocide thus become frames for understanding it. The Holocaust was characterized by systematized coercive channelling of targeted groups to conveyer belt mass murder, organized akin to an industrial *grand projet*. Austrian architects and German engineering firms constructed the 'death factories', as Arendt termed the extermination camps, for maximum efficiency. Attempts by genocide scholars to theorize and develop typologies have not moved beyond the linkage of state and genocide. It is nearly always a totalitarian or authoritarian state that they have in mind, as linking democracy and genocide generally falls outside the paradigms employed by most. Fein, for instance, developed a typology of genocides in which she identified four types: ideological, retributive, developmental or despotic (Fein 1990). Chalk and Jonassohn distinguished between those that seek to implement an ideology, eliminate a threat (real or perceived), acquire wealth, or spread terror, while also arguing for a much looser definition that included social and political groups (Chalk and Jonassohn 1990). However, as we discuss below, these paradigms are challenged by the linking of Western colonialism and racism, democracy and nation-state building, and genocide.

The attempt to link genocide with nationalism has necessitated a further retraction into history. Mann fixes the relationship between genocide and the modern state in the nineteenth century, shifting the explanation away from an emphasis on the totalitarian state and the notion of the Holocaust as the ultimate form of genocide. He points to the role of nationalist and democratization ideologies that emerged largely in the middle of the nineteenth century in generating organic conceptions of the nation and the state. Nationalism entwined the demos with the dominant ethnos, leading to forms of democratic nation state-building that, according to Mann, produced wholesale inter-group violence. This he termed the 'dark side of democracy' (Mann 2005). Critiques of Mann argue that he has revealed the 'dark side' of the nation-state not democracy, but this deflects from Mann's robust use of historical evidence to demonstrate the interdependent origins of exclusivist nationalist ideologies in democratic modern state-building, and of the role of this kind of ideologically motivated violence in the pre-totalitarian state era.

The relationship between genocide and modern state formation is retracted even further into history by Levene who argues that the earliest genocides occur in a small coterie of states at the forefront of the modern revolution in the sixteenth to eighteenth centuries – England (the conquest and settlement of Ireland and other colonies), revolutionary France (the repression of the Vendée revolt), and the USA (extermination of native Americans). Moreover, these genocides adhere to the same diverse forms as more recent genocides – with racial, ethnic, religious, and political factors playing a role. For Levene, genocide should be understood as an intrinsic part of the historical process of modernization. The birth of the modern state during the Age of Enlightenment occurred in tandem with the formation of the international system (its birth is generally dated to the Treaty of Westphalia of 1648). Geopolitical and economic competition between states in an increasingly internationalized context drove a race for modernization which impelled some states to target for genocide populations perceived to be threats or obstacles to their power. The success of the most advanced modernizing states – England, France, USA – was founded on genocide. This success had demonstration effects on other modernizing and colonizing powers for which genocide often became a response to uneven historical development. For Levene, modern genocides are most likely to occur in states undergoing a systemic crisis where the dominant ideology favours a radical and speedy modernizing social transformation (the collapse of the Ottoman Empire, Germany after the First World War, Stalinist Russia in the 1930s) (Levene 2005a, 2005b). A mentality of betrayal by a targeted group is a powerful undercurrent in such crises: the 'stab in the back' by Jews in Germany in 1918–19; the 'kulaks' grain strike' in 1927–8; the Armenians as an 'enemy within' in 1915; the Tutsi insurgency against Rwanda in 1994.

For classic studies of genocide, however, such as those by Kuper and others, the focus on modernity and the state as the key factors of causation is too restrictive. As Kuper's famous aphorism about genocide put it: 'the word is new, the crime ancient' (Kuper 1981). Kuper argued that the essential structural base for genocide is the plural society based on persistent and pervasive cleavages between its segments. Such societies have a variety of synonyms: deeply divided societies, communally fragmented societies, multi-ethnic societies, composite societies, segmented societies and internally colonized societies, and so on. The strong historical correlation between genocidal conflicts and plural societies (as for example in India on partition, or in Bangladesh, or in Rwanda and Burundi) suggested a symbiotic relationship. This is not to say that genocide is inevitable in plural societies, as their history shows otherwise, but only that the presence of a diversity of racial, ethnic and/or religious groups that are politically, economically, socially and/or culturally distinct, organized and competing as segments, offers the necessary conditions for domestic genocide. In extremis the plural society is characterized by systemic inequalities, discrimination and segregation. Such societies are often polarized into dominant and subordinate groups, with rigidity in power distribution that reflects the group inequality. Conflict tends to follow the lines of cleavage and inequality, generating zero-sum politics, where grievances can be generalized into identity politics and systemic challenges. These structural conditions are likely to be conducive to genocidal conflict because they facilitate the framing of resent and scapegoats, directing mass violence against collectivities and allowing whole communities of the 'enemy' group or 'other' to be targeted for annihilation.

The 'intentionalist' studies stress the role of radical, fundamentalist, usually Apocalyptic, ideologies in fomenting genocide. Intent must be organized and systematic, not an individual spontaneous epiphenomenon. Attributing intention to destroy whole groups of people is highly dangerous as it can itself result in crude stereotyping. For Semelin, ideologies of genocidal intent are concerned with 'identity, purity and security' (Semelin 2007). These are, in essence, ideologies of racial superiority based on the construction of 'us vs them' antagonistic relationships between groups, notions of insiders and outsiders, with destructive paranoid fantasies of mass violence and conspiracy theories framing the 'other' as 'enemies within'. Developments in the arts and sciences in the late nineteenth and early twentieth centuries – Darwinism and eugenics, research on disease and its causes (vermin, contamination, bacteria and bacilli), and the concern with 'national character' in European historiography – coincided with the rise of nationalist ideologies that stressed the organic concept of the state, people, culture and territory. Stone refers to this phenomenon as 'biopower' (Stone 2008). This was also an era of mass epidemics in the growing urban centres. The obsession within racist ideologies of finding scapegoats, the excessive valuing of ethnic authenticity and purity, denouncing 'mixing' and defending against contamination from 'outsiders' to the group resonated with society-wide phobias. But it would be a mistake to connect the dehumanizing frames inherent in genocide to one historical era. Dehumanization, whatever the time or context, necessitates the use of non-human ascriptive labels: Nazi extermination of Jewish 'vermin', Soviet 'liquidation' of 'kulak spiders', Pol Pot's crushing of 'worms', the Hutu killing of 'cockroaches'.

History suggests that it is not only structure or a crisis/war time context that is important for the occurrence of genocide but also that charismatic leadership is pivotal. For some it is so pivotal that the crime is named for the leader: 'Hitler's Holocaust', 'Stalin's Great Terror'. For genocide is not only infused with Apocalyptic fears but is orchestrated by a Messianic design for the remaking of society, the state, and the wider world, whatever the costs. The impetus may come from intellectual leaders – Cato's constant plea for Rome to destroy its strategic enemy Carthage ('*Carthago delenda est*'), Gokälp's romanticizing of the Anatolian Turks as an authentic core ethnie for national regeneration; it may involve a leader deluded by a 'divine mission' to transform the nation – Cromwell, Hitler; and revolutionary leaders bent on rapid social transformation – Stalin's 'Year of the Great Turn', Pol Pot's 'Year Zero'; or it may simply reflect a broader elite's racism and strategic anxieties and ambitions, as in US elites' framing of native Americans as a group as an obstacle to the 'Divine Providence' and 'Manifest Destiny' of US expansionism in the early nineteenth century.

Mass society has also its role to play. The logistics of organizing the deportation to extermination camps of some six million Jews, one million Sinti and Roma, and hundreds of thousands of other targeted groups (homosexuals, communists, trade unionists) by the Nazis between 1939 and 1945 required societal involvement on an immense scale. The genocide of the Jews in Eastern Europe also in many cases was characterized by barbaric personalized killing (especially in Latvia, Poland, Belarus and Ukraine) not dissimilar to the immediacy of the machete-wielding goriness of the Rwanda genocide of 1994. The study of process allows us to differentiate between forms of participation, violence and barbarity that precede or precipitate genocide, and genocide proper. It is the mass of 'ordinary' citizens who become engaged. This may generally involve assisting the state with the process of identification, exclusion, dehumanization, and ultimately extermination. Studies of the participatory process vary in how they locate mass participants, but the driving questions have a tendency to stereotype and simplify categories. To what extent are they 'bystanders' or 'perpetrators'? (Hilberg 1993). Can we identify the violent elite of 'willing executioners' and who are they? (Goldhagen 1996). In reality intentions and levels of participation can be blurry. Even in a relatively undeveloped rural society like Rwanda, forms of modern technology (in this case, radio) can facilitate a genocidal mass mobilization (Prunier 1995). Equally, we should not overlook the role of envy, resentment and greed in grassroots genocide, as Gross's study of the murder of the Jews of Jedwabne by their Polish neighbours in 1941 reminds us (Gross 2001). Sometimes, as in Nazi Germany, most citizens will be insulated by one or more removes from the actual killing, but may still be enthusiasts. Rwanda was a case of mass killing by the masses. Although separated by 50 years and a huge disjuncture in levels of modernity, the kill rate in pre-modern Rwanda also significantly exceeded that of the peak period in the Nazis' industrial extermination process (estimates indicate 500,000–800,000 Rwandan Tutsi were murdered over three and a half months in April to July 1994, compared with some 400,000 Hungarian Jews murdered at Auschwitz in April to June 1944). Modern forms of mass communication provide an immediate translation of leadership ideology to mass society, a facilitation of command and control of the process, and a capacity for the instantaneous repetition of propaganda for emulation, that are among the most distinctive features of genocides in the twentieth century. By the late twentieth century technological advances in mass communications have become not only a significant part of the causation of genocide but are also critical to its disclosure, if not prevention and punishment, through the publicity of mass media (for example, in the Balkans, Rwanda and Darfur), and the use of technology to internationally track, detain and forensically build a trial case against suspected perpetrators.

But how far can we plausibly pursue historical retraction in the study of genocide? By the modern criteria of what constitutes genocide, there is no logical reason to determine it as a modern phenomenon. Baumann, Arendt, Mann and Levene, and others, offer us good grounds for understanding why genocides occurred in the particular historical eras that concern them. There may be no particular relationship between genocide and the twentieth century, but equally, as Kuper reminds us, there is no logical reason for the modern definitions to exclude cases from the pre-Modern, or even ancient era (for example, Mongol massacres across Eurasia in the thirteenth and fourteenth centuries, Caesar's destruction of 'barbaric' Gallic civilization, the Roman Republic's destruction of Carthage). The lessons from the distant past remain of value. After all, Thucydides' *Melian Dialogue* concerning the Athenian Empire's genocidal annihilation of Melos in 416 BC – a case not unlike Srebenica – frequently features in modern US and UK military officer training on war crimes and genocide. This reminds us that genocide is a recurrent feature of war. To be precise, genocide characterizes those wars where the 'laws and norms' of war have been refuted by one or other party. The decision to deny an opponent in a conflict (whether inter-state war or internal armed conflict) the legitimacy and protections afforded by the laws and norms of war is generally a strategic decision that is operationalized tactically at low levels, and is one that is often configured by racism and/or religious zeal. Such behaviour is nearly always reciprocated by other parties to a conflict, as is evident on a grand scale from the responses to Hitler's direction of a race war against Slavs on the Eastern Front, and Japanese genocidal acts in South-East Asia. There are numerous historical cases of anticolonial resistance, guerrilla wars and insurgencies, where states refused to recognize armed resistance as being worthy of the protections of the laws and norms of war. That lack of recognition, the delegitimizing and demonizing of opponents tends to result in non-compliance with the combatant–noncombatant distinction in the use of force, thus leading to war crimes and indiscriminate civilian casualties. The decision can also arise, however, from tactical responses to resistance, military frustrations, and opportunities for rape and plunder. History provides numerous examples of cities reduced in this manner (the British Army's sacking of Badajoz in 1812; the Japanese Army's 'Rape of Nanking' in 1937; the Wehrmacht's obliteration of the Warsaw Uprising in 1944; the Russian military assault and destruction of Grozny by aerial bombing in late 1994 to early 1995, and many others).

The relationship between military culture and genocide has been most extensively studied in the case of Germany, as if the Clausewitzian idea of 'total war' was uniquely German. The German Empire's displacement and extermination of the Herero and Nama peoples at the beginning of the twentieth century (1904–07) in what is today Namibia is often presented as the 'first' modern genocide. Hull locates the intentionality for 'absolute destruction' (genocide in this case) within the 'developmental logic' of German military culture, which encouraged a doctrinal fixation on a strategy of 'annihilation' and the overriding 'military necessity' to achieve victory at all costs through extreme solutions. The doctrine laid the foundations of what became 'total war' in the Second World War: rapid and unrestrained action against an enemy, without distinction of civilians or soldiers, including a repertoire of savagery – of laying waste, reprisals, summary justice, mass killings, and even genocide (Hull 2005). Not for the first time, however, a people were annihilated less by direct killings than by forced starvation and neglect in concentration camps.

But, how distinctively brutal was German military culture? Parallels could be drawn with other contemporaneous episodes of systematic mass killing by militaries, such as the US repression of the Philippines rebellion (1899–1902). There was certainly murderous neglect by the British military and civil authorities of Boer civilians who died by the tens of thousands in concentration camps during the 'Boer War' (1900–02). Race is an obvious vital point of distinction in explaining the different levels of barbarity or restraint and deadly outcomes. The Herero and Nama were black. The USA pursued a colonial 'race war' where Filipinos were generally dehumanized akin to blacks and native Americans in the USA proper (Kramer 2006). The US military's savagery in crushing resistance in the Philippines differed little from the German military, except that the scale was greater – some half a million war casualties, and perhaps as many again perished through disease and neglect. Moroever, US military policy had direct antecedents in the genocidal campaigns against native American peoples. In contrast, the comparative British restraint during the Boer War was rather exceptional, and can be attributed to the fact that the Boers were white descendants of Europeans. Distinguishing a brutal exceptionalism in German military culture is myopic. The idea of 'total war' may have been first coherently theorized in Germany, but it is inherent in modern ideas about warfare. Truman referred to the two atom bombs dropped on Japan as a 'rain of ruin', and there is no doubt that more would have been used as soon as constructed in order to bring about the capitulation of Japan. Does this indicate genocidal 'intention' by the USA? Almost certainly it does, since this class of weapon is by the very nature of its effects genocidal. There is no more 'total' war, than atomic or nuclear war.

Military culture and behaviour can be more appropriately disaggregated into forms which generally accept the laws and norms of war, and those which do not. Military practices developed by the colonial powers to combat anticolonial resistance in the nineteenth and early twentieth centuries – concentration camps for whole populations, relocation and displacement of peoples, land seizures, all punctuated by massacres and occasionally genocide – fall into the latter category. This bifurcation of military culture continued to be evident in the military repertoire of what was later in the twentieth century termed 'counterinsurgency'. The racism and brutality of British military policy against the Mau-Mau rebellion in Kenya and the Chinese communist insurgency in Malaya, French policy against the Algerian revolt, and later US policy in Vietnam built on lessons learned in the nineteenth century. A similar pattern is evident also in another great European colonial power, Russia. It is unsurprising that Russian military vehicles in the military campaigns in Chechnya in 1994–6 and 1999–2004 often bore the legend 'Ermolov', for General Ermolov's genocidal campaigns against the peoples of the North Caucasus in the 1820s fit well within the overall pattern of practices of military conquest established by other European colonial powers.

The evolution of a culture of non-restraint and non-discrimination in German military doctrine undoubtedly contributed to German complicity in the Armenian genocide in 1914–18 in which at least one million Armenians were murdered, starved or died from neglect and forced marches in a campaign of deportation and extermination pursued by the Ittihadist Turkish military regime determined to build an exclusivist Turkish nation out of the collapsing Ottoman Empire. Turkey's refusal to recognize the Armenian genocide is perhaps the most illustrative, but far from being the only one, where a state enforced collective amnesia, censorship and self-censorship, surrounds genocide. States rarely promote a historical narrative of their genesis and development that throws light on genocidal episodes. Post-Second World War Germany is a notable exception to this rule, as the study of the Holocaust features prominently in the educational curriculum from an early age, and the German state has made immense efforts to compensate and commemorate victims. In sharp contrast, other European colonial powers, notably Britain, France, Spain, Portugal and Netherlands, or the USA, have yet to undergo a *vergangenheitsbewaltigung* (actively coming to terms with the past) as pervasive as that of post-war Germany. In February 2008 Australian Prime Minster Kevin Rudd made an official apology to the indigenous peoples of Australia for 'past mistreatment', setting in motion a process of reparation. However, while admitting that forcible transfer of children from one group to another had occurred there was no recognition that this was genocide under Article II of the Convention (Australia 2008). In the case of Turkey, however, the censoring of the past has reached heights where not only careers are threatened but prosecution, forced exile, and murder face those who recognize the Armenian genocide. Conscious of the shame attached to the term genocide, successive Turkish governments have pressured foreign states, including the USA and many European states, into using alternative terminology such as the 'tragic events of 1915' to disguise the genocide. The use of euphemisms and metaphors by perpetrators to cloak genocide is not uncommon, and to some extent could be understood as reflecting shame. The minutes of the Wannsee Conference of 1942, where the Nazis organized the 'Final Solution' to the 'Jewish Question', referred to 'emigration' and 'transportation' to the East. Stalin spoke of the 'liquidation of the kulaks as a class'. British Bomber Command labelled its mass killing of German civilians through area bombing in the Second World War as 'dehousing'.

The discussion of the causation of genocide so far has largely focused on the question of threat perception, or what Realists term the 'security dilemma' – whether and how states or dominant ethnie (and they could be majorities or minorities) perceive other groups to be a threat that requires the mass physical extermination of that group. The threat is generally claimed to be one that is posed to a state-building project, and by extrapolation to the geopolitical power of a state vis-à-vis other states. These are interdependent existential threats. The state-building group fears that the purity and power of its state is threatened by the presence of a hostile group, to which the answer is to annihilate that group. Focusing on this formula, with the state as the unit of analysis, overlooks other significant dynamics and rationales for genocide. The threat perception may also be ethnic, cultural, or religious and assume transnational forms. The emergence of a transnational 'globalized' form of Islamist extremism since the mid-1990s, as most clearly articulated by the militant Salafism of Al Qaeda, has employed claims of 'massacres' against Muslims in diverse places including Lebanon, Bosnia-Herzegovina, Chechnya, Kashmir, Somalia, Burma, etc. to legitimize an armed struggle against the 'Judeo-Christian alliance' of the USA, Israel, and the 'West' (Bin Laden 1996).

The materialist rationale for genocide might be often quite narrow and explicit – land greed, conquest and forced seizure, and settler colonialism. Recent scholarship on genocide has more systematically and rigorously analysed and highlighted Lemkin's interest in the connection between genocide and colonialism (Moses 2008). A persuasive case has been made for the colonial 'land grabbing' origins of the modern conception of genocide. A pattern of genocide has emerged historically in places where land greed has become infused with religious bigotry, and where the racist and religious ideologies of coercive colonial conquest combine with settler colonialism (Kiernan 2007). European philosophers have debated since the sixteenth century on the morality of colonial occupation and barbarism, including the physical and 'cultural' genocides of indigenous societies versus their rights – all conducted under the rubric of the *mission civilisatrice* (Fitzmaurice 2008). Historically, settler colonists and the settler colonial mentality of forced acquisition have been the driving forces for the dehumanization and displacement of peoples, the logical conclusion of which is genocide. The interaction of religion and the interests of settler colonialists is most illuminating when the core elements of both are the basis for an overriding state ideology as in the US ideology of 'Providence' and later 'Manifest Destiny', and the Zionist biblically rooted claims to Palestine. In these and other cases genocidal massacres were employed as a terrorizing land-clearing device. While state leaderships have often attempted to disguise the motivations of racism and religious bigotry within the more legitimate ideological wrappings of security or national interests, it is generally only the exceptionally fanatical leader who openly expresses clarity of genocidal intent. Cromwell saw his massacres of the Irish as a 'judgement of God' on 'Papists' that would force them 'to Connaught or Hell'. Hitler's demand for 'living space' (*Lebensraum*) for Germany in the East was also intended to obliterate 'Jewish Bolshevization'. Yet, even great democrats can articulate deeply genocidal instincts. How different the Jefferson Memorial would look if it inscribed his damnation of the native Americans: 'to pursue them to extermination'. To be fair to Jefferson, this and a few comments of similar ilk were made in the aftermath of massacres of settlers by native Americans, and unlike many of his contemporaries, Jefferson recognized that genocide was part of the 'Anglo' culture of colonial occupation, from Ireland to Asia. For some scholars, ethnic competition for land was a factor in the Rwanda genocide, as it is in Darfur. A sole focus on threat perception and security dilemmas, however, distracts us from the role of state ambitions and material interests. Elites may exaggerate a threat and thereby provide a discourse to legitimize acts which may, in fact, have an ulterior motive, whether it is the pursuit of material interests – seizing and colonizing lands from another group; or imposing ideological hegemony – as in racial purity, or counter communism.

Conclusion

Theoretical and explanatory frameworks for understanding genocide are weak both as regards the looseness of definitions and determining its causes. Examining the main genocides of the modern era – say since the French Revolution – reveals a diverse list of states from all regions of the world, representing all cultures, all ideological trends, rich and poor, and all regime types from democracies, to empires, authoritarian and totalitarian states. There is much of merit in the observation that genocidal states/societies have been the ones with the greatest complexes about security and position internationally, and political and cultural coherence internally. A focus on wars and other crisis contingencies, and leaderships who articulate this anger and resentment by seeking a radical transformation of domestic politics and foreign policies, is important but not sufficient to explain genocide. Observing the social contexts in which genocide occurs appears to confirm Kuper's pointing to the segmented composition of societies as the structural foundation for genocide. However, most societies are structured pluralistically, and most have no experience of genocide. So the question remains what makes some societies genocidal and others not? Much of the scholarship on genocide, generated from the USA and informed by liberal norms, is overly focused on the relationship between genocide and twentieth-century totalitarian and authoritarian states. As Kuper, Mann and others have argued, genocide affects all historical periods and regimes, including democracies. If we further take into account the role of state strategic ambitions, ideological and material interests, racism, imperialism and settler colonialism, and forms of inequality and group competition, we come closer to explaining why state/societal resentments against specific groups can turn genocidal. Ideologies of racial superiority that are connected to power and territory, in particular, however explicit or implicit, are likely to be an important motivation and justification for genocide.

There may be a 'banality of evil', as Arendt put it, in the conduct of genocide, however, genocide is not a product of banality, but of extraordinary political, economic and social conditions. What genocide studies have proven unable to do is to provide a general model which would allow us to forecast when state anxieties and societal antagonisms reach the threshold of toxicity where they unleash genocide.

Further reading

Charny, I. W. ed. (2000) *Encyclopedia of Genocide*, 2 vols, Santa Barbara: ABC-CLIO.
Gellately, R. and Kiernan, B. eds (2003) *The Specter of Genocide. Mass Murder in Historical Perspective*, Cambridge: Cambridge University Press.
Kiernan, B. (2007) *Blood and Soil. A World History of Genocide and Extermination from Sparta to Darfur*, Yale: Yale University Press.
Kuper, L. (1981) *Genocide: Its Political Use in the Twentieth Century*, London: Penguin.
Moses, A. D. ed. (2008) *Empire, Colony, Genocide. Conquest, Occupation, and Subaltern Resistance in World History*, Oxford: Berghahn.

References

Australia (2008) Apology to Australia's Indigenous Peoples by Prime Minister Kevin Rudd, MP; available at http://www.australia.gov.au/about-australia/our-country/our-people/apology-to-australias-indigenous-peoples.
Arendt, H. (1951) *The Origins of Totalitarianism*, New York: Harcourt, Brace and Co.

Baumann, Z. (1989) *Modernity and the Holocaust*, Cambridge: Polity Press.

Bell-Fialkoff, A. (1993) 'A Brief History of Ethnic Cleansing', *Foreign Affairs*, 72, 3: 110–121.

Benhabib, S. (2005) 'On the Alleged Conflict between Democracy and International Law', *Ethics and International Affairs*, 19, 1: 85–100

Bin Laden, O. (1996) 'A Declaration of Jihad against the Americans Occupying the Land of the Two Holy Sanctuaries' in B. Lawrence ed. *Messages to the World. The Statements of Osama Bin Laden*, London: Verso: 23–30.

Blair, T. (1999) The Doctrine of the International Community; Transcript available at http://www.pbs. org/newshour/bb/international-jan-june99-blair_doctrine4-23/.

Cambodia (2007) Extraordinary Chambers in the Courts of Cambodia, Office of the Co-Prosecutors, Statement of the Co-Prosecutors, Phnom Penh, 18 July 2007; available at http://www.yale.edu/cgp/ downloads/Statement_of_Co-Prosecutors18-July-2007.pdf.

Chalk, F. and Jonassohn, K. eds (1990) *The History and Sociology of Genocide: Analyses and Case Studies*, New Haven: Yale University Press.

Chinkin, C. (1994) 'Rape and Sexual Abuse of Women in International Law', *European Journal of International Law*, 5: 326–341; available at http://www.ejil.org/pdfs/5/1/1246.pdf.

Clinton, W. (1999) Press Conference by the President, The White House, June 25, 1999; available at http://clinton6.nara.gov/1999/06/1999-06-25-press-conference-by-the-president.html.

Conquest, R. (1987) *The Harvest of Sorrow. Soviet Collectivization and the Terror-Famine*, New York: Oxford University Press.

Fein, H. (1990) *Genocide: A Sociological Perspective*, London: Sage Publications.

Fein, H. (2001) *Denying Genocide. From Armenia to Bosnia*, London: London School of Economics and Political Science, Department of Government, Series: Occasional Papers in Comparative and International Politics 1.

Fitzmaurice, A. (2008) 'Anticolonialism in Western Political Thought: The Colonial Origins of the Concept of Genocide' in A. Dirk Moses ed. *Empire, Colony, Genocide. Conquest, Occupation, and Subaltern Resistance in World History*, Oxford: Berghahn: 55–80.

Goldhagen, D. J. (1996) *Hitler's Willing Executioners, Ordinary Germans and the Holocaust*, New York: Knopf.

Gross, J. T. (2001) *Neighbors. The Destruction of the Jewish Community in Jedwabne, Poland*, Princeton: Princeton University Press.

Harff, B. and Gurr, T. R. (1988) 'Toward Empirical Theory of Genocides and Politicides: Identification and Measurement of Cases since 1945', *International Studies Quarterly*, 32: 359–371.

Harff, B. and Gurr, T. R. (1996) 'Victims of the State: Genocides, Politicides and Group Repression from 1945 to 1995' in A. J. Jongman ed. *Contemporary Genocides: Causes, Cases, Consequences*, Leiden: PIOOM/University of Leiden: 33–58.

Hilberg, R. (1993) *Perpetrators, Victims, Bystanders. The Jewish Catastrophe 1933–1945*, New York: Harper.

Hull, I. V. (2005) *Absolute Destruction: Military Culture and the Practices of War in Imperial Germany*, Ithaca, New York: Cornell University Press.

Human Rights Watch (1993) *Genocide in Iraq. The Anfal Campaign Against the Kurds*. A Middle East Watch Report, Human Rights Watch, New York; available at http://www.hrw.org/reports/1993/iraqanfal/.

International Court of Justice (2015) *Application of the Convention on the Prevention and Punishment of the Crime of Genocide (Croatia v. Serbia)*, 3 February 2015, Judgement; available at http://www.icj-cij.org/ docket/files/118/18422.pdf.

International Criminal Tribunal for Former Yugoslavia (2001) *The Prosecutor versus Radislav Krstic, Case No. IT-98-33-T*, Judgement, 2 August 2001; available at http://www.icty.org/x/cases/krstic/tjug/en/ krs-tj010802e.pdf.

International Criminal Tribunal on Rwanda (1998) *The Prosecutor versus Jean-Paul Akayesu, Case No. ICTR-96-4-T*, Judgment, 2 September 1998; available at http://www.unictr.org/sites/unictr.org/files/ case-documents/ictr-96-4/trial-judgements/en/980902.pdf.

Kiernan, B. (2007) *Blood and Soil. A World History of Genocide and Extermination from Sparta to Darfur*, Yale: Yale University Press.

Kramer, P. A. (2006) *The Blood of Government. Race, Empire, the United States and the Philippines*, Chapel Hill: The University of North Carolina Press.

Kuper, L. (1981) *Genocide: Its Political Use in the Twentieth Century*, London: Penguin.

Kuper, L. (1984) *International Action Against Genocide*, London: Minority Rights Group.

Kuper, L. (1985) *The Prevention of Genocide*, New Haven: Yale University Press.

Lemkin, R. (1933) *Acts Constituting a General (Transnational) Danger Considered as Offences Against the Law of Nations*. Additional explications to the Special Report presented to the 5th Conference for the

Unification of Penal Law in Madrid (14–20 October 1933); available at: http://www.preventgenocide. org/lemkin/madrid1933-english.htm.

Lemkin, R. (1944) *Axis Rule in Occupied Europe: Laws of Occupation – Analysis of Government – Proposals for Redress*, Carnegie Endowment for International Peace, Washington, DC; available at http://www.pre ventgenocide.org/lemkin/AxisRule1944-1.htm.

Levene, M. (2005a) *Genocide in the Age of the Nation State vol. 1: The Meaning of Genocide*, London: I.B. Tauris.

Levene, M. (2005b) *Genocide in the Age of the Nation State vol. 2: The Rise of the West and the Coming of Genocide*, London: I.B. Tauris.

Mann, M. (2005) *The Dark Side of Democracy. Explaining Ethnic Cleansing*, Cambridge: Cambridge University Press.

Moreno-Ocampo, L. (2008) *International Criminal Court, Prosecutor's Statement on the Prosecutor's Application for a Warrant of Arrest under Article 58 Against Omar Hassan Ahmad Al Bashir*, The Hague, 14 July 2008; available at http://www.icc-cpi.int/NR/rdonlyres/A2BA9996-67C3-4A5F-9AD2-B20A7FD2D176/ 277757/ICCOTPST20080714ENG.pdf.

Morris, B. (2003) *The Birth of the Palestinian Refugee Problem Revisited*, Cambridge: Cambridge University Press.

Moses, A. D. (2008) 'Modernity and the Holocaust', *Australian Journal of History & Politics*, 43, 3: 441–445.

Neumann, F. (1942) *Behemoth. The Structure and Practice of National Socialism*, London: Victor Gollancz Ltd.

Nuremberg Trial Proceedings (1945a) *Vol. 1, Charter of the International Military Tribunal, 8 August 1945*; available at http://avalon.law.yale.edu/imt/imtconst.asp#art22.

Nuremberg Trial Proceedings (1945b) *Vol. 1, Indictment, 18 October 1945*; available at http://avalon.law. yale.edu/imt/count3.asp.

Petrovic, D. (1994) 'Ethnic Cleansing – An Attempt at Methodology', *European Journal of International Law*, 5: 342–359.

Potsdam Agreement (1945) *The Berlin (Potsdam) Conference, July 17–August 2, 1945(a) Protocol of the Proceedings, August 1, 1945*; available at http://avalon.law.yale.edu/20th_century/decade17.asp.

Prunier, G. (1995) *The Rwanda Crisis, History of a Genocide 1959–1994*, New York: Columbia University Press.

Prunier, G. (2005) *Darfur. The Ambiguous Genocide*, London: Hurst.

Rome Statute (1998) Of the International Criminal Court, 17 July 1998 (entered into force on 1 July 2002); available at http://www.icc-cpi.int/NR/rdonlyres/EA9AEFF7-5752-4F84-BE94-0A655EB30E16/0/ Rome_Statute_English.pdf.

Schabas, W. A. (2003) 'National Courts Finally Begin to Prosecute Genocide, the "Crime of Crimes"', *Journal of International Criminal Justice*, 1, 1: 39–63.

Scheer, R. (1995) 'Born of Blind Faith – Robert McNamara believed he would ascend in a meritocracy. And with good reason. So what went so "terribly wrong"?', *Los Angeles Times*, 16 May 1995; available at http://articles.latimes.com/1995-05-16/news/ls-2273_1_robert-mcnamara?pg=4.

Semelin, S. (2007) *Purify and Destroy. The Political Uses of Massacre and Genocide*, New York: Columbia University Press.

Stone, D. (2008) 'Biopower and Modern Genocide' in A. Dirk Moses ed. *Empire, Colony, Genocide. Conquest, Occupation, and Subaltern Resistance in World History*, Oxford: Berghahn: 162–179.

The Trial of Adolf Eichmann (1961) *District Court Sessions, Session No. 1, 11 April 1961*.

United Nations (1946) *United Nations General Assembly, Resolution 96 (1) 11 December 1946*; available at http://www.un.org/documents/ga/res/1/ares1.htm.

United Nations (1947) *Economic and Social Council, Draft Convention on the Crime of Genocide, E/447 26 June 1947*; available at http://www.un.org/.

United Nations (1948) *United Nations General Assembly, Convention on the Prevention and Punishment of the Crime of Genocide, New York, 9 December 1948*; available at http://treaties.un.org/doc/Treaties/1951/ 01/19510112%2008-12%20PM/Ch_IV_1p.pdf.

United Nations (2005) *Report of the International Commission of Inquiry on Darfur to the United Nations Secretary-General, Geneva 25 January 2005*; available at http://www.un.org/News/dh/sudan/com_inq_darfur.pdf.

Whitaker Report (1985) *United Nations Economic and Social Council Commission on Human Rights Sub-Commission on Prevention of Discrimination and Protection of Minorities, Thirty-eighth session, Item 4 of the provisional agenda, E/CN.4/Sub.2/1985/6–2 July 1985. Revised and updated report on the question of the prevention and punishment of the crime of genocide, Prepared by Mr. B. Whitaker*; available at http://www. preventgenocide.org/prevent/UNdocs/whitaker/.

12

DEBATING PARTITION

Brendan O'Leary

Introduction: the standard justification

Political partition may usefully be defined as a *fresh* political border cut through at least one community's national homeland with the goal of resolving conflict (see Talbot and Singh 2009; applying the approach suggested in O'Leary 2007). Political partition is therefore distinct from adjacent phenomena, such as *secessions*, which are attempted within existing recognized units (O'Leary 2001: 54; 2005; O'Leary 2007 defends this definition), or from *border adjustments*, such as those that occur after a shift in the course of a river bed, or from a shift in maritime boundaries following the immersion of an island, i.e. where the placements of people are not at stake.

Explanations of partitions, both in particular and in general, are recurrent in political science and history (e.g. Fraser 1984; Hasan 1993, 2002; Mansergh 1997), but this chapter focuses on the arguments used to justify them, drawing mostly from the twentieth-century cases of Ireland, India, Palestine and Cyprus. Just as no one is a relentless advocate of divorce at the slightest hint of disagreement between couples, so there are no relentless advocates of partition at the slightest hint of national or ethnic conflict. Partitionists, however, are obliged to use rhetoric. This phrasing is not disparaging. Long ago the Stagirite taught the world that rhetorical argument must be advanced when we are uncertain of our premises but must nevertheless persuade ourselves of the best choice of policy (Aristotle, *Rhetoric*). The most powerful arguments for resolving antagonisms through partition may be labelled, in order, as "historicist"; "last resort"; "net benefit"; "better tomorrow"; and "realist rigour".

The "historicist" argument

Historicists assume that history is necessarily evolving in a given direction (Popper 1976 [1957]), and conclude that we should aid the inevitable by giving it a nudge. Some insist that once nationalist, ethnic or communal conflicts pass a certain threshold, they will end in partition (e.g. Galbraith 2006; Kaufmann 1998). They may detect such tendencies in residential, educational and employment segregation, in the formation of nationalist, ethnic or communal parties, or in the overheating of political systems with the demands of what

W.H. Auden's poem on "Partition" satirizes as "peoples fanatically at odds, With their different diets and incompatible gods" (Auden 1976).

Historicism may shape policy because it is seen as both informed and realistic. That partition is inevitable, or is already happening, that facts have already been established "on the ground", are assumptions that may persuade policy makers that the process should be speeded up to reduce the pain. In 1993 advocates of the partition of Bosnia *and* of "population transfers", John J. Mearsheimer and Robert A. Pape, maintained, "transfer is already occurring. ... The only question is whether it will be organized, as envisioned by partition, or left to the murderous methods of the ethnic cleansers" (Mearsheimer and Pape 1993). Another partitionist argues that "ethnic wars always separate the warring communities", so it is not a question of "whether the groups will be separated but how" (Kaufmann 1998: 123). It is a tempting argument when extensive expulsions are afoot by militias, paramilitaries or police, but there is no confirmed social science law that *all* segregation – voluntary or forced – leads inevitably to the break-up of states. Not only has no one identified clear thresholds of violence (absolute or proportional to population) beyond which partition (or separation more broadly) becomes inevitable, but also simple comparative evaluations of recent conflicts show that there can be peace without separation (Carment and Rowlands 2004: 369 ff.)

The "last resort" argument

This argument acknowledges that alternative strategies exist to manage or resolve national, ethnic or communal conflicts, such as federalism, consociation, arbitration, or integration, and accepts that these alternatives should be attempted before partition is considered. But, if these options fail, so the argument goes, partition should be chosen to avoid genocide or large-scale ethnic expulsions (universally acknowledged to be the worst possible outcomes). Partition, in short, should be pursued as public "triage". Exponents of this argument often invoke the "security dilemma" (Jervis 1968; Johnson 2008; Kaufmann 1996a, 1996b, 1998; Posen 1993). The claim is that in conditions of emergent anarchy, e.g. when an empire or a regime is collapsing, the relations among ethnic groups become akin to those of individuals in a Hobbesian state of nature. One distrustful community will seek to enhance its security, which will enhance the insecurity of the other communities, creating a vicious and escalating cycle of insecurity. Ethnic groups with strong and durable identities will be mobilized for war in conditions of insecurity, and will attack ethnic islands of the other community, or protect their own by expelling others. Partition is justified, in these conditions, because it ends the imperatives to cleanse and rescue, and renders war unnecessary to achieve mutual security. In Auden's poem the partitionist lawyer, Radcliffe, is told "It's too late/For mutual reconciliation or rational debate/The only solution now lies in partition" (Auden 1976). The logic and the modelling and the poetic satire are neat, but critics rightly suspect the underlying psychology and sociology.

The "net benefit" argument

A third line of argument need not presume the empirical existence of an ethnic security dilemma, or justify partition only when it is absolutely necessary to prevent genocide or large-scale expulsions. Instead, it suggests that partition should be chosen when, on balance, it offers a better prospect of conflict reduction than maintaining the existing borders. The suggestion is that partition is desirable in its own right as a preventative strategy; it need not be the option of last resort. The net benefit argument was maintained in the last years of

British imperial rule by the leading politicians of minorities who opposed independence within existing colonial borders – by Ulster unionists in Ireland, who were prepared to abandon their fellow unionists elsewhere in Ireland; by Zionists in Israel who then thought some sovereign Israeli land was better than hoping for Eretz Israel; and by the Muslim League in India, which decided that southern Muslims would have to fend for themselves. Here it was argued that partition was justified to prevent a loss of freedom – it was not then maintained that genocide and ethnic expulsions were going to be carried out by Irish, Indian or Palestinian nationalists. Some consider partition an appropriate and prudent pre-emptive policy choice simply where there are ethnically intermixed populations, which are capable of sustained pogroms, massacres, expulsions and genocide. The argument, of course, tends to license too many partitions: after all, of which groups could it be said that they are incapable of genocide? Organized extermination has occurred in every continent, in all periods of human history, within every major religious civilization, and in all political systems (though under some more than others) (Chirot and McCauley 2006).

The "better tomorrow" argument

The historicists, the triagists, and the utilitarian calculators jointly maintain that after partition there will be a reduction in violence and conflict recurrence. New more homogenized polities will have better prospects of stable democratization, of political development, and of better relations in general. The analogy is with divorce. After the trauma is over, the former partners will conduct themselves better because their interests will not interfere so intimately with one another's identity, pride and emotions. This argument predicts a better tomorrow based on key counterfactual assumptions, namely, that without partition there will be more conflict and conflict recurrence; and that more heterogeneous polities have poorer prospects of democratization, political development and inter-group relations. One author even claims that the evidence from Ireland, India, Palestine and Cyprus confirms that partitions reduce violence and conflict recurrence, and that the post-partitioned entities were no less democratic or culturally exclusive than their precursors (Kaufmann 1998)!

The "realist rigor" argument

The tough-minded partitionist maintains that any possible difficulties with partition flow from irresolution – a thoroughgoing revision of borders, which fully separates the relevant antagonistic communities, is what is required. Good fences make good neighbors; bad fences provoke disputes. Policy makers must devise borders – and provide incentives for controlled population movements – that will create sufficient homogeneity that the incentives for national, ethnic, religious and communal violence are radically reduced. Another and better cut will be advocated to rectify the surgery if it was botched the first time.

To work, the rigorous realists maintain that partition must lead to radical demographic restructuring, reducing the military and political significance of the new minorities. Mearsheimer and Pape and subsequently Mearsheimer and Steven Van Evera (1995) argued for the partition of Bosnia, "shrinking it to save it", as they put it. They deemed unworkable the alternative federal formula developed under the plan proposed by former US Secretary of State Cyrus Vance and former UK Foreign Secretary David Owen, and criticized the 1995 Dayton settlement, negotiated and effectively dictated by US diplomats, as "an unfinished peace", precisely because it did not arrange a three-way partition of Bosnia between

Muslims, Serbs and Croats, but just an incomplete two-way split between the recently constructed Muslim-Croat federation and Republika Srpska.

These five standard arguments for partition are political and moral. They are not on their face simple apologias, or excuses for land-grabbing, or indeed for dereliction, though, of course, they may provide cover for such actions. Indeed I have carefully avoided selecting pro-partitionist arguments which are obviously racist, sectarian or civilizationist in order to present partitionism in its best light.

These five arguments are only partially testable. One accepts historicist philosophies, or approaches, or one does not – Popper's critique (1976 [1957]) of historicism is convincing to this author even though his history of ideas is not always accurate. The leap from demographic trends to assumptions of future political behavior by pro-partitionists is not scientific; the same trends may be compatible with a range of political relationships – from genocide to federal or consociational co-existence. The "realistic rigor" thesis is probably not testable at all because, confronted by the evidence of catastrophe, partitionists will claim that the tragedies lie in the imperfection of the attempted project rather than the idea itself. Though there is now an interesting literature which tests partitionist claims (Sambanis 2000; Chapman and Roeder 2007; Sambanis and Schullhofer-Wohl 2009), not all of the above arguments are testable, and, at least on my definition of partition, the number of twentieth-century cases that were not rapidly reversed is pretty small, making large-N testing problematic (the existing literature usually conflates partitions and secessions in order to get a larger N). Many partitionists' claims, however, are at least implicitly empirical. Partitionists implicitly predict either a linear or an exponential relationship between the degree of national and ethnic heterogeneity of a place and the security dilemmas that provoke violence (false). They insist "restoring civil politics in multi-ethnic states shattered by war is impossible because the war itself destroys the possibilities for ethnic cooperation". They insist that the "stable resolution of ethnic civil wars is only possible when opposing groups are demographically separated into defensible enclaves" (Kaufmann 1996b: 137). These arguments suggest that it is foolish to insist on maintaining unviable multinational polities.

The modalities of partitionists

The above partitionist arguments do not tell us who should execute the deed, or how they should go about their work. Partitionists who are not mere annexationists come in two general types – proceduralists and paternalists, though they may come in fusions. Proceduralists favour justice and agreement, while paternalists favor imposition in others' interests – they put order before justice.

Proceduralists advocate consultation with the "affected parties", to achieve as much reciprocal consent on the new border as possible, and try to establish rules to which reasonable partitions should conform. They see roles for commissions, and particularly judges and technical experts, in determining appropriate boundaries. The British Empire was a procedural partitionist. It set up boundary commissions in twentieth-century Ireland, Palestine, and India. The UN attempted to be a proceduralist in Palestine in 1947.

Honest proceduralists reject any partition proposal that does not meet fairness and feasibility requirements. Some proceduralists are less honest, and claim that it is not they or their governments who partition. Mountbatten declared in his radio broadcast of 3 March 1947, which announced the plan to partition India, that "I felt it was essential that the people of India themselves should decide this question of partition" (Ahmed 1999: 119). He ordered the legislative assemblies of Bengal and the Punjab (excluding European members) each to

141

meet in two parts, one representing "the Muslim majority" districts, the other the rest of the relevant province. The districts were to be defined, not by the past votes for the members, but by reference to the 1941 census. A simple majority in either part would be sufficient to trigger partition of the relevant region. (In the Punjab the new West section of the Assembly voted against partition by 99 votes to 27, while the new East voted in favour by 50 votes to 22 (Ahmed 1999: 121). Punjab therefore had 121 assembly members' votes against and 67 for, but under Mountbatten's rule the partition process continued.)

Arend Lijphart has specified the requirements of a fair partition (Lijphart 1984). A partition can be acceptable where it is negotiated by all the affected groups rather than imposed; when it involves a fair division of land and resources; and where it results in homogeneous, or at least substantially less plural, independent states. The major difficulty with this reasonable conception of a principled partition is the sheer unlikelihood of the first requirement: non-imposition. The affected parties – politicians and their publics – are not likely to agree unanimously, and even if representative politicians did concur, it is unlikely that all the adversely affected people will agree, even if offered significant compensation. Partitions involving the movement of people or of their sovereign territory are simply not likely to proceed with technical agreement and political consensus.

Lijphart's other criteria offer feasible benchmarks against which to evaluate the fairness of partitions of bi-national or multi-national polities. The Radcliffe "Award" in Bengal in 1947 almost perfectly met Lijphart's second and third criteria. West Bengal, an area of 28,000 square miles, was to contain a population estimated at 21.19 million people, of whom 29% were Muslims. East Bengal, to become East Pakistan, an area of 49,000 square miles, contained a population of 39.11 million, of which 29.1% were Hindus (Chatterji 1999: 191). West Bengal was to get 36.6% of the land to accommodate some 35.1% of the Bengal population, while East Bengal was to get 63.6% of the land to accommodate 64.8% of the population. The ratio of the majority to the minority populations was almost identical, and the resulting entities more homogenous than their predecessor, partitioning a polity with a Muslim:Hindu ratio of 56:44 into two with 70:30 majority: minority ratios. But we might equally conclude that Radcliffe created two large Northern Irelands out of Bengal, and very few regard the bloody Indian partition as a success story.

Jan and Birgitta Tullberg have also proposed procedural criteria for a fair partition (Tullberg and Tullberg 1997). They conflate partition with secession, but then so too do most of their critics (e.g. Rothchild 1997). The Tullbergs believe that borders should be drawn to leave as few people as possible in the "wrong" state, advocating that an equal number of people from each group should be wrongly placed after a partition. The partitioning border also ought to be as "natural" as possible. They also propose rules for "transfers": in a binary partition each state should be responsible for accepting people of its own nationality; each individual may emigrate to the "right" state; and each state should be entitled to evict members of the other group. The Tullbergs' critics have little difficulty in picking out the difficulties with these proposals (e.g. Lustick 1997; McGarry and Moore 1997; Ryan 1997). Why should an equal number of "wrongly" placed people be regarded as a fair outcome, as opposed to an equal ratio of "wrongly" to "rightly" placed people in each jurisdiction? Surely fairness should include proportionality, not just absolute numbers? The notion of "natural" borders is highly problematic – even if common among politicians and mass publics. Lastly, the proposed transfer rules are appalling – and illegal under international law. They license ethnic expulsions, and incentivize them. The proposals also give insufficient recognition to the importance of the integrity of the territorial homeland in the eyes of at least one community: for whom it is not the rules of partition with which they disagree, but the very idea, which is equivalent to a discussion of the modalities under which they are to be executed.

Paternalists, by contrast, assume that the local parties or communities are incapable of reaching a reasonable agreement, except perhaps after protracted wars that end in stalemate. They propose that a sufficiently powerful outsider should determine a partition, one that will be durable, and reduce conflict as much as possible – and quickly. A settlement that addresses security imperatives is more important than meeting participation requirements or considerations that might flow from abstract social justice. Paternalists usually advise or lobby great or regional powers. "Better rough justice than none" is their outlook. For contemporary Kosova, Mearsheimer argued both that partition is the only viable strategy for anything that resembles peace in the long term – the best, as he put it, of a handful of really lousy alternatives. His premise was that multi-ethnic states do not (or cannot?) survive, especially, he claims, in Europe. Interventions to hold multi-ethnic states such as Bosnia together will not work "unless we [the USA] stay there forever" (Mearsheimer 1999a, 1999b). American realists are not against multinational or multi-ethnic states, in principle, but believe, correctly, that there is a general American tendency to underestimate the power of nationalism; and a dogmatic American faith that other multi-ethnic societies can integrate themselves as America's immigrants have (Mearsheimer and Van Evera 1995: 21).

Anti-partitionist arguments

Let us now consider the most powerful rebuttals of partitionist arguments. Anti-partitionists include nationalists and multi-nationalists. Nationalists reject the rupturing of their national territories; multi-nationalists reject the historicist assumptions of homogenizers and their negative assessments of the prospects for co-existence. They share common appraisals of how partitions are perverse, of how they jeopardize existing relationships, and of the impossibility of achieving fair partitions. Their arguments include (i) the rejection of the rupturing of national unity; (ii) advocacy of the possibilities of constructive bi- and multi-nationalism; (iii) the practical impossibility of just partitions; (iv) the high likelihood of worsening violence; (v) the elusive mirage of homogenization without expulsions; (vi) the damage to the successor states; and (vii) the failure to make a clean or elegant cut, all of which jointly render the surgical and the triage claims highly suspect.

The rupturing of national territorial unity is protested by those who hold that partition is a violation of the right to self-determination, of the right to territorial integrity of the entity that is being partitioned. This complaint is usually accompanied by the claim that partition is being proposed or executed in the interests of privileged minorities, and that it is especially brutal in its impact on what will now become border communities. In all cases the nationalists observe that "border communities" which were previously not "border" communities may suffer most – the Sikhs of the Punjab; the Irish nationalists of south Armagh, Tyrone, Fermanagh, Derry city and Newry; and the peoples among divided cities, for example those of Jerusalem (between 1948 and 1967) and Nicosia.

In the twentieth century partitions were rejected by most of the affected majority nationalists whose national homelands were freshly cut. Irish, Indian, Palestinian and Cypriot nationalists argued that partition was a violation of national self-determination, and directly contravened the expressed preferences of the relevant majorities in their national territories. Bosniaks made the same claim – though ethnic Bosniaks were just a plurality in the former Yugoslav republic. Indian nationalists, for example, argued that their nation had a long past, had been treated as an entity by the British Empire, prepared for self-government as such, and that India as a whole was the appropriate unit for self-determination (Nehru 1989). The Muslim League's claim that there were two nations and not one in the subcontinent was treated as false, proven by Congress's own Muslim voters and politicians, and dismissed as being made very late in the day – in the vested interests of privileged elites, regrettably manipulating communal passions. Until the end, many Congress leaders regarded Jinnah's endorsement of the two-nation thesis as a bargaining posture. Cypriot nationalists likewise insist that the partition of Cyprus, and the proclamation of the Turkish Republic of Northern Cyprus, violated Cyprus's integrity and its right to self-determination and sovereign independence – entrenched in treaties between the UK, Turkish, Greek and Cypriot governments. They complain that the UK's resistance to Greek demands for decolonization and *enosis* (union) with Greece led the imperial power in the 1950s to mobilize the Turkish minority in their support, especially within the police and the army, and that this encouraged Turkish Cypriots to demand *taksim*, the partition of Cyprus between Greece and Turkey (Anderson 2008). Cypriot nationalists see the "counter-nationalism" of the Turkish minority as manipulated or rooted in past privilege, believing that the British had played Greek and Turkish Cypriots against one another (Hitchens 1997; Kyle 1984).

Advocacy of bi-nationalism

Only disputing their premises plausibly rebuts nationalist anti-partition arguments. That involves either insisting that within the pre-partitioned entities there was more than one nation with a right to self-determination, or rejecting national self-determination arguments completely (an intellectual move not evaluated here because partitionists do not reject the idea of nation-states).

The bi-national or multi-national case is that pluri-national arrangements must be properly exhausted before partition is considered genuinely as a last resort. Multi-nationalists maintain that if one were to accept that there were two nations in Ireland, India, Palestine and Cyprus, or three in the case of Bosnia Herzegovina, no automatic case for partition followed. Instead they observe that partitionists must insist on the undesirability, infeasibility or insecurity of bi-national, federal, consociational or confederal arrangements. It is just assumed by partitionists that such options are or were impossible, and often this claim obscures more creative modes of co-existence. In three British imperial cases most of the relevant minority – Ulster Unionists, the Muslim League, and Zionists – appeared unwilling to propose or experiment with such formulae. Their veto of alternative formulae, backed by force, was rendered more effective by the declarations of the imperial power that they would not coerce the relevant minorities. These minorities' leaders sought partition either before, or coterminous with, the withdrawal of the imperial power, and refused or blocked all other options. That partition was "a last resort", or a regrettable choice "when all else had failed", therefore usually rings hollow. In Cyprus, by contrast, before independence a generous constitutional arrangement was negotiated for Turkish Cypriots, but arguably one that was so generous in its over-representation of the minority that it was bound to provoke Greek Cypriot resentment.

The impossibility of just partition. Anti-partitionists argue that, even if partition should be an option of last resort when clashing nationalities have rejected bi-national or multi-national forms of shared rule and self-rule, that does not justify any partitions, but only fair or just partitions. The latter, however, demand the wisdom of Solomon, which by definition is rare. They require not just wisdom, but a great or regional power that is well-governed if they are to be procedurally proper (all of which seems an unlikely combination).

International procedures, including World Court jurisprudence, have peaceably addressed some border disputes between states. Typically, however, these arise from ambiguities in historic treaties or legislative documents (for example, disputes between the Netherlands and Belgium, Burkina Faso and Mali, Honduras and El Salvador, and over the Aouzou desert strip – at issue between Chad and Libya). Or, they involve maritime jurisdictions (for example the recently concluded negotiations over the Timor Gap, disputes between Norway and Great Britain, and between the USA and Canada in the Gulf of Maine). Or, they are occasioned by natural geographical changes in terrain and river beds (e.g. through "avulsion") (Prescott 1996). Legal procedures are not, however, appropriate for what is at stake in political partitions. From 1945 until 2009 only two disputes where homelands were arguably at stake, both involving marginal islands, have been settled by the International Court of Justice, one being the Minquiers and Ecrehos Islands located between the English-speaking Channel Islands and French Normandy. It remains to be seen whether the Permanent Court of Arbitration at The Hague has successfully determined the borders of Abyei (Arbitral Tribunal 2009). It remains an issue between Northern and Southern Sudan, despite the South having seceded in the wake of the 2011 referendum.

According to the *Book of Kings* Solomon did not partition the famously disputed baby, but adopted a procedure, the threat of partition, to establish its true mother. No such procedure is likely to work well amid mass ethno-nationalist politics. The credible threat of partition will likely provoke pre-emptive action, in the form of ethnic expulsions, to establish "facts on the ground". These repercussions are more likely than the disputing parties coming to their senses. Kaufmann and partitionists therefore get the causality wrong: it is partitionists who generate a self-fulfilling security dilemma. The credible threat of partition flows from decisions of a state or imperial authority – or of known plans by paramilitaries that have state support. It is they who occasion the "security dilemma", not the mere presence of hetero-geneous populations. It was partition which occasioned extensive violence in Northern Ireland between 1920 and 1922; and "it was the *escalating possibility* of partition, and the tensions that unleashed, which caused the August 1946 violence in Calcutta and the subsequent 'security dilemma' [of the] Hindus and Muslims of Bengal" (Bose 2002: 179).

Partitionists usually come from among the self-appointed, as with most paternalists, and are unlikely to be impartial. The Peel Commission, which first proposed the partition of Palestine, exceeded its terms of reference, at the prompting of Professor Coupland, who became the chief enthusiast and crafted the text. The outgoing imperial power determined the proce-dures for partition in Ireland and India, and handed over some established groundwork for the UN Partition plan for Palestine. In Ireland partition was executed unilaterally in 1920 before the UK negotiated with Ireland's elected Sinn Féin government. An invading Turkish Army in 1974 determined the fresh cut in Cyprus, stopping at a line that the Turkish government had proposed in 1965 and which had been rejected by the UN mediator Galo Plaza (Kliot and Mansfield 1997: 503).

Anti-partitionists observe that boundary commissions usually give the pivotal power to the relevant big power. Thus the Irish Boundary Commission of 1924–5, and the 1947 Radcliffe Commissions in Punjab and Bengal, had British appointees as the decisive chairs. With some exceptions, the local appointees acted as partisan champions of the ethno-national or religious communities that they were appointed to represent – though they were con-strained to make their arguments persuasive, and to make their proposals as consistent as possible with the commissions' terms of reference. If the local nominees to boundary com-missions are bound to act to some degree as ethno-national champions, then that places the burden of decision upon the organizers and chairs of such commissions: in Auden's words,

Radcliffe was told "We can give you four judges, two Moslem and two Hindu/To consult with, but the final decision must rest with you" (Auden 1976). The key difficulty for such chairs is what we might call Solomon's agenda. That can be defined by the following questions.

i   *Which should be the units around which new boundaries should be drawn?* One cannot have elections to determine who should be among the electorates that have the final say. The Irish Free State thought that a plebiscite should be conducted in all the Poor Law jurisdictions in Northern Ireland – excepting in Belfast and County Antrim, whereas unionists insisted that the six counties of the northeast be treated as a bloc. Relatedly,

ii *Should there be subunit opt-outs?* If unit A opts to be with one state, but B, a concentrated minority within A, wants to go with another, may it opt out?

iii *How should units' preferences be determined?* If there is agreement on the units of determination, then how should the new boundary respect popular preferences? Should this be done through local plebiscites, or through determining people's presumed preferences through their ascriptive identities as recorded in census data (that may be unreliable)? If there are to be plebiscites, what rule should be adopted for determining whether a given unit goes to one jurisdiction or another: a simple majority of those voting, an absolute majority of registered voters, a weighted majority? And, if working from census data, who should count: adults, or adults and children?

iv *Should local popular preferences be considered just one criterion to be balanced among others?* How important should be matters such as the maintenance of *contiguity* (at issue in the formation of Pakistan, and in the redistricting of West Bengal); *preserving a cultural heartland* (at issue in the division of Sikh sacred sites in the Punjab, in the placement of Jerusalem, and at issue in proposals to partition Kosova); *retaining a unit within an economic, geographical hinterland or infrastructure* (at issue in the location of Derry and Newry in Ireland, and in the waterways and canals of the Punjab); or *ensuring militarily secure borders* (at issue in every partition)?

v   *If non-preferential factors are to be considered in designing new borders, should local popular preferences be subordinated to these other considerations, and, if so, which ones – and who should make that determination?*

vi *Should there be constitutional amendments to ratify the commission's proposals or referendums, and should there be provisions to enable their subsequent revision?*

Given the difficulties in Solomon's agenda it is not surprising that Radcliffe, the man who drew the partition of Bengal and the Punjab, refused to be interviewed on his work for the rest of his life (Ahmed 1999; Chatterji 1994, 1999): "Return he would not/Afraid, as he told his Club, that he might get shot" (Auden 1976). Radcliffe's commission worked fast, and it mattered; its resolutions were implemented. The commission chaired by Richard Feetham in 1924 to consider adjustments in the light of article 12 of the Anglo-Irish Treaty did not work in a hurry, and eventually made no difference to the line of partition in Ireland. But Feetham's judgment of his terms of reference shaped the commission's outcome: "the Commission is not to reconstitute the two territories, but to settle the boundary between them. Northern Ireland must, when the boundaries have been determined, still be recognizable as the same provincial entity" (Hand 1969; O'Callaghan 2000). South Down, the location of a *new* reservoir to supply Belfast, not yet finished, incredibly became an argument for maintaining the existing border because Feetham maintained that, whenever there was a clash, that economic and geographic factors had to trump local popular wishes. This case, of a failed commission, vividly demonstrates the procedural conundrums attached to boundary commissions, and the unpredictable consequences of giving judges vague terms of reference. It is difficult to imagine impartiality in the appointment and management of a boundary commission – an empire or regional power has its own interests, and their officials will take great care over appointments to such bodies.

The likelihood of disorder and violence. Anti-partitionists turn the tables on the subject of violence. They maintain that partitions encourage ethnic expulsions; trigger partially chaotic breakdowns in order, leading to flight, opportunist killing, rapes, and looting; lead to more violence than that which preceded them; have domino effects; contribute to post-partition wars, and insecurities; and set precedents that lead to demands for re-partitions. Their case is that partitions are perverse: they achieve the exact opposite of what they nominally intend.

In raw numbers of dead and forcibly displaced, the critics are correct across the cases of India, Palestine, Ireland and Cyprus. The partition of India was accompanied by a death toll, variously credibly estimated at between 200,000 (Moon 1998) and 500,000 (Khosla 1989; Kumar 1997). (Figures of up to two million are also cited.) Involuntary and expelled cross-border refugees and displaced persons may have approached 15 million. The scale and intensity of the brutal coercion, rape, abduction of women, looting, family fragmentation, and resettlement pains were individually and collectively appalling. The partition of Palestine and the war that accompanied Israel's declaration of independence led to the deaths of approximately 6,000 Israeli Jews, and over 10,000 Arabs, and to the expulsion and flight of over 750,000 Palestinians, who became homeless refugees, whom Israel refused to allow to return, and whom the Arab states refused to integrate. As a by-product of the partition, and of Israel's war of independence, over half a million Jews were expelled from surrounding Arab states. In the Turkish invasion and partition of Cyprus 6,000 Greek Cypriots were killed and 2,000 reported missing, and some 1,500 Turks and Turkish Cypriots were killed. After the partition more than 10,000 Greek Cypriots were pressurized into leaving Northern Cyprus, on top of the nearly 160,000 who had already fled before the invading Turkish army. The partition of Ireland was accompanied by the least violence amid twentieth-century partitions, in raw numbers and taking into account the scale of the population. But the deaths accompanying the formation of Northern Ireland between 1920 and 1922 have been estimated at between 232 and 544 (O'Leary and McGarry 1996: 21) and either figure is much higher than the death toll in Ulster before the partition. Moreover, thousands of Catholics were expelled from their jobs and their homes in Belfast and fled south; and thousands of Protestants also emigrated from independent Ireland. It therefore beggars belief that Kaufmann (1998) argues that in all these cases partition successfully reduced violence! He compares post-partition internal violence in the new units with the violence that accompanied the partition – which begs the appropriate evaluative question because it discounts the conflict immediately caused by the partition itself. In Cyprus significant inter-communal killings between 1960 and 1974 preceded the partition (Loizos 1988) but Kaufmann's argument is only made convincing by failing to count the costs of the partition itself.

At bottom, claims such as Kaufmann's are counterfactual not factual: his claim is that without partition the conflicts would have been worse. In three of the cases – Ireland, India, and Palestine – Kaufmann maintains that it was independence from Britain, and the collapse of its military and policing authority, rather than partition, that caused large-scale violence. This is simply unconvincing. Had the imperial authority transferred power to a single central authority then the security dilemma would surely have had less resonance than one accompanying partition and the formation of two new governments. Partitionists inevitably have to defend the historical record of partitions through counterfactual propositions: partition was not the problem *per se*, but rather the particular partition was defective in key respects. Kaufmann, for example, regards the leaving of intermixed populations as potential triggers of future insecurity. The reason the Cypriot partition, according to his criteria, was "better" than any of the others was because of the planned and implemented ethnic expulsion that accompanied it. Kaufmann's argument shows it is easy to slip from a defense of partition as a last resort to tacit support for ethnic expulsions, or "population transfers" in the standard euphemism.

Partitions are especially perverse when they have domino effects – triggering post-partition wars. Security dilemmas now take an inter-state rather than merely inter-communal form. The Arab-Israeli wars of 1956, 1967, and 1973, and the Israeli-Lebanese wars, show that the partition of Palestine was not the end of conflict in the region. India and Pakistan have fought three wars, in 1948, 1965 and 1971, triggered by two regions troubled by the repercussions of the 1947 partition: Kashmir in the first two, and East Bengal in the third. Radcliffe did not partition Jammu and Kashmir. Instead, the UK left it to its princely head, as with all other princely states, to determine its future. Princely self-determination was Great Britain's last contribution to the theory of partition management. Under coercive pressure from Pakistan, its Hindu ruler took his majority Muslim province into the Indian Union. (Bose (2002: 183–9) documents Kaufmann's errors in understanding what happened in Kashmir.) War was triggered, leaving Kashmir divided by a line of control and with a UN presence. India and Pakistan still confront one another over what Pakistanis are inclined to call the "unfinished business" of partition, but now with each state in possession of nuclear arms. A thousand miles divided the Pakistan that resulted from partition – a security nightmare for any armed forces. Its internal divisions proved deeper than geographical non-contiguity: East Pakistan's Bengalis experienced discrimination and domination at the hands of West Pakistan's power elite, and when the latter refused to allow authentic federalism or authentic democratization, and engaged in genocide, the secession of Bangladesh was fought for, and won, in 1971, with the aid of a decisive Indian intervention. Conflict in and over Northern Ireland, though it never took the form of inter-state war, was not resolved before 1998, or 2007, depending upon your point of view (Taylor 2009). The partition of Cyprus is maintained by the presence of the Turkish Army, and by UN peacekeeping forces in buffer zones. It threatens war between Turkey and Greece, two NATO "allies", while the non-recognition of the Turkish Republic of Northern Cyprus affected the complex diplomacy attached to the accession to the European Union of Cyprus (as a whole). Official Cyprus is now within the EU and has the ability to help veto Turkey's accession. These post-partition inter-state tensions (Cyprus and Ireland) and inter-state wars (in the Middle East and South Asia) hardly inspire confidence that partition offers a "realistic" settlement of security dilemmas.

The receding goal of homogenization. Critics of partition maintain that the only thing they "are unlikely to produce is ethnically homogeneous … states" (Horowitz 1985: 589). This argument may seem compelling. Post-partition India and Pakistan were both vast, populous and multi-ethnic, and remained multi-religious; and West Pakistan experienced a fresh infusion of linguistically differentiated refugees. Post-partition Israel was left with a significant Palestinian Arab minority, and soon had waves of new Jewish refugees of diverse ethnic formation. Its subsequent settler colonial infusion policies in the West Bank and Gaza hardly aided the homogenization of the occupied territories. Northern Ireland was left with a unionist and cultural Protestant/nationalist and cultural Catholic ratio of 67:33 that has since shifted to 60:40, and may have moved past 55:45 toward parity. Horowitz's argument, however, needs to be qualified by considering religious not ethnic homogenizing. Pakistan is certainly proportionally more Islamic than India, even though India had, and still has, the largest minority Muslim population in the world. (The secession of Bangladesh led to an irony: Muslims in India separately outnumber those in Bangladesh and Pakistan.) In Ireland, ethnicity and religion were fused in many people's identities, but the Irish Free State was more Catholic than pre-partition Ireland, and Northern Ireland was more Protestant than historic Ulster. Israel was more Jewish, and the West Bank and Gaza, more Muslim and Christian, than pre-partition Palestine. The units of post-partition Cyprus are very ethnically, linguistically and religiously homogenized by comparison with pre-1974 Cyprus.

Critics of partition establish their point more effectively when they say that partition *alone* is unlikely to generate the presumably desired homogenization. The rigorous realists rely on a tacit assumption: the necessity of expulsions. Consider just twentieth-century European ethno-national and ethno-religious history. None of the new European states created after 1919 – after the collapse of the Czarist, Hohenzollern, Habsburg and Ottoman Empires – came close to being mono-national because of the Versailles settlement, or the settlements at other chateaux in the Paris region, or because of other subsequent border adjustments before 1939. Of the seven that survived in some form after the Second World War their proportion of national minorities fell from 25% in the 1930s to 7.2% in the 1970s, a radical homogenization. But only a small proportion of this change was the consequence of border adjustments. The rest has to be accounted for by genocide, expulsion and assimilation (Coakley 1992a, 1992b; Horak 1985: 4). The dark nights of Nazism, the Second World War, and Stalinism – not partitions – "tidied up" Europe's states.

Partitions are never enough for rigorous homogenizers. They must pursue voluntary or quasi-voluntary "transfers", and are driven to condone or organize expulsions, while post-partition states may pursue policies of control that encourage potentially or actively disloyal minorities to emigrate, while encouraging inward immigration of the "right" people to ensure the demographic advantage of the *Staatsvolk*. Partitions without comprehensive expulsions generate two kinds of orphaned minorities: former prospective majorities, and formerly dominant minorities. The former are often double losers – they may have never shared in the self-government of their community as part of a majority, and now they are in another jurisdiction. Former prospective majorities and formerly dominant minorities may both become part of irredentist movements, or campaign for a further partition.

Damage to successor states. Anti-partitionists maintain that partitions generate new security crises of an inter-state form, but also cause significant economic disruption, and not just because they may be accompanied by communal conflict and warfare, and sudden flows of refugees. They disturb established monetary and exchange networks, increase transactions costs, enhance the likelihood of protectionism, and provide incentives for smuggling and other border-related criminal activity. They have led to the depreciation of significant capital investments in transport, as roads, railways and canals, and ports and airports, have their original functions terminated or significantly damaged, and to losses that may flow from failure to cooperate in agriculture, water management, and energy production and distribution. The new post-partition entities have common functional and infrastructural interests flowing from their shared pasts. So they usually end up, ironically, by considering post-partition cross-border functional cooperation, or confederal arrangements – which put in question part of the necessity of partition in the first place. Great Britain accompanied the partition of Ireland with a proposed Council of Ireland, intended to link the Belfast and Dublin parliaments, and it insisted that the Irish Free State share a common crown and membership of the "British Commonwealth of Nations".

Of the cases considered here the Irish Free State has had, in the long run, the most successful post-partition experience in state building, development and democratization. But its early years were deeply affected by the civil war that accompanied its inception – and that might have been avoided had there been no partition. Ireland's comparative homogenization, through its integration and assimilation of its formerly dominant minority, the Anglo-Irish, suggests it was a beneficiary of the partition it opposed. But this perspective neglects the costs of partition for Irish state building, especially in economic development. The new state began life without the industrial base of Belfast, and with a larger Protestant minority, the long cultural sway of the Catholic Church over public policy in Ireland might have been less, and terminated earlier. Northern Ireland, by contrast, has been persistently unstable. Between the 1920s and the 1960s it was operated under a control system. Since the 1960s its conflict made the UK the most internally politically violent established European democracy (O'Leary and McGarry 1996: ch. 3; and 1). Post-partition Pakistan is acknowledged as a developmental disaster. The story of post-partition Palestine is known to the world. The unrecognized Turkish Republic of Northern Cyprus has an unenviable reputation for corruption. There is a pattern here: one entity (Ireland; India; Israel; and Greek Cyprus) has done better than the other. Triage has certainly not been equally good for all. In the separation of Siamese twins the record appears to show that at least one of the twins has been badly lamed.

On the failure to make a clean or elegant cut. Partitionists do not have an easy time in creating new maps. Not only do their maps bleed, but also they do not look good – look at the shape of West Bengal, or the meandering border of Northern Ireland. One can argue that partitions worsen the "compactness" of the post-partition entities by contrast with their precursors. Compactness here refers to the physical solidity of a state – something that once was widely believed to have implications for its military security, and arguably still affects popular assumptions about the right shape of a state, however much academicians reject the thesis of "natural boundaries". It was once argued that an ideal state is a circle, with a capital at its centre, a form that has multiple communications, control and security advantages (Galnoor 1991, 1995: 26ff.). The most compact state, a perfect circle, would have an index score of 1; a square state would score well too, as would a pentagon or a hexagon. It is possible to think of partitions where the compactness scores of at least one entity have "improved". Hungary, as it emerged from the partition of the Austro-Hungarian Empire, became fairly compact, with a score of 1.5, by comparison with its former shape. But, the Peel Commission (1.8) and the UN Partition plans for Palestine (3.3) would both have worsened the compactness of the Jewish state by comparison with mandate Palestine (1.5), and the Israel that emerged from the 1949 armistice lines had a worsened index (2.1). Pakistan, of course, in two discontinuous entities, achieved no compactness. Northern Ireland's new borders created adverse security and transport connections because its compactness was worse than that of Ireland as a whole. The potency of argument of this kind is questionable to those who think that globalization has abolished geography. Compactness may, however, have less salience for military security and communications than it once had. And compactness is far more complex to measure, assess and use in evaluation than was once thought (Niemi et al. 1990).

Conclusion

The partitionist and anti-partitionist arguments just considered are universal; they recur in response to, or in the aftermath of any proposed or actual partition. I have deliberately not biased the evaluation of either partitionists or anti-partitionists by attributing racist, chauvinist or sectarian claims or motivations to their exponents – though these are part of the historical record, and no doubt part of the future. The claim is that these are typically the best arguments that accompany actual partitions as well as the best arguments that accompany the defeats of proposals to have partitions. The arguments themselves must enter any rounded historical explanations of why partitions do or do not occur. When partitions occur the arguments of partitionists have been compelling for at least one powerful agent, but they may not be sufficient to explain why they occur, especially given that the rebuttals of partitionist arguments seem more generally compelling – and are now internationally endorsed in international law.

Anti-partitionists, the foregoing evaluation suggests, have better arguments, judged by realistic, political and moral criteria. When partition threatens, the appropriate slogan should not be John Lennon's "Give Peace a Chance", nor Edward Luttwak's "Give War a Chance" (Luttwak 1999), but rather "Give power-sharing a chance". Contemporary Northern Ireland suggests, and even Lebanon and Iraq may in future suggest, that complex power-sharing settlements are possible even after protracted ethno-national wars (Kerr 2006; O'Leary 2009; Weller, Metzger and Johnson 2008). They are at least as feasible as partitioning intermingled populations and less likely to risk mass deaths.

Partitions deserve their poor press. They have not generated better security environments. Most have been biased toward privileged or dominant minorities – pushing conflict downstream. Partition processes and post-partition arrangements have been worse than those predicted by supporters of partition for at least one successor unit. Partitionists are generally forced to argue that the pathologies of their preferred partition were the result of an imperfect design or of insufficient rigor, a response that is unfalsifiable, and unconvincing. Prudence therefore mandates opposing partition as a tool of international public policy-making, and placing the burden of proof on its advocates.

For those of who us who are not historicists there can be no certainty that there will be no further partitions – partitionist plans have been proposed in the last two decades for Quebec, Bosnia, Kosova, Sri Lanka, Burundi, and Rwanda, Afghanistan, and Iraq (Galbraith's 2006 advocacy of the partition of Iraq may be usefully compared with my own reflections (O'Leary 2009 – see especially 142–7).) Moreover, it cannot be known in advance that there will never be any case where partition truly is a better policy option for the affected peoples than the alternatives. But the standard for making that argument should be that partition is demonstrably the best way to prevent genocide, or large-scale ethnic expulsions, or their recurrence – after reflecting that proposing partition may enhance the risk of genocide and ethnic expulsions. Note carefully, the arguments surveyed here are not intended to hold any sway against the merits of peaceful negotiated secessions within recognized boundaries (see Young 1997a and 1997b for a good discussion of the commonalities of peaceful secessions). There are good and bad secessions, but, by contrast, it is hard to find a good twentieth-century partition. What the argument here suggests is that the novelty of proposing and implementing a fresh sovereign border may destabilize existing inter-group relations in ways that may take generations to repair. By contrast, because secession takes place within a recognized border it may be easier to accomplish a soft landing to the crisis that promotes it.

This chapter has not discussed the reversibility of partitions (see O'Leary 2007: 905–6 for some speculations). It is sufficient to observe here that if the evidence suggests that one should generally oppose partitionist arguments, it does not mean that one should necessarily support all efforts to reverse partitions; and even the practical feasibility of overturning a partition does not mean that it is necessarily the best political option. The reunification of Ireland and of Cyprus under confederal and consociational formulae *may* be in the material and collective long-run interests of all the majorities of the affected peoples. By contrast, reunification in historic Palestine or South Asia is less obviously in the interests of the affected peoples. Nor has this chapter extensively discussed explanations of partitions (see O'Leary 2007), which are rooted in the competition between the nation-state form and its rivals and the forces which underpin nationalism in modernity (Gellner 1983). Nor has this chapter attempted to synthesize the results of the large N literature with the detailed comparative case histories that have helped clarify the materials provisionally summarized here, partly because the author believes that much of these discussions are at cross-purposes given the lack of scholarly clarity in coding what is to count as a partition – as opposed to a secession.

References

This chapter is a revised portion of a keynote address to the conference Mapping Frontiers, Plotting Pathways, Armagh, 19–20 January 2006, which revised a section of a long paper presented at the Keough Conference on Partition and Memory: Ireland, India and Palestine, University of Notre Dame, 6–9 December 2001. I am grateful to J. McGarry (as always), to participants at both conferences, and to K. Adeney, S. Bose, S. Deane, A. Goldstein, G.W. Jones, J.A. Hall, R. Kumar, N. Kasfir, A. Lijphart, I. Lustick, T. Mabry, M. Moore, J. Nagel, R. Smith and S. Wolff.

Ahmed, I. 1999. "The 1947 Partition of Punjab: Arguments Put Forth Before the Punjab Boundary Commission by the Parties Involved." In *Region and Partition: Bengal, Punjab and the Partition of the Subcontinent*, ed. I. Talbot and G. Singh. Karachi: Oxford University Press.

Anderson, P. 2008. "The Divisions of Cyprus." *London Review of Books*, April 24.

Arbitral Tribunal. 2009. "Final Award: In the Matter of an Arbitration Before a Tribunal Constituted in Accordance with Article 5 of the Arbitration Agreement Between the Government of the Sudan and the Sudan People's Liberation Movement/Army on Delimiting Abyei Area and The Permanent Court of Arbitration Optional Rules for Arbitrating Disputes Between Two Parties Of Which Only One Is a State, July 22." ed. *Permanent Court of Arbitration*. The Peace Palace, The Hague.

Aristotle. Aristotle's *Rhetoric*, A Hypertextual Resource compiled by Lee Hunnicutt; available at http://rhetoric.eserver.org/aristotle/.

Auden, W. H. 1976. *Collected Poems, edited by Edward Mendelson*. New York: Random House.

Bose, S. 2002. *Bosnia after Dayton: Nationalist Partition and International Intervention*. New York: Oxford University Press.

Carment, D. B. and Rowlands, D. 2004. "Vengeance and Intervention: Can Third Parties Bring Peace Without Separation?" *Security Studies* 13(4): 366–393.

Chapman, T. and Roeder, P. G. 2007. "Partition as a Solution to Wars of Nationalism: The Importance of Institutions." *American Political Science Review* 101(4): 677–691.

Chatterji, J. 1994. *Bengal Divided: Hindu Communalism and Partition, 1932–1947*. Cambridge, England; New York, NY: Cambridge University Press.

Chatterji, J. 1999. "The Making of a Borderline: The Radcliffe Award for Bengal." In *Region & Partition: Bengal, Punjab and the Partition of the Subcontinent*, ed. I. Talbot and G. Singh. Karachi: Oxford University Press.

Chirot, D. and McCauley, C. 2006. *Why Not Kill Them All?* Princeton, NJ: Princeton University Press.

Coakley, J. 1992a. "The Resolution of Ethnic Conflict: Towards a Typology." *International Political Science Review* 13(4): 343–358.

Coakley, J. ed. 1992b. *The Social Origins of Nationalist Movements: The Contemporary West European Experience*. London: Sage.

Fraser, T. G. 1984. *Partition in Ireland, India, and Palestine: Theory and Practice*. New York: St. Martin's Press.

Galbraith, P. W. 2006. *The End of Iraq: How American Incompetence Created a War Without End*. New York: Simon and Schuster.

Galnoor, I. 1991. "Territorial Partition of Palestine: The 1937 Decision." *Political Geography Quarterly* 10(4): 382–404.

Galnoor, I. 1995. *The Partition of Palestine: Decision Crossroads in the Zionist Movement*. Albany, NY: State University of New York Press.

Gellner, E. 1983. *Nations and Nationalism*. Oxford: Basil Blackwell.

Hand, G. J. ed. 1969. *Report of the Irish Boundary Commission 1925*. Shannon.

Hasan, M. ed. 1993. *India's Partition: Process, Strategy and Mobilization*. Delhi: Oxford University Press.

Hasan, M. ed. 2002. *The Partition Omnibus: Prelude to Partition: The Indian Muslims and the Imperial System of Control 1920–1932, The Origins of the Partition of India 1936–1947, Divide and Quit, Stern Reckoning*. New Delhi: Oxford University Press.

Hitchens, C. 1997. *Hostage to History: Cyprus from the Ottomans to Kissinger.* London: Verso.

Horak, S. M. 1985. "East European National Minorities, 1919–1980." In *Eastern European National Minorities, 1919–1980: A Handbook.* Littleton, CO: Libraries Unlimited.

Horowitz, D. 1985. *Ethnic Groups in Conflict.* Berkeley: University of California Press.

Jervis, R. 1968. "Co-operation under the Security Dilemma." *World Politics* (January): 167–213.

Johnson, C. 2008. "Partitioning to Peace: Sovereignty, Demography, and Ethnic Civil Wars." *International Security* 32(4): 140–170.

Kaufmann, C. 1996a. "Intervention in Ethnic and Ideological Civil Wars: Why One Can be Done and the Other Can't." *Security Studies* 6(1, Autumn): 62–100.

Kaufmann, C. 1996b. "Possible and Impossible Solutions to Ethnic Civil Wars." *International Security* 20(4): 136–175.

Kaufmann, C. 1998. "When All Else Fails: Ethnic Population Transfers and Partitions in the Twentieth Century." *International Security* 23(2, Fall): 120–156.

Kerr, M. 2006. *Imposing Power-Sharing: Conflict and Coexistence in Northern Ireland and Lebanon.* Dublin: Irish Academic Press.

Khosla, G. D. 1989. *Stern Reckoning: A Survey of the Events Leading up to and following the Partition of India.* Delhi: Oxford University Press.

Kliot, N. and Mansfield, Y. 1997. "The Political Landscape of Partition: The Case of Cyprus." *Political Geography* 16(6): 495–521.

Kumar, R. 1997. "The Troubled History of Partition." *Foreign Affairs* (Jan–Feb).

Kyle, K. 1984. *Cyprus.* London: The Minority Rights Group.

Lijphart, A. 1984. "Time Politics of Accommodation: Reflections – Fifteen Years Later." *Acta Politica* 19(1): 9–18.

Loizos, P. 1988. "Intercommunal Killing in Cyprus." *Man (NS)* 23(4): 639–653.

Lustick, I. S. 1997. "The Illusion of a Radical Solution to Cultural Conflict When 'We' and 'Them' Are Part of 'Us'." *Politics and the Life Sciences* (September): 262–264.

Luttwak, E. N. 1999. "Give War a Chance." *Foreign Affairs* 78(4): 36–44.

Mansergh, N. 1997. "The Prelude to Partition: Concepts and Aims in India and Ireland." In *Nationalism and Independence: Selected Irish Papers*, ed. D. Mansergh. Cork: Cork University Press.

McGarry, J. and Moore, M. 1997. "The Problems with Partition." *Politics and the Life Sciences* (September): 18–19.

Mearsheimer, J. J. 1999a. "Remarks in 'Policy Forum: The Balkan War: What do We Do Now?'" *Cato Policy Report* XX1 (4, July–August): 5–8.

Mearsheimer, J. J. 1999b. "The Case for Partitioning Kosovo." In *NATO's Empty Victory: A Postmortem on the Balkan War*, ed. T. G. Carpenter. Washington DC: Cato Institute.

Mearsheimer, J. J. and Pape, R. A. 1993. "The Answer: A Three-Way Partition Plan for Bosnia and How the US Can Enforce It." *The New Republic* (June 14): 22–28.

Mearsheimer, J. J. and Van Evera, S. 1995. "When Peace Means War." *The New Republic* (December 18): 16–21.

Moon, P. 1998. *Divide and Quit: An Eye-witness Account of the Partition of India.* New edn. Delhi: Oxford University Press.

Nehru, J. 1989. *The Discovery of India.* New Delhi: Signet Press.

Niemi, R. G., Grofman, B., Carlucci, C. and Hofeller, T. 1990. "Measuring Compactness and the Role of a Compactness Standard in a Test for Partisan and Racial Gerrymandering." *Journal of Politics* 52(4, November): 1155–1181.

O'Callaghan, M. 2000. "'Old Parchment and Water': The Boundary Commission of 1925 and the Copperfastening of the Irish Border." *Bullan: An Irish Studies Journal* 4(2): 27–55.

O'Leary, B. 2001. "Introduction: The Elements of Right-Sizing the State." In *Right-Sizing the State: The Politics of Moving Borders*, ed. B. O'Leary, I. Lustick and T. Callaghy. Oxford: Oxford University Press.

O'Leary, B. 2007. "Analyzing Partition: Definition, Classification and Explanation." *Political Geography* 26(8): 886–908.

O'Leary, B. 2009. *How To Get Out of Iraq with Integrity.* Philadelphia, PA: University of Pennsylvania Press.

O'Leary, B. and McGarry, J. 1996. *The Politics of Antagonism: Understanding Northern Ireland.* 2nd expanded edn. London; Atlantic Heights, NJ: Athlone.

Popper, K. R. 1976 [1957]. *The Poverty of Historicism.* London: Routledge and Kegan Paul.

Posen, B. 1993. "The Security Dilemma and Ethnic Conflict." *Survival* 35(1): 27–47.

Prescott, V. 1996. "Contributions of the United Nations to Solving Boundary and Territorial Disputes, 1945–1995." *Political Geography* 15(3/4): 287–318.

Rothchild, D. 1997. "Secession Is a Last Resort." *Politics and the Life Sciences* 16(2): 270–272.

Ryan, S. 1997. "Between Separation and Unity." *Politics and the Life Sciences* 16(2): 268–270.

Sambanis, N. 2000. "Partition as a Solution to Ethnic War: An Empirical Critique of the Theoretical Literature." *World Politics* 52(July): 437–483.

Sambanis, N. and Schullhofer-Wohl, J. 2009. "Is Partition a Solution to Civil War?" *International Security* 34(2): 82–118.

Talbot, I. and Singh, G. 2009. *The Partition of India*. Cambridge: Cambridge University Press.

Taylor, R. ed. 2009. *Consociational Theory: McGarry and O'Leary and the Northern Ireland Conflict*. London: Routledge.

Tullberg, J. and Tullberg, B. S. 1997. "Separation or Unity? A Model For Solving Ethnic Conflicts." *Politics and the Life Sciences* 16(2): 237–248.

Weller, M., Metzger, M. and Johnson, N. eds. 2008. *Settling Self-Determination Disputes: Complex Power-Sharing in Theory and Practice*. Leiden; Boston: Martinus Nijhoff.

Young, R. A. 1997a. "How Do Peaceful Secessions Happen?" *Canadian Journal of Political Science* 27(4): 773–794.

Young, R. A. 1997b. "How Do Peaceful Secessions Happen?" In *Wars in the Midst of Peace: The International Politics of Ethnic Conflict*, ed. D. B. Carment and P. James. Pittsburgh: University of Pittsburgh Press.

13

IRREDENTAS AND SECESSIONS

Adjacent phenomena, neglected connections[1]

Donald L. Horowitz

To think about something makes it necessary to identify and isolate it, to fix upon it and, in fixing upon it, to reify it. Even before conscious conceptualization occurs, even in the selection of phenomena for study, concepts creep in. The more careful the thinking, the more precise the identification of the phenomena for study, the greater the isolation of one phenomenon from its neighbours, even its near neighbours. When the careful thinker says, 'I mean to include *this* and to exclude *that*' the precision that makes any careful thinking possible may come at a price. Less careful but perhaps more nimble thinkers – namely, those actors whose behaviour forms the subject of social-science thinking – have a way of putting back together what careful thinkers pull apart.

Secessions and irredentas are near neighbours that can be pulled apart for analysis, properly in my view, but with points of contact and even, at times, a degree of interchangeability that might permit groups to choose one or the other and that also makes it necessary to treat the two phenomena together, in order to have a full view of each, By and large, the two have not been treated together. They have either been treated in isolation or mentioned in the same breath without an appreciation of their connections. When, however, secessions and irredentas are considered together, some rather startling conclusions emerge. Since the two phenomena are sometimes alternatives to each other, the frequency of each is, in part, a function of the frequency of the other. Furthermore, the strength of a given movement may be, in part, a function of the possibility that the alternative movement may arise. Indeed, the fate of a movement, at least in the sense that it manages to extract concessions from a central government, may depend on which course it takes.

Two distinct phenomena

Secession and irredentism are definable in distinct terms, even if we restrict ourselves solely to ethnically motivated movements. Secession is an attempt by an ethnic group claiming a homeland to withdraw with its territory from the authority of a larger state of which it is a part. Irredentism is a movement by members of an ethnic group in one state to retrieve ethnically kindred people and their territory across borders.

It will quickly be noted that disparate subphenomena are subsumed in the definition of secession propounded here. The definition might be sufficiently elastic to embrace the activity of a group that merely seeks regional autonomy or creation of a federal system and control of its own state as a component of such a system. This was the aim of the Federal party in Sri Lanka until at least 1972 and of the Liberal party in the Sudan until 1958. The same definition of secession might also comprehend the activity of an ethnic group occupying a discrete territory within a state in an existing federal system but aiming to carve a new state out of its portion of the existing state. The Telangana movement in Andhra Pradesh is one of several such movements in India.[2] Nigeria has had many comparable movements, beginning with the United Middle Belt Congress in the 1950s. Finally, and most relevantly for connections to irredentism, this definition of secession certainly includes attempts to form separate, independent, internationally recognised states out of existing sovereign entities, as in the unsuccessful war for Biafra and the successful war for Bangladesh. In this definition, secession thus entails several forms of greater or lesser withdrawal from existing units.

Similarly, irredentism, as defined here, contains two subtypes: the attempt to detach land and people from one state in order to incorporate them in another, as in the case of Somalia's recurrent irredenta against Ethiopia, and the attempt to detach land and people divided among more than one state in order to incorporate them in a single new state – a 'Kurdistan', for example, composed of Kurds now living in Iraq, Iran, Syria, and Turkey. Both forms of reconstituted boundaries would qualify as irredentist.

Despite their elasticity, the definitions of the two phenomena are conceptually distinct. Irredentism involves subtracting from one state and adding to another state, new or already existing; secession involves subtracting alone.

Moreover, the distinction between secessions and irredentas seems to capture some important differences in political phenomena on the ground; it is not merely a figment of the imagination of analysts. A glance at the relative frequency of the two phenomena hints at this. There are possibilities aplenty for secession and irredentism in the postcolonial world of Asia, Africa, and the Middle East. Most states are ethnically heterogeneous; of these, most have territorially compact minorities. Likewise, many ethnic groups are divided by territorial boundaries. Consequently, secession and irredentism are both abundantly plausible possibilities in the contemporary world. The necessary conditions, if not the sufficient conditions, for both are present, but the two phenomena are by no means proportionately represented in relation to the possibility of their occurrence. In spite of predictions to the contrary,[3] there have been remarkably few irredentas in the postcolonial states, but there have been a great many secessionist movements.

Withdrawal alone attracts many more adherents to action than does withdrawal coupled with the aim of reincorporation in another state. This seeming puzzle becomes even more perplexing when additional facts are added to the comparison. Consider just two. First, although secession is common, the victory of secessionist movements is extremely uncommon. Victory requires external assistance, which is rarely forthcoming in a volume and duration sufficient to win the war and create the new secessionist state. The Bangladesh example was until the 1990s conspicuous by its exceptional character. The improbability of success, however, has not deterred a significant number of secessionist groups. Second – again contrary to forecasts that wealthy regions would be more likely secessionists[4] – secessionist regions are disproportionately ill favoured in resources and per capita income.[5] Not infrequently, groups attempt to withdraw from states from which their region actually receives a subsidy.

Counterintuitively, then, in numbers that are both absolute and relative to the possibilities, secession is much more frequent than irredentism, and this despite the enormous obstacles to success and the disadvantages most secessionist regions would face were they to succeed. By contrast, irredentism is rare, even though the first subtype of the definition of irredentism would usually involve the armed forces of one state in retrieving kinsmen across borders from another. Although irredentism would often carry with it military resources often denied secessionists, that advantage does not appear to increase the frequency of irredentas. Some behavioural features must therefore be associated with one phenomenon that are not associated with the other. Otherwise, the disparate incidence of the two phenomena cannot be explained.

This suffices to demonstrate the utility of distinguishing between secessions and irredentas. In fact, there is a whole spectrum of phenomena worth distinguishing. At one end, there are international border disputes that have no ethnic component and are therefore not irredentist. Latin American history is filled with such disputes.[6] At the other end of the spectrum, there are territorially compact groups that nevertheless do not wholly dominate their region, which is ethnically heterogeneous. Although they may not aspire to secession, they may well aspire to homogeneity and take violent steps toward that end. A good many ethnic riots produce a stream of refugees of the victim group, which in turn fosters increased territorial segregation. Violence that increases homogenization is, to be sure, a frequent prelude to secession or irredentism – it may be that for the Albanians in the Kosovo province of Yugoslavia,[7] but it need not be and probably is not for groups like the Assamese in India.

Having delimited the two phenomena and argued that, on the face of it, the delimitation seems useful, I now propose to put back together what I have pulled apart. I adhere to the utility of the secession–irredentism distinction, and I continue to think the differential incidence of the two is partly explicable in terms that are peculiar to the dynamics of each.[8] Nevertheless, I intend to show that there are some fairly close connections between the two as well. For example, one reason there are few irredentas may be that many groups that have a choice between irredentism and secession find the latter the more satisfying choice. Indeed, the potential for irredentism may increase the frequency and strength of secession, but not vice versa. In short, while it makes a difference which course of action a group is embarked upon, my aim here is to elucidate the neglected interrelations between secessions and irredentas where both are possible.

Two related phenomena

The connections between secessionist and irredentist movements can be divided into three sets of issues. The first relates to the convertibility of the two types of movement. The second involves the relative frequency of secessions and irredentas. The third concerns the relative strength of the movements. These three issues are, as we shall see, closely related to each other.

The convertibility of claims

To speak seriously of interchangeability – of the possibility that a movement may become either secessionist or irredentist or that it may move from one category to the other – is to limit ourselves to those territorially compact ethnic groups that span borders. Not all secessionists are in this category. Bengalis are found on the Indian side of the border as well as on what is now the Bangladesh side and what was before 1971 the East Pakistan side, but Ibo (except for some migrants to other countries) are entirely contained within Nigeria's boundaries. The Bengalis might have become either irredentist or secessionist, but the Ibo had no irredentist option. Although a great many groups do span borders, a good many others are in the Ibo category.

Violence is frequently convertible from one form to another. Countries that experience political violence of one sort are likely to experience violence of another sort.[9] Relatively spontaneous violence often gives way at later stages to more organised violence. Riots, for example, are a common forerunner of secessionist movements; for transborder ethnic groups, it stands to reason that if conditions are not propitious for irredentism, those groups may turn to secession, and vice versa.

Underpinning the convertibility of movements is the mutability of ethnic-group claims, of international relations, and of transborder ethnic affinities. Groups (and states) are not born irredentist or secessionist; they can and do move back and forth from integrated participation in the state of which they are a part to a posture of secession or irredentism.

To begin with, whether a group is integrationist or secessionist depends, in large measure, on its assessment of its prospects in the undivided state. The Ibo were the most prominent proponents of one Nigeria. With a considerable investment in human capital, they had migrated all over Nigeria in their quest for employment. Perhaps one Ibo in four or five lived outside the Eastern Region before 1966. But when recurrent violence, culminating in the massacres of September–October 1966, drove the Ibo back to the east, then and then only did the Ibo become secessionist. Meanwhile, the Hausa travelled in the opposite direction, from their openly secessionist inclinations of mid-1966 to their strong role in suppressing the Biafra secession and preserving an undivided Nigeria.

The Ibo and Hausa were not alone in altering their collective objectives. The Sri Lankan Tamils are as reluctant a group of secessionists as may be found, but secessionist some did become, especially after the bloody anti-Tamil riots of 1983.[10] The southern Sudanese, on the other hand, were divided and, even when not divided, were ambiguous about what they wanted during the civil war of 1963–1972. For some groups, the dominant theme was a settlement within the Sudan; for others, it was southern independence. At times, one or another of these themes was ascendant; at other times, both were heard simultaneously, even from the same speaker. In 1972, an abrupt settlement of the war, on terms of regional autonomy, was reached. Following the resumption of hostilities in the southern Sudan in the 1980s, guerrillas fighting in the south declared as their goal the democratization of the entire country, rather than merely the liberation of the southern Sudan.[11] Like the Nigerians, the southern Sudanese have, at various times, moved in various directions.

That flexibility extends to irredentism; it is no secret that many Kurds advocate the creation of a Kurdistan out of portions of several independent states. During most of the post-World War II period, however, regional autonomy and secession, rather than irredentism, have been the stated Kurdish objectives.[12] There is an obvious reason for this. Kurds in Iraq have required assistance from Iran to make any claim effective. From time to time, Iran has provided substantial aid. Without any doubt, no such aid could be expected for a movement that pursued the irredentist objective of unification of all the Kurds, including those in Iran.

To put the point sharply, the propensity for an irredentist ideology to emerge among an ethnic group to be retrieved is directly related to the likelihood that the putative irredentist state will espouse a similar irredentist ideology. That propensity is inversely related to the likelihood that the emergence of an irredentist claim will produce denial of the international assistance that would be accorded to secessionists or, even worse, will produce suppression of the irredentists.

To make matters more complex, it is not merely ethnic groups that are fickle in their objectives. State policies supporting or opposing secessions and irredentas also change. In 1975, Iran abruptly terminated military assistance to Kurds in Iraq and eventually closed its border to them, thereby dooming their movement. In 1987, India ceased its assistance to Sri

Lankan Tamil secessionists, reached an agreement with the Sri Lankan government providing for Tamil regional autonomy instead, and attempted to suppress by force armed, Tamil guerrillas in Sri Lanka itself. Periodically, Somalia, perhaps the most persistently irredentist state in the postcolonial world, has embarked upon a policy of détente with Ethiopia, which at other times is the target of its irredenta.[13] State policy in pursuit of irredentism tends to be inconstant.

That inconstancy drives some potential irredentists to secession instead. For a time in the 1970s, it seemed as if the connections between the Malaysian state of Sabah and the Moro National Liberation Front (MNLF) in the Philippines might support an attempt to link the two politically. The ethnic identity of the chief minister of Sabah was Suluk, as was that of a good many Philippine Muslims engaged in the combat, and the chief minister had relatives across what had always been a permeable water boundary. But there are Malaysians of Suluk origin only in Sabah, and they are a distinct minority even there. No leaders in Kuala Lumpur were Suluk. Eventually, the chief minister was voted out of office, and the remote possibility of irredentism was stillborn. The MNLF never turned its struggle in an irredentist direction.

The southern Philippine example brings us to one final aspect of convertibility: the convertibility of ethnic affinities. To define irredentism as an attempt to retrieve kindred people across boundaries is to assume that kindred people know each other, that kinship and ethnicity are firm. It is by now well established, however, that ethnic identity is variable over time and over context. Consider, for example, the case of Malays in southern Thailand. There is no doubt whatever that migration and interchange between them and Malays in the northern Malaysian states of Kedah and Kelantan have been considerable, and there are still family ties across the border.[14] To most Malays, however, the 'Pattani Malays' of southern Thailand seem rather foreign, and their distance is accentuated by the Indonesian origin of many Malays in southern Malaysian states. One of the major problems with irredentism is that the ethnic affinity of the core of a putative irredentist state may not extend to people at and beyond the periphery, and those are the very people who are to be retrieved.

The relative frequency of movements

Like some of the other forces conducive to the convertibility of movements, the variability of group affinities across borders extends also to the relative frequency of secessionist and irredentist claims. Because of the common reluctance of people at the centre to see nominally kindred people on the periphery as truly members of the same ethnic group, and for many other reasons as well, irredentist action on the part of the potential retrieving state is distinctly uncommon. I shall not rehearse all of these reasons here, because they have been laid out carefully elsewhere.[15] I shall merely touch on a few that bear on the comparative frequency of secessions and irredentas.

For several reasons, the foreign-policy goals of most putative irredentist states (apart from the actual goal of retrieval) can be achieved better by encouraging secessionist movements by groups located in antagonistic states than by encouraging irredentism. For one thing, there is the easy reversibility of the policy. As the Iranians demonstrated in 1975, aid to secessionists can be terminated abruptly in return for a quid pro quo. Carefully rationed Malaysian assistance to the Moro secessionists in the Philippines helped persuade the Philippine government to abandon its claim on the Malaysian state of Sabah. Ethiopia has helped southern Sudanese secessionists in order to discourage Sudanese help for secessionists in Ethiopia. Typically, when the objectives are achieved, the aid is terminated – which is one reason why there are many wars fought by secessionists, but few that they win. Even the government of India was able to reverse its policy of support for the Tamil secessionists in Sri Lanka in return for a regional autonomy agreement. The Sri Lankan Tamils are a kindred people, which many secessionists who receive aid are not,[16] but there was no irredentist claim advanced on their behalf. Aid to irredentists, however, is underpinned by an ideology of common fate that hardly lends itself to abrupt termination. Indeed, when the Somali regime did disengage from war in the Ogaden, the decision helped precipitate the Somali coup of 1969, because kindred groups in the armed forces did not wish to abandon Somalis of the Darood subgroup on the Ethiopian side of the border.

If adjacent states find irredentism unattractive, the feeling is reciprocated by many discontented, territorially compact, transborder ethnic groups. Groups like these, with the potential to be retrieved, find retrieval by the putative irredentist state undesirable. This may be because that state is poorer or less prestigious or more authoritarian than the state in which they are now encapsulated. Baluch would rather be in Pakistan or be independent than be in Afghanistan, even if Afghanistan were at peace. Toubou in northern Chad might equally prefer several alternative fates to merger in Libya. Ethnic affinity across borders is not enough by itself to make merger attractive.

One reason fostering the reluctance to be incorporated is so obvious that it has escaped notice altogether: the interests of political leaders of a potentially secessionist region. They are generally willing to accept independence, even though independence often means an economic position for their state that is inferior to the one it enjoyed as part of an undivided state, partly because with independence they will no longer have to compete for leadership positions with all the other political leaders in the undivided state. By partitioning their area within sovereign boundaries, they also keep out competition for leadership. The ready willingness of so many backward regions to attempt secession soon after independence owes something to the interests of leaders who felt unable to compete in the wider arena.

The same logic applies to the response to the prospect of annexation in an adjacent, albeit ethnically kindred, state. Irredentism will re-merge not just populations but leadership pools. True enough, the ethnic affinities of the annexing and the annexed peoples may be more felicitous, but for leaders this may be more, rather than less, dangerous. If there is a sharp disparity of ethnic identification between the population of a given region and the population of the rest of the state in which it is currently merged, leaders of the group dominant in the region at least face no external challenge to their leadership of that group from leaders of the population in the remainder of the undivided state; by the same token, they are unable to aspire to leadership positions in the undivided state. This is the presecession situation. In the postsecession situation, those leaders still face no external challenge to their leadership, but now their group leadership becomes state leadership, for the region has achieved sovereignty. If, instead of secession, the choice is merger into an existing, adjacent state via irredentism, regional leaders have not achieved sovereignty and also are no longer immune from external challenge. Quite the opposite. Ethnic affinities across the irredentist border open the way to challenges to their leadership from ethnically kindred leaders of the annexing state.

There are also, of course, wider opportunities for leaders of the annexed region in the larger irredentist state as a whole, but these are more circumscribed than they might at first appear. First, leaders from the newly annexed region must break into what is likely to be a crystallized political situation and do so from a merely regional base, with at best imperfect knowledge of the new state and its political patterns. Second, because ethnic affinities are rarely undifferentiated, the newly annexed area stands every chance of being regarded as at least subethnically different in composition (in dialect, accent, family ties, or customs) – in short, as truly peripheral[17] – and its people, cousins though they are, are likely to be viewed as rustics who lived too long under an alien regime. So the position of the annexed region as peripheral newcomer is an enormous impediment to the national-level ambitions of its leaders, should irredentism succeed.

Given this structure of opportunities and constraints, is it not obvious that secession will be the preferred alternative of most ethnic leaders in separatist regions? Of course, leadership interests are not always overriding. Leaders may be, and sometimes are, overruled by an avalanche of mass ethnic sentiment.[18] Moreover, the particular structure of opportunities and constraints will vary from one situation to another, and some regional leaders may prefer irredentism to secession, just as many prefer continuation of the region in the undivided state of which it is currently a part.[19] But where withdrawal from that state is the preferred option, most leaders, most of the time, will think in terms of becoming leaders of the sovereign state, rather than risking reincorporation into another, larger state, the behaviour of which toward a newly annexed region is, in any case, impossible to foretell. Overall, leadership interests are a major explanation for the frequency of secession and the infrequency of irredentas.

Reluctance to be annexed by an adjacent state may also derive from the heterogeneity of the irredentist state. Even assuming transborder ethnic affinities are intact, the retrieving state may contain a plurality of ethnic groups, so that a decision in favour of irredentism will not necessarily be a decision resulting in ethnic self-determination, much less domination in the new state. The Ewe and the Bakongo (of the Democratic Republic of Congo [Kinshasa] and the Republic of Congo [Brazzaville]) are in this position. Even if adjoining states containing other Ewe and Bakongo wished to retrieve them – which they do not – the presence of still other powerful ethnic groups in the retrieving state would deter acceptance of the offer.

Moreover, such potentially irredentist groups – the Kurds are also among them – cannot practically go the alternative route and opt for multiple secessions, carving out of several existing states a new, homogeneous Ewe, Bakongo, or Kurdish state. One secession is difficult enough; it has long odds. But multiple secessions threaten the very governments whose aid across borders is the indispensable component of success. I have already noted the unwillingness of the Kurds in Iraq to take a position regarding Kurds in Iran that would have precluded Iranian assistance. The same applies to all such transborder groups; for this reason, potential irredentists are much more likely to engage in their own separate secessions.

As a matter of fact, virtually everything I have said thus far points in the same direction. If claims are convertible from secession to irredenta and vice versa, if transborder affinities are imperfectly developed, if state policy is at best inconstant, and if there is frequently a reluctance to retrieve or to be retrieved, the sum of all of this is a powerful structural bias against the incidence of irredentism. What that means is that discontented groups will tend to look favourably on secession, rather than on irredentism, where both are possible. The Malays of southern Thailand, who might have become irredentist but find no such invitation from across the Malaysian border, are likely to find secession an attractive alternative. As noted earlier, the many compact groups that do not span borders do not, by definition, have an irredentist option. In practice, neither do most of the many transborder groups have an irredentist option.

In short, all else being equal, the fewer the irredentas, the larger the number of secessionist movements. And since irredentas are rare, secession is by far the more frequent movement of territorially compact ethnic groups. The opposite conclusion also seems likely: ceteris paribus, if for some reason the various inhibitions on irredentism were to decline and irredentism were to become more common, there would also be fewer secessionists.

That is not to say that there is only a finite amount of ethnic discontent available or a finite number of movements possible among territorially compact ethnic groups. It is only to make the important point that the two types of movement are closely related and frequently are plausible alternatives to each other. The behaviour of many groups in one direction or another is structured by the availability or absence of the other option. Since there is no reason to think the inhibitions on irredentism will in fact decline – particularly because irredentism, unlike secession, depends on the presence of two willing parties whose interests and affinities are rarely identical – secession is likely to remain by far the more common movement.

The strength of movements

The strength of secessionist and irredentist movements – and their prospects for success – may be affected in various ways by whether they choose one or the other alternative and by whether the other possibility lurks in the background. If a transborder group attempts secession, the states hosting its population may combine to suppress the movement, as Iran and Pakistan have both suppressed the Baluch movement. If the groups adjacent to the border choose separate secessions at different times, the neighbouring governments may, on the contrary, provide assistance to the secessionists in the country across the border, on the Ethiopia–Sudan model. If, on the other hand, a movement becomes irredentist and one of the transborder segments seeks incorporation in the neighbouring state, it is quite possible that the two states will be at war over this issue.[20] So the range of possibilities simultaneously affects prospects for the discontented ethnic groups and for relations between the states of which they are a part. The form of the movement thus has consequences, and the likely consequences presumably have a reciprocal influence on the form the movement takes and the objectives it proclaims.

Whether secessionists receive any significant support from the state across the border will depend, in considerable measure, on the international interests of that state and its objectives with respect to its neighbour. Where interests are perceived to be in conflict, at least some help can generally be expected, as Pakistan's receptivity to the Sikh independence movement shows. But where irredentism is in the background – even in the very remote background, as in India's relations to the Sri Lankan Tamils (despite Sinhalese suspicions of worse) – more support can be expected, at least for a time. Indeed, because of external help of various kinds, from various sources, both the Sikh and the Sri Lankan Tamil movements engaged in armed warfare far out of proportion to the underlying and at best ambivalent sentiments of their putatively secessionist populations. The armed militants had their way because of international connections.

Where, however, irredentist sentiment is more strongly felt in the putative retrieving state, warfare may be initiated even if – and perhaps *because* – the authorities in the putative irredentist state are unsympathetic to the irredentist objective. I am thinking here of the warfare that made Bangladesh independent. To be sure, there were several reasons why India intervened in East Bengal in 1971. There was an unparalleled opportunity to dismember Pakistan and install a friendlier government on the eastern frontier. There was the burden of refugees and the prospect of long-simmering guerrilla warfare across borders under circumstances that might later become more favourable to Pakistan. Pakistan's retaliation for inevitable Indian assistance to the guerrillas might prove painful. But, above and beyond all the other reasons, there were incipient claims in West Bengal for the unification of all Bengalis, east and west. Had this movement succeeded, the Hindu–Muslim balance in India would have been altered permanently, and India would have assumed the burden of supporting a very poor dependent state. An independent Bangladesh was far preferable to a growing demand for a Bengali irredenta. Consequently, India's willingness to go to war to secure Bangladesh's independence was likely coloured by the alternative (and undesirable) possibility of irredentism. The success of the war produced a fait accompli, an independent Bangladesh that ended the irredentist clamour the government of India had no wish to encourage,

If this analysis is correct, it shows that the only successful secession from 1945 to 1991 was the result of a secessionist war conducted in the growing shadow of a potential irredenta. And if this is so, the example shows again, not merely how the two phenomena are related, but how the reluctance of states to espouse irredentist claims drives ethnic movements toward secession – in this case, secession augmented by military force that an irredenta-shy regime committed in time to forestall an irredentist movement it had no wish to encourage.

The choice of movement and the bases of action

In explaining the relationship between secessions and irredentas. I have not gone all the way back to account for the emergence of movements for ethnoterritorial separatism in the first instance. To do this would require much greater explication of the course of ethnic relations within the undivided state. There is now quite a wide range of theorizing on the emergence of such movements, some more inward looking, emphasizing intraethnic history, myths of origin, and connections to land, others more outward looking, emphasizing interethnic changes within the present territory.[21] What is rare is a general theory that accounts for whether ethnoterritorial separatism will take a secessionist or irredentist course. The two are typically bracketed together in the literature, as if the emergence of one or the other were a matter of no consequence or a happenstance event.

We have seen, however, that secessions and irredentas are convertible under some circumstances, but not perfectly interchangeable at all. Their widely differential frequency shows how much more attractive secession is overall. To the participants, it obviously matters enormously which course is chosen, and it follows that the conditions associated with each course can, in principle, be specified. As they make such choices, group members and leaders resort to an array of perceptual and calculative considerations. Who are our true cousins? In which territorial unit are my political ambitions more likely to be fulfilled? Who will deploy force against us if we go in one direction or another? Neither secession nor irredentism is a spontaneous, unorganized movement, so it is hardly surprising that the strategic choice should have a heavy overlay of calculations of rational interest.

Such a conclusion should not, however, displace the role of the emotional discomfort that is customarily felt in conflict-prone interethnic relations or the perceptions of ethnic affinity and disparity that define group boundaries – neither of which is properly subsumed in any sensible scheme based wholly on rational interest. Indeed, even as we explain the preference for secession over irredentism on understandable calculative grounds, we elide an element of choice that belies the dominant role of calculation: if nearly every secession is doomed to failure, why do secessionist movements continue to arise? Until we are able to specify the mix of givens and chosens, of passionate and calculative behaviour, with greater precision, we shall continue to bracket related ethnic phenomena, the choice of which is neither an unpredictable event nor a matter of indifference to the participants.

Notes

1 This article was originally published in *Irredentism and International Politics*, edited by Naomi Chazan. Copyright © 1991. Lynne Reinner Publishers Inc. Reproduced here by permission of the publisher.

2 On 9 December 2009, the Indian government announced that it would start the process of creating a separate Telangana state. This was followed by serious unrest in the existing state of Andhra Pradesh, prompting the government on 24 December 2009 to make any further action dependent on a political consensus in the existing state.

3 Rupert Emerson, *From Empire to Nation* (Cambridge, MA: Harvard University Press, 1960), p. 105.

4 Immanuel Wallerstein, *Africa: The Politics of Independence* (New York: Vintage, 1961), p. 88.

5 Donald L. Horowitz, 'Patterns of Ethnic Separatism', *Comparative Studies in Society and History* 23, 2 (April 1981): 165–195, at p. 194.

6 As Jacob Landau pointed out at the conference to which this chapter in its original form was a contribution.

7 Subsequent developments in the former Yugoslavia confirm this assessment from two decades ago: Kosovo is now an independent state, recognized by over 50 members of the UN following its unilateral declaration of independence on 17 February 2007.

8 Donald L. Horowitz, *Ethnic Groups in Conflict* (Berkeley and Los Angeles: University of California Press, 1985), ch. 6, 'The Logic of Secessions and Irredentas'.

9 Ted Robert Gurr, *Why Men Rebel* (Princeton, NJ: Princeton University Press, 1970), pp. 4–5.

10 The military defeat of the Tamil Tigers by the Sri Lankan government in spring 2009 may have put at least a temporary end to any further secessionist impulses among some Tamils.

11 The 2005 Comprehensive Peace Agreement for Sudan includes an option for independence for the South. In late 2009, North and South reached an agreement on the terms of a referendum on the future status of the South in 2011.

12 Joane Nagel, 'The Conditions of Ethnic Separatism: The Kurds in Turkey, Iran, and Iraq', *Ethnicity* 7, 3 (September 1980): 279–297; George S. Harris, 'Ethnic Conflict and the Kurds', *The Annals* 433 (September 1977): 112–124.

13 While Somalia subsequently experienced a complete state collapse and has not had a functioning government for almost two decades now, irredentist impulses have kept resurfacing regularly.

14 David J. Banks, *Malay Kinship* (Philadelphia: Institute for the Study of Human Issues, 1933), pp. 25–28.

15 Horowitz, *Ethnic Groups in Conflict*, pp. 281–288, a section entitled 'Irredentism: Prerogative of the Few'.

16 Ibid., pp. 274–275.

17 This is not necessarily a reflection of the actual historical role of the region now regarded as peripheral.

18 Here, however, it should be borne in mind that the leadership interests are likely to be disproportionately important. Once the matter comes down to secession or irredentism, it will probably also come to fighting, and the leaders will negotiate access to the crucial arms.

19 For a discussion of the many African groups divided by boundaries, see A.I. Asiwaju, ed., *Partitioned Africans* (New York: St. Martin's Press, 1985).

20 This point is based on Myron Weiner's comments at the conference to which this chapter in its original form was a contribution.

21 Compare, for example, Anthony D. Smith, *The Ethnic Revival in the Modern World* (Cambridge: Cambridge University Press, 1981), pp. 64–66, with Ronald Rogowski, 'Causes and Varieties of Nationalism; A Rationalist Account', in Ronald Rogowski and Edward A. Tiryakian, eds., *New Nationalisms of the Developed West* (Boston: George Allen & Unwin, 1985), pp. 87–107.

Further reading

Emerson, Rupert, *From Empire to Nation* (Cambridge, MA: Harvard University Press, 1960).

Gurr, Ted Robert, *Why Men Rebel* (Princeton, NJ: Princeton University Press, 1970).

Horowitz, Donald L., *Ethnic Groups in Conflict* (Berkeley and Los Angeles: University of California Press, 1985).

Horowitz, Donald L., 'Patterns of Ethnic Separatism', *Comparative Studies in Society and History* 23, 2 April 1981.

Smith, Anthony D., *The Ethnic Revival in the Modern World* (Cambridge: Cambridge University Press, 1981).

Wallerstein, Immanuel, *Africa: The Politics of Independence* (New York: Vintage, 1961).

14

CONFLICT PREVENTION

A policy in search of a theory or a theory in search of a policy?

David Carment, Martin Fischer, Joe Landry and Sean Winchester

Introduction

Through an evaluation of both theory and policy, this chapter advances our understanding of why prevention remains both necessary and possible. Apart from this introduction, the chapter unfolds in five sections. In the first section, we discuss the conceptual aspects of prevention theory and policy. In the second section we engage in a broad discussion of ethnic conflict, and how its analysis can contribute to effective structural prevention. In the third section, supported by evidence from recent preventive activities by regional organizations and civil society, we assess conflict prevention policy in its operational guise, thus identifying key contributions to the field and opportunities for innovation. We conclude with some direction for future research and implications for policy.

Despite the fact that development practitioners, foreign policy makers, security specialists, civil society and even the private sector, have historically approached ethnic conflict prevention from different directions, they have, over time through cooperation as well as through support for extensive research and policy networks, developed a much better understanding of what conflict prevention entails and how it can be comprehensively applied. As a result, we have seen a virtual explosion in tool kits, early warning methodologies, frameworks for impact assessment and project evaluation, handbooks for practitioners, specialized funding envelopes, and multinational task forces. Donor agencies, foreign policy departments, defence departments, regional organizations and international financial institutions have all taken up the need for conflict prevention mainstreaming. Structural, as well as operational initiatives have been put in place, prevention centres and units within governments and intergovernmental organizations established, and collaborative research projects undertaken.

In short, the gap between rhetoric and reality, which loomed large at century's end, has been narrowed. Does this mean that more effective conflict prevention is now within reach? The answer is both yes and no. On the one hand, while there has been considerable deepening of capabilities through structural prevention and specialized departments within government agencies, in the absence of effective monitoring and evaluation methodologies, it is difficult to determine if these initiatives have lived up to the rhetorical claims.

Bridging the gap

Much of the necessary conceptual and theoretical brush-clearing on conflict prevention has been conducted over the years by a number of think tanks in Europe and North America, publishing key findings on, among other things, the phases of conflict, tools and techniques for monitoring and assessment, political will and response strategies. In an important and early contribution to the field, Michael Lund (1999) examined the issues of conflict prevention impact assessment and the improvement of techniques and methods for conflict prevention. In doing so, he provides an all-inclusive definition of conflict prevention that is a useful point of departure for this chapter. Lund suggests that:

> conflict prevention entails any structural or interactive means to keep intrastate and interstate tensions and disputes from escalating into significant violence and to strengthen the capabilities to resolve such disputes peacefully as well as alleviating the underlying problems that produce them, including forestalling the spread of hostilities into new places. It comes into play both in places where conflicts have not occurred recently and where recent largely terminated conflicts could recur. Depending on how they are applied, it can include the particular methods and means of any policy sector, whether labelled prevention or not (e.g. sanctions, conditional aid, mediation, structural adjustment, democratic institution building etc.), and they might be carried out by global, regional, national or local levels by any governmental or non-governmental actor.
>
> *(Lund 1999: 3)*

It is obvious that a broad definition has both advantages and disadvantages. For example, in some instances the term conflict prevention is qualified by the antecedents 'violent' or 'deadly' as if to suggest that some conflicts may be constructive and are not in need of immediate attention or are at least less threatening. Others have taken conflict prevention to mean the task of addressing latent, underlying, or structural features, which, under certain conditions, have the potential to become deadly. Still others equate preventive diplomacy with conflict prevention, although that too is overlaid with conceptual ambiguity since preventive diplomacy carries with it connotations of crisis management, statecraft and the use of force in order to prevent the escalation of organized and wide-scale violence.

Is conflict prevention an *ad hoc action-oriented operational* approach to emerging and potential problems or is it a medium- and long-term pro-active *structuralist* strategy intended to create the enabling conditions for a stable and more predictable international environment? Kalypso Nicolaïdis (1996) provides a useful conceptual framework for determining how preventive diplomacy and long-term structural approaches relate. Preventive diplomacy is seen as an operational response. It is premised on incentive structures provided by outside actors to change specific kinds of undesirable behaviour. Preventive diplomacy is therefore targeted and short-term and the preventive action taken relates directly to changes in conflict escalation and conflict dynamics. In this regard outside actors can seek to influence the course of events and try to alter or induce specific behaviour through coercive and operational threats and deterrents or through less coercive strategies of persuasion and inducement. Operational prevention or preventive diplomacy has now come to refer to a response generated by a state, a coalition of states or a multilateral organization – often represented by eminent envoys – intended to address the rapid escalation of emergent crises, disputes and inter-state hostilities. Preventive diplomacy entails primarily, but not exclusively, ad hoc forms of consultation using non compartmentalized and non-hierarchical forms of information gathering, contingency planning and short-term response mechanisms. The risks are proximate and analysis and action are combined at once in rapid succession.

Of course, operational and structural approaches are not mutually exclusive activities. Shifting attitudinal change necessarily entails a concerted movement toward, and investment in, both strategic operational responses and long-term approaches. Though not exclusively, conflict prevention *is* more and more often being associated with structural transformations achieved through developmental aid and with indeterminate processes that may take years if not decades to achieve. Ultimately, conflict prevention is a strategy intended to identify and create the enabling conditions for a stable and more predictable international security environment.

The need for timely and correct analysis

When it comes to prevention of ethnic conflict, policy makers must know what to look for at the outset of their engagement. However, several problems arise in translating analysis into action. Misdiagnosis can create 'situational ambiguity' in which there is uncertainty about cause and effect, creating a perception of high risk with little or no potential for lasting impact. Under conditions of uncertainty, policy makers employ the phrase 'the absence of political will' to rationalize their inactions. According to Woocher (2001), Jentleson (2003) and Ivanov and Nyheim (2004), among others, political will is largely a 'smoke-screen' for either not taking the time to get the analysis right or not fully understanding the kinds of capabilities that could be deployed to address the problem.

As Suhrke and Adelman (1996) showed long ago in their careful assessment of the failure to respond to the genocide in Rwanda, that breakdown was due in large part to strategies of 'passing the buck' and 'waffling' by lead actors who actively encouraged situational ambiguity to discredit clear-cut analyses that would initiate decisive responses. The media played its part by wilfully engaging in misdiagnosis, interpreting the conflict as a complex humanitarian disaster rather than the politically motivated agenda of leaders whose carefully laid out plans included genocidal intent (Suhrke and Adelman 1996; Jentleson 2003).

Twenty years later, little research has been done to 'unbundle' the political will problem and its relationship to analysis. Several task forces on genocide prevention in Canada and the USA have been established but it remains to been seen what impact their recommendations will have on either ongoing or future risks (Albright and Cohen 2008).

In sum, forging a relationship between analysis and political will is complex but not insurmountable. The donor community, non-governmental organizations (NGOs) and the private sector need analytical tools. Investments in the development of local capacity are also crucial because NGOs and local actors are, by design, a crucial and necessary part of the analysis and response chain of responsibilities (Schnabel and Carment 2004). For example, investments by government agencies led to the Peace and Conflict Impact Assessment (PCIA) initiative, which sought to create a series of tools to aid in programming and policy decision-making. However these initiatives were never fully implemented. Though not concerned with ethnic conflicts *per se*, the PCIA initiative's focus on early warning and early response, driven by objective analysis and risk assessment, clearly has much in common with current efforts to enhance monitoring and assessment capability. These approaches assume that a demand-side oriented approach to analysis and response is better suited to local capacity building given that various frameworks could be adapted to local needs (Nyheim 2008). Localized approaches also have another distinct advantage. Active and applied conflict prevention can easily be perceived as a serious threat to a state's sovereignty – and so political resistance is unavoidable. In part because of the unwillingness to allow outsiders to 'meddle in their affairs', there has been much rhetoric and advocacy and sadly little specific in tackling conflict prevention within the UN. Thorough training, mainstreaming capacity building is required to enhance preventive thinking. This does not just happen by itself or overnight, but can only be the result of deliberate action, collaboration and commitment from governments.

As Ouellette (2004) argues, financial capacity building might be seen as an easy shortcut between analysis and prevention. However, earmarking funds or creating a central fund to support preventive measures, is only part of the story. As with any government policy, the development of conflict prevention policy is constrained by various systemic, political, and bureaucratic factors. These factors include the characteristics of the existing expenditure management system; the bifurcation of policy and budget; the fact that ends are chosen to fit available means; and poor horizontal integration across agencies and ministries. In the case of conflict prevention, these problems are further compounded by the diversity of situations and the range of tools needed to address any given conflict. Establishing a sustainable financial regime capable of supporting both operational and structural prevention requires a framework that allows for clear priority setting and operational doctrine (Ouellette 2004).

In answer to this challenge, a notable convergence has taken place between research and policy interventions that deal with conflict on the one hand and with development on the other. Hot conflicts have become primarily a poor country affair, and extreme under-development a problem of countries at war. It is now impossible to think seriously about development without considering conflict, and conversely to think of conflict without considering development. Such a convergence has spawned a number of research initiatives, and a growing willingness on the part of development agencies from the World Bank and the Development Aid Committee of the Organization of Economic Co-operation and Development (OECD), to the UK's Department for International Development (DFID), to make conflict a standard preoccupation of their work.

Evaluating the operational prevention of ethnic conflict

Turning now to the operational dimensions of ethnic conflict prevention, in the early 1990s it became increasingly evident that the United Nations, governments and most regional organizations were not up to the task of operational prevention. The problems, as highlighted above, were primarily bureaucratic but, as Michael Lund showed, a core issue was also attitudinal. His various analyses have helped dispel the sometimes prevailing assumption that operational prevention is an idealist notion that cannot succeed in a world driven by re-active – not proactive – notions of conflict management (Lund 1996a, 1996b, 2005). There are in sum, intrinsic benefits of systematic preventive thinking as reflected in serious commitments to mainstream operational prevention by numerous international organizations. To evaluate this assumption we look at recent evidence indicating that, on the operational side of the equation, some progress has been made.

An Agenda for Peace (A/47/277-S/2411, 1992), the *Brahimi Report* (A/55/305-S/2000/809, 2000) and the *High Level Panel on Threats, Challenges and Change* (A/59/565, 2004) all sought to bring operational prevention to the attention of the UN and its member states. As Carment and Fischer (2009) suggest, 'there is little doubt that conflict prevention has won the rhetorical battle, judging by the various reports released within the last several years'. But does it work?

To answer this question, we suggest that a much wider range of tools is available to external and internal actors than simply preventive diplomacy. Operational conflict prevention measures can be grouped into four sets of hands-on action: first, political measures such as mediation with muscle, that is the creation of institutional mechanisms through regional and international organizations; second, economic measures such as sanctions; third, military measures such as preventive peace operations; fourth, civil society-led initiatives such as network building and forums for dialogue.

Political measures and instruments

Political measures and instruments aimed at preventing ethnic conflict may include the establishment of national and regional mechanisms and institutions, direct preventive diplomacy activities (see Jentleson 1999, 2003) such as mediation, fact-finding, establishing good offices, initiating peace conferences, sending envoys, the creation of back channels, message carrying as well as problem-solving and confidence-building workshops, talks initiated by faith leaders and cross-group discussions. While there is an abundance of examples for each of these activities, it is at times hard to pinpoint if and when exactly they were successful at preventing the outbreak of ethnic conflict. In this vein, reference has been made to efforts undertaken by former UN Secretary General Kofi Annan to curb the post-election violence in Kenya in late 2007 and early 2008.

On 27 December 2007 Kenya held its fourth multi-party elections. Violence erupted between supporters of the different parties after the Election Commission of Kenya prematurely declared President Kibaki as the winner (see Dagne 2008; Nicoll and Delaney 2008). Many observers described the violence as being based on ethnic differences between the President's Kikuyu and the Luo and Kalenjin ethnic groups, supporters of the opposition leader Raila Odinga. Initial efforts by the African Union (AU) and European Union (EU) to curb the violence and bring about a negotiated settlement between the two parties failed. It was only 'after intense mediation by a panel of eminent Africans led by the former United Nations Secretary General, Kofi Annan, [that] a power-sharing agreement was reached between the Kibaki government and the opposition party led by Odinga' (Kwaja 2009: 43). It is widely believed that without the mediation efforts led by Annan, the ethnic violence would have escalated into full-blown civil war (see Romero, Kimenyi and Dercon 2008). The Annan-led mediation effort was undertaken under the umbrella of the AU's *Panel of the Wise*, which was established as part of the AU's Peace and Security Council as 'a panel of five eminent African personalities to engage in conflict prevention diplomacy' (Cilliers and Sturman 2004: 98). It serves as an example of an initiative originating directly from a regional organization's political organ.

There have been two other prominent examples of Responsibility to Protect (R2P) being invoked in high level policy discussions in recent years. The first and most obvious is the case of Libya in 2011, wherein the UN Security Council (UNSC) approved the use of force in order to protect civilians who were deemed to be at risk of massacre by Ghaddafi's forces. In this case even the typically non-interventionist states, Russia and China, allowed the resolution to pass. However after the North Atlantic Treaty Organization (NATO) mission shifted its mandate from merely protecting civilians that were immediately at risk, to deposing the entire Ghaddafi regime, both the Russians and the Chinese (among others) felt that they had been hoodwinked into supporting a Western military engagement, which was never their intention. This case of buyer's remorse then led to the subsequent stalemate which has characterized the civil war in Syria for a number of years now. Countries which are unwilling to support intervention into the affairs of a sovereign nation have willingly blocked any attempt to implement R2P in the case of Syria. Whether or not this will become an international norm remains to be seen; however one can be sure that cases such as Libya will no longer be receiving a rubber stamp via the UNSC. For these reasons regional organizations have become critical in approaches to conflict prevention.

Indeed, most regional organizations have included conflict prevention in their core mandates and have developed some political, civilian and military preventive capacities (see Carment and Fischer 2009; contributions in Schnabel and Carment 2004 volume 1; Wulf 2009). Dorn (2004) suggests that the EU played a crucial role in preventing a full-blown ethnic war in Macedonia in the mid-1990s. Based on its early prevention experience in the Balkans, the EU has created a host of different mechanisms to coordinate and increase the effectiveness of the various civilian and military resources at its disposal. As is the case with other regional organizations, the Organization for Security and Co-operation in Europe (OSCE) and EU have focused their political measures and instruments on the prevention of conflict stimulated by ethnic motives. Since the release of the International Commission on Intervention and State Sovereignty's report *The Responsibility to Protect* (R2P) in 2001, much of the academic and policy discussion relating to ethnic conflicts in general and genocides in particular has been focused on the tools and mechanisms detailed in the R2P.

The R2P agenda's threshold for the direct involvement in identity-based conflicts is fairly high. While much attention has been paid to the R2P's reactive component, Bellamy (2008) argues that the preventive pillar of the R2P has been largely overlooked. Instead of tying the R2P and conflict prevention together, the 2005 World Summit Outcome document (A/RES/60/1) shifted its focus on early warning by fully supporting the office of the Special Adviser on the Prevention of Genocide. The Special Adviser's mandate was defined by the Secretary General to include, among other responsibilities, the collection 'of existing information [...] on massive and serious violations of human rights and international humanitarian law of ethnic and racial origin that, if not prevented or halted, might lead to genocide' and to 'act as a mechanism of early warning to the Secretary General, and through him to the Security Council, by bringing to their attention situations that could potentially result in genocide' (S/2004/567, 2004).

Building on the work of Carment and Fischer (2009) we revisit the question of how seven regional organizations implement R2P's preventive principles. Here, we depart from a specific focus on the R2P's preventive pillar and broaden the framework's scope to reflect the position of regional organizations toward the prevention of ethnic conflict in general.

Regional organizations continue to pay insufficient attention to the prevention of ethnic conflict. We suggest two main reasons for this. First, many regional organizations continue to lack the operational capacity to prevent ethnic conflicts prior to violence erupting. Donors have for some time focused on mainstreaming conflict prevention by conducting training in conflict risk assessment and the development of conflict prevention policy (see contributions in Schnabel and Carment 2004 volumes 1 and 2). Second, as long as regional organizations are unwilling to institutionalize the prevention of ethnic conflicts, political will problems will continue to undermine possible capacity-building successes (see Lund 2000). The prevention of ethnic conflict requires substantial financial investments as well as long-term political commitments to develop effective operational structures. As long as the process of 'formulating and promoting a shared set of ideas and a common moral commitment' (Lund 2000: 23) is hampered by the lack of political will, regional organizations will struggle with the operational prevention of ethnic conflict.

For example, it is no secret that the African continent faces a wide variety of challenges, including being home to the greatest number of active conflicts (both state and non-state) and the highest number of battle deaths of any region in the world. The AU hence plays a vital role in ensuring that R2P principles are acted upon swiftly. The AU charter provides explicit guidelines for dealing with peace, security and human rights issues, using R2P-related language, specifically outlined in article 4(h) which reads, 'the right of the Union to intervene in a Member State pursuant to a decision of the Assembly in respect of grave circumstances, namely: war crimes, genocide and crimes against humanity'. The adoption of this principle indicates a willingness to at least consider sovereignty as not only a right, but also a responsibility.

In terms of conflict prevention, the AU has activities that fall under both 'structural prevention' and 'operational prevention'. The former refers to longer term mitigation of root causes of conflict, whereas the latter refers to shorter term crisis de-escalation. The most important body for conflict prevention in the AU is the Peace and Security Council (PSC). The council is made up of 15 elected members, with ten elected for two year terms and five for three year terms. It functions as a decision making body and aims to act in a similar fashion to the UN Security Council, however there are no vetos, and resolutions are passed by 2/3 majority rule. In practice the AU is one of the few Regional Organizations (ROs) examined that have managed to mobilize operational peacekeeping missions, a fact that – despite its other shortcomings – puts it far ahead of the other ROs examined in this chapter.

For its part the Economic Community of West African States (ECOWAS) was developed initially to help foster economic integration in the region, with goals similar to that of the EU. However it has become a major player on the continent not only in economic development but also in terms of conflict prevention and early warning. The early warning system – ECOWAS Early Response Network (ECOWARN) – developed and used by ECOWAS members is discussed in more depth later in this chapter, but suffice it to say here that, after the conflicts in Liberia and Sierra Leone, the capacity of the organization to monitor and prevent conflict saw a marked improvement. The Protocol on the Mechanism for Conflict Prevention adopted in 1999 helped to systematize the regional protocol for dealing with conflicts, before, during and after onset.

During the past decade ECOWAS has proved itself a critical partner in quelling national and sub-national level tensions during and after elections; for instance Guinea, Côte d'Ivoire and Guinea-Bissau required intervention on multiple levels when political crises emerged. Along with the AU, ECOWAS has come to take on a much more active role in conflict prevention and de-escalation than many analysts would have imagined even a few years ago. At the same time, the relationship between the UNSC and ECOWAS is unclear. In the past, military interventions have relied on Western funding as well as logistical and military support. Nigerian support for the organization has also begun to wane, revealing some of the key shortcomings of the current arrangement. The ethno-religious violence that broke out in 2012 in Central African Republic is one example of where ECOWAS and the AU 'failed' to implement the protection mandate of R2P, indicating that these regional bodies are still unable to intervene swiftly even in obvious cases of widespread ethnic violence. Nevertheless, the importance of the successes seen in implementing R2P principles in the region should not be understated, especially in terms of precedence for other regional organizations to look to.

Turning now to South East Asia we examine the South Asian Association for Regional Cooperation (SAARC) made up of eight countries, namely Afghanistan, Bangladesh, Bhutan, India, Maldives, Nepal, Pakistan, and Sri Lanka. It is evident that the region has major issues with ethnic conflict and civil unrest; however as an organization there is little interest in pursuing multilateral conflict prevention or R2P principles. In the charter it is noted that 'bilateral and contentious issues shall be excluded from the deliberation of the Association'.

171

Moreover, none of the official documents produced by the organization contain a reference to R2P, and a search for 'intervention' brings up a litany of references to the principle of non-intervention. While disappointing for proponents of regional solutions to conflict and crimes against humanity, given the disparate nature of the member nations as well as the contentious political and military relationships between many of the dyads included in the group, this reluctance to embrace a policy that can be seen as violating sovereignty in any way does not come as a surprise. Until regional tensions are managed, progress in this area is doubtful. Perhaps as a silver lining, major combat operations in Sri Lanka and ongoing unrest in Nepal have both died down in the past few years; an optimist may see this period as a window for SAARC to begin discussing its role as a player in maintaining regional peace and security.

In a similar vein as SAARC, the other main Asian RO examined here – the Association of Southeast Asian Nations (ASEAN) – has not made progress towards adopting any type of R2P framework. As scholars and analysts have noted, ASEAN has not incorporated the principle into its official charter, nor has it been discussed as a mainstream issue at organizational summits. To be sure, efforts have been made to formalize the security aspirations of the organization.

For example, the ASEAN (Political) Security Community was established in 2003 with the goal of 'explor[ing] innovative ways to increase its security and establish modalities for the ASEAN Security Community, which include the following elements: norms-setting, conflict prevention, approaches to conflict resolution, and post-conflict peace building'. Despite the apparent invocations of R2P principles in this document, iron-clad sovereignty and the non-interference principle rule the day in practice. At the same time, six ASEAN countries (Singapore, Malaysia, Indonesia, the Philippines, Vietnam and Myanmar) participated in the 2009 General Assembly debate on the report implementing the Responsibility to Protect. During the debate, all of these member states reaffirmed the fundamentals of R2P, while also emphasizing that it should not be renegotiated or broadened, but rather adopted as is and applied under strict conditions. Based on this debate and other evidence, Bellamy and Drummond (2011) argue that ASEAN nations are willing to adopt R2P principles with modifications wherein 'a new norm is made consistent with established norms in a manner that alters both the new norm (R2P) and those more established norms (non-interference)'.

The rapid economic development of the region means that there are few failing and extremely fragile states in the region. In turn, most national governments feel that their internal issues with political violence or terrorism will not devolve into instability warranting international action. ASEAN leaders tend to focus on the intervention aspect of R2P, rather than the preventative and assistive aspects. Asian leaders look upon the experience of Libya in 2011 with suspicion and worry that the third pillar can be tainted by political and military goals, particularly on the part of the Security Council's Permanent Members

That being said, there are some opportunities for R2P to enter into the ASEAN framework. An early warning system would be a step in the right direction and would be welcomed by member states, although capacity to implement and run such a system is still an issue. A limited form of post-conflict peace building (agreed to by all parties) may be another viable entry point for R2P. Finally, the establishment of the ASEAN Inter-Governmental Commission on Human Rights has been subject to debate, and it does not have the power to enforce any binding resolutions, yet it could be a vehicle to build greater awareness of R2P principles in the Southeast Asian community.

The EU has a mandated interest in conflict prevention and provides a great deal of funding and capacity-building efforts towards this end. Since the conflicts in the Balkans following the end of the Cold War, the EU has strived to become a leader in the field of conflict prevention and R2P. The 2001 Gothenburg European Council laid the groundwork for this role, with the provision of four main areas of priority: 1) Set clear political priorities for preventive actions; 2) Improve its early warning, action and policy coherence; 3) Enhance its instruments for long- and short-term prevention; and 4) Build effective partnerships for prevention. In developing its capacity for conflict prevention around the globe, the EU works closely with NATO and the OSCE to form arguably the most effective partnership in terms of its ability to predict conflict and intervene swiftly. Indeed, the EU is seen as being the only major power of the twenty-first century to unambiguously support this concept.

The EU's conflict prevention platform has evolved over the past decade. After the 2005 UN World Summit, EU members (especially France and Britain) were keen to formalize the EU's stance on R2P; however the language adopted had to satisfy the sceptics, particularly in the global south. For these reasons the emphasis was placed on the prevention of conflict rather than on the right of humanitarian intervention. Further, members of the UNSC were not willing to give up their power to review situations on a 'case by case' basis, meaning that principles for the universal application of R2P were not on the radar at this time. The EU viewed R2P as a legal concept that required norm building through diplomatic channels and multilateral cooperation over time. R2P was invoked by EU members in the aftermath of the 2008 cyclone Nargis in Myanmar, providing a unique example of how a humanitarian crisis caused by disaster could also fall under the purview of R2P; this concept remains controversial however.

Indeed, the 2009 Secretary General's report pushed the notion that the most important aspect of R2P is prevention of atrocities, downplaying the interventionist aspects of the norm. This move was seen as positive by the EU because it allowed for a broader discussion on the role of civilian crisis management without it being seen as a Western concept used primarily for political purposes. As the Libya crisis unfolded in 2011, the true nature of R2P and its motivations were under the microscope. Resolution 1973 represented 'the first time that the Security Council has authorized the use of military force for human protection purposes against the wishes of a functioning state' (UN Security Council 2011). Here the EU position was very fuzzy, in that France and Britain were strongly in support of the intervention, while Germany was not. Nevertheless, with Germany abstaining from the vote, Resolution 1973 passed and the torch of responsibility was now passed to NATO.

NATO stands in a unique position as it is a regional military alliance as opposed to a multi-lateral intergovernmental body as many of the other organizations examined here are. The Libya intervention has brought the role of NATO into the wider discussion of R2P and its applicability as an international norm. In just one month after the crisis began, NATO had mobilized a large coalition, closed down airspace and begun attacking military targets. Many emerging powers and members of the Global South were not happy with the NATO actions in Libya, which used the clause 'all necessary measures' to justify the broader intervention and eventual regime change which was conducted under the auspices of Resolution 1973. While the intervention was widely heralded as a success in the West, subsequent analyses have indicated that perhaps more harm than good resulted from the operations overall.

The OSCE remains one of the most important regional actors when it comes to ethnic conflict prevention. When the OSCE was first formed at the end of the Cold War, it was expected to emerge as the most important regional security organization; however tensions between Russia and its Western members led to the emergence of NATO and the EU as the key fora for Western security interests. It is tightly linked to the EU, with EU member states making up nearly half of the OSCE participating countries, and contributing more than two-thirds of its operating budget. The OSCE and the EU both operate in areas of geographical and functional overlap. Human rights, democracy promotion, and responses to civilian crises are all areas in which both organizations work.

The OSCE, however, has remained an integral player in regional security efforts and also acts as a vehicle for conflict prevention and management. In terms of R2P, the OSCE Conflict Prevention Centre is probably the most important acting body. The centre employs a strategy of minimizing structural risks of conflict by promoting democracy and human rights (such as election monitoring, police missions, dispute settlement, etc.). In addition, the centre conducts early warning and analysis activities, although these activities are subject to secrecy due to the potentially politically sensitive nature of the information collected. The OSCE – as a consensus based organization – is subject to the political realities of its member states, and therefore has lost stature over time.

The 2014 crisis in Ukraine has offered a unique opportunity for the OSCE however. With its placement as a linkage point between Europe and Russia, it has been able to fulfil an important role as an impartial election monitor during the tense situation faced in the eastern parts of Ukraine. The Special Monitoring Mission to Ukraine was deployed on request by the Ukrainian government and following a consensus vote by all 57 OSCE participating states. As this chapter was going to print, the elections in Ukraine had been undertaken peacefully with the support of the OSCE and international election monitoring missions. This is a positive development in Russia–EU relations. Some have even argued that the OSCE represents an entry point to a 'pan-European society', yet only time will tell whether that is a possibility or merely wishful thinking.

Economic measures

A central element of the UN Charter's mechanisms for the maintenance of international peace and security is the use of sanctions as set out in Article 42. A variety of sanction mechanisms including arms embargos and individual travel sanctions (see contributions in Brzoska 2001), the freezing of financial assets (see Biersteker, Eckert and Romaniuk 2001) as well sanctions on specific natural resources such as oil and diamonds are available to the UN. Escribà-Folch (2010) argues that economic embargos imposed by international organizations are the most effective type of coercive conflict management measure and have a shortening effect on the duration of intrastate conflicts. The UN Security Council has frequently reverted to economic sanctions targeted at natural resources to manage ethnic conflicts (see Cortright and Lopez 2000), most prominently perhaps in the post-conflict phase in Liberia in the early 1990s and as a tool to prevent the escalation of ethnic violence in the Côte d'Ivoire starting in 2004 (see Eriksson 2008).

Beginning with the initial decision to impose targeted sanctions on Côte d'Ivoire in 2004, the aim was to prevent a return to full blown ethnic conflict and achieve a settlement through democratic means (see Wallensteen, Eriksson and Strandow 2006; Tamm 2002). A series of UN Security Council resolutions imposed a comprehensive sanctions regime on the country. This regime included an arms embargo, travel ban and the freezing of financial assets (initially imposed through S/RES 1572 in November 2004) and later included sanctions on rough diamonds (S/RES 1643 in December 2005). In its assessment of the Ivorian sanction regime (S/2006/204), the Expert Panel responsible for the evaluation concluded that the sanctions had 'the effect of preventing a return to pre-war production levels' (Wallensteen, Eriksson and Strandow 2006: 13). Although the (rebel) New Forces were able to diversify their revenue sources, we suggest that, in combination with other elements of the comprehensive sanctions regime, the restrictions placed on diamonds did in fact contribute to preventing the renewed outbreak of ethnic conflict in Côte d'Ivoire.

Civil society initiatives

NGOs play an essential role in the global advancement of conflict prevention. Many of these NGOs operate at relatively high levels of engagement, where they primarily lobby international and regional organizations, but a growing number have begun to make themselves heard at the local level. The ability to engage actors at the local level is particularly important in areas that lack strong national or regional support for conflict prevention, such as Southeast and Northeast Asia, because it can help to build a grassroots consensus in favour of the norm. Once these local organizations are engaged, it becomes much easier to adapt the normative framework for domestic consumption and build the pressure needed for change.

These tasks range from advocacy for human rights and the protection of civilians, the provision of humanitarian aid, strengthening of local civil society, to concrete conflict prevention measures such as the facilitation of dialogue and problem-solving workshops. Recognizing the broad spectrum of roles that NGOs in general play in the prevention of ethnic conflict, in this part we pay particular attention to operational activities by organizations rooted in civil society (CSOs). Barnes (2006: 27) argues that CSOs can engage in the prevention of ethnic conflict in three ways: first, there are responses rooted in a specific civil society sector, for example trade unions, youth groups, women's associations or faith communities; second, CSOs can focus on working toward structural/policy changes in national, regional and global systems; third, local CSOs as well as ad-hoc coalitions of concerned citizens can target specific emerging conflict situations. Our focus will be two-fold as we first return to the discussion of mechanisms that contributed to preventing the escalation of the post-election violence in Kenya into full-blown ethnic conflict and then briefly present efforts to build a global civil society network for the prevention of armed conflict.

Various civil society led efforts worked alongside the high-level Annan-led mediation undertaken to prevent the escalation of ethnic violence after the December 2008 elections in Kenya. One of these initiatives was a movement called *Concerned Citizens for Peace* (CCP), a group of five eminent Kenyans, two former generals, two civil society activists, and led by Ambassador Bethual Kiplagat (see Abdi 2008). The group's preventive activities occurred on three levels (Abdi 2008: 9–11). First, upstream activities aimed at supporting the top-level mediation and dialogue process. The five members were able to access key national and international politicians and engage them in preventive action (see Fisher and Zimina 2009). Second, middlestream efforts supported mid-level public and private institutions and key individuals by mobilizing the government and public institutions as well as the media. For example, using national, regional and local media, CCP members made public appeals for the cessation of violence. Third, downstream activities targeted local-level programmatic actions by key individuals, groups and institutions to transform local violence, mobilize for change and offer practical support for confidence-building and healing. CCP was able to mobilize an extensive national network of peace resources that made important contributions to preventing the further escalation of violence.

In recent years, efforts have been undertaken to establish and strengthen a global network of CSOs working in the field of preventing ethnic conflict. The Global Partnership for the Prevention of Armed Conflict (GPPAC) is made up of nearly 1,000 NGOs working in the field of conflict prevention. Wolter (2007: 75) argues that by creating a 'knowledge based regime of prevention [...] GPPAC is becoming a driving force for effective UN/government/CSO partnerships'. GPPAC's Early Warning Response working group seeks to bring together partners working on civil society based preventive actions. By facilitating dialogue and producing action-oriented analysis the working group seeks to enhance the capacity of CSOs. One of the most effective initiatives in this regard has been the International Coalition for the Responsibility to Protect (ICR2P). Founded in 2009, this coalition of 82 local, regional and international NGOs has members that operate in every major region of the globe. Its ability to connect local norm entrepreneurs with transnational activists has done much to support the diffusion of R2P. The Asia-Pacific Centre for the Responsibility to Protect, for example, is a member of ICR2P that has sought to actively promote the idea of R2P with local civil society organizations. It has held a number of workshops and training sessions in countries within the Asia-Pacific region and has even ranked CSOs based on their likelihood of supporting R2P initiatives in the future. Other methods of engagement include the development and dissemination of R2P 'toolkits', the promotion of NGO/CSO coalitions and network structures, and coordination with national R2P focal points. This third approach is common across West and East Africa, where national governments and ROs are generally supportive of R2P, but has met with only limited success in Asia and Latin America.

In addition to their role as transnational advocates, NGOs are also directly involved in the implementation of preventative initiatives. Their activities in this area include rule of law strengthening, conflict mediation, human rights monitoring and a wide range of related projects. One of the most promising initiatives in recent years has been the development of an entirely new generation of early warning technologies (EWTs). These new, fourth generation EWTs have attempted to address the 'warning-response gap' inherent in earlier generations of technology by developing horizontal linkages between communities at-risk. In common use since 2008, these new early warning systems focus on two-way communication via mobile technologies to ensure that information can be used by civilians in a timely manner. The open source platform developed by Ushahidi, for example, allows individuals to upload violent incidents to online crisis-maps within moments of their occurrence. This information can help civilians to avoid conflict zones during their day-to-day activities or to flee from an area before trouble has arrived. Similarly, the emergence of new SMS-based applications, such as Kenya's PeaceTXT, has facilitated near instantaneous communication between networks of mobile phone users. Conflict-affected areas can now be blanketed in messages urging peace and restraint prior to the outbreak of violence or in messages of warning once it has begun. These technologies are still undergoing a process of refinement, and may possess risks of abuse due to the lack of centralized vetting systems, but they represent a crucial step forward in the area of conflict early warning.

Despite the growing influence of these NGO developed technologies, most of the early warning systems that exist at the regional or sub-regional level remain centralized and vertically structured. Examples of these systems include the AU's Continental Early Warning System (CEWS), ECOWAS' ECOWARN and the Intergovernmental Authority on Development's (IGAD) Conflict Early Warning and Response Mechanism (CEWARN). Although these systems continue to be plagued by political indecision, bureaucratic inefficiencies and weak linkages to local actors, steps are currently being undertaken to increase their effectiveness. The AU's Continental Early Warning System (CEWS) network, for example, has made steady improvements to its ability to collect, analyse and disseminate information over the past several years. It continues to suffer from a number of major gaps, which are to be expected given the ambitious scale of the project, but they appear to be slowly closing over time. At the sub-regional level, these top-down reform efforts are being complemented by NGO-driven efforts to improve the responsiveness of CEWS' constituent components. The grassroots support provided by the West African Network for Peacebuilding (WANEP) to ECOWARN has strengthened its ability to monitor issues at the local level and the involvement of the Information and Communication Technologies for Peace Foundation (ICT4Peace) with Intergovernmental Authority on Development (IGAD) has helped it to explore horizontal communication methods. Lest these issues be misconstrued as being wholly African-centric, it is worth noting that the EU has also encountered considerable difficulties developing an effective early warning and early response capacity. It is currently funding a number of studies on this topic through the Initiative for Peacebuilding (IfP), a consortium of NGOs led by International Alert, but it is still a long way away from developing a viable, top-down response mechanism.

Conclusion

Our conclusions relate to directions for future work, not only to make conflict prevention effective but to ensure that it is sustainable. Three areas merit particular attention.

Integrating findings and methodologies across communities

There is a lot of good, mostly complementary, analysis both in academe and advocacy circles. Some analysis and research finds its way into the policy community, but not much of it is linked together in a formal institutionalized way with ongoing and secure funding. When it is used, risk analysis tends to be drawn on in an *ad hoc, secretive* and *selective* way. As a result, key findings remain underutilized and researchers have little incentive to collaborate among themselves and with the policy community. More hazardous is a trend within government, towards individually tailored in-house analytical tools with each department advocating a distinct set of indicators, tool kits and set of assumptions about causal connections that support their agendas. While this approach might be helpful in mainstreaming prevention of ethnic conflict within these departments to the extent that it forces decision makers to ask questions about causality (that they might not have considered before), it also poses challenges to inter-departmental coordination and inter-donor harmonization.

Linking analysis to response

There remains a need for effective strategies that link analysis to policy. It has been argued, many times before, that a key problem in improving the prevention of ethnic conflict is not the availability of information or for that matter, the absence of early warning information, but a clear understanding of how to make diagnosis policy relevant. Risk analysis and early warning need to be practicable, standardized and accessible. In other words, the absence of a clear understanding of how specific information fits within the operational capacities of the end user is the most significant constraint on effective conflict prevention. Properly understood policy relevant diagnosis combines real time dynamic analysis with structural information, matches the analysis to the operational capacity of the end user and provides an evaluative framework for assessing policy impact.

Making prevention pay

Political will, or more specifically its absence, is the number one justification for inaction. Making prevention pay means that the costs (and risks) of inaction must be fully calculated and clearly communicated. This also means that institutional incentive structures must be developed to ensure better coordination across departments and between governments. Pooling of resources is one way to assist in the process of identifying costed options but this must be achieved at both the micro and macro level. Coordination means that programme officers from different departments should work effectively together as a problem-solving team and not in isolation. Making prevention pay applies to the private sector as well. While it is not without controversy, the suggestion that the private sector, in particular the mining and resource extraction sectors, has a role to play in conflict prevention is well founded both on analytic as well as ethical and commercial grounds.

In this chapter, we have pointed to some of the challenges and opportunities of preventing ethnic conflict through structural and operational response mechanisms. For conflict prevention to move from rhetorical catchphrases to effective action, all involved actors, national, regional and local governments, the UN, regional and civil society organizations, research institutions and the private sector, still have much more room to improve their analysis of emerging ethnic tensions, to take seriously warning signals and engage in appropriate preventive action. Only after this gap has been closed can we say that the concept of conflict prevention has moved from theory to policy.

Further reading

Berdal, M. R. and Malone, D. (eds) *Greed and Grievance: Economic Agendas in Civil Wars*. Boulder: Lynne Rienner, 2000.
Jentleson, B. *Preventive Diplomacy and Ethnic Conflict: Possible, Difficult, Necessary*. La Jolla: Institute on Global Conflict and Cooperation, 1996.
Lake, D. and Rothchild, D. (eds) *The International Spread of Ethnic Conflict: Fear Diffusion and Escalation*. Princeton: Princeton University Press, 1998.
Schnabel, A. and Carment, D. (eds) *Conflict Prevention, from Rhetoric to Reality: Opportunities and Innovations*, 2 Vols. Lanham: Lexington Press, 2004.
Schnabel, A. and Carment, D. (eds) *Conflict Prevention: Path to Peace or Grand Illusion*. Tokyo: United Nations University Press, 2003.
The Conflict Prevention Network. *The Impact of Conflict Prevention*. Baden-Baden: Nomos Verlagsgesellschaft, 1999/2000.

References

A/47/277-S/2411. An Agenda for Peace. Preventive Diplomacy, Peacemaking and Peace-Keeping. Report of the Secretary-General. New York City: United Nations, 1992.
A/55/305-S/2000/809. Report of the Panel on United Nations Peace Operations. New York City: United Nations, 2000.
A/59/565. A More Secure World: Our Shared Responsibility. Report of the High-Level Panel on Threats, Challenges and Change. New York City: United Nations, 2004.
S/RES 1572. The Situation in Côte d'Ivoire. New York City: United Nations Security Council, 2004.
S/2004/567. Outline of the Mandate for the Special Adviser on the Prevention of Genocide. New York City: United Nations Security Council, 2004.
A/RES/60/1. The World Summit Outcome Document. New York City: United Nations, 2005.
S/RES 1643. The Situation in Côte d'Ivoire. New York City: United Nations Security Council, 2005.
S/2006/204. Update Report of the Group of Experts Submitted Pursuant to Paragraph 2 of Security Council Resolution 1632(2005) Concerning Côte d'Ivoire. New York City: United Nations Security Council, 2005.
Abdi, D. Ibrahim. *Working for Peace in Conflict Systems in Kenya: Addressing the Post-Election Crisis 2008*. Berghof Research Center for Constructive Conflict Management, 2008.

Albright, M. and Cohen, W. *Preventing Genocide: A Blueprint for US Policy Makers*. Washington, DC: The American Holocaust Museum, The American Academy of Diplomacy, United States Institute for Peace, 2008.

Barnes, C. *Agents for Change: Civil Society Roles in Preventing War and Building Peace*. The Hague: Global Partnership for the Prevention of Armed Conflict, 2006.

Bellamy, A. J. 'Conflict Prevention and the Responsibility to Protect'. *Global Governance: A Review of Multilateralism and International Organizations* 14.2(2008): 135–156.

Bellamy, A. J. and Drummond, C. 'The Responsibility to Protect in Southeast Asia: Between Non-interference and Sovereignty as Responsibility'. *The Pacific Review* 24.2(2011): 179–200.

Biersteker, T. J., Eckert, S. E. and Romaniuk, P. *Targeted Financial Sanctions: A Manual for Design and Implementation*. Providence, RI: Watson Institute for International Studies, 2001.

Brzoska, M. (ed.) *Smart Sanctions: The Next Step*. Baden-Baden: Nomos Verlagsgesellschaft, 2001.

Carment, D. 'Nato and the International Politics of Ethnic Conflict: Perspectives on Theory and Policy'. *Contemporary Security Policy* 16.3(1995): 347–359.

Carment, D. and Fischer, F. 'R2P and the Role of Regional Organisations in Ethnic Conflict Management, Prevention and Resolution: The Unfinished Agenda'. *Global R2P* 1.3(2009): 261–290.

Cilliers, J. and Sturman, K. 'Challenges Facing the AU's Peace and Security Council'. *African Security Review* 13.1(2004): 97–104.

Cortright, D. and Lopez, G. A. *The Sanctions Decade: Assessing UN Strategies in the 1990s*. Boulder: Lynne Rienner Publishers, 2000.

Dagne, T. *Kenya: The December 2007 Elections and the Challenges Ahead*. Washington, DC: Congressional Research Service, 2008.

Dorn, W. 'Early and Late Warning by the UN Secretary-General of Threats to the Peace: Article 99 Revisited', in A. Schnabel and D. Carmen (eds) *Conflict Prevention, from Rhetoric to Reality: Opportunities and Innovations*. Lanham: Lexington Press, 2004: 305–344.

Eriksson, M. *Operational Conflict Prevention and the Use of Targeted Sanctions: Conditions for Effective Implementation by the EU and UN*. New York City: Center for International Cooperation, 2008.

Escribà-Folch, A. 'Economic Sanctions and the Duration of Civil Conflicts'. *Journal of Peace Research*, 47.2(2010): 129–141.

Fisher, S. and Zimina, L. 'Just Wasting Our Time? Provocative Thoughts for Peacebuilders', in B. Schmelzle and M. Fischer (eds) *Peacebuilding at a Crossroads*, Berghof Handbook Dialogue Series, no. 7. Berlin: Berghof Research Center, 2009: 11–35.

International Commission on Intervention and State Sovereignty. *The Responsibility to Protect*. Ottawa: International Development Research Centre, 2001.

Ivanov, A. and Nyheim, D. 'Generating the Means to an End: Political Will and Integrated Responses to Early Warning', in A. Schnabel and D. Carmen (eds) *Conflict Prevention, from Rhetoric to Reality: Opportunities and Innovations*. Lanham: Lexington Press, 2004: 163–176.

Jentleson, B. *Opportunities Missed, Opportunities Seized: Preventive Diplomacy in the Post-Cold War World*. Lanham: Rowman & Littlefield, 1999.

Jentleson, B. 'The Realism of Preventive Statecraft', in D. Carment and A. Schnabel (eds) *Conflict Prevention: Path to Peace or Grand Illusion?* Tokyo: United Nations University Press, 2003: 26–46.

Kwaja, C. 'Do the People Have Faith in Electoral Democracy? Lessons from Kenyan 2007 Presidential Elections'. *African Journal of Political Science and International Relations* 3.2(2009): 38–45.

Lund, M. *Preventing Violent Conflicts: A Strategy for Preventive Diplomacy*. Washington, DC: US Institute of Peace Press, 1996a.

Lund, M. 'Early Warning and Preventive Diplomacy', in C. A. Crocker, F. O. Hampson and P. Aal (eds) *Managing Global Chaos*. Washington, DC: US Institute of Peace Press, 1996b: 379–402.

Lund, M. 'Improving Conflict Prevention by Learning from Experience: Context, Issues, Approaches and Findings'. Conflict Prevention Network Annual Conference, 1999. First draft available at: http://pdf.usaid.gov/pdf_docs/Pnacl861.pdf (Accessed 3 September 2015).

Lund, M. 'Creeping Institutionalization of the Culture of Prevention?' *Preventing Violent Conflict. The Search for Political Will, Strategies and Effective Tools*. Report of the Krusenberg Seminar. Ed. Stockholm International Peace Research Institute (SIPRI). Stockholm, 2000.

Lund, M. 'Greed and Grievance Diverted: Why Macedonia Has Avoided Inter-Ethnic Civil War', in P. Collier and N. Sambanis (eds) *Understanding Civil War*. Washington, DC: World Bank, 2005.

Nicolaïdis, K. 'International Preventive Action: Developing a Strategic Framework', in R. I. Rotberg (ed.) *Vigilance and Vengeance*. Washington, DC: Brookings Institution Press, 1996: 23–69.

Nicoll, A. and Delaney, J. *Violence in Kenya. Continuing Crisis.* International Institute for Strategic Studies, 2008.

Nyheim, D. 'Can Violence, War and State Collapse Be Prevented? The Future of Operational Conflict Early Warning and Response Systems'. Joint Room Document 1 of the DAC Network on Conflict, Peace and Development Cooperation (CPDC) & the DAC Fragile States Group, 2008.

Ouellette, A. 'Conflict Prevention and Financial Capacity Building', in A. Schnabel and D. Carment (eds) *Conflict Prevention from Rhetoric to Reality: Opportunities and Innovations.* Lexington: Lexington Books, 2004: 341–358.

Romero, R. G., Kimenyi, M. S. and Dercon, S. 'The 2007 Elections, Post-Conflict Recovery and Coalition Government in Kenya'. IIG Briefing Paper 1. Improving Institutions for Pro-Poor Growth, Oxford University, 2008.

Schnabel, A. and Carment, D. *Conflict Prevention from Rhetoric to Reality.* 2 vols. Lanham: Lexington Books, 2004.

Suhrke, A. and Adelman, H. *The International Response to Conflict and Genocide: Lessons from the Rwanda Experience.* Copenhagen, Denmark: Joint Evaluation of Emergency Assistance to Rwanda, 1996.

Tamm, I. J. *Diamonds in Peace and War: Severing the Conflict–Diamond Connection.* Cambridge: Carr Center for Human Rights, 2002.

UN Security Council, Security Council Resolution 1973 (2011) on the Situation in the Libyan Arab Jamahiriya, 17 March 2011. Available at: http://www.refworld.org/docid/4d885fc42.html (Accessed 18 September 2015).

Wallensteen, P., Erikson, M. and Strandow, D. *Sanctions for Conflict Prevention and Peace Building. Lessons Learned from Côte d'Ivoire and Liberia.* Uppsala: Uppsala University. Department of Peace and Conflict Research, 2006.

Wolter, D. 'UN: Effective Partnership between the UN, Member States and Civil Society to Promote Human Security', in P. van Tongeren and C. van Empel (eds) *Joint Action for Prevention. Civil Society and Government Cooperation on Conflict Prevention and Peacebuilding.* The Hague: Global Partnership for the Prevention of Armed Conflict, 2007: 74–77.

Woocher, L. 'Deconstructing Political Will: Explaining the Failure to Prevent Deadly Conflict and Mass Atrocities'. *Journal of Public and International Affairs* 12(2001): 179–206.

Wulf, H. (ed.) *Still under Construction. Regional Organisations' Capacities for Conflict Prevention.* Duisburg: Institute for Development and Peace, 2009.

15

MANAGING AND SETTLING ETHNIC CONFLICT

Asaf Siniver

Introduction

The management of ethnic conflict, either by local elites or external actors such as individual states and international organizations, rarely results in the resolution of the conflict or the dissipation of rival ethnic claims and grievances. Conflicts characterised by ethnic and cultural rivalries are the most common type of conflict, most notably in Africa, Asia, the Middle East and Europe (Bercovitch and Fretter 2004: 46; Wallensteen and Sollenberg 1999). Importantly, the significance of a group's ethno-cultural identity cannot be dismissed as a guise to power-seeking. Depending on their historical and geographical experiences, ethnic groups are highly diverse in their aspirations and claims. Minority groups within existing political communities may seek access to power and equal rights (for example, Israeli Arabs), indigenous groups such as the Mayans and the Chiapas may resist attempts by the state to assimilate them, whereas the Basque people can be described as ethnonationals who strive for self-determination and even independence (Gurr 2000). Most contemporary conflicts need external assistance in order to be brought under control, and accordingly such strategies of conflict management may involve diplomacy (for example negotiation and mediation), legal methods (arbitration, adjudication) and even the use of military force. However due to the intricate nature of some ethnically generated conflicts, we may at best hope to manage, or regulate them, rather than resolve them. Accordingly conflict management can be defined as the limitation, mitigation and containment of conflict without necessarily solving it. Importantly, conflict management is distinct from conflict resolution, where the emphasis is placed on resolving the underlying incompatibilities which have caused the conflict, rather than simply containing them. Conflict management and resolution are separate but related mechanisms which need to be used at different stages in the 'conflict cycle'; managing a conflict may take a long time and must foster conditions which are amenable to the successful resolution of the conflict (Tanner 2000).

The choice of strategies depends on the nature of the conflict and the identity of the warring parties, as well as the identity of any third party and its available resources and nature linkage to the conflict. This chapter will examine the efficacy of such strategies employed by third parties in their efforts to manage and settle ethnically generated conflicts in recent years. The primary purpose of conflict management is to slow, or stop the escalation of violence and to create conditions which are conducive to peaceful reconciliation between the warring parties. Accordingly conflict management is understood as a dynamic social process, in which external and internal actors employ an array of strategies to reduce the rival parties' economic, political and humanitarian costs and enhance their mutual benefits through cooperation and compromise.

There is much debate however, not only about which strategies work best and under what conditions, but whether intervention by third parties is desirable in the first place. Attempts by external actors to settle violent ethnic conflicts, some of which are fuelled by 'ancient hatreds', may sometimes compound, rather than solve the problem, given their priorities and objectives may not necessarily be compatible with those of the warring parties (Lake and Rothchild 1996). In broad terms there are three schools in the study of the causes of conflict and in turn the desirable role that third parties should play in managing it: realist approaches which emphasise the security of the state; liberal, governance-based approaches which focus on the role of third parties in shaping and developing linkages between state and society; and social-psychological approaches which are concerned with societal or human security (Hampson 2001: 388). Importantly, these approaches are not necessarily mutually exclusive, but rather offer complementary elements which together may offer the best route to the understanding and successful managing of ethnic conflicts.

Realist approaches

While all realist interpretations of the causes of ethnic conflict and the role of third parties in managing it are rooted in similar assumptions about state-centrism and the rationality of the actors involved, they offer different emphases on power sharing and the use of force as means to an end. For 'hard' realists, the dynamics of ethnic conflicts are rather similar to the processes which shape interstate rivalries, that is to say that they are motivated by, and act in accordance with the security dilemma (Collins 2007). Accordingly the need to maintain a balance of military power between the warring parties is imperative – rather by supporting the weaker side with arms or withholding resources from the stronger side. In extreme cases, direct intervention on behalf of a third party is necessary to maintain such balance in military power (Betts 1994; Van Evra 1994). Military intervention may be carried by a single state (the United Kingdom in Sierra Leone in 2000) or be a multilateral effort of international organisations (the United Nations in Mozambique in 1992–4), and regional organisations (NATO in the Balkans in the 1990s). Whether these strategies involve military aid to one party and sanctions on the other, or coercive military intervention for the purpose of ending the fighting, the emphasis here is often placed on creating new geopolitical boundaries, most notably through partition, rather than seeking political accommodation or reconciliation (Kaufmann 1996, 2007). However this approach to the settlement of ethnic conflict is often criticised for assuming that just and mutually acceptable territorial partition is a readily available solution to ethnic rivalries. Examples from Israel/Palestine, Cyprus, Kosovo, and most recently Iraq, suggest that in some cases the competition over territory is a zero-sum game and where alternative forms of intervention may be necessary (Downes 2006; Pischedda 2008). Accordingly 'softer' approaches of realism to ethnic conflict management advocate the use of non-coercive forms of third party intervention such as mediation, the provision of good offices and other confidence-building measures (Bercovitch 2002; Princen 1992; Zartman and Touval 1996). Moreover, these activities are not limited to the great powers, but are being taken by a wide range of states and international organisations, though with various degrees of success in managing such conflicts (Siniver 2006; Touval 1994; Zartman 1995). Nevertheless, mediation by third parties with different resources and strategies creates opportunities for non-territorial solutions such as power-sharing, political accommodation and other socio-political mobilisation mechanisms to drive the parties towards the settlement of the conflict. While these strategies offer an attractive, non-coercive alternative to direct military inter-vention by third parties, they can only be effective as long as the rival ethnic groups accept the identity of the mediator and indeed the strategies employed. Thus even when mediation is undertaken by great powers, the ultimate power in the mediation process lies with the disputing parties. Furthermore, these attempts by third parties must take place under the most propitious circumstances of timing, or 'ripeness' of conflict to optimise the likelihood of success (Zartman 1985).

Liberal approaches

Governance-based approaches to conflict management have their roots in the Kantian notions of liberalism and just governance. Thus while variants of realism emphasise the use of force and balancing strategic security dilemmas as keys to manage conflicts, liberal approaches stress the importance of creating democratic institutions and mechanisms of governance. Here causes of ethnic conflict are understood as the lack of the authority and legitimacy of plur-alistic structures, violations of human rights and the breakdown of the rule of law. In addition to the reconstruction of political and security institutions, other reforms may include the establishment of truth and reconciliation tribunals in order to restore faith in the judicial process and to install a new cooperative and peaceful environment, as has been demonstrated in South Africa, East Timor, Haiti, and El Salvador (Hayner 2006; Kingston 2006; Mani 2005). Thus in order to achieve these objectives, third parties must engage not only at the state level with local governments, but perhaps more importantly with grass-roots actors, civil society leaders and the private sector. Like softer versions of realism, here too the role of third party may be assumed not only by the great powers, but by inter-governmental and non-governmental organisations. These organisations have the advantage of apparent neutrality and the emphasis on alleviating the humanitarian suffering, however they may lack the clout and resources which are often accompanied by the great power intervention. Particularly with reference to the working of the United Nations in this field, the need to achieve first a wide consensus about the objectives and the contours of the settlement may hinder the effectiveness of the operation (Annan 2005). Still, this approach has a strong normative component in that the intervening outside party must stand by those in the conflict who are committed to the liberal-democratic way. This raises obvious problems of neutrality for the mediator and indeed may damage the effectiveness of the entire approach on grounds of hypocrisy and bias. This has been demonstrated recently in the American and European support for the moderate and secular Fatah government in the West Bank, compared to the isolation and sanctioning of the militant Hamas government in Gaza. The most acute result of this policy has been the worsening of the humanitarian situation of Palestinian civilians in the Gaza Strip (Pace 2009). Indeed this normative crusade in the name of liberal-democracy has been criticised repeatedly for not only failing to appreciate the difficulties in introducing democratic practices in unstable and torn societies with no democratic experience but also for emphasising procedural and institutional priorities while neglecting the importance of an engaged and informed civil society. In extreme cases this may lead to a return to violence and political instability (Mansfield and Snyder 1995; Tocci 2007). Finally, while the advance of various confidence-building measures, such as elections and power-sharing, are important techniques to reduce violence and increase cooperation, they cannot alter the basic fears and perceptions which are embedded in individuals and ethnic groups.

Social-psychological approaches

The important contribution of social-psychological approaches to the study and practice of ethnic conflict management is the added dimension of image formation of the other. In other words, here the key to understanding the root causes of ethnic conflicts is not in the security dilemma or the breakdown of state authority, but rather in the development and reinforcement of 'enemy images', or the 'us versus them' mentality (Stein 2005). These images and identities are formed by individuals and groups, political elites and the general public, and they relate to either tangible experience or certain beliefs about the behaviour of the other group. This basic need to establish individual and societal identity is most commonly achieved by differentiating 'us' from 'them'. Obviously, identity differentiation does not necessarily and invariably lead to violent conflict. The critical components which combine with these social images to cause violence are mostly environmental, namely the domestic and international conditions which may help to facilitate the formation of enemy images (Coleman and Lowe 2007; Lake and Rothchild 1996; Ross 1995). Accordingly any efforts by third parties to successfully manage the conflict must first address the embedded anxieties and identities which inform the rival groups' images of each other. Strategies designed to change these entrenched identities may range from reconciliation processes to special problem-solving workshops, as well as the development of systems which are compatible with the relevant local culture and norms (Kaufman 2006). These efforts are targeted at the local level, rather than the state, and the third party must assume a neutral role with emphasis on communicating and facilitating strategies. Individuals and non-governmental organisations are best suited to perform these activities as they often possess the required sensitivity, local expertise and perceived impartiality which are needed to lead the rival parties out of conflict. Successfully managing ethnic conflicts according to this social-psychological framework seems a particularly difficult task given the kind of knowledge and sensitivity which is required of the third party. Since conflict is caused by deep-rooted stereotypes and ethnocentric views of the other, it does not necessarily follow a rational pattern, and instead must be understood as a subjective and context-dependent social process. Third parties therefore need to engage with a cross-section of society on both sides and help change perceptions and attitudes without imposing new ones in the process. These strategies are best carried out in small informal groups which are composed of middle-range elites, such as academics, retired politicians and officials who can still influence policy but are removed from decision-making (Hampson 2001: 396). Nevertheless, third parties may find it difficult to access the local groups and may be prevented from intervening on the grounds of suspected biased or poor credentials. Moreover, even if these activities prove successful, their impact on society at large is not guaranteed. Unless high-level officials are informed and engaged with the process, these programmes will have limited effect, particularly in areas which are inaccessible or dangerous due to ongoing fighting. Most acutely however, is the question whether these programmes can indeed change for the long run deeply embedded images and attitudes which have been hardened over a long period of time and through personal experience.

Assessing the efficacy of conflict management strategies

As noted above, the first hurdle to successful outside intervention lies in the imperviousness of some conflicts to external efforts to bring an end to violence. This resistance derives most commonly from the parties' perceptions about the characteristics of the conflict and the associated stakes (Stedman 1996). Humanitarian intervention is perhaps the most visible manifestation of operations designed to address these issues. It can be defined as

> the threat or use of force across state borders by a state (or a group of states) aimed at preventing or ending widespread and grave violations of the fundamental human rights of individuals other than its own citizens, without the permission of the state within whose territory force is applied.
>
> *(Holzgrefe 2003: 18)*

However, despite the large number of such missions in recent years, their record of success is mixed. Interventions in Northern Iraq, Somalia, Bosnia, Rwanda, Kosovo, East Timor and Darfur (to name a few) have failed to produce a definite protocol for such missions. Inevitably, the conduct and efficacy of these activities breaks down to the question of the right of the international community to intervene in intrastate conflicts, followed by questioning the desirable characteristics of such interventions if they are indeed necessary. The principle of state sovereignty is embedded in international law, and calls for external intervention, even on humanitarian grounds, invariably raise important legal and ethical questions. Nevertheless, while non-intervention is still the norm in international relations, the post-Cold War period has witnessed a definite rise in the number and range of third party interventions as the demise of the Soviet Union has removed the strategic constraints which had previously restricted the potential for ethnic clashes. The concern over the increasing failure of governments to protect their people and the rise in conflicting ethno-national claims of neighbouring ethnic groups has led former United Nations Secretary General Boutros Boutros-Ghali to assert that 'the time of absolute and exclusive sovereignty has passed' (1992: 9). Others have similarly supported the need for a more proactive engagement. According to Teson, 'foreign armies are morally entitled to help victims of oppression … provided that the intervention is proportionate to the evil which it is designed to suppress' (1998: 15). In recent years greater emphasis has been placed on defining the appropriate boundaries for interventions. Hoffman, for example, identifies two categories where intervention may be necessary: first, where there is a threat to international peace by 'dangerous' states, as was demonstrated in the cases of Somalia, Haiti, and the plight of the Kurds in northern Iraq. Second, where there are massive violations of human rights, including the forcible expulsion of minorities and ethnic cleansing, such as in cases like Rwanda, Kosovo, and East Timor (Hoffman 1998: 161–164). A recent attempt to establish norms of intervention was manifested in the International Commission on Intervention and State Sovereignty's framework of *The Responsibility to Protect*. This concept is designed to provide a legal and ethical basis for humanitarian interventions, as well as authorise military interventions in cases where the primary objective is to prevent human suffering. Moreover, it is suggested that in order to establish consistency in norms and operations the United Nations must assume a primary role in authorising and coordinating such interventions (MacFarlane, Thielking and Weiss 2004). Despite its many organisational and institutional faults, the United Nations (UN) is the only body in world politics which maintains, albeit not always successfully, the image of communal values and shared responsibility. Nevertheless, there are still some who object to the legitimisation of humanitarian interventions for several reasons. As noted above, realists argue against humanitarian interventions as they not only challenge the principle of state sovereignty, but they enhance the national interest, and in some cases can even damage the state's reputation abroad (as in the case of American intervention in Somalia in the early 1990s). Moreover, they argue that states have no moral duty to intervene on behalf of the citizens or ethnic groups in other states, and that inevitably states will apply selective measures in their choices of intervention, which will lead to accusations of hypocrisy and double-standards. This was evident when Western states failed to respond quickly and effectively to the genocide in Rwanda, or to the plight of Bosnian Muslims. Finally, pluralists point to the problem of forming an international consensus on what principles should guide these interventions. Described as *rule consequentionalism*, opponents of humanitarian intervention argue that international peace and order are better served by upholding the principle of non-intervention than by authorising humanitarian interventions in the absence of a consensus about the relevant criteria for intervention. Inevitably, these decisions are made by those who possess the power and the will to carry out these missions (Welsh 2006: 52–68). This brings us back to the importance of multilateral missions, ideally led by the UN. Even though individual states are likely to respond more quickly and decisively to an emerging humanitarian crisis, the more an intervention is removed from the narrow interests of the big powers or neighbour states the more likely it is to be perceived as just and appropriate. This last point is often measured by the proportionality of the mission to the danger it posed in the first place. Proportionality here means that human suffering must be met with humanitarian response that is not to do more harm to human rights than the harm the intervention is aimed to prevent. However assessing the proportionality of the response is a difficult task, as it does not entail ameliorating the level of violence displayed by the warring parties, but rather providing a morally appropriate response. This is problematic since two similar cases of human rights abuse may necessitate different 'proportional' responses, depending on the relevant sociopolitical and cultural contexts. Similarly the task of assessing the success of humanitarian intervention is a difficult one. When evaluating success we must first ask 'success for whom?' There are various parties involved in such operations, each with different sets of objectives and desirable outcomes depending on how they view the conflict. Thus for example the UN (or 'the international community') may seek long-lasting peace and order, whereas the rival groups may be less preoccupied with respecting human rights and more with regaining territory; the primary goal of the civilians caught in the middle may be to return to their homes, whereas the third parties who intervene in the conflict may be more concerned about the safety of their personnel. In some cases success for one party to the conflict may come at a loss for another. Accordingly the US mission in Somalia had successfully limited its engagement after the initial setback, but this came at the expense of order and protection for the local population. Moreover, in assessing the success of interventions it is useful to distinguish between the short- and long-term outcomes of the mission; indeed the outcomes of such operations are as significant as the motivations to engage in the first place. Thus while in the short term the immediate suffering of civilians or the fighting between rival groups may be ended successfully, the long-term and underlying causes of mutual fears and dilemmas must also be addressed. External actors must not withdraw quickly once the alleviation of human rights abuse has been achieved. To prevent the resumption of violent ethnic conflict, there must be a long-term commitment to addressing the underlying causes of the conflict through a combination of political, social and economic reforms (Walzer 1995). These two different interpretations of success have their respective benefits, but inevitably they are at tension with each other and implicate different forms of intervention. Broadly, interventions of limited objectives and short duration have a stronger military component, whereas non-armed humanitarian interventions are more likely to engage with long-term objectives in order to address the underlying causes of conflict. Notwithstanding the evident differences between cases of humanitarian intervention, some generic criteria for success are applicable to all cases of intervention. We may identify three criteria for determining success, namely the fulfilment of the missions' mandate as specified by the Security Council resolution; the resolution of the underlying disputes of the conflict; and the contribution to the maintenance of international peace and security. It is important to note, however, that often UN mandates are the result of political bargaining between different actors, the result of which may be overly vague or flexible, which makes the fulfilment of the conditions set in the mandate an unattainable task. Other criteria of success, such as the abatement of conflict or at very least the discouragement of violence, invariably need to be judged based on their longevity, which opens up the question of how long a time frame should be considered in assessing the outcome (Bratt 1996; Diehl 2008: 118–123).

In addition to humanitarian and military interventions, third parties often assume the role of mediators in their efforts to manage violent ethnic conflicts. While mediation is often over-looked as an integral mechanism of conflict management, compared to the high profile of peacekeeping missions, it has in fact proved to be the most popular form of contemporary conflict management. It was present in nearly 60 per cent of international and intrastate disputes between 1945 and 2003 (Bercovitch and Fretter 2004: 29), while nearly half of all post-Cold War crises were mediated by third parties (Beardsley et al. 2006: 59). While definitions of and approaches to mediation vary, it is commonly understood as the intervention of a third party in the dispute of two or more parties, for the purpose of improving the nature of interaction between the disputants (Kressel and Pruitt 1989). Importantly, it is distinct from other forms of intervention by its voluntary, non-forceful and non-coercive nature. Nevertheless, third parties can exercise a significant amount of leverage on the parties in order to draw them closer to reconciliation. Zartman and Touval (1996) suggest that mediators may call upon up to five sources of leverage. The first, *persuasion*, is the ability to depict a more favourable alternative to the present conflict. The second, *extraction*, is the ability to produce a favourable position from each party. The third, *termination*, is the ability to withdraw – or threaten to withdraw – from the mediation process. The fourth, *deprivation*, is the ability to deprive one or both disputants of resources. The final source, *gratification*, is the ability to reward the parties for 'good' behaviour. Rather than describing the full range of mediator activities, these particular sources of leverage seem consistent with a select mediation strategy, one that is based upon tactics of manipulation (as opposed to pure communication or formulation), where mediation is viewed as a process of 'three-cornered bargaining' (Touval 1982: 16) in which the mediator has a clearly defined stake. This is not to suggest, however, that third parties who do not possess the necessary resources to conduct such bargaining are powerless and hence less effective as mediators. Here mediators are depicted as rational third parties who offer their services to disputants upon the basis of self-interest and shrewd cost-benefit calculations (Zartman and Touval 1996: 446). While it is especially apparent in the conduct of individual states (great and small), these rational calculations can also be found in the motivations of international organisations and other non-state actors, who maintain certain norms that they wish to uphold beyond the principle of peaceful settlement (Zartman and Touval 1996: 452). Indeed mediation is particularly important to the United Nations' and non-governmental organisations' conflict management. Compared to military and humanitarian interventions it is a cost-effective and flexible strategy which can successfully support other mechanisms of conflict management and resolution. However, here too assessing success is not an easy task. It is possible to identify two broad contending conceptualisations of mediation success. The first approach offers seemingly objective criteria which assess the ultimate consequences of the mediation effort. These criteria are often defined broadly to compensate for the idiosyncratic nature of different conflicts, and accordingly link success with objective and observable signposts, such as cease-fire, peace treaty or other tangible political settlements, as well as the opening of a dialogue and a marked reduction in the level of violence (Kriesberg 1991; Touval 1982). This measurement of success is problematic as it fails to account for the effectiveness of mediation. The 1993 Oslo Accords between Israelis and Palestinians is one example of an objective mediation success (a binding political agreement), although it cannot be said to have been effective in ending the bloody conflict between two peoples. The second measurement of mediation success attempts to bridge this gap between results and perceptions. While the first approach eschews any discussion of the subjective interpretations of the disputants or the mediator to the bargaining process, this approach explains mediation success by focusing on the process of communication as a means of changing attitudes, largely outside the structures of formal negotiation. Successful mediation is defined here in terms of the (subjective) perceptions of the disputants and the mediator regarding their respective efforts to accomplish their aims as they were outlined at the initiation of the process (Hopmann 1995; Smith 1985).

Conclusion

Despite the real differences between the various strategies of conflict management, evidence suggests that best practice would entail both military and diplomatic components. Third party mediation is more effective when it is backed by actors who possess the will and the power to change the status quo, and conversely military intervention alone is less likely to produce a long-lasting settlement without a viable political process (this partly explains the failure of US and UN missions in Somalia and Haiti). Moreover, in their actions third parties must possess staying power and remain fully engaged during negotiations and military operations. History suggests that most modern conflicts do not resolve themselves, and that some type of external intervention is necessary to bring them under control. While the ultimate responsibility to change modes of behaviour and to reform systems of governance lies with the parties themselves, it is clear that without armed and non-armed interventions by individual states and international organisations many more ethnic conflicts would spiral out of control and bring more human suffering.

Further reading

Byman, D. 2002. *Keeping the Peace: Lasting Solutions to Ethnic Conflicts*. Baltimore: Johns Hopkins University Press.
Crocker, C. A., Hampson, F. O. and Aall, P. (eds) 2001. *Turbulent Peace: The Challenges of Managing International Conflict*. Washington, DC: United States Institute of Peace.
Crocker, C. A., Hampson, F. O. and Aall, P. (eds) 2001. *Leashing the Dogs of War: Conflict Management in a Divided World*. Washington, DC: United States Institute of Peace.
Lake, D. A. and Rothchild, D. 1996. 'Containing Fear: The Origins and Management of Ethnic Conflict', *International Security*, 21(2): 41–75.
Schneckener, U. and Wolff, S. (eds) 2004. *Managing and Settling Ethnic Conflicts: Perspectives on Successes and Failures in Europe, Africa, and Asia*. Basingstoke: Palgrave.

References

Annan, K. 2005. *In Larger Freedom: Towards Development, Security and Human Rights for All: Report of the Secretary General*. New York: United Nations.
Beardsley, K., Quinn, D., Biswas, B. and Wilkenfeld, J. 2006. 'Mediation Style and Crisis Outcomes', *Journal of Conflict Resolution*, 50(1): 58–86.
Bercovitch, J. (ed.) 2002. *Studies in International Mediation*. London: Palgrave Macmillan.

Bercovitch, J. and Fretter, J. 2004. *Regional Guide to International Conflict and Management from 1945 to 2003*. Washington, DC: CQ Press.

Betts, R. 1994. 'The Delusion of Imperial Intervention', *Foreign Affairs*, 73(6): 20–33.

Boutros-Ghali, B. 1992. *An Agenda for Peace*. New York: United Nations.

Bratt, D. 1996. 'Assessing the Success of UN Peacekeeping Operations', *International Peacekeeping*, 3(4): 64–81.

Coleman, P. and Lowe, J. 2007. 'Conflict, Identity, and Resilience: Negotiating Collective Identities within the Israeli and Palestinian Diasporas', *Conflict Resolution Quarterly*, 24(4): 377–412.

Collins, A. 2007. 'Comparing and Contrasting Realist and Constructivist Interpretations of the Ethnic Security Dilemma'. Paper presented at the 48[th]Annual Convention of the International Studies Association, Chicago.

Diehl, P. 2008. *Peace Operations*. Cambridge: Polity.

Downes, A. 2006. 'More Borders, Less Conflict? Partition as a Solution to Ethnic Civil Wars', *SAIS Review*, 26(1): 49–61.

Gurr, T. R. 2000. *Peoples versus States: Minorities at Risk in the New Century*. Washington, DC: United States Institute of Peace.

Hampson, F. O. 2001. 'Parent, Midwife, or Accidental Executioner? The Role of Third Parties in Ending Violent Conflict', in C. A. Crocker, F. O. Hampson and P. Aall (eds), *Turbulent Peace: The Challenges of Managing International Conflict*. Washington, DC: United States Institute of Peace, 387–406.

Hayner, P. 2006. 'Truth Commissions: A Schematic Overview', *International Review of the Red Cross*, 862: 295–310.

Hoffman, S. 1998. *World Disorders: Troubled Peace in the Post-Cold War Era*. Lanham, MD: Rowman and Littlefield.

Holzgrefe, J. L. 2003. 'The Humanitarian Intervention Debate', in J. L. Holzgrefe and R. O. Keohane (eds), *Humanitarian Intervention: Ethical, Legal, and Political Dilemmas*. Cambridge: Cambridge University Press.

Hopmann, P. T. 1995. 'Two Paradigms of Negotiation: Bargaining and Problem Solving', *Annals of the American Academy of Political and Social Science*, 542: 24–47.

Kaufman, S. 2006. 'Escaping the Symbolic Politics Trap: Reconciliation Initiatives and Conflict Resolution in Ethnic Wars', *Journal of Peace Research*, 43(2): 201–218.

Kaufmann, C. 1996. 'Intervention in Ethnic and Ideological Civil Wars: Why One Can be Done and the Other Can't', *International Security*, 6(1): 62–101.

Kaufmann, C. 2007. 'What Have We Learnt About Ethnic Conflict? What Can We Do in Iraq?', *Harvard International Review*, 28(4): 44–50.

Kingston, J. 2006. 'Balancing Justice and Reconciliation in East Timor', *Critical Asian Studies*, 38(3): 271–302.

Kressel, K. and Pruitt, D. 1989. *Mediation Research*. San Francisco: Jossey-Bass.

Kriesberg, L. 1991. 'Formal and Quasi-Mediators in International Disputes: An Explanatory Analysis', *Journal of Peace Research*, 28(1): 19–27.

Lake, D. and Rothchild, D. 1996. 'Containing Fear: The Origins and Management of Ethnic Conflict', *International Security*, 21(2): 41–75.

MacFarlane, N., Thielking, C. and Weiss, T. 2004. 'The Responsibility to Protect: Is Anyone Interested in Humanitarian Intervention?', *Third World Quarterly*, 25(5): 977–992.

Mani, R. 2005. 'Balancing Peace with Justice in the Aftermath of Violent Conflict', *Development*, 48(3): 25–34.

Mansfield, E. and Snyder, J. 1995. 'Democratization and the Danger of War', *International Security*, 20(1): 5–38.

Pace, M. 2009. 'Paradoxes and Contradictions in EU Democracy Promotion in the Mediterranean: The Limits on EU Normative Power', *Democratization*, 16(1): 39–58.

Pischedda, C. 2008. 'Partition as a Solution to Ethnic Conflict', *The International Spectator*, 43(4): 103–122.

Princen, T. 1992. *Intermediaries in International Conflict*. Princeton, NJ: Princeton University Press.

Ross, M. 1995. 'Psychocultural Interpretation Theory and Peacemaking in Ethnic Conflicts', *Political Psychology*, 16(3): 523–544.

Siniver, A. 2006. 'Power, Impartiality and Timing: Three Hypotheses on Third Party Mediation in the Middle East', *Political Studies*, 54(4): 806–826.

Smith, W. P. 1985. 'Effectiveness of the Biased Mediator', *Negotiation Journal*, 1(4): 363–372.

Stedman, S. 1996. 'Negotiation and Mediation in Internal Conflict', in M. Brown (ed.), *The International Dimensions of Internal Conflict*. Cambridge, MA: MIT Press, 341–376.

Stein, J. G. 2005. 'Image, Identity, and the Resolution of Violent Conflict', in M. Evangelista (ed.), *Peace Studies: Critical Concepts in Political Science*. New York: Taylor and Francis, 364–389.

Tanner, F. 2000. 'Conflict Prevention and Conflict Resolution: Limits of Multilateralism', *International Review of the Red Cross*, no. 839: 541–558.

Teson, F. 1998. *Humanitarian Intervention: An Inquiry into Law and Morality*. New York: Transnational Publishers.

Tocci, N. 2007. *The EU and Conflict Resolution: Promoting Peace in the Backyard*. London: Routledge.

Touval, S. 1982. *The Peace Brokers: Mediators in the Arab–Israeli Conflict, 1948–1979*. Princeton, NJ: Princeton University Press.

Touval, S. 1994. 'Why the UN Fails', *Foreign Affairs*, 73(5): 44–57.

Van Evra, S. 1994. 'Hypotheses on Nationalism and War', *International Security*, 18(4): 5–39.

Wallensteen, P. and Sollenberg, M. 1999. 'Armed Conflict, 1989–1998', *Journal of Peace Research*, 36(5): 593–598.

Walzer, M. 1995. 'The Politics of Rescue', *Social Research*, 62(1): 53–66.

Welsh, J. 2006. *Humanitarian Intervention and International Relations*. London: Oxford University Press.

Zartman, I. W. 1985. *Ripe for Resolution: Conflict and Intervention in Africa*. New York: Oxford University Press.

Zartman, I. W. 1995. *Elusive Peace: Negotiating an End to Civil Wars*. Washington, DC: Brookings Institution.

Zartman, I. W. and Touval, S. 1996. 'International Mediation in the Post-Cold War Era', in C. A. Crocker, F. O. Hampson and P. Aall (eds), *Managing Global Chaos: Sources of and Responses to International Conflict*. Washington, DC: United States Institute of Peace, 445–461.

16
MULTILATERAL FRAMEWORKS FOR CONFLICT RESOLUTION

Eva Sobotka

Introduction

In examining conflict resolution and peacekeeping efforts since the Cold War, this chapter focuses on the evolution of approaches in multilateral conflict resolution, set in the current era of security challenges and changes. The first section of this chapter outlines a) developments in conflict resolution from peacekeeping to the emergence of multilateral conflict resolution frameworks in the United Nations (UN) context, including the post 2009 UN New Horizon Strategy[1] era and the greater involvement of the European Union; b) broader multilateral collective endeavours in conflict management that include the participation of civil society groups such as non-governmental organisations (NGOs), professional bodies, private companies and task-specific international agencies. It also examines the role of regional organisations, individual states and international organisations working in dedicated coalitions that deal with non-traditional as well as traditional conflicts. In examining multilateral approaches concerning conflict resolution that have been applied in El Salvador and Mozambique, it illustrates early peacekeeping, peace making and conflict prevention/resolution approaches. The second section of the chapter analyses the multidimensional character of conflict resolution, the functions of various actors and their potential impact on conflict resolution within multilateral frameworks. This section also discusses examples of conflicts where new approaches to conflict resolution have been implemented, including the role of regional organisations, such as the Organization for Security and Co-operation in Europe (OSCE), the African Union (AU) and the European Union (EU). Lastly, acknowledging critiques made following the high-profile failures in peacekeeping in Somalia, Rwanda and Bosnia and Herzegovina, which caused member states to place stringent conditions upon UN operations, the chapter takes a close look at reform efforts to close a gap between expectations and availability of resources in conflict resolution in a political context of new threats, actors and forms of conflict.

The evolution of conflict resolution frameworks

Following the end of the Cold War, fundamental changes in the nature of the international system have ushered in new thinking with respect to approaches to conflict resolution and existing institutions adapting their missions, doctrines and expanding their membership (Heinbecker and Goff 2005; Saunders 1999: 7; Talbott 2008: 15). One cause of the change was identified as being the strengthening of the internationalisation of international relations and the recognition of a duty on the part of the international community to maintain international peace and thus secure the elementary security of individuals in a post Cold War world increasingly fraught with ethnic and nationalist conflict (Bigo 2003: 185). Initially, the late 1980s and 1990s marked a new era of the United Nations as the global mechanism through which conflict could be monitored, managed and resolved. The number of increasingly internal, violent conflicts around the world soared, in which the majority of victims were civilian and where identity conflicts and poverty became common (Fleitz 2002: 16; Gurr 2002). The institution had some notable successes in different parts of the world – Namibia, Mozambique, Cambodia, El Salvador and more recently in East Timor. However, UN collective efforts fell fatally short of effective action in Bosnia and Herzegovina, Somalia, Rwanda and Haiti. In face of the post 2001 'war on terror', and the consequent United States of America (US) decision to attack Iraq and Afghanistan, the conflict resolution agenda was further marginalised. A trend in linkages between local and regional security and national security in different corners of the world, and the prevention and resolution of conflicts became more prominent in international relations. With the 2000 Brahimi report, a series of institutional adjustments were identified as being necessary in order to maximise internal UN support for more effective peacekeeping and peacebuilding. The institution moved towards more collaborative efforts in conflict resolution, combining efforts, actors and approaches (Stedman 2007: 933–44).

The UN is designed to serve as both first and last resort in dealing with threats to peace. Since 1945, peacekeeping has been the method of operation mostly applied by the United Nations in its efforts to resolve conflicts and secure lasting peace. The UN Charter commits states to the maintenance of international peace, justice and human rights, including social progress. These goals are also achieved through assistance in early intervention in conflict. Article 33(1) of the Charter requires that parties to any dispute seek a solution by negotiation, enquiry, mediation, conciliation, arbitration, and resort to regional agencies or apply any other peaceful means of their own choice. The UN Secretary General is mandated by the General Assembly and the Security Council to undertake and maintain efforts including the appointment of special representatives and envoys, good offices, fact-finding missions, and other peaceable means to assist parties in the resolution of disputes prior to their escalation. Preventive diplomacy is intended to be proactive, although traditionally the international community has taken only a reactive stance to conflict.

Since the UN Charter does not provide an explicit definition of peacekeeping, its meaning was established in an *ad hoc* fashion through specific situations and deployments. Chapter VI and Chapter VII of the UN Charter provide a basis for understanding this term: Chapter VI refers to approaches of peaceful settlement while Chapter VII enables the enforcement of decisions, should the Security Council decide to do so. Chapter VII also sanctions the use of armed force if necessary. The decision of the Security Council to intervene is dependent on the agreement of the five permanent members, which is not always guided by the normative criteria of human rights protection or humanitarian need (Weiss 1996: 62). The provisions for regional organisations under Chapter VIII of the UN Charter were intended to provide an option through which the Security Council could mandate action and thus proceed with collective responsibility for peace and security between the UN and the regional organisations. Article 53 of the UN Charter provides for the possibility that disputes are first addressed by regional organisations, as long as the Security Council authorises it. However, the unwillingness of states in the Security Council to support action, whether directly or indirectly through authorisation for regional organisations during the Cold War, has limited the ability of the UN and other actors to undertake collective action. That said, during the initial phases of conflict, the humanitarian agencies of the UN have played more independent roles, working with local and government actors to support initiatives aimed at crisis alleviation, of which assessment missions, diplomatic initiatives, support for civil society initiatives, and emergency aid are just a few examples.

The first ever UN peacekeeping mission was the Emergency Force (UNEF), which was dispatched to the Sinai Peninsula in response to the 1956 Suez crisis. Its role was to observe the ceasefire, and the withdrawal of British, French and Israeli forces. The mission was successful and set a precedent for other UN missions, creating a role for unarmed and neutral forces in keeping sides of the conflict away from each other by creating a buffer zone between them. A set of principles was established to guide future UN missions. Through trial and error during the Cold War, the international community adapted and amended principles of peacekeeping, developed by UNEF into a set of minimum conditions for deployment of UN peacekeeping missions (Allen 1996: 137–141; Hansen, Ramsbotham and Woodhouse 2001: 3). These principles can be summarised as acceptance, impartiality and the minimum use of force. While acceptance means that parties to a dispute consent to the deployment of a peacekeeping force and agree to cooperate with it, impartiality refers to the importance of traditional peacekeeping troops being acceptable to the warring parties and having no stake in their dispute. Peacekeepers are bound to employing only minimum use of force and are permitted to use force only in self defence. In the words of the former UN Secretary General Boutros Boutros-Ghali: 'peacekeeping can rightly be called the invention of the United Nations' (Boutros-Ghali 1992: 14).

During the Cold War, peacekeeping missions were deployed to mediate inter-state con-flicts and their number rose to a total of 14 in the period 1945–1990. In a number of conflict situations, the United Nations created multinational military forces to supervise a truce or administer arrangements that had been established as part of the conflict's resolution. Such peacekeeping forces were an important part of many efforts at conflict resolution, and by the 1990s they had become an accepted resource for conflict management in global affairs. United Nations peacekeeping forces were sent to the Sinai Peninsula following the Suez crisis (1956–67); the Congo (1960–64); West Irian Jaya (1962–63); Cyprus (1964–90s); the Sinai again (1973–79); the Golan Heights in Syria (1974–90s); southern Lebanon (1978–90s); territories in the former Yugoslavia (beginning in 1992); Cambodia (beginning in 1992); Mozambique (beginning in 1992); and Somalia (beginning in 1993). Although traditional peacekeeping missions must be multilateral, they do not have to be conducted by the UN. One of the most successful peacekeeping missions deployed, in the period 1945–90, was the Multinational Force Organisation (MFO), a non-UN multilateral operation in the Sinai Peninsula created to help verify the terms of the 1979 Israel–Egypt Camp David Accords.

The United Nations provided mechanisms for dealing with conflicts, either avoiding war or assisting in bringing it to an end. These mechanisms were less effective, however, with conflicts involving the major powers, who exercise a veto in the Security Council. The United Nations also had only limited jurisdiction to become involved in civil wars and the internal affairs of member states. Nevertheless, within these limits the United Nations per-formed important services in conflict resolution. At the end of the Second World War, there were issues that needed resolutions based on international agreement. Although the United Nations was active in helping to resolve many conflicts, critics noted that its effectiveness was limited by the ability of the superpowers to restrict UN actions (Fleitz 2002). Although the

Table 16.1 Selected traditional peacekeeping missions (1945–90)

Peacekeeping mission	Start/End	Authorised size	Total cost (million $)
UNMOGIP (India/ Pakistan)	1948–	102	163
UNTSO (Palestine)	1948–	572	592
UNEF I (Sinai/Gaza Strip)	1956–67	6,073	214
UNOGIL (Lebanon)	1958	591	4
ONUC (Congo)	1960–64	19,828	400
UNSF (W. New Guinea)	1962–63	1,576	26
UNYOM (Yemen)	1963–64	189	2
UNFICYP (Cyprus)	1964	1,257	980
UNIPOM (India/ Pakistan)	1965–66	96	2
UNEF II (Sinai/Suez)	1973–79	6,973	446
UNDOF (Golan Heights)	1974–	1,454	732
UNIFIL (Lebanon)	1978–	7,000	3,240
UNIMOG (Iran/Iraq)	1988–91	399	190
UNGOMAP (Afghanistan)	1988–90	50	14

Source: United Nations Department of Peacekeeping Operations

International Court of Justice has limited jurisdiction, its rulings and advisory opinions played an important role in resolving some conflicts and further defining the rights and obligations of states under international law.

During the Cold War there was little official interest in employing non-military means such as mediation, 'good offices' or pre-emptive diplomatic engagement to promote negotiated alternatives to violence and political upheaval (Wohlforth 1998: 650–80; Waltz 2000: 5–41). Although nuclear deterrence was underpinned by diplomacy and the credible threat to use force, the dominant powers in a bipolar international system sought to 'manage' their conflicts in order to avoid a loss of face or strategic setbacks and to prevent their conflicts from escalating 'out of control'. Whereas they had little interest in using the tools of negotiation, mediation and preventive statecraft more broadly to promote durable settlements, the East–West conflict found expression in proxy wars – initially in Greece, then in Korea, Vietnam, southern Africa, Central America, Afghanistan and other places – but, with the exception of those in Korea and Vietnam, these wars were generally limited in scale and scope. While lip service was paid to the role of collective security instruments, such as the United Nations, in resolving conflicts, it was clear that the ability to freeze or manage conflicts lay with the powerful states, not with international or regional organisations. The UN's conflict management potential was confined to those cases where there was some measure of East–West tolerance or consensus, and its actions consisted mainly of good offices, electoral support in decolonisation processes, and 'traditional' peacekeeping operations in consensual settings such as Cyprus, Israel/Egypt (the Sinai Desert), or Israel/Syria (the Golan Heights) (Gaddis 1986; Goldgeier and McFaul 1992; Buzan and Waever 2003).

As the Cold War came to an end, the world's attention shifted from tracking superpower rivalry to witnessing the outbreak on nearly every continent of civil wars that habitually spilled over state boundaries to contaminate entire regions. Global security was redefined in local and regional terms, and the tasks undertaken to provide security widened to protecting civilians from massacre by their own governments as well as shoring up weak states threatened by struggles among factional militias.[2] The demand for assistance on the part of the United Nations by the international community increased, aiding in the end of the Iran–Iraq War of the 1980s; mediating conflicts in Cambodia, Angola, and Western Sahara in 1988; assisting in the Soviet withdrawal from Afghanistan in 1989; and monitoring the elections that brought an end to the civil war in Nicaragua in 1990. Formal observer groups were among the most important mechanisms created by the United Nations to help monitor agreements. Major United Nations observation missions played a role in Palestine (1948), India and Pakistan (1949), Lebanon (1958), Yemen (1963), the Dominican Republic (1965), Afghanistan (1988), the Iran–Iraq cease-fire (1988), and Kuwait (1991).

In addition, the United Nations was the organisational framework for two major military mobilisations in response to aggression. This function was limited by Cold War rivalries, which meant that either the US or the Soviet Union could prevent the UN response to North Korean attacks. However, in 1950, when North Korea invaded South Korea, the Soviet Union was temporarily boycotting the United Nations. This enabled the Security Council to pass without veto the appropriate resolutions calling on member states to contribute forces for a UN police action to stop the aggression, with the US providing the major source of military power for the action. The second major United Nations military response was in 1990, when Iraq invaded Kuwait. In the Persian Gulf War of 1990–91, the US again provided the major source of military power, and the United Nations provided the international authority for the multinational response to Iraqi aggression. Such multilateral action had become possible by the end of the Cold War.

Post-Cold War peacekeeping and conflict resolution during the 1990s

When assessing the opportunities for UN-led missions, we must first acknowledge how the world of conflict management has changed since the end of the 1980s and the beginning of the 1990s. As Monty Marshal and Ted Robert Gurr have both noted, international conflict reached its peak during this period, as measured by both the number of international conflicts and the number of fatalities or war-related deaths in those conflicts (Gurr 2002: 41–62; Marshall 2002: 66). At the beginning of 1988, as the Cold War was coming to its end, there were only five operations active in the field: three in the Middle East, a small observer mission in Kashmir and UNFYICYP I in Cyprus. Between 1996 and 1998, 29 operations were created, compared to the establishment of only 13 operations undertaken between 1948 and 1987 and none between 1979 and 1988.

In addition, the increase in operations has brought about a diversification in the nature of such endeavours. In *An Agenda for Peace*, then UN Secretary General, Boutros Boutros-Ghali, recommended strengthening and making more efficient, within the frameworks and provisions, the capacity of the United Nations for *preventive diplomacy*, for peace-making and peacekeeping (Boutros-Ghali 1992: 1). Traditional state-centric approaches to conflict resolution are deemed to be no longer suitable. The function of missions has evolved into a multiplicity of tasks, while the composition of missions has become more diverse. Hence, contemporary practice and theory of peacekeeping has become more *multi-lateral, multi-dimensional, multi-national* and *multi-cultural*. The recognition of long-term approaches, and the centrality of governance, institutional capacity, as well as economic development is not limited to the UN, but is reflected in other types of engagements, such as allied forces' ten year long engagement in Afghanistan.

The second generation of conflict resolution techniques contributed to the notion of human security as opposed to state security. The emergence of the concept of responsibility to protect as focused on human security, a concept that places the individual at the centre, rather than the state, underpins the logic of external intervention aimed at strengthening local capacity in running the economy and institutions, and providing safety for the population. This allowed for the inclusion of non-state actors and attempted to address the root causes of the conflict, focusing on conflict transformation. The complexity of arrangements concerning multilateral peacekeeping today requires the involvement of various levels of actors in an operation: two or more conflicting parties, peacekeepers, the UN, regional and international organisation or institutions, civil society, international financial institutions, corporations and influential private individuals, usually acting under the umbrella of a foundation or peace institute. Similarly, the terms of multilateralism or multiculturalism in conflict resolution require that a peacekeeping force is formed from a diverse range of nations or agencies, each of which will bring its own understanding, resources, and political influence in conflict resolution. As a result of the evolving normative framework, peacebuilding has become increasingly central to international efforts in conflict prevention and post-conflict reconstruction, but also in furthering economic development. In short, multilateral conflict resolution takes place in a dense institutional environment and in an international context that is marked by conceptual synergy and that emphasises coordination and cooperation in peacebuilding. That requires economic and political but also operational engagement on the part of primarily civilian and also in some circumstances military actors.

The first such multidimensional operation, the United Nations Transition Assistance Group (UNTAG) was deployed in Namibia at the end of the Cold War. Although a detailed assessment of the UN's mediated interventions in the 1980s and 1990s is outside the scope of this chapter, and there is an obvious temptation to focus on the UN's negotiation failures, we can point to a few cases where the UN did succeed through its mediated interventions in promoting a peaceful settlement of major conflicts. The conditions of these successful cases are also instructive about the potential strengths that the UN can bring to a negotiating table. As is shown by the three case studies below, over the years the UN has developed a more nuanced approach to (ethnic) conflict resolution.

El Salvador (1991–95)

The resolution of this conflict is a good example of the emerging multidimensional and multilateral approach to peacekeeping. The Special Representative of the Secretary General Alvaro de Soto played a key role in leading the parties to a negotiated settlement (Hume 1994: 45). The fundamentally different political position of parties to the conflict made the political settlement a subject of intensive negotiation, despite the fact that a military stalemate helped to bring the parties to the negotiating table. The government's goal was to end the war, whereas the goal of the Farabundo Martí National Liberation Front (FMLN) was to change Salvadorian society entirely, starting with intensive demilitarisation. The UN was an outside mediator, and was able to replace the diminishing influence of the US and the former Soviet Union upon the warring parties. Through the UN, which was perceived as neutral, both sides turned to the UN negotiator, Alvaro de Soto, who was

---

a trusted source of proposals, reframing the meaning of concessions, creating a sense of urgency, imposing deadlines and resorting to sanctions, if necessary. In maintaining its independence when undertaking these tasks, the Special Representative also enjoyed the support of 'allies' – Colombia, Mexico, Spain and Venezuela – who lent their support when negotiations were running into difficulties.

Mozambique (1992–94)

The special representative of the UN Secretary General, Aldo Ajello, who was responsible for overseeing the implementation of the General Peace Agreement, played a critical role in mediating, when one of the parties threatened not to fulfil their commitments (Ajello 1999). While the peace accords were negotiated between Marxist-led government party Front for the Liberation of Mozambique (FRELIMO) and the opposition guerrilla movement the Mozambique Resistance Movement (RENAMO), with the assistance of Sant'Egidio, a Catholic organisation, and the direct support of Italian government, implementation of the General Peace Agreement, which was signed in 1992, was undertaken by the United Nations (Bartoli 1999: 256). When the RENAMO candidate, Alfonso Dhlakama, threatened that he would pull out of the UN supervised general election in 1993, because he feared that the process was not fair, the special representative intervened and thus helped the general election to maintain its credibility. The special representative convinced all parties that the election would be fair and that the UN supervision and monitoring commission would inquire into all irregularities of the election.

Since the early 1990s a number of terms have been applied and suggested for the extension of international responsibility and administration of war torn societies. Some scholars have adopted UN terminology or 'interim administration' and 'transitional arrangements', which refers to the temporary assumption of governmental functions by the UN over territories and peoples that have been left in a conflict-torn environment, for instance, because of civil war, crimes against humanity, territorial disputes, and environmental disaster (Caplan 2005: 16–41). Others have referred to comprehensive peacebuilding efforts, which are derived from former UN Secretary General Boutros Boutros-Ghali's *An Agenda for Peace*. The term signifies the readiness of the UN to take on increasing responsibilities in such complicated operations through the 1990s as is evident from the gradual drift from traditional peacekeeping to wider peace-enforcement, humanitarian intervention and, ultimately, the civil, political, social and economic reconstruction of entire societies (Pugh 1997: 20).

Partnering in conflict management in the twenty-first century

A number of studies have noted a decline in the outbreak and lethality of conflict.[3] At least one report attributed this trend to UN engagement; others pointed to the embrace of notions of human security and a growing acceptance of the normative 'responsibility to protect'. At the same time, according to data published by the University of Maryland, the steady decline in the number of active conflicts levelled off towards the end of the twentieth century, but the current trend seems to be an upturn in armed conflict and violence in many countries. Many of the peace agreements that were concluded in the 1980s and 1990s to end sectarian strife have either failed, or are barely holding together, as in the cases of Nepal, Sudan and Colombia.[4] Many countries continue to suffer chronic instability because of persistent social, political and economic problems. This produces conflict patterns that are multi-dimensional, featuring a range of traditional and emerging features – sectarian and factional strife, criminal networks, human rights abuses, state-building crises and regional rivalries. The annual 'Failed (Fragile) State Index', developed by the Fund for Peace and Foreign Policy magazine, identifies some 60 countries as being at risk of political and economic collapse.[5]

The UN is currently running 16 peacekeeping operations, with an annual budget of US$7.06 billion.[6] Ongoing work on the coordination of peacebuilding tasks and activities resulted in the establishment of the UN Peacebuilding Commission in 2005, as an effort of the international community to streamline efforts, focus on post-conflict scenarios and develop a set of best practices. In 2009, the UN New Horizon initiative was developed as a contribution to a dialogue aimed at reinvigorating the peacekeeping partnership and identifying a common future vision of United Nations peacekeeping. The New Horizon document stated that, in order to contribute to a broader peacebuilding effort, the Department of Peace Keeping Operations (DPKO) and the Department of Field Support (DFS) should develop a coherent strategy to guide the early peacebuilding tasks of peacekeeping operations. Since 2009, there have been a number of developments that have helped to clarify the early peacebuilding tasks and comparative advantage of peacekeepers, and to improve mission transition processes by which peacebuilding roles are transferred to national or international partners. More recently, attention has also been given to addressing the socioeconomic dimensions of peacekeeping, addressing human rights abuses, empowerment, the development of institutions and local ownership. The Security Council has held a number of debates related to peacebuilding, which have helped to reinforce the nexus of peacekeeping and peacebuilding and to move away from a traditional sequential approach in peacekeeping. The 2011 report of the Special Committee on Peacekeeping Operations (a/65/19) made similar statements aimed at strengthening the conceptual understanding of peacekeeping and peacebuilding linkages. An informal DPKO and DFS document on the peacekeeping/peacebuilding nexus, produced in 2010 and circulated to Member States, lays out three important roles of peacekeepers in (a) helping national authorities to articulate priorities, (b) enabling efforts by others, and (c) implementing directly a limited set of actions.[7] Similar developments in concepts for peacebuilding and peacekeeping have taken place within regional organisations such as the Organisation of American States (OAS), the EU, and non-governmental organisations (e.g. Amnesty International, International Crises Group, the Carter Center), and individuals have become increasingly involved in various aspects of conflict resolution. Entities have moved towards comprehensive approaches to conflict management; shrinking budgets due to austerity and decreasing willingness to intervene with military engagement have prompted some states to push for reforms within the UN in strategic directions of the peacekeeping operations.[8] Whereas over the last ten years the EU and UN developed closer cooperation in planning, training, delivering and reforming justice and security together, there are still challenges, such as maintaining the right balance between available capabilities and capacities in supporting each other's efforts in peace-building (Tardy 2013). UN–EU cooperation has become a steady feature of the conflict and crisis management, in particular in the last ten years. While the EU works with the UN in most of its missions and contributes to covering its costs (36.8% of the UN peacekeeping budget), EU member states are less willing to provide manpower (Tardy 2013: 3). The typology of financial and troop contributions has led to a dichotomy between two categories of states (Western/Northern vs. Southern), that is now characteristic for peacekeeping operations, which does not contribute to shared understanding of peacekeeping efforts.

Actors and their role in multilateral frameworks for conflict resolution

The 1990s began with a hopeful phase in which the UN set out to implement the expanded conception of peace-making envisioned in Boutros Boutros-Ghali's *An Agenda for Peace*, with notable peacebuilding operations in areas with recent peace settlements, including Cambodia, Namibia, Angola, Mozambique and El Salvador. A general model for UN peacebuilding has emerged from these cases. It calls for military measures to secure the demobilisation, disarmament and cantonment of opposing forces; constitutional measures to implement elections and establish a transitional government; governance measures to support civilian government and infrastructure, including training and, if necessary, supervision of local police; human rights measures; the return of refugees; and the restoration of war damaged infrastructure. At first, this model appeared to have striking successes, and in some cases such as Namibia and Mozambique, a peaceful transformation from war was indeed achieved. In others, however, such as Angola and Cambodia, violent conflict resumed.

While international interventions have in these cases seemed to have halted 'ethnic' wars, the extent of transformation of the underlying conflict remains limited. Ethno-nationalist leaderships remain and settlements based on the realities of ethnic divisions hardened during wartime have preserved these divisions during peace time. These high profile cases, of course, involved imposed settlements, achieved after considerable vacillation on the part of a divided international community. More impressive have been the cases in which conflicts were prevented even before they became violent. Here, real changes in the context of the conflict and in the structure of the societies have resulted in some impressive transformations. In the case of Estonia, for example, a potential ethnic conflict was averted in part through the well-known interventions of the OSCE High Commissioner on National Minorities, supported by the EU and Scandinavian governments. In part, the transformed economic context served to create incentives for the Russian-speaking community. Moreover, an additional key factor was the introduction of an electoral system that created incentives for cross-ethnic voting, thus resulting in a transition from ethnic politics to a politics of economic and regional interest groups. Non-Estonian politicians were included in the party lists of Estonian parties, and the Estonian Centre Party won support from Russian-speakers as a vehicle for promoting their interests. This is a particularly striking success for the conflict management and ethnic accommodation approaches, made possible by the transformation of the Estonian context after 1991.

Several problems still remain with regard to the UN's preventive capacity. Although both the UN Charter and the 1988 Declaration on the Prevention and Removal of Disputes and Situations and on the Role of the UN in the Field urged the UN to become involved 'early in a dispute or a situation' or 'at any stage of a dispute or a situation', the fact is that most disputes do not reach the Security Council's agenda until they have escalated into armed conflict (Peck 1998: 70). Ultimately, decision for action has rested with member states.

The engagement of human rights organisations and humanitarian agencies has become more visible since the 1980s and 1990s. These agencies were increasingly drawn into the costly business of rebuilding war-torn societies, and were responding to the acute humanitarian need, by targeting development and human rights monitoring programmes specifically towards peacebuilding. In some cases, their activities supported UN peacebuilding operations, for example in Mozambique, where donors helped to keep the elections on schedule and supported the transformation of RENAMO into a political party. In other cases, development aid was channelled to directly mitigate conflict, as when donors supported refugees in neglected parts of Somalia with the intention of reducing discontent in a politically unstable area. Programmes designed to support the re-integration of child soldiers or the rehabilitation of agricultural land are further examples of development tasks that can readily have a peace-building component. Capacity-building and support for indigenous conflict handling capacity are also crucial.

Development aid can, of course, have unintended as well as intended consequences; in some circumstances, aid is captured by the parties to the conflict, which then sustains the fighting. Although development agencies are increasingly important and influential in this field, they generally see their role as principally to support and encourage the work of others, rather than to take prime responsibility for transforming particular conflicts (this role is still seen as a new and untested function). Most of the conflict transformation work has, therefore, been left to NGOs (Collier 2007; Lederach 2001). In addition to NGOs, international financial institutions have begun to incorporate conflict resolution and post-conflict recon-struction departments within their organisations, most importantly the World Bank's Post-Conflict Reconstruction Unit. This shift is in part the result of a more holistic approach to peace and conflict resolution that has led various scholars and practitioners to link conflict with issues of human rights and development (Holtzman, Elwan and Scott 1998).

Table 16.2 Functions of multidimensional peacekeeping operations

Component	Function
Military component	Monitoring and verification of cease-fires Cantonment Disarmament and demobilisation of combatants Overseeing the withdrawal of foreign forces Mine-awareness education and mine-clearance Provision of security for UN and other international organisations Provision of activities in support of the peace process
Civilian police component	Crowd control Establishment and maintenance of judicial system Law enforcement Monitoring, training and advising local law enforcement authorities on organisational, administrative and human rights issues
Civilian component	Political element: Political guidance on overall peace process Assistance in the rehabilitation of existing political institutions Promotion of national reconciliation Electoral element: Monitoring and verification of all aspects and stages of the electoral process; coordination of technical assistance Education of the public about electoral processes and provision of help in the development of grass-roots democratic institutions Human rights element: Human rights monitoring Investigating of specific cases of human rights violation Awareness raising of human rights Humanitarian help element: Provision of humanitarian aid (food and other emergency relief supplies) Implementation of refugee repatriation programmes Resettlement of displaced persons Reintegration of ex-combatants

Source: Hansen, Ramsbotham and Woodhouse 2001

Collective threats to security are best met by collective responses, yet the presence of strong norms regarding sovereignty and non-interference has limited the ability of states to collectively deal with conflicts, let alone engage in prevention (Brems Knudsen and Bagge Laustsen 2006). Demand for UN intervention, particularly in the form of peacekeeping operations, has strained the resources available to that organisation. Conflicts in the post-Cold War period have tested the UN's capabilities to the limit, and the failures in Somalia, Rwanda and Bosnia and Herzegovina have led to critical assessments of the UN's role (Betts 1994: 25; Rieff 1994: 17; Luttwak 1999). The genocide in Rwanda, where approximately 800,000 people were killed between April and July of 1994, was described as one of the 'most abhorrent events of the twentieth century' (United Nations 1999a; United Nations 1999b). A year later, in one of the worst war crimes committed in Europe since the end of the Second World War, the Bosnian town of Srebrenica, which had been designated the world's first ever civilian safe area under Security Council Resolution 819 (16 April 1993), fell to Serb militias. As many as 8,000 Muslims were killed under the eyes of the UN peacekeeping forces deployed in the area.

In light of such failures in peacekeeping, the concept of peace support operations (PSO) has evolved as an expression of the reluctance of states to deploy forces and provide resources in conflicts for which they are inadequately prepared and supported. This new way of thinking is best exemplified by Wilkinson who argues that, in a world marked by civil wars, collapsed states and declining respect for international and humanitarian law, the wider peacekeeping concepts developed in the 1990s are in need of updating (Wilkinson 2000).

During the 1990s, the debate surrounding conflict resolution increasingly advocated a more innovative approach. Today, multilateral conflict resolution frameworks involve a broad range of functions and actors, who make use of a wide repertoire of practices. The operations are multilateral and multidimensional, incorporating military and civilian police and other civilian components. The civilian police component has become an increasingly important player in conflict resolution. Operating under the auspices of the UN Security Council, international police monitors assist in the creation of secure environments and in the maintenance of public order. Finally there is a civilian component, which consists of intergovernmental organisations (IGOs), or agencies, regional organisations and non-governmental organisations, international organisations, foundations, etc. With respect to their mandates, the civilian component can be further divided to include subcomponents, such as political, electoral, human rights and a humanitarian mandate. Following on from this, it is arguable that the use of Australian forces to lead the peace operations in East Timor in 1999 (see below) and the deployment of British forces in Sierra Leone in 2000 constitute examples of such multilateral and multidimensional operations.

East Timor

UN involvement in East Timor dates back to the UN General Assembly Resolution in 1960, when East Timor was added to the UN's list of non-self governing territories. When Portugal, which administered the territory, decided to establish a provisional government in 1974, a civil war broke out between those who sought independence and those who wanted union with Indonesia. Indonesia annexed East Timor in 1976. For years afterwards, the UN conducted negotiations with Indonesia and Portugal to resolve the status of East Timor. A set of agreements was reached in 1999, confirming East Timor as holding 'special autonomy status' within the territory of Indonesia. In the same year, a multinational force led by Australia was deployed to protect the United Nations Mission in East Timor (UNAMET). Further to a general election in 2001 and independence in 2002, the UN has continued its presence with a successor mission known as the United Nations Mission of Support in East Timor. It is responsible for helping to maintain security in the country and providing core administrative assistance to the new government (Ramesh 2001: 118).

Another relevant example of the early application of the multilateral approach to conflict resolution, including peace support operations to conflict resolution, is the intervention of the UN in the conflict in Kosovo.

Kosovo

Conflict resolution in Kosovo falls under the category of humanitarian intervention and the creation of international trusteeship (Brems Knudsen and Bagge Laustsen 2006). Like traditional peace-keeping (Chapter VI of UN Charter), the Charter's basis for humanitarian intervention is ambiguous, lying somewhere in the grey zone between Chapter VI and Chapter VII. Here we can speak of a third generation of conflict resolution operations, which involve the application of all the principles of traditional peacekeeping (consent, partiality and absence of use of force). In addition, such intervention may involve further tasks, such as capturing criminals, gathering evidence of war crimes and effectively helping to rebuild the country's administrative institutions.

With the adoption of UN Security Council Resolution 1244 of 10 June 1999 and the establishment of UNMIK, the UN and its partners, NATO, the OSCE and the EU became responsible for the territory, the people and the society of Kosovo. For the first time in recent history, the UN administered an entire territory. To facilitate the implementation of the mandate, the operation was divided into four pillars each managed by a different organisation: Civil Administration (UNMIK), Humanitarian Assistance (UNHCR),[9] Institution Building (OSCE) and Economic Reconstruction (EU). The overall strategy in Resolution 1233 involved five phases. During the first phase, an interim civil administration controlled by UNMIK was to be established. The interim administration was to be strengthened and a gradual transfer to the population of Kosovo was to begin during the second phase, while preparation for election was initiated. The holding of elections was to constitute the third phase, leading to the establishment of provisional administration in the fourth phase. In the fifth phase, the conflict in Kosovo has been finally resolved and the overall administration of the territory transferred to a permanent civil administration directed and controlled by the local population. The largest obstacle to the consolidation of democratic peace in Kosovo is inherent in the structure of the UN operation: the unresolved end-status of the territory. It is clearly stated in Resolution 1244 that Kosovo is a legal part of Yugoslavia and Yugoslavia then and Serbia today has no intention of allowing Kosovo to leave the Federation. The Kosovo Albanians nevertheless continued to demand the creation of an independent state.

Conclusion

By the 1990s it was clear that international community still could not prevent wars, but that the international conflict resolution mechanisms of the United Nations were more effective than those that had been available to the League of Nations. At the end of the twentieth century, such mechanisms were an accepted part of the structure of global political power. New impetus to lateral thinking on conflict resolution, going beyond the state-centred approach to a multidimensional approach has taken place. During the Cold War conflict resolution activities of the UN operated in permissive environments but, since 1988, peace-keeping has had to adapt to semi-permissive, non-consensual environments or hostile environments, where multilateral and multinational approaches in conflict resolution/settlement have become a predominant feature.

As we have seen, there are many examples of an increase in understanding by member states that multilateral approaches to peacekeeping and conflict prevention are, from a long-term perspective, a much more effective solution. The use of multilateral conflict resolution will gain currency with the increasing use of these concepts by the UN and regional organisations, such as the EU, OSCE or the African Union or the Economic Community of West African States (ECOWAS). By their very nature, regional organisations have a more concentrated focus on a specific area, thus allowing the UN to focus its limited resources on the emergence of conflicts outside the purview of areas falling under regional systems. In the meantime, the capacity of these collective security arrangements must be increased through the sharing of both resources and experience by the UN and regional organisations.

Notes

1 A New Partnership Agenda: Charting a New Horizon for UN Peacekeeping. Department of Peace-keeping Operations and Department of Field Support New York, July 2009: http://www.un.org/en/peacekeeping/documents/newhorizon.pdf.
2 See, for example, Hampson 2008: 229–43; Report of the Secretary General's High-level Panel on Threats, Challenges and Security, A More Secure World: Our Shared Responsibility: http://www.un.org/en/peacebuilding/pdf/historical/hlp_more_secure_world.pdf.
3 See, for example, the conflict database of the Uppsala Conflict Data Program and the International Peace Research Institute, Oslo (http://www.prio.no/CSCW/Datasets/Armed-Conflict), which record the decline in conflicts from 1991 to 2006.
4 For an overview of ongoing armed conflict see http://en.wikipedia.org/wiki/List_of_ongoing_armed_conflicts and http://www.cfr.org/global/global-conflict-tracker/p32137#!/.
5 Fund for Peace Failed (Fragile) States Index: http://library.fundforpeace.org/fsi14-overview.
6 Peacekeeping Fact Sheet as of 31 December 2014: http://www.un.org/en/peacekeeping/resources/statistics/factsheet.shtml.
7 Fifth annual progress report on the implementation of the global field support strategy, UN Secretary General 2014: http://www.un.org/en/ga/search/view_doc.asp?symbol=A/69/651. For current orga-nigram of UN peacekeeping structure please see: http://www.un.org/en/peacekeeping/documents/dpkodfs_org_chart.pdf.
8 See Franco-British non-paper on Peacekeeping, January 2009.
9 United Nations High Commissioner for Refugees.

Further reading

Bercovitch, J. and Jackson, R. 2009. *Conflict Resolution in the Twenty-first Century*. Ann Arbor: University of Michigan Press.
Collier, P. 2007. *The Bottom Billion*. Oxford: Oxford University Press.
Fleitz, F. H., Jr. 2002. *Peacekeeping Fiascos of the 1990s: Causes, Solutions and U.S. Interests*. Westport: Praeger Publishers.
Gurr, T. R. 2002. 'Containing Internal War in the Twenty-First Century', in F. O. Hampson and D. M. Malone (eds) *From Reactions to Conflict Prevention: Opportunities in the UN System*. Boulder, CO: Lynne Rienner.
Ramsbotham, O., Woodhouse, T. and Miall, H. 2011. *Contemporary Conflict Resolution*, 3rd edn, Cambridge: Policy Press.

References

Ajello, A. 1999. 'Mozambique: Implementation of the 1992 Peace Agreements', in C. A. Crocker, F. O. Hampson and P. Aall (eds) *Herding Cats: Multiparty Mediation in a Complex World*. Washington, DC: Institute of Peace Press.

Allen, J. 1996. *Peacekeeping: Outspoken Observations by a Field Officer*. Westport, CT: Praeger.

Bartoli, A. 1999. 'Mediating Peace in Mozambique: The Role of the Community of Sant'Egidio', in C. A. Crocker, F. O. Hampson and P. Aall (eds) *Herding Cats: Multiparty Mediation in a Complex World*. Washington, DC: Institute of Peace Press, 245–274.

Betts, R. K. 1994. *The Delusion of Impartial Intervention. Foreign Affairs* 73(1): 20–33.

Bigo, D. 2003. 'A Fresh Look at Conflicts', in M.-C. Smouts (ed.) *The New International Relations*. Paris: Fondation nationale des sciences politiques Centre d'études et de recherches internationales, 171–198.

Boutros-Ghali, B. 1992. 'An Agenda for Peace', UN Document A/47/277. 17 June 1992.

Brems Knudsen, T. and Bagge Laustsen, C. 2006. *Kosovo between War and Peace*. New York: Routledge.

Buzan, B. and Waever, O. 2003. *Regions and Powers: The Structure of International Security*. Cambridge: Cambridge University Press.

Caplan, R. 2005. *International Governance of War-Torn Territories: Rule and Reconstruction*. Oxford: Oxford University Press.

Collier, P. 2007. *The Bottom Billion*. Oxford: Oxford University Press.

Fleitz, F. H., Jr. 2002. *Peacekeeping Fiascos of the 1990s: Causes, Solutions and U.S. Interests*. Westport: Praeger Publishers.

Gaddis, J. L. 1986. 'The Long Peace: Elements of Stability in the Postwar International System', *International Security* 10(4): 99–142.

Goldgeier, J. M. and McFaul, M. 1992. 'A Tale of Two Worlds: Core and Periphery in the Post-Cold War Era', *International Organization* 46(2): 467–491.

Gurr, T. R. 2002. 'Containing Internal War in the Twenty-First Century', in F. O. Hampson and D. M. Malone (eds) *From Reactions to Conflict Prevention: Opportunities in the UN System*. London: International Peace Academy.

Hampson, O. 2008. 'Human Security and International Relations', in P. Williams (ed.) *Security Studies: An Introduction*. London: Routledge.

Hansen, W., Ramsbotham, O. and Woodhouse, T. 2001. *Hawks and Doves: Peacekeeping and Conflict Resolution*. Berlin: Berghof Handbook for Conflict Transformation.

Heinbecker, P. and Goff, P. (eds) 2005. *Irrelevant or Indispensable? The United Nations in the 21st Century*. Waterloo, Ont.: Wilfred Laurier University Press.

Holtzman, S., Elwan, A. and Scott, C. 1998. *Post-Conflict Reconstruction: The Role of the World Bank*. Washington, DC: World Bank.

Hume, R. C. 1994. *The United Nations, Iran and Iraq: How Peacekeeping Changed*. Bloomington: Indiana University Press.

Lederach, P. 2001. 'Civil Society and Reconciliation', in C. A. Crocker, F. O. Hampson and P. Aall (eds) *Turbulent Peace: The Challenges of Managing International Conflict*. Washington DC: United States Institute of Peace, 841–854.

Luttwak, E. 1999. 'Give War a Chance', *Foreign Affairs* 78(4).

Marshall, M. G. 2002. 'Measuring the Societal Impact of War', in F. O. Hampson and D. Malone (eds) *From Reaction to Conflict Prevention: Opportunities for the UN System*. Boulder, CO: Lynne Rienner for the International Peace Academy.

Peck, C. 1998. *Sustainable Peace: the Role of the UN and Regional Organisations*. New York. Carnegie Commission the Prevention of Deadly Conflict.

Pugh, M. 1997. *The UN, Peace and Force*. London: Frank Cass.

Ramesh, T. 2001. 'Cambodia, East Timor and the Brahimi Report', *International Peacekeeping* 8(3): 115–124.

Rieff, D. 1994. 'The Illusion of Peacekeeping', *World Policy Journal* 11(3): 1–18.

Saunders, H. H. 1999. *A Public Peace Process*. New York: Palgrave.

Stedman, S. J. 2007. 'UN Transformation in an Era of Soft Balancing', *International Affairs* 83(5): 933–944.

Talbott, S. 2008. *The Great Experiment: The Story of Ancient Empires, Modern States, and the Quest for a Global Nation*. New York: Simon & Schuster.

Tardy, T. 2013. *Partnering in Crisis Management: Ten Years of UN–EU Cooperation*. Paris: European Union Institute for Security Studies, http://www.iss.europa.eu/publications/detail/article/partnering-in-crisis-management-ten-years-of-eu-un-cooperation/.

United Nations. 1999a. Security Council Resolution 1259 (1999), on the International Tribunal for the Former Yugoslavia and Rwanda, appointment of the Prosecutor.

United Nations. 1999b. Security Council Resolution 1241 (1999), International Tribunal for Rwanda.

United Nations Department of Peacekeeping Operations. http://www.un.org/en/peacekeeping/resour ces/statistics/factsheet.shtml.

Waltz, K. W. 2000. 'Structural Realism after the Cold War', *International Security* 25(1): 5–41.

Weiss, T. G. 1996. 'Collective Spinelessness: UN Actions in the Federal Republic of Yugoslavia', in R. H. Ullman (ed.) *The World and Yugoslavia's Wars*. New York: Council on Foreign Relations.

Wilkinson, P. 2000. 'Peace Support Under Fire: Lesson from Sierra Leone'. *International Security Information Service*. Briefing Papers, 2 June.

Wohlforth, C. W. 1998. 'Reality Check: Revising Theories of International Politics in Response to the End of the Cold War', *World Politics* 50(4): 650–680.

17

POST-CONFLICT RECONSTRUCTION IN ETHNICALLY DIVIDED SOCIETIES

Monika Heupel

Introduction

Post-conflict reconstruction first appeared on the agenda of the United Nations (UN) and multilateral development agencies in the early and mid-1990s. With the end of the Cold War, many proxy wars in developing countries came to an end and other conflicts in weak and failing states escalated, so that new strategies were needed to create the conditions for self-sustaining peace in post-conflict settings. In this context, the UN and other global and regional agencies exploited their new scope of action to devise reconstruction strategies und build up respective capacities. Over the years, commonly accepted principles and a 'standard operating procedure' (Ramsbotham 2000) developed that guided efforts at stabilizing peace processes in the aftermath of armed conflict or war.

Two decades after the end of the Cold War, a rich body of research on post-conflict reconstruction has emerged. Earlier work predominantly concentrated on conceptualizing the term post-conflict reconstruction and describing and debating what measures were and should be initiated within the scope of reconstruction endeavours (e.g. Kühne 1996). Later studies increasingly centred on exposing the flawed liberal bias of the 'standard operating procedure' of post-conflict reconstruction and suggesting alternative approaches (most notably Paris 2004). Within the research on post-conflict reconstruction, the question of ethnically divided societies holds particular significance. With the number of ethnic conflicts on the rise since the early 1990s (Wolff 2006) and ethnic conflicts being more difficult to settle and durably pacify than non-identity conflicts (Hartzel and Hoddie 2003), a great number of scholars engaged in debating what measures were most suitable to lay the foundations for stable peace in the aftermath of armed conflict or war in ethnically divided societies.

The purpose of this chapter is to provide a brief overview of the state of the art of post-conflict reconstruction in ethnically divided societies. It gives a description of the 'standard operating procedure' of post-conflict reconstruction, reviews the main perspectives on post-conflict reconstruction in ethnically divided societies and presents the arguments of the critics of the conventional approach to post-conflict reconstruction. The conclusion summarizes the key points and marks out avenues for further research.

Post-conflict reconstruction

Post-conflict reconstruction – or post-conflict peacebuilding – is defined as 'activities undertaken on the far side of conflict to reassemble the foundations of peace and provide the tools for building on those foundations something that is more than just the absence of war' (United Nations 2000: II.A). Reconstruction activities in the aftermath of armed conflict or war are usually divided into four fields of activity that address security-related, political, psychosocial and socioeconomic problems of post-conflict societies respectively. It is commonly assumed that progress in all four fields of activity is required to render post-conflict reconstruction effective (Hamre and Sullivan 2002). Also, progress in each field of activity is assumed to depend on progress in the other fields, with the provision of security frequently being considered the necessary precondition for progress in other fields (Schwarz 2005).

Security-related reconstruction refers to the (re-)transfer of the monopoly of force to the state. The build-up of the state monopoly of force normally involves the disarmament and demobilization of private and parastatal combat units (Ball 2001; Knight 2004). In many cases, security-related reconstruction also requires security sector reform. A core element of security sector reform in post-conflict states is the integration of members of all relevant warring parties and societal groups into national security institutions. Other elements are the establishment of civilian control of the military and the police, as well as the reduction of the military to providing external security (Bryden and Hänggi 2005; Pauwels 2000). Frequently, security-related reconstruction also involves the temporary deployment of multilateral peacekeeping forces that tend to be increasingly endowed with robust mandates. Peace-keeping forces can monitor and enforce cease-fire agreements and provide an environment that is secure enough to carry out other reconstruction efforts. Thus, they are meant to ease the security dilemma that is presumed to prevent or at least complicate peace-time cooperation among formerly opposing parties (Feil 2002; Walter 1997, 1999).

Political reconstruction refers to the promotion of the rule of law and to the (re-)building of democratic institutions in post-conflict societies. Oftentimes, political reconstruction first and foremost requires the composition of a constitution that embodies basic principles and norms as well as actionable rights (Samuels 2005). Rule of law promotion involves the establishment of a judicial system that is open to every citizen and shielded against political influence (Carothers 1998; Mani 1998). Democracy promotion is based on the assumption that stable democracies are less likely to become embroiled in internal armed conflict or war (Ellingsen and Gleditsch 1997). Democracy promotion usually draws upon a procedural and a substantive understanding of democracy. Thus, it aims to create formal democratic institutions and hold free and fair elections, as well as strengthen civil society organizations and foster acceptance of the values that underpin democratic orders (Barnes 2001; Ottaway 2003).

Psychosocial reconstruction refers to reconciliation both between civilians and former combatants and between different social groups. Given the high number of civilian casualties in many of today's armed conflicts and wars, psychological reconstruction is believed by many to be both highly relevant and particularly difficult (see Bigombe, Collier and Sambanis 2000; Schnabel 2002). Truth commissions that provide a forum for perpetrators to acknowledge their wrongdoings and for victims to recount their stories and possibly forgive the perpetrators are believed to have the potential to facilitate reconciliation in the aftermath of armed conflict or war (Hayner 2002; Rotberg and Thompson 2000). Furthermore, tribunals such as the international tribunals for the former Yugoslavia and Rwanda and the hybrid tribunals for Sierra Leone and Cambodia are assumed to make reconciliation possible through a decollectivization of guilt (Bassiouni 2002; Meron 1999). More recent studies, however, increasingly question whether truth-telling mechanisms and war crimes tribunals really contribute to reconciliation and point to counterproductive side effects (Graybill 2004; Mendeloff 2004)

Socioeconomic reconstruction, finally, refers to the improvement of the socioeconomic wellbeing of civilians and former combatants in post-conflict societies. In the immediate aftermath of armed conflict or war, the provision of humanitarian assistance often takes centre stage. It is also frequently necessary to clear landmines and (re-)build infrastructure to enable refugees and internally displaced persons to return to their homes and resume agricultural production or other economic activities (Chimni 2002; Black and Gent 2006). Assisting former combatants to (re-)integrate into civilian life and take up work that enables them to support themselves and their dependants is considered to be particularly important. That way, former combatants are assumed to have fewer incentives to take up arms again and more incentives to support the peace process (see Humphreys and Weinstein 2007). In the mid and long run, socioeconomic reconstruction aims at the creation of sustainable economic growth and the reduction of social inequality, acknowledging that low levels of development (Collier and Hoeffler 2004) and high levels of social inequality (Boyce 1996; Nafziger and Auvinen 2002) can be important sources of armed conflict and war. The 'standard operating procedure' in this regard is the introduction of a free market economy, normally with the help of macroeconomic structural adjustment programmes (Collier, Hoeffler and Söderbom 2008; Mendelson Forman 2002).

Post-conflict reconstruction in ethnically divided societies

Research on post-conflict reconstruction in ethnically divided societies forms part of the broader research on post-conflict reconstruction. It draws heavily on the insights of the long-standing research on the causes and dynamics of conflict in pluralistic societies as well as on broader theoretical insights of several disciplines. The growing interest in post-conflict reconstruction in ethnically divided societies after the end of the Cold War has been inspired by the rising number of ethnic conflicts and by a growing perception among scholars and policymakers that ethnic divisions replaced the ideological fault lines of the Cold War as the dominant factor of conflict. Moreover, post-conflict reconstruction turned out to be more difficult after ethnic wars than after non-identity wars (Doyle and Sambanis 2000; Hartzell and Hoddie 2003), thus making research on the preconditions for successful reconstruction in ethnically divided societies all the more imperative. One can discern three main perspectives on post-conflict reconstruction in ethnically divided societies that each relate to a specific field of the above specified reconstruction activities: a (neo-)realist perspective underlines the importance of security-related measures, an institutionalist perspective points to the value of balanced political institutions, and a constructivist perspective highlights the significance of reducing the political salience of ethnic divisions.

Scholars in the *(neo-)realist* tradition argue that the concept of the security dilemma can be used to explain the behaviour of non-state actors in anarchical environments. Traditionally, the security dilemma concept describes a situation in which two states that do not wish to harm each other end up going to war against each other. The dilemma arises because the anarchical structure of the international system compels states to make worst case assumptions and rely on self-help strategies to increase their security, which in turn decreases the security of other states (Herz 1951). The same dilemma, the argument goes, occurs before the outbreak or in the aftermath of ethnic conflicts if a state fails to provide security throughout its territory. Hence, ethnic groups can equally be caught up in a situation in which they cannot trust one another and thus feel compelled to introduce measures that decrease the security not only of other parties but eventually also their own security (Posen 1993; Roe 1999; Snyder and Jervis 1999).

The application of the security dilemma concept to ethnic conflicts prompts scholars in the neo-realist tradition to make rather grim predictions for the success of many of the post-conflict reconstruction measures summarized above. However, they come to different conclusions on how to surmount the challenges posed by the security dilemma in post-conflict settings. Some argue that warring factions might sign a ceasefire or peace agreement but are unlikely to disarm and agree to power-sharing formulas if there are no credible guarantees that all factions will abide by the terms of the agreement. A necessary precondition for the success of post-conflict reconstruction is therefore the presence of peacekeeping forces that are prepared to enforce the agreement and can thus provide such guarantees (Doyle and Sambanis 2000; Hampson 1996; Walter 1997, 1999). By contrast, other scholars call for the geographic separation of ethnic groups. They claim that, due to the security dilemma, cross-ethnic political appeals are unlikely to resonate in the aftermath of armed conflict or war. Accordingly, they consider the creation of ethnic enclaves, with or without independent sovereignty, to be a suitable way to reduce both incentives and opportunities for armed conflict or war (Kaufmann 1996, 1998; Mearsheimer and Van Evera 1995; for a criticism see Jenne 2012).

Many scholars who draw on *institutionalist* insights assert that the establishment of consociational democracy facilitates post-conflict reconstruction of ethnically divided societies (Hartzell and Hoddie 2003). This is based on the assumption that the needs and interests of all relevant groups must be accommodated to prevent the recurrence of armed conflict or war in pluralistic societies. Therefore, it is crucial to develop power-sharing mechanisms and/ or agree upon group autonomy rights to give all relevant groups the opportunity to participate in rulemaking (see Gurr 1993; Lijphart 1977, 2004). Power-sharing typically refers to centralized joint rule and consensus-based decision-making of all relevant (ethnic) groups in divided societies. A narrow conception corresponds to power-sharing provisions in the executive and legislative branch, such as all-party governments or the right of all parliamentary factions to veto decisions. A broader power-sharing conception refers to proportional representation of all relevant groups, not only in the executive and the legislature but also in the public administration, the judiciary and the security institutions (Hartzell and Hoddie 2003; Lijphart 1977, 2004; Reynal-Querol 2002; Schneckener 2002; Sisk 1996). Territorial group autonomy provisions imply the introduction of federal structures in divided societies with geographically concentrated (ethnic) groups. Non-territorial group autonomy provisions relate to the granting of minority rights, for instance related to religion, education and language, to (ethnic) groups that are not geographically concentrated (Coakley 1993; Ghai 2000).

Horowitz and Reilly also draw on institutionalist insights but arrive at different conclusions on how voting systems ought to be designed in ethnically divided societies to contribute to the prevention or re-escalation of violent conflict. According to them, power-sharing provisions that guarantee proportional representation of all relevant ethnic groups in decision-making are counterproductive in that they reinforce ethnic divisions and reward radical parties. Instead, they recommend alternative vote systems that require voters to rank candidates according to their preferences, thus encouraging parties to bid for support from different constituencies. Alternative vote systems consequently reward moderate parties and facilitate coalition-building across ethnic divides (Horowitz 1991, 1993; Reilly 1997, 2001).

Finally, scholars that draw on *constructivist* theory point to the social construction of ethnic identities and maintain that it is of particular importance to address the symbolic and emotional roots of ethnic conflicts to cultivate stable peace in post-conflict settings. Rational approaches, they argue, err in assuming that ethnic identities are fixed and cannot be transformed. Proposals such as the geographical separation of ethnically defined groups or the institutionalization of power-sharing mechanisms and group autonomy rights are therefore flawed because they build on the faulty assumption of unchangeable ethnic identities. Moreover, such proposals hold risks in that they institutionalize ethnic cleavages in post-conflict societies (Kaufman 2006; Simonsen 2005). Consequently, rather than institutionalizing ethnic divisions in post-conflict societies, steps should be taken to reduce the salience of such divisions and facilitate a redefinition of identities and attitudes (Long and Brecke 2003; for a critical appraisal see Walker 2012).

There are several propositions on how to facilitate identity-related and attitudinal changes in ethnically divided societies that emerge from armed conflict or war. Some scholars underline the potential of problem-solving workshops that bring together representatives of conflicting groups and social scientists to engage in informal communication (Kelman and Cohen 1976). Others consider truth and reconciliation commissions to be a promising tool to make identity-related and attitudinal changes possible (Hayner 2002; Kaufman 2006). Others point out that multi-ethnic armies can help former combatants develop a professional identity that complements their ethnic identity (Gaub 2012). Again others suggest to promote societal cleavages that cut across ethnic divisions in order to de-ethnicize politics and lay the foundation for multicultural democracy in post-conflict settings. According to this view, members of ethnic groups are supposed to become aware of the fact that they share interests with members of other ethnic groups if they define their identity and interests not only along ethnic but also along regional, gender, class and other lines. The long-term objective, eventually, is not the suppression of ethnic identities but the creation of an overarching national identity (Kymlicka 1995; Simonsen 2005).

'Liberal internationalism' and its critics

Throughout much of the 1990s, research on post-conflict reconstruction was primarily concerned with mapping out how specific reconstruction strategies could be designed to be effective and thus widely took a problem-solving approach. In the late 1990s, however, when more and more efforts at post-conflict reconstruction in homogenous and ethnically divided societies alike faltered and failed (Tschirgi 2004), scholars increasingly challenged the appropriateness of the normative underpinnings of 'liberal internationalism' or the 'liberal peace', which are generally used to denote the 'standard operating procedure' of post-conflict reconstruction. In their view, post-conflict reconstruction was based on the assumption that the introduction of Western-style democracy and free market economy would help states emerging from armed conflict or war to lay the groundwork for self-sustaining peace. Yet, while democracy and market economy were indeed correlated with a low risk of violent conflict, political and economic liberalization engendered competition and were therefore not qualified to stabilize countries that lacked reliable institutions for the peaceful management of conflicts in the immediate aftermath of violence. The disillusioning success rate of post-conflict reconstruction since the end of the Cold War can consequently, at least in part, be attributed to untimely liberalization (David 1999; Paris 1997, 2002, 2004; Richmond 2006).

Some scholars endeavoured to flesh out why *premature democratization* in post-conflict situations was risky. They showed that states undergoing a transformation from autocracy to democracy are more susceptible to armed conflict or war than stable autocracies or mature democracies. States in limbo between autocracy and democracy are considered to be particularly at risk because the process of democratization enables societal groups to gather and voice their demands while the governing regime is frequently not yet in a position or willing to accommodate such demands (Ellingsen and Gleditsch 1997; Mousseau 2001; Paris 1997, 2004). The heightened vulnerability of democratizing states to violent conflict also applies to states with ethnically divided societies. What is more, there are indications that the pacifying effect of maturing democracies is less pronounced in ethnically divided societies than in homogenous societies (Mousseau 2001). The introduction of democracy in multi-ethnic societies, it is argued, is likely to stimulate political competition along ethnic lines, facilitate ethnic mobilization and thus foment ethnic conflict. Especially premature elections are a gamble, given that ethnic groups often perceive elections as zero-sum games and may resort to violent means if elections produce undesirable results (Diamond, Linz and Lipset 1995; Horowitz 1994; Huntington 1997). More recently, it has been asserted that particularly first and second elections after periods of no voting run the risk of giving rise to ethnic civil wars (Cederman, Gleditsch and Hug 2013).

Other scholars claim that the *hasty introduction of free market economies* in post-conflict societies is likewise risky. They assert that states that are about to introduce free market economy (and are at middle levels of development) are exposed to a higher risk of armed conflict or war than states that are less open to the world economy (or less developed) or that are already well integrated into the world economy (or highly developed). The causal explanation of this relation is that the introduction of free market economy, often guided by externally imposed neoliberal structural adjustment programmes, and integration into the global economy, give rise to social inequality in war-shattered societies and create losers that may resort to violent means to assert themselves (Bussmann and Schneider 2007; Cooper 2005; Mousseau 2001; Paris 1997). As in the relation between the degree of democratization and the risk of violent conflict, the relation between economic openness (and development) and the risk of violent conflict equally applies to ethnically divided societies. Processes of economic development create more issues that societal groups can compete for and thus heighten the risk of group conflicts (Horowitz 1985; Mousseau 2001), especially where post-conflict states have yet to institutionalize social safety nets. Moreover, horizontal inequality between ethnic groups renders societies more prone to armed conflict or war as it produces grievances that can be used by 'ethnic entrepreneurs' to mobilize followers along ethnic lines (Chua 2003; Gurr and Moore 1997; Humphreys 2003; Stewart 2002).

In light of the negative side-effects of precipitated political and economic liberalization, many critics of the conventional approach to post-conflict reconstruction call for what has become known as 'strategic liberalization' (Paris 1997). Proponents of 'strategic liberalization' share the normative underpinnings of 'liberal internationalism' but argue for a gradual and controlled implementation of its ambitious agenda and, as a consequence, long-term commitment by external actors. Instead of focusing on holding (premature) elections, they emphasize constitution-building and recommend delaying elections until disarmament and demobilization efforts have made progress, civil society organizations whose agendas cut across dominant cleavage lines have developed, and electoral systems have been crafted with mechanisms that reward moderate parties (Paris 1997, 2004; Zakaria 1997). To absorb the negative side-effects of economic liberalization in fragile post-conflict situations, proponents of 'strategic liberalization' suggest adjustment policies that avoid economic shocks and allocate resources to those who are negatively affected by adjustment programmes (Paris 1997, 2004). Other critics of the 'liberal internationalist' approach to post-conflict reconstruction question whether external actors have the right and the ability to engage in far-reaching social engineering in post-conflict societies (Chandler 2006). Rather, they demand that local actors have a greater stake in deciding the constitutional foundations of the political system and the parameters of the approach to peacebuilding (Chandler 2006; Richmond and Franks 2007).

Conclusion

The body of research on post-conflict reconstruction in general and on reconstruction in ethnically divided societies has grown substantially during the past two decades. Until the late 1990s, most studies followed a 'problem-solving' approach and concentrated on spelling out what specific reconstruction strategies proved effective. Over the years, more and more scholars focused on the normative underpinnings of the 'standard operating procedure' of post-conflict reconstruction and the flaws of their execution. At the same time, a field of research that specifically dealt with post-conflict reconstruction in ethnically divided societies developed and generated insights that enriched the broader debate on post-conflict reconstruction in general.

To further enhance our understanding of the determinants of effective post-conflict reconstruction in ethnically divided societies, future research should first and foremost strive to overcome some of the divides that separate the different perspectives on reconstruction from each other. Firstly, proponents of the conventional 'liberal internationalist' approach to post-conflict reconstruction and proponents of 'strategic liberalization' should engage more seriously with each other and spell out more clearly under which conditions individual approaches prove most promising. Secondly, scholars who draw on different theoretical insights to account for the effectiveness of post-conflict reconstruction in ethnically divided societies should likewise make greater efforts to pool their findings. While it is true that some of the measures put forward by the different approaches countervail one another, it is worthwhile to examine more closely which measures can be combined under particular circumstances; an interesting attempt in this regard is to draw on perspectives as diverse as realism, rational choice, constructivism, the Copenhagen School and social psychology to apply the security dilemma concept to the study of ethnic conflicts (Tang 2011). Research on post-conflict reconstruction in ethnically divided societies has come a long way and has produced theoretically interesting and practically relevant insights. Yet, bringing together insights from different normative and theoretical perspectives will certainly expand our understanding of what makes post-conflict reconstruction in ethnically divided societies work.

Further reading

Hartzell, C. and Hoddie, M. (2003) 'Institutionalizing peace: power sharing and post-civil war conflict management', *American Journal of Political Science*, 47(2): 318–332.

Kaufman, S.J. (2006) 'Escaping the symbolic politics trap: reconciliation initiatives and conflict resolution in ethnic wars', *Journal of Peace Research*, 43(2): 201–218.

Paris, R. (1997) 'Peacebuilding and the limits of liberal internationalism', *International Security*, 22(2): 54–89.

Simonsen, S.G. (2005) 'Addressing ethnic divisions in post-conflict institution-building: lessons from recent cases', *Security Dialogue*, 36(3): 297–318.

Walter, B. (1997) 'The critical barrier to civil war settlement', *International Organization*, 51(3): 335–364.

References

Ball, N. (2001) 'The challenge of rebuilding war-torn societies', in C. A. Crocker, F. O. Hampson and P. Aall (eds) *Turbulent Peace: The Challenges of Managing International Conflict*, Washington: United States Institute of Peace Press.

Barnes, S.H. (2001) 'The contribution of democracy to rebuilding postconflict societies', *The American Journal of International Law*, 95(86): 86–101.

Bassiouni, M.C. (2002) 'Accountability for violations of international humanitarian law and other serious violations of human rights', in M.C. Bassiouni (ed.) *Post-conflict Justice*, Ardsley: Transnational Publishers.

Bigombe, B., Collier, P. and Sambanis, N. (2000) 'Policies for building post-conflict peace', *Journal of African Economies*, 9(3): 323–348.

Black, R. and Gent, S. (2006) 'Sustainable return in post-conflict contexts', *International Migration*, 44(3): 15–38.

Boyce, J. (ed.) (1996) *Economic Policy for Building Peace: The Lessons of El Salvador*, Boulder and London: Lynne Rienner.

Bryden, A. and Hänggi, H. (eds) (2005) *Security Governance in Post-conflict Peacebuilding*, Münster: LIT Verlag.

Bussmann, M. and Schneider, G. (2007) 'When globalization discontent turns violent: foreign economic liberalization and internal war', *International Studies Quarterly*, 51: 79–97.

Carothers, T. (1998) 'The rule of law revival', *Foreign Affairs*, 77(2): 95–106.

Cederman, L.-E., Gleditsch, K.S. and Hug, S. (2013) 'Elections and ethnic civil war', *Comparative Political Studies*, 36(3): 387–417.

Chandler, D. (2006) 'Back to the future? The limits of neo-Wilsonian ideals of exporting democracy', *Review of International Studies*, 32: 475–494.

Chimni, B.S. (2002) 'Refugees and post-conflict reconstruction: a critical perspective', *International Peacekeeping*, 9(2): 163–180.

Chua, A. (2003) *World on Fire: How Exporting Free Market Democracy Breeds Ethnic Hatred and Global Instability*, New York: Doubleday.

Coakley, J. (ed.) (1993) *The Territorial Management of Ethnic Conflict*, London: Frank Cass.

Collier, P. and Hoeffler, A. (2004) 'Greed and grievance in civil war', *Oxford Economic Papers*, 56: 563–595.

Collier, P., Hoeffler, A. and Söderbom, M. (2008) 'Post-conflict risks', *Journal of Peace Research*, 45(4): 461–478.

Cooper, N. (2005) 'Picking out the pieces of the liberal peaces: representations of conflict economies and the implications for policy', *Security Dialogue*, 36(4): 463–478.

David, C. (1999) 'Does peacebuilding build peace? Liberal (mis)steps in the peace process', *Security Dialogue*, 30(1): 25–41.

Diamond, L., Linz, J.J. and Lipset, S.M. (1995) *Politics in Developing Countries: Comparing Experiences with Democracy*, Boulder: Lynne Rienner.

Doyle, M.W. and Sambanis, N. (2000) 'International peacebuilding: a theoretical and quantitative analysis', *American Political Science Review*, 94(4): 779–801.

Ellingsen, T. and Gleditsch, N.P. (1997) 'Democracy and armed conflict in the third world', in K. Volden and D. Smith (eds) *Causes of Conflict in the Third World*, Oslo: North South Coalition and PRIO.

Feil, S. (2002) 'Building better foundations: security in post-conflict reconstruction', *The Washington Quarterly*, 25(4): 97–109.

Gaub, F. (2012) *Military Integration After Civil Wars: Multiethnic Armies, Identity and Post-Conflict Reconstruction*, New York: Routledge.

Ghai, Y.P. (ed.) (2000) *Autonomy and Ethnicity: Negotiating Competing Claims in Multi-ethnic States*, Cambridge: Cambridge University Press.

Graybill, L.S. (2004) 'Pardon, punishment, and amnesia: three African post-conflict methods', *Third World Quarterly*, 25(6): 1117–1130.

Gurr, T.R. (1993) *Minorities at Risk: A Global View of Ethnopolitical Conflicts*, Washington DC: United States Institute of Peace Press.

Gurr, T.R. and Moore, W.H. (1997) 'Ethnopolitical rebellion: a cross-sectional analysis of the 1980s with risk assessment for the 1990s', *American Journal of Political Science*, 41(4): 1079–1103.

Hampson, F.O. (1996) *Nurturing Peace: Why Peace Settlements Succeed or Fail*, Washington DC: United States Institute of Peace Press.

Hamre, J. and Sullivan, J.R. (2002) 'Toward postconflict reconstruction', *The Washington Quarterly*, 25(4): 85–96.

Hartzell, C. and Hoddie, M. (2003) 'Institutionalizing peace: power sharing and post-civil war conflict management', *American Journal of Political Science*, 47(2): 318–332.

Hayner, P.B. (2002) *Unspeakable Truths: Facing the Challenge of Truth Commissions*, New York: Routledge.

Herz, J.H. (1951) *Political Realism and Political Idealism*, Chicago: Chicago University Press.

Horowitz, D.L. (1985) *Ethnic Groups in Conflict*, Berkeley: University of California Press.

Horowitz, D.L. (1991) *A Democratic South Africa? Constitutional Engineering in a Divided Society*, Berkeley: University of California Press.

Horowitz, D.L. (1993) 'Democracy in divided societies', *Journal of Democracy*, 4(4): 18–38.

Horowitz, D.L. (1994) 'Democracy in divided societies', in L. Diamond and M.F. Plattner (eds) *Nationalism, Ethnic Conflict, and Democracy*, Baltimore: Johns Hopkins University Press.

Humphreys, M. (2003) 'Economics and Violent Conflict', Cambridge: Harvard University. Online. Available online at: http://www.idrc.ca/uploads/user-S/10588054981Humphreys_Essay.pdf (Accessed 12 March 2009).

Humphreys, M. and Weinstein, J.M. (2007) 'Demobilization and reintegration', *Journal of Conflict Resolution*, 51(4): 531–567.

Huntington, S.P. (1997) 'Democracy for the long haul', in L. Diamond, M.F. Plattner, Y. Chu and H. Tien (eds) *Consolidating the Third Wave Democracies*, London: Johns Hopkins University Press.

Jenne, E.K. (2012) 'When will we part with partition theory? Flawed premises and improbable longevity of the Theory of Ethnic Partition', *Ethnopolitics*, 11(3): 255–267.

Kaufman, S.J. (2006) 'Escaping the symbolic politics trap: reconciliation initiatives and conflict resolution in ethnic wars', *Journal of Peace Research*, 43(2): 201–218.

Kaufmann, C. (1996) 'Possible and impossible solutions to ethnic wars', *International Security*, 20(4): 136–175.

Kaufmann, C. (1998) 'When all else fails: ethnic population transfers and partitions in the 20th century', *International Security*, 23(2): 120–156.

Kelman, H.C. and Cohen, S.P. (1976) 'The problem-solving workshop: a social-psychological contribution to the resolution of international conflicts', *Journal of Peace Research*, 2(13): 79–90.

Knight, M. (2004) 'Guns, camps and cash: disarmament, demobilization and reinsertion of former combatants in transitions from war to peace', *Journal of Peace Research*, 41(4): 499–516.

Kühne, W. (1996) *Winning the Peace: Concept and Lessons Learned of Post-conflict Peacebuilding*, Ebenhausen: Stiftung Wissenschaft und Politik.

Kymlicka, W. (1995) *Multicultural Citizenship*, Oxford: Clarendon Press.

Lijphart, A. (1977) *Democracy in Plural Societies: A Comparative Exploration*, New Haven: Yale University Press.

Lijphart, A. (2004) 'Constitutional design for divided societies', *Journal of Democracy*, 15(2): 96–109.

Long, W.J. and Brecke, P. (2003) *War and Reconciliation: Reason and Emotion in Conflict Resolution*, Cambridge: MIT Press.

Mani, R. (1998) 'Conflict resolution, justice and law: rebuilding the rule of law in the aftermath of complex political emergencies', *International Peacekeeping*, 5(3): 1–25.

Mearsheimer, J.J. and Van Evera, S. (1995) 'When peace means war', *New Republic*, 18: 16–21.

Mendeloff, D. (2004) 'Truth-seeking, truth-telling, and postconflict peacebuilding: curb the enthusiasm?' *International Studies Review*, 6: 355–380.

Mendelson Forman, J. (2002) 'Achieving socioeconomic well-being in postconflict settings', *The Washington Quarterly*, 25(4): 125–138.

Meron, T. (1999) *War Crime Law Comes of Age*, Oxford: Oxford University Press.

Mousseau, D.Y. (2001) 'Democratizing with ethnic divisions: a source of conflict?' *Journal of Peace Research*, 38(5): 547–567.

Nafziger, E.W. and Auvinen, J. (2002) 'Economic development, inequality, war, and state violence', *World Development*, 30(2): 153–163.

Ottaway, M. (2003) 'Promoting democracy after conflict: the difficult choice', *International Studies Perspectives*, 4(3): 314–322.

Paris, R. (1997) 'Peacebuilding and the limits of liberal internationalism', *International Security*, 22(2): 54–89.

Paris, R. (2002) 'International peacebuilding and the "mission civilisatrice"', *Review of International Studies*, 28(4): 637–656.

Paris, R. (2004) *At War's End: Building Peace after Civil Conflict*, Cambridge: Cambridge University Press.

Pauwels, N. (ed.) (2000) *War Force to Work Force: Global Perspectives on Demobilization and Reintegration*, Baden-Baden: Nomos.

Posen, B.R. (1993) 'The security dilemma and ethnic conflict', *Survival*, 35(1): 27–47.

Ramsbotham, O. (2000) 'Reflections on UN post-settlement peacebuilding', *International Peacekeeping*, 7(1): 169–189.

Reilly, B. (1997) 'Preferential voting and political engineering: a comparative study', *Journal of Commonwealth and Comparative Politics*, 35(1): 1–19.

Reilly, B. (2001) *Democracy in Divided Societies: Electoral Engineering for Conflict Management*, New York: Cambridge University Press.

Reynal-Querol, M. (2002) 'Ethnicity, political systems, and civil wars', *Journal of Conflict Resolution*, 46(1): 29–54.

Richmond, O.P. (2006) *The Transformation of Peace*, London: Palgrave.

Richmond, O.P. and Franks, J. (2007) 'Liberal hubris? Virtual peace in Cambodia', *Security Dialogue*, 38(1): 27–48.

Roe, P. (1999) 'The intrastate security dilemma: ethnic conflict as a tragedy', *Journal of Peace Research*, 36(2): 183–202.

Rotberg, R.I. and Thompson, D. (eds) (2000) *Truth v. Justice: The Morality of Truth Commissions*, Princeton: Princeton University Press.

Samuels, K. (2005) 'Post-conflict peace-building and constitution-making', *Chicago Journal of International Law*, 6(2): 1–20.

Schnabel, A. (2002) 'Post-conflict peacebuilding and second-generation preventive action', *International Peacekeeping*, 9(2): 7–30.

Schneckener, U. (2002) 'Making power-sharing work: lessons from successes and failures in ethnic conflict regulation', *Journal of Peace Research*, 39(2): 203–228.

Schwarz, R. (2005) 'Post-conflict peacebuilding: the challenges of security, welfare and representation', *Security Dialogue*, 36(4): 429–446.

Simonsen, S.G. (2005) 'Addressing ethnic divisions in post-conflict institution-building: lessons from recent cases', *Security Dialogue*, 36(3): 297–318.

Sisk, T. (1996) *Power Sharing and International Mediation in Ethnic Conflicts*, Washington DC: United States Institute of Peace Press.

Snyder, J. and Jervis, R. (1999) 'Civil war and the security dilemma', in B. Walter and J. Snyder (eds) *Civil Wars, Insecurity and Intervention*, New York: Columbia University Press.

Stewart, F. (2002) 'Horizontal inequalities as a source of conflict', in F.O. Hampson and D.M. Malone (eds) *From Reaction to Conflict Prevention: Opportunities for the UN System*, Boulder and London: Lynne Rienner.

Tang, S. (2011) 'The security dilemma and ethnic conflict: toward a dynamic and integrative theory of ethnic conflict', *Review of International Studies*, 37(2): 511–536.

Tschirgi, N. (2004) 'Post-conflict peacebuilding revisited: achievements, limitations, challenges', paper prepared for the WSP International/IPA Peacebuilding Forum Conference, New York, 7 October 2004.

United Nations (2000) 'Report of the Panel on United Nations Peace Operations (Brahimi Report)', A/55/305-S/2000/809, 21 August 2000.

Walker, K. (2012) 'Resolving debates over the status of ethnic identities during transitional justice', *Contemporary Political Theory*, 11: 68–87.

Walter, B. (1997) 'The critical barrier to civil war settlement', *International Organization*, 51(3): 335–364.

Walter, B. (1999) 'Designing transitions from civil war: demobilization, democratization, and commitments to peace', *International Security*, 24(1): 127–155.

Wolff, S. (2006) *Ethnic Conflict: A Global Perspective*, Oxford: Oxford University Press.

Zakaria, F. (1997) 'The rise of illiberal democracy', *Foreign Affairs*, 76(6): 22–43.

PART III

18

DEEPENING DEMOCRACY

The role of civil society

Ian O'Flynn and David Russell

Introduction: democracy and civil society

There is more to democracy than the responsibilities and decisions of elected representatives. This is as true for societies deeply divided along ethnic lines as for any other kind of society. Democracy means rule by the people, which, in turn, assumes that ordinary people can hold representatives to account and make them responsive to their preferences and opinions. Yet according to one reading of democracy, representatives need only be held accountable for the positions and policies they adopt at election time. If voters are dissatisfied with the way in which their interests have been served, they can use their franchise to register that dissatisfaction in the hope of bringing about a change in power (Schumpeter 1942; Riker 1982).

Critics argue that this is an overly reductive understanding of democracy – ordinary people ought, they argue, to be more involved in political life. They should not be merely passive recipients of decisions made in their name, who patiently (or frustratedly) wait for the periodic opportunity to pass judgement on the performance of the government of the day. On the contrary, a flourishing democracy must strive, on this alternative view, towards achieving greater levels of public participation enabling ordinary people to engage in meaningful deliberation that can inform decision making on an ongoing basis (Barber 1984; cf. Warren 2001). In this vein, John Stuart Mill famously argued that when an ordinary person participates in political life, he is

> called upon, while so engaged, to weigh interests not his own; to be guided, in case of conflicting claims, by another rule than his private partialities; to apply, at every turn, principles and maxims which have for their reason of existence the common good: and he usually finds associated with him in the same work minds more familiarised than his own with these ideas and operations, whose study it will be to supply reasons to his understanding, and stimulation to his feeling for the general interest. He is made to feel himself one of the public, and whatever is for their benefit to be for his benefit.
>
> *(Mill 1999: 255)*

One might agree with Mill that political participation raises the moral character by obliging people to take a broader and more encompassing view of public issues than that of their own special interest. However, if participation is to be effective or constructive, it must be organised. The various associations that make up civil society (e.g., churches, universities, trade unions, employers' associations, environmental groups, etc.) provide ordinary people with multiple formal and informal channels that enable them to build affinities and mobilise for common purposes, to coordinate their actions through discussion and to reach for new ideas and practices. But, in principle, the associations of civil society can do much more than enable people to engage with and learn from one another. They can also enable them to talk to government, either directly through their own efforts or through channels and institutions established specifically for that purpose. In doing so, they can exercise greater control over the conditions under which they live and act – in effect, to be self-determining – and hence increase the quality of their democracy (Young 1999: 149–150).

The implications for societies deeply divided along ethnic lines are encouraging. If the members of conflicting ethnic groups really could engage within civil society, they might come to see that others can have reasons to hold their views as firmly as they hold theirs, and perhaps even realise that they share many interests in common (e.g., housing, employment, social security, education, economic development, etc.). The pursuit of those interests may sit uneasily with their ethnic commitments. But they might still lead people to realise that life is a complex affair and that their political representatives should be responsive to that complexity. In short, it might lead them to realise that public opinion, or indeed their own interest, need not necessarily break down along ethnic lines. Accordingly, as Larry Diamond argues, a rich and pluralistic civil society 'tends to generate a wide range of interests that may cross-cut, and so mitigate, the principal polarities of political conflict' (Diamond 1999: 245). This not only encourages tolerance and a healthy respect for difference, but, in principle, allows representatives much more room to build the sorts of composite compromises that are necessary to address difficult political questions.

This, of course, is the theory. In practice, however, the ability of ordinary people to engage in deliberation with one another through civil society associations may be limited. Where ethnic groups are concentrated in different parts of a country, they may have little or no meaningful contact with each other. But even in cases where groups are intermingled, ordinary people may still find themselves leading parallel lives or living within parallel social spheres – for example, people may typically marry within their own community, send their children to separate schools, engage in different cultural activities, speak a different language and so forth. In this kind of situation, it may seem meaningless to speak of 'civil society' in the singular (O'Leary 2005: 10). Each group may contain a plethora of civil society associations. Yet there may be little communication between organisations from different sides of the ethnic divide or little attempt to combine resources, even when they are concerned with the same issues and with achieving similar outcomes. Instead, they may operate within discrete social spheres, advocate on behalf of discrete publics, and even lobby separate government institutions.

The seriousness of this worry cannot be gainsaid. The experience of physical, social or political separation may indeed mean that, even if ordinary people do participate in associational life, they may still fail to think beyond the boundaries of their own ethnic group or enlarge their sympathies so as to take a broader or more inclusive view of public issues. If this were always to hold true, then we might rightly despair of the prospects for strengthening democracy in deeply divided societies. In this chapter, we argue to the contrary. It may not be possible to create civil society associations where none exist. But weak civil society associations can sometimes be strengthened through sensitive and appropriate forms of strategic intervention. But this is not all. Just as it is possible to create institutions that facilitate power sharing between the representatives of different ethnic groups, it is possible to create institutions that facilitate participation and deliberation between ordinary people, both within and across different ethnic groups, and that enable them to effectively channel their views and opinions to government.

Civil society defined

People participate in civil society organisations for all sorts of reasons and to all sorts of ends (Galston 2000: 67). One useful way of exploring the phenomenon of civil society, and how people participate within it, is by analysing the component parts of the definition put forward by Larry Diamond. According to Diamond, civil society 'is the realm of organised social life that is open, voluntary, self-generating, at least partially self-supporting, autonomous from the state, and bound by a legal order or set of shared rules' (Diamond 1999: 221). While Diamond is primarily concerned with the role that civil society organisations can play in transitions from authoritarian rule to democracy, his definition can be put to good use with respect to the understanding of the particular challenges that deeply divided societies present.

To begin with, Diamond claims that civil society is *the realm of organised social life*. Naturally, social life can take many different forms and may be more or less organised. It may also have nothing at all to do with politics. Yet if civil associations are to have any real political influence, they must be effectively organised. There are at least three obvious reasons that explain why this is so. Civil associations must be effectively organised so that their members can successfully (1) exchange information and evaluate alternative perspectives, (2) formulate a coherent political outlook or perspective on public issues, (3) mobilise sufficient numbers to influence political decisions (cf. Young 1999: 149). Of course, this still leaves us wondering what might distinguish civil associations from other forms of organised social life, such as the family on the one hand or political parties on the other (Galston 2000).

According to Diamond, what marks civil associations out as distinctive is *their open and voluntary character*. The underlying ideal here is quintessentially liberal, and may be stated thus. Individuals should be free to move between associations, as and when they please. This freedom leads to the creation of an ever larger number of associations, which in turn advances the cause of democracy – the more that people are free to move, and the more associations there are for them to move to, the more space there is for the expression of diverse interests (Walzer 2004: 75). Of course, the difficulty with this liberal ideal is that, in practice, many civil associations cannot plausibly be described as 'open'. Some religious groups provide a good example, since they may exclude people not born into the religion (cf. Warren 2001: 96–103). However, even religious groups of this sort can plausibly be described as voluntary, since it is always possible to leave the group. This may be extremely difficult (Green 1999: 266). However, saying that something is difficult is not the same as saying that it is impossible.

A further defining feature is that, although they aim to influence political decisions, civil associations do not seek to take control of government (Schmitter 1997: 240). Admittedly, the line between influence and control can be hard to draw. But at least as far as democracy is concerned, one way in which we might seek to draw that line is by asking whether, or to what extent, an association sees itself as *autonomous from the state*. Civil associations do not seek to represent the complete set of interests of their members or of society at large. In other words, civil associations are not hegemonic, but instead seek to represent particular interests at particular times. Again, as Diamond points out, this partiality is crucial to generating one of the most important consequences of a truly civil society: the profusion of different organisations and, for individuals, multiple organisational ties that cut across and complicate existing cleavages and generate moderating cross-pressures on individual preferences, attitudes and beliefs.

(Diamond 1999: 223)

At the same time, the relation between state and civil society remains highly complex. Civil associations must be *at least partially self-supporting* because otherwise they may become overly dependent on governmental support which, in turn, may compromise their independence. When this happens, civil associations may lose the freedom to advance their own interests in their own way. Perhaps more worryingly still, they may lose the ability to stand as a critical check on the behaviour of elected representatives. This risks undermining one of the principal arguments for civil society, namely the purported benefits of a more participatory model of democracy. The worry here may not be such a problem with respect to powerful associations that have significant resources of their own. But for weaker groups, who often speak for the most vulnerable or marginalised members of society, the threat to freedom is very real.

None of this is to ignore or deny the fact that civil society will often contain illiberal and intolerant groups whose members refuse to be *bound by a legal order or set of shared rules.* Groups of this sort have no place within a modern democratic order, since they are not willing to respect the institutions of state, work within the rules and procedures by which politics operates, or be bound by the decisions of elected representatives. Fundamentally, a *civil* association is one which respects the equal standing of other people within a democratic order. It may disagree with them, or have conflicting interests, but it nevertheless accepts that, as far as democracy is concerned, no one is automatically entitled to get his or her way but must instead seek to convince or persuade rather than merely outmanoeuvre or defeat (O'Flynn 2007: 740–743; cf. Przeworski 1993: 62).

Difficulties with civil society

So what should we make of this general definition when set within the context of a society deeply divided along ethnic lines? For some, the idea that civil associations might have an important role to play in deepening democracy in such contexts is at best questionable, since, as Brendan O'Leary puts it, 'there is more than one society and their relations may be far from civil' (O'Leary 2005: 10). In this section, we analyse this basic criticism along two interlinking dimensions: the 'positional dimension' concerns how associations are constituted and operate, and how they see themselves in relation to other civil associations and the state; the 'dispositional dimension' concerns how they formulate and articulate their interests, and how they interact with other civil associations and the state.

The positional dimension

In one sense, O'Leary is wrong to claim that 'there is more than one society'. There is only ever one civil society, albeit made up of different and sometimes conflicting associations. However, in another sense, what marks a deeply divided society out as distinct is the degree to which associations are exclusive rather than inclusive: in the main, membership tends to be drawn from particular ethnic groups rather than from across society as a whole. Consequently, the deliberations that go on within those associations will tend to conform to what Cass Sunstein calls 'the law of group polarization' (Sunstein 2002). That law refers to a statistical regularity which allows us to predict that when people from the same background meet to discuss an issue of importance to them, they will move toward a more extreme point in the direction indicated by the median point of their prior views and opinions (Sunstein 2002: 176). Of course, the mere fact of moving in a more extreme direction is neither good nor bad in itself. But if people only engage in discussion and debate with members of their own ethnic group, they may view every issue as an ethnic issue and hence fail to recognise the importance to democracy of exposing themselves to alternative views.

Under such conditions, civil associations may differ little in their constitution from political parties; after all, the usual mode of party organisation in deeply divided societies is ethnicity. Indeed, they may explicitly attach themselves to such parties and consciously view themselves as part of a larger political project. Thus, for example, John McGarry and Brendan O'Leary argue in this vein that the political preferences of civil society in Northern Ireland do not

> significantly differ from those of its political parties. The most popular civil society organizations in Northern Ireland, the Orange Order and Gaelic Athletic Association, are solidly unionist and nationalist, respectively. True, several, and sometimes admirable, smaller, peace and conflict-resolution organizations reach across the national divide and seek to promote a transcendent identity, but just as many ... are nationalist or unionist groups that want an honourable bi-national compromise.
>
> *(McGarry and O'Leary 2009: 67–68)*

When this occurs, civil associations, however 'honourable' they may be, fail to generate networks that cross ethnic divides or, in the worst cases, to provide an antidote to violence (cf. Kaldor 1999: 61). Instead, they become part of a hegemonic programme that seeks to take control of government and hence lose a key defining feature of a truly civil association, namely its autonomy from the state. Naturally, this may do little or nothing to foster mutual understanding or respect between groups or across society as a whole, or to bridge the gaps of political conflict and thereby deepen democracy (but see Keane 2003: 160–161).

If civil associations are constituted and positioned in such a way that, as a realm of organised social life, ordinary people only ever get to talk to others like themselves, participation may be of little practical benefit (Varshney 2002: 46–51). They will not be informed enough to arrive at reasonable opinions or to make constructive representations to government. On the contrary, there may even be a case for saying that civil associations should be expressly positioned and constrained so that their members' deliberations are shepherded into within-bloc channels where they can do little damage (Lijphart 1977: 41–44; O'Leary 2005: 10; but see Dryzek 2005: 222ff.). In these circumstances, critics would, of course, be right to argue that our primary concern should be with the creation of democratic institutions that enable elected representatives to deliberate away from the glare of public scrutiny and to arrive at compromises that they can then go on to sell to their constituents (Barry 1975: 486).

The dispositional dimension

As the term suggests, civil associations are partly defined by their civility. Here, 'civility' may plausibly be understood as the willingness to explain our political views on terms that are accessible to everybody and could in principle be accepted by anyone. This disposition is often lacking in deeply divided societies, however. Many groups are extremely uncivil in their dealings with others from across the ethnic divide and may even be uncivil in their dealings with government when decisions do not go their way (O'Leary 2005: 10). For example, Ashutosh Varshney describes how so-called 'peace committees' in the Indian city of Aligarh do not seek to build bridges but to protect co-religionists from the possibility of violent attack by other communities. 'They don't facilitate communication with the other communities; they simply raise the perception of risk and harden those who participate in them' (Varshney 2002: 124). Groups of this sort do not see themselves as bound by a legal order or set of shared rules, but instead act outside the rule of law and show little or no respect for social morality.

It is important to understand what is *not* being said here. Some scholars argue that civil associations are defined by their ability to transcend traditional ties, including ethnicity. This argument has been most forcefully put by Ernest Gellner, who claimed that civil society is a distinctly modern phenomenon, based strictly upon open and voluntary associations. On this reading, the concept of civil society therefore excludes associations that are explicitly ethnic, particularly those that are closed to outsiders (Gellner 1995). Yet Gellner's treatment of the concept of civil society seems unduly narrow. For example, it would be odd to think that the Catholic Church, which is clearly a traditional association, is not part of civil society. After all, it is autonomous from the state, it enables ordinary people to gather together and deliberate about public issues, it calls on government to account for its decisions and so forth. More generally, it would be odd to think that taking pride in one's ethnic group and working for the group made one, *ipso facto*, 'uncivil' (Varshney 2002: 43).

What makes a civil association 'civil' is not how it is constituted or the interests that it serves, but how it seeks to engage with other civil associations and government. As Diamond points out, civil associations do not aim to represent the complete set of interests of any particular group of people or of society as a whole. Rather, different associations represent different aspects of the same interest – for example, the Catholic Church will have one view on the issue of abortion, a women's organisation will have another, and a professional medical association will have another still (Diamond 1999: 223). At some level, an association may claim to offer an encompassing perspective or worldview. However, as long as that association is willing to recognise that there are other valid perspectives, and that democracy demands that those perspectives deserve a hearing, the association can be legitimately classed as 'civil'. This is as true for ethnic associations as it is for any other kind of civil association.

Ethnic associations need not be uncivil in their dealings with other associations and government. Yet as far as deeply divided societies are concerned, the fact of the matter is that many associations are not so disposed. They tend to make maximalist or uncompromising demands, are often inward looking and insular in their thinking, and may even align themselves with powerful militant interests. Hence, the problem is not so much that they speak in 'ethnically toned voices', but that they do not speak to people with a different point of view or countenance what they have to say (cf. O'Leary 2005: 10). This incivility serves to reinforce exclusive identities and reify narrow interests, and does nothing to generate new ideas or encourage people to take the broader view. Otherwise put, insofar as there is little willingness to communicate, ordinary people have no way of testing and verifying whether those who think differently from them can be trusted (Putnam 2000: 134–147). Obviously, under such conditions, the capacity of civil society to promote meaningful deliberation and deepen democracy is severely impaired.

Potential solutions

Addressing the positional and dispositional difficulties attaching to civil associations in societies deeply divided along ethnic lines is no easy matter. Yet given the important role that those associations may play in deepening democracy, every effort should be made to develop and implement appropriate solutions. The comparative politics literature stresses the importance to democracy of designing political institutions that can enable politicians from different ethnic groups to share power with one another. But there is also an important body of research that points to the benefits of creating institutions that can enable ordinary people to talk to and learn from one another, thereby encouraging them to formulate views and opinions that bridge ethnic divisions, and that in principle make it easier for politicians at the governmental level to make the comprises upon which stable democracy inevitably depends. Underpinning this latter body of research is one basic, but nonetheless profound, observation: politicians can negotiate binding agreements and even enforce them, but only ordinary people can change human relationships (Lederach 1997; Saunders 2001). Of course, one should not exaggerate: macro political institutions are vitally important and can also assist in shaping attitudes and behaviour. Nevertheless, the fact remains that deepening democracy is the responsibility of everyone in society, not simply the responsibility of politicians (Walzer 2004: 83).

One would not expect negotiations between politicians from different ethnic groups to occur in the absence of facilitating conditions – for example, the presence of external parties who are willing to act as impartial mediators, or agreed institutions and procedures that structure the negotiation process itself (Zartman 1995; du Toit 2003). By the same token, one should not expect meaningful deliberation to occur across civil associations, or between civil associations and government, in the absence of appropriate support. That support should involve a dual-track process. First, it should involve strengthening *inclusive* associations whose members come from different sides of the ethnic divide, and second, it should involve conduits that enable *exclusive* associations whose members are drawn from different ethnic groups to talk to one another. In both cases, financial or material support may come from the state or from the international community, although matters must be handled carefully (Lederach 1997: 94–95).

The state or the international community may actively seek to support civil associations whose memberships are cross cutting. They may legitimately see such associations as 'schools for democracy' which offer ordinary people the opportunity to talk to those who are different from themselves and to learn to couch their views in terms that those can in principle accept. In other words, in seeking to offer such support, they can try to overcome the positional and dispositional difficulties discussed above. However, there is a risk that the state or the international community will make funding conditional upon pursuing an agenda that transforms civil associations into a set of regulatory agencies. This need not be a deliberate strategy, but its effect is to compromise the autonomy of those associations it chooses to support (Belloni 2001: 176). Moreover, in choosing to support such associations, the state or international community may end up alienating ordinary people by supporting associations that do not seem immediately relevant to them. Thus, in his discussion of the case of Bosnia, Roberto Belloni argues that 'Bosnians are often uneasy about and confused by the term "civil society" and its frequent equation to civilised society'. As he goes on to point out, most Bosnians 'rightly think of themselves as intelligent and educated people', not least of all because 'there already exists a long history of Bosnian multi-ethnicity, inherited from the Ottoman and Yugoslav periods, that differs from the liberal version of "civility" and makes the "civilising" mission of the international community suspicious' (Belloni 2001: 169).

Thus, on the one hand, it is vitally important to support civil associations whose members come from different sides of the ethnic divide, since those associations can have a vital role to play in building bridges and in deepening democracy. But, on the other hand, it is vitally important not to promote or impose any model of 'civil association' that is at odds with the way in which ordinary people generally tend to understand the term. Consequently, it is also necessary to foster dialogue between civil associations whose memberships are exclusive. In a deeply divided society, levels of social integration will be low. As we noted in our introductory remarks, the members of different ethnic groups often have little or no meaningful contact with one other and often live their lives within parallel social spheres. This not only affects who joins which civil associations, but also delimits the opportunities they will have to engage with those who think differently to them. In other words, it affects how associations are positioned in relation to one another and how they are positioned in relation to the state, as well as the types of dispositions their members are likely to display.

A second track, then, involves the creation of institutions that serve as conduits which enable civil associations whose members are exclusively drawn from one or other side of the ethnic divide to become better informed about the views of others in society and hence to arrive at greater levels of mutual understanding and respect. In so doing, the hope is that ordinary people from different ethnic groups will have the space and opportunity to develop their own sense of what 'civil society' ought to mean, given the circumstances in which they actually find themselves. The role that the state or the international community can play here carries less risk than along the first track, since support is not provided directly to civil associations but is instead channelled indirectly through facilitating institutions. A good example of the kind of institution that is at issue here is the Community Relations Council in Northern Ireland which was created by the British government to promote better relations between members of the two conflicting ethnic groups, Irish nationalists and British unionists. More specifically, its purpose is to promote reconciliation and mutual trust, to develop opportunities for social learning across division, to facilitate constructive debate throughout society, and to encourage greater acceptance and respect for cultural diversity (*Interim Strategic Plan* 2007).

Thus, the point of this two-track approach is to change how the members of ethnic groups are positioned in relation to one another and, correspondingly, the dispositions that they are likely to develop or display. However, as we have already indicated, it is also important to consider how civil associations are positioned in relation to the state. Just as it is possible to create conduits that enable the members of different ethnic groups to talk to one another, it is also possible to create conduits that enable associations to talk to government and hence to have their views and opinions factored into the decision-making process. The creation and maintenance of such conduits enables a more consultative and inclusive form of political engagement to develop – one that enables civil associations to take part in deliberation with, and inform the thinking of, politicians at the governmental level. A good example of the sort of conduit that is at issue here is the Office of the Status of Women in South Africa, the major objective of which is 'to influence and shape government policy in order to ensure that gender issues are integrated into the overall policies of government' (Harris and Reilly 1998: 326).

The vital point to note about this latter sort of conduit is that they help to maintain a sense of distance between state and society. They allow civil associations to talk to government, but without getting caught up in the actual business of making decisions. This 'decoupling of the deliberative and decisional moments' not only enables civil associations to preserve their autonomy, but also allows their members to discuss political issues without constantly having to worry about what any final decision might mean for the future of their particular ethnic group (Dryzek 2005: 220). This sense of increased distance can take some of the heat out of democratic politics by enabling ordinary people to realise that every issue does not have to be framed as an ethnic issue or treated as a potential site of ethnic conflict.

Taking the heat out of the deliberations that go on within civil society also opens up the space for exploratory interchange across difference (Dryzek 2005: 220; cf. Foley and Edwards 1996: 39). Over time, it may therefore foster a greater sense of trust among ordinary people, a greater willingness to defend their views and opinions on terms that others might in principle accept, and hence a greater capacity to work together for the sake of a common future. Crucially, this civilising potential of civil society may not only serve to shape the dispositions of ordinary people in more positive directions, but also to reinforce democratic institutions by making it easier for politicians to compromise across ethnic lines. As such, civil associations may have a vital role to play in deepening democracy – not as an alternative to political engagement at the governmental level, but as a vital supplement to it.

Conclusion

As we have argued in this chapter, civil associations can have a vital role to play in deepening democracy in deeply divided societies. Yet that role is heavily contingent upon whether ordinary people from different sides of the ethnic divide have the opportunity to deliberate together within appropriate institutional structures. Insofar as those structures can be fostered and sustained, ordinary people can come to learn more about one another and perhaps also develop a greater sense of respect for the views of those with whom they fundamentally disagree. This can give politicians from different ethnic groups the confidence – and indeed the mandate – to compromise with one another and hence, in the longer run, to work for the good of society as a whole. In sum, civil associations can help foster those very things that are in shortest supply in deeply divided societies but which are critical for peace and stability.

Further reading

Belloni, R. (2008) 'Civil Society in War-to-Democracy Transitions', in A. Jarstad and T. Sisk (eds), *From War to Democracy*. Cambridge: Cambridge University Press, pp. 182–210.

Cinalli, M. (2005) 'Below and Beyond Power Sharing: Relational Structures across Institutions and Civil Society', in I. O'Flynn and D. Russell (eds), *Power Sharing: New Challenges for Divided Societies*. London: Pluto, pp. 172–187.

Cox, M. (ed.) (2008) *Social Capital and Peace-building: Creating and Resolving Conflict with Trust and Social Networks* (Routledge Studies in Peace and Conflict Resolution). London: Routledge.

Devic, A. (2006) 'Transnationalization of Civil Society in Kosovo: International and Local Limits of Peace and Multiculturalism', *Ethnopolitics* 5(3): 257–273.

Edwards, M. (2004) *Civil Society*. Cambridge: Polity Press.

Orjuela, C. (2003) 'Building Peace in Sri Lanka: A Role for Civil Society?' *Journal of Peace Research* 40(2): 195–212.

References

Barber, B. (1984) *Strong Democracy: Participatory Politics for a New Age*. Berkeley: University of California Press.

Barry, B. (1975) 'Review Article: Political Accommodation and Consociational Democracy', *British Journal of Political Science* 5(4): 477–505.

Belloni, R. (2001) 'Civil Society and Peacebuilding in Bosnia and Herzegovina', *Journal of Peace Research* 38(2): 163–180.

Diamond, L. (1999) *Developing Democracy: Toward Consolidation*. Baltimore: Johns Hopkins University Press.

Dryzek, J. (2005) 'Deliberative Democracy in Divided Societies: Alternatives to Agonism and Analgesia', *Political Theory* 33(2): 218–242.

Du Toit, P. (2003) 'Rules and Procedures for Negotiated Peacemaking' in J. Darby and R. MacGinty, (eds), *Contemporary Peace Making: Conflict, Violence and Peace Processes*. Basingstoke: Palgrave Macmillan, pp. 65–76.

Foley, M. and B. Edwards (1996) 'The Paradox of Civil Society', *Journal of Democracy* 7(3): 38–52.

Galston, W. (2000) 'Civil Society and the "Art of Association"', *Journal of Democracy* 11(1): 64–70.

Gellner, A. (1995) *Conditions of Liberty: Civil Society and Its Rivals*. Harmonsworth: Penguin.

Green, L. (1999) 'Internal Minorities and their Rights', in W. Kymlicka (ed.), *The Rights of Minority Cultures*. Oxford: Oxford University Press.

Harris, P. and Reilly, B. (eds) (1998) *Democracy and Deep-Rooted Conflict: Options for Negotiators*. Stockholm: International Institute for Democracy and Electoral Assistance.

Interim Strategic Plan (2007) Belfast: Northern Ireland Community Relations Council. Available at http://www.community-relations.org.uk/filestore/documents/IntSP0710.doc [accessed 14. 04. 2009].

Kaldor, M. (1999) *New and Old Wars: Organised Violence in a Global Era*. Cambridge: Polity Press.

Keane, J. (2003) *Global Civil Society?* Cambridge: Cambridge University Press.

Lederach, J. (1997) *Building Peace: Sustainable Reconciliation in Divided Societies*. Washington, DC: United States Institute of Peace.

Lijphart, A. (1977) *Democracy in Plural Societies: A Comparative Exploration*. New Haven, CT: Yale University Press.

McGarry, J. and O'Leary, B. (2009) 'Power Shared After the Deaths of Thousands', in R. Taylor (ed.), *Consociational Theory: McGarry and O'Leary and the Northern Ireland Conflict*. London: Routledge, pp. 15–84.

Mill, J.S. (1991 [1861]) 'Considerations on Representative Government', in J. Gray (ed.), *John Stuart Mill: On Liberty and Other Essays*. Oxford: Oxford University Press, pp. 203–467.

O'Flynn, I. (2007) 'Review Article: Divided Societies and Deliberative Democracy', *British Journal of Political Science* 37(4): 731–751.

O'Leary, B. (2005) 'Debating Consociational Politics: Normative and Explanatory Arguments', in S. Noel (ed.), *From Power Sharing to Democracy: Post-Conflict Institutions in Ethnically Divided Societies*. Montreal and Kingston: McGill-Queen's University Press, pp. 3–43.

Przeworski, A. (1993) 'Democracy as a Contingent Outcome of Conflicts', in J. Elster and R. Slagstad (eds), *Constitutionalism and Democracy*. Cambridge: Cambridge University Press, pp. 59–80.

Putnam, R. (2000) *Bowling Alone: The Collapse and Revival of American Community*. New York: Simon & Schuster.

Riker, W. (1982) *Liberalism Against Populism*. San Francisco: W. H. Freeman.

Saunders, H. (2001) *A Public Peace Process: Sustained Dialogue to Transform Racial and Ethnic Conflicts*. Basingstoke: Palgrave Macmillan.

Schmitter, P. (1997) 'Civil Society East and West', in L. Diamond, M. Plattner, Y. Chu (eds), *Consolidating the Third Wave Democracies: Themes and Perspectives*. Baltimore, MD: Johns Hopkins University Press, pp. 240–262.

Schumpeter, J. (1942) *Capitalism, Socialism and Democracy*. New York: Harper and Row.

Sunstein, C. (2002) 'The Law of Group Polarization', *The Journal of Political Philosophy* 10(2): 175–195.

Varshney, A. (2002) *Ethnic Conflict and Civil Life: Hindus and Muslims in India*. New Haven, CT: Yale University Press.

Walzer, M. (2004) *Politics and Passion: Towards a More Egalitarian Liberalism*. New Haven, CT: Yale University Press.

Warren, M. (2001) *Democracy and Association*. Princeton: Princeton University Press.

Young, I. (1999) 'State, Civil Society, and Social Justice', in I. Shapiro and C. Hacker Cordón (eds), *Democracy's Value*. Cambridge: Cambridge University Press, pp. 141–162.

Zartman, W. (1995) 'Dynamics and Constraints in Negotiations in Internal Conflicts', in W. Zartman, (ed.), *Elusive Peace: Negotiating an End to Civil Wars*. Washington, DC: Brookings Institute, pp. 3–29.

19

HUMAN RIGHTS AND ETHNOPOLITICS

Joseph Marko

Introduction: how to reconcile political unity, legal equality with cultural diversity?

Any overview on the intricate relationship between human rights and ethnopolitics first has to give an exposition of the epistemological problems and ideological underpinnings in understanding the 'meaning' of these concepts. It goes without saying that the claim of universal human rights raised by the American Declaration of Independence in 1776 never mirrored social and political 'reality'. To put it in a nutshell, the European history of state-formation and nation-building can be summarized in theory by two 'ideal-types' of the relationship of the concepts of 'state' and 'nation' – namely, the 'French' model of a 'state-nation' based on 'cultural indifference' and the 'German' model of the 'nation-state' by constructing 'ethnic difference' and ascribing political and legal significance to it.

The French, or rather the 'Jacobin' model of a 'state-nation' is firmly based on the notion of popular sovereignty exercised by 'abstract' citizens, who are equal before the law irrespective of their diversity due to gender, economic or social status, or 'ethnic' or 'national' origin, and a complementary doctrine of 'national' sovereignty, based on the original concept of 'territorial indivisibility' stemming from monarchic inheritance law. In conclusion, the 'imagination' of an 'other' people within the French nation is inconceivable with the consequence that cultural and political pluralism of groups, formed on an ethnic basis and claiming rights as such, is prohibited and social upward mobility is only possible through assimilation into 'la civilisation française'.

The model of the 'ethnicized' nation-state is normatively based on the so-called 'nationality principle' with an 'ethnically' conceived nation based on the ideal of cultural/ethnic homogeneity in contrast to the 'civic' nation based on ethnic indifference. Hence, the individual person is no longer conceived of as an 'abstract' citizen, but defined by its membership in a certain ethnic group. However, nowhere can we find a state whose population is culturally homogenous in terms of religion or language as cultural markers. The fact of cultural diversity is thus translated by the nationality principle into an 'ethnic difference' of groups and their power relations based on the categorical distinction of majority/minority. In effect, this model has led to suppression, expulsion from the territory and genocide as the history of the twentieth century amply demonstrates.

Is the lesson provided by history thus, that ethnic conflict with these effects can only be avoided either through assimilation, i.e. by giving up one's cultural identity, or institutional segregation and/or territorial separation since ethnic diversity as such seems to be the major root cause of ethnic conflict? All 'primordialist' social and political theories following this assumption are based on the epistemological trap of a 'naturalization of difference'. The twin-ideologies of racism and ethno-nationalism make use of this strategy for their policy pre-scriptions by legitimizing segregation or partition as the 'natural' consequence of the allegedly biologically or culturally predetermined, i.e. 'natural', trait of ethnicity. Hence, as long as ethnicity is 'seen' as a 'primordial "given" of human existence' (Smith 1991: 39 and 20) which stands in dichotomical opposition to political unity and legal equality, ethnic diversity must be tamed or at least tempered by a strong state and 'muddling through' is indeed the best that can be achieved for re-construction or reconciliation after a violent ethnic conflict (Canovan 1996: 83–100; Levy 2007).

In contrast to primordial theories, however, it has to be stressed that we 'construct' social, political and legal categories such as 'people' or 'nation' through three analytically distinct, though, in practice, intimately linked steps:

- on the epistemological level, we have to make a choice based on the binary code of identity/difference;
- on the normative level, we again have to make a choice based on the binary code of equality/inequality; and
- on the empirical level, we make a choice based on the binary code of inclusion/exclusion.

Hence, all forms of racism and ethno-nationalism are based on the same structural code, which is characterized by the unilinear equation of identity=equality=inclusion, or, the other way round, difference=inequality=exclusion. Only if the ideologically constructed and in no way 'natural' antagonism of equality and difference is transformed into a triadic structure of identity, equality and diversity without the alleged predetermination for conflict or coop-eration, institutional diversity management becomes possible in order to reconcile political unity, legal equality and cultural diversity within one social and political system.

The problem of definition and the 'right to self-determination of peoples'

With regard to the function of law, i.e. to regulate and limit the exercise of power, con-ventional juridical wisdom will tell us that one must first define what or who should later be protected by law. However, all efforts to establish a 'general' definition of the term 'minority' as the 'object' of protection, which would universally be recognized under public international law have so far failed. The defining element simply cannot be an 'objective' criterion, the subjective will of persons or the number of the members of a group, but has always to do with power relations. Consequently the first Organization for Security and Co-operation in Europe (OSCE) High Commissioner on National Minorities, Max van der Stoel, declared, 'Even though I may not have a definition of what constitutes a minority, I would dare to say that I know a minority when I see one.'

Moreover, when looking back into the history of the twentieth century, the critical question arises: What else distinguishes a 'people' with a right to self-determination from an 'ethnic or national minority' but the (re-)drawing of territorial boundaries by the victorious parties of a war? Moreover, is it even theoretically possible to reconcile the *prima facie* mutually excluding principles of state sovereignty and self-determination of peoples?

A first important test case came to the fore already after the First World War with the dispute between Finland and Sweden concerning the legal status of the Åland Islands, inhabited by Swedish speakers. In 1920 the dispute was brought before the League of Nations' Council which appointed a Commission of Rapporteurs, concluding that the Åland Islanders were not a 'people', but simply a 'minority' without a right to self-determination. However, at the same time, the Commission also addressed the question of oppression through a government and concluded that oppression would indeed be a factor allowing a minority to secede, but only as a 'last resort when the state lacks either the will or the power to enact and apply just and effective guarantees' (Report 1921) for religious, linguistic and social freedom. Thereby the Commission, through a functional interpretation, opened the way to reconcile the seemingly antagonistic principles of state sovereignty and self-determination of peoples by reference to the human rights aspect of democratic governance, thereby de-constructing the alleged dichotomy through a transformation of the problem into a triadic structure.

The principle of self-determination of peoples, explicitly enshrined in the UN-Charter, became legally entrenched by the UN General Assembly Resolution 1514 in 1960 'Granting of Independence to Colonial Countries and Peoples' and the respective Articles 1 of the UN's International Covenant on Civil and Political Rights (ICCPR) and the International Covenant on Economic, Social and Cultural Rights (ICESCR) of 1966. The same triadic structure of state sovereignty–self-determination of peoples–human rights as an element of democratic governance can then be found in the provisions concerning the principle of equal rights and self-determination of peoples of the 'Declaration on Principles of International Law Concerning Friendly Relations and Co-operation Among States in Accordance with the Charter of the United Nations', annexed to UN General Assembly Resolution 2625 of 1970. But due to the political premises of the Cold War, the mainstream of public international law scholars was of the opinion that the right to self-determination and the principle of uti possidetis juris for the establishment of frontiers of newly independent states were only applicable within the colonial 'context', but not in Europe.

With the disintegration of the Socialist Federal Republic of Yugoslavia in the course of 1991, the problem of self-determination returned to the European continent. In November 1991 Lord Carrington asked the meanwhile established European Community arbitration commission, the so-called Badinter Commission, to deliberate on the questions whether the Serb population in Croatia and Bosnia-Herzegovina had the right to self-determination and whether the internal boundaries between Croatia, Serbia and Bosnia-Herzegovina could be regarded as frontiers in terms of public international law. In Opinions Nr. 2 and 3 of 11 January 1992, the Commission responded that Serbs in Croatia had only a right to minority protection and confirmed the principle of uti juris possidetis as a 'general principle' of public international law. Despite strong criticism of these legal opinions (Ratner 1998; Stokes 2009), they contribute in a substantive way to the further legal development by making clear that self-determination and uti possidetis are no longer restricted to a 'colonial context' and that the prohibition of use of force does not only apply to international borders, but also internal borderlines and thus invokes the uti possidetis principle and its functional logic: 'territorial adjustments' by use of force shall never be recognized.

Also Security Council Resolution 1244 in 1999 did, initially, not reward the use of force by Serb authorities and the insurgent Kosovo Liberation Army by referring to the right of territorial integrity of the Federal Republic of Yugoslavia and promising only 'substantial autonomy' to Kosovo until a 'final settlement' of the conflict could be reached. The unilateral declaration of independence by the Kosovo Assembly in February 2008 and the recognition of Kosovo as a new state can hardly be justified except for the illegal obstruction of UNMIK (United Nations Interim Administration Mission in Kosovo) administration in Northern Kosovo by all Serb governments since 1999 in upholding parallel institutions and thereby trying to prepare the ground for a territorial separation of Kosovo as well as the exclusion of Kosovo Albanians from the right to vote and to participate in the referendum of the Serb constitution of 2006 (Muharremi 2008; Marko 2008).

In conclusion, the use of force in international relations (Grey 2000; Gazzini 2005; Hofmann 2003) is combined with two legal-dogmatic problems, which go hand in hand in practice: unilateral and/or violent secession and humanitarian intervention by third parties. With regard to the legality of secession and humanitarian intervention there are two conflicting approaches: lawyers of public international law, methodically anchored in strict legal positivism, simply deny the legality with reference to the text of the principles and rules of the UN-Charter and their interpretation in light of the 'original intent'. Lawyers preferring a method of contextual/functional interpretation will also deny the legality, except for certain exceptions as 'ultima ratio'. It is then a matter of hotly disputed facts what will be recognized as 'ultima ratio'. It is beyond doubt for proponents of this approach that (attempted) genocide will be a situation which allows the use of force by external intervention. It is, however, less clear and disputed whether also ethnic cleansing allows the use of force and where the empirical and legal borderline between genocide and ethnic cleansing can be drawn. The interpretation of genocide by international criminal courts (Schabas 2000; International Court of Justice 2007) is rather narrow and requires specific intent which can hardly ever be proven, thus scholarly literature vehemently argues to 'criminalize' also ethnic cleansing as a separate criminal offence (Mulaj 2008: 163–170; Hofmann 2003: 146).

It goes hand in hand with these developments that a new doctrine is also emerging in international law. After the illegal North Atlantic Treaty Organization (NATO) intervention in Kosovo 1999, the Canadian Government established an independent International Commission on Intervention and State Sovereignty (ICISS) with the task to reconcile intervention for humanitarian purposes and sovereignty. This commission produced a report with the programmatic title 'The Responsibility to Protect' (ICISS 2001).

Hence, sovereignty does not only include a right of states to territorial integrity and non-intervention, but also a responsibility to protect their own populations. Only if the state concerned is unable or unwilling or itself the perpetrator, it becomes the responsibility of the international community to act in its place. This new principle was then adopted by the UN General Assembly at its World Summit in 2005. Under the heading 'Responsibility to protect populations from genocide, war crimes, ethnic cleansing and crimes against humanity', paragraphs 138 and 139 summarize the new obligations following from this doctrine through measures of prevention, reaction and rebuilding (UN GA 2005). However, it remains to be seen how this new doctrine will be transformed into 'hard' public international law.

Legal standard setting: from minority protection to human rights protection and back?

After the Second World War, there was a dramatic shift of the paradigm from the protection of the 'special' rights of minorities as ethnic groups to the notion that it is 'essential' and appropriate to protect individuals and their 'general' human rights, as can be seen in the developments in the legal standard setting processes within the United Nations as well as the

Council of Europe (Thornberry 1991; Pentassuglia 2002). The ethnic issue was not totally neglected, but it was expected that the protection of human rights in combination with the principle of non-discrimination on grounds such as, inter alia, 'race, sex, language, religion, or national origin' in the language of Article 14 of the European Convention on Human Rights (ECHR) of 1950 would be much more functional instead of a special and group rights approach. Due to the experience with both totalitarian ideologies of Nazism and Bolshevism, for Western style democracies individual human rights and their effective protection against violation by public authorities through judicial enforcement remained the 'essence' of liberalism and democratic governance until the end of the Cold War.

At the European level the breakdown of communist regimes in Central, Eastern and Southeastern Europe in 1989 brought again a swing of the pendulum back to the minority protection paradigm as can be seen from various international documents. The chapter on national minorities of the Commission on Security and Cooperation in Europe (CSCE) Copenhagen Meeting 1990 sets the tone by referring in the preamble to 'cultural diversity and the resolution of questions relating to national minorities' through 'respect for the rights of persons belonging to national minorities as part of the universally recognized human rights' as 'an essential factor for peace, justice, stability and democracy'. Hence, no longer is assimilation into an ethnically homogeneous or indifferent nation-state the underlying premise of minority protection, but cultural diversity as such is recognized as a basic value for democratic governance. From this perspective, human and minority rights are no longer opposite approaches, but minority rights are seen as part of an all-embracing human rights regime and human and minority rights are seen not only as an essential element of liberal democracy, but also as a necessary pre-condition for peace and stability. And finally, the provisions require states to take affirmative action measures to protect and promote the (different) 'ethnic, cultural, linguistic and religious identity' of minorities, i.e. the groups as such, and not only to abstain from discrimination. Following this declaration, the CSCE/OSCE member states established a High Commissioner on National Minorities (HCNM) as 'early warning' and conflict prevention mechanism at their Helsinki meeting in 1992. Within the Council of Europe, the Parliamentary Assembly took the lead and adopted Recommendation 1201 on an additional protocol on the rights of minorities to the ECHR, which included in Article 1 not only a definition of 'national minority', but would have rendered also a judicial enforcement mechanism through the European Court of Human Rights.

However, a backlash followed suit. Due to the political and ideological resistance of many unitary states within the Council of Europe (CoE), such an additional protocol was not adopted by the CoE Committee of Ministers (CoM). Instead, the European Charter for Regional and Minority Languages and the Framework Convention for the Protection of National Minorities were adopted as a 'substitute'. Despite early criticism with regard to vague language, weak obligations and only a political supervision by these instruments (Benoît-Rohmer 1996: 40–44), any assessment of the activities of the HCNM and the monitoring mechanism of the Framework Convention for the Protection of National Minorities after more than a decade must come to the conclusion that they have established a rather effective 'pan-European' minority protection regime. All of the opinions of the expert committees and the conclusions and recommendations of the CoM offer a massive corpus of text, which is already characterized as 'soft jurisprudence' (Lantschner 2009), consisting of legally binding 'minimum standards', 'emerging standards' and 'best practices'. In conclusion, the political monitoring mechanism can be seen as an advantage today, which has helped to overcome the political deadlocks in legal standard setting. In addition, the permanent dialogue between the organs of the CoE and governments and minority organizations, and the political pressure following from the publication of all documents must be seen as a long-term benefit which could also lead to a change of attitudes of majority populations in terms of the acceptance of cultural diversity.

However, despite this rather optimistic assessment, in particular if compared to other regions of the world, there are some leftovers. So far the EU has not incorporated a specific minority protection provision into its primary law due to strong resistance from the above mentioned states. Article 13 of the EC Treaty and the corresponding EC-Directives are still an expression of the anti-discrimination approach and the burning banlieux in French cities as well as the electoral success of right wing populist or even extremist parties all over Europe prove the constantly pressing problem of the integration of new minorities. Nevertheless, 'effective participation, full and effective equality and promotion of national minorities' identity and culture' as the 'three corners of a triangle which together form the main foundations of the Framework Convention' are fundamental values, which reflect a shift of the paradigm from 'national minority' protection as means of conflict 'resolution' in the context of state sovereignty and the European nation-state models to the 'management' of ethnic diversity, where 'old' and 'new minorities' can also serve as a bridge for peaceful cooperation based on the functional prerequisites of (internal) 'autonomy', in order to preserve and promote cultural diversity and 'integration' in order to enhance social cohesion and to stabilize political unity within, between and beyond states.

Human and minority rights in the life cycle of ethnic conflict

The pre-conflict phase: ethno-mobilization and prevention

Against all forms of primordial theories it follows from the epistemological analysis of the preceding section as well as from a careful comparative analysis of empirical case studies of ethnic conflict around the globe that cultural diversity as one of the possible 'structural' causes does not automatically have to lead to tensions or even violent conflict. In addition to political, socio-economic or perceptual underlying causes, there have to be internal or external 'proximate' causes which enable the outbreak of conflict. Internal causes are 'bad leaders' or 'predatory' elites who control their own community for their own, individual political and/or economic interest, are ready to spoil legitimate government also by use of force and are not willing to compromise. External causes are usually 'bad' neighbours either by diffusion, when conflicts spill over, or by escalation through direct military intervention or (in)direct support of insurgent parties and their militias.

Why do leaders then choose war over peace and how do fears and threats translate into violence? The general hypothesis of the constructivist-instrumentalist approach goes that 'ethnic entrepreneurs' in a 'fear-producing environment', such as a government breakdown, shifts in political power balances between groups and/or changes in control over economic resources and accompanying shifts in the balance of rival external patrons, (mis)use the 'feeling' that only my own group can protect me against the 'others' for triggering a political process of ethno-national mobilization. Hence in a situation of regime change or weak or failed states, they create or make recourses to the 'we-feeling' of their group and transform economic, political or cultural tensions into an ethnic conflict over identity and/or territory, in short they create a political or even physical 'security dilemma'. Hence, the creation of we–they antagonisms and enemy stereotyping through political or religious leaders, intellectuals and in the media has to serve as an 'early warning' indicator that such perceived or already real security dilemmas are engineered. Political and legal disputes over the 'justification' of claims and counter-claims concerning basic human and minority rights such as freedom of expression and association and more special identity rights with regard to the use of the minority languages and scripts for names, topographical indications, and/or as 'second', additional, but equal official language in education, administration and before courts are the next serious indicators that the process of ethno-mobilization by transforming competing rights and interests into ethnically perceived, antagonistic identity conflicts is in full swing. The more one group challenges the status quo and the less another is prepared to allow changes, the more likely it is that conflict will rapidly escalate into violence. Finally, recourse to 'extra-constitutional' means such as 'illegal' referenda on establishing territorial autonomies or the abolition of existing autonomy regimes and the formation of para-military formations already require the question whether it is high time for external mediation, arbitration or even intervention.

Conflict and conflict settlement

It goes without saying that ethnic conflicts over territory and identity, when they indeed have become 'primordial' so that the physical existence of members of groups, because of their group characteristics, is endangered in reality, may lead to gross violations of human and minority rights, in the worst case to ethnic cleansing and genocide. Mass killings, raping, torture in detention camps, and expulsion from the territory are part of the agenda of ethnic entrepreneurs in pursuing their ethno-nationalist policies. The central question then is, how to stop violence? Through external mediation, sanctions or, in the final analysis, military intervention? The legal-dogmatic problem of 'humanitarian intervention' and the use of force by external actors in 'civil' wars has been discussed above. What concerns here is the perspective of conflict management and resolution.

As we have experienced in the wars in Croatia and Bosnia and Herzegovina in the 1990s, mediation in the framework of the UN- and EU-led Yugoslavia conference was a total failure. The international community, being ill-prepared, ill-equipped and lacking political will, did always 'too little, too late' in order to prevent the outbreak of violence or to stop violence. But even after military intervention the question arises, how is it possible to negotiate for sustainable peace and not only a cease-fire? In other words, what encourages ethnic entrepreneurs to give up their rational choice for a politics of violence and how is it possible to deal with the legacy of violent conflict not only in terms of security guarantees and institutional arrangements, but also concerning the damages for the political culture, i.e. the mix of fear, hate and ensuing distrust and thus the lack of societal solidarity and loyalty vis-à-vis state institutions following violent conflict? But why should 'radical' claims for secession or partition be given up, since there is no military solution possible for self-determination conflicts in terms of long-term peace? Why should there be a 'rational' interest in stability, if a 'frozen conflict' based on permanent international crisis-management allows predatory elites to enrich themselves and their clientele through state controlled 'privatization' and organized crime, which might even be supported by an external strong patron? Moreover, an ethic of self-restraint of political leaders and tolerance of the people as a precondition for peace-building is exactly the problem after violent conflict. The absence of tolerance and mutual trust is exactly the definitional essence of 'severe ethnic divide'. Insofar, also the theoretical battles between accommodationists and integrationists do not really help (McGarry, O'Leary and Simeon 2008).

Nevertheless, there are some general lessons to be learned from negotiations on the terms of peace-settlements and the effects of the structure of their provisions, based on the assumption that tolerance and trust must and can be created by institutional design and law-enforcement. First, to denounce one of the parties of ethnic conflict as 'terrorists', as was the case on the eve of the fully fledged war between Serb authorities and the Kosovo Liberation Army in Kosovo, simply pours oil onto the flames. The same is true, on the other hand, if the 'international community' shies away from simply calling ethnic cleansing and attempted genocide by state authorities or agents controlled by them, what it is, namely an international crime. Hence, there is a dialectic of necessary impartiality and taking sides which can only be resolved, if the dichotomy between 'realists' and 'idealists' in international relations theory and diplomacy is overcome by a firm commitment to international legal standards and their implied value judgements. It goes without saying that this needs also more legal clarity through a better international criminal law regime as argued above.

Any attempt to exclude 'radicals' and their positions from the framework for negotiation and to accommodate only the interests of moderate parties in the settlement agreement, is bound to fail. As can be seen from case studies on Northern Ireland (McGarry and O'Leary 2008) and Bosnia-Herzegovina (Marko 2013), the former will always try to spoil the peace-building process by continuing ethno-national mobilization and recourse to illegal means or even violence. Post-conflict reconstruction efforts will then resemble permanent crisis management rather than stable peace-building.

Wolff also argues (Wolff 2007: 149–151) that the 'velvet divorce' of the Czech Republic and Slovakia, the dissolution of the Soviet Union and the Israel–Palestine conflict demonstrate that separation and independent statehood are (potentially) viable solutions provided that they are consensual and well managed. There are, of course, the general moral and legal implications with this view that partition after violent conflict would reward and legitimize ethnic entrepreneurs' politics of violence in the end and, at least in the European context, forced population transfer is prohibited by Article 3 of Protocol Nr. 4 ECHR. However, it is also contestable that partition is a viable solution in terms of political stability. First, new states created by partition are not automatically homogenous so that 'new' minorities are created which will be, in the logic of ethno-nationalism as basis for territorial partition, dominated and suppressed, thereby creating new conflicts. Hence, partition makes sense in the ethno-nationalist logic only if it goes hand in hand with population transfer, which has been termed the 'Lausanne principle' after the international agreement concluded between Greece and Turkey in 1923. However, studies on the partition between India and Pakistan, Cyprus, etc., reveal that population transfer is never voluntary, but always forced and does not lead, neither in the short nor long run, to the acclaimed security for peoples in their new country and regional stability between states (Kumar 1999; Clark 2007).

All post-conflict activities for political unity have to address the '4 Rs', rehabilitation, restitution, and reconciliation, and thereby also address old and new root and proximate causes in order to prevent a relapse into a conflict cycle. Hence, in order to be able to reconcile peace *and* justice from the very beginning, any interim settlement agreement should reflect a 'creative ambiguity' along the following lines:

- The content of a settlement agreement must contain rules on immediate security guarantees and a new institutional framework where conflicting interests can be accommodated so that the incentives for non-violence and compromise outweigh benefits expected from a further politics of violence.
- At the same time, it is necessary to entrench and enforce rules on human and minority rights protection and transitional justice, in case of previous ethnic cleansing in particular, through the right to return to the home of origin and the restitution of property in

conjunction with an obligation of authorities to take affirmative action to reverse the effects of ethnic cleansing.

- Moreover, rules are needed to stop ongoing ethno-mobilization by the respective agents in government, political parties, media, and education to break the danger of 'intergenerational vengeance' and a conflict cycle.
- As far as procedure and time-lines are concerned, the rules should enable flexibility for the re-negotiation of institutional arrangements in order to be able to 'temper' the saliency of ethnicity for the entire political system in progressing from corporate to liberal power-sharing and, finally, to integration under an impartial internal umpire, as the case law of the Constitutional Court of Bosnia-Herzegovina can demonstrate (Marko 2013).

Finally, the international legal community and institutions must be ready for a long-term commitment. Any public exit strategy with the announcement of deadlines will only invite the warring parties to compromise on the surface, but to spoil in reality any implementation of the settlement in the expectation that they have only to wait and see the withdrawal of the international military and/or civilian presence.

The post-conflict phase: reconstruction and reconciliation

In the immediate aftermath of conflict, reconstruction efforts by implementation of the peace settlement have to have priority. However, as can particularly be seen from the 'democratization' efforts of the OSCE in Bosnia and Herzegovina, early and repeated elections every second year, which have been free, but not fair, only legitimize the 'radical' ethno-nationalist parties and their leaders, thereby enabling them, on the basis of the corporate power-sharing arrangements of the Dayton constitution, to form a cartel of power and to hinder or even block reforms to overcome the institutional weaknesses and to strengthen the rule of law. The general lesson for reconstruction is that effectiveness of institutions and rule of law must be given priority over democratization. Moreover, as the riots in Kosovo in March 2004 against Serb and Roma communities demonstrated, the vigilance with regard to security issues cannot be given up, so that an international military presence with a robust and extended mandate including police tasks and civil–military cooperation will be necessary also for long-term peace-building.

The second important task is economic reconstruction in order to get rid of aid-dependency and to trigger sustainable economic development. More often than not economic aid does not reach the people who are in need immediately after conflict because the control over economic aid and its distribution by the warring parties becomes a proximate cause for ongoing conflict. Moreover, what happens when partition and a politics of divide and rule are not effectively tackled can be observed again in Bosnia-Herzegovina, where the power to legislate in economic affairs rests almost exclusively with the Entities. Thus it was so far impossible to create a common economic legal system as precondition for a functioning common market even within the country, let alone to integrate into the European Union.

As far as reconciliation is concerned, the climate of revenge, fear and hatred must be overcome to create the preconditions for mutual trust and cooperation not only on the elite level, but also in the minds and attitudes of people. However, as we can see in particular in the Balkans, instruments of transitional justice, such as international and national criminal courts in order to sanction individual guilt for genocide, crimes against humanity and war crimes as well as truth commissions, face the problem that victims and perpetrators proclaim a different 'truth' with regard to past events. Knowledge of facts and events, even if established by independent courts, does not necessarily translate into moral or political acknowledgement (Marko-Stöckl 2008). As long as there is either my truth against your truth, as one of the International Criminal Tribunal for the Former Yugoslavia indictees stated in defence, there will be ongoing and 'competing narratives of resentment and blame'. The same phenomenon can be observed in education. A moratorium in history teaching for ten years as it was foreseen in the Erdut Agreement in 1995 for the peaceful reintegration of Eastern Slavonia will thus not help to overcome the we–they dichotomy which has been characterized as an important indicator for ethno-mobilization in the pre-conflict phase. Hence, as long as ethno-national stereotypes, myths of victimhood and hate can be spread, the vicious circle of 'intergenerational vengeance' cannot be broken. The new approach of 'positive history' and 'multiperspectivity' of history textbooks are first steps in order to de-construct the we–they dichotomy and to prepare the ground for the insight that it is necessary to find a consensus on the past, not in terms of collective guilt, but as collective responsibility for reconciliation and a peaceful living together in the future.

Conclusion

When is it possible to renegotiate the (interim peace) settlement and its institutional design of corporate power sharing in order to democratize the entire political system without opening Pandora's Box for a new round of conflict? And when is an exit for ending international territorial administration possible? These two problems are again intimately linked. Until this very day, intransigent, obstructionist and predatory political elites are in power in both Bosnia-Herzegovina and Kosovo, hindering reforms to make institutions and public services more effective. 'Representativeness', however, cannot be decreed by international supervisory mechanisms, but needs a reform of the entire system of intermediary organizations, in particular of political parties, based on the acceptance of both leaders and electorate. In conclusion, only when the party system is transformed so that governmental institutions are representative of and accountable for the economic prosperity and well-being of the 'entire population without discrimination according to ethnic or national origin', to paraphrase the UN General Assembly's Friendly Relations Declaration, will the relapse into ethnic conflict become unlikely and endogenous cultural diversity management possible. This would be the perfect point in time to end international territorial administration and to hand over the exercise of sovereign power to the people and their leaders.

Further reading

Bell-Fialkoff, A. (1996) *Ethnic Cleansing*, St. Martin's Press, New York.
Clark, B. (2007) *Twice a Stranger: How Mass Expulsion Forged Modern Greece and Turkey*, Granta Books, London.
Grey, C. (2000) *International Law and the Use of Force*, Oxford University Press, Oxford.
International Commission on Intervention and State Sovereignty (2001) *The Responsibility to Protect*; available at http://www.iciss.ca/pdf/Commission-Report.pdf (accessed 3 September 2015).
Kaufman, S. (2001) *Modern Hatreds. The Symbolic Politics of Ethnic War*, Cornell University Press, Ithaca-London.
Mulaj, K. (2008) *Politics of Ethnic Cleansing. Nation-State Building and Provision of In/Security in Twentieth Century Balkans*, Lexington Books, Plymouth.

References

Benoît-Rohmer, F. (1996) *The Minority Question in Europe. Texts and Commentary*, Council of Europe Publishing, Strasbourg.

Canovan, M. (1996) *Nationhood and Political Theory*, Edward Elgar, Cheltenham.

Clark, B. (2007) *Twice a Stranger: How Mass Expulsion Forged Modern Greece and Turkey*, Granta Books, London.

Gazzini, T. (2005) *The Changing Rules on the Use of Force in International Law*, Manchester University Press, Manchester.

Grey, C. (2000) *International Law and the Use of Force*, Oxford University Press, Oxford.

Hofmann, R. (2003) 'The Use of Force in Minority-Majority Relations: An International Law Perspective', in F. Daftary and S. Troebst (eds), *Radical Ethnic Movements in Contemporary Europe*, Berghahn Books, New York-Oxford: 133–149.

International Commission on Intervention and State Sovereignty (2001) *The Responsibility to Protect*; available at http://www.iciss.ca/pdf/Commission-Report.pdf (accessed 3 September 2015).

International Court of Justice (2007) Bosnia and Herzegovina v. Serbia and Montenegro, Judgment of 26 February 2007; available at http://www.icj-cij.org/docket/index.php?p1=3&p2=3&case=91&p3=4 (accessed 3 September 2015).

Kumar, R. (1999) *Divide and Fall? Bosnia in the Annals of Partition*, Verso, London.

Lantschner, E. (2009) *Soft Jurisprudence im Minderheitenrecht. Standardsetzung und Konfliktbearbeitung durch Kontrollmechanismen bi- und multilateraler Instrumente*, NOMOS, Baden-Baden.

Levy, J. (2007) 'Contextualism, Constitutionalism, and Modus Vivendi Approaches', in A.S. Laden and D. Owen (eds), *Multiculturalism and Political Theory*, Cambridge University Press, Cambridge: 173–197.

Marko, J. (2008) 'The New Kosovo Constitution in a Regional Comparative Perspective', *Review of Central and East European Law*, 33: 437–450.

Marko, J. (2013) 'Ethnopolitics and Constitutional Reform in Bosnia-Herzegovina', in O. Listhaug and S. Ramet (eds), *Bosnia-Herzegovina since Dayton: Civic and Uncivic Values*, Longo Editore, Ravenna, 49–80.

Marko-Stöckl, E. (2008) 'My Truth, Your Truth – Our Truth? The Role of Truth Commissions and History Teaching for Reconciliation', *European Yearbook of Minority Issues*, vol. 7, Martinus Nijhoff, Leiden.

McGarry, J. and O'Leary, B. (2008) 'Consociation and its Critics: Northern Ireland after the Belfast Agreement', in S. Choudhry (ed.), *Constitutional Design for Divided Societies. Integration or Accomodation?*, Oxford University Press, Oxford, 369–408.

McGarry, J., O'Leary, B. and Simeon, R. (2008) 'Integration or Accomodation? The Enduring Debate in Conflict Regulation', in S. Choudhry (ed.), *Constitutional Design for Divided Societies. Integration or Accommodation?*, Oxford University Press, Oxford, 41–88.

Muharremi, R. (2008) 'Kosovo's Declaration of Independence: Self-Determination and Sovereignty Revisited', *Review of Central and East European Law*, 33: 401–455.

Mulaj, K. (2008) *Politics of Ethnic Cleansing. Nation-State Building and Provision of In/Security in Twentieth Century Balkans*, Lexington Books, Plymouth.

Pentassuglia, G. (2002) *Minorities in International Law*, Council of Europe Publishing, Strasbourg.

Ratner, S. (1998) 'Ethnic Conflict and Territorial Claims: Where Do We Draw a Line?', in D. Wippmann (ed.), *International Law and Ethnic Conflict*, Cornell University Press, Ithaca-London, 112–112.

Report (1921) Submitted to the Council of the League of Nations by the Commission of Rapporteurs, The Aaland Island Question, League Doc. B7.21/68/106, 28.

Schabas, W.A. (2000) *Genocide in International Law*, Cambridge University Press, Cambridge.

Smith, A. D. (1991) *National Identities*, Penguin, London.

Stokes, G. (2009) 'Independence and the Fate of Minorities, 1991–1992', in C. Ingrao and T.A. Emmert (eds), *Confronting the Yugoslav Controversies. A Scholars' Initiative*, Purdue University Press, West Lafayette, 103–107.

Thornberry, P. (1991) *International Law and the Rights of Minorities*, Clarendon Press, Oxford.

UN GA (2005) United Nations General Assembly Resolution A/60/1 of 20 September 2005.

Wolff, S. (2007) *Ethnic Conflict. A Global Perspective*, Oxford University Press, Oxford.

20

TERRITORIAL APPROACHES TO ETHNIC CONFLICT SETTLEMENT

John McGarry and Brendan O'Leary

Introduction

Governments that seek to accommodate mobilized national, ethnic, linguistic or religious communities have a range of institutional strategies at their disposal if they do not wish to permit secession.[1] They may promote *consociation* or *centripetalism*, which accommodate plural communities through power-sharing within central or regional institutions. They may promote group-based self-government, sometimes termed *corporate* or *cultural autonomy*. They may also seek accommodation through territorially based autonomy, that may be described as '*territorial pluralism*' (McGarry, O'Leary and Simeon 2008). The latter entails four distinctive institutional arrangements: *pluralist federation, decentralization within a union or unitary state, federacy,* and *cross-border territorial arrangements*, the last of which can be combined with any of the first three. Territorial pluralism assists geographically concentrated national, ethnic, linguistic, or religious communities. It is not relevant for small, dispersed communities, including immigrant communities, for whom self-government is infeasible or undesirable. Territorial pluralism should be distinguished not just from group-based (non-territorial) autonomy, but also from territorial self-government based on 'administrative', or 'geographic' criteria, including regional components of the state's majority community.[2] Contemporary territorial pluralism originated as a conflict-regulating strategy in the mid-nineteenth century, with the creation of pluralist federations in Switzerland and Canada. It has become particularly fashionable, at least in liberal democracies, in recent decades (Gurr 1993a, 1993b; Hannum 1989, 1990, 1993, 1996; Lapidoth 1997; Weller and Wolff 2005). Within the past quarter-century, several democratic states, including Belgium, the United Kingdom, Italy, and Spain, formally either unitary or union states, have transformed themselves into states in which some nationalities enjoy some territorial autonomy. Even France, the home of the Jacobin model of centralized government, has established a regional assembly for the Corsicans, though the extent of its autonomy is minimal (Daftary 2001). Elsewhere, territorial pluralism has been implemented in response to nationalist disputes in Bosnia-Herzegovina, Indonesia (Aceh and Irian Jaya), Iraq (Kurdistan), and Sudan (the South). It is frequently mooted to resolve ongoing conflicts in Azerbaijan (Nagorno-Karabakh), Cyprus, Georgia (Abkhazia, South Ossetia), Moldova (Transnistria), and Nepal (the Terai and other regions). Territorial pluralism allows nationalities, big or small, some autonomy within existing states. It has significant support in the academy, and among political elites from minority communities. International organizations, including the United Nations, the Organization for Security and Co-operation in Europe (OSCE), and the European Union (EU), have seen it as a possible solution to the tension between the desire of nationalities for autonomy and the desire of states to maintain their territorial integrity.

Mapping the varieties of territorial pluralism

Devolution/decentralization in a union or unitary state

The central authorities of a unitary or union state can devolve or decentralize power to one or more regions, and can give different or asymmetrical degrees of autonomy to each region (McGarry 2010). The amount of self-government devolved can be substantial, and the devolved powers may sometimes exceed the powers of states within some federations, or of some federacies. A fundamental, and defining, feature of decentralization and devolution is that within the relevant political systems there is a monistic conception of sovereignty, in which the central authorities retain the right to alter unilaterally the grant of autonomy or rescind it altogether. The central authorities are also able to change the boundaries of the autonomous region, and may retain the right to continue legislating for it, even within those jurisdictional responsibilities that have been devolved.

For example, in 1998, the United Kingdom's Westminster Parliament established a parliament in Scotland, and assemblies in Northern Ireland and Wales, after referendums in the respective entities. Scotland and Northern Ireland were given extensive powers of primary legislation, while the powers of the National Assembly of Wales were restricted to secondary legislation. In the Scotland Act Westminster clearly retains sovereignty,[3] though some British academics believe it would be difficult for Westminster to act unilaterally within the Scottish parliament's sphere of responsibility, or to reduce or rescind its autonomy (Bogdanor 2003: 225–228). Northern Ireland's Agreement went further, creating, as we argue below, a federacy, but did not prevent the UK government (at least within its legal interpretations) from unilaterally suspending Northern Ireland's political institutions four times between 2000 and 2007, the fourth suspension lasting for over four years. It did so in response to a perceived political impasse between unionist and Irish republican politicians. Its actions were a breach of the Agreement in Ireland's readings of the relevant treaties, but reflected the continuing strength of the view within Westminster that parliament's sovereignty cannot be restricted (O'Leary 2001a, 2001c, 2008a).

To take another example, whereas India is usually considered a federation, it does not describe itself as such, but rather as a 'union state', and its constitution has a number of important features akin to those of devolution in a unitary state. Article 249 of the Indian constitution allows the Union parliament, by a two-thirds vote in the upper house (Rajva Sabha), to make laws in the national interest with respect to any matter enumerated in the 'States list', while Article 250 allows the federal parliament to make laws on any item included in the States list during an 'emergency', the existence of which is determined by the federal government under Article 352. These provisions mean that there are, constitutionally, no exclusive state jurisdictions in India. Article 250 has been used by parliament on several occasions to shift powers from the states to the concurrent list and to the 'Union' list. Article 356, 'President's Rule', allows Delhi to take over the government of a state, a provision that has been used 100 times since 1950 (Mathew 2005: 169). The Indian Union authorities are able, after a consultative process, to redraw state boundaries and to establish new states, a power that has been used on numerous occasions.

From the perspective of pluralist accommodation and political stability, devolution is said to have certain advantages. It gives the state's central authorities the flexibility to correct experiments that have gone wrong, and to intervene to protect regional minorities or to take measures to restore order. The UK's belated decision to abolish Northern Ireland's autonomy in 1972 was taken after clear evidence that this had failed spectacularly, giving rise to sustained ethnocratic government by the Ulster Unionist Party and, by 1969, pogroms by the majority amid a quasi-insurrection by Northern Ireland's Irish nationalist minority. Later, after the restoration of a Northern Ireland Assembly, the UK's suspension of Northern Ireland's institutions between 2000 and 2007 was seen as necessary to address a political stalemate, and to protect moderate politicians against radicals. Canada has used its unilateralist powers to accommodate newly mobilized regional nationalities who demanded regional autonomy, while the use of President's Rule in India has usually been justified as necessary to restore quiet.

These advantages, however, are deeply ambiguous. Devolution leaves ultimate power in the hands of the state's central authorities, which often means its dominant nationality, religion or linguistic community. India's federal authorities have used their power, not just to protect minorities within states but to control (larger) minorities that possess their own states, including the Sikhs of Punjab and Muslims of Kashmir (Singh 1993, 1995, 2001). Even interventions that are aimed ostensibly at promoting the rights of small minorities within regions may be motivated by a desire to rein in the larger minorities who control the regions in question.

Devolution also suggests a hierarchy of authority within the state, with the relevant regional institutions firmly subordinate to the centre, a status unlikely to sit well with nationalities that seek a pluri-national partnership of equals. Thus, Canada's indigenous nations have long insisted that they possess an 'inherent' right to self-government, one that cannot be bestowed by anyone. It is also not difficult to imagine nationalities, particularly after armed conflicts, being wary of an autonomy settlement that can be unilaterally altered or rescinded by the state's central authorities. In such contexts, the most popular choice for non-dominant nationalities is not devolution but pluralist federation, federacy, or independence. In Cyprus, even moderate Turkish Cypriots insist on a 'bi-zonal, bi-communal federation' to give them both a share in Cyprus's sovereignty and guaranteed autonomy. Irish republicans rejected the Government of Ireland Act of 1920 in part because it maintained Westminster's 'undiminished' sovereignty, and accepted the 1998 Agreement only because they believed it had qualified UK sovereignty, rendering the new institutions an act of Irish self-determination.

There are ways to protect regional minorities, who might be abused by nationalities who control autonomous territorial governments, short of granting overriding powers to the state's central authorities. Constitutionalized agreements can provide for regional-level power-sharing; or for a regional-level bill of rights, which includes protection for minorities and individuals; and for cantonisation within regions, which results in some level of autonomy for smaller nationalities. Northern Ireland's 1998 Agreement sought to prevent a recurrence of the abuses that occurred between 1921 and 1972, not by relying on Westminster, which had not intervened to protect the nationalist minority until 1969, but by extending autonomy with consociational guarantees, other equality provisions within Northern Ireland, and a bi-governmental oversight role for the UK and Republic of Ireland.

Pluralist federation

In a federation, sovereignty is divided between a federal (not central) government and the federation's constituent units (provinces, states, Länder, cantons, republics, entities). Each unit of government has exclusive responsibility for certain functions, and the division of powers is entrenched in a written constitution. Neither the federal government nor the constituent units can change the constitution unilaterally – there is an amending formula that involves the assent of both. It is for this reason that India cannot be constitutionally regarded as a formal federation. The Indian constitution permits the Union parliament to make laws with respect to any matter under the jurisdiction of the states, and the Union government to take over the government of a state. In federations, an impartial judicial tribunal decides constitutional disputes.

Federations standardly imply bicameral federal legislatures. In the chamber of the states (provinces, entities, etc.) the smallest component units are usually disproportionately represented, i.e. over-represented. In addition to entrenching regional self-government, therefore, federations normally provide for a regional role in the decisions of the federal governmental institutions. In federations, autonomous units usually cover the entire state's territory, with exceptions sometimes made for capital city regions. The degree of self-government enjoyed by minorities in federations varies: some are less 'non-centralized' than others. While federations offer more secure autonomy than devolved polities, they do not necessarily offer more autonomy. Northern Ireland, a devolved government of the United Kingdom between 1921 and 1972, had many powers, including policing powers that were at least as wide-ranging as those enjoyed by the states of the United States of America.

Federations can be formed from previously independent states (including from a confederation of independent states) or through separate ex-colonies deciding to 'come together' (Stepan 1999). This route was followed in Switzerland and the USA. It is the route that some hope (and more fear) that the European Union is embarked upon. But a federation can also develop out of a unitary state, in an effort to 'hold together', as has happened in the case of Belgium, and may happen in the United Kingdom and Spain. It is currently thought that new federations are more likely to be of the 'holding-together' rather than of the 'coming-together' variety, an observation that should please Eurosceptics (Linz 1997). Stepan has noted a third type of federation, one 'put together' by force. He cites the Soviet Union, established by Red Army troops (Stepan 1999). More recently, while many Bosniaks (Bosnian Muslims) consider their federation as springing from a unitary state, many Bosnian Serbs and Croats (as well as outsiders) see it as forced together by the international community. The prospects for such federations, under conditions of democracy, are not good (McGarry and O'Leary 2005).

Not all federations are pluralist. A minimal criterion for a pluralist federation is that it has some internal boundaries that respect nationality, ethnicity, language or religion. By this standard, Canada, Belgium and Switzerland are pluralist federations. While India has the formal characteristics of a union state, in other respects, primarily its move towards more linguistically homogeneous states, it resembles a pluralist federation. Beyond this minimalist conception, pluralist federations vary. Full pluralist federations entail three complementary arrangements. First, they involve not just a constitutionally entrenched division of powers, which cannot be rescinded unilaterally by the federal authorities, but also substantive autonomy, and a reasonable allocation of fiscal resources. Second, a full pluralist federation has consensual, indeed consociational, rather than majoritarian decision making rules within the federal government, i.e. inclusive executive power sharing and representative arrangements in the federal government, and proportional principles of representation and allocation of public posts and resources (O'Leary 2005). Consensual federations create strong second chambers representing the constituent regions and have strong regional judiciaries and a regional role in the selection of federal judges. They do not create strong single-person presidencies, or senates that are mirror images of the house of representatives. Third, full pluralist federations are pluri-national. They recognize a pluralist rather than a monist conception of sovereignty. The pluri-national character of the federation may be recognized in the state's constitution, or through its flag and symbols, or through official bilingualism or multilingualism that treats the federation as a multi-homeland, a partnership between or among distinct peoples. Iraq's 2005 Constitution stipulates in Article 3 that it is a 'country of many nationalities'. Article 4 makes Arabic and Kurdish the country's two official languages, while Article 12 (1) stipulates that 'the flag, national anthem, and emblem of Iraq shall be fixed by law in a way that represents the components of the Iraqi people'. A pluri-national federation involves collective territorial autonomy for the partner nations.

There are few examples of federal constitutions that are fully pluralist in design. Iraq is an uncompleted example, and its future is uncertain (McGarry and O'Leary 2007; O'Leary 2007). Any viable federation of the European Union will have to be fully pluralist. Pluralist federation enjoys some advocacy among contemporary academics. A federation or pluralist federation is distinct from a confederation, though the two are sometimes confused. The former is a state with shared citizenship and a single international personality, while the latter is a union or alliance of (independent) states, established usually for a limited set of purposes, such as defence or economic cooperation. The (federal) governments of federations have a direct role in the lives of their citizens, while confederal authorities normally interact with the citizens of their member-states indirectly – through the governments and bureaucracies of these states. As confederations are generally much looser unions than federations, they are more likely to have decision-making rules based on unanimity. It is also (formally) easier to leave a confederation.

The distinction between a pluralist federation and confederation, however, is not as clear as it once was. Some pluralist federations allow their constituent units a role in international relations. Both Canada and Belgium permit constituent units with French-speaking populations to sit in 'La Francophonie', the league of French-speaking states (Leonardy 2000). Canada's Supreme Court, has, in effect, ruled that each of its provinces now has a constitutional right to secede, providing certain procedures are followed. From the other direction, the European Union, which originated as a confederation, has developed some federal characteristics. Since the Maastricht Treaty, there has been EU citizenship, and the 'Eurocracy' in Brussels is increasingly having an impact, though not clearly a 'direct' impact, on the lives of these citizens. The EU's dominant decision-making rule has also been shifting from unanimity to qualified majority rule within the con/federal institutions.

Federacy

When a nationality seeks guaranteed autonomy, but there is no general desire among the dominant nationality for a federation, the state can establish a federacy, that is, it can enter into a bilateral arrangement in which secured autonomy is offered to a part of the state only (Rezvani 2003). The primary difference between federacy and devolution is that the grant of self-government is constitutionally guaranteed and cannot be revoked by the centre unilaterally. The primary difference between federacy and federation is that a federacy normally applies to a part of the state's territory, and normally a small part (in population), whereas federation involves state-wide autonomy arrangements. Where part of a federation's territory enjoys a special guaranteed status and a distinct type of autonomy, as in Puerto Rico's relationship with the USA, federation and federacy co-exist.

The full and proper implementation of Northern Ireland's 1998 Agreement will create a federacy. While the Agreement's institutions are the subject of ordinary Westminster legislation, like those in Scotland and Wales, they are also entrenched in an international treaty between the United Kingdom and Ireland. Moreover, the UK government, as part of the Agreement, repealed the Government of Ireland Act, 1920, including S. 75, which asserted the 'supreme authority' of the Westminster parliament, and explicitly recognized the people of the island of Ireland's 'right of self-determination', including their right, voting separately, North and South, to bring about a united Ireland. The reasonable reading of the Agreement is that the UK government and parliament cannot exercise power in Northern Ireland in a way that is inconsistent with the Agreement, without breaking its treaty obligations and without denying Irish national self-determination. This fact was obscured by the actions of the UK government between 2000 and 2002, when it unilaterally suspended Northern Ireland's political institutions. The Irish government chose not to challenge these breaches of the Agreement because of the need to maintain good working relations with Britain and to avoid dangerously polarizing politics within Northern Ireland. Nonetheless, since 1998, the United Kingdom has been composed of two unions, the Union of Great Britain and the Union of Great Britain and Northern Ireland, each of which has a different constitutional basis (O'Leary 1999a, 1999b).

Cross-border territorial links

The three types of territorial pluralism discussed thus far grant self-government to a nationality within the borders of a particular state. They are suited toward nationalities, such as the Scots or Welsh, who mostly live within a single state's territory. In some cases, however, nationalities are separated from their national kin by international borders. Their kin may be the dominant community in the neighbouring state, or a minority. Such minorities exist all over Europe and elsewhere too. They are part and parcel of 'the Macedonian syndrome' (Weiner 1971). They include the Basques of France and Spain, Northern Ireland's Irish nationalist minority, the Hungarian minorities of Serbia, Slovakia, and Romania, the Croats and Serbs of Bosnia and Herzegovina, as well as the Serbs of now independent Kosovo, the Albanians of Macedonia, and the German-speaking (Austrian) community in South Tyrol. In these cases, devolution, pluralist federation or federacy are necessary but insufficient to establish 'collective' national autonomy. What may be sought in addition are cross-border political institutions that allow cooperation between the different parts of the national community. Within these areas of cooperation, the nation can be said to be collectively self-governing.

There are few examples of such institutions. Most states remain wedded to the traditional 'Westphalian' system of discrete sovereign states, and are reluctant to consider cross-border institutions. The fear is that such institutions will promote irredentism. Indeed, states are very often opposed to giving even autonomy within state boundaries to minorities that have national kin on the other side of a frontier, and particularly when these kin control a neighbouring state, i.e. the fear of irredentism usually blocks even devolution, pluralist federation, or federacy, never mind cross-border institutional links.

However, at least within the European Union, where relations between states are friendly, irredentism is weak, and traditional notions of state sovereignty may be weakening, such cross-border institutions are becoming possible, though they are not uniformly accepted. The most far-reaching example stems from Northern Ireland's Good Friday Agreement of 1998. In addition to creating a federacy, the Agreement provides for political institutions linking Northern Ireland (part of the United Kingdom) with the Republic of Ireland (O'Leary 1999a, 1999b). The most important is a North–South Ministerial Council (NSMC), a body comprised of Ireland's government and the Northern Ireland Executive. In addition, the Agreement led to the establishment of six all-Ireland 'implementation' bodies, which were given the task of cooperating to develop joint policies over inland waterways, food safety, trade and business development, special EU programmes, the Irish and Ulster Scots languages, and aquaculture and marine matters. The driving force behind Ireland's trans-border institutions was the fact that autonomy for Northern Ireland alone would not have satisfied the aspiration of even moderate Irish nationalists. All of their elected politicians insisted on such cross-border links.

Distinguishing territorial pluralism from other forms of autonomy

Territorial pluralism should be distinguished from non-territorial forms of autonomy, such as personal autonomy, and what is called, variously, corporate, segmental, cultural, and national cultural autonomy, and from forms of territorial self-government that do not accommodate nationalities or minorities.

From personal and corporate (non-territorial) autonomy

Conventional liberal individual or human rights, such as freedom of religion, expression or association, protect personal autonomy. These rights extend to individuals, but permit minorities the freedom to practise their community's culture in the private sphere. Thus freedom of religion allows religious minorities to worship together; freedom of expression allows minorities to establish media in their own language; and freedom of association facilitates minority civic associations and political parties. Corporate autonomy, by contrast, involves minority-based public self-government. While personal autonomy can facilitate the formation of minority-based political parties, which can then demand public accommodation, corporate autonomy entails representative public institutions, which may be permitted to tax their members and to exercise public authority with respect to cultural matters.

Corporate autonomy was used by the Ottomans originally to manage religious diversity (Braude and Lewis 1982; Coakley 1994: 299). From the fifteenth century, Greek Orthodox, Armenian Catholic, Jewish and Muslim communities administered their own affairs in religion, education and family law. With the growth of national sentiment, these religious millets later split into linguistically based units (Laponce 1993). An equivalent of the millet, the *kahal*, was introduced in the old Polish-Lithuanian Commonwealth, where it was used to give autonomy to the Jewish community. The millet system has contributed to the current legal systems in India, Israel and Lebanon, where different religious communities have autonomy over family law.

Corporate autonomy was proposed by the Austro-Marxists, Karl Renner and Otto Bauer, as a solution to the nationalities question in the disintegrating Austro-Hungarian Empire (Bauer 2000; McGarry and Moore 2005; Stouurzh 1991). Although their proposals were not widely implemented in Austria-Hungary, there were limited attempts to apply them in Moravia, Galicia and Bukovina (Coakley 1994: 300). A much more significant application of corporate autonomy occurred in inter-war Estonia, where a Cultural Autonomy Law was passed in 1925, which enabled ethnic groups numbering at least 3,000 to establish cultural councils capable of taxing group members, and exercising jurisdiction over a wide range of cultural activities, including education, culture, libraries, theatres, museums and sport (Coakley 1994: 307). Other consociational systems – in Belgium, the Netherlands and Lebanon – have allowed degrees of corporate autonomy to various religious and secular communities (Lijphart 1977: 41–44). More recently, Belgium has sought to manage its ethno-linguistic communities through a mixture of consociational power sharing, territorial pluralism, and corporate autonomy. The French and Flemish-language communities have non-territorial jurisdiction over French and Flemish-speakers in Brussels (Lijphart 1977: 184–185). In New Zealand, the Maori Council supervises matters of interest to Maoris throughout the country (Coakley 1994: 309). Corporate autonomy has been proposed as a way of accommodating the significant proportion of Canada's indigenous population that lives in urban regions (Royal Commission 1996).

The demise of Marxism–Leninism in Eastern Europe led to a partial resurgence in the popularity of corporate autonomy. Unlike Lenin, who railed against the idea of corporate autonomy, the new rulers of the region appear to see it as preferable to territorial pluralism, which they see as dangerous and destabilizing. In 1993, Estonia reintroduced its inter-war arrangements for corporate autonomy. In the same year, Hungary passed an Act 'On the Rights of National and Ethnic Minorities' (Krizsan 2000: 248). In 1996, the Russian parliament adopted the National Cultural Autonomy Act, which allows individuals to form National Cultural Associations, with rights over culture, language, education and the media, as well as the right to represent the interests of minorities to state (federal, republic and local) institutions. By mid-1999, 227 National Cultural Associations (NCAs) had been registered (160 local, 60 regional and seven federal).

The arguments for corporate autonomy institutions most frequently used by public authorities in Eastern Europe are of the peace-and-stability sort. They fear the secessionist dangers of territorial pluralism, but recognize the need to accommodate the linguistic, religious or cultural diversity of their populations. In Russia, where territorial pluralism was more vibrant in the early 1990s than it is now, corporate autonomy has been promoted as an alternative or at least as a countervailing force. The first politician to recommend it in the post-communist era, Gavril Popov, linked it with a proposal for scrapping Russia's system of territorial pluralism, and restoring the Tsarist system of ethnically neutral administrative regions (Codagnone and Fillipov 2000: 275). Some have speculated that the country's adoption of 'national cultural autonomy' is aimed at replacing territorial pluralism over the long run (Goble 2000). Certainly Presidents Putin and Medvedev have combined corporate autonomy with the undermining of Russia's system of territorial pluralism.

The idea that corporate autonomy will suffice as a way to manage the concerns of nationalities has become, apparently, a 'veritable mantra' among East European intellectuals (Kymlicka 2001: 365). It is an argument that has some support among western states and international organizations. Since the Copenhagen Document of 1990 suggested territorial autonomy as an option for the accommodation of minorities, there has been a steady retreat in support for it in international documents, in part as a result of conflicts arising from the break-up of Yugoslavia and the Soviet Union. These documents are now more likely to stress corporate rather than territorial methods of accommodation.

Corporate autonomy has some advantages over territorial pluralism. As Karl Renner observed, membership in a corporately defined autonomous community can be voluntary, which means that only those who identify with the group are governed by it. It offers one way, therefore, to prevent territorially based governance discriminating against minorities, or generating a government that lacks widespread allegiance. Corporate autonomy is clearly useful for nationalities that are too dispersed or few in number to exercise, or to aspire to, territorial autonomy. There is some evidence that Estonia's inter-war arrangements for corporate autonomy improved the position of its dispersed minorities: it 'did much to reconcile the Germans to life within the Estonian state' (Coakley 1994: 307); and Jews appear to have been happy with Estonia's autonomy arrangements. Dispersed groups, like the Roma of Hungary and Russia, stand to benefit from those countries' arrangements for corporate auton- omy, as these will provide institutions and resources that they currently lack. In Canada, cor- porate autonomy has enabled Francophones outside Quebec to maintain some control over their own schools. The natives who live in Canada's cities would also benefit from it, as it is difficult to see how plans for giving self-government to native reserves address their situation. However, for dispersed nationalities, which do not have the demographic basis to reproduce their culture and identity, such schemes may just make assimilation gentler rather than stop it.

Even large territorially concentrated nationalities may find corporate autonomy, or even personal autonomy, better than the alternatives on offer. The Kurds in Turkey would benefit significantly from genuine freedom of association and expression, as well as from controlling publicly funded schools in the Kurdish language. This would represent a considerable advance over the Kemalist regime of coercive assimilation to which they have been subjected (Gunter 1990; Romano 2006). However, it is highly unlikely that large and territorially concentrated nationalities will be satisfied with personal or corporate autonomy, particularly if they have enjoyed territorial autonomy in the past. Many of the public powers such nationalities seek, including over the economy, policing, population influxes, and language planning, require control over territory.

Corporate autonomy fails, just as significantly, to consider the vital relationship that most mobilized nationalities have with their homeland or 'national territory'. For many groups, there is a conception of a 'homeland', a geographical area with symbolic and emotional significance, which is not captured simply by provisions for cultural self-government over members. This relationship to the land is evident in the discourse of the indigenous people, but is found among all mobilized nationalities, including Scots, Catalans or Uighurs (Connor 1986). Nationalists seek not just self-government, but self-government over their national homeland.

While a minority religious community may survive without controlling territory, particularly if the state is neutral on religion, there are reasons for doubting that a linguistic community can do so. A language will prosper best if it has a territorial basis in which that language is the primary medium of social and economic exchange, and a principal language of work, business and social interaction. Corporate autonomy, usually limited to control over schools, even when combined with some kind of official status for the minority language within state-wide public institutions, arguably does not suffice. Territorial autonomy may be required, in which the minority can promote its language as the public language, including in the workforce, as the Québécois have done in Quebec. The contrasting fortunes of linguistic minorities with territorial autonomy and non-territorial autonomy can be observed by looking at the Swedes of Finland. The Åland Islanders, who enjoy territorial autonomy, including control over demographic influxes, and who have promoted their language in the public sphere, have been able to reproduce their culture and their identity. By contrast, Swedish-speakers on the Finnish mainland, territorially concentrated and beneficiaries of language rights but not territorial autonomy, have not fared nearly as well (Alcock 1991: 13).

Territorial self-government regimes that do not accommodate nationalities and minorities

There are two kinds of federation that are consistent with policies of integrating, assimilating, or controlling minorities, rather than accommodating them. The first are what we have described as 'national federations', to distinguish them from the pluralist variety (McGarry and O'Leary 2005). National federations are usually relatively centralized, as it is their federal governments that are normally seen as representing the 'national' will. An unambiguous national federation exists where the federation-wide majority is a majority in every federal unit, as in the USA, Germany, Australia, or the Latin American federations of Mexico, Brazil and Venezuela. In each of these cases, the decision to establish federations had nothing to do with the accommodation of minorities but was taken for other reasons, such as to provide for accessible (regional) government in a large country (Brazil, Australia, and the USA); to coax previously independent units into joining a union without extinguishing their identity/existence (USA and English Canada); or to protect against the concentration and abuse of power (Germany, USA). Indeed, the establishment of national federations has often been accompanied by purposive steps, where necessary, to prevent minorities from becoming self-governing. As the USA, to take the most prominent case, expanded south-westward from its original homo-geneous (except for black slaves) 13 colonies, it was decided that no territory would receive statehood unless minorities were outnumbered by White Anglo-Saxon Protestants (WASPs). Sometimes, the technique employed was to gerrymander state boundaries to ensure that Indians or Hispanics were outnumbered, as in Florida. At other times, as in Hawaii and the south-west, statehood was delayed until the region's long-standing residents could be swamped with enough WASP settlers. The American authorities were even sceptical of immigrant groups concentrating in particular locations lest this lead to ethnically based demands for self-government, and grants of public land were denied to ethnic groups in order to promote their dispersal (Gordon 1964). In line with nation-building aims, minorities were required to conform to the culture and identity of the Anglo-Saxon core. In the case of blacks in the southern states for a century after slavery was abolished, American federalism facilitated con-trol rather than assimilation: African Americans would have been better served by centralized political structures than they were by the restoration of federalism after the failure of recon-struction. Control was largely dismantled as a result of the combined intervention, starting in the 1950s, of the federal judicial, executive and legislative branches of government.

A more ambiguous national federation exists where ethnic, religious, linguistic, or national minorities are spread out across a number of federal units, in some of which they may be majorities. National federations of the unambiguous kind may be impractical in some cases – where the minority in question is so large that it is difficult to construct the federation's internal boundaries to deny them majority status in any federal unit. In these cases, a second-best 'national federal' strategy draws internal boundaries across minority communities rather than between or among them, i.e. preventing the minority from exercising *collective* self-government within its own single unit. Integrationists argue that the advantage of this strategy is that it breaks up the minority's national or 'ethnic' solidarity, promotes intra-group divisions, and inter- or trans-group alliances, thus promoting a single overarching national identity coterminous with the state (Roeder 2007). This thinking appears to have inspired the Nigerian military nation-builders who divided Nigeria's original three republics, dominated by the Ibo, Yoruba, and Hausa-Fulani, respectively, into nine, 12, and, eventually, 36 republics. Similar thinking is also popular among Sinhalese nation-builders in Sri Lanka, though they tend to shy away from any use of the term 'federation', preferring the language of decen-tralization and devolution. Such national federations, in which minorities are divided across several units without their consent, and as a result of purposive 'nation-building' by military dictators, external interventionists, or majority elites, need to be carefully distinguished from federations in which such patterns emerge organically. In Switzerland, the German and French linguistic communities are divided across several cantons, but this is a result of

Switzerland's history and the unwillingness of cantons with the same language to merge. This makes Switzerland an example of a pluralist federation, but a pluri-lingual rather than a pluri-national federation.

The second type of federation, which is not pluralist, is the 'sham' or pseudo-pluralist variant. A sham pluralist federation exists where the state is organized ostensibly as a federation, and nationalities are majorities within federal units, but there is no genuine self-government. Such federations exist when federal units are either not autonomous, i.e. the formal constitutional division of powers/rule of law is ignored in practice; or there is no democracy (freedom of expression; freedom of association; regular competitive elections and other attributes necessary to produce self-government).

The USA is the paradigmatic example of a national federation, while the Soviet Union was the most prominent sham pluralist federation. Though its state structure was federated from early on, real power lay in the tightly centralized Communist Party (the CPSU), which operated according to the principle of 'democratic centralism'. The Union Republics were therefore not autonomous. Their legislatures (the Soviets), though in theory elected by local populations, were rubber-stamp bodies nominated by the CPSU. Key institutions, including the army and police, were controlled by Moscow. No effective judicial review existed to decide on the division of rights and functional spheres between the centre and the republics (Lieven and McGarry 1993). Communism has no monopoly on sham federations. Nigeria and Pakistan during their long bouts of military dictatorship have been sham federations, and Putin's Russia, in which governors are appointed by the centre, and regional parties banned from competing in Russian elections, has moved substantially in this direction.

Under what conditions is territorial pluralism likely to offer sustainable conflict settlements?

Given the mixed record of territorial pluralism, the proper question for political scientists is not whether it is bound to fail or succeed, but under what conditions it is likely to succeed or fail. At least some of the following conditions matter, although further rigorous empirical testing is required to assess the explanatory validity of these propositions.

First, history matters, even if it is not destiny. Past coercion and conquest, totalitarian or authoritarian governments, and the historic maltreatment of nationalities, render free political accommodation more difficult. Democratization may lead to the springtime of the oppressed nations – as they break free, rejecting the uncertainties of territorial pluralism for the potential security of independence. Territorial pluralism therefore stands a better chance if it emerges from past voluntary alliances, and in conjunction with democratization. Historically dominant nationalities, with poor track records of accommodation, find it difficult to persuade other nationalities that they can make credible commitments.

Second, and relatedly, the long-term survival of territorial pluralism is more likely when there are 'nested' or 'complementary' identities among the territorially concentrated nationalities, i.e. where there is some sense of allegiance to the whole state as well as to the national homeland. This in turn is facilitated by the acceptance of pluri-nationalism by the state's central or federal authorities and, where relevant, its dominant community. Nested identities are unlikely to exist where the relevant regional nationality has been harshly treated by the state, or where violent wars have raged. Critics of territorial pluralism, such as Roeder, may be correct to argue that secession, what he incorrectly terms 'partition', is one of the most sensible options after many civil wars. Equally, complementary identities may be less likely to exist, or more difficult to nurture, if a region was forcibly incorporated, or reincorporated, into the state, rather than voluntarily acceding. The Baltic republics were the most eager secessionists in the former Soviet Union, and the Serbs of Republika Srspka are no champions of Bosnia and Herzegovina. The importance of complementary identities suggests that states should react early to popular demands for territorial pluralism, before relations between nationalities deteriorate. One problem here is what Tim Sisk calls the 'timing paradox'. While early accommodation is more likely to work, state authorities may not be likely to recognize the need for concessions until relations have polarized and it is too late (Sisk 1996). But the adoption of territorial pluralism in the United Kingdom, Spain, Canada, Belgium, India, and Switzerland indicates central authorities are sometimes capable of engaging in self-denying prophecies.

Third, some successful cases of territorial pluralism suggest that, at least with sizable nationalities, autonomy should be accompanied by consociational power sharing within central or federal institutions. Such arrangements prevent majoritarianism by the dominant nationality, and make it more likely that minorities have a stake in the state. It is a mistake to consider autonomy a simple substitute for inclusive state institutions. Power sharing may be entrenched in laws or constitutional documents, or, less attractively from the minority's perspective; it may be the result of political conventions or of general election results (that leave minorities holding the balance of power in central legislatures). Inclusive federal governmental institutions and conventions have helped keep the Canadian, Swiss Indian, and Belgian federations together. Spain's autonomy regime has been at its most cordial when minority nationalities have enjoyed influence in Madrid. Conversely, there is evidence that the absence, or collapse, of inclusive federal or central institutions has contributed to breakdown and secession. Nigeria's breakdown into civil war and attempted secession in 1966–67, followed a coup which led to the centre becoming the preserve of Ibo officers and a counter-coup in which these officers were overthrown (Suberu 2001). Much of Nigeria's post-1970 conflict, including sectarian warfare between Muslims and Christians and the rise of violent separatism in the oil-rich Delta area, has also been traced to the lack of inclusiveness at the level of the centre (Suberu and Diamond 2002).

Fourth, the success of territorial pluralism appears to be linked to the nature of the state's diversity. Federations with a strong dominant nationality, or a *Staatsvolk*, are less likely to break apart than those without (O'Leary 2001b). This is partly because such dominant communities can deter or prevent secession, and yet may be secure enough, as the English have shown, to implement territorial pluralism. The Russian Federation is more likely to stay together than the former Soviet Union, as the Chechens have discovered, in part because it has more Russians: Russians constitute 80 per cent of the Russian federation's population, but were only 50 per cent of the Soviet Union's population. Other prominent cases of states that fell apart, like Yugoslavia, or collapsed into civil war and military dictatorship, like Nigeria, lacked a *Staatsvolk*, or even a majority community. But what the *Staatsvolk* does with its dominance may be as important as its mere existence. When it coerces, supports a totalitarian party or religion, maltreats minority nationalities, or supports centralist coups and putsches it will generate antagonistic rather than complementary identities. When it is liberal, democratic, rights respecting, and open toward accommodation then territorial pluralism has a better prospect of finding cooperative partners.

Fifth, the number of autonomous units matters, though not in obvious ways. Two unit, or dyadic, pluralist federations have an abysmal track record (Vile 1982), with Serbia and Montenegro merely the latest casualty. This may be because divisions in dyadic federations always take place along the same axis, with floating coalitions rendered very difficult. Belgium's continuing survival may owe something to the fact that it is not a dyadic federation of Flanders and Wallonia. Brussels' existence as a separate unit may have prevented the secession of Flanders. Canada's stability may be helped by the fact that it is not a two-unit federation of Quebec and English Canada. Pointing to the advantage of a multiple balance of power is not, however, an argument for imposing it through a Machiavellian strategy of subdividing regional units belonging to distinct national communities. But if a multiple balance of power develops organically, as has happened in Canada, it is helpful. Some dominant communities may accept the division of their territory into several regions, provided their aspiration to collective self-government can be expressed within the union, or federal-level, institutions. Minority nationalities, however, are likely to resist any imposed partition of their autonomous region, as Iraq's Kurds would surely have done had the USA or Baghdad sought to partition Kurdistan (O'Leary, McGarry and Salih 2005).

Sixth, economic prosperity, appropriately dispersed, enhances the prospects of territorial pluralism. It may allow redistribution from wealthy regions to the less wealthy, binding the latter to the state without incurring the rancour of the former. The counter-example of India, until recently not an example of deepening prosperity, suggests that material – or shared – prosperity is a facilitative, not a necessary condition for stable territorial pluralism. The converse hypothesis is that severe distributive conflicts – over natural resources or fiscal or tariff or subsidy policies – especially if they coincide with national, ethnic, linguistic or religious allegiances may overload territorial pluralist states.

Seventh, the prospects for the success of territorial pluralism are enhanced, even in otherwise unfavourable circumstances, where international agents, including nearby powerful states, have a strong interest in holding the relevant state together. Bosnia-Herzegovina is not destined to fail, as long as NATO and the European Union are determined that it should not. If Iraq's federation survives, in spite of the complete absence of a warm Iraqi identity among Kurds and their genocidal treatment by Saddam's regime, it will partly be because the USA, Turkey and Iran are strongly opposed to an independent Kurdistan. The only scenario in which an independent Kurdistan looks feasible is if the rest of Iraq collapses – i.e. if it becomes clear that Iraq has no Arab or Shia *Staatsvolk* capable of holding it together. Kurdistan's political leadership is presently intending to make Iraq work, as a pluralist federation, because autonomy under the 2005 constitution offers a better and more certain future than a bid for formal independence (O'Leary 2008b).

Conclusion

This analysis has made an effort to provide a detached treatment of territorial pluralist arrangements. Such arrangements offer no panacea; politics never ends; and territorially pluralist arrangements have their pathologies or sore-spots. But territorial pluralism has strong, frequently more important benefits. It offers some prospects of accommodating multiple nationalities, religions, languages, and ethnicities, with consent and justice. It rejects coercive assimilation and control (repression). It involves, more controversially, the rejection of integration, i.e. the idea that mobilized nationalities can be satisfied with individual (personal autonomy) rights and that they do not require public institutional accommodation of their nationality, culture and identity. Integration is, arguably, the west's dominant method of conflict regulation, but there is little evidence that it can work in pluri-national places. Support for territorial pluralism involves rejecting the view that sizable mobilized nationalities will, given a free choice of options, be satisfied with corporate forms of autonomy. We have also suggested that there is no *a priori* reason why territorial pluralism should be any more discriminatory than other territorially based institutions, including those of formally integrationist states. We have not suggested that territorial pluralism guarantees stability or unity. We have suggested it is the best inoculation against secession presently available as institutional medicine in pluri-national places. Governments that do not try territorial pluralism may preside over the deaths of their states.

Notes

1 States do constitutionalize the right of secession – the right was embedded for Soviet Socialist Republics in the constitution of the USSR (1936, 1977), though no one anticipated it would be exercised. Ethiopia's constitution embeds the right (Art. 47, S.2.). The United Kingdom's treaty with the Government of Ireland lays down the rules under which Northern Ireland may leave the Union to join Ireland. Canada's Supreme Court and the Canadian federal parliament, while not explicitly conceding that Quebec has the right of secession under Canada's constitution, have laid down protocols under which a referendum mandating secession would lay binding negotiating requirements on the federal government.
2 What distinguishes 'territorial pluralism' from the expression 'federal political systems' used by Watts and Elazar (Elazar 1987; Watts 1996; Watts 1998), is that it is focused on territorial autonomy for national, ethnic, linguistic or religious minorities, and 'territorial pluralism' does not apply the word 'federal' beyond its legitimate semantic extension.
3 Scotland Act 1998, S. 28 (7).

References

Alcock, A. 1991. Finland: The Swedish-speaking Community. In *Minorities and Autonomy in Western Europe*, edited by M. R. Group. London: Minority Rights Group.

Bauer, O. 2000. *The Question of Nationalities and Social Democracy*, edited by E. Nimni. Translated by J. O'Donnell. Minneapolis: University of Minnesota Press.

Bogdanor, V. 2003. Asymmetric Devolution: Toward a Quasi-Federal Constitution? In *Developments in British Politics* 7, edited by P. Dunleavy, et al. New York: Palgrave. 222–241.

Braude, B. and Lewis, B. eds 1982. *Christians and Jews in the Ottoman Empire: The Functioning of a Plural Society*. Two vols. Vol. II: *The Arabic-Speaking Lands*. New York: Holmes and Meier.

Coakley, J. 1994. Approaches to the Resolution of Ethnic Conflict. *International Political Science Review* 15(3): 298–314.

Codagnone, C. and Fillipov, V. 2000. Equity, Exit and National Identity in a Multinational Federation: The "Multicultural Constitutional Patriotism" Project in Russia. *Journal of Ethnic and Migration Studies* 26(2): 263–288.

Connor, W. 1986. The Impact of Homelands upon Diasporas. In *Modern Diasporas in International Politics*, edited by G. Sheffer. London: Croom Helm. 16–46.

Daftary, F. 2001. The Matignon Process and Insular Autonomy as a Response to Self-determination Claims in Corsica. Paper read at Association for the Study of Nationalities, New York.

Elazar, D. 1987. *Exploring Federalism*. Tuscaloosa: University of Alabama.

Goble, P. 2000. A New Kind of Autonomy, *RFE/RL Russian Federation Report*, 2/17 (10 May)

Gordon, M. 1964. *Assimilation in American Life: The Role of Race, Religion and National Origins*. New York: Oxford University Press.

Gunter, M. M. 1990. *The Kurds in Turkey: A Political Dilemma*. Boulder, CO: Westview Press.

Gurr, T.R. 1993a. *Minorities at Risk: A Global View of Ethnopolitical Conflicts*. Washington DC: United States Institute of Peace Press.

Gurr, T.R. 1993b. Settling Ethnopolitical Conflicts. In *Minorities at Risk: A Global View of Ethnopolitical Conflicts*, edited by T. Gurr. Washington DC: United States Institute of Peace Press.

Hannum, H. 1989. The Limits of Sovereignty and Majority Rule: Minorities, Indigenous Peoples and the Rights to Autonomy. In *New Directions in Human Rights*, edited by E. Lutz, H. Hannum and K. J. Burker. Philadelphia: University of Pennsylvania Press.

Hannum, H. 1990. *Autonomy, Sovereignty, and Self-determination: The Accommodation of Conflicting Rights*. Philadelphia: University of Pennsylvania Press.

Hannum, H. 1993. *Documents on Autonomy and Minority Rights*. Dordrecht and Boston: M. Nijhoff.

Hannum, H. 1996. *Autonomy, Sovereignty, and Self-determination: The Accommodation of Conflicting Rights*. rev. edn. Philadelphia: University of Pennsylvania Press.

Krizsan, A. 2000. The Hungarian Minority Protection System: A Flexible Approach to the Adjudication of Ethnic Claims. *Journal of Ethnic and Migration Studies* 26(2): 247–262.

Kymlicka, W. 2001. Reply and Conclusion. In *Can Liberal Pluralism be Exported? Western Political Theory and Ethnic Relations in Eastern Europe*, edited by W. Kymlicka and M. Opalski. Oxford: Oxford University Press. 345-414.

Lapidoth, R. E. 1997. *Autonomy: Flexible Solutions to Ethnic Conflicts*. Washington, DC: United States Institute of Peace Press.

Laponce, J. 1993. The Government of Dispersed Minorities: From Constantinople to Ottawa. In *Divided Nations*, edited by T. Kozma and P. Drahos. Budapest: Education Publishing.

Leonardy, U. 2000. Treaty Making Powers and Foreign Relations of Federated Entities. In *Federal Practice: Exloring Alternatives for Georgia and Abkhazia*, edited by B. Coppieters, D. Darchiashvili and N. Akaba. Brussels: VUB University Press. 151–168.

Lieven, D. and McGarry, J. 1993. Ethnic Conflict in the Soviet Union and its Successor States. In *The Politics of Ethnic Conflict Regulation: Case Studies of Protracted Ethnic Conflicts*, edited by J. McGarry and B. O'Leary. London: Routledge. 62–83.

Lijphart, A. 1977. *Democracy in Plural Societies: A Comparative Exploration*. New Haven: Yale University Press.

Linz, J. 1997. Democracy, Multinationalism and Federalism, working paper 1997/103. Paper read at Juan March Institute, June, Spain.

Mathew, G. 2005. India. In *Handbook of Federal Countries, 2005*, edited by A. Griffiths. Montreal & Kingston: McGill-Queen's University Press. 166–182.

McGarry, J. 2010. Asymmetric Autonomy in the United Kingdom. In *Asymmetric Autonomy and the Settlement of Ethnic Conflicts*, edited by M. Weller and K. Nobbs. Philadelphia: University of Pennsylvania Press, ch. 6.

McGarry, J. and Moore, M. 2005. Karl Renner, Power-Sharing and Non-Territorial Autonomy. In *National Cultural Autonomy and its Contemporary Critics*, edited by E. Nimni. London: Routledge. 74–94.

McGarry, J. and O'Leary, B. 2005. Federation as a Method of Ethnic Conflict Regulation. In *From Power Sharing to Democracy: Post-Conflict Institutions in Ethnically Divided Societies*, edited by S. Noel. Montreal & Kingston: McGill-Queen's University Press. 263–296.

McGarry, J. and O'Leary, J. 2007. Iraq's Constitution of 2005: Liberal Consociation as Political Prescription. *International Journal of Constitutional Law* 5 (4 (October)): 670–698.

McGarry, J., O'Leary, B. and Simeon, R. 2008. Integration or Accommodation? The Enduring Debate in Conflict Regulation. In *Constitutional Design for Divided Societies: Integration or Accommodation*, edited by S. Choudhry. Oxford: Oxford University Press. 41–88.

O'Leary, B. 1999a. The Nature of the Agreement. *Fordham Journal of International Law* 22(4): 1628–1667.

O'Leary, B. 1999b. The Nature of the British-Irish Agreement. *New Left Review* 233 (January–February): 66–96.

O'Leary, B. 2001a. Agreement is Not Devolution in Unitary State. *Irish Times*, October 11, 16.

O'Leary, B. 2001b. An Iron Law of Nationalism and Federation? A (Neo-Diceyian) Theory of the Necessity of a Federal Staatsvolk, and of Consociational Rescue. *Nations and Nationalism* 7(3): 273–296.

O'Leary, B. 2001c. The Belfast Agreement and the Labour Government: How to Handle and Mishandle History's Hand. In *The Blair Effect: The Blair Government 1997–2001*, edited by A. Seldon. London: Little, Brown & Company. 448–488.

O'Leary, B. 2005. Power-Sharing, Pluralist Federation and Federacy. In *The Future of Kurdistan in Iraq*, edited by B. O'Leary, J. McGarry and K. Salih. Philadelphia: University of Pennsylvania Press. 47–91.

O'Leary, B. 2007. Iraq's Future 101: The Failings of the Baker-Hamilton Report. *Strategic Insights* VI (2 (March)).

O'Leary, B. 2008a. Complex Power-Sharing in and Over Northern Ireland: A Self-determination Agreement, a Treaty, a Consociation, a Federacy, Matching Confederal Institutions, Inter-Governmentalism and a Peace Process. In *Settling Self-determination Disputes: Complex Power-sharing in Theory and Practice*, edited by M. Weller and B. Metzger. Leiden & Boston: Martinus Nijhoff. 61–124.

O'Leary, B. ed. 2008b. *The Kurdistan Region: Invest in the Future. An Official Publication of the Kurdistan Regional Government*. Washington DC: Newsdesk Media.

O'Leary, B., McGarry, J. and Salih, K. eds 2005. *The Future of Kurdistan in Iraq*. Philadelphia: University of Pennsylvania Press.

Rezvani, D. R. 2003. Federacy: The Dynamics of Semi-Sovereign Territories. Unpublished manuscript.

Roeder, P. 2007. *Where Nation-States Come From: Institutional Change in the Age of Nationalism*. Princeton, NJ: Princeton University Press.

Romano, D. 2006. *The Kurdish Nationalist Movement: Opportunity, Mobilization and Identity*. Cambridge: Cambridge University Press.

Royal Commission. 1996. *Royal Commission on Aboriginal Peoples*. Ottawa: Department of Indian and Northern Affairs.

Singh, G. 1993. The Politics of Ethnic Conflict Regulation: Case Studies of Protracted Ethnic Conflicts. In *Ethnic Conflict in India: A Case Study of Punjab*, edited by J. McGarry and B. O'Leary. London & New York: Routledge. 84–105.

Singh, G. 1995. The Punjab Crisis Since 1984: A Reassessment. *Ethnic and Racial Studies* 18 (3 (July)): 476–493.

Singh, G. 2001. Resizing and Reshaping the State: India from Partition to the Present. In *Right-Sizing the State: The Politics of Moving Borders*, edited by B. O'Leary, I. S. Lustick and T. Callaghy. Oxford: Oxford University Press. 138–167.

Sisk, T. 1996. *Power Sharing and International Mediation in Ethnic Conflicts*. Washington, DC: Princeton University Press.

Stepan, A. 1999. Federalism and Democracy: Beyond the U.S. Model. *Journal of Democracy* 10(4): 19–34.

Stouurzh, G. 1991. Problems of Conflict Resolution in a Multi-Ethnic State: Lessons from the Austrian Historical Experience. In *State and Nation in Muti-Ethnic Societies: The Breakup of Multinational States*, edited by U. Ra'anan, M. Mesner, K. Armes and K. Martin. Manchester: Manchester University Press. 67–80.

Suberu, R. T. 2001. *Federalism and Ethnic Conflict in Nigeria*. Washington DC: United States Institute of Peace Press.

Suberu, R. and Diamond, L. 2002. Institutional Design, Ethnic Conflict Management and Democracy in Nigeria. In *The Architecture of Democracy: Institutional Design, Conflict Management and Democracy*, edited by A. Reynolds. Oxford: Oxford University Press. 400–428.

Vile, M. J. C. 1982. Federation and Confederation: The Experience of the United States and the British Commonwealth. In *Political Co-operation in Divided Societies: A Series of Papers Relevant to the Conflict in Northern Ireland*, edited by D. Rea. Dublin: Gill & Macmillan. 216–228.

Watts, R. L. 1996. *Comparing Federal Systems in the 1990s*. Kingston, Ontario: Institute of Intergovernmental Relations/Queen's University.

Watts, R. L. 1998. Federalism, Federal Political Systems, and Federations. *Annual Review of Political Science* 1: 117–137.

Weiner, M. 1971. The Macedonian Syndrome: An Historical Model of International Relations and Political Development. *World Politics* 13(4): 665–683.

Weller, M. and Wolff, S. eds 2005. *Autonomy, Self Governance and Conflict Resolution: Innovative Approaches to Institutional Design in Divided Societies*. London: Routledge.

21

ETHNIC ACCOMMODATION IN UNITARY STATES

Frans Schrijver

Introduction

The unitary state is the most prevalent state system worldwide, and just like federal states, many of the world's unitary states are places of ethnic conflict. We can connect the common distinction of state systems between unitary and federal states (Elazar 1997) with ethnic conflicts in two ways: in the first place, it provides a context, a state structure as arena in which ethnic conflicts are fought and solutions are introduced. Ethnic conflicts are located somewhere, and whether they are located in unitary or federal states matters; difference in state structures influence the actors in the conflict. Secondly, the distinction between unitary and federal is part of the accommodation of ethnic conflict itself. Federalism is not just a context, but is itself an instrument of pacification and managing ethnic difference (McGarry and O'Leary 1994). And, arguably also the unitary state has been used as instrument in response to ethnic conflicts and tensions. Particular historical examples of unitary states have been specifically designed to create national unity and end ethnic conflict by merging rival ethnic identities into one homogenous state identity. The French republic, with its state organisation as 'instruments of unity' (Lacoste 1997) aimed at standardisation and uniformity as introduced after the 1789 revolution, is perhaps the most well-known example of the unitary state as instrument of ethnic homogeneity. However, to regard all unitary states as such would be a simplification, and unitary states can be contexts for the recognition and accommodation of ethnic differences too.

This chapter discusses ethnic accommodation within unitary state structures, and therefore does not pay attention to those modes of ethnic conflict regulation that go beyond the unitary state, like federalisation or secession. A unitary state can be a starting point for those policies, but both do not regulate ethnic conflict *within* the unitary state. This chapter also does not discuss more crudely coercive tactics of dealing with ethnic difference like genocide or mass-population transfer. While they have been historically applied in unitary states, they certainly do not *accommodate* ethnic difference.

Ethnicity is a concept used widely throughout the social sciences, but it is also one of the hardest to define, with lively debates over its meaning (Hale 2004). In contrast to essentialist and primordialist (e.g. Shils 1957; Geertz 1967) views on ethnicity, this chapter builds on the understanding that ethnicity is not a natural aspect of humanity, but constructed, situational, context-dependent and contested (Barth 1969; Nagel 1994). It is particularly that contested nature of ethnicity and ethnic identification and recognition that is related to those situations that are meant with 'ethnic conflict'. Individuals may have a range of groups they belong to, several of which can be defined as 'ethnic groups'. Sometimes these ethnic identities can overlap, but in contexts of ethnic conflict identification with both groups in conflict with each other becomes mutually exclusive.

In a context of ethnic conflict ethnicity is relational as well; ethnic groups identify themselves as such not alone but in relation to one another, distinguishing themselves from other ethnic groups. But, just as much as the distinction from other groups is central to the existence of ethnicity, ethnic groups should not be regarded as homogenous. Not every member of an ethnic group feels loyalties or a sense of belonging to that group to the same extent, not every member has the same ideas about what it is that distinguishes the group from other groups, not every member has the same view on the history or the political and cultural future of the group, and not every member is to the same degree mobilised in ethnic conflicts.

According to Smith (1995: 7) what distinguishes federations is not necessarily their level of decentralisation, but that in federations regional autonomy is protected by the constitution. Unitary states may be decentralised, but lack that constitutional guarantee. This means that the *degree* of decentralisation is not necessarily what distinguishes federations from unitary states. When we consider federalism as a method of ethnic conflict accommodation, that step is often placed on an 'autonomy continuum', with increasing levels of decentralisation between complete centralism and secession (Paddison 1983). On such a continuum federations are normally placed between a regionalised or decentralised unitary state and a confederation. This implies that federations allow more regional autonomy than decentralised unitary states. But because the unique distinguishing feature of a federation is its constitutional guarantee of regional autonomy, and not the degree or nature of autonomy, that is not always the case. For instance, the Basque Country and Scotland have high degrees of autonomous regional policy-making powers within a unitary state (Spain and the United Kingdom respectively), without having the constitutional guarantee of that autonomy that a federation would give.

The division between federal and unitary states is not fixed, and states can move from one category to the other. Historic examples abound of confederations and federations that moved towards more centralisation (e.g. the Republic of United Netherlands evolving into a unitary republic and then kingdom after 1795) (Elazar 1982). More recently shifts in the opposite direction of decentralisation are more prevalent. Sometimes such shifts are slow step-by-step processes of decentralisation, positioning states 'in between' a unitary state and a federation. Spain for example has been described as being in a process of 'federalisation' since the death of its dictator Francisco Franco in 1975, with the incremental introduction of regional autonomies, partially constitutionally recognised (Moreno 2001).

Finally, although in most federations the whole state territory is divided into sub-state regions, federal states, provinces or Länder, that is not necessarily the case. In some situations only part of the country is federalised, while the rest has remained a unitary state, creating a situation of asymmetrical autonomy (Keating 1998). Unitary states can be decentralised asymmetrically too, with political or cultural regional autonomy applied to only a part of the state's territory. This is for instance the case if particular arrangements to facilitate and stimulate a regional language only apply to the region where that language is historically spoken. Asymmetrical decentralisation is very common, especially in reaction to demands of ethnic groups and as a method to accommodate ethnic conflict.

Regionalised unitary states

In unitary states regionalisation (Loughlin 1993) – the devolution of decision-making powers to regional authorities – is one of the most common ways to accommodate ethnic conflict, applying territorial autonomy principles similar to federalisation. Especially when an ethnic minority group lives concentrated in one particular area, has historical connections to that territory (for instance an era of independence), and claims regional autonomy or independence, regionalisation is a prevalent solution. Often regional devolution is considered a compromise solution, falling short of federalisation or secession, but giving an ethnic minority more say over its territory than centralisation. The general drift of those who propose regionalisation from a central government perspective as an effective reaction to claims by separatists is formulated by Bogdanor (1999: 194) writing, rather cynically, that 'it might well be that the best way to strengthen national unity is to give way to them a little as to better to disarm them'. For example, New Labour's 1997 British general election manifesto defended its proposal for devolution stating that 'the Union will be strengthened and the threat of separatism removed' (Labour Party 1997). Similarly, in 1981 French Minister of the Interior Gaston Deferre defended President Mitterand's proposal for regionalisation claiming that 'The regionalisation will maintain the national unity ... If we give all the French regions the statute that the *Parti Socialiste* proposes, the majority of the regional demands will be satisfied. That will calm down the situation in the regions concerned' (cited in Huguenin and Martinat 1998: 22, author's translation). Such propositions are based on the idea that most people who might otherwise support separatism will be satisfied with a compromise that offers regional autonomy and the recognition of regional distinctiveness. But even if some ethnic movements or political parties aim for full independence, the majority of the ethnic group they claim to represent or the regional population as a whole may not want to go as far. In such cases regional devolution may be an attractive way to accommodate the demands of a regionally concentrated ethnic minority, and isolate extremists (e.g. Gurr 1993; McGarry and O'Leary 1994; Rudolph and Thomson 1985).

There is no unambiguous evidence that regionalisation (or federalisation for that matter) in itself pacifies an ethnic conflict, either in the long or short term. In Northern Ireland the introduction of a directly elected regional Northern Irish Assembly was part of the 1998 Belfast Agreement and the relatively successful peace process. In contrast, the establishment of the Basque Country as 'autonomous community' in 1979 did not pacify the conflict even in the short term. ETA did not accept the compromise solution and decided to continue its bombing campaign more or less unchanged. This shows that regionalisation as instrument of ethnic conflict resolution needs to comply with certain conditions, such as full involvement and agreement of all major actors, to be successful in the short term.

Whether regionalisation pacifies ethnic conflicts in the long run is even more questionable. While regional autonomy does introduce institutions that facilitate the democratic discussion of grievances and peaceful expression of political claims, those regional institutions can also function as a platform for the deepening of ethnic cleavages. Van der Wusten and Knippenberg (2001) have stressed the recursive dimension of ethnic conflicts, where one stage or 'episode' of the conflict ends with institutional re-arrangement and re-positioning of relevant actors, but also with a new political agenda for a next round of ethnic politics. In that light regionalisation, like any instrument of ethnic conflict accommodation, can be seen as the outcome of a cycle of ethnic conflict. However, the outcome of one cycle also shapes the starting conditions of a new round of ethnic conflict. Especially the introduction of regional autonomy provides a regional ethnic minority with opportunities to emphasise ethnic distinction and mobilise support for further claims for autonomy or full independence (Schrijver 2005, 2006). This refers to the institutionalisation process of a region (Paasi 1991), and the importance of the presence of regional institutions for the development of ethno-regional consciousness.

Discussing the accommodation of ethnic conflict, Juan José Linz comments that 'federalism might create a temporary stability, a framework in which further demands can be articulated and additional rights can be granted, but it is unlikely to be a once and for all stable, durable solution' (1997: 22). This would apply even more to a halfway solution as regionalisation. Regionalisation changes political infrastructures, providing regional ethnic movements with a base from which to challenge the central government and put forth further claims (Máiz 2003). It is much easier for regionally concentrated ethnic groups to get elected, form part of a government, and use this to mobilise support at the regional than at state level. In the United Kingdom devolution has offered the Scottish National Party in Scotland and Plaid Cymru in Wales opportunities to take on governing responsibilities at regional levels, and become more respectable, established political parties. However, those new political opportunities, and especially the possibility to become a mainstream political party at regional level, do inspire a moderation of the movement as well (Schrijver 2006). In order to profit from the opportunities offered by regional elections, and appeal to more voters, ethnic movements often moderate their main aims, and aim to distance themselves from extremists. This suggests that regionalisation perhaps is no way to end a conflict, but at least channel it into a continuation by democratic means and with more moderate claims. Apart from its effectiveness as conflict resolution instrument, there is a moral case to be made for regionalisation (and federalisation) in a democracy, if a clear majority of the region's population is in favour, expressed in a regional referendum.

Finally, it should be noted that regionalisation is not always about ethnic difference and the accommodation of the territorial demands of ethnic minorities. That has been the perspective here, but there are many other possible motivations for regionalisation, ranging from local administration efficiency, obstacles against totalitarianism, and the influence of supranational organizations, to central government budget cuts and reactions to global economic restructuring (Sharpe 1993; Bullmann 1997; Macleod and Jones 2007).

Consociational democracy and state-wide power-sharing

Regionalisation (and federalisation) recognises the link between ethnic group and territory, but not all ethnic conflict is about claims to regional territories, and not all ethnic groups live concentrated in a particular 'homeland'. An instrument of ethnic conflict accommodation allowing non-territorial forms of autonomy and power-sharing between ethnic groups is consociationalism (Lijphart 1969, 1977), which as discussed elsewhere in the volume, is often applied to the state as a whole, not just a particular region associated with an ethnic minority.

With regard to consociationalism of crucial importance is the cooperation between elites representing all segments of society. For his concept of consociational democracy Lijphart clearly drew on the system of *verzuiling* ('pillarization') in his native country, the Netherlands (Knippenberg 1999). During much of the twentieth century Dutch politics, and society in general, was characterised by coalition-building, negotiation, and cooperation at elite level of those representing deeply divided segments ('pillars') of society. However, it should be noted that in Lijphart's example of the Netherlands these different segments of society were not generally recognised as different ethnic groups, but based on ideological and religious cleavages (Protestant, Catholic, Socialist and Liberal). Arguably, therefore, Lijphart's concept of consociationalism was in the core not a system of ethnic conflict accommodation, but introduced as an alternative model of representative democracy, in contrast to other models of democracy (e.g. the Westminster model), designed to deal with pluralism in a very broad sense.

But, Lijphart (1977) did argue the applicability of consociationalism to societies where ethnic conflict was an issue, using case-studies of Belgium, Lebanon and Malaysia. Since then consociational power-sharing has found a prominent place in ethnic conflict resolution literature. Consociationalism has been applied in unitary states such as Burundi (Lemarchand 2007), and in regions within unitary states like in Northern Ireland (McGarry and O'Leary 2004) and South-Tyrol (Markusse 1996; Wolff 2008). As instrument of ethnic conflict accommodation consociationalism differs markedly from assimilationist approaches. As Donald Horowitz (1985: 569) writes, consociationalism assumes 'that it is necessary for ethnically divided states to live with ethnic cleavages rather than wish them away'. Consociationalism is based on the presence of institutions that secure the distinctiveness and internal autonomy of segments of society, and give all segments access to decision-making at the centre. And whereas territorial autonomy approaches (federalisation or regionalisation) leave the door open for secession (and arguably create the geographical infrastructure for partition), consociationalism aims for an enduring solution of power-sharing at state-level and within existing state boundaries. This aim for a stable democracy in a plural society is on the one hand achieved through the facilitation of sub-societies with their own institutions (political parties, newspapers, schools, sports clubs, etc.), and on the other hand top-down ethnic conflict accommodation through elite cooperation. Proportional representation ensures that the connection between a grand coalition at elite level and the segments of society at grassroots level is not lost, and each segment and their leaders have access to power at nation-state level.

Despite significant criticism of consociationalism's effectiveness (Barry 1975; Deschouwer 1994; Horowitz 1985) it remains one of the most advocated models of democratic regulation of ethnic conflict. However, most concrete cases where its application has been noted more recently (see McGarry and O'Leary (2006) on Northern Ireland, Caspersen (2004) on Bosnia-Herzegovina, and Wilson (2003) on Sri Lanka) are regarded as adapted versions of consociationalism or hybrids with other models, and have diverged from Lijphart's original. Consociationalism involves the establishment of institutions that guarantee internal autonomy for each constituent group. Those institutions are organised mostly territorially in federations and in regionalised unitary states. However, consociationalism also requires non-territorial power-sharing mechanisms among elites, which can exist at state-level in federations (e.g. Belgium, Deschouwer 2006), but just as well in unitary states like Lijphart's original example the Netherlands. In some unitary states this may involve consociational arrangements without territorial segmentation, for instance through the political, cultural and social pillarisation and radical electoral proportional representation of the Netherlands, or the prescribed balance between Hutu and Tutsi representation in central and local government of Burundi (Lemarchand 2007). However, the territorial segmentation and consociational institutionalisation in federations and regionalised unitary states may provide more stability than non-territorial consociationalism. Many consociational arrangements in unitary states have not survived beyond temporary, transitional or post-conflict settlements (e.g. South Africa, Lebanon, Rwanda, and Colombia).

Democracies with ethnic majority dominance

While consociationalism is built around cooperation and compromise resulting from proportionality and access to power of all ethnic groups in a state, there are many democratic systems where one ethnic group dominates one or more others, coined 'ethnic democracies'

(Smith 1996; Smooha 1990; Smooha and Hanf 1992). Ethnic democracies give individual citizens access to political and civil rights, but preserve collective political and cultural rights to the dominant ethnic majority. This applies to multi-ethnic democracies where state institutions do not constitute a neutral set of rules, but are controlled by one of the constituent ethnic groups. In some cases this situation can persist for a long time, with far-reaching institutionalisation of the ethnic dominance over the state.

Ethnic democracy is a form of what has been called hegemonic control (Lustick 1979; McGarry and O'Leary 1994), which also applies to authoritarian, imperial and partially democratic societies. Historically, ethnic control by a hegemonic group has been the most common way of dealing with ethnic and cultural plurality. The suppression of ethnic minorities (and sometimes majorities) through coercion or threats of coercion has been commonplace, achieving varying degrees of stability. However, the combination of democratisation and the advance of the age of nationalism meant other solutions replaced durable ethnic hegemony as system of choice. On the one hand, nationalism and the idea that state and nation should coincide resulted in attempts to eradicate ethnic plurality, through instruments ranging from assimilation to genocide. On the other hand, in other contexts individual and collective civil and political rights of liberal democracy introduced opportunities for ethnic minorities to gain (limited) access to power or political and cultural autonomy. Still, hegemonic control has retained a presence, especially in non-democratic or partially democratic states. South Africa between 1948 and 1990 was a clear example of ethnic hegemonic control, with full access to democracy, citizenship and civil rights restricted to a white minority.

In states where the principles of liberal democracy apply to the whole population, ethnic minority control like in South Africa under apartheid is much rarer. A functioning democracy tends to either give minorities some access to power, or establish majority rule. The latter means that a majority ethnic group controlling the state institutions with limited influence for one or more minority ethnic groups is rather common in democratic societies. For instance, in Israel (Smooha 1990) a Jewish majority has dominance over an Arab minority, in post-communist Estonia (Pettai and Hallik 2002) the Estonian majority allows limited influence for an ethnic Russian minority, while in relatively recent history there were clear situations of majority ethnic control in functioning democracies in Northern Ireland, the Southern United States, and of aboriginal populations in Canada, Australia and the USA. In such situations of ethnic democracy the dominance of one group is institutionalised, and the dominant ethnic group gains power disproportionate to its size. This is in contrast to consociationalism where proportionality is a key element in maintaining a power balance between the different segments of society. The most well-documented case of ethnic democracy is Israel, where Arabs with Israeli citizenship can vote in elections, but enjoy restricted political and social rights in practice, for instance through the exclusion of political parties that negate the principle that 'the State of Israel is the state of the Jewish people', and through the exemption of Israeli Arabs from mandatory military service, thereby excluding them from the social rights tied to and symbolic importance of military service (Peled 1992).

The dominance of one group in ethnic democracies is reflected in a control of political decision-making, monopolisation of positions in government, and the establishment of a structure of governance favourable to the leading ethnic group. But it is also manifested through incorporation of de facto ethnic inequality in unwritten rules, and through a monopolisation of state symbols by one ethnic group. That is the case when for instance the language, religion, cultural symbols such as national holidays, and national aspirations of the hegemonic ethnic group also become those of the state as a whole, with little room for the national ambitions or iconography of minority ethnic groups at state level. Take for instance the adoption of Estonian as the only official language of Estonia and of the initially restrictive language requirements for naturalisation and electoral candidates, despite the presence of a substantial Russian minority (Pettai and Hallik 2002). This institutionalisation of ethnic dominance can create a situation where the de jure existing political rights and civil liberties of a liberal democracy covering the whole population become restricted de facto for ethnic minority groups.

In an ethnic democracy – in contrast to non-democratic or partially democratic forms of ethnic hegemonic control – there are democratic procedures in place for ethnic minorities to negotiate better terms of coexistence. However, a situation of ethnic democracy can only survive through a strict interpretation of democracy as majority rule with little minority influence. Although this raises questions of injustice, some have advocated ethnic control as a relatively stable settlement for ethnic conflicts. Ian Lustick argues that 'certain forms of control may be preferable to the chaos and bloodshed that might be the only alternatives', in 'particular situations and for limited periods of time' (1979: 344). Whether it is indeed possible in a democracy to introduce ethnic control for a limited amount of time is doubtful, considering that it might be tempting for the majority ethnic group to cling to its hegemonic position as long as possible. In reality what is introduced as a temporary solution can easily turn into a stable and permanent settlement, as retreating from the status quo into a solution requiring more compromise might become less and less appealing to the dominant majority. Apart from that, proponents of consociationalism, federalisation or regionalisation would argue that very rarely 'chaos and bloodshed' are truly the only alternatives to hegemonic control.

Assimilation and the quest for national unity

The instruments of ethnic conflict accommodation discussed above work under the assumption that the most effective way to deal with ethnic conflict is by facilitating existing ethnic differences, or at least acknowledging them. In contrast, assimilation policies aim to eradicate ethnic differences in society, to take away the basis for ethnic conflict. Assimilation is a process whereby an ethnic group gives up the cultural identity and sense of belonging that distinguishes it from other groups (Gordon 1964), and either adopts those of another ethnic group or of a newly created transcendent ethnic identity. This mostly is the outcome of unequal power relations and often involves some form of coercion. It should, however, be distinguished from other methods that aim to do away with existing ethnic differences by making ethnic minorities 'disappear', such as genocide, ethnic cleansing and population transfer.

Assimilation as used here is a form of social integration, and both have been mostly discussed in relation to immigration. The particulars of ethnic conflict related to immigrants are briefly touched upon below, but assimilation has been widely applied to deal with non-immigrant ethnic minorities as well. The merger of several ethnic groups into an overarching national identity, often modelled on that of a dominant group, has been commonplace in historical processes of nation-building. The classic example of France, and the nineteenth-century process of turning 'peasants into Frenchmen' described by Weber (1976), demonstrates that assimilation can in the long run be rather successful. With the exception of parts of Corsica, the French republic managed to assimilate most of its many constituent regional identities into one French nation. However, any success achieved through assimilation policies should be set against the coercion that is needed to make groups give up their identity. French unity was not achieved without force, just as the russification of non-Russian parts of the Soviet Union could only be achieved by violent means.

Often assimilation through coercion is counterproductive, because it is exactly the threat of the disappearance of a minority culture that makes ethnic minorities rebel and causes ethnic conflict. The use of force against an established ethnic group in order to force them to abandon their way of life can provide references and memories to be used in the mobilization of resistance for generations afterwards. Take for example sympathy for Basque separatist organisation ETA among significant sections of the population, partly as a result of the attempts in Spain under Franco to oppress Basque cultural distinctiveness (Lecours 2008). In Iraq, attempts using brute force to eradicate a Kurdish cultural identity have been similarly unsuccessful (O'Leary and Salih 2006).

Social integration policies can be more benign, often aiming to take away obstacles to interaction between ethnic groups and reducing socio-economic inequalities along ethnic lines that can go hand in hand with ethnic segregation. Assimilation goes further, aiming to make cultural differences within a society disappear, or fuse different cultures into one common culture. Because changing a person's culture, way of life and group identifications takes time, assimilation is always a long process, mostly taking several generations of inter-marriage and nation-building. It requires consistent efforts of what Michael Billig (1995) has called 'banal nationalism', the constant and habitual production and reproduction of nations in everyday life. As Billig writes, 'for such daily reproductions to occur, one might hypothesize that a whole complex of beliefs, assumptions, habits, representations and practices must also be reproduced' (1995: 6). This 'banal' reproduction of nationalism applies to the everyday maintenance of existing nations and their populations, but also certainly to the process of assimilation of minority ethnic groups into a national majority culture.

Ethnic conflict and immigration

The different ways in which ethnic conflict is accommodated in unitary states discussed above mostly deals with long-established groups that often claim a territory within the state as their homeland. Examples would be the Basques, Québécois, Kurds, or Hutus. But the discussion of assimilation as response to ethnic conflict already showed that in public and academic debates concepts like 'ethnicity' and 'minority' are also associated with immigrants. And just like 'native' ethnic groups can get into conflict with each other, there can be tensions between a native ethnic majority and immigrant ethnic minorities. In both cases there can be a similar connection between ethnicity and access to political power, and claims for political and cultural autonomy from both national minorities and immigrants.

Regarding political or cultural claims of both types of ethnic minority as a threat to national unity, in many cases hegemonic state actors tend to treat national minorities and immigrants in a broadly similar way. In France for instance both the claims for cultural autonomy of national minorities like the Bretons and Corsicans and of immigrant minorities are denied with reference to risks of '*communautarisme*' (Schnapper 2004), submitting the individual members of a group to the norms of a cultural minority community. According to this logic, the state should be culturally neutral, and any recognition of minorities (both native and immigrant) and facilitation of their culture would diverge from that neutrality. However, one could question whether the state can indeed be neutral through a strict application of Western liberal democracy, and in practice this restriction of recognition of cultural expression is applied much less strictly to that of the dominant majority.

In contrast, some, like the political philosopher Will Kymlicka, argue for a differential treatment of immigrants and national minorities, suggesting that while the formation of an autonomous societal culture is viable for territorially concentrated national minorities, this is not appropriate for immigrant groups, who 'lack the territorial concentration or historical institutions needed to sustain a vibrant societal culture' (Kymlicka 2001: 54, see also Kymlicka 1995).

The debate over whether or not claims of national minorities should be met with the same state response as those of immigrant minorities reaches a particular level of complexity in the case of immigration into the territories of national minorities (Carens 2000; Zapata-Barrero 2007). Territories like Quebec, Catalonia, Flanders, and Scotland are not only the regions or 'homelands' of ethnic minorities within their respective states, but also increasingly places of immigration. In those situations an established ethnic conflict can be further complicated, with the ethnic minority at state level (Catalans, Flemish, etc.) turned into an ethnic majority at regional level, facing a choice of responses to immigrant ethnic minorities themselves. In federal states this may involve far-reaching choices over immigration policy, but in unitary states this will mostly be limited to minor adaptations of state-wide immigration policies. Take for instance the arrangement in federal Canada that allows the government of Quebec to apply its own immigration selection criteria, and recruit immigrants from French-speaking countries, compared to the introduction in the unitary United Kingdom of the option for immigrants in Wales to take citizenship tests in Welsh.

Conclusion

The enormous variation of unitary states worldwide means that it is impossible to distinguish a single type of response to ethnic conflict chosen by unitary states. It is true that the ideal-typical unitary state emphasises the importance of the protection of the unity of the state, its territory, and its single and homogenous nation, and views ethnic conflict and claims of ethnic minorities as a threat to that unity. It follows that the stereotypical unitary state response to ethnic conflict and difference is one of assimilation with the elimination of ethnic difference as objective, or accommodation from a perspective of 'damage control'. But, although some states come close to that ideal-type, the ethnically and nationally completely homogenous state does not exist. Some unitary states have followed pluralist policies that provide ethnic minorities with far-reaching degrees of autonomy, whereas some of the most brutal policies aimed at the eradication of ethnic difference have been used in federal states.

Ethnic conflict has produced two sovereign states and new members of the United Nations in the twenty-first century at the time of writing: Montenegro and Timor-Leste. Both are unitary states, as is the overwhelming majority of new independent states that emerged from the break-up of the Soviet Union and Yugoslavia. The choice for a unitary state system often reflects a desire to maintain, or establish, national unity after gaining independence. However, many of those states that were born out of ethnic conflict are in turn confronted with ethnic minorities within their own borders, and the need to formulate policies in response to their political and cultural claims. These situations offer fruitful case studies for the further exploration of the dynamics and tensions of dealing with plurality in unitary states.

References

Barry, B. (1975) The Consociational Model and its Dangers. *European Journal of Political Research*, 3: 393–412.

Barth, F. (1969) *Ethnic Groups and Boundaries: The Social Organization of Culture Difference*. Boston: Little, Brown, and Co.

Billig, M. (1995) *Banal Nationalism*. London: Sage.

Bogdanor, V. (1999) *Devolution in the United Kingdom*. Oxford: Oxford University Press.

Bullmann, U. (1997) The Politics of the Third Level. In: C. Jeffery, ed. *The Regional Dimension of the European Union: Towards a Third Level in Europe?* London: Frank Cass, pp. 3–19.

Carens, J. (2000) *Culture, Citizenship and Community*. New York: Oxford University Press.

Caspersen, N. (2004) Good Fences Make Good Neighbours? A Comparison of Conflict-Regulation Strategies in Postwar Bosnia. *Journal of Peace Research*, 41: 569–588.

Deschouwer, K. (1994) The Decline of Consociationalism and the Reluctant Modernization of Belgian Mass Parties. In: R. S. Katz and P. Mair, eds. *How Parties Organize: Change and Adaptation in Party Organizations in Western Democracies*. London: Sage, pp. 80–108.

Deschouwer, K. (2006) And the Peace Goes On? Consociational Democracy and Belgian Politics in the 21st Century. *West European Politics*, 29(5): 895–911.

Elazar, D. J. (1982) Federalism, Centralization, and State Building in the Modern Epoch. *Publius*, 12(3): 1–9.

Elazar, D. J. (1997) Contrasting Unitary and Federal Systems. *International Political Science Review*, 18(3): 237–251.

Geertz, C. (1967) *Old Societies and New States: The Quest for Modernity in Asia and Africa*. New York: Free Press.

Gordon, M. M. (1964) *Assimilation in American Life. The Role of Race, Religion, and National Origins*. New York: Oxford University Press.

Gurr, T. R. (1993) *Minorities at Risk: A Global View of Ethnopolitical Conflicts*. Washington DC: United States Institute of Peace Press.

Hale, H. E. (2004) Explaining Ethnicity. *Comparative Political Studies*, 37: 458–485.

Horowitz, D. L. (1985) *Ethnic Groups in Conflict*. Berkeley: University of California Press.

Huguenin, J. and Martinat, P. (1998) *Les Régions. Entre l'État et l'Europe*. Paris: Le Monde-Editions.

Keating, M. (1998) What's Wrong with Asymmetrical Government? *Regional and Federal Studies*, 8(1): 195–218.

Knippenberg, H. (1999) The Ethnicity of National Integration: Religion, Education and Politics in the Netherlands. *The Netherlands Journal of Social Sciences*, 35(1): 37–52.

Kymlicka, W. (1995) *Multicultural Citizenship*. Oxford: Oxford University Press.

Kymlicka, W. (2001) *Politics in the Vernacular: Nationalism, Multiculturalism and Citizenship*. Oxford: Oxford University Press.

Labour Party (1997) *New Labour: Because Britain Deserves Better*. London.

Lacoste, Y. (1997) *Vive la Nation. Destin d'une idée géopolitique*. Paris: Librairie Arthème Fayard.

Lecours, A. (2008) Violence as Politics: ETA and Basque Nationalism. In: S. M. Saideman and M.-J. Zahar, eds. *Intra-State Conflict, Governments and Security*. London: Routledge, pp. 120–137.

Lemarchand, R. (2007) Consociationalism and Power Sharing in Africa: Rwanda, Burundi, and the Democratic Republic of the Congo. *African Affairs*, 106(422): 1–20.

Lijphart, A. (1969) Consociational Democracy. *World Politics*, 21(2): 207–225.

Lijphart, A. (1977) *Democracy in Plural Societies: A Comparative Exploration*. New Haven: Yale University Press.

Linz, J. J. (1997) Democracy, Multinationalism and Federalism. Madrid: Fundación Juan March Working papers.

Loughlin, J. (1993) Nation, State and Region in Western Europe. In: L. Bekemans, ed. *Culture: Building Stone for Europe 2002*. Brussels: European Interuniversity Press, pp. 229–248.

Lustick, I. (1979) Stability in Deeply Divided Societies: Consociationalism versus Control. *World Politics*, 31(3): 325–344.

Macleod, G. and Jones, M. (2007) Territorial, Scalar, Networked, Connected: In What Sense a 'Regional World'? *Regional Studies*, 41(9): 1177–1191.

Máiz, R. (2003) Politics and the Nation: Nationalist Mobilisation of Ethnic Differences. *Nations and Nationalism*, 9(22): 195–212.

Markusse, J. (1996) *Zuid-Tirol: de pacificatie van een multi-etnische region*. Utrecht: Koninklijk Nederlands Aardrijkskundig Genootschap.

McGarry, J. and O'Leary, B. (1994) The Political Regulation of National and Ethnic Conflict. *Parliamentary Affairs*, 47(1): 94–115.

McGarry, J. and O'Leary, B. (2004) *The Northern Ireland Conflict: Consociational Engagements*. Oxford: Oxford University Press.

McGarry, J. and O'Leary, B. (2006) Consociational Theory, Northern Ireland's Conflict, and its Agreement. Part 1: What Consociationalists Can Learn from Northern Ireland. *Government and Opposition*, 41(1): 43–63.

Moreno, L. (2001) *The Federalization of Spain*. London: Frank Cass.

Nagel, J. (1994) Constructing Ethnicity: Creating and Recreating Ethnic Identity and Culture. *Social Problems*, 41(1): 152–176.

O'Leary, B. and. Salih, K. (2006) The Denial, Resurrection and Affirmation of Kurdistan. In: B. O'Leary, J. McGarry and K. Salih, eds. *The Future of Kurdistan in Iraq*. Pennsylvania: University of Pennsylvania Press, pp. 3–46.

Paasi, A. (1991) Deconstructing Regions: Notes on the Scales of Spatial Life. *Environment and Planning*, 23: 239–256.

Paddison, R. (1983) *The Fragmented State: The Political Geography of Power*. Oxford: Blackwell.

Peled, Y. (1992) Ethnic Democracy and the Legal Construction of Citizenship: Arab Citizens of the Jewish State. *American Political Science Review*, 86(2): 432–443.

Pettai, V. and Hallik, K. (2002) Understanding Processes of Ethnic Control: Segmentation, Dependency and Co-optation in Post-communist Estonia. *Nations and Nationalism*, 8(4): 505–529.

Rudolph, J. R. and Thompson, R. J. (1985) Ethnoterritorial Movements and the Policy Process: Accommodating Nationalist Demands in the Developed World. *Comparative Politics*, 17(3): 91–311.

Schnapper, D. (2004) La République face aux communautarismes. *Études*, 400: 177–188.

Schrijver, F. (2005) Regionalism in Galicia after Regionalisation. *Tijdschrift voor Economische en Sociale Geografie*, 96(3): 275–286.

Schrijver, F. (2006) *Regionalism after Regionalisation: Spain, France and the United Kingdom*. Amsterdam: Amsterdam University Press.

Sharpe, L. J. (1993) *Rise of Meso Government in Europe*. London: Sage.

Shils, E. (1957) Primordial, Personal, Sacred, and Civil Ties. *British Journal of Sociology*, 8: 130–145.

Smith, G. (1995) *Federalism: The Multiethnic Challenge*. London: Longman.

Smith, G. (1996) The Ethnic Democracy Thesis and the Citizenship Question in Estonia and Latvia. *Nationalities Papers*, 24(2): 199–216.

Smooha, S. (1990) Minority Status in an Ethnic Democracy: The Status of the Arab Minority in Israel. *Ethnic and Racial Studies*, 12(3): 389–413.

Smooha, S. and Hanf, T. (1992) The Diverse Modes of Conflict-Regulation in Deeply Divided Societies. *International Journal of Comparative Sociology*, 33(1–2): 26–47.

Van der Wusten, H. and Knippenberg, H. (2001) The Ethnic Dimension in Twentieth Century European Politics: A Recursive Model. In: G. Dijkink and H. Knippenberg, eds. *The Territorial Factor: Political Geography in a Globalising World*. Amsterdam: Vossiuspers, pp. 273–291.

Weber, E. (1976) *Peasants into Frenchmen: The Modernization of Rural France, 1870–1014*. Stanford: Stanford University Press.

Wilson, A. J. (2003) Sri Lanka: Ethnic Strife and the Politics of Space. In: J. Coakley, ed. *The Territorial Management of Ethnic Conflict*. London: Frank Cass, pp. 173–198.

Wolff, S. (2008) Complex Power Sharing as Conflict Resolution: South Tyrol in Comparative Perspective. In: J. Woelk, F. Palermo and J. Marko, eds. *Tolerance through Law: Self-governance and Group Rights in South Tyrol*. Leiden: Martinus Nijhoff, pp. 329–370.

Zapata-Barrero, R. (2007) Setting a Research Agenda on the Interaction Between Cultural Demands of Immigrants and Minority Nations. *Journal of Immigrant and Refugee Studies*, 5(4): 1–25.

22

NATIONAL CULTURAL AUTONOMY

David J. Smith

Introduction

In the first two to three decades after the Second World War it was widely, though mistakenly assumed that ethnicity had ceased to be a significant factor in European politics. Increasingly challenged from the 1970s, this view lost any remaining credence following the end of the Cold War. Since the turn of the 1990s, ethnic politics has been a particular focus of attention in relation to the former communist countries, where the policies of the previously existing regimes are widely seen as having strongly institutionalized ethno-cultural understandings of nationhood. The economic turbulence of the late socialist period, a collective memory of past oppressions and the absence of any strongly rooted tradition of democratic institutions all created fertile terrain for ethnic conflict, which emerged in several of the countries created or reconstituted following the demise of the USSR and the former Yugoslavia. To outside eyes, the bloodshed that has occurred in Croatia, Bosnia, Chechnya, Kosovo and elsewhere has invited parallels with the period from 1878–1945, when the region's 'national question' contributed in no small measure to the outbreak of two World Wars. This focus on con-flictual dynamics of ethnicity, however, has obscured past multinational legacies within the region, including some original models for the management of ethnic diversity within a single territorial state framework.

A good example is the concept of National Cultural Autonomy (NCA – also known as non-territorial cultural autonomy), which was first devised at the turn of the twentieth century by the Austrian Social Democrats Karl Renner (1870–1950) and Otto Bauer (1881–1938). These 'Austro-Marxists' sought to transform the then Habsburg Monarchy into a democratic multinational federation based on 'personal, not territorial characteristics' (Renner 2005: 32). Their ideas also attained widespread currency within the western provinces of the neigh-bouring tsarist empire. Renner and Bauer's vision was soon overtaken by the tumultuous events of 1914–1923, which precipitated the collapse of the region's polyethnic empires. In Central Europe, these gave way to a belt of new, putatively national states. Further east there emerged the Union of Soviet Socialist Republics, which (in line with Stalin's famous 1913 definition of the nation and Lenin's previous repudiation of Austro-Marxism) gave territorial recognition to the former subject ethnicities of the tsarist empire. The USSR could, however, in no way be considered a genuine federation, and it ultimately served to institutionalize both territorial-political and personal ethno-cultural models of nationhood as well as the tension between them (Brubaker 1996: 35–36). The NCA concept was nevertheless carried over into the 'New Europe' of the post First World War era: during the 1920s it informed laws on minority rights adopted by Estonia and Lithuania and also became the guiding principle of the European Nationalities Congress, a transnational lobby group that sought to reform the League of Nations and challenge the primacy of the indivisibly sovereign nation-state within international relations (Smith and Hiden 2012). These pre-1914 and inter-war developments could easily be dismissed as a quaint experiment belonging to a bygone age. However, in the post-1945 period, NCA has been applied as a facet of federally based political arrangements in Belgium and Canada and as an arrangement catering for indigenous peoples in a range of settings (Coakley 1994; Chouinard 2013; Salat et al. 2014). Since 1991, national minority legislation based on the NCA principle has also been adopted in a number of former communist states in Central and East Europe.

'Austro-Marxism' and the origins of NCA

As Aviel Roshwald (2001: 5) has observed, the rise of nationalism as an ideology and political movement during the late nineteenth and early twentieth centuries exerted a centrifugal force within the ethnically complex territories of Central and Eastern Europe. This posed a challenge not just for imperial rulers, but also for those liberal and socialist circles that were committed to halting rising demands for national territorial sovereignty amongst the empires' subject nationalities and realizing universalist principles of democracy and social equality within existing territorial boundaries. Whereas orthodox Marxists tended to dismiss the entire concept of nationality as a form of bourgeois false consciousness, Renner and Bauer's everyday experience of politics in late Imperial Austria convinced them that demands for cultural recognition by the various nationalities would have to be addressed if the solidarity of the socialist movement was to be maintained. In 1899, Renner set out his vision in an article entitled 'Staat und Nation'. Bauer followed suit with *The National Question and Social Democracy*, published in 1907. A lawyer by training, Renner saw the rule of law as integral to solving the 'national question'. By making each 'national group' a 'collective juridical subject in the constitutional order' (Bowring 2005: 191) and according cultural autonomy on this basis, ethnicity would cease to be a bone of political contention. In this way, it would be possible to engineer a shift towards 'a more progressive agenda of political action unhampered by nationalist division' (Schwarzmantel 2005: 64).

The novelty of NCA lies above all in its non-territorial approach to the issue of national self-determination. The model is founded on the 'personality principle', which holds that 'totalities of persons are divisible only according to personal, not territorial characteristics' (Renner 2005: 32). Under Renner's scheme, the state would allow representatives of national groups to set up public corporations and elect their own cultural self-governments. Bauer in particular argued that ethno-national groups are, to a large extent, historically developed communities of fate and character and thus bear something of an inherited, deterministic quality. A democratic approach to the issue nevertheless dictated that ethnicity – rather like religion – be treated as a matter of personal conviction and 'a feature of the legal status of the individual' (Renner 2005: 22). In an extension of the 'personality principle', membership of the proposed public corporations was to be on the basis of individuals freely determining their ethnicity and voluntarily enrolling on a national register. Those signing up in this way would be eligible to elect the representatives of the cultural self-government, but would also be liable to pay cultural taxes to the corporation, to supplement funding provided by state and municipal authorities. Once constituted, the cultural self-governments could assume full control over schooling in the relevant language and other issues of specific concern to the group. The jurisdiction of the aforementioned bodies would not be confined to particular territorial sub-regions of the state, but would extend to all citizens who professed belonging to the relevant nationality, regardless of where they lived.

Territory had 'a significant role to play as an organisational principle' within Renner's federal scheme, which envisaged the subdivision of the Habsburg realms into eight economic regions. However, the personality principle alone could form 'the constitutive principle which brings about the separation of the nationalities and the union of individuals' (Renner 2005: 29). In the highly complex ethnic environment of Central and Eastern Europe, any effort to resolve the national question solely on the basis of territorial sovereignty for different groups was doomed to failure, for regardless of how territorial boundaries were drawn, national and political space would never be entirely congruent. A system of non-territorially based representation was therefore necessary to cater for those citizens who wished to preserve their distinct ethnic identity but who constituted a cultural minority within their region of residence. Otherwise, the territorial principle would dictate that 'if you live in my territory, you are subject to my domination, my law and my language!' (Renner 2005: 27–28). Oppression of minorities, rather than equal rights, would continue to be the order of the day, and national conflicts would be localized, but not definitively regulated.

Inter-war experiments and debates

Contemporary critics frequently dismissed the entire NCA vision as 'utopian'. However, as Renner asked in his original article, why should it be seen as any more so than German and Czech national programmes based on territorial sovereignty? The rightness of this view was confirmed after 1918, when attempts to realize national self-determination on a territorial basis simply recreated the problems of the old empires in miniature: each of the 'successor states' in the region contained significant ethnic minority populations. The NCA principle did, however, live on within the three Baltic States. These states rested on the concept of self-determination for the ethnic Estonian, Latvian and Lithuanian nations; however, the specific circumstances of their creation ensured that aspects of federalist thinking from the late and immediate post-tsarist period were carried over into the new constitutional provisions that they adopted.

Thus, the 1918 declarations of Baltic independence were addressed to everyone residing within the boundaries of the new states. In the case of Latvia, the 1922 constitution made reference to a single political 'nation of Latvia', while stating that ethnic Latvians were only one of a number of 'sovereign and autonomous' ethnic communities entitled to preserve their distinct cultural heritage, religion and language (Plakans 1995: 127). In 1925, Estonia adopted a law giving citizens declaring belonging to the country's largest ethnic minorities the right to establish their own public-legal corporations, on the basis of voluntary enrolment on a national register. If a number of citizens equivalent to 50% of the designated minority (as recorded under the latest census) could be enrolled, the national register formed the basis for elections to a cultural council, in which at least half of those belonging to the register had to take part. Once the cultural council was in place a 2/3 majority vote by its members was then required in order to implement cultural autonomy and appoint a cultural self-government with control over schools teaching in the relevant minority language and other cultural matters pertaining to the minority in question. As Karl Aun (1949: 241) has observed, the constituency of minority cultural self-governments in Estonia thus derived from 'the deliberate personal will of individual nationals living within the state territory'. Once cultural autonomy had been established, everyone enrolled on the national register was required to pay additional taxes to the cultural self-government. This supplemented existing funding provided by the state, which continued to exercise a broad supervisory role. Anyone unwilling to fulfil this added obligation, however, could withdraw from the respective national register by means of a simple written declaration. If the number of those enrolled on the register fell to a figure below 50% of those who declared belonging to the relevant minority under the census, the state could dissolve the institutions of minority self-government.

Estonia's 1925 law on cultural autonomy was promptly implemented by the country's German and Jewish minorities, whose small size and dispersed settlement meant that existing municipalities were not always obliged to offer them native-language schooling. The 1925 legislation was, however, highly complex. In order to implement and sustain it, minority activists necessarily had to be able to draw upon considerable financial and human resources. In this respect, Estonia's German and Jewish communities were also more socio-politically cohesive, and generally more highly educated and better-off than other minorities eligible for cultural autonomy. In this regard, the fact that Estonia's Russian population never implemented the law was mainly down to the unwillingness of a predominantly rural and impoverished population to pay additional taxes for the purposes of education, particularly when the state already provided publicly funded Russian-language schooling in those municipalities where Russians lived compactly (Smith 1999). This was compounded by political infighting amongst the ethnic Russian political elite, and the sheer practical difficulties of enrolling 45,000 ethnic Russian voters onto a national register, all this in the face of high levels of illiteracy in rural areas.

The failure by Estonia's Russians to implement NCA obviously undermined arguments that were made regarding the more general applicability of this model to Central and Eastern Europe's diverse ethno-national groups. Such arguments were frequently advanced from 1925 onwards by the European Nationalities Congress (ENC). Established largely on the initiative of ethnic Germans from Estonia and Latvia, the ENC lobbied the League of Nations for the establishment of a pan-European guarantee of minority rights based upon the NCA principle. In 1931 the League Minority Secretariat did produce a highly dismissive report on NCA.

Of greatest concern to League officials was the profoundly 'anti-modernist' character of Baltic legislation. The NCA scheme was very much at odds with prevailing Western orthodoxies, which regarded the unitary, 'atomist-centrist' model of nation-statehood as the only viable template for the future development of Central and Eastern Europe. In the aftermath of the First World War, the League of Nations and the dominant Western European powers at its heart had espoused the concept of minority rights in their dealings with the new successor states. Minority protection treaties stipulated that persons belonging to 'non-titular' ethnic minorities should enjoy equal treatment as well as certain positive rights relating to the practice of their language and culture, such as the right to receive primary education in their mother tongue and to form their own *private* cultural organizations. Any violation of these provisions – which fell far short of the autonomy accorded in Estonia and Latvia – could be reported to the League of Nations by means of a petition. In reality, however, the minority procedures of the League were such as to ensure that the sovereignty of individual states was scrupulously respected and upheld Minorities, by contrast, were reduced to objects rather than subjects of international law.

In sum, the minority provisions of the peace settlement were envisaged as little more than a transitional stage in a process leading to the eventual assimilation of non-titular national groups into a single dominant societal culture. Any suggestion of creating public institutions for minorities as an intermediary between individual citizens and the state was therefore distrusted and seen as likely to undermine the sovereignty and cohesion of new countries by encouraging the formation of 'states within states'. According to one League official

> the 'complete' solution to the minorities problem rests on the development, in countries of mixed population, of a spirit of national tolerance and liberalism, a development which will be no less long and painful than that which took place in the sphere of religious tolerance, but which will become all the more difficult if a system of separatism in certain branches of the common life of the state becomes generalised.
>
> *(Krabbe 1931: 47)*

The activists of the Minorities Congress retorted that in the specific context of Central and Eastern Europe, where (ethno-)national mobilisation had preceded the formation of the modern state, cultural self-government was essential precisely in order to *forestall* the potential emergence of irredentist nationalism. In support of their arguments, they pointed to the example of Estonia, where practical experiences of NCA during 1925–1930 had shown previous fears of a 'state within a state' to be wholly exaggerated. Policies predicated on assimilation, by contrast, seemed only to be fuelling ethnic antagonism and conflicts across the region.

While League officials were certainly misguided in their support for assimilation, they were right to underline the importance of a shared public space uniting all ethnic groups living within a particular territory. Cultural autonomy may help to encourage loyalty to a state, but it is obviously not the be-all and end-all in the construction of an integrated multi-ethnic political community. Equally, if not more important are guarantees of equal rights and opportunities for all citizens, regardless of ethnicity, the possibility for all ethnic groups to participate meaningfully in decision-making and the emergence of a cross-ethnic civil society that ensures continuous dialogue across community boundaries. In the absence of this, there is a potential danger that cultural autonomy could reinforce ethnic particularity and become conducive to ghettoization and marginalization of particular groups, particularly if ethnic and socio-economic boundaries coincide.

Renner and Bauer's original proposals set out to 'cut in two the sum of the activities of the state, separating national and political matters' and 'organize the population twice; once along the lines of nationality, the second time in relation to the state, and each time in administrative units of different form' (Springer 1906: 201). When it came to the sphere of the state, it was envisaged that German would function as a common language of administration, while the state would exercise broad supervision of all schools in order to ensure the attainment of common standards across the various nationally organized systems of education. Generally, however, the proposals were vague on how inter-ethnic interaction was to be ensured. The assumption here was, broadly speaking, that a socialist order would be established, guaranteeing the equality of all citizens regardless of ethnicity and thereby removing any remaining scope for disputes between different nationalities.

The successor states that emerged in the region between Germany and the USSR were – with the partial and ambiguous exceptions of Czechoslovakia and Yugoslavia – configured as unitary nation-states. Political decision-making power was necessarily weighted towards the 'titular' ethnic majority, even in countries like Estonia, where non-titular minorities had been granted considerable cultural autonomy. League of Nations procedures were supposed to offer guarantees against any 'nationalizing' practices on the part of these states, but these procedures were, as already noted, essentially toothless. This explains why the European Nationalities Congress lobbied so hard for a change to League Institutions that would give minority representatives subjectivity alongside representatives of state governments. The ultimate aim was to end the primacy of the indivisibly sovereign state within the international system and to create a Europe of Nationalities alongside the existing Europe of territorial states. Yet the minority activists that headed the Congress in the late 1920s also realized that the ethnic harmony so essential to European unity could not be engendered through negotiations at the state level – it had to be fostered more organically from below. The Congress leaders thus urged representatives of minority groups to eschew all talk of border revisions and to engage positively with the political process within the states they inhabited. Only in this way would they win the trust of the ethnic majority and engender a more inclusive and multicultural concept of political community.

The inter-war period, however, represented a thoroughly unpropitious context for realizing the Congress vision of a Europe 'beyond the nation-state'. In a situation where the 'national question' was essentially viewed as a security rather than a cultural issue, it was hard to counteract the power of ethnic politics within the new states. Not surprisingly, the NCA system was to the profound distaste of nationalists, not just amongst the titular ethnic majority, but also within minority communities themselves. Even though Baltic German activists within Estonia played a key role in pushing through the 1925 NCA law, more conservative and reactionary circles within this ethnic group dismissed the model as unworthy of a group that had traditionally constituted the political, economic and cultural elite within the territories concerned.

Estonian nationalists for their part were aggrieved that under the 1925 law, persons born into the now titular ethnic group were still able to opt for German nationality and/or cultural orientation – this following decades of struggle for cultural recognition within the old empires and the creation of a sovereign Estonian Republic. As was the case in neighbouring Latvia, calls to create a more 'complete' nation-state persisted throughout the 1920s and later intensified during the Great Depression, when attention was drawn to the prominent position that minority groups still occupied within the local economy. The authoritarian regimes that were installed in Estonia and Latvia during 1934 significantly restricted the individual freedom to choose nationality and language of instruction, while seeking to prioritise the needs of the titular ethnicity within the economic sphere. This 'nationalizing' turn was frequently justified not only by reference to past injustices, but also to perceptions of external threat following the rise to power of Hitler in Germany and the penetration of Nazi influences into the Baltic German milieu.

NCA in post-Cold War Europe

The experiments of the 1920s, however, cannot simply be dismissed as an interesting historical footnote. As already noted above, NCA has since 1945 become a feature of arrangements catering for ethnic diversity in some of the longer-established Western democracies. In the original formative context of Central and Eastern Europe, meanwhile, the model has found its way back onto the political agenda following the end of the Cold War, as post-communist governments and international organizations (OSCE, Council of Europe) have again grappled with minority issues in many respects similar to those which arose after 1918. While ethnic conflict has not been as generalized as many predicted it would be in the immediate aftermath of the wars in former Yugoslavia, discussions of ethno-cultural diversity in the region have to this day remained securitized, with many states fearing that minority claims might pose a challenge to their overall societal cohesion and territorial integrity. Against this background, approaches to minority autonomy based on personal characteristics have been regarded as potentially less contentious than the territorially based alternatives which have – in recent decades – become a feature of some longer-established democracies in the West. NCA has thus been applied across a variety of contexts in Central and Eastern Europe since the 1990s, though with mixed results.

What Aviel Roshwald (2008) has termed the 'dilemma of ethno-cultural diversity' – how to ensure equal treatment and adequate cultural recognition for different ethnicities without undermining state cohesion – became immediately apparent in the former USSR following the start of Gorbachev's *perestroika* in the late 1980s. Here, as part of an effort to contain growing ethno-national tensions, reformers broke with long-standing Leninist precepts and advocated the introduction of a parallel system of NCA alongside pre-existing ethno-territorial structures, to better accommodate 'non-titular' nationalities living within individual Soviet republics. While the Soviet regime was unable to arrest the disintegration of the USSR, this thinking was carried over into the post-Soviet Russian Federation, where it led ultimately to the NCA law adopted in 1996 (a development neatly characterized by Bill Bowring (2002) as 'Austro-Marxism's last laugh'). In the view of its initiators, this law would cater for the needs of non-ethnically Russian citizens (in practice the vast majority) who either lacked entirely or resided outside a designated territorial homeland 'of their own' (Tolz 2001: 249–256). It would also help to counter centrifugal, 'nationalizing' trends at the level of Russia's constituent national republics and thus serve overall to reinforce a sense of belonging to a single multi-ethnic Russian (*Rossiiskii*) state community based on Russia's existing borders.

On the basis of the law, more than 700 federal, regional and local-level NCAs were established in Russia during the period 1996–2009 (Osipov 2010: 42). Most commentators, however, would question the extent to which these embody a genuine form of minority autonomy, given the very limited resources and competences possessed by NCA bodies. Rather, they see the law as affording little more than symbolic cultural recognition for non-Russian nationalities, which is consistent with an inherited Soviet legacy of 'culturalising the social' (Osipov 2010, 2013). While recognition in itself should not be seen as unimportant, the remit of the law does not encompass key issues such as anti-discrimination and social exclusion. Moreover, the absence of any meaningful right of participation in decision-making means that minority communities remain ill-placed to resist current moves towards greater centralization and homogenization by a political regime that itself faces a growing challenge from ethnic Russian nationalism.

A similar 'symbolic' understanding has been ascribed to Estonia's current law on national-cultural autonomy, adopted in 1993 (Aidarov and Drechsler 2011). Whilst often hailed as a 'restoration' of its famous 1925 predecessor, the law in fact provides little more than a basic framework, within which the legal status, competences and provision for funding of autonomous institutions remain ill-defined. This framework has been adopted (following a protracted process) by Estonia's numerically small and dispersed Finnish and Swedish minorities. Spokespersons for the much larger Russian population have, however, seen three separate attempts to register an NCA rejected by the state, on the grounds that those advancing the proposals were not sufficiently representative of the broader community. This view appears to have some foundation, in so far as many activists amongst the Russian population have voiced scepticism towards NCA and have focused their attentions on other issues such as the status assigned to Soviet-era migrants and their descendants (many of whom still lack full citizenship and are therefore excluded from the official definition of 'national minority').

Parliamentary discussions during 1993 in any case made it clear that the law was intended as a vehicle for smaller minorities rather than something catering for the Russian-speaking part of the population. The sheer size of the latter means that Russian autonomy is seen in official circles as potentially detrimental to the project of restoring a unitary national state, whilst also (in a highly securitized context of inter-state relations) opening up the possibility of undue external influence from Russia. In the final analysis, it seems that the principal motive behind the original adoption of the law was to boost the external image of the restored Estonian state, by connecting symbolically with an inter-war tradition of multiculturalism. The practical impact has, however, been limited.

In early 2005 the inter-war Estonian model of cultural autonomy was invoked as an example in discussions on a new draft minority law in Romania. Mindful of ethnic Romanians' historically rooted sensitivities over Transylvania, the ethnic Hungarian initiators of the draft felt that a proposal to grant a non-territorial form of autonomy to Hungarians and other minorities living in this region (and in Romania more broadly) would stand a better chance of being accepted by parliament. The draft law, however, has at the time of writing failed to make it onto the statute book, as a majority of deputies felt that the proposed powers to be accorded to minority self-governments contravened the terms of the Romanian constitution (Decker 2008). The lack of progress on the law further attests to the securitized under-standing that is still attached by the majority to any proposal for autonomy (be it territorial or non-) within the context of Romania's unitary state. As a further issue, one can also point to the fact that the NCA model has not been universally embraced by ethnic Hungarian political activists within the country, a section of whom continue to insist on a territorially based form of autonomy for the Szeklerland region where Hungarians constitute a significant share of the local population. The latter fact brings into focus the question of whether NCA actually has the potential to serve as a 'catch-all' model applicable to all minorities (both territorially dispersed and non-), with authors such as Will Kymlicka (2008: 52) arguing that in the case of more compactly settled ethnic communities 'the link between national identities and territory' runs very deep 'and is central to self-understanding, histories and aspirations'. Here, though, one can point to the contrasting case of Serbia, where a law on NCA introduced in 2009 has been implemented by a large, mobilized and territorially compact Hungarian community, albeit within the overall territorial framework of an autonomous and multinational province of Vojvodina in which institutionalized ethno-cultural diversity forms part of the Yugoslav political legacy.

Arguably the most successful example of contemporary NCA can be found in Hungary, which in 1993 became the first of the post-socialist states to adopt a national minority law along these lines. Given the very small proportion of national minorities within Hungary's population, the introduction of a minority law proved relatively uncontroversial, while the territorially dispersed nature of minority settlement lent itself to non-territorial autonomy. The law was also adopted partly with an eye to gaining membership of European international organizations, and to the needs of Hungarians living in neighbouring countries, which, it was hoped, might follow Hungary's example by adopting corresponding laws towards their own non-titular minorities. Introduced amidst much fanfare, the 1993 law has since been widely implemented: as many as 1,200 minority self-governments – half of them Roma – have been established. The Hungarian case has, however, highlighted a number of practical issues surrounding the implementation of cultural autonomy, issues which will seem familiar to anyone familiar with the NCA debates of the 1920s.

Central to Renner and Bauer's original scheme was of course the entry of one's name on a national register. Memories of negative historical experiences, however, (including forced migration of Germans after the Second World War and (involuntary) Slovak–Hungarian population exchanges) meant that minority representatives were unwilling to support a law on this basis (Dobos 2008: 121). This issue was perhaps of greatest concern to Hungary's Roma. Subject to past persecution by dint of their ethnicity and mostly disadvantaged in socio-economic terms, many Roma have feared that asserting their own cultural identity might lead to their being identified as a caste apart and singled out for differential treatment (Dobos 2008: 122). Consequently, the original law adopted in 1993 specified that local-level minority cultural self-governments were to be elected by all voters within a particular district, regardless of ethnic provenance. In certain instances, this provision has boosted the system of minority self-government, since it has opened up the possibility for so-called 'sympathy votes' from other voters who do not belong to a particular minority group but nevertheless feel well-disposed towards it. On the other hand, it has at times eroded the legitimacy of elected self-governments: even where voters from other groups are well-disposed, they are not necessarily well-versed in the affairs of the relevant minority or its representatives. This necessarily led to flawed outcomes, as far as the representativeness of particular minority self-governments was concerned. For instance, a tendency was observed whereby most votes flowed to the first name indicated on the alphabetically arranged list of candidates. This had predictable consequences in terms of the behaviour of particular groups when drawing up their electoral lists.

Since candidates for minority self-governments were also not required to publicly declare their ethnicity, the 1993 law also opened up scope for so-called 'ethnobusiness' – the manipulation of the system by political entrepreneurs who had little obvious affiliation to the minority group concerned. In some cases, those putting themselves forward as 'German' or 'Romanian' representatives were actively seeking to acquire the benefits of office in terms of social capital and finances; in another case concerning the Roma, the local Hungarian population was able to engineer the election of mostly non-Roma candidates to a 'Roma' minority government, thereby thwarting the establishment of a genuinely representative minority body (Dobos 2008: 124). As a result of these anomalies, the cultural autonomy law was eventually amended in 2005, and an obligatory system of enrolment on national registers – for candidates and voters alike – was introduced. The reform also introduced a new system of proportional representation for the election of local minority self-governments, after complaints that the previous single majority voting system had served to exclude entire interest groups from the structures that were supposed to be speaking on behalf of an entire local minority (Dobos 2008: 125). In line with recommendations from the Council of Europe, the Act on National Minorities was further amended in 2011, and now incorporates more detailed regulations governing the legal status and competences of minority self-governments and their rights of advocacy in relation to state and municipal authorities. As in the case of Russia, however, there remains a debate over the extent to which the law provides for substantive representation as opposed to mere symbolic recognition of national minorities. The capacity of this framework to address issues of central concern to the Roma, such as poverty and discrimination, remains especially open to question (Smith 2013).

Conclusion

By way of conclusion, one can say that NCA has had most obvious relevance and appeal for smaller and more dispersed minority populations living in Central and Eastern Europe, which could otherwise not aspire to autonomy on a territorial basis. Whether the model could serve as a 'catch-all' alternative to territorial autonomy, however, remains more questionable: in this sense, NCA may be best regarded as a complement to rather than a substitute for the kind of territorial arrangements that have been established for larger minority populations living in some established democracies, or else as an interim approach introduced as part of an incremental devolution of power within an overall process of democratization and inter-communal dialogue. The still unconsolidated 'stateness' of many Central and East European countries (and the continued context of geopolitical instability within the region) means that proposals for any form of minority autonomy are often politically sensitive. In those cases where variants of NCA have been adopted following the end of communism, the arrangements in place have often borne only a nominal resemblance to the original model propounded by Renner and Bauer. As the latter foresaw in their original work, however, the difficulty of applying the culturally homogenizing, indivisibly sovereign nation-state model to this region became painfully apparent between the Wars, and the longer-term viability of this approach appears similarly questionable in today's setting. In this respect, as the OSCE Commissioner for National Minorities Max Van der Stoel (1999: 172) observed back in 1999, insufficient attention has still been paid to non-territorial forms of autonomy as part of a package of targeted minority rights in CEE. As European governments and international organizations continue to grapple with the question of how to embed ethnicity within a liberal democratic framework of state and supranational institutions, Renner and Bauer's original ideas – as well as the 1920s debates and experiences around NCA – still seem well worth revisiting.

Further reading

Aun, K. (1949) *On the Spirit of the Estonian Minorities Law* (Stockholm: Societas Litteratum Estonica in Svecia).

Bauer, O. (2000) *The Question of Nationalities and Social Democracy* (Minneapolis: University of Minnesota Press).

Hiden, J. (2004) *Defender of Minorities. Paul Schiemann 1876–1944* (London: Hurst and Co).

Nimni, E., Osipov, A. and Smith, D. J. (eds) (2013) *The Challenge of Non-Territorial Autonomy: Theory and Practice* (Oxford, Bern, Berlin, Brussels, Frankfurt am Main, New York and Vienna: Peter Lang).

Renner, K. (1899/2005) 'State and Nation', in E. Nimni (ed.) *National Cultural Autonomy and its Contemporary Critics* (London and New York: Routledge).

Salat, L., Constantin, S., Osipov, S. and Székely, I. (eds) (2014) *Autonomy Arrangements around the World: A Collection of Well and Lesser Known Cases* (Cluj-Napoca: Romanian Institute for Research on National Minorities).

Smith, D. J. and Cordell, K. (eds) (2008) *Cultural Autonomy in Contemporary Europe* (London and New York: Routledge).

Smith, D. J. and Hiden, J. (2012) *Ethnic Diversity and the Nation State: National Cultural Autonomy Revisited* (London: Routledge).

References

Aidarov, A. and Drechsler, W. (2011) 'The Law and Economics of the Estonian Law on Cultural Autonomy for National Minorities and of Russian National Cultural Autonomy in Estonia', *Halduskultuur*, 12(1): 43–61.

Aun, K. (1949) *On the Spirit of the Estonian Minorities Law* (Stockholm: Societas Litteratum Estonica in Svecia).

Bowring, B. (2002) 'Austro-Marxism's Last Laugh? The Struggle for Recognition of National Cultural Autonomy for Rossians and Russians', *Europe-Asia Studies*, 54(2): 229–250.

Bowring, B. (2005) 'Burial and Resurrection: Karl Renner's Controversial Influence on the "National Question" in Russia', in E. Nimni (ed.) *National Cultural Autonomy and its Contemporary Critics* (Abingdon and New York: Routledge): 191–206.

Brubaker, R. (1996) *Nationalism Reframed: Nationhood and the National Question in the New Europe* (Cambridge and New York: Cambridge University Press).

Chouinard, S. (2013) 'Is There a Right to Non-Territorial Autonomy in Canada? The Case of Institutional Completeness and Minority Language Rights', in E. Nimni, A. Osipov and D. J. Smith (eds) (2013) *The Challenge of Non-Territorial Autonomy: Theory and Practice* (Oxford, Bern, Berlin, Brussels, Frankfurt am Main, New York and Vienna: Peter Lang).

Coakley, J. (1994) 'Approaches to the Resolution of Ethnic Conflict: The Strategy of Non-territorial Autonomy', *International Political Science Review*, 15(3): 309–326.

Decker, C. (2008) 'The Use of Cultural Autonomy to Prevent Conflict and Meet the Copenhagen Criteria: The Case of Romania', in D. J. Smith and K. Cordell (eds) *Cultural Autonomy in Contemporary Europe* (London and New York: Routledge).

Dobos, B. (2008) 'The Development and Function of Cultural Autonomy in Hungary', in D. J. Smith and K. Cordell (eds) *Cultural Autonomy in Contemporary Europe* (London and New York: Routledge).

Krabbe, L. (1931) 'L'autonomie culturelle comme solution du problème des minorités. Note de M. Krabbe au date du 18 Nov 1931', League of Nations Archives, Geneva, R2175 4 32835.

Kymlicka, W. (2008) 'National Cultural Autonomy and International Minority Rights Norms', in D. J. Smith and K. Cordell (eds) *Cultural Autonomy in Contemporary Europe* (London and New York: Routledge).

Osipov, A. (2010) 'National Cultural Autonomy in Russia: A Case of Symbolic Law', *Review of Central and East European Law*, 35: 27–57.

Osipov, A. (2013) 'Non-Territorial Autonomy during and after Communism: In the Wrong or Right Place?' *Journal of Ethnopolitics and Minority Issues in Europe*, 12(1): 7–26.

Plakans, A. (1995) *The Latvians: A Short History* (Stanford: Hoover Institution Press).

Renner, K. (2005) 'State and Nation', in E. Nimni (ed.) *National Cultural Autonomy and its Contemporary Critics* (Abingdon and New York: Routledge): 15–48.

Roshwald, A. (2001) *Ethnic Nationalism and the Fall of Empires: Central Europe, Russia and the Middle East 1914–1923* (London and New York: Taylor and Francis).

Roshwald, A. (2008) 'Between Balkanisation and Banalisation: Dilemmas of Ethno-cultural Diversity', in D. J. Smith and Karl Cordell (eds) *Cultural Autonomy in Contemporary Europe* (London and New York: Taylor and Francis).

Salat, L., Constantin, S., Osipov, A. and Székely, I. G. (2014) *Autonomy Arrangements Around the World* (Flensburg: European Centre for Minority Issues).

Schwarzmantel, J. (2005) 'Karl Renner and the Problem of Multiculturalism', in E. Nimni (ed.) *National Cultural Autonomy and its Contemporary Critics* (Abingdon and New York: Routledge): 63–73.

Smith, D. J. (1999) 'Retracing Estonia's Russians: Mikhail Kurchinskii and Inter-war Cultural Autonomy', *Nationalities Papers*, 27(3): 455–474.

Smith, D. J. (2013) 'Non-Territorial Autonomy and Political Community in Contemporary Central and Eastern Europe', *Journal of Ethnopolitics and Minority Issues in Europe*, 12(1): 27–55.

Smith, D. J. and Hiden, J. (2012) *Ethnic Diversity and the Nation State: National Cultural Autonomy Revisited* (London: Routledge).

Springer, R. (pseudonym of K. Renner) (1906) *Grundlagen und Entwicklungsziele der österreichischen-ungarischen Monarchie* (Vienna).

Tolz, V. (2001) *Russia: Inventing the Nation* (London: Arnold).

Van der Stoel, M. (1999) *Peace and Stability through Human and Minority Rights: Speeches by the OSCE High Commissioner on National Minorities* (Baden-Baden: Nomos Verlagsgesellschaft).

23

CENTRIPETALISM

Benjamin Reilly

Introduction

Centripetal approaches to conflict management seek to foster peaceful politics by encouraging cooperation, accommodation and integration in divided societies. These goals are broadly shared with other approaches to conflict management, such as the scholarly orthodoxy of consociationalism, discussed elsewhere in this volume. However, the specific institutional recommendations to achieve these goals differ significantly from orthodox prescriptions. Centripetalists believe that the best way to manage democracy in divided societies is not to replicate existing ethnic divisions in the legislature and other representative organs, but rather to put in place institutional incentives for cross-ethnic behaviour so as to encourage accommodation between rival groups. As such, they typically reject elite-driven approaches such as consociationalism, and instead seek to dilute the ethnic character of competitive politics and instead promote outcomes which favour the political centre. To do this, centripetalists place a premium on promoting cross-ethnic electoral behaviour to make politicians reliant on the votes of different ethnic communities to gain election. In so doing, they advocate political institutions which can help to break down the salience of ethnicity rather than fostering its representation.

As a shorthand for a political system or strategy designed to focus competition at the moderate centre rather than the extremes, centripetalism is so named because 'the explicit aim is to engineer a centripetal spin to the political system – to pull the parties towards moderate, compromising policies and to discover and reinforce the centre of a deeply divided political spectrum' (Sisk 1996: 19). Prominent centripetal scholars such as Donald Horowitz (1985, 1991) argued that deeply divided societies such as post-apartheid South Africa needed to foster intercommunal moderation by promoting multi-ethnic political parties to encourage inter-group accommodation. In the same vein, my own work has highlighted how centripetal reforms centred around cross-cutting electoral incentives have lowered electoral violence in highly fragmented states such as Papua New Guinea (Reilly 2001).

The competing claims around different institutional models of ethnic conflict management have spawned a prodigious political science debate, and also have had a significant impact on institutional designs in a range of post-conflict societies. While proponents of both consociational and centripetal approaches can point to some successes (and more failures), developments over the past decade have seen a bifurcation in terms of the 'real world' experience of each model. On the one hand, high profile attempts at post-conflict peace-building such as in Bosnia, Northern Ireland and more recently Iraq have all adopted broadly consociational political settlements. On the other hand, a range of emerging democracies in Africa, Asia and Latin America have chosen centripetal reforms when refashioning their own domestic institutions. This chapter examines the key institutional elements of centripetalism as a model of political engineering in these developing democracies.

Centripetalism compared

In terms of political engineering, centripetalists and consociationalists both focus on core democratic institutions such as political parties, electoral systems, and cabinet governments, and on the territorial division of state powers via federalism. However, their specific recommendations regarding each of these institutions differ enormously. In terms of the development of political parties and party systems, for instance, the two approaches are almost diametrically opposed. Consociationalists favour parties which represent social cleavages explicitly, via 'bonding' rather than 'bridging' strategies – that is, parties which 'focus upon gaining votes from a narrower home-base among particular segmented sectors of the electorate' (Norris 2004: 10). The ideal consociational party system is one in which individual parties are based around clear social cleavages, and in which all significant social groups, including minorities, can 'define themselves' into ethnically based political parties. Only through parties formed around segmental cleavages, consociationalists contend, can political elites negotiate delicate ethnic issues effectively.[1]

Centripetalists reject this elite-driven approach, and the reification of ethnicity which goes with it. Rather than 'making plural societies more truly plural' (Lijphart 1977: 42) as consociationalism proposes, centripetalists instead seek to dilute the ethnic character of competitive politics and promote multi-ethnic outcomes instead. Instead of focusing on the fair representation of each ethnic group via ethnically defined political parties, for instance, centripetalists place a premium on promoting multi-ethnic parties or coalitions and cross-ethnic activity. In so doing, they emphasise the importance of institutional designs which encourage cooperation, accommodation and integration across ethnic divides, helping to break down the salience of ethnicity rather than fostering its representation institutionally. In direct opposition to consociational theory, centripetalism maintains that the best way to manage democracy in divided societies is not to replicate existing ethnic divisions in the legislature and other representative organs, but rather to *depoliticise* ethnicity by putting in place institutional incentives for cross-ethnic behaviour which can also help promote more fluid cross-cutting identities.

Both consociational and centripetal proposals for conflict management focus on electoral systems, political parties and other mechanisms of representation as offering the most potential for effective political engineering. Again, however, centripetal recommendations tend to run sharply counter to the prevailing orthodoxy. Perhaps the clearest distinction between centripetalism and other approaches is found in their contrasting recommendations regarding the design of electoral systems. One of the most fundamental relationships in political science is that between electoral systems and the representation of minorities. Proportional representation (PR) is frequently advocated as a key reform in ethnically plural societies to ensure fair representation of minorities and majorities alike. However, because PR systems encourage smaller parties they tend to fragment the party system and can encourage parties to craft their appeals around narrow sectarian interests, such as ethnicity – precisely because they can be secure in gaining seats by appealing to a relatively narrow section of society. In addition, there is a difference between representation and power: a minority can be fairly represented in a legislature but remain completely shut out of political power in government.

For this reason, centripetalists often see PR as a cause of rather than a solution to problems of ethnic politics. Instead of focusing on minority representation, they recommend electoral rules which can make politicians reciprocally dependent on the votes of members of groups other than their own, and which more broadly favour multi-ethnic political parties rather than ethnically exclusive ones. Specific institutional reforms to achieve such outcomes include the use of cross-regional or vote-transfer electoral systems, political party laws which require pan-national party organisation, and legislative selection procedures which promote median, centrist outcomes. These and other kinds of institutions give parties and candidates electoral incentives to 'pool votes' across ethnic lines, centripetalists contend, and can thus encourage vote-seeking politicians to reach out across the ethnic divide and, in so doing, help to take the heat out of ethnic politics (Horowitz 1985, 1991).

In an earlier book on electoral engineering for divided societies (Reilly 2001), I examined the record of centripetalism as a conflict management strategy, and identified three facilitating components which seem to recur across different countries and contexts:

i   the presentation of *electoral incentives* for campaigning politicians to reach out to and attract votes from a range of ethnic groups other than their own, thus encouraging candidates to moderate their political rhetoric on potentially divisive issues and forcing them to broaden their policy positions;
ii the presence of multi-ethnic *arenas of bargaining* such as parliamentary and executive forums, in which political actors representing different identity groups have an incentive to come together and cut deals on reciprocal electoral support, and hence perhaps on other more substantial policy issues as well; and
iii the development of *centrist, aggregative and multi-ethnic political parties* or coalitions of parties which are capable of making cross-ethnic appeals and presenting a complex and diverse range of policy options to the electorate.

These components of centripetalism should, ideally, be self-reinforcing: parties and candidates that adopt conciliatory policy positions and make compromises in the search for electoral victory will be more likely to pick up a broader share of votes than those who choose to maintain a more narrowly focused, sectarian approach. If the votes gained by so doing can outweigh the votes lost to the extremes by being moderate (a big if in deeply divided societies), then electoral rewards should accrue to those who occupy the political centre. To attract such support, candidates may need to make cross-ethnic appeals and demonstrate their capacity to represent groups other than their own. In other cases, where a moderate or non-ethnic 'middle' of the electorate exists, candidates may need to move to the centre on policy issues to attract these voters, or to accommodate fringe issues into their broader policy. Either way, elected candidates will be dependent to some extent upon the votes of groups other than their own core support base for their electoral success, and can thus be expected to serve the needs of these groups as well as their own ethnic group if they are to establish a reputation and gain re-election. In short, those candidates who can successfully sell themselves as a good median choice should, under sensitively designed electoral systems, be rewarded with a greater vote share than those with more polarised support.

By what specific institutional designs can such desirable outcomes be encouraged in divided societies, where cooperation across social cleavages is, by definition, lacking? One approach is to structure electoral processes so as to require successful candidates to gain support across different regions of a country, thus helping to break down the appeal of narrow parochialism or regionalism. Another is to give campaigning politicians incentives to seek the second-preference votes of electors from rival ethnic groups under electoral systems which allow the expression of a gradation of political preferences. A third is to mandate some degree of multi-ethnicity within political parties and other representative bodies, via requirements that compel parties to put forward heterogeneous candidate lists or organise on a cross-regional basis, thus making parties themselves a potential site for multi-ethnic bargaining. While having different impacts, all these examples of centripetal institutional design seek to nudge the basis of representative democracy in divided societies away from the politics of ethnic solidarity and towards more inter-ethnicity. The following section discusses some empirical examples of each approach.

Centripetalism in practice

The 'distribution requirement' applied at presidential elections in Nigeria, Kenya and Indonesia is an example of the first kind of approach, which seeks to encourage cross-regional politics by requiring winning presidential candidates to gain not just a majority of the vote, but a spread of votes across different parts of the country, in order to be elected. Distribution requirements have been mostly used for presidential elections in large, ethnically diverse states in order to ensure that winning candidates receive a sufficiently broad spread of electoral support, rather than drawing their votes from one region only. Nigeria, for instance, requires a president to win a majority overall and at least one-third of the vote in at least two-thirds of all states. The Kenyan constitution provides a similar threshold, requiring successful candidates to win a plurality of the vote overall as well as one-quarter of valid votes cast in at least five of the eight provinces. In Indonesia, the election law provides a two-stage process to ensure such broad-based support: only parties or coalitions controlling 20 per cent of parliamentary seats or winning 25 per cent of the popular vote in the preceding parliamentary elections are eligible to nominate a presidential candidate. The candidate must then gain a nationwide majority and at least 20 per cent of the vote in over half of Indonesia's 33 provinces to avoid a run-off.

There is disagreement amongst scholars as to the utility of devices, with some interpreting them as impotent or even harmful interferences with the democratic process, while others see them as important mechanisms for muting ethnic conflict and ensuring the election of broad, pan-ethnic presidents (Sisk 1996: 55). The empirical evidence to date reflects this divergence of opinion. In both Kenya and Nigeria, problems have arisen with the operation of such systems when no candidate has met the required cross-national vote spread. But despite these problems, distribution requirements have remained a feature of national electoral politics, and in Nigeria have been extended to parliamentary elections as well as via reforms that make national party registration dependent on their vote shares at local elections (Bogaards 2008: 54). In Indonesia, the world's largest Muslim country and third-largest democracy, distribution laws have proved more successful, with the two most recent presidents each gaining the broad support required in the electoral law for their election victory. As centrist moderates, Presidents Susilo Bambang Yudhoyono (in 2009) and Joko Widodo (in 2014) both easily amassed the necessary spread of votes across the archipelago in their first-round election victories. For similar reasons, distribution requirements have also been proposed (but not enacted) for presidential elections in Iraq (Wimmer 2003: 122).

For parliamentary elections, a more direct and potentially more powerful centripetal approach to electoral system design is to use vote-transfer electoral systems such as the alternative vote (AV) or the single transferable vote (STV), which ask voters to declare not only their first choice candidate, but also their second, third and subsequent choices amongst all candidates standing. Under AV rules, if no-one gains an outright majority, these votes are transferred according to their rankings in order to elect a majority-supported winner. STV, as a proportional system, uses a quota rather than a majority threshold for election, but the same basic principle applies. While the best known examples of such vote-transfer systems are the established democracies of Australia and Ireland, such systems have also been used in a number of ethnically divided democracies, including Papua New Guinea, Northern Ireland and Fiji, as well as for one-off elections in Estonia and Bosnia. AV and STV systems also have a history of use in several Canadian provinces and US cities. Related systems include the supplementary vote used for presidential elections in Sri Lanka and London mayoral elections, and variants of the Borda count which are used for parliamentary elections in Nauru and some seats in Slovenia (Reilly 2004). STV also has a well-established record of use in intra-parliamentary elections, such as the selection of upper houses in India and a number of other South Asian democracies.

Because they enable politicians to make deals for reciprocal vote transfers with their rivals, in ethnically diverse societies such systems can present vote-maximising candidates with incentives to seek secondary preference votes from groups other than their own, so as to ensure the broadest possible range of support for their candidacy. To obtain such cross-ethnic support, candidates may need to behave accommodatively on core issues, tempering their rhetorical and policy positions so as to attract broader support. There is evidence of this practice occurring in very different types of multi-ethnic societies including Papua New Guinea, Fiji, and Northern Ireland at different times.[2] However, the utility of using such systems in deeply divided societies remains a subject of debate: the accommodation-inducing potential of 'preference-swapping' is dependent on a range of facilitating conditions, including a competitive party system, an ethnically heterogeneous electorate and a degree of moderate sentiment existing in the community at large. For this reason, critics have pointed to the difficulties of inducing accommodation via electoral engineering, and questioned whether vote transfers have indeed promoted moderate outcomes in bi-polar societies such as Northern Ireland and Fiji.[3]

Other centripetal electoral reforms seek to undercut the logic of ethnic politics by requiring political parties to present ethnically mixed slates of candidates for 'at-large' elections, thus making voter choice contingent, at some level, upon issues other than ethnicity. In multi-ethnic societies as diverse as Singapore, Lebanon and Djibouti, electoral laws require parties to include ethnic minorities on their candidate lists in multi-member districts. As the electorate comprises voters from all groups in a given district, some degree of cross-ethnic voting is thus inevitable. However, these kinds of stipulations are often more tokenistic than substantive. In Singapore, for instance, parties and alliances contesting the 15 multimember districts designated as 'Group Representation Constituencies' must include one or two candidates from designated ethnic minorities on their ticket – an arrangement which requires only a minimal degree of cross-ethnic voting, while guaranteeing that nine seats in the Singaporean parliament will be occupied by Malays, and six by Indians or other minorities. The island states of the Comoros and Mauritius use similar measures to ensure ethnic minority representation via 'best loser' schemes for members of under-represented groups or parties.

In Africa, a variety of cross-voting schemes to ameliorate ethnic divisions have been proposed over the years. An elaborate racial cross-voting scheme was included in the 1961 Rhodesian constitution to allow black voters to cast a vote in white electoral units and vice versa, as a means of moderating the potential election of extremists in either camp. However, the qualifications for each voter roll were based on a mix of income, property, and education qualifications which seemed designed to maintain the economic superiority of whites, and few black electors ever registered or voted in the two elections (1962 and 1965) held under the 1961 constitution.[4] There is also the intriguing case of the 'constituency pooling' model proposed (but never implemented) in Uganda. According to Bogaards (2003), this was first introduced in the Ugandan electoral law of 1971 as a means of overcoming regional, ethnic, and religious differences and encouraging the creation of national political parties. Under this proposal, candidates would stand for election in four different electoral districts at the same time: their 'basic' district and three 'national' districts. The candidate receiving the largest overall percentage of votes, combining both the 'basic' constituency and 'national' constituencies, would win the seat. Unfortunately for comparative purposes, Idi Amin seized power in a military coup and cancelled the elections.

Fiji provides another, even more complex, example of mandated cross-voting in the shape of the political system which existed there from independence in 1970 until the ethnically motivated coup of 1987. As in Lebanon, the ethnic balance of the 52-seat parliament was pre-determined, with 22 seats reserved for Fijians, another 22 reserved for Indo-Fijians, and the remaining eight seats reserved for 'General Electors' (i.e. Europeans, Chinese and other minorities). In addition, 23 electorates were designated as 'national' seats which required voters from one ethnic community to vote for candidates from a different community, in order to ensure that elected members from these seats would have to draw a degree of cross-communal support from all groups. Like the abortive Ugandan cross-voting model, the Fijian system required each elector to cast no less than *four* votes: one for their communal (co-ethnic) representative, and one each for a 'national' candidate from each of the other three designated communal groups. An indigenous Fijian voter, for example, would vote for a Fijian candidate in his or her communal electorate, and then cast three additional votes – one for a Fijian, one for an Indo-Fijian and one for a General Elector – in the appropriate national electorates.

Other cross-voting schemes mix centripetal and communal incentives. Lebanon's 'confessional' political system, in which both parliamentary seats and key executive offices are allocated on a sectarian basis, is perhaps the best-known example. To do this, the composition of Lebanon's 128-seat national assembly is pre-ordained according to communal ratios, with an even split between Christians and Muslims, as well as specified seat balances for Sunni, Shi'a, Maronite, Druze and other confessional groups within each religious community. Key executive offices such as the presidency, prime ministership, and the parliamentary speaker are also allocated on a confessional basis. Elections are contested by inter-confessional electoral alliances which must match the pre-ordained confessional structure of each multi-member electoral district. In practice, this requires electors to engage in a degree of cross-voting by choosing candidates who hail from outside as well as within their own confessional identity group. But the Lebanese model also has real drawbacks, fixing ethnic identities in place and making communal affiliation the basis of the entire political system (Salloukh 2006).

Similarly complex schemes for cross-communal voting have been a part of transitional constitutions in Cyprus, Bosnia, Northern Ireland and no doubt elsewhere. In addition, informal patterns of ethnic vote pooling have been identified in the electoral politics of a number of ethnically plural states, such as Malaysia and Sri Lanka. Despite a mixed record of success, the fact that so many different countries and conflicts have made recourse to the basic ideas of cross voting, often without reference to or apparent knowledge of the experience of others, is a testament to the recurring appeal of this idea. Indeed, schemes for cross-voting featured in eighteenth-century constitutional debates in France and the USA as a means of tempering the 'interests and passions' of different social groups and classes in order to 'induce a tendency to encourage the common interest' in representative bodies (Elster 2013).

A related but distinct approach to centripetal political engineering has featured direct attempts to shape the nature of political parties and party systems. In particular, efforts to foster large, aggregative parties, and discourage sectional or minority ones, have been a distinctive feature of the 'third wave' of democratisation (Reilly and Nordlund 2008). Again, one of the clearest examples is to be found in Indonesia – the world's most populous emerging democracy and largest Muslim country. There, parties must establish an organisational network across a set proportion of provinces (initially one-third, then two-thirds and now 60 per cent of all provinces), as well as offices in at least half of the districts or municipalities within these provinces, before they are allowed to contest the election, while a separate threshold has also been introduced to limit splinter parties. These rules are intended not just to make it difficult for regionally based or secessionist movements to organise and promote the development of nationally focused political parties, although an exception was made for local parties in Aceh under the terms of the 2005 peace deal there (Hillman 2010). The party law thus shares a common centripetal logic with Indonesia's presidential electoral system, which also includes (weaker) incentives for cross-regional support.

Political party engineering is also popular in other regions. In Africa, some 22 countries include requirements that parties have a national presence (Bogaards 2008: 48–66). But such exhortations are typically accompanied by overt bans on ethnic parties, and tend to have little impact on actual party development. In Latin America, ethnic parties are not a major issue, but there have been similar attempts to encourage aggregative and nationally oriented parties with a cross-regional organisational base in Colombia, Ecuador, Guatemala, Nicaragua, Honduras, Mexico, and Peru. In Mexico, for example, parties must have at least 3,000 affiliates in ten out of the 32 states, or one-third of federal districts, while in Ecuador and Peru, parties must meet officially inscribed membership levels in at least half of all provinces. However Ecuador, which introduced spatial registration rules in the 1970s to combat party fragmentation, also provides a cautionary tale. There, the introduction of spatial rules helped consolidate the party system, but at the cost of wiping out parties representing the country's indigenous minority, which relied on regionally concentrated Amerindian support (Birnir 2004).

As these divergent examples suggest, political engineering and institutional design to encourage centripetal outcomes is an uncertain process fraught with what some have characterised as an 'iron law' of unintended consequences (Bastian and Luckham 2003). But despite this, and the uncertain experience of some measures to promote cross-ethnic politics, centripetal political engineering remains popular, particularly in new democracies. The attractiveness of such reforms can be explained by several factors. Theoretically, centripetalism draws upon core political science ideas about the nature of social cleavages, particularly Seymour Martin Lipset's (1960) classic arguments about the virtues of cross-cutting cleavages for democracy. The kinds of cross-voting schemes discussed above, for instance, all hinge on the idea that reinforcing social cleavages is a problem, and that general interests need to be given priority over group interests. Normatively, the virtues of political aggregation and centrism are advocated (sometimes instinctively) by policymakers schooled in the Anglo-American tradition of two-party politics. Empirically too, most centripetal reforms are more compatible with the development of aggregative, centrist party systems than alternatives such as consociationalism. Indeed, to many 'third wave' reformers, the integrative politics of fluid ethnic attachments and mass parties found in the immigrant societies of the USA, Australia and Canada represents the potential benefits of centripetalism of multi-ethnic societies. But the 'settler society' context of these new world democracies is very different from the deep-rooted hostilities found in parts of Africa, Asia or indeed Europe.

Critiques

Centripetalism has attracted significant criticism on empirical and conceptual grounds. Empirically, critics point to the paucity of centripetal models in the real world; the limited application of cross-voting electoral systems, distribution requirements and other favoured devices; the difficulty in both forming and sustaining multi-ethnic political parties and coalitions in divided societies; and the ambiguous real-world experience of particular institutions such as the alternative vote.[5] The empirical record is indeed mixed, and there are problems for both advocates and detractors of centripetalism in defining and measuring a clear criterion for success, as indeed there is for consociationalism. For example, should 'success' be classified as moderation of outcomes, the absence of violence, or macro-level political stability? All three approaches are present in the literature, especially in critiques of centripetalism's empirical record. However, many of these critiques focus on the experience of a few high-profile cases such as Northern Ireland or (recently) Fiji, but tend to ignore other larger but less well-known examples of centripetalism in action such as Indonesia or Papua New Guinea. For instance, the re-introduction of AV laws in Papua New Guinea and the subsequent reduction in electoral conflicts at the 2007 national elections has yet to be incorporated into comparative discussions of centripetalism. Neither has the success of the peacemaking process in Bougainville, which includes a number of centripetal reforms such as cross-voting reserved seats for women, youth and ex-combatants as well as AV parliamentary and presidential elections.[6]

As noted above, centripetalism is also criticised for being essentially majoritarian in nature. As the logic of centripetalism is focused above all on the potential benefits of *aggregation* – of votes, of opinions, of parties – at one level, this is correct. G. Bingham Powell, for example, notes that political aggregation lies at the heart of what he calls the 'majoritarian vision' of democracy: 'the majoritarian view favours much greater aggregation, while the proportional view emphasises the importance of equitable reflection of all points of view into the legislature' (Bingham Powell 2000: 26). For this reason, critics of centripetalism have often identified the majoritarian nature of its institutional recommendations as a key weakness.[7] Centripetalists respond that they favour 'a majoritarian democracy that will produce more fluid, shifting majorities that do not lock ascriptive minorities firmly out of power' (Horowitz 1991: 176). In other words, while centripetalism is indeed a majoritarian model, it is a majoritarianism of broad-based parties and inclusive coalitions – not a majoritarianism of 'ins' and 'outs', of ethnically defined majorities and minorities.

Following the same logic, centripetalists ideally favour an aggregative party system, in which 'one or two broadly-based, centrist parties fight for the middle ground' (Diamond 1996: 239), and therefore endorse the development of multi-ethnic parties or coalitions. Over time, it is argued, the presence of such party constellations can serve to depoliticise social cleavages and foster more fluid, cross-cutting affiliations. In practice, this means that rather than advocating proportional elections, as per the scholarly orthodoxy, centripetal approaches instead favour an aggregative majoritarianism, with more emphasis on the *process* by which different groups work together than strict fairness of *outcomes*. Sometimes, the potential for vote-pooling is latent but still consequential. This can be seen in Sri Lanka, where the more ethnically inclusive presidential candidates backed by Tamil and Muslim minorities won freely conducted elections in 1994 and 2015, even though preference votes were not counted in either case.

Interestingly, the majoritarian themes of the centripetal approach and their emphasis on aggregative, 'bridging' political parties are increasingly echoed by the scholarly literature on the political economy of development (Persson and Tabellini 2000). Both literatures, for example, advocate aggregative political institutions, majoritarian electoral processes and broad-based 'catch-all' parties or coalitions. These same recommendations are also prominent in the 'developmental state' literature on the optimum political arrangements for economic reform in new democracies (Haggard and Kaufman 1995). More recent contributions from Persson and Tabellini (2005) and Rock (2013) have reached similar conclusions, suggesting a growing convergence amongst different political science sub-disciplines on the benefits of aggregative and centripetal institutions for political development and stability.

Conclusion

In practice, centripetalism, like other political engineering models, is best seen as an ideal type rather than a coherent, all-encompassing prescription. Indeed, in many cases of conflict management, a mixture of recommendations from different models can be and is applied. Thus a number of constitutional settlements and peace deals cited above including Bosnia, Fiji, Lebanon and Northern Ireland feature a mixture of centripetal, consociational and communal models of ethnic conflict management.

One explanation for this is the fact that, despite differences, there is some agreement on a number of broader issues. For instance, there is a general consensus on the capacity of political institutions to change political outcomes, and hence on the utility of political engineering. Common ground is also found in the central role ascribed to political parties and electoral systems as key institutional variables influencing the reduction – or escalation – of communal tensions in ethnically diverse societies. A third area of agreement is the broad acceptance of the need in divided societies to deal with the political effects of ethnicity directly, rather than wishing them away. At a minimum, this means some type of government arrangement that gives all significant groups access to power, either directly or indirectly. For this reason, consociationalists and centripetalists broadly agree on the desirability of some form of power sharing for divided societies, even as they disagree on the means to achieve it (Jarstad 2008).

The contemporary experience of these different approaches has varied depending on the severity of the conflicts at stake. In deeply divided post-war scenarios such as Bosnia, Northern Ireland and most recently Iraq, consociationalism remains the dominant approach. However, this trend is partly driven by the United Nations' standard model of post-conflict democratisation, which favours the use of PR elections and power-sharing governments in the immediate aftermath of a conflict (Reilly 2008). Elsewhere, in less catastrophic cases, the trend in many regions has been away from the ethnically based approach of consociationalism towards more fluid, centripetal models. Thus, there has been a marked shift away from consociationalism and towards centripetalism in many parts of the developing world, particularly in Asia and the Pacific, in recent years.[8]

Notes

1 See Lijphart 1995. Similarly, consociationalists also favour ethnic federalism. As with political parties, a key presumption is that constituent units should be as ethnically homogeneous as possible in order to maximise each group's control over their own interests and resources.
2 See Reilly 2001, chaps 4–6.
3 For a recent example, see Coakley and Fraenkel 2009.
4 See Bowman 1973, pp. 34, 174.

5 See Lijphart 1991; Fraenkel 2001; Lijphart 2004; Fraenkel and Grofman 2004; McCulloch 2013.
6 For a partial exception, see Reilly 2007.
7 Lijphart 1991, 2004.
8 See Reilly 2006, 2011.

Further reading

Horowitz, D. L. (2000) *Ethnic Groups in Conflict*, rev edn, Berkeley CA: University of California Press.
McCulloch, A. (2014) *Power-Sharing and Political Stability in Deeply Divided Societies*, Abingdon and New York: Routledge.
Pippa, N. (2004) *Electoral Engineering: Voting Rules and Political Behavior*, Cambridge: Cambridge University Press.
Reilly, B. (2001) *Democracy in Divided Societies: Electoral Engineering for Conflict Management*, Cambridge: Cambridge University Press.
Sisk, T. D. (1996) *Power Sharing and International Mediation in Ethnic Conflicts*, Washington DC: United States Institute of Peace Press.

References

Bastian, S. and Luckham, R. (2003) 'Conclusion. The Politics of Institutional Choice', in Bastian, S. and Luckham, R. (eds), *Can Democracy Be Designed? The Politics of Institutional Choice in Conflict-Torn Societies*, London: Zed Press.
Bingham Powell, G. (2000) *Elections as Instruments of Democracy: Majoritarian and Proportional Visions*, New Haven CT and London: Yale University Press.
Birnir, J. K. (2004) 'Stabilizing Party Systems and Excluding Segments of Society? The Effects of Formation Costs on New Party Foundation in Latin America', *Studies in Comparative International Development*, 39(3): 3–27.
Bogaards, M. (2003) 'Electoral Choices for Divided Societies: Multi-Ethnic Parties and Constituency Pooling in Africa', *Commonwealth & Comparative Politics*, 41(3): 59–80.
Bogaards, M. (2008) 'Comparative Strategies of Political Party Regulation', in Reilly, B. and Nordlund, P. (eds), *Political Parties in Conflict-Prone Societies: Regulation, Engineering and Democratic Development*, Tokyo: United Nations University Press.
Bowman, L. (1973) *Politics in Rhodesia*, Cambridge MA: Harvard University Press.
Coakley, J. and Fraenkel, J. (2009) 'Do Preference Transfers Assist Moderates in Deeply Divided Societies? Evidence from Northern Ireland and Fiji', paper presented at the Annual Meeting of the American Political Science Association, Toronto, September.
Diamond, L. (1996) 'Toward Democratic Consolidation', in Diamond, L. and Plattner, M. F. (eds), *The Global Resurgence of Democracy*, Baltimore MD and London: Johns Hopkins University Press.
Elster, J. (2013) *Securities Against Misrule: Juries, Assemblies, Elections*, New York: Cambridge University Press.
Fraenkel, J. (2001) 'The Alternative Vote System in Fiji: Electoral Engineering or Ballot-Rigging?', *Commonwealth and Comparative Politics*, 39(1): 1–31.
Fraenkel, J. and Grofman, B. (2004) 'A Neo-Downsian Model of the Alternative Vote as a Mechanism for Mitigating Ethnic Conflict in Plural Societies', *Public Choice*, 121: 487–506.
Haggard, S. and Kaufman, R. (1995) *The Political Economy of Democratic Transitions*, Princeton NJ: Princeton University Press.
Hillman, B. (2010) Political Parties and Post-Conflict Transition: The Results and Implications of the 2009 Parliamentary Elections in Aceh, Centre for Democratic Institutions Policy Paper 1/10, Canberra: Centre for Democratic Institutions.
Horowitz, D. L. (1985) *Ethnic Groups in Conflict*, Berkeley CA: University of California Press.
Horowitz, D. L. (1991) *A Democratic South Africa? Constitutional Engineering in a Divided Society*, Berkeley CA: University of California Press.
Jarstad, A. (2008) 'Power-Sharing: Former Enemies in Joint Government', in Jarstad, A. K. and Sisk, T. D. (eds), *From War to Democracy: Dilemmas of Peacebuilding*, Cambridge: Cambridge University Press.
Lijphart, A. (1977) *Democracy in Plural Societies*, New Haven: Yale University Press.
Lijphart, A. (1991) 'The Alternative Vote: A Realistic Alternative for South Africa?', *Politikon*, 18(2): 91–101.

Lijphart, A. (1995) 'Self-Determination Versus Pre-determination of Ethnic Minorities in Power-Sharing Systems', in Kymlicka, W. (ed.), *The Rights of Minority Cultures*, Oxford: Oxford University Press.

Lijphart, A. (2004) 'Constitutional Design for Divided Societies', *Journal of Democracy*, 15(2): 96–109.

Lipset, S. M. (1960) *Political Man: The Social Bases of Politics*, New York: Doubleday.

McCulloch, A. (2013) 'Does Moderation Pay? Centripetalism in Deeply Divided Societies', *Ethnopolitics*, 12(2): 111–132.

Norris, P. (2004) *Electoral Engineering: Voting Rules and Political Behavior*, New York: Cambridge University Press.

Persson, T. and Tabellini, G. (2000) *Political Economics: Explaining Economic Policy*, Cambridge MA: MIT Press.

Persson, T. and Tabellini, G. (2005) *The Economic Effects of Constitutions*, Cambridge MA: MIT Press.

Reilly, B. (2001) *Democracy in Divided Societies: Electoral Engineering for Conflict Management*, Cambridge: Cambridge University Press.

Reilly, B. (2004) 'The Global Spread of Preferential Voting: Australian Institutional Imperialism?', *Australian Journal of Political Science*, 39(2): 253–266.

Reilly, B. (2006) *Democracy and Diversity: Political Engineering in the Asia-Pacific*, Oxford: Oxford University Press.

Reilly, B. (2007) 'Political Engineering in the Asia-Pacific', *Journal of Democracy*, 18(1): 58–72.

Reilly, B. (2008) 'Post-Conflict Elections: Uncertain Turning Points of Transition?', in Jarstad, A. K. and Sisk, T. D. (eds), *From War to Democracy: Dilemmas of Peacebuilding*, Cambridge: Cambridge University Press.

Reilly, B. (2011) 'Political Reform and the Demise of Consociationalism in Southeast Asia', in Croissant, A. and Bünte, M. (eds), *The Crisis of Democratic Governance in Southeast Asia*, New York: Palgrave Macmillan.

Reilly, B. and Nordlund, P. (eds) (2008) *Political Parties in Conflict-Prone Societies: Regulation, Engineering and Democratic Development*, Tokyo: United Nations University Press.

Rock, M. T. (2013) 'East Asia's Democratic Developmental States and Economic Growth', *Journal of East Asian Studies*, 13(1): 1–34.

Salloukh, B. (2006) 'The Limits of Electoral Engineering in Divided Societies: Elections in Postwar Lebanon', *Canadian Journal of Political Science*, 39(3): 635–655.

Sisk, T. D. (1996) *Power Sharing and International Mediation in Ethnic Conflicts*, Washington DC: United States Institute of Peace Press.

Wimmer, A. (2003) 'Democracy and Ethno-Religious Conflict in Iraq', *Survival*, 45(4): 111–134.

24

CONSOCIATIONALISM

Stefan Wolff and Karl Cordell

Introduction

John Stuart Mill's scepticism with regard to the possibility of democracy 'in a country made up of different nationalities' (Mill 1861: 230) is perhaps the best-known and most widely cited scholarly reflection of a phenomenon empirically all too often observable as violent ethnic conflict. Yet, Mill's scepticism has not, to date, resulted in either ever more homogeneous democratic states or in the inability of heterogeneous countries to become democratic polities. Rather, Mill's dictum has been taken up as a challenge by scholars and practitioners of institutional design in divided societies to find stable and democratic ways in which democracy and diversity can be married. The answers given in theory and practice are vastly different, and a debate thus continues unabated over which institutional design is best able to provide sustainable democracy in ethnically heterogeneous societies.

One such answer is 'consociational democracy,' prominently associated with the work of Arend Lijphart, as well as more recently with that of John McGarry and Brendan O'Leary. Lijphart began to examine this particular type of democratic system in greater detail for the first time in the late 1960s, when making reference to the political systems of Scandinavian countries and of the Netherlands and Belgium (Lijphart 1968, 1969). He followed up with further studies of political stability in cases of severely socially fragmented societies, eventually leading to his ground-breaking work *Democracy in Plural Societies* (Lijphart 1977). The phenomenon Lijphart was describing, however, was not new. As a pattern of social structure, characterizing a society fragmented by religious, linguistic, ideological, or other cultural segmentation, it had existed and been studied (albeit not as extensively) long before the 1960s. These structural aspects, studied among others by Lorwin (1971), were not the primary concern of Lijphart, who was more interested in why, despite their fragmentation, such societies maintained a stable political process, and identified the behaviour of political elites as the main, but not the only, reason for stability. Furthermore, Lijphart (1977: 25–52) identified four features shared by consociational systems – a grand coalition government (between parties from different segments of society), segmental autonomy (in the cultural sector), proportionality (in the voting system and in public sector employment), and minority veto. These characteristics, more or less prominently, were exhibited by all the classic examples of consociationalism: Lebanon, Cyprus, Switzerland, Austria, the Netherlands, Belgium, Fiji, and Malaysia. Some of these consociations have succeeded, such as in Switzerland, Austria, the Netherlands, and others have experienced varying degrees of failure, including Lebanon, Cyprus, Fiji, and Malaysia. Similarly, Bosnia and Herzegovina continues to teeter on the edge of outright failure, kept alive as much as anything else by the lack of clearly identifiable and mutually acceptable alternatives to the current domestic and regional territorial settlements in place across the western Balkans. This predicament neatly illustrates the importance that Lijphart attached to the existence of overarching loyalties and the sustainability of consociational settlements. He also noted the importance of a number of other factors, including there being only a small number of political parties in each societal segment, that ideally such segments be of about equal size, complemented by the existence of some cross-cutting cleavages as an avenue for moderating segmental isolation. This latter point is important, as the absence of cross-cutting cleavages seems to be a commonality in those countries in which consociation has not succeeded. In addition to Cyprus and Lebanon being examples of failed consociation, Belgium's continued experience of protracted government formation brings it close to failure, albeit clearly not with the same violent aftermath that consociational failures in Cyprus and Lebanon experienced. It is striking to note that in all three examples society had at some point become polarized around a single fault line: respectively an ethno-religious, linguistic and religious cleavage.

Lijphart's assumptions and prescriptions did and do, of course, not go unchallenged. Major criticisms of the consociational approach question its compatibility with both democracy and justice and argue that consociationalism has a poor track record of even achieving sustainable peace (Wolff 2011). Lijphart and other advocates of consociational approaches to the political accommodation of cultural diversity responded in two ways – by offering a robust defence of their views and by gradually developing consociational theory further. Lijphart himself engaged his critics most comprehensively in his book on *Power Sharing in South Africa* (1985: 83–117) and in his contribution to Andrew Reynolds's *The Architecture of Democracy* (Lijphart 2002: 39–45). In the latter, he also offers a substantive revision of his original approach, now describing power sharing and autonomy (i.e. grand coalition government and segmental autonomy) as primary characteristics, while relegating proportionality and minority veto to 'secondary characteristics' (2002: 39). Yet, in relation to his grand coalition requirement, Lijphart maintains his earlier position that such executive power sharing means 'participation of representatives of all significant groups in political decision making' (2002: 41).

Subsequent developments of consociational theory, especially by John McGarry and Brendan O'Leary (McGarry 2006; McGarry and O'Leary 2004a, 2004b; O'Leary 2005a, 2005b), whilst acknowledging the importance of Lijphart's oeuvre have made one important modification in particular in this respect. O'Leary contends that 'grand coalition' (in the sense of an executive encompassing all leaders of all significant parties of all significant communities) is not a necessary criterion; rather, he demonstrates that what matters for a democratic consociation 'is meaningful cross-community executive power sharing in which each significant segment is represented in the government with at least plurality levels of support within its segment' (O'Leary 2005a: 13, and below).

In order to appreciate fully the breadth and depth of consociational theory, it is useful to examine John McGarry and Brendan O'Leary's *The Northern Ireland Conflict: Consociational Engagements* (2004a, a collection of their joint and individual writings on this conflict from 1987 to 2002), in particular its co-authored introduction on the lessons that Northern Ireland holds for consociational theory more broadly. The arguments put forward by McGarry and O'Leary here have also been rehearsed elsewhere (e.g. McGarry and O'Leary 2006a, 2006b; as well as in a volume by Rupert Taylor published in 2009). These arguments are offered as a basis for a broad discussion among scholars on the merits of consociation (and other techniques of conflict settlement).

McGarry and O'Leary maintain that Northern Ireland and its 1998 Agreement, 'highlights six important weaknesses in traditional consociational theory' (McGarry and O'Leary 2004b: 5). These are the failure to address the role of external actors; the trans-state nature of some self-determination disputes and the necessary institutional arrangements to address them; the increasing complexity of conflict settlements in which consociational arrangements form an important element but require complementary mechanisms to deal with 'the design of the police, demilitarization, the return of exiles to their homes, the management of prisoners, education reform, economic policy, and the promotion of language and other group rights' (McGarry and O'Leary 2004b: 13); terminological and conceptual inaccuracies, primarily associated with Lijphart's grand coalition requirement; the merits of preferential proportional electoral systems, i.e. the single transferable vote (STV); and the allocation of cabinet positions by means of sequential proportionality rules, i.e. the d'Hondt mechanism. In dealing with these weaknesses, McGarry and O'Leary offer both refinements of, and advancements to, traditional consociational theory. The refinements relate, first, to the technical side of consociational institutions, where the authors recommend STV instead of list-proportional representation (PR) as an electoral system as it militates against the proliferation of micro-parties. Second, McGarry and O'Leary elaborate the usefulness of sequential proportionality rules, such as the d'Hondt mechanism or the Sainte-Laguë method, in the allocation of cabinet positions in order to avoid protracted bargaining between parties and increase parties' incentives to remain part of cross-communal coalitions.

That to one side, and to return to the main theme, the advancements to traditional consociational theory offered here, as well as elsewhere (e.g. O'Leary 2005a, 2005b; McGarry 2006), are a significant step forward in that they address both long-standing criticisms of consociationalism and a gap between consociational theory and conflict resolution practice. McGarry's and O'Leary's observations on external actors bring consociational theory in line with an established debate in international relations on the role of third parties in conflict resolution (see, for example, contributions in Otunnu and Doyle 1998; Walter and Snyder 1999; Carment and Schnabel 2003; Diehl and Lepgold 2003; Weller and Wolff 2005; Mattes and Savun 2009; Curtis 2013; Hartzell and Hoddie 2015). Equally importantly, their discussion of the provisions in the 1998 Agreement that go beyond domestic institutions and address the specific 'Irish dimension' of the Northern Ireland conflict reflect a growing awareness among scholars and practitioners of conflict resolution that many ethnic conflicts have causes and consequences beyond the boundaries of the states in which they occur and that for settlements to be durable and stable, these dimensions need addressing as well. In the case of the 1998 Agreement for Northern Ireland, McGarry and O'Leary highlight three dimensions: cross-border institutions which formalize cooperation between the Northern Ireland Executive and the Irish government (the so-called North–South Ministerial Council) and renew British–Irish inter-governmental cooperation (the British–Irish Inter-governmental Conference); the explicit recognition by the two governments of the right to self-determination of the people in Northern Ireland and the Republic, i.e. the possibility for them to bring about, in separate referenda, a united Ireland if that is the wish of respective majorities; and new institutions of regional cooperation, incorporating the UK and Irish governments, and the executive organs of the other two devolved regions in the UK and its three dependent island territories in the Channel and the Irish Sea.

These arrangements have earlier precedents in the history of conflict settlement in Northern Ireland, but they are not unique to this case alone. Institutions of cross-border cooperation have been utilized as part of comprehensive peace settlements elsewhere as well – for example, in South Tyrol and Bosnia and Herzegovina – and exist, of course, in less conflict-prone situations as part of arrangements between sovereign states and/or substate entities – for example, in the EU's Euroregions (cf. Danspeckgruber 2005; Nauclér 2005). If we elaborate these points, we find that the divergent fortunes of South Tyrol and Bosnia and Herzegovina vindicate the point made by O'Leary and McGarry (forthcoming) about the importance of external actors. The positive support given by both Italy and Austria to the Autonomy Statute for South Tyrol has been crucial in the process of facilitating the accom- modation of South Tyroleans within wider Italian society, and in diffusing what could have become a very nasty conflict. With regard to Bosnia and Herzegovina, we find the opposite to be true. Here, the relevant kin states, namely Croatia and Serbia, pay little more than lip- service to the agreements that established their neighbour, and consciously or otherwise, encourage separatism that could still bring about the collapse of state structures in Bosnia and Herzegovina.

As far as the possibility of future status changes are concerned, such possibilities are not unique to Northern Ireland or indeed the 1998 Agreement. In recent Northern Ireland history, a so-called border poll took place in 1973 but was almost completely boycotted by Nationalists and Republicans. There had been an initial British commitment to hold such polls at ten-year intervals, but this was unceremoniously and quietly abandoned when it was seen to have inadvertently strengthened the hand of hardliners within the Unionist spectrum. Farther afield, the people of the Autonomous Republic of Gagauzia in Moldova would have a one-off opportunity to exercise their right to (external) self-determination if Moldova were to join Romania. In turn, the Comprehensive Peace Agreement for Sudan of 2005 offered the people in the South a referendum on independence in 2011 (cf. Weller 2005), which resulted in the creation of the Republic of South Sudan later that same year, while the Bougainville Peace Agreement of 2001 included a clause that envisages a referendum on independence to be held in Bougainville after 10–15 years, but which still has not been held as of the time of writing (May 2015). Crucially, in all these situations, the signatory parties have committed to respecting the outcome of these referenda, although in the case of Sudan whether the (former) antagonists have rigorously stuck to the terms of the overall agreement is open to question (Kupferberg and Wolff 2015; Wolff 2012).

The more recent writings by Lijphart, McGarry, and O'Leary also indicate a clear move from corporate toward liberal consociational power sharing. Corporate consociationalism, however, is still evident to some extent in political practice: for example, Bosnia and Herzegovina, under the original Dayton Accords, Northern Ireland under the 1998 Agree- ment, Lebanon under the National Pact and under the 1989 Ta'if Accord, Cyprus under the 1960 constitution and the rejected Annan Plan of 2004 all display features of predetermined arrangements based on ascriptive identities. The main difference between the two is that a 'corporate consociation accommodates groups according to ascriptive criteria, and rests on the assumption that group identities are fixed, and that groups are both internally homogeneous and externally bounded,' while 'liberal [...] consociation [...] rewards whatever salient political identities emerge in democratic elections, whether these are based on ethnic groups, or on sub-group or trans-group identities' (McGarry 2006: 3; see also Lijphart 1995; O'Leary 2005a). This is another important modification of consociational theory that addresses one of its more profound, and empirically more valid, criticisms, namely that (corporate) consociations further entrench and institutionalize pre-existing, and often conflict-hardened, ethnic identities, thus decreasing the incentives for elites to moderate (e.g. Horowitz 1985: 566–576; 1991: 167ff.; 2003: 119). Once again Lebanon provides a useful example. Here ethno-religious identities are so entrenched within the fabric of the state that it is virtually impossible legally to leave one community and join another. Similarly, although in Northern Ireland the Good Friday Agreement of 1998 has certainly delivered at one level, at another it has not. The political centre has collapsed, and social segregation appears at best not to have eased. In fact, given the political programmes of the two dominant parties, the pro-union Democratic Unionist Party and Sinn Féin and their mutually exclusive profiles with regard to fundamental issues of identity and sovereignty, it makes little sense for them to promote integration, as opposed to co-operation across the divide. In short, neither has any interest, rhetoric to one side, in devising a programme that might glean significant support from across the ethno-sectarian divide. In the case of Lebanon in the 1970s, elites both fed and succumbed to pressures from below, eventually causing the collapse of a political settlement, elements of which had first emerged in 1926 and had remained impervious to alteration despite the demographic changes that had occurred within Lebanese society in the intervening years. Although extreme in terms of its consequences, the example of Lebanon demonstrates the need for consocational frameworks to be supple and responsive to the processes of broader change. Fortunately, there is no sign of such failure being apparent in Northern Ireland. However, as stated, neither is there any real sign that mental and physical barriers are diminishing.

Beyond power sharing? The complementarity of power sharing with other conflict settlement approaches

Power sharing is commonly used as a shorthand for the consociational approach and vice versa (e.g. Jarstad 2008, 2009; also, Binningsbø 2013). In fact, it combines power sharing with a number of other features of designing governance institutions. The core power-sharing element of consociationalism is the grand coalition, in Lijphart's terminology, or meaningful jointness in O'Leary's and McGarry's. Proportionality serves as both an enabling mechanism (PR election system or some other non-majoritarian and/or preferential voting system and/or seat allocation formula) and a resource distribution and allocation mechanism (public funding, public sector jobs, increasingly also natural resource revenues). The minority veto in its various forms from a simple straight-forward ability of a group to veto an executive decision, legislative act, or judicial ruling to qualified or concurrent voting procedures in decision-making bodies is essentially a guarantee mechanism to prevent the unilateral abrogation of a particular consociational settlement. Segmental autonomy (different types of territorial and non-territorial self-governance) is the final component of consociational political systems in their ideal-typical form, meant to minimize the number of issues that are subject to joint decision making.

The relationship between power sharing and self-governance, now widely seen as the two primary characteristics of consociationalism, raises a broader issue, namely the extent to which the consociational approach is compatible with other approaches to, and principles of, conflict management in ethnically plural societies and with which mechanism it needs to be complemented for achieving sustainable peace.

In order to illuminate these issues of compatibility and complementarity further, let us begin with a discussion of territorial self-governance (as one particular example of how to institutionalize segmental autonomy) which has a specific theoretical and empirical significance within consociationalism (Wolff 2009).

The liberal consociational approach, in line with its corporate predecessor, places significant value on territorial self-governance, but emphasizing that the self-governing territory should define itself from the bottom up, rather than be prescribed top-down. Within this context, the example of Iraq is as illuminating as it is tragic. John McGarry (2006: 6–7) explains how this process of self-definition was supposed to have worked with regard to the city of Kirkuk: as enshrined in the Iraqi constitution:

> Kirkuk can choose to join Kurdistan if its people want. Governorates in other parts of the country are permitted to amalgamate, forming regions, if there is democratic support in each governorate. In this case, a twin democratic threshold is proposed: a vote within a governorate's assembly and a referendum.

Today Kirkuk lies within Kurdish controlled Iraq, not as the result of the exercise of self-determination as provided for by the Iraqi constitution, but by virtue of the Peshmerga's force of arms and the desperate need of the Iraqi government to form a tactical alliance with the Peshmerga against the Islamic State. In a general sense, what Iraq teaches us is that for consociational and especially power-sharing mechanisms to succeed, politicians need to have regard for those outside their immediate communities and to view politics as something other than a zero sum game: in today's Iraq the ghastly consequences of the politics of hubris and vainglory are all too obvious.

Liberal consociationalists also support the principle of asymmetric devolution of powers, i.e. the possibility for some self-governing entities to enjoy more (or fewer) competences than others, depending on the preferences of their populations (cf. McGarry 2007). However, in order to be genuine, self-governance needs to be complemented with what liberal consociationalists term 'shared rule', i.e. the exercise of power at and by the centre and across the state as a whole. Yet, we must distinguish between theory and practice. For example, Russia is characterized by asymmetric devolution of powers and indeed purports to be federal in character. However, the practice of politics in Russia tells us that presidential (and prime-ministerial) caprice and whim count for more than does the constitution. While grand coalitions, proportionality, and minority veto rights continue to be favoured by liberal consociationalists, when it comes to power sharing, the emphasis is on cooperation and consensus among democratically legitimized elites, regardless of whether they emerge on the basis of group identities, ideology, or other common interest. They thus favour parliamentary systems, while acknowledging the merit and frequency of collective or rotating presidencies in existing functioning consociations, proportional (PR list) or proportional preferential (STV) electoral systems, decision-making procedures that require qualified and/ or concurrent majorities, and have also advocated, at times, the application of the d'Hondt rule for the formation of executives (cf. Lijphart 2004; O'Leary 2005a; O'Leary, Grofman and Elklit 2005).

This means that liberal consociationalists prefer what O'Leary refers to as 'pluralist federations,' in which co-sovereign sub-state and central governments have clearly defined exclusive competences (albeit with the possibility of some concurrent competences) whose assignment to either level of authority is constitutionally and, ideally, internationally protected, in which decision making at the centre is consensual (between self-governing entities and the centre, and among elites representing different interest groups), and which recognize, and protect the presence of different self-determined identities (O'Leary 2005b). This preference for pluralist federations, however, remains context-dependent, and is not per se part of liberal consociational thinking. In some circumstances, e.g. where ethnic communities are not ethnonationalist (i.e. demanding their own governance institutions), it is quite possible that a unitary state with power sharing at the centre will suffice as a mechanism to settle conflicts.

In order to protect individuals against the abuse of power by majorities at the state level or the level of self-governing entities, liberal consociationalism offers two remedies – the replication of its core institutional prescriptions within the self-governing entity, and the establishment and enforcement of strong human and minority rights regimes at both the state and sub-state levels. Canada provides us with a good example of such practices. Not only is the state federal, but Quebec enjoys a unique relationship with the remainder of the federation, and with the creation of Nunavut, special (administrative) provision for at least some of Canada's indigenous peoples exists within a federal framework that is re-enforced by a robust minority rights regime. As the example of Canada further shows, the rights of communities – minorities and majorities alike – are best protected in a liberal consociational system if its key provisions are enshrined in the constitution and if the interpretation and upholding of the constitution is left to an independent and representative constitutional court whose decisions are binding on executive and legislature (cf. O'Leary 2005b: 55–58).

This extensive discussion of how and why territorial self-governance complements power sharing and how the coherent implementation of both mechanisms, in combination with other principles, renders consociationalism compatible not just with peace but also with justice and democracy illustrates that the key to liberal consociational prescriptions of institutional design in divided societies is the emphasis on the protection of self-determined (rather than predetermined) identity groups through ensuring both their representation and effective participation in decision making especially in the legislature and executive. The underlying assumption here is that representation and participation together will ensure that different identity groups recognize that their aims can be achieved, and interests protected, by political means and do not require recourse to violence. This point also re-enforces our earlier comment that consociations are most vulnerable either to violence or effective disintegration when the consociation has been constructed in a society that either lacks cross-cutting cleavages or where none emerge over time.

The examples of Belgium and Lebanon are instructive with regard to this point. Although both possessed the ingredients necessary for the development of cross-cutting cleavages, both failed to do so. In Belgium society became polarized around a linguistic fault-line. Lebanon is more complex and for reasons of brevity we can say that, confessional fault lines to one side, society eventually became and remains polarized with regards to differing attitudes towards Lebanon's relationship with Syria. In the case of Lebanon, civil war resulted, and in the case of Belgium, it could be argued that a post-consociational system is now in place that has full separation as its probable logical conclusion.

A striking feature of contemporary conflict resolution *practice* is that a large number of actual and proposed settlements involve a broad range of different conflict settlement mechanisms compatible with liberal consociational prescriptions, as empirically illustrated by Weller and Metzger (2008) and Wolff (2011). This reflects the assumption that a combination of consociational and other mechanisms can indeed provide institutional solutions that are both acceptable to negotiators and conducive to accommodating conflict parties in an institutional framework in which they can settle their disputes by peaceful means. The need to combine a range of different mechanisms has been increasingly understood by practitioners of conflict resolution and has led to an emerging practice of conflict settlement that can be referred to as 'complex power sharing.' The term 'complex power sharing' was first used and conceptualized in a research project funded by the Carnegie Corporation of New York ('Resolving Self-determination Disputes through Complex Power Sharing Arrangements'). There, complex power-sharing regimes were distinguished 'in that they no longer depend solely on consociational theory, or solely upon integrative theory,' involve international actors that 'are often key in designing, or bringing experience to bear upon, the structure of the eventual agreement, or its implementation,' and 'consider a far broader range of issues [...] and [...] address structural issues as diverse as economic management, civil-military relations and human and minority rights, and [...] do so at many different levels of government,' thus recognizing 'that at different levels of government, different strategies may be more, or less, applicable, and consequently more, or less, successful, in engendering peace and stability' (Kettley, Sullivan and Fyfe 2001: 4–5; also Weller 2008). In a somewhat similar vein, O'Leary (2005a: 34–35) uses the term 'complex consociation.'

Complex power sharing, thus, describes a practice of conflict settlement that requires a relatively complex institutional structure across different layers of authority from the centre down to local government units and that cannot be reduced to autonomy/(ethno-)federation, (traditional) models of power sharing, centripetalism, or power dividing, but rather represents a combination of them. Bosnia and Herzegovina provides us with a good example of such practices, and also neatly illustrates the short-term advantages and long-term drawbacks of such practices. However, liberal consociationalism, both as a theory and a set of policy pre-scriptions, is open to incorporation of elements from other approaches, including, for example, centripetalism and territorial pluralism. Within a liberal consociational framework, there is room (and a recognized need) for a range of strategies not traditionally part of the core consociational prescription, including a strong role for judicial entrenchment and enforce-ment mechanisms, and universally applicable and enforceable human rights legislation. Liberal consociationalism is also open to a vertical division of power on the basis of non-ascriptive, i.e. non-ethnic, criteria without ruling out that self-determined entities on that basis emerge and desire territorial or corporate self-governance.

Yet, liberal consociationalism is not synonymous with complex power sharing, even though it offers a promising point of departure for a new research agenda on conflict resolution theory. In order to make a significant contribution to existing debates, a theory of complex power sharing would need to accomplish several tasks. First, most existing theories of conflict resolution are consequence-focused, i.e. they seek to explain why certain institutional designs offer the prospect of sustainable peace and stability, while others do not. They do this by offering normative and pragmatic accounts of the desirability and feasibility of particular institutions in divided societies, but these are not always, let alone successfully, grounded in theories of conflict, nor are the assumptions made about the drivers of conflict always fully spelt out. Yet it is essential to understand the causes of conflict before viable prescriptions for its resolution can be offered. This is not to suggest that any single theory of conflict will be able to explain every distinct conflict, but rather that more reflection is needed about what institutions can address what causes. Fear requires a different response than deprivation, and people driven to violence by their desire for power need to be dealt with in a different way than those who fear the loss of their culture.

In other words, a theory of complex power sharing would need to explain why we find empirically a greater mix of institutions than existing theories recommend. Factoring in causes of conflict is one aspect of this, but two others are equally important. The first one has been examined at some length already and relates to the process of settlement, that is, the structure of negotiations and the nature of the different actors participating in them (e.g. Horowitz 2002, 2008; Eklund, O'Leary and Williams 2005; Galbraith 2005). The second one is a more careful consideration of 'objective' factors that might privilege certain institutions in their presence. For example, as O'Leary and McGarry illustrate in the case of Northern Ireland, the fact that this region is territorially distinct and clearly delineated, ethnically mixed, and that its two major groups have strong preferences for links with different actors outside their region created a path toward a regional consociation embedded in two cross-border arrangements – the North–South Ministerial Council and the Council of the British Isles (cf. McGarry and O'Leary 2004b). McGarry, O'Leary and Simeon (2008) also briefly discuss structural conditions under which integration (in this essay's terminology: mechanisms of centripetalism and power dividing) and accommodation (in this essay's terminology: mechanisms of territorial self-governance and power sharing) are appropriate conflict settlement strategies, while Wolff (2013) develops an argument based on structural factors more systematically and applies it to a broader range of cases.

Apart from the question of why complex power-sharing settlements emerge, a proper theory of conflict resolution also needs to be able to explain why they fail or succeed, i.e. it needs to identify the conditions under which they can provide long-term peace and stability in divided societies. Ultimately, this can only be done empirically and thus requires a definition of what can be considered complex power-sharing settlements, the identification of relevant cases, and their analysis against standards of success and failure. On the basis of such a comprehensive theory of complex power sharing that enables us to understand why they emerge and why they succeed or fail, sensible policy recommendations for conflict settlement can be made.

References

Binningsbø, H. M. (2013) Power Sharing, Peace and Democracy: Any Obvious Relationships? *International Area Studies Review*, 16(1): 89–112. doi: 10.1177/2233865912473847.

Carment, D., and Schnabel, A. (eds) (2003) *Conflict Prevention: Path to Peace or Grand Illusion?* Tokyo: United Nations University Press.

Curtis, D. (2013) The International Peacebuilding Paradox: Power Sharing and Post-conflict Governance in Burundi, *African Affairs*, 112(446): 72–91. doi: 10.1093/afraf/ads080.

Danspeckgruber, W. (2005) Self-governance plus Regional Integration: A Possible Solution to Self-determination Claims. In M. Weller and S. Wolff (eds) *Autonomy, Self-governance and Conflict Resolution: Innovative Approaches to Institutional Design in Divided Societies*. London: Routledge, pp. 26–48.

Diehl, P. F. and Lepgold, J. (eds) (2003) *Regional Conflict Management*. Lanham: Rowman and Littlefield.

Eklund, K., O'Leary, B. and Williams, P. R. (2005) Negotiating a Federation in Iraq. In B. O'Leary, J. McGarry, and K. Salih (eds) *The Future of Kurdistan in Iraq*. Philadelphia: University of Pennsylvania Press, pp. 116–142.

Galbraith, P. W. (2005) Kurdistan in a Federal Iraq. In B. O'Leary, J. McGarry, and K. Salih (eds) *The Future of Kurdistan in Iraq*. Philadelphia: University of Pennsylvania Press, pp. 268–281.

Hartzell, C. A. and Hoddie, M. (2015) The Art of the Possible: Power Sharing and Post-Civil War Democracy, *World Politics*, 67(01): 37–71. doi: 10.1017/S0043887114000306.

Horowitz, D. L. (1985 [2000]) *Ethnic Groups in Conflict*. Berkeley: University of California Press.

Horowitz, D. L. (1991) *A Democratic South Africa? Constitutional Engineering in a Divided Society*. Berkeley: University of California Press.

Horowitz, D. L. (2002) Constitutional Design: Proposals versus Processes. In A. Reynolds (ed.) *The Architecture of Democracy*. Oxford: Oxford University Press, pp. 15–36.

Horowitz, D. L. (2003) Electoral Systems and Their Goals: A Primer for Decision-Makers, *Journal of Democracy*, 14(4): 115–127.

Horowitz, D. L. (2008) Conciliatory Institutions and Constitutional Processes in Post-conflict States, *William and Mary Law Review*, 49: 1213–1248.

Jarstad, A. K. (2008) Power Sharing: Former Enemies in Joint Government. In A. K. Jarstad and T. D. Sisk (eds) *From War to Democracy: Dilemmas of Peacebuilding*. Cambridge: Cambridge University Press, pp. 105–133.

Jarstad, A. K. (2009) The Prevalence of Power-Sharing: Exploring the Patterns of Post-Election Peace, *Africa Spectrum*, 44(3): 41–62.

Kettley, C., Sullivan, J. and Fyfe, J. (2001) Self-determination Disputes and Complex Power Sharing Arrangements: A Background Paper for Debate. Cambridge: Centre of International Studies. Available at: http://www.intstudies.cam.ac.uk/centre/cps/download/background1.pdf. Accessed 4 March 2009.

Kupferberg, K. and Wolff, S. (2015) Sudan: Successful Constitutional Reform Spurs Localized Violence. In A. J. Kuperman (ed.) *Constitutional Design and Conflict Management in Africa*. Philadelphia, PA: University of Pennsylvania Press, pp. 96–114.

Lijphart, A. (1968) Typologies of Democratic Systems, *Comparative Political Studies*, 1(1): 3–44.

Lijphart, A. (1969) Consociational Democracy, *World Politics*, 21(2): 207–225.

Lijphart, A. (1977) *Democracy in Plural Societies*. New Haven: Yale University Press.

Lijphart, A. (1985) *Power Sharing in South Africa*. Berkeley: University of California Press.

Lijphart, A. (1995) Self-determination versus Pre-determination of Ethnic Minorities in Power Sharing Systems. In W. Kymlicka (ed.) *The Rights of Minority Cultures*. Oxford: Oxford University Press, pp. 275–287.

Lijphart, A. (2002) The Wave of Power Sharing Democracy. In A. Reynolds (ed.) *The Architecture of Democracy: Constitutional Design, Conflict Management and Democracy*. Oxford: Oxford University Press, pp. 37–54.

Lijphart, A. (2004) Constitutional Design for Divided Societies, *Journal of Democracy*, 15(2): 96–109.

Lorwin, V. R. (1971) Segmented Pluralism: Ideological Cleavages and Political Cohesion in the Smaller European Democracies, *Comparative Politics*, 3(January): 153–156.

Mattes, M. and Savun, B. (2009) Fostering Peace After Civil War: Commitment Problems and Agreement Design, *International Studies Quarterly*, 53(3): 737–759. doi: 10.1111/j.1468–2478.2009.00554.x.

McGarry, J. (2006) Iraq: Liberal Consociation and Conflict Management (Draft working paper, ms. in author's possession).

McGarry, J. (2007) Asymmetrical Federal Systems, *Ethnopolitics*, 6(1): 105–116.

McGarry, J. and O'Leary, B. (2004a) *The Northern Ireland Conflict: Consociational Engagements*. Oxford: Oxford University Press.

McGarry, J. and O'Leary, B. (2004b) Introduction: Consociational Theory and Northern Ireland. In J. McGarry and B. O'Leary, *The Northern Ireland Conflict: Consociational Engagements*. Oxford: Oxford University Press, pp. 1–60.

McGarry, J. and O'Leary, B. (2006a) Consociational Theory, Northern Ireland's Conflict and its Agreement: Part 1. What Consociationalists Can Learn from Northern Ireland, *Government & Opposition*, 41(1): 43–63.

McGarry, J. and O'Leary, B. (2006b) Consociational Theory, Northern Ireland's Conflict and its Agreement: Part 2. What Critics of Consociation Can Learn from Northern Ireland, *Government & Opposition*, 41(2): 249–277.

McGarry, J., O'Leary, B. and Simeon, R. (2008) Integration or Accommodation? The Enduring Debate in Conflict Regulation. In S. Choudhry (ed.) *Constitutional Design for Divided Societies: Integration or Accommodation?* Oxford: Oxford University Press, pp. 41–88.

Mill, J. S. (1861) *Considerations on Representative Government*. New York: Liberal Arts Press.

Nauclér, E. (2005) Autonomy and Multilevel Governance: Experiences in Nordic and Continental European Cooperation. In M. Weller and S. Wolff (eds) *Autonomy, Self-governance and Conflict Resolution: Innovative Approaches to Institutional Design in Divided Societies*. London: Routledge, pp. 98–116.

O'Leary, B. (2005a) Debating Consociational Politics: Normative and Explanatory Arguments. In S. Noel (ed.) *From Powersharing to Democracy*. Montreal: McGill-Queen's University Press, pp. 3–43.

O'Leary, B. (2005b) Powersharing, Pluralist Federation, and Federacy. In B. O'Leary, J. McGarry, and K. Salih (eds) *The Future of Kurdistan in Iraq*. Philadelphia: University of Pennsylvania Press, pp. 47–91.

O'Leary, B., Grofman, B. and Elklit, J. (2005) Divisor Methods for Sequential Portfolio Allocation in Multi-Party Executive Bodies: Evidence from Northern Ireland and Denmark, *American Journal of Political Science*, 49(1): 198–211.

O'Leary, B. and McGarry, J. (forthcoming) Power-sharing Executives: Consociational and Centripetal Formulae and the Case of Northern Ireland, *Ethnopolitics*.

Otunnu, O. A. and Doyle, M. W. (eds) (1998) *Peacemaking and Peacekeeping for the New Century*. Lanham: Rowman and Littlefield.

Taylor, R. (ed.) (2009) *Consociational Theory: McGarry & O'Leary and the Northern Ireland Conflict*. London: Routledge.

Walter, B. and Snyder, J. (eds) (1999) *Civil Wars, Insecurity and Intervention*. New York: Columbia University Press.

Weller, M. (2005) Self-governance in Interim Settlements: The Case of Sudan. In M. Weller and S. Wolff (eds) *Autonomy, Self-governance and Conflict Resolution: Innovative Approaches to Institutional Design in Divided Societies*. London: Routledge, pp. 158–179.

Weller, M. (2008) Settling Self-determination Conflicts: An Introduction. In M. Weller and B. Metzger (eds) *Settling Self-determination Disputes: Complex Power Sharing in Theory and Practice*. Leiden: Martinus Nijhoff, pp. xi–xvii.

Weller, M. and Metzger, B. (2008) *Settling Self-determination Disputes: Complex Power Sharing in Theory and Practice*. Leiden: Martinus Nijhoff.

Weller, M. and Wolff, S. (2005) (eds) *Autonomy, Self-governance and Conflict Resolution: Innovative Approaches to Institutional Design in Divided Societies*. London: Routledge.

Wolff, S. (2009) Complex Power-sharing and the Centrality of Territorial Self-governance in Contemporary Conflict Settlements, *Ethnopolitics*, 8(1): 27–45.

Wolff, S. (2011) Post-Conflict State Building: The Debate on Institutional Choice, *Third World Quarterly*, 32(10): 1777–1802. doi: 10.1080/01436597.2011.610574.

Wolff, S. (2012) South Sudan's Year One: Managing the Challenges of Building a New State, *RUSI Journal*, 157(5): 46–54.

Wolff, S. (2013) Conflict Management in Divided Societies: The Many Uses of Territorial Self-Governance, *International Journal on Minority and Group Rights*, 20(1): 27–50. doi: 10.1163/15718115-02001003.

25

PLAYING THE ETHNIC CARD

Sandra Barkhof

In this chapter, we shall focus on analysing the differences between liberal democratic and authoritarian systems with regards to ethnic policy. In particular we will stress the persistence of authoritarian practices with regards to ethnicity and ethnic minorities in both established liberal democracies and in 'new democracies', especially the ones that have emerged from former Eastern Europe communist systems. We shall explore the extent to which the 'ethnicity card' is used and manipulated by the established elites to further their own interests and goals. Finally, this chapter will discuss the role of ethnic movements in the transition from authoritarian to democratic rule.

Liberal democracies and authoritarian systems: some comparisons

It has been argued elsewhere in this volume that one of the basic principles of liberal democracy is equality, whereby each member of a liberal democracy has essentially the same protected rights, freedoms and liberties including the freedom of speech, press, religion, assembly and so forth. At the other end of the political spectrum we find authoritarian regimes, which are usually characterised by infringements of these civil liberties and political rights. Authoritarian regimes often implement some sort of limitations on political competition (indeed such competition might be missing completely), employing the overt use of coercion, and often according an important role to ideology. In between the idealised notions of 'democracy' and 'autocracy', which hardly ever exist in their pure form, we find various political systems that need to be classified as hybrid or transitional systems. Some states can be described as 'semi-authoritarian' which may respect some civil liberties but have only 'show' elections. Others are often referred to as 'competitive authoritarian regimes', which (in contrast to true authoritarian regimes) actually have weak legislatures that serve as focal points for opposition (Way 2006: 148). Some states, including many of the new states emerging from the former USSR, especially in Central Asia, still linger in a transitional phase between the former authoritarian communist system and an aspired democratic system (whereby sometimes this 'aspiration' is little more than a legitimisation for continued authoritarian practices as shall be discussed below). On the other hand, while some authoritarian systems use limited 'liberal' policies such as mass participation to legitimise their rule, many of the established western liberal democracies feature exclusive or restrictive political policies that clash with their general liberal democratic framework. We shall discuss examples of this in relation to ethnic minority policy in this chapter.

Ethnic minorities and authoritarian systems

Authoritarian states are often unable to cope with ethnic tensions or conflict in non-violent ways. As pointed out above, authoritarian regimes lack meaningful competitive elections and division of power. Stability in these regimes means the rooting out of opposition and pre-servation of the privileges of the ruling elite. Their strategy with regards to ethnic minorities is often enforced assimilation or even expulsion or elimination of minority groups (non-nationals). Using such measures, strong autocratic regimes may be able, for some time at least, to suppress ethnic or ethno-national movements.

Authoritarian regimes can also be associated with minority ethnic dominance, whereby an ethnic minority occupies a privileged position and access to political power, which is exercised despite the fact that the ruling ethnicity is demographically outnumbered. The goal of such elites is to keep the circle of power as small as possible in order to maximise the benefits associated with that position of power. This includes suppressing the dominant ethnicity and excluding it from political power, a strategy that is becoming more and more difficult to sustain given the general global trend towards democratic transition (Kaufmann and Haklai 2008: 746). Thus dominant minority regimes have become rarer and are now largely limited to authoritarian and semi-authoritarian regimes. Historically, some of these regimes emerged from colonialism, whereby either the white settlers formed this dominant minority or they appointed a favoured minority to have exclusive access to political power and administration. An example would be Iraq where the British created Iraq out of three former provinces of the Ottoman Empire. They installed Faisal, an allied Syrian leader, as king and included the minority Sunni Arab elites in the administration, who then came to dominate military and administrative authority at least until the revolution in 1958 (Farouk-Slugett and Slugett 1987: 12). Another example is of course South Africa, where the white settlers formed the privileged minority that dominated political power.

Maintaining minority dominance usually has to rely on extensive use of coercive measures and exclusion of the majorities from political decision making and representation. Again, we can refer to South Africa where under Apartheid policies the large majority of non-whites were disenfranchised. Usually, such measures needed to go hand in hand with extensive military and security police presence to ensure the marginalisation of the rest of the population, including the suppression of any form of political opposition or activism. This policy has been more successful in some cases than in others. Maintaining a large scale military and police presence costs money, and those regimes without the necessary resources struggled to maintain order and their position (Kaufmann and Haklai 2008: 751). Thus oil rich regimes such as Saudi Arabia and Syria had more access to resources and thus fared better than for example Burundi, where numerous uprisings and revolts occurred until an internationally brokered agreement in 2003 (the Burundi Global Peace Accords of November 2003) paved the way for a fitful transition to a more democratic system (Rothchild 2007: 83).

Coercion, however, is not the only way to maintain minority rule. Many autocratic regimes have used concepts of national and ethno-national ideology to broaden their support base. The vehicle for this is often the construction of a one-party state with vast networks of associations to extend the outreach of the party and thus the ruling elite (similar to the fascist networks of Nazi Germany or Mussolini's Italy). Party membership and association can mean better access to social welfare provisions, education etc., thus providing incentives for people to identify with and support the state. The message used to legitimise the regime was often worded along nationalist or ethno-nationalist lines, thus using the 'ethnic card' as a tool to control the majority. To encompass both the minority and the majority ethnicity, it is necessary to appeal to a 'higher order'. For example, respective regimes in Iraq, Syria, Jordan and Egypt have often attempted to promote a Pan-Arab identity, making their nation the leaders for a wider idea. Such supra-ethnic ideologies are often coupled with a continued domestic suppression of the majority ethnicity (Kaufmann and Haklai 2008: 754).

Seemingly, some new states, especially parts of the former USSR in Central Asia, have reverted to authoritarianism, partly because the legacies of commingled ethnic groups, convoluted borders and emerging national identities all posed severe challenges to the stability in Central Asia (Roudik 2007: 154). In addition, Schatz (2005: 232) points to the importance and continued significance of sub-ethnic clans and kinship politics, which further complicate the transition in the post-communist period. For example, Schatz (2005: 232) notes that sub-ethnic clans were among the main actors as Tajikistan descended into civil war in the 1990s, while in Uzbekistan local identities related to kinship dominate rural areas, thus adding to the multi-ethnic dynamic in the region.

To take the example of Uzbekistan, after the fall of communism, an authoritarian presidential system emerged. Some opposition parties were allowed to give the illusion of democracies, but these parties all supported the ruling party (People's Democracy Party, PDP). Other opposition groups including ethnic opposition groups have been restricted or prohibited, in order to ensure inter-ethnic 'harmony' in the country (Kubicek 1998: 32). The political elite hereby portrayed themselves as guardians of the motherland (although President Karimov announced in 2005 a move away from the presidential system, giving more powers to the Prime Minister and the other branches of government).

A similar situation arose in Kazakhstan, where the post-independence political system could at first be characterised as 'semi-democratic authoritarianism', although after 1995 most observers would describe it as a typical authoritarian regime as the consolidation of presidential power under Nazarbaev began (Oka 2009: 4). The emergence of a delegative democracy meant that an elected president ruled practically unrestricted, and many members of the ruling elite believe that popular participation is overrated and that the popular will should instead be shaped through ideological indoctrination (Brill Olcott 2002: 21). The argument is that democratisation would bring with it ethnic mobilisation, which may result in political instability since the different claims of the various ethnic groups would be difficult to reconcile, especially given the acute socio-economic crisis in many of the Central Asian states (Kubicek 1998: 35–36). Again, opposition including ethnic opposition has been curtailed to avoid ethnic or national tensions and conflict and to preserve national unity. Kazakhstan is unique among the former Soviet Republics as the only one without a majority nationality. After independence, the main risk to Kazakh domination of state organs was considered to be opposition by ethnic Russians (Oka 2009: 3). Considering that ethnic Kazakhs make up under half of the population, the ruling elite gave priority to the consolidation of the political community and creating Kazakh patriotism rather than to establishing democracy. Subsequently, the new constitution in 1993 defined the state as a 'self-determined Kazakh nation' (Alexandrov 1999: 99).

Ethnic diversity in liberal democracies

The basis of political systems or states is usually the 'nation', a somewhat contentious and ambiguous concept that has been analysed in greater detail in previous chapters. In modern

European political theory, the constitutional concept of a sovereign nation has always been trapped between *ethos* and *demos*. In the political sense, the nation is the entity living in the state's territory and under its administrative control. This conflicts with the ethnic concept of nation, which reflects the differences and often tensions between different ethnic groups living in a state's territory (Přibáň 2004: 417). Ethnic minorities hereby often claim a nationality that is somewhat different from that of the core ethnic group in the state (Gallagher 2005: 32).

In general, there are different ways in which states can respond to ethnic diversity. Eide (2004: 60) broadly categorised these approaches as a) assimilation and integration or b) separation and exclusion. The former is normally associated with liberal democracies, the latter with authoritarian regimes. Ideally, the liberal democratic state should make no distinction between different ethnic groups, seeking to encompass all of them in the form of a common civil society whereby all members should share sovereignty as citizens eligible to vote and be represented in government. In addition, liberal democracies should protect ethnic minorities either through positive minority rights and/or anti-discriminatory measures. The accommodation of ethnic diversity thus becomes an intrinsic part of the modern liberal-democratic reality (Přibáň 2004: 418–419). However, as Riggs (1995) points out, democratic government in itself does not automatically resolve ethnic conflicts, and liberal democracies, for various reasons, do not or cannot always adhere to the norms they aspire to, as will be illustrated by the following examples.

Common strategies of ethnic policy in liberal democracies include seeking to assimilate minority groups by non-coercive means. An easy way to accommodate the concerns and issues of ethnic minorities is to empower them within the established political system and for example permit political organisation thus paving the way for legislative representation. The success of ethnic minorities hereby depends to some degree on the political and electoral system. Political systems based on proportional representation (PR) usually make it easier for ethnic minorities to gain representation than those where only one candidate per district is elected (for example First Past the Post in UK national elections), especially if an ethnic minority is dispersed. Thus ethnic minorities have a greater chance of access to political power as part of a governing coalition in PR systems than in majoritarian systems (Koslowski 1994: 392).

Political representation, however, is a political right based on citizenship, and many liberal-democratic states employ citizenship laws that can lead to exclusion of ethnic minorities from political rights and political representation. In general, we need to distinguish between countries employing citizenship laws based on the principles of *jus sanguinis* (ancestral lineage) and those using the principle of *jus soli* (birthplace). Ireland and the UK are often cited as examples of countries using the principle of *jus soli* for both ascription of citizenship and naturalisation. On the European continent, as Koslowski (1994: 371) points out, *jus sanguinis* became the norm for ascription, although the rules governing naturalisation tended to vary greatly. Germany used to be a prime example of a liberal democracy (after 1949) where the principle of *jus sanguinis* (in place since 1913) governed both ascription of citizenship and naturalisation leading to the existence of a) an understanding of nationhood as an ethno-cultural concept and b) a growing number of permanent resident aliens without political citizenship rights. Since *jus sanguinis* also applied to naturalisation, 'alien' status was in effect hereditary, for example the majority of the children of Turkish migrant workers born in Germany were unable to acquire German citizenship. Thus the German citizenship laws challenged the liberal-democratic framework of the state by denying political rights to a considerable ethnic minority despite the fact that many of Germany's 'aliens' belong now to the third generation born in Germany. As Radtke (1997: 253) explains, without political rights, the migrant workers (and their children) needed (German) advocates and became an enduring topic of discourse for the majority, who often labelled migrants as either illegitimate participants in the social welfare system or as victims of discrimination.

After 1992, Germany (and other EU member states based on *jus sanguinis*) were themselves challenged by the new EU citizenship which is, in the case of local and European Parliament elections, based on *jus soli*, that is every EU citizen can vote for local and European elections in their EU country of residence, even if they are 'aliens' in that country and cannot vote there in national elections. In this changing European political climate, with its encroachment on national sovereignty and changing understanding of the role of the nation-state (at least within the EU), it is perhaps not surprising that since the early 1990s, there has been a general move towards some form of *jus soli* in many European countries. In Germany, as pointed out above, the existence of large numbers of permanent aliens led to demands for easier access to citizenship. As *The New York Times* (1997) stated, one in five babies born in Germany were 'foreign'. Thus, naturalisation policies were revised through the amended Nationality Act (2000, further amended in 2007) and the Immigration Act (2005). Now children born in Germany to foreign parents may acquire German citizenship if certain conditions are met, although they have to decide between the ages of 18 and 23 if they wish to retain German nationality or the nationality of their parents. Furthermore, foreigners have now the right to become naturalised after eight years of habitual residence (15 years previously) if they meet certain conditions including adequate knowledge of the German language.

On the other hand, however, some countries such as France have moved in the opposite direction. In France, ascription used to be based on *jus sanguinis*, while *jus soli* was used extensively in naturalisation, thus reflecting a more state-centred and assimilationist national self-understanding than in ethno-cultural Germany (Brubaker 1996: 169). Thus, a person born in France to foreign parents, used to acquire French citizenship by virtue of place of birth. However, by the 1980s, this policy led to the existence of large immigrant communities, generating a rightist campaign for more restrictive naturalisation laws. In 1993, the French government pushed through a bill that eliminated the automatic extension of French citizenship and nationality to children of foreigners once they reach the age of 18. Under the new legislation, children of foreigners have to apply for French citizenship between the ages of 16 and 21.

Citizenship policies are not the only form of disenfranchisement in liberal democracies, which can also occur through indirect measures including cumbersome electoral registration, disproportionate electoral districts (a feature of pre-1972 Northern Ireland), poll taxes or literary tests as in the southern states of the USA prior to 1965, which can make it difficult or near impossible for certain groups to vote or gain representation. Such indirect techniques can maintain a de facto dominant ethnicity and discrimination against ethnic minorities or other foreigners. Both post-communist Latvia and Estonia have been criticised for denying citizenship and thus political rights to ethnic Russians who have failed to pass language tests or other bureaucratic hurdles (Jurado in Kaufmann and Haklai 2008: 759–760).

Ethnic movements

On the other hand, because democracy permits freedom of speech and association, it also enables discontented people including ethnic minorities to organise themselves and lobby their interests. Thus ethnic movements tend to flourish in democracies, especially in new democracies where ethnic minorities have, for the first time, the opportunity to express their demands. Ethnic movements also have opportunities in weak authoritarian regimes, where the governing elite is unable to handle or suppress demands. In addition, ethnic movements tend to be especially active among ethnic groups living in enclaves (territorially concentrated). Here, the main aim of ethnic movements is often to achieve a degree of autonomy or self-determination.

An example is the German speaking South Tyrol, which became part of Italy after the First World War. Since 1945, the German minority in South Tyrol has often been cited as one of the most successful forms of ethnic mobilisation, in the form of the *Südtiroler Volkspartei* (SVP, South Tyrolean People's Party). The SVP represented the German minority's fight against the enforced 'Italianisation' of the region and for the protection of German ethnic minority rights (although the German 'minority' continued to constitute around two thirds of the population in South Tyrol after 1945). As Panayi (2000: 161) points out, the German population of South Tyrol became completely politicised in the process, and the SVP regularly took over 90% of the German vote. A final agreement with the Italian government was signed in 1992 resulting in the autonomy of the region, an exemplary success for a regional ethnic movement in Europe, which managed to safeguard its main aims (self-determination and language protection for the German ethnic group). Other examples of autonomy, whereby the ethnic group can administer its own domestic affairs, include for example the Swedish-speaking Åland islands in Finland, Greenland (granted autonomy by Denmark in 1979), and a number of regions in Spain including the Basque and Catalan regions. Here again, we note the importance of ethno-nationalist political parties and movements in achieving ethnic minority rights.

New democracies and ethnic policy

So far, we have looked largely at established liberal democracies in Western Europe. There is, however, also a host of new democracies, which have emerged out of authoritarian regimes. Therefore, we shall now shift focus toward former Eastern and Central European communist countries. It is often argued that transitional regimes or newly democratised regimes, especially in multi-ethnic countries, are particularly prone to ethnic tensions as ethnic groups redefine their identity in political terms thereby challenging the existing elites and processes. Ethnonationalist movements played an important role in the break-up of communism and the former USSR. After 1985, there were protests in almost every Soviet Republic against official policies of Russification including the suppression of local languages and cultures (Inder Singh 2001: 33). Perestroika allowed for the expression of strong nationalist pressures, with some ethno-national groups such as Latvians, Lithuanians, Estonians or Georgians calling for independence. Ukrainian nationalism, for example, developed in stages during and since the Stalin era. In 1980 a Ukrainian Patriotic Movement was founded, and by 1989 around 30,000 national and cultural organisations had developed, many of them calling for independence (Panayi 2000: 165), which was achieved in 1991. In the three Baltic States, to give another example, popular ethno-nationalist movements and parties, such as the Estonian National Front or the Latvian Popular Front, played an equally important role in achieving independence.

The emerging democratic systems in the former European communist bloc found themselves under pressure to condemn the abandoned past, codify future aims and principles and commit the nation and the new constitutional institutions to these principles (Přibáň 2004: 409). Part of this transitional process involved the rebuilding of political identities and civil society, which was necessarily comprised of these new principles as well as older civil and ethnic traditions. An important part of the constitution-making processes and rebuilding of political identity was the rebuilding of national identity in the sense of a cultural and ethnic identity, much of which had previously been manipulated or suppressed by the communist regimes. Thus, in East-Central Europe, we often find very close links between civil and ethnic politics.

For instance the new Hungarian constitution of 1989, although based internally on a civic concept of nationhood, also contains an article (Article 6/3) which makes a constitutional commitment to ethnic Hungarians living outside of Hungary's borders (causing negative reactions from surrounding states with large Hungarian minorities). In addition, in 1993, Hungary adopted new citizenship legislation based on the principles of *jus sanguinis* meaning that the main prerequisite for the acquisition of Hungarian citizenship would be Hungarian descent (although political rights were at the same time also guaranteed to ethnic minorities living in Hungary). The 'ethnic card' was played again under Prime Minister Viktor Orbán (1998–2002), when ethnic Hungarians living outside Hungary were granted special access to Hungary's social welfare. Originally intended to be a political symbol of the cohesion of ethnic Hungarians and their identification with the Hungarian state, the legislation was widely criticised by the EU and neighbouring countries due to its alleged inherent ethno-national discrimination and potential violation of other states' sovereignty. Nevertheless, the legislation came into force in 2002, albeit in slightly modified and limited form. Afterwards, the conservative party led by Orbán (after 2002 in the opposition) continued to campaign for granting Hungarian citizenship to ethnic Hungarians in neighbouring countries, although a referendum on this failed in 2004. As this example shows, Hungary's transition to liberal-democracy remains influenced by ethnic concepts of the nation (Přibáň 2004: 424).

We have already discussed the role of ethnic movements and parties in securing or pressing for minority ethnic rights. A prime example of this in the new democracies of Eastern Europe would be the Slovak parties that emerged after the 1989 Revolution in the former Czechoslovakia, demanding Slovak autonomy or even independence. The most prominent, the Movement for a Democratic Slovakia (MDS) negotiated the so-called 'Velvet Divorce' which came into effect in 1993. Shortly after the separation into the Czech Republic and Slovakia, both states drafted new constitutions, which displayed a different understanding of 'the nation'. In Slovakia, the constitution addressed primarily the ethnic Slovaks thus opening opportunities for ethnic marginalisation, which did occur under Prime Minister Vladimír Mečiar (1994–1998), leader of the HZDS (Movement for a Democratic Slovakia), who used historical resentment and recent fears of Hungarian nationalism to isolate the Hungarian minority in Slovakia. Mečiar, whose party governed together with the extreme nationalists (the SNS) and the 'reds' (the extreme left Association of Workers of Slovakia), pursued a two-track ethnic minority policy. On the one hand they successfully negotiated reconciliation with Hungary, while internally a series of anti-Hungarian measures were passed (Fowkes 2002: 125). It was only after 1998, that a more balanced legislation protecting ethnic minorities was implemented based on the special section of the Slovak constitution which protects ethnic and minority rights. The example shows how Mečiar used the 'ethnic card' to address populist fears of Hungarian nationalism as part of a much bigger political agenda and political power struggles in Slovakia (Přibáň 2004: 426).

The Czech Constitution of 1992 on the other hand largely ignores ethnic diversity and defines nationhood almost exclusively in terms of citizenship and civil society while also including a section on the protection of ethnic and minority rights. It has been argued that this approach in itself was an 'ethnic card', played in view of the accession negotiations with the EU, which would have been hindered by ethnic conflict and ethno-national tensions.

This civic interpretation of nation has however not prevented local discrimination against the Roma minority in the 1990s, which was highlighted by the so-called 'Bratinka report' in 1997, which identified anti-Romani discrimination as a crucial problem in the Czech Republic (Vermeersch 2006: 83). This illustrates that the adoption of a civic concept of nationhood does not necessarily prevent discriminatory policies, while on the other hand the adoption of an ethnic concept of nationhood does not rule out a cooperative and inclusive ethnic policy as in the case of Slovakia after 1998 (Přibáň 2004: 428). Nevertheless, Miller, Grodeland and Koshechkina (2001: 181) note that general inter-ethnic alienation was comparatively high in both the Czech Republic and Slovakia, with over 90 per cent of the population exhibiting unfavourable feelings towards the Roma.

As a final point, before we move on to authoritarian regimes, it must be noted that in some cases, where the transition to democracy has mobilised marginalised ethnic communities to pursue a more equitable treatment, this has led to the implementation of reactive policies by the established elites or more privileged communities. A frequent reaction is one of a turn toward neo-traditionalist or ultra-nationalist ideas and parties, sometimes aiming to subordinate minority communities. Explicit ethnic nationalism tends to persist mostly among far-right and ultra-nationalist parties who use the 'ethnic card' in the form of ethno-nationalist ideas largely to appeal to populist fears of immigration and multiculturalism. In Bulgaria, the far right Ataka (Attack) party has risen in popularity since 2005 (with the slogan 'Bulgaria back to the Bulgarians'), while in Romania, the Greater Romania Party has attracted many Romanian voters with its anti-minority slogans, attacking ethnic Hungarians, Roma, Jews and others. In Hungary, the far right Movement for a Better Hungary came in third in the European elections of 2009, and in Slovakia, the Slovak National Party joined the ruling government in 2006.

Such a nationalist-rightist reaction, however, is by no means restricted to new democracies. We have already noted the role of rightist campaigners in changing citizenship laws in France from inclusive naturalisation to more exclusive policies. Similar rightist parties exist for example in the UK and Germany, lobbying for example for stricter immigration controls. In the Netherlands, the Dutch Freedom Party with its anti-immigration policy was the second strongest party there in the 2009 European elections and in the UK, the British National Party won its first ever seat in the European parliament in the same election. Thus we witness a general rise of rightist nationalist parties across Europe, which is of course linked to the prevailing economic crisis. Rightist parties often use the 'ethnic card' in the form of arguments of 'ethnic minority threat to scarce economic resources' to mobilise voters, especially during times of economic downturn and in new democracies with weakly developed market economies. Stefanovic (2008: 1214) suggests that the success of the transition to democracy may be helped considerably by the development and maintenance of efficient welfare systems which might reduce the electoral appeal of authoritarian ultra-nationalists.

Conclusion

This chapter has analysed some aspects of ethnic policy in liberal-democratic and authoritarian systems. We have seen that on the one hand, liberal democracy entails the policies of compromise and negotiation and thus in theory a reconciliation of ethnic and state claims (Brown 1996: 309). However, many liberal democracies operate ethnic policies that either directly or indirectly promote exclusivity. We must hereby distinguish between politically and ethnically exclusionary policies. Liberal democracies, especially majoritarian systems or those operating citizenship systems based on *jus sanguinis*, often produce more ethnically exclusive societies than some semi-authoritarian regimes. In addition, the 'ethnic card' is popular with both nationalist and liberal democratic elites and, as we have seen, is used widely in the domestic sphere, for example during election campaigns, and within the international context in terms of foreign policy with regard to other states and indeed international organisations.

Further reading

Cordell, K. (1999) *Ethnicity and Democratisation in the New Europe*, London, New York: Routledge.

Daftary, F. and Troebst, S. (eds) (2005) *Radical Ethnic Movements in Contemporary Europe*, Oxford, New York: Berghahn Books.

Fowkes, B. (2002) *Ethnicity and Ethnic Conflict in the Post-Communist World*, Basingstoke: Palgrave.

Guibernau, M. and Rex, J. (eds) (1997) *The Ethnicity Reader*, Oxford, Malden: Polity Press.

Hutcheson, D. S. and Korosteleva, E. A. (eds) (2006) *The Quality of Democracy in Post-Communist Europe*, London, New York: Routledge.

Inder Singh, A. (2001) *Democracy, Ethnic Diversity, and Security in Post-Communist Europe*, Westport: Praeger.

Panayi, P. (2000) *An Ethnic History of Europe since 1945*, Harlow: Pearson Education Ltd.

References

Alexandrov, M. (1999) *Uneasy Alliance: Relations between Russia and Kazakhstan in the Post-Soviet Era, 1992–1997*, Westport: Greenwood Press.

Brill Olcott, M. (2002) *Kazakhstan: Unfulfilled Promise*, Washington: Carnegie Endowment for International Peace.

Brown, D. (1996) Ethnicity, Nationalism and Democracy in South-East Asia. In: Hutchinson, J. and Smith, A. D. (eds) *Ethnicity*, Oxford, New York: Oxford University Press.

Brubaker, R. (1996) Civic and Ethnic Nations in France and Germany. In: Hutchinson, J. and Smith, A. D. (eds) *Ethnicity*, Oxford, New York: Oxford University Press.

Eide, A. (2004) The Role of the United Nations Working Group on Minorities. In: Council of Europe Publishing (ed.), *Mechanisms for the Implementation of Minority Rights*, Strasbourg: Council of Europe.

Farouk-Slugett, M. and Slugett, P. (1987) *Iraq since 1958: From Revolution to Dictatorship*, London: Kegan Paul International.

Fowkes, B. (2002) *Ethnicity and Ethnic Conflict in the Post-Communist World*, Basingstoke: Palgrave.

Gallagher, T. (2005) Conflicts between East European States and Minorities in an Age of Democracy. In: Daftary, F. and Troebst, S. (eds), *Radical Ethnic Movements in Contemporary Europe*, Oxford, New York: Berghahn Books.

Inder Singh, A. (2001) *Democracy, Ethnic Diversity, and Security in Post-Communist Europe*, Westport: Praeger.

Kaufmann, E. and Haklai, O. (2008) Dominant Ethnicity: From Minority to Majority, *Nations and Nationalism*, 14(4): 743–767.

Koslowski, R. (1994) Intra-EU Migration, Citizenship and Political Union, *JCMS: Journal of Common Market Studies*, 32(3): 369–402.

Kubicek, P. (1998) Authoritarianism in Central Asia: Curse or Cure? *Third World Quarterly*, 19(1): 29–43.

Miller, W. L., Grodeland, A. B. and Koshechkina, T. Y. (2001) *A Culture of Corruption. Coping with Government in Post-Communist Europe*, Budapest, New York: CEU Press.

Oka, N. (2009) Ethnicity and Elections under Authoritarianism: The Case of Kazakhstan, IDE Discussion Paper No. 194.

Panayi, P. (2000) *An Ethnic History of Europe since 1945*, Harlow: Pearson Education Ltd.

Přibáň, J. (2004) Reconstituting Paradise Lost: Temporality, Civility, and Ethnicity in Post-Communist Constitution-Making, *Law & Society Review*, 38(3): 407–432.

Radtke, F.-O. (1997) Multiculturalism in Welfare States: The Case of Germany. In: Guibernau, M. and Rex, J. (eds), *The Ethnicity Reader*, Oxford, Malden: Polity Press.

Riggs, F. W. (1995) Ethnonational Rebellions and Viable Constitutionalism, *International Science Review*, 16(4): 375–404.

Rothchild, D. (2007) Executive Power-sharing Systems: Conflict Management and Conflict Escalation? In: Guttieri, K. and Piombo, J. (eds), *Interim Governments: Institutional Bridges to Peace and Democracy?* Washington: United States Institute of Peace Press.

Roudik, P. (2007) *The History of the Central Asian Republics*, Westport: Greenwood Press.

Schatz, E. (2005) Reconceptualizing Clans: Kinship Networks and Statehood in Kazakhstan, *Nationalities Papers*, 33(2): 231–254.

Stefanovic, D. (2008) The Path to Weimar Serbia? Explaining the Resurgence of the Serbian Far Right after the Fall of Milosevic, *Ethnic and Racial Studies*, 31(7): 1195–1221.

The New York Times (1997) Redefining German Citizenship, 10 April; http://www.nytimes.com/1997/04/10/opinion/redefining-german-citizenship.html.

Vermeersch, P. (2006) *The Romani Movement: Minority Policy and Ethnic Mobilization in Contemporary Central Europe*, Oxford, New York: Berghahn Books.

Way, L. A. (2006) The Sources and Dynamics of Competitive Authoritarianism in the Ukraine. In: Hutcheson, D. S. and Korosteleva, E. A. (eds), *The Quality of Democracy in Post-Communist Europe*, London, New York: Routledge.

PART IV

26

THE KURDS

A nation divided, a nation without a state

Bill Park

Introduction

The Kurds are frequently referred to as the world's largest contiguously located ethno-linguistic or cultural group without a state of their own. They also constitute the fourth largest ethnic group of the Middle East region, after Arabs, Persians and Turks. Given the absence of reliable, up-to-date and ethnically based censuses in the four countries across which the majority of Kurds are dispersed – Turkey, Iraq, Iran and Syria – the size of the Kurdish population cannot be given with any precision. The Kurdish population of the four main countries of residence is usually put at around 30 million, around half of them living in Turkey, where they are reckoned to constitute around 20 per cent of its inhabitants. Kurds make up a similar percentage of Iraq's smaller population, whereas in Iran and Syria the Kurdish population is usually put at 10 per cent or less. There are also small Kurdish populations in Armenia, Georgia, Russia and Lebanon, many of them descended from Kurds fleeing Turkish and Persian oppression during the twentieth century. Assimilation and inter-marriage, and the emergence of significant Kurdish diasporas – notably in western Europe, where perhaps a million and a half Kurds reside, half of them in Germany – adds to the imprecision.

Although the Ottoman rulers recognised the distinctiveness of their usually semi-autonomous Kurdish subjects and of a place they happily referred to as 'Kurdistan', the breakup of what remained of the Ottoman Empire at the end of the First World War did not give birth to a Kurdish state. In part this was because Kurdish national identity was not at the time deemed sufficiently developed or unified (Gunter 2007: Jwaideh 2006), but it also did not accord with the interests of the main imperial powers in the region, the UK and France (McDowall 1997: 115–146). Kurdish self-determination has since been fiercely opposed by those states that did emerge from the post-Ottoman map-redrawing exercise and that embarked on determined nation- and state-building projects – Turkey, Iraq and Syria – that provoked a greater Kurdish consciousness. Iran has been no less determined in its state-building, and although generally more inclusive of its myriad non-Persian minorities, it has also stimulated Kurdish identity politics (Stansfield 2014; Vali 2014). Primarily for reasons of *realpolitik*, external powers have generally been unwilling to seriously revisit the Kurds' lack of a homeland of their own. In any case, some Kurds have shown little interest in challenging the existing political arrangements – for example, up to half of the votes in Turkey's predominantly Kurdish southeast go to the ruling Islamist Justice and Development Party (*Adalet ve Kalkınma Partisi* – AKP), rather than its ethnically based Kurdish electoral rivals (Satana 2012: 174–177).

Some observers stress the diffuse and heterogeneous nature of the Kurds as an ethnic group. Linguistically, Kurdish is related to Persian, but it is not a unified language. Of the two major Kurdish dialects, around three-quarters of all Kurds speak Kurmanji, which is found in Turkey, Syria, and the northernmost Kurdish areas of Iraq and Iran. Most Iraqi Kurds speak the other main dialect, Sorani, which is not invariably intelligible to Kurmanji speakers. Other dialects spoken by Kurds include Zazaki, Gorani and Kermanshahi (White 1995). Of course, many Kurds also speak the language of their host country and are thus bilingual, while some no longer speak Kurdish at all. This is partly a consequence of official restrictions on the use of Kurdish, but has also resulted from migration and assimilation. For example, it is estimated that around half of all Kurds in Turkey no longer inhabit the traditionally and predominantly Kurdish southeast of the country, but have migrated to towns and cities in Turkish-speaking areas of the country. It is believed that the largest concentration of ethnic Kurds anywhere – as many as three million people – is found in Istanbul (Saracoglu 2010). An additional consequence of their dispersal is that Kurdish is written in the Arabic script in Iraq and Syria, in the Persian script in Iran, and in the modern Turkish (Latin) script in Turkey. In religious terms too, although the majority of Kurds are Sunni Muslims, it is reckoned that about a quarter of Turkey's Kurds adhere to Alevism, a syncretic Sufi-inflected branch of Shia Islam (although not all Alevis regard themselves, and nor are they invariably regarded, as Muslims). Some of Turkey's Alevi Kurds might identify with the approximately one-fifth of the Turkish population that is Alevi, rather or in addition to stressing their Kurdish identity (White 2003). There are also Yazidi, Christian and Jewish Kurds – the majority of this latter group now constitute a 200,000 strong Israeli community of Kurdish Jews.

The region from which Kurds originate and in which they mostly reside – which henceforth we will call 'Kurdistan' – is land-locked and mostly characterised by deep valleys and high mountain ridges. Communication and interaction in such a terrain can be difficult, even today. This geography has contributed to the clan and tribal structure that has traditionally been a feature of Kurdish society (van Bruinessen 1992). For much of Kurdish history this geographical fragmentation and isolation has hindered modernity, and helped preserve a feudal social and economic order. That the Kurdish region is geographically located at the intersection of the Persian, Arab and Turkish worlds has meant that Kurdish tribes have often been recruited to defend the frontiers of a succession of political formations and empires – the Ottoman, and various Persian and Arab entities – against encroachment from neighbours. These experiences earned Kurds a warlike reputation, but also meant that Kurds were often pitted against each other on behalf of competing non-Kurdish powers. In more recent times, the creation of a map that failed to respect local Kurdish transit routes or tribal or ethnic networks has encouraged smuggling as an economic activity, rendering the region's borders porous. Added together, and whether fairly or not, these features of Kurdish life have generated a reputation for violence, feuding, lawlessness, and general ungovernability. Kurds have been seen as difficult to subordinate, and equally difficult to unite. Intra-Kurdish struggles such as the civil war fought in the mid-1990s between the two leading Iraqi Kurdish political parties (Bengio 2012: 211–215; Gunter 1996), or the tensions between Turkey's Kurdistan Workers' Party (PKK) and the state-recruited and funded 'village guards' (McDowall 1997: 421–424), or today's rivalry for the leadership of Kurdish nationalism between the feudally based and politically and socially conservative Massoud Barzani, President of the Kurdistan Regional Government (KRG), and Abdullah Öcalan, head of the secular and leftist Kurdistan

Communities Union (KCK), incorporating the PKK and its Syrian and Iranian affiliates, have all tended to reinforce this impression of disputatiousness.

A number of recent developments have combined to present the Kurds with new opportunities to advance the cause of self-determination, but also with new risks. These developments include: the emergence of the KRG after the 1991 expulsion of Iraqi forces from Kuwait, and its further institutionalisation in the wake of the US-led 2003 war to overthrow the Ba'athist regime in Baghdad; the factionalised and sectarian nature of Iraqi politics that developed in the wake of the 2003 invasion and that threatens the very survival of Iraq as a state; the threat to Syria's territorial integrity as a consequence of the civil war that broke out there in 2011 – not least through the establishment in 2013 of three self-governing Kurdish cantons in the north of the country, known as *Rojava*; the rise of Islamic State (IS) and the additional challenges it poses to the region's political and territorial arrangements, and the role Kurds have played in confronting it; and Turkish regional ambitions, its relationship with the KRG, and its attempts to address its domestic Kurdish travails. The remainder of this chapter will trace and analyse these developments, and explore the extent to which they have encouraged centrifugal and centripetal tendencies amongst the Kurds of the region. Might circumstances bring the Kurds, together or separately, around shared agendas of enhanced self-government, or autonomy? Or – again together or separately – might they move in parallel towards secession and even the aspiration to establish an encompassing pan-Kurdish state? Alternatively, will the shocks the region is currently undergoing offer new spoils and fractures which will serve only to accentuate their existing differences, and perhaps add some new ones? If so, what might that tell us about the state of Kurdish 'nationhood'?

The Kurdistan Regional Government of Iraq

Contrary to the 1920 Treaty of Sèvres, which had been signed by the Ottoman regime and which hinted at the possible establishment of a Kurdish state, the British as the mandated power annexed Mosul to what in 1932 became the otherwise primarily Arab independent state of Iraq (Tripp 2007: 30–74). Kurds had generally fought alongside Turks in the years preceding the establishment of the Turkish Republic, and the Republic's leaders had wanted the former Ottoman *miliyet* of Mosul to be incorporated into its territory, which would have meant that a large easy majority of Kurds would have been living within one set of state boundaries (Park 2005: 14–15). This might have had interesting implications for Turkey's subsequent evolution. Iraq's Kurds reacted in a variety of ways, either dispersing into the country's leftist movements, gravitating towards Kurdish nationalism, or remaining loyal to their tribes. One such tribal leader, Mullah Mustafa Barzani, launched a series of revolts, which ultimately obliged him and his followers to flee across the border into Iran (McDowall 1997: 290–295). Here his forces were instrumental in enabling Iranian Kurdish nationalists to proclaim the Kurdish Republic of Mahabad in 1946. This short-lived Republic benefitted from the weakness of the Iranian government and the Soviet presence in the country in the wake of the Second World War. However, with Moscow's withdrawal from Iran, Mahabad fell to Iranian troops within a year, and Barzani and his followers went into exile in the Soviet Union (Eagleton 1963).

When a military coup in 1958 led to the recognition of Kurdish national rights within Iraq, Barzani returned. Kurdish cooperation with Baghdad did not last long, and in 1961 another Kurdish revolt broke out. Barzani's aims included Kurdish autonomy, control over Kirkuk, that Kurdish be made an official language of Iraq, and a share of the country's oil revenues – aims which are almost exactly replicated by the KRG today. The leaders of the

1968 Ba'athist coup sought an end to the revolt, and in 1970 an agreement was signed which recognised Kurdish as an official language, offered a measure of autonomy, guaranteed Kurdish participation in Iraq's government, cultural rights, economic assistance, and a census in Kirkuk – again, not dissimilar to Erbil's current demands. Bad faith on both sides again led to a resumption of fighting, in which the Kurds received assistance from Iran and from Washington, which felt obliged to support the Shah and which was unhappy with the Ba'athist regime's tilt towards Moscow. However, in 1975, the Shah withdrew his support for the Kurds in return for a settlement of Iran's boundary with Iraq. Barzani again went into exile, this time in Iran (Yildiz 2007: 15–24), while in Iraq the regime ramped up its policy of the Arabisation of Kurdish areas and began the evacuation of Kurdish villages along the Turkish and Iranian borders.

The 1975 defeat also brought to a head tensions within the Iraqi Kurdish leadership, many of whom had opposed Barzani's uncompromising stance, associated him with nepotism and corruption, and resented his Machiavellian behaviour. Jalal Talabani established the Patriotic Union of Kurdistan (PUK), while a reconstituted Kurdish Democratic Party (KDP) emerged under the leadership of Mustafa Barzani's son, Massoud. With the outbreak of the Iran–Iraq war in 1980, these and other Kurdish groups were almost as inclined to fight each other as they were the forces of Saddam Hussein's regime, and it wasn't until 1986 that a Kurdish National Front was formed that unambiguously sided with Tehran against Baghdad (Sherzad 1992). A consequence was a resort to what could be regarded as genocidal behaviour on the part of the Ba'athist regime. This involved the use of chemical weapons on Halabja and elsewhere in Iraq's Kurdish-populated areas, and the wider 'Anfal' campaign in which entire villages were destroyed and their inhabitants killed. The campaign resulted in an estimated 180,000 Kurdish deaths and three thousand razed villages (Yildiz 2007: 25–33).

The emergence of the KRG

This experience has left a lasting effect on Iraq's Kurdish population and their attitude towards Baghdad, as became clear at the tail end of the US-led military expulsion of Iraqi forces from Kuwait in April 1991. Before the conflict was formally brought to an end, Kurdish forces rose up against the regime and captured most of the Kurdish-populated areas, including Kirkuk. However, the Iraqi army soon went on the counter-offensive, retaking most of the territories that had been briefly held by the *peshmerga*. Kurds feared retribution as punishment for their uprising and thousands fled towards the Turkish and Iranian borders. However, Turkey refused to open its borders or provide aid and shelter. Nor, in a rehearsal of its approach to the beleaguered Syrian Kurds of Kobane in 2014, would Ankara allow Kurds from Turkey to come to their aid. To avoid a looming humanitarian disaster, a no-fly zone north of the 36th parallel was imposed by US, UK and French aircraft operating out of the NATO air base at Incirlik in Turkey. It enabled the refugees to return to their home towns and villages, where they could receive relief provisions under 'Operation Provide Comfort (OPC)'. 'OPC' averted a humanitarian disaster (Yildiz 2007: 34–43), but skirmishes between Kurdish and Iraqi government forces broke out as talks between the Kurds and Baghdad on the future relationship between them stalled. Saddam's surprising and somewhat precipitate response to a warning from the allied coalition to avoid the excessive use of force was to withdraw both his military and the civil administration from the three predominantly Kurdish governorates. Baghdad also imposed a severe economic embargo on the Kurdish region. Iraq's Kurds, led primarily by the two main parties in the region, the KDP and the PUK, had little alternative but to establish their own rudimentary administration, which in

1992 became the KRG. It has evolved to become the closest Kurds have ever been to having a state of their own, and it was born under the cover of international protection (Stansfield 2003; Natali 2010).

Even so, it was not an auspicious start. To overcome the effects of Baghdad's embargo, and of UN sanctions that applied to Iraq in its entirety, the KRG initially relied primarily on smuggling and extortion from traders at border crossing posts (most of whom crossed in from Turkey, and were obliged to pay into the KDP's coffers). In time, UN and NGO relief programmes – although not reconstruction and capacity-building efforts, which would have suggested a violation of Iraq's sovereignty – and agreements struck with neighbouring countries such as Turkey, Iran, and Syria, and with other parts of Iraq, enabled the restoration of some kind of functioning, though largely informal, economic order. Matters improved still further after the 1996 introduction of the Oil-for-Food Programme, although this was still aimed at relief rather than economic reconstruction and development. Although many Kurds benefitted, and continued to do so after Saddam's overthrow, the self-enrichment of the Iraqi Kurdish elite and the extreme inequalities that characterise the KRG today can be traced back to this period of external dependency.

In May 1992 elections were held for a Kurdish National Assembly, which produced a roughly equal vote tally for the KDP and PUK, who then went on to establish a power-sharing government on a 50:50 basis. In fact, the two parties functioned as two distinct administrative and political entities, based on patronage and nepotism, such that it cannot be said that Iraqi Kurdistan enjoyed a single unified government. Indeed, the two parties, each with their own *peshmerga* units, fought a civil war from 1994 until a peace deal was brokered by the USA in 1998, in part over the distribution of the spoils from various rackets and aid programmes. During this conflict, Iran aligned itself with the PUK while in 1996 the KDP went so far as to recruit the services of the Iraqi army to help in the expulsion of PUK-controlled *peshmerga* units from Erbil, the seat of the KRG's nominal government. As a reminder of the prior appeal of religion over ethnicity for some Kurds, Islamic groups, and especially the Islamic Movement of Kurdistan (IMK), also engaged in the fighting and for a time controlled its own slice of territory. Once the conflict was brought to an end, the KDP and PUK reverted to positions very close to those they had initially occupied, running two administrations, the KDP from Erbil and the PUK from Suleymaniya.

The civil war reinforced the image of the Kurds as chronically fragmented and prone to tribalised feuding in pursuit of short-term tactical and personal gains. Even the no-fly-zone and the opportunity it afforded for greater self-determination, which operated until the 2003 US-led invasion of Iraq, could not protect the Kurdish leaderships from the pursuit of their own personal interests and rivalries. In fact, there is little reason to doubt that the Iraqi Kurdish leadership generally aspired to self-government and even independence from Iraq, but the political and social structures of the region and squabbles over the distribution of such funds as were available resulted in internecine feuding rather than a unified confrontation with Baghdad.

In any case, the Kurdish leadership appreciated that, given the opposition of Baghdad, Ankara, Tehran and Washington to the idea of an independent Kurdistan, and in light of its landlocked geography, independence was not yet an option that could be realistically entertained. In fact, the Kurdish leadership had participated, if unenthusiastically, in the US-sponsored search for an eventual alternative to the Ba'athist regime via the Iraqi National Council. This period also saw regular Turkish military interventions into Iraqi Kurdistan as part of Ankara's ongoing battle with the PKK, many of whose fighters used the inaccessible Qandil Mountains in Iraqi Kurdistan as their rear base. KRG *peshmerga* – and especially those of the KDP – frequently cooperated with the Turkish troops (Robins 2003: 312–342). For Iraq's Kurdish leadership, the PKK offered an alternative repository for Kurdish nationalist sympathies, a challenge to their political and economic control, and posed a threat of further destabilisation. Even so, this period saw the beginnings of linguistic, cultural, institutional and political 'Kurdification' and 'de-Arabisation' of the region, a transformation that progressively gained momentum. Kurdistan was evolving into 'the other Iraq', as its actual and perceived separateness from Baghdad grew, and its relative tranquility and political and economic progress contrasted starkly with Arab Iraq's worsening disorder.

With the adoption of a new US-sponsored constitution in 2005, the KRG's autonomy also acquired a more formal sanction. Article 117 of the constitution recognised the KRG as a distinct entity in an Iraqi federal political system. It was granted control over its own security forces, the right to develop new energy fields within its territory, and the right to enact its own legislation where this did not impact on Iraq's foreign policy or financial authority. It was also entitled to 17 per cent of the annual federal budget, although various clauses and areas of dispute have in practice reduced this to something more like 13 per cent. In any case, foreign aid now expanded massively, and although the KRG did not receive such a big share as before the invasion, it was nevertheless now awash with money for infrastructure and development projects of all kinds. The KRG was beginning to look more and more like a 'normal' state. It drafted a new constitution, has a parliament, government, flag, national anthem, police and border forces of its own. It conducts what amounts to a foreign policy of its own, and introduced notions of rights, freedoms and good governance. In 2006 the KDP and PUK administrations merged into a unified government structure – although power was still shared on a roughly 50:50 basis and the two parties retained control over their own patronage networks, economic resources and *peshmerga* units. Even so, the new electoral laws in the KR produced in 2006 a Kurdish National Assembly (KNA) consisting of 14 political parties (Danilovich 2014). Again, as in 1991, in the aftermath of the 2003 invasion the Kurdistan region found itself being nudged towards greater self-governance as a consequence of external intervention.

The KRG and Baghdad

Even so, and not least due to the US presence in and tutelage over Iraq, the Kurds were also significant participants in Iraq's central government. KDP and PUK nominated candidates constituted the major elements in one unified Kurdistani List in the 2005 national elections. They also provided the Iraqi president (in the form of the PUK leader Jalal Talabani), the foreign minister, a deputy prime minister and a number of other official posts in the federal government. In the absence of alternatives and so long as Iraq functioned to Kurdish satisfaction, the Iraqi Kurdish leadership would not bid for independence. However, it soon became clear that, post the 2003 invasion, the only part of Iraq that did function was the Kurdistan region. As Arab Iraq descended into an increasingly violent sectarian polarisation and resistance to the coalition presence, Iraqi Kurdistan stood out by virtue of its stability, economic advancement, and relatively progressive political and social life.

Not only was Iraq descending into chaos, but Baghdad and Erbil also proved incapable of settling the differences between them. Chief of these involved Kurdish claims to additional territories where there were – or had been, before the Arabisation policies of the Ba'athist regime – significant numbers of Kurdish inhabitants. Much of this debate centred on the city and oil-rich governorate of Kirkuk, sometimes referred to by Iraqi Kurds as their 'Jerusalem'. Article 140 of the new Iraqi constitution provided for a resettlement of Arabs back to their regions of origin and a resettlement of Kurds who had been expelled from the disputed territories, to be followed by a census and referendum to determine the final status of these territories. Although some Arabs subsequently left and many Kurds returned, many of these disputed areas remain demographically complex, and the subject of claims from other groups, notably a substantial Turkmen community that was vociferously championed by Ankara. Baghdad's opposition to the KRG's claims has been unwavering, and although Kurdish political control over many of the disputed areas, including Kirkuk, has been considerable, Erbil has not been in a position to organise a census or referendum in the absence of Baghdad's cooperation, and has perhaps been reluctant to do so in any case given the uncertain outcome in some areas (International Crisis Group Middle East Report 103, 2011).

In any case, the situation on the ground was rendered more complex still by the events triggered by the rise of the *jihadist* IS. An IS advance on Mosul in June 2014 forced the flight of the Iraqi army and generated a large-scale refugee problem throughout northern Iraq as a consequence – including the flight of a million or more displaced persons to Iraqi Kurdistan, most of them Arabs. This number has been augmented by the quarter of a million Syrian refugees – mostly of Kurdish ethnicity – that have also sought shelter in Iraqi Kurdistan. The Kurdish *peshmerga* immediately took control of the territories vacated by the Iraqi army, and thereby expanded their area of control by up to 40 per cent. Immediately after Mosul's fall, Barzani called for preparations to be put in train for a referendum on the Kurdistan region's independence, and declared that with the Kurdish takeover there was no longer any need to negotiate the status of the disputed territories. This was a stark demonstration of Kurdish aspirations, or at least those of the KDP leadership, but Barzani was soon overtaken by events (Hiltermann 2014). The Kurds almost immediately lost much of their newly acquired territory to another IS advance, and were obliged to enter into an uneasy cooperation with the Iraqi army and Shia militias in a joint attempt to push back the IS presence. The USA and its western allies also embarked on a prolonged bombing campaign aimed at the eventual destruction of IS, and began training and arming Kurdish as well as Iraqi federal forces. IS advances also helped trigger a change of government in Baghdad, involving the ousting of the uncompromising Prime Minister Nuri al-Maliki and his replacement by a more accommodating 'government of national unity' – in which again there was a senior and substantial Kurdish presence – led by Haider al-Abadi. However, none of this resolved either the status of the disputed territories or the direction that Iraqi Kurdish self-determination might take.

The other major issue that contributed to the tension between Erbil and Baghdad involved the right of the Kurds to develop and market the energy resources found within the KRG's territory. Erbil insists that it has the constitutional right to initiate the development of new fields within the areas it controls, and has signed Production Sharing Contracts (PSCs) with a large number of energy companies, including the US oil giants ExxonMobil and Chevron. Some estimates suggest that the Kurdish north possesses as much as a quarter of Iraq's total oil reserves, which would make the KRG equivalent to the world's tenth most oil-rich country, roughly on a par with Nigeria or Libya. There are too substantial quantities of gas. This would comfortably provide sufficient income to enable independence. The problem is how to market it in the face of Baghdad's opposition. The KRG was already trucking small supplies of oil to Iran and Turkey when, in early 2014, it began exporting oil to the Turkish port of Ceyhan via a newly constructed pipeline which joined the existing and Baghdad-owned pipeline on the Turkish border. Partly for this reason, Baghdad withheld the 17 per cent of the national budget due to Erbil, which made the Kurds still more determined to achieve self-sufficiency. The oil was difficult to market due to Baghdad's threat of legal action and US opposition to the trade. In any case, the Turkish authorities abided by the understanding that only 17 per cent of the proceeds were due to Erbil, and deposited the remainder in a Turkish bank pending an energy agreement between Erbil and Baghdad (Park 2014: 22–31). This issue too was soon overtaken by the events described above, as the new government in Baghdad and the Kurdish authorities sought to resolve their differences in a more constructive fashion.

Turkey's Kurdish problem, and the Kurds' Turkish problem

In general terms, the problem for Iraq's Kurds has been their incorporation into a primarily Arab state. The majority population has not denied the existence of the Kurds, but Arab nationalist ideology and the country's centralising and authoritarian instincts have obstructed Baghdad's capacity or willingness to embrace the Kurds as no less Iraqi than the country's Arab citizens. Furthermore, in Iraq the Kurdish flame has been kept alive by traditional leadership structures rooted in a fairly unchanged – at least until very recently – feudal and clan-based society. This contrasts significantly with the experiences of Turkey's Kurdish population. The Turkish Republic was established in 1923 out of the ruins of the Ottoman Empire and was recognised by the Treaty of Lausanne through the efforts of Kemal Ataturk and his followers. Unlike the Treaty of Sèvres, no mention was made of the Kurds in Lausanne, who were not even allowed to send a delegation to the talks. Only non-Muslim groups – Greeks, Armenians, and Jews – were defined as minorities in the new Turkish state, which remains the case to this day. Within a few years and especially in the wake of a Kurdish revolt in 1925, it soon became evident that the new republic was to be defined by its Turkishness and characterised by an intense Turkish nationalism, such that not only the Kurdish language but even Kurdish ethnic distinctiveness was denied. Official policy was to regard the Kurds as 'mountain Turks' who, through their geographical isolation, had forgotten how to speak Turkish properly. The Kurdish language was banned, as were Kurdish first names, place names, and any reference to 'Kurdistan' – a term which, under Ottoman rule, had been in normal usage (McDowall 1997: 184–213, 395–417; Natali 2005: 70–116).

Unsurprisingly, the republic's history has been punctuated by Kurdish revolts, persistent unrest, and alienation. The first major uprising was led by Sheik Said in 1925, which led to his execution and that of 52 of his followers, the deaths of thousands of Kurds, and the destruction of hundreds of villages. Another revolt, centring on Mount Ararat in 1929, led to even fiercer reprisals by the Turkish state. A law was passed which decriminalised the murder of Kurds by state officials. The Kurdish city of Dersim – now called Tunceli – was earmarked for total evacuation. In the revolt that ensued in 1932 and that was not quelled until 1938, the city was bombed from the air. In an echo of the fate of Armenians during the First World War, millions of Kurds were force-marched westwards and settled in primarily Turkish-inhabited areas. Turkish speakers – often from the Balkans, Caucasus or Central Asia – were settled in traditionally Kurdish-inhabited locations, just as Kurds had replaced Armenians in much of eastern Anatolia just a couple of decades earlier. Martial law remained in place in Dersim until 1946; indeed, the entire region east of the Euphrates was declared out-of-bounds to foreigners until 1965.

The devastation in the region, combined with its economic backwardness and neglect, also caused millions of Kurds to move either into nearby but not always predominantly Kurdish cities, such as Gaziantep and Malatya, or further afield. This economic migration has continued ever since, intensified by Turkey's economic dynamism and rapid urbanisation of the past few decades, such that Istanbul now contains the world's largest concentration of ethnic Kurds, estimated to be three million strong. Around half of all Turkey's Kurds no longer live in the country's traditionally Kurdish southeast. These demographic shifts contributed to the 'de-tribalisation' of Kurdish society in Turkey, and to Kurdish assimilation into Turkish culture. Many Kurds in Turkey speak no Kurdish at all, and disguise or are even uninterested in their Kurdish heritage. This contrasts with the circumstances of Kurds in Iraq. From around the 1960s hundreds of thousands of Turkey's Kurds migrated to western Europe in search of better economic prospects and political and social freedoms. Other Kurds, from Turkey and elsewhere, have gained political asylum in Europe and further afield. This Kurdish diaspora has since contributed greatly to keeping the Kurdish culture and language alive, and to highlighting the continued repression of Kurds and Kurdishness in Turkey. It was mainly Turkish Kurds who established the Kurdish Parliament in Exile in The Hague in 1995, as well as as MED-TV, and its successors MEDYA-TV and, after that was closed down, ROJ-TV, which broadcasts from Denmark to the Kurds of the Middle East.

The Kurdistan Workers' Party

For all Turkey's supposed democratisation and westernisation since the end of the Second World War, its evolution is replete with the banning of a succession of Kurdish political parties and of Kurdish journals, and the detention of Kurdish activists – typically for no more than declaring themselves to be Kurdish or referring to 'Kurdistan'. Traditional feudally based Kurdish leaders in Turkey were sometimes co-opted into the regime, assimilated, lost their influence as a result of social and economic change, or were otherwise silenced. Indeed, assimilation was the fate of many Kurds, further encouraged along this path both by Turkey's economic development as well as by the risks of continuing the struggle. The succession of military coups and interventions, and the inclination of even democratically elected Turkish governments to securitise the Kurdish question and give the security forces a free hand in addressing it, intensified the repression, despair and alienation. As with Turkey's oppositional politics in general and the left in particular, during the 1970s and 1980s Kurdish political and cultural dissidence was pushed underground.

In 1978 the PKK emerged from Turkey's rich underground leftist undercurrents (Jongerden and Akkaya 2011). Led by a non-Kurdish speaking Ankara University student, Abdullah Öcalan, the PKK's ideology is both Kurdish and leftist, although over the years it has come to demand 'democratic autonomy' rather than complete independence. It is highly disciplined, and Öcalan enjoys an almost cult-like status among his followers. Öcalan went into exile in Syria in 1980, and gained support from a Syrian regime always looking for opportunities to undermine Turkey. The PKK embarked on its armed campaign in 1984, prompted by the severe crackdown on both Kurdish and leftist activism that followed the 1980 military coup. Again, the Turkish state responded with its characteristic repressiveness, and a 'dirty war' broke out that involved unexplained disappearances and assassinations, the deployment of *agents provocateurs*, mass graves, the forced evacuation and destruction of around 3,000 villages, torture, and the widespread detention of journalists, students, writers and human rights activists deemed by the authorities to be sympathetic to the Kurdish cause. Turkey's southeast was in effect under military occupation, with at least one-third of Turkey's substantial army located there at any one time. The conflict has mostly been fought inside the region, with occasional terrorist attacks in western Turkey, and at least 40,000 lives have been lost, most of them on the Kurdish side. The fighting was at its most intense during the 1990s, and martial law was not finally lifted across the whole of Turkey's southeast until 2002 (McDowall 1997: 418–444; Sarihan 2013; Tezcur 2014).

A particular feature of the conflict was the establishment of the so-called 'village guards' in the 1980s. These are local Kurdish militia, paid by the state, sometimes derived from particular villages or clans, and sometimes joining up as a result of intimidation by the security forces. The 'village guards' have often been involved in some of the 'dirty war' aspects of the conflict, and have frequently been targeted by the PKK. They are believed to number somewhere between 50,000–90,000 – and indeed are possibly more numerous than the combined total of full-time and part-time PKK fighters, although all such numbers are estimates. In any case, their exchanges with the PKK have added an intra-ethnic dimension to the conflict. Unsurprisingly, the disbandment of the 'village guard' system is one of the central demands of the PKK and its political representatives today. Kurdish Islamists have also fought the PKK. In 1993 Kurdish Hizbollah was formed from pre-existing Kurdish Islamist movements, possibly at the behest of the security forces as an element in the Turkish 'deep state's' campaign against the PKK. It is believed to be responsible for the deaths of hundreds of PKK activists, but was targeted by the security forces in 2000 as a response to the kidnapping of a number of businessmen. Although it was decided in 2002 to end the armed struggle, Islamist movements have continued throughout to be a feature of Kurdish politics and society in Turkey, and mostly stand in opposition to the PKK. In 2012 the Huda-Par was formed to electorally contest with the PKK-aligned Peace and Democracy Party (BDP). In October 2014 there were deadly clashes between PKK and Huda-Par supporters during the disturbances surrounding the siege of the Syrian Kurdish town of Kobane. In Turkey as in Iraq, Islamism is an important feature of Kurdish politics and society.

The Turkish state's struggle with its own Kurdish problem has always been impacted by regional circumstances. With the establishment of the allied no-fly zone over northern Iraq, the PKK made increasing use of the Qandil Mountains in Iraqi Kurdistan, basing as many as half their fighters there. This prompted around 30 Turkish military incursions and air attacks against PKK bases in northern Iraq during the 1990s, with some cross-border operations involving as many as 50,000 troops. Turkish forces were often aided by the KDP and PUK, who feared the implications for the KRG's autonomy and stability of repeated Turkish incursions, who were motivated by their growing economic dependence on Turkey, and who disliked the challenge posed by the PKK's ideology and its potential appeal to Iraqi Kurds. Constrained from entering northern Iraq by the US post-2003 occupation of Iraq, Turkey nevertheless resumed occasional cross-border incursions in 2007. Even so, PKK units remain in northern Iraq to this day, and even became involved in the defence of Iraqi Kurds against the threat posed by Islamic State in 2014. In particular, the PKK's role in defending northern Iraq's Yezidi minority from IS was seen by Iraqi Kurdish leaders as an encroachment into their domain and contributed to the tension between the KRG authorities and the PKK and its affiliates.

Turkey's 'peace process'

Öcalan was expelled from Syria in 1998 in response to a Turkish military threat to Damascus, and was captured in Kenya in 1999 despite the protection afforded him by Greece. Syria agreed to end its support for the PKK, which called a ceasefire. However, the PKK again resorted to violence from 2004 onwards and continued, with occasional interruptions until 2013, heralding a new attempt to negotiate an end to the conflict. In fact, the ruling AKP, which garners up to half the Kurdish vote in Turkey's southeast and is thus in electoral competition with the Kurdish People's Democracy Party (HDP, formerly BDP), has acknowledged past mistakes in Turkey's Kurdish policies, has been keen to desecuritise the

Kurdish issue and to reach a political solution. For example, restrictions on Kurdish-language broadcasting were relaxed, and the first state-run Kurdish-language television station commenced broadcasting in 2011.

A 'peace process' that commenced in 2009 was brought to a swift end by clashes between PKK fighters and Turkish soldiers, the banning of the BDP, and the arrests of hundreds of Kurdish activists. This led to an intensification of violence which in 2011 alone resulted in around 400 deaths. However, after Turkish Prime Minister Recep Tayyip Erdoğan admitted that secret talks had been taking place between government officials and Abdullah Öcalan, confined to the prison island of Imrali in the Marmara Sea, in March 2013 Öcalan called for a ceasefire and for dialogue. A few weeks later PKK fighters crossed into northern Iraq, although it was widely suspected that some remained in Turkey. Negotiations followed but have made little progress. This is partly a consequence of electoral considerations in Turkey, but also indicated that the two sides were far apart. The government appeared wary of provoking a Turkish nationalist backlash, while it was evident that there were divisions on the Kurdish side. It remains uncertain that Ankara will be able to accede to Kurdish demands for 'democratic autonomy' (which would presumably involve considerable devolution), a lowering of the electoral threshold, an amnesty for Kurdish fighters and prisoners, the disbandment of the 'village guards', the recognition of Kurdish as a co-equal language (with Turkish) of the Republic, and Öcalan's freedom (Gunter 2014; Tezcur 2013). In the meantime, many Kurds believed that Turkish security forces were using the ceasefire to strengthen their facilities in Kurdish areas, while the Kurds appeared to set about establishing 'parallel government' structures in Turkey's southeast.

The Syrian Kurdish moment

In any case, developments in Syria in 2014 threatened Turkey's 'peace process' altogether. Turkey's refusal to come to the aid of Kurdish defenders of Kobane, just across the Syrian border from Turkey, against an IS onslaught, and suspicions that Turkey was aiding Islamists whilst obstructing Kurds, led to widespread disturbances throughout Turkey in which over 40 people lost their lives. Given the symbiotic relationship between the PKK and the main Syrian Kurdish force, the Democratic Union Party (PYD), the threat posed to Turkey's 'reconciliation process' by Ankara's hostility to the PYD was evident. The emergence of the PYD as the leading Syrian Kurdish element was unexpected. Syria's Kurds had long been notoriously fractured, but in the chaos that followed the majority Sunni Arab revolt against the Alawite and Ba'athist regime in 2011 the PYD emerged as the most organised and militarily most effective of Syria's disparate Kurdish groups, some of which threw in their lot with the mainly Arab opposition to Damascus (Gunter 2014). Syria's Kurds did not live in geographically contiguous areas, and in early 2013 the PYD established three geographically distinct self-governing cantons, called Rojava. To Ankara this implied the establishment of PKK-controlled havens on its southern border.

Significant Kurdish populations could also be found in Aleppo and Damascus. This dispersal had added to the disunity of Syria's Kurds (International Crisis Group Middle East Report 136, 2013; Kurdwatch Report 8, 2011), as some assimilated, others were isolated and largely passive, while since 1962 others were regarded by the regime as refuges from Turkish repression and hence denied Syrian citizenship – in effect, they were stateless people, numbering around 300,000. This policy was justified by the fact that some of Syria's Kurds descended from Kurds fleeing Turkey during the 1920s and thus could be regarded as not indigenous to Syria. However, the designation of 'statelessness' was largely arbitrary and aimed at eroding

Kurdish sentiment. It was accompanied by the Arabisation of the areas bordering Turkey and Iraq. It was also part and parcel of a wider policy of repression towards the Kurds, which restricted their civil, political and cultural rights in the interests of nation-building and regime survival (Lynch and Ali 2015). This did not inhibit the Damascus regime from using the Kurdish card against its Turkish neighbour from time to time, while Öcalan expressed his gratitude for the protection Damascus afforded him by publicly embracing the Syrian view of the transitory status of many of the country's Kurds.

The mainstream Syrian opposition has resisted the idea of Kurdish autonomy in any post-Assad political arrangements, which has inhibited the PYD from aligning with it. The PYD has undoubtedly prospered both from its seamless relationship to the PKK, which provided fighters and arms, and from the preference on the part of the regime's forces to engage with its more numerous and hostile Sunni Arab rather than its Kurdish opponents. Indeed, Syrian regime forces chose not to contest PYD control over the Kurdish enclaves, a gesture which could yet prove to have consequences as far-reaching as Saddam Hussein's decision to withdraw the Iraqi state's presence in Kurdish Iraq. These factors have reinforced Ankara's opposition to the PYD, and its view that it is in league with the regime. Although there were skirmishes between PYD and regime forces, most of the fighting conducted by Syria's Kurds has been with the more *jihadist* elements of the Syrian opposition. This culminated in the IS onslaught against the Syrian Kurdish town of Kobane, nestled up against the Turkish border from where units of the Turkish army passively observed the fighting. Unable to elicit Ankara's cooperation, which was widely suspected of both aiding the *jihadist* elements of the opposition and of at best doing nothing to assist Kurdish resistance, the US declared the PYD to be a non-proscribed organisation, unlike its PKK sister, and was obliged to air-drop arms to Kobane's Kurdish defenders and to use non-Turkish military bases from which to conduct air strikes against the IS forces besieging Kobane.

The KDP leadership has been scarcely better disposed towards the PYD than was Ankara. Barzani had sought to incorporate the PYD into a coalition of Syrian Kurdish groups, the Kurdish National Council (KNC), in the hope that the pro-KDP elements could then curtail if not control the PYD's autonomy and capacity. Initially, Erbil offered no assistance to the PYD forces, and even obstructed them from using KRG territory in any way. It was undoubtedly the case that the PYD leadership was determined to dominate the Syrian Kurdish effort, and these KDP–PYD differences offer yet another example of Kurdish disunity even in the face of both great danger and great opportunity. However, US pressure and pan-Kurdish popular outrage in Turkey and Iraq as well as in Syria itself eventually led both to the KRG-sponsored creation of a power-sharing council in October 2014 in an attempt at greater political coordination between the various Syrian Kurdish groups, and to the remarkable transit of a small but relatively heavily armed group of Iraqi Kurdish *peshmerga* forces via Turkey in order to assist the defence of Kobane. The PYD's unease at what it thought was a bid by Barzani to take over the leadership of the Syrian Kurds was evident, and further Kurdish power struggles relating to Syrian Kurdistan, or Rojava, can be expected.

The Kurdish moment?

The struggle for Kurdish self-determination is replete with repression, disappointments and betrayals. Even so, some now see what could be a historic turning point in Kurdish fortunes. The emergence of the KRG and Turkey's relationship with it, the threat to the territorial integrity of Iraq and Syria, the rise of IS and the consequent western support for the Kurds of

Rojava as well as of northern Iraq, and the Turkish 'reconciliation process', all raise the prospects of a reordering of the region's politics in favour of the Kurds, and even of a redrawing of the map. Western sympathy for the Kurds has been strengthened by their emergence as the most credible opposition to IS, as well as to what appears as their relative attachment to more democratic and secular political values. Kurdish forces are being trained and armed by western countries, there are calls for the PKK to be removed from the EU's proscribed list and for closer diplomatic and economic relationships with the KRG, and continuing pressure on Turkey to take steps to resolve its Kurdish issue. The unanimous vote to support the Kurds of Kobane in the KRG's KNA, the appearance of Iraqi Kurdish *peshmerga* alongside their PYD brethren in Syria, the uproar amongst Turkey's Kurds against Ankara's refusal to come to the aid of Kobane, and the role played by PKK and PYD fighters in Sinjar and Makhmur in Iraq Kurdistan, have all contributed to and are testimony to the intensification of a genuine and palpable pan-Kurdish sentiment.

Nevertheless, it would be foolish to make predictions amidst such dramatic turmoil and unpredictability, and one or two more sobering observations are worth noting. First, many of the advances that Kurds have made in recent years, and even some of the false dawns in earlier times too, have essentially been made more as by-products of developments that are external to the Kurdish struggle. This is true of the KRG's emergence, which was made possible by first the weakening and then the overthrow of the Ba'athist regime in Baghdad by US-led interventions, as well as Rojava's in more recent times, where the PYD exploited the opportunity presented by the Assad regime's fight for survival against its primarily Sunni Arab opponents. The short-lived Mahabad Republic, and transient Kurdish 'successes' in Iran at the end of the First World War and in Iraq after the 1958 coup, all accompanied moments of weakness on the part of the central authorities. It should also be noted that Baghdad has never fully reconciled itself to the KRG's autonomy. While the current government of Haider al-Abadi appears to be more accommodating towards Erbil, it nevertheless seeks to ensure that the KRG's energy policy is subordinate to or at least not in opposition to the interests of Iraq as a whole. Furthermore, there is no indication that Baghdad is ready to concede on the territorial issue. Of course a Baghdad that is powerless to physically obstruct KRG control of the disputed territories might be obliged to acquiesce in it, but this impotence might not endure forever. In any case, the numerous and usually Iranian-backed Shia militias and the Sunni and Turkmen inhabitants of Kurdish-controlled areas in northern Iraq could offer credible resistance to Kurdish domination, and it is reasonable to expect this could be forthcoming once the IS threat is brought under greater control. Arab opposition to Kurdish autonomy is as rife in Syria as it is in Iraq. Much depends on the outcome of the Syrian civil war. The emergence of a federalised Syria to include Alawite, Christian, Druze and other self-governing cantons is at least a possibility, but one that would at best be only reluctantly and perhaps only temporarily embraced by Syria's Sunni Arab majority. In short, the Kurdish fate continues to depend heavily on the evolution of developments in the region more widely.

Nor are the Kurds' neighbours or the USA and its allies likely to welcome a redrawing of the region's map. Tehran still hopes for a unified Iraq in which it can exercise influence through the Shia majority there, and has been unnerved by the close relationship that developed between Erbil and Ankara. In any case, the assistance Tehran afforded the KRG in the face of the IS threat, which contrasted with Ankara's inactivity, has restored Iranian influence in Iraqi Kurdistan. An ever more independent KRG would either stoke intense Turkish–Iranian rivalry for influence, or could encourage cooperation against Iraqi Kurdish ambitions. Like Turkey, Iran is exercised by the potential impact on its own Kurds of enhanced Kurdish autonomy elsewhere. Although culturally there is more overlap between Iran's Persian majority and the roughly 10 per cent of the country that is ethnically Kurdish, and Iran's Kurds have rarely been on the receiving end of the kind of brutality and marginalisation that their Turkish, Iraqi and even Syrian counterparts have experienced, Tehran has nevertheless been unprepared to extend significant rights or self-government (Natali 2005: 117–159; Stansfield 2014). This is in part a consequence of Tehran's sensitivity to Iran's complex multi-ethnic make-up, but is also linked to the country's nation-building project. In any case, as many as two-thirds of Iran's Kurds are Shia, and they have traditionally been relatively comfortable with Tehran's rule. Furthermore, although the majority of Iranian Kurds live adjacent to the Turkish and Iraqi borders, many of these areas are ethnically mixed. Some of Iran's Kurds are located in the far north of the country and have been somewhat isolated from the main currents of Kurdish identity politics. Overall, Iran's Kurds have been as fragmented, and often as passive, as their Syrian counterparts. In recent years, the most determined Iranian Kurdish force has been the Party for Freedom and Life in Kurdistan (PJAK), also aligned with the PKK and which since 2004 has fought a relatively low-key battle against Iranian security forces. Like the PKK it uses Iraq's Qandil Mountains as a rear base, a fact which has encouraged Turkish–Iranian security cooperation against them. A major Iranian offensive in 2011 led to a ceasefire, but occasional acts of violence, and Iranian repression of Kurdish activists, persist.

Conclusion

After its initial opposition to the KRG and the threat its existence was deemed to pose to Turkey's unitary nature, Ankara emerged as the KRG's chief economic and political partner, and as the outlet for its energy resources (Park 2014). A growing KRG dependence on Turkey was an inevitable concomitant of this, which among other things involved cooperating with Ankara against the PKK and the PYD. It is possible that a complete collapse of the Iraqi state could persuade Turkey to acquiesce to Kurdish independence in northern Iraq, but such a development would probably increase Ankara's determination to divide Iraq's Kurds from their Turkish counterparts, and to weaken the PKK and its affiliates. Weaning Turkey's Kurds away from their attachment to the PKK might best be achieved by extending the political rights of Turkey's Kurdish citizens, but it is not self-evident that Ankara is prepared to take sufficient steps in this direction nor that it would necessarily succeed in pacifying the more nationalistic Kurds if it did. However, even were a violent struggle to reignite in Turkey, it does not follow that the Iraqi Kurdish leadership would support their Kurdish brethren. The same argument applies to Syrian and Iranian Kurds too – Erbil might well leave them to fight their own battles.

The USA is also unlikely to support Iraqi Kurdish independence so long as some semblance of an Iraqi unitary state survives. For all Washington's role in enabling the emergence of the KRG, it has remained steadfast in its commitment to the Baghdad government, and in general has long been disinclined to support Kurdish aspirations that could threaten the existing territorial and political arrangements in the region (Charountaki 2011), particularly in the face of opposition from NATO member Turkey. The USA opposed the export of Kurdish oil via Turkey in the face of Baghdad's opposition, did little to help resolve either the budgetary or territorial differences between Erbil and Baghdad, and invested far more in the federal armed forces than in the KRG's *peshmerga*, despite the excesses of the al-Maliki government. The USA remains committed to the survival of an Iraq that it gave birth to, and does not want to appear responsible for its breakup. For that reason too, the PKK is likely to remain on the

US list of proscribed terrorist organisations. This is true for the EU too, although the rise in the profile of the Kurds and the decline in Turkey's reputation could see those positions challenged. International support for a Kurdish state remains very weak, and Kurds in each of the four states in which they reside might do well to be prepared for future western diplomatic passivity in the face of Turkish, Iranian or Arab governments capable of suppressing them.

Above all, what could well be the emergence of an unprecedented level of pan-Kurdish sentiment may not convert itself into a unified pan-Kurdish political movement. The PKK and its Iranian and Syrian affiliates do represent a network, organisation, and ideology that straddles the region's borders, but they do not represent all or even the majority of Kurds in their respective countries. The Iraqi Kurdish leadership, and especially that of the KDP, will continue to regard them as rivals, even as enemies. This in part stems from ideological differences, in part from the exigencies in Erbil of running a quasi-state and the concomitant requirement to protect state interests, and in part from deeper tribal cleavages and the 'tribalisation' of Kurdish politics. But it also reflects the competing and contradictory loyalties that continue to undermine the emergence of a more unified Kurdish identity. Tribe, region, religion, ideology, patronage and power all continue to play a major part in Kurdish political behaviour. Even in the midst of the turmoil that has shaken the region's political arrangements in recent years, these fissures have been powerful and determining.

Yet there can be no stability for the region, and for Turkey, Iraq, Syria and Iran, if Kurdish aspirations remain unmet. This is now even truer than it has ever been. Each of these four states has stoked Kurdish identity and resistance by seeking to suppress it. The KRG will not disappear, and nor will Kurdish activism and struggle in Turkey, Syria and Iran. Only time will tell whether this will eventually result in some redrawing of the region's map, in the emergence of one or many Kurdish statelets living in competition or harmony with each other, in the adoption of more inclusivity and/or devolution by some or all of the states affected, or in continued attempts to deny Kurdish self-determination. If the latter, then we can anticipate more Kurdish outbursts at moments of weakness or transition. Whatever the eventual outcome, the Kurdish story suggests that the undeniable existence of an ethnic group, combined with a readiness to struggle for greater self-determination, need not necessarily lead to the emergence of a unified national state.

Further reading

Allsopp, H., *The Kurds of Syria: Political Parties and Identities in the Middle East* (London: I.B. Tauris, 2015).
Bengio, O., *The Kurds of Iraq: Building a State within a State* (Boulder, CO, and London: Lynne Rienner, 2012).
Bilgin, F. and Sarihan, A. eds, *Understanding Turkey's Kurdish Question* (Lanham and Plymouth: Lexington Books, 2013).
McDowall, D. *A Modern History of the Kurds* (London: I.B. Tauris, 2003).
Romano, D. and Gurses, M. (eds), *Conflict, Democratization, and the Kurds in the Middle East* (New York: Palgrave Macmillan, 2014).
van Bruinessen, M., *Agha, Shaikh and State: The Social and Political Structures of Kurdistan* (London: Zed Books, 1992).

References

Bengio, O., *The Kurds of Iraq: Building a State within a State* (Boulder, CO, and London: Lynne Rienner, 2012).
Charountaki, M., *The Kurds and US Foreign Policy: International Relations in the Middle East since 1945* (London and New York: Routledge, 2011).

Danilovich, A., *Iraqi Federalism and the Kurds: Learning to Live Together* (Farnham and Burlington: Ashgate, 2014).

Eagleton, W., *The Kurdish Republic of 1946* (London: Oxford University Press, 1963).

Gunter, M. M., 'The KDP–PUK Conflict in Northern Iraq', *Middle East Journal*, 50 Spring 1996: 225–241.

Gunter, M. M., 'The Modern Origins of Kurdish Nationalism', in M. M. A. Ahmed and M. M. Gunter (eds), *The Evolution of Kurdish Nationalism* (Costa Mesa, CA: Mazda Publishers, 2007), pp.1–17.

Gunter, M. M., *Out of Nowhere: The Kurds of Syria in Peace and War* (London: Hurst and Co., 2014).

Hiltermann, J., 'Kurdish Independence: Harder than it Looks', *New York Review of Books*, 10 July 2014.

International Crisis Group Middle East Report 103, *Iraq and the Kurds: Confronting Withdrawal Fears*, 28 March 2011.

International Crisis Group Middle East Report 136, *Syria's Kurds: A Struggle within a Struggle*, 22 January 2013.

Jongerden, J. and Akkaya, A. H. 'Born from the Left: The Making of the PKK', in M. Casier and J. Jongerden (eds), *Nationalism and Politics in Turkey: Political Islam, Kemalism and the Kurdish Issue* (London and New York: Routledge, 2011), pp.123–142.

Jwaideh, W., *The Kurdish National Movement: Its Origins and Development* (Syracuse, New York: Syracuse University Press, 2006).

Kurdwatch Report 8, Who is the Syrian Opposition? The Development of Kurdish Parties, 1956–2011, December 2011.

Lynch, M. and Ali, P., Buried Alive: Stateless Kurds in Syria, *Refugees International*, January 2006; www.refworld.org/docid/47a6eba80.html, accessed 29 April 2015.

McDowall, D., *A Modern History of the Kurds* (London: I.B. Tauris, 1997).

Natali, D., *The Kurds and the State: Evolving National Identity in Iraq, Turkey, and Iran* (Syracuse, New York: Syracuse University Press, 2005).

Natali, D., *The Kurdish Quasi-state: Development and Democracy in Post-Gulf War Iraq* (Syracuse, New York: Syracuse University Press, 2010).

Park, B., Turkey's Policy towards Northern Iraq: Problems and Perspectives, Adelphi Papers 374, London: International Institute of Strategic Studies, 2005.

Park, B., *Turkish-Kurdish Regional Government Relations after the US Withdrawal: Putting the Kurds on the Map?* Strategic Studies Institute, US Army War College, March 2014.

Robins, P., *Suits and Uniforms: Turkish Foreign Policy since the Cold War* (London: Hurst and Co., 2003).

Saracoglu, C., *Kurds of Modern Turkey: Migration, Neoliberalism and Exclusion in Turkish Society* (London: I.B. Tauris, 2010).

Sarihan, A., 'The Two Periods of the PKK Conflict: 1884–1999 and 2004–2010', in F. Bilgin and A. Sarihan (eds), *Understanding Turkey's Kurdish Question* (Lanham and Plymouth: Lexington Books, 2013), pp. 89–102.

Satana, N. S., 'The Kurdish Issue in June 2011 Elections: Continuity or Change in Turkey's Democratization?' *Turkish Studies*, 13(2) June 2012: 169–189.

Sherzad, A., 'The Kurdish Movement in Iraq; 1975–1988', in P. G. Kreyenbroek and S. Sperl (eds), *The Kurds: A Contemporary Overview* (London: Routledge, 1992), pp.134–142.

Stansfield, G. R.V., *Iraqi Kurdistan: Political Development and Emergent Democracy* (New York and Abingdon: RoutledgeCurzon, 2003).

Stansfield, G., 'Kurds, Persian Nationalism, and Shi'i Rule: Surviving Dominant Nationhood in Iran', in D. Romano and M. Gurses (eds), *Conflict, Democratization, and the Kurds in the Middle East* (New York: Palgrave Macmillan, 2014), pp.59–84.

Tezcur, G. M., 'Prospects for Resolution of the Kurdish Question: A Realist Perspective', *Insight Turkey*, 1(2) Spring 2013: 69–84.

Tezcur, G. M., 'The Ebb and Flow of Armed Conflict in Turkey: An Elusive Peace', in D. Romano and M. Gurses (eds), *Conflict, Democratization, and the Kurds in the Middle East* (New York: Palgrave Macmillan, 2014), pp.171–188.

Tripp, C., *A History of Iraq* (Cambridge: Cambridge University Press, 2007).

Vali, A., *Kurds and the State in Iran: The Making of Kurdish Identity* (London and New York: I.B. Tauris, 2014).

van Bruinessen, M., *Agha, Shaikh and State: The Social and Political Structures of Kurdistan* (London: Zed Books, 1992)

White, P. J., 'Ethnic Differentiation among the Kurds: Kurmanci, Kizilbash and Zaza', *Journal of Arabic, Islamic and Middle Eastern Studies*, 2, November 1995: 67–90.

White, P. J., 'The Debate on the Identity of "Alevi Kurds"', in P. J. White and J. Jongerden (eds), *Turkey's Alevi Enigma: A Comprehensive Overview* (Leiden and Boston: Brill, 2003), pp.17–32.

Yildiz, K., *The Kurds in Iraq: The Past, Present and Future* (London and Ann Arbor: Pluto Press, 2007).

27

NO MORE CONFLICTS

Accounting for détente in the Great Lakes Region

David E. Kiwuwa

Introduction

Africa in general still registers onto the world's mental map as a tinderbox of violent conflicts perhaps evidenced by the 70 wars fought on the continent since the 1980s (Englebert and Dunn 2013: 267). The Great Lakes Region (GLR) in particular, Daley notes, has registered approximately 11 wars in the Democratic Republic of Congo (DRC) since 1960, five in Burundi, two in Rwanda and about six in Uganda (Lemarchand 1999: Daley 2006a, 2006b: 303; Gleditsch 2009: 597). Evidentially, diverse scholarship has identified the region with the notorious Uganda's Lord Resistance Army (LRA), their crude brutality and sexual enslavement of captives, with the DRC's plethora of militias such as the *mai mai*, M23 fighters, with Rwanda's Federal Forces for the Liberation of Rwanda (FDLR) Hutu militias and *genocidaires*, with Burundi's National Liberation Forces (FNL) and general regional fragility amidst a phenomenal gift of natural resources (Collier and Hoeffler 1998, 2000; Henderson and Singer 2000; Lemarchand 2009; Strauss 2012a, 2012b; Omeje and Hepner 2013; Englebert and Dunn 2013). While this could be critiqued as oversimplification of Africa and the GLR situation in particular, there is no denying that there is still some grain of truth in the observation. Most recently however, there is an unmistakable positive change in the durability of political stability and security, an emerging kind of détente in the region both within and between states (Strauss 2012a: 184). What primarily explains this rapprochement? This chapter offers a general examination of conflicts dynamics in the GLR, briefly interrogating the nature of conflicts, their causes and consequently accounts for the emergent thaw.

The GLR is a complex geopolitical space that has been a focus of significant scholarly and policy research (Lemarchand 1994, 2000; Prunier 1995; Melvern 2000; Mamdani 2001; Nzongola-Ntalaja 2002; Allen and Vlassenroot 2010; Reyntjens 2010). From a minimalist standpoint, the GLR is a cluster of countries contiguous to the African Great Lakes and rift valley, sharing distinct ecological and demographic traits (Chretien 2003: 23; Khadiagala 2006: 1). It consists of six countries: DRC (formerly Zaire), Kenya, Tanzania, Uganda, Burundi and Rwanda. Peculiarly, the International Conference on the Great Lakes Region appears to have extended this reach to include countries as far afield as Angola, Zambia, Central African Republic, Congo and Sudan. As it is not my intention to debate the appropriateness of this redefinition, I will confine my focus to the original parameters. In this context, it is clear that not all of the GLR states have been caught up in the cycle of violence and political instability or at the very least been affected to the same extent. Notably, all have played a part in one way or another in affecting geopolitical security dynamics and political stability in the region though not all have had equal or determinative roles. This leaves a cluster of countries that are caught up in the discourse of violence or what I refer to as the 'axis of conflict': the DRC, Uganda, Burundi, Rwanda and by association (South) Sudan which will be our primary focus. A general interrogation of existing scholarship, while disagreeing on many things concerning the Great Lakes, at least appears to agree that this unique geopolitical space is characterized by weak state structures, porous borders and a proclivity for violence resulting in an expanded and interconnected spatial zone of conflict. This in turn has led on one occasion or another to transnational insecurity and political instability (Chazan et al. 1999; Lemarchand 2009: 4; Prunier 2009b; Reyntjens 2010; Williams 2011: 41).

New wars in the Great Lakes

Between 1990 and 2006, the GLR witnessed some of the most virulent intra- and interstate conflicts amongst which was allegedly 'Africa's first world war' (Prunier 2009a, 2009b; Reyntjens 2010: 194). But these are what Kaldor (1999) has termed the 'new wars', which she argues represent a fundamental departure from previous wars, noting that whereas the conflicts in the Cold War epoch were largely ideological, the new wars are more informed by variables less tinged by ideological nuances. Instead, these are wars characterized by state structural dysfunctionality, social transformation informed by globalization and liberal economic forces, by competition over natural resources and illegal commercial entrepreneurship, communal/private militias, criminal warlords and ethnic disputes (Duffield 2001: 118; Newman 2004; Williams 2011). Another alleged distinctive factor among 'new wars' is the increasing targeting of civilians as objects of war. For 'behavior that was proscribed according to the classical rules of warfare and codified in the laws of war ... such as atrocities against non-combatants, sieges and destruction of historic monuments now constitutes an essential component of the strategies of the new mode of warfare' (Kaldor 1999: 8). Conflicts in the region therefore are not only markedly brutal towards civilians but are also highly convoluted due to a noticeable interconnectedness in a number of spheres. To the casual observer, the GLR is palpably a tinderbox of ethnic primordial tensions that ultimately resulted in genocide in Rwanda, ethnic warfare and cleansing in DRC and Burundi and most recently ethnic political violence in Kenya and South Sudan (Lemarchand 2009: 5). Consequently, this absurd and recurring tragedy in the region excluding Darfur has accounted for approximately six million victims with millions more displaced.

Conflict typology

Before briefly examining the underlying causes of these conflicts, it is pertinent to interrogate their structural differences. Admittedly, there are many classifications of conflict based on causality, actors, duration, scope, intensity and goals, with noticeable overlaps, all of which have fundamental impacts on the very conduct, organization and dynamics of a given conflict (Ramsbotham and Woodhouse 1996: 40). Here we shall conceptualize conflicts along two dimensions: geographical scope and intensity. By geographical scope, we imply a conflict zone of coverage: the territorial parameters within which a particular conflict is actively operationalized – domestic (intrastate), regional or international (interstate). Intrastate conflict therefore denotes a situation of acute dissonance that embodies domestically oriented actors and whose theatre of often violent action is confined within given state boundaries. On the other hand, interstate conflicts are assumed to be wars involving at least two sovereign states in sustained combat precipitated by a complex set of causal variables (Galtung 1965; Levy 1989; Herbst 1990; Sarkees and Wayman 2010). In the context of force or concentration, there are low and high intensity conflicts (Ramsbotham and Woodhouse 1996; Ramsbotham, Woodhouse and Miall 2005; Molloy 2001). Low intensity conflicts here denotes a limited politico-military struggle to attain political, military, social, economic or psychological objectives often confined to a specific geographical space and characterized by limitations of armaments, tactics and level of force. Not only is such conflict most evident in developing countries but it is often drawn out and extends from diplomatic, economic and psychological pressure to terrorism and insurgency (Molloy 2001: 16). Potentially, this conflict may involve parties with asymmetrical capabilities, for instance state versus non-state actors, and is directed towards change of the internal power or relational structure of a given state. Historical evidence suggests that intrastate low intensity conflicts have been predominant in Africa with over 30 countries of the 54 having experienced one or more such conflicts since the 1960s (Clapham 1998; Reno 1998; Doyle and Sambanis 2000). High intensity conflicts on the other hand are those that entail high levels of force and may often involve parties with symmetrical capabilities. These conflicts are often though not always fought between states. The rationale for this type of conflict can range from territorial dispute, to ideological dominance, security or altering the internal political governance of a state, as the case of the Uganda–Tanzania 1979 conflict attests. Clearly, inter- and intrastate, low and high intensity conflicts have been evident in the GLR with their causes as complex and dialectical as the region itself.

Domestic (intrastate) conflicts

In the twenty-first century, 95 per cent of conflicts in the world have been intrastate of which the GLR and the conflict axis states in particular have experienced a disproportionate number. Broadly, what accounts for these conflicts? Arguably, this is the most contested scholarship due to the fact that on the one hand there have been efforts to provide a grand (macro) narrative as to the general causes of conflicts, while on the other, a micro approach emerged to push back against this 'neat box' treatment (Mitchell 1981; Holsti 1983; Homer-Dixon 1994; Stewart 2002; Dixon 2009; Williams 2011: 8). Evidently, the most common albeit passionately contested grand narrative *was* Collier and Hoeffler's 'greed vs grievance' thesis (1998; Collier 2000b, 2007). It attempted to frame conflicts as a result of two rational motivations: either greed or grievance suggesting that human beings are rational actors and will most *often* engage in behaviour that is calculated to adduce maximum benefits which are wealth and/or power. As such, conflicts are caused when economically oriented individuals/groups pursue self-interested actions to maximize utility in a situation of finite supply. Simply, the institutionalization of violence in African states and not least GLR is primarily driven by the 'silent force of greed' or pursuit of profit more than the 'loud discourse of grievance' (Collier 2000a: 101; Berdal and Malone 2000). This attempt to draw a clear dichotomy for causation is certainly problematic as seeking to establish causal discontinuities inevitably overlooks the real picture that more realistically places causation along a causal continuum (Berdal 2003, 2005). However, there is a pragmatic acknowledgement of the explanatory value of the greed–grievance narrative though with a caveat that in and by itself is insufficient in explaining complex causation of conflicts in the GLR across time and space (Ballentine and Sherman 2003; Nathan 2008). As such, a micro approach that employs a more meticulous and systematic disaggregation of individual conflicts for meaning and explanation is more appropriate. Employing a multiplicity of theories such as Galtung's structural violence thesis that points to the violence of poverty and powerlessness as causation, or Gurr's relative deprivation theory that speaks to 'actors' perception of discrepancy between their value expectations and their value capabilities; the gap between that to which people believe they are rightfully entitled and that which they think they are capable of getting and keeping' may offer methodical insight into causes of individual conflicts (Gurr 1970: 24; see also Galtung 1965; Cohen 1974: 94; Sandole 1993; Dixon 2009). A close reading of these theories therefore will demonstrate that the GLR conflicts are both complex and multi-causal where greed, grievances and other intrinsic factors combine to cause and *sustain* conflicts. What follows next is a country by country brief overview of the conflict dynamics, actors and potential causal explanations which are by no means exhaustive.

Statistically, the DRC, the biggest state in the conflict axis, has been undoubtedly the epicentre of violence in the GLR since the overthrow of its long-standing leader Joseph Mobutu in 1997 (Baregu 2006: 59; Prunier 2009a, 2009b). Very early on in its independence, the country was flung straight into civil wars with secessionist forces in the East: Katanga and South Kasai. It is plausible to argue in the context of this timing that the legacy of violence in the DRC was partially a direct consequence of colonialism where newly independent states experienced an institutional vacuum unable to marshal bureaucratic and coercive force competencies to either run a relatively functional state apparatus or amply project power and authority across their entire territory. For instance at independence, of the 20 million people, the DRC (the size of Western Europe) had only 17 graduates! This example of monumental incapacity resulted in the failure of state building exacerbating the already difficult challenge of nation building. The post-Cold War systemic challenges of the 1990s saw a number of regime breakdowns and Mobutu's 32 years (1965–97) kleptocratic regime suffering from terminal structural dysfunctionality as manifested in neopatrimonialism was no exception. His overthrow was facilitated in no small measure by the Rwanda–Uganda alliance in support of a local uprising, Alliance Democratic Forces for the Liberation of Congo (AFDL), whose grievances were purportedly democratic in aspiration, advocating human rights, good governance and economic prosperity, while greed as it became apparently clear was not far behind (Prunier 2009b; Reyntjens 2010: 102). Mobutu's overthrow marked the beginning of a very convoluted conflict cycle that witnessed some of the most sustained violence in the GLR perpetrated by states and non-state actors alike (Daley 2006a, 2006b; Stearns 2011). While various armed outfits rebelled against the state setting up their bases in the eastern part of the country, particularly Katanga, Province Orientale, Ituri and the Kivus, the conflicts fluctuated on the basis of Kinshasa's willingness to compromise and/or the prerogative of external backers. Most notorious were the *Mai Mai*, *Hema* and *Lendu* self-help militias set up by local warlords and tribal leaders or politically motivated fighters for the express purpose of wreaking havoc on rival factions and central government authority. Against the rising tide of violence in the region, these groups not only became particularly active as organized self-protection forces, they elsewhere dabbled in wide scale pillaging, exploitation and plunder of natural resources that enriched and funded the institutionalization of violence. Given the extremely weak nature of DRC state institutions, its vast mineral wealth and the central authority disconnect and remoteness from the east, its being unable to exert any meaningful control created a vacuum that was to be exploited by what Reyntjens refers to as 'entrepreneurs of insecurity'. The implication was the privatization and criminalization of public spaces and proliferation of general insecurity and violence (Reyntjens 2010: 221). More recently (2013), former fighters from the Tutsi dominated National Congress for the Defence of the People (CNDP), having been integrated into the national army, mutinied and took control of areas close to the border with Rwanda as the March 23 Movement (M23) causing major havoc and temporarily capturing the major eastern town of Goma. In addition, marauding rebels from Rwanda's ex-Rwandan Defence Forces (FAR) fighters, Hutu militias and Uganda's own rebel elements all fought turf wars against local tribal militias and routinely terrorized local population adding to the DRC Eastern mayhem.

To the east of DRC, Uganda has equally experienced its share of internal conflicts with the most recent and noteworthy being the armed insurgency of the Lord's Resistance Army. This pseudo Christian insurgency terrorized northern Uganda driven by a lofty agenda of replacing the government of Museveni with a regime based on the biblical Ten Commandments (Akhavan 2005; Ssenyonjo 2005; Allen and Vlassenroot 2010). The LRA are what Olson (2000) calls 'roving bandits' owing to their modus operandi: no permanent bases nor desire to capture and hold territory and relying largely on opportunistic attacks and plundering civilian populations for self-sustenance. The insurgency arose primarily from a coalescing of defeated military elements of previous regimes dissatisfied with the new political dispensation of the National Resistance Movement/Army as victors of the 1981–86 guerrilla war. Likewise, it attracted elements from disaffected communities of northern Uganda whose grievances were not only economic and political marginalization but also military brutalization for being on the losing side of the aforementioned war (Acker 2004; Ssenyonjo 2005: 410). The conduct of the insurgency grew in international notoriety due to its markedly indiscriminate brutality towards civilians who were direct targets of the LRA's scorched earth strategy. At its height, the LRA with its notorious messianic leader Joseph Kony routinely abducted and forcefully conscripted civilians (many minors), burnt and mutilated its victims, sexually enslaved abductees and terrorized northern Uganda for over two decades with victims numbering in their thousands. It is notable that the intensity of its violence ebbed and flowed according to the government counter-insurgency campaigns and the dictates of LRA external backers, notably the Sudanese Government (Reno 1998; Prunier 2004). Similarly, the country was faced with another south-western based insurgency, aka Allied Defence Forces (ADF), an Islamic religious entity whose agenda while mostly opaque equally wrought destruction and low level insecurity. These two armed insurgencies have largely characterized though not exclusively defined the intrastate violence in Uganda for the last 25 years.

Rwanda to the south perhaps is the poster child of the tragedy of the Great Lakes. While the country had been relatively stable with no major internal or external security threat since the Tutsi purges (1959–73), the civil war that broke out in 1990 motivated by a number of grievances (right of Tutsi refugee return, inequality, human rights, governance etc.) and the subsequent 1994 genocide, marked an absurd turn of events (Melvern 2000; Williams 2011; Kiwuwa 2012). It has been claimed that between 800,000 and a million lives were lost during this implosion accompanied by unimaginable destruction (Strauss 2004). Expectedly, the security and political post war recovery was slow and haphazardly calibrated given the challenges. Nevertheless, the Tutsi dominated Rwanda Patriotic Front/Army military victory and consequent exile of the Hutu dominated Habyarimana regime brought a relative degree of imposed stability and avoided overt wide-scale insecurity in the country. Expectedly, the immediate post genocide security challenge was from the defeated Rwanda Armed Forces, now the Armed Forces for the Liberation of Rwanda, who re-organized in order to pursue subversive military incursions. This internal threat was short lived and expressly and militarily dealt with (Prunier 2009a: 268). Increasingly, the challenge to internal political stability would emanate not so much from insurgent forces but from the civilian population. Drawing from structural violence theorists, while there is minimal physical violence, its ever present potential and continuing structural dysfunctionality including internal disquiet due to perceived growing authoritarianism, powerlessness and poverty have become a greater concern (Galtung 1969, 1990). Equally, an ever present security threat allegedly from FDLR forces sheltering in the DRC since the genocide has been a constant and utmost priority for Kigali and a key reason for its constant intervention and incursion into its neighbour.

Further to the south, Burundi, like its 'twin' neighbour to the north, has since the 1970s experienced both bitter inter- and intraethnic conflicts between the Hutu and Tutsi and later amongst the Hutu. These conflicts oscillated between low and high intensity depending on various political dynamics at play (Lemarchand 1970, 1998, 2009). Contextually, while these conflicts could be framed as primarily ethnic, it is also notable that poor governance, political exclusion and socio-economic defects were equally critical as catalysts, and one could consider ethnicity as only incidental to the proceedings (Ball 2002: 34; Prunier 2009a: 59). Although a transitional regime was inaugurated in 1994 following the death of the country's president along with that of Rwanda in a plane crash, Burundi was also plagued by sustained insurgency, deliberate political sabotage and routine wide scale violence. It took yet another regionally brokered effort, the Arusha Peace and Reconciliation Agreement of 2000, to establish a more structured and lasting power sharing framework and prepare Burundi for democratic transition. Under the auspices of the African Union Mission in Burundi, the Pretoria Protocol on Political, Defence and Security Power Sharing signed in October 2003 and the Pretoria Protocol on Outstanding Issues signed a month later engendered an emergence of relative peace and stability (Howard 2008; Takeuchi 2013: 50). For a while now, the former rebels' currently democratically elected ruling party (the National Council for the Defence of Democracy and the Forces for the Defence of Democracy, CNDD-FDD) have managed to make some progress towards general political stability and security enabling a return to relative normalcy. Increasingly, however, this ruling party has become a de facto one-party system characterized by the end of dialogue with the opposition especially the Front for Democracy (FRODEBU) and the Movement for Solidarity and Development. Looking at current trends, the government's authoritarian drift has seen a resumption of armed hostilities evidenced by the recent spike in violence perpetrated by FNL rebels and other marginalized groups. It is possible that if political space is routinely restricted, reversion to wide scale violence is inevitable.

Interstate (regional) conflict

Comparatively, while interstate wars were not uncommon in the rest of the world, they were a rarity in Africa, a situation perceived as anomalous. That said, Africa has witnessed a small number of interstate conflicts since the 1960s. These have primarily involved two states, for instance Libya versus Chad, Ethiopia versus Somalia, Tanzania versus Uganda, South Africa versus the frontline states and Ethiopia versus Eritrea. In the GLR there have been only two interstate wars since independence: the 1979 Tanzanian intervention in Uganda and the 1996/98 wars in the DRC which former US Assistant Secretary of State Susan Rice called the 'First African world war' (Hartung and Moix 2000; Reyntjens 2010: 198; Stearns 2011). The multistage war of DRC regimes' survival drew in armies from eight countries: Angola, Zimbabwe, Chad, Namibia, Sudan on the side of the DRC government, while rebel forces – the Movement for the Liberation of Congo (MLC) and the Rally for Congolese Democracy (RCD-G, RCD-ML, RCD-N) – were supported by Uganda, Rwanda and Burundi (Prunier 2009a: 181; Reyntjens 2010: 196). This was the first regionalized conflict structured along a complex interaction of localized rebellions and the clash of regional states' interests was further exacerbated by weak institutional state structures and international indifference or at worst complicity (Adebajo 2006: 149; Prunier 2009a: 73; Reyntjens 2010: 58; Englebert and Dunn 2013: 285). A number of authors have attempted to explain why six of the eight states above joined the theatre of war by noting that countries experiencing internal civil wars are twice as likely to engage in external wars (Gleditsch and Salehyan 2007; Gleditsch, Salehyan and Schultz 2008; Beardsley 2011). That said, for Uganda's Museveni, DRC intervention was allegedly needed in order to maintain a check on security threats posed by Sudanese supported LRA and Rwanda's defeated genocidal forces (*interahamwe*), and curtail ADF activities while at the same time seeking to *stabilize* a neighbour whose economic relevance to Uganda was arguably worth millions of dollars in direct trade (Museveni 1999; Clark 2000; Prunier 2004). Rwanda's rationale was presumably security, humanitarian and economic interests. Zimbabwe's interests were largely those of a straightforward profiteer, while Chad, Angola and Namibia were caught up in a complex web of regional security, political alliances and vested economic interests. For the local militias such as the Union Patriotic Congolese (UPC) or the *mai mai* their motivation oscillated between local grievances and simple war profiteering (Lemarchand 2009: 24; Reyntjens 2010: 195–201).

Interestingly, the DRC conflict gave rise to a *conflict within a conflict*: where Uganda and Rwanda in 1999 and 2000 engaged in direct and proxy military confrontation inside DRC territory on three occasions for the control of Kisangani (Samset 2002; Prunier 2009a; Reyntjens 2010: 207). The end of the original war through the Lusaka Peace Accord and subsequent agreements suspended but did not resolve conflict proceedings. As such, shortly after, Ituri in Eastern DRC became a proxy theatre of war, this time between erstwhile allies. Rising distrust and animosity since the second Congo war saw Uganda accuse Kigali of supporting a new Uganda rebel group, the People's Redemption Army (PRA), based in the Ituri region and intent on destabilizing its western regions, while Rwanda's counter accusation was that Kampala was supporting ex-FAR and *Interahamwe* militias in North Kivu and preparing a destabilization campaign of its western provinces. By the end of 2001, a new peak of tension had to be de-escalated through British government intervention leading to the establishment of a verification mechanism of the claims traded by the two governments (Schraeder 2006: 163; House of Congress 2003). While pressure from Britain, the USA and South Africa resulted in the eventual withdrawal of foreign forces from the DRC, the tensions and conflict, despite de-escalation, took on a Cold War aspect. Although bilateral tensions persisted for a while between the DRC and Rwanda, the DRC and Uganda, with Uganda declaring Rwanda a hostile state, today all these tensions have greatly receded precipitating some level of détente (Borzello 2001).

Realizing détente

This part of the chapter accounts for the emergent relative peace in the GLR. As earlier demonstrated, between 1990 and 2006 the region saw a litany of intra- and interstate conflicts of varying intensity but the situation today couldn't be remarkably more different with open aggression, mutual bitterness, distrust and subversive behaviour giving way to relatively normal bilateral relations, regional security and political stability. The persistent internal wars have also since receded to occasional banditry especially in Burundi, the DRC and south-west Uganda with Kony's LRA abandoning the region altogether for the remote Central African Republic. How do we account for the above 'détente'?

To understand the emergence of this thaw, I will seek to provide an overarching explanation of the shift in intrastates status quo and secondly offer a more comprehensive inter-regional explanation. States have sought to resolve conflicts differently either through pure coercive force, traditional mechanisms, negotiations, mediations or a multiplicity of approaches (Lederach 1997, 2000; Bercovitch, Kremenyuk and Zartman 2009). How successfully a conflict is resolved depends on how well the contradictions or incompatibilities that precipitated the conflict are understood and therein addressed to a mutually agreeable conclusion. To escape what some have referred to as the conflict trap, states emerging momentarily from violent conflicts are soon confronted by the very structural causation of the same such as under-development, poverty, inequality and discrimination, needing to address challenges beyond physical violence (Collier et al. 2003). As Walter (2004) has cautioned, countries that achieve a fleeting negative peace will in the succeeding ten years regress into conflicts if structural problems are not addressed, giving currency to the claim that absence of physical violence does not imply presence of peace. Therefore to borrow from Galtung's work (1965), a recalibrated conflict resolution approach entails some kind of systemic transformation that calls for increase in justice and equality, addressing the culture of violence in the social system, a systematic elimination of oppression and equity in resources distribution with each of these actions mutually reinforcing. Burton (1990: 182) points to societal transformation as 'fundamental social and political changes made to correct inequities and injustice to provide all groups with their fundamental human needs'. This may include the restructuring of social institutions as well as a redistribution of power from high-power groups to low-power groups. In relation to international conflict, Wallensteen (1991: 130) argues that 'a successful case of conflict transformation is one where the parties, the issues, and the expectations are changed so that there is no longer a fear of war arising from the relationship'. Hence two level changes are envisaged: in the parties and the nature of the conflict (micro) and in the socio-political system (macro) within which the conflict is embedded (Väyrynen 1991: 163).

How then is intrastate détente to be understood? On a broader level, conflict resolution here has been a combination of both traditional approaches and 'newer' thinking on conflict resolution. This has seen the employment of both brute force/coercive means in some way along with efforts to address structural violence (Bercovitch, Kremenyuk and Zartman 2009: 55). Hence, individual state military apparatus has been crucial in facilitating and securing their relative security thereby bringing about negative peace while a number of domestic developments have emerged to address the systemic/structural foundation of conflicts, hence realizing some relative level of positive peace. This I argue, is in response to the observation that long-term conflict resolution ought to go beyond mere establishing or enforcement of positive peace but rather pursue a broader socio-political and economic transformation of society. Equally, a far reaching development is perhaps located within the much examined 'democratic peace theory' in which it is claimed that democracies are more peaceful internally than they are in their relations with each other (Levy 1988; Huth and Allee 2002). Now, taking this proposition as largely true, and with most GLR states either willingly or under some kind of external prodding to embrace some level of democratic practice, their behaviour externally and internally is predicted to change from coercion, aggression and zero sum politics to negotiation, compromise and give and take, from exclusion to inclusion and a general elite externalization of domestic peaceful practices. For instance, with the DRC since the end of the war having held two presidential elections amongst other political reforms, Uganda having been on the election circuit since 1996, Rwanda and Burundi with two electoral cycles each since 2003 and 2006 respectively, the evidence seems to point towards the adoption of some liberal democratic behaviour that has an inbuilt mechanism to relatively forestall internal and external violent conduct (Holtzman, Elwan and Scott 1998: 22). There is already a broad consensus that poverty and underdevelopment strongly correlate to conflict. Therefore, the aggressive pursuit of economic development through internal economic reforms, securing inward investment, developing a supportive infrastructural network and ensuring an equitable distribution of resources go a long way in assuaging grievances and/or their violent expression. The high economic growth rates in the GLR averaging six per cent year on year have translated into a general increase in income per capita and reduction in poverty levels, and above all an unwillingness or lack of motivation for non-state actors to pursue violent articulation of grievances.

The greatest change perhaps has been evident at the regional level. For the last ten years or so there has been a marked improvement in regional political stability and security denoting a new era of interstate détente. Accounting for this thaw is the shadow of the International Criminal Court (ICC), a 'capitalist peace' shifting regional dynamics, the role of the United Nations, US foreign policy re-adjustment, and strengthened aid conditionality.

It is not often possible to draw a clear linkage between conflict resolution and criminal courts yet it is exactly what The Hague-based ICC has occasioned. Conflict transformation entails changing behaviour considered central to resolving or forestalling conflicts. In this context, the recent history of the ICC can be traced from the tragic circumstance of the proliferation of post-Cold War conflicts and their conduct. More particularly, the resort to violence and subsequently its indiscriminate use against civilians or elsewhere referred to as 'war crimes' and 'crimes against humanity' has appeared to shake the world's conscience into action. Relatedly, the absence of political will and judicial capability to bring to account purveyors of violence and perpetrators of gross crimes within local jurisdiction has contributed to the emergence and operationalization of the ICC as an extra-territorial judicial body (Roht-Ariazza 1999; Cilliers, Gumedze and Mbadlanyana 2009). Increasingly, the ICC has emerged as an international legal architecture to address and examine culpability in often convoluted conflicts. The threat of personal criminal culpability especially towards those who bear leadership and enabling culpability for actions that are tantamount to crimes against humanity is seen as potentially dissuading. As such, indicting and bringing charges against war lords such as the DRC's Thomas Lubanga (UPC), Jean Pierre Bemba (MLC), Katanga (*Ngiti* militia), Joseph Kony and the LRA leadership or former or sitting presidents including Al Bashir of Sudan and Kenya's Kenyatta has sent out an unambiguous message that personal responsibility will be apportioned with regard to conflict excesses without exception (Akhavan 2005: 404; van der Vyver 2010; Clarke 2012). It has long been argued within the broader field of conflict resolution that accountability in situations where society has experienced wide-scale violence and harm positively correlates with enduring conflict transformation and peace. Inversely, impunity gives rise to entrenchment of repetitive cycles of political violence in the absence of prohibitive counter measures like criminal culpability (Goldstone 1997: 107; Hughes, Schabas and Thakur 2007). This is such that perpetrators, especially those in 'command responsibility' for widespread violence or crimes against humanity, will bear no personal culpability for their actions and therefore precipitate repetitive cycles of violence at no personal cost. Criminal culpability or threat of such against individuals or their agents is therefore meant not only to protect civilians from wanton harm but to act as a deterrent to expressing grievances through violence (Wilkins 2001: 86; Clarke 2012: 310). To this extent, the emergence of the ICC in general, and the 2003 precedent-setting LRA case referral for jurisdiction in particular, sent a strong signal against impunity and pointed to an appropriation of judicial architecture as conflict resolution in the GLR.

With the LRA's Dominic Ogwen indicted and currently held in The Hague, the deterrence nature of this court cannot be overemphasized. Although prosecution successes are still minimal with only three indictees brought to this court found guilty (Lubanga, Bemba and

Katanga) not to mention increasing criticism from Africa alleging discriminatory targeting of Africans, its deterrent nature is unmistakably evident. In fact, the heightened rhetoric against the court especially from African leaders and political elites demonstrates a growing unease about the ramifications and reach of such a court to bring to account originally unaccountable leaders and warlords whose excesses often went unpunished but ironically rewarded with political appointments, the cases of Bemba (MLC), Laurent Nkunda and Lubanga being instructive (Daley 2006b: 313; Reno 2007; Reyntjens 2010). Although Kony used the fear of prosecution at the ICC as an excuse not to sign a 2010 Juba Peace Treaty unless Uganda withdrew its ICC referral, as the former court prosecutor Louis Campo rightly noted, the very existence of the court is a deterrent or at the very least casts a legal shadow which potential perpetrators of violence should be right to be wary of (Ssenyonjo 2005: 424). This therefore may account for the decrease of widespread violence in the GLR, notwithstanding recent instances of sporadic violence by rogue actors in the eastern part of the DRC and Central African Republic.

The capitalist peace thesis portends that mutually dependent trade partners are less likely to engage in interstate conflicts (Gartzke 2007; Schneider and Gleditsch 2013). By implication, economic regional cooperation has been critical to encouraging rapprochement by which GLR states have invested in stronger and deeper bilateral and multilateral economic cooperation. Equally, Murdoch and Sandler (2004) have argued that conflicts have a negative contagion effect on neighbours' economic well-being. It has not been lost on the political leaders of the region that any sustainable economic development of a given state geared towards addressing structural violence can only be achieved within a peaceful environment fully taking advantage of mutually beneficial regional markets. A report from a think tank notes that all South Sudan's regional neighbours will collectively lose approximately US$53 billion as a result of that civil war (Frontier Economics 2015). To this end, the deeper economic and political integration drive by the East African Community (EAC) has seen better cooperation between Kigali and Kampala, further vindicating Granger's causality test that points to trade producing reduction of conflict. The EAC fast track integration pursued by Kenya, Uganda and Rwanda has seen much better working relations between Kigali and Kampala signalled by a number of bilateral and trilateral agreements including mutual economic, security and defence pacts. Of special note is the June 2013 Kampala tripartite accord signed during a summit between the three heads of state that sought to realize a single tourist visa, a single customs territory launched in 2013 as well as a joint railway line project, oil pipeline, and use of national identity cards as travel documents (*All Africa* 2014). The wide gauge railway network intended to connect Kenya, Uganda and Rwanda railway transport infrastructure is a signature project for renewed cooperation. Equally, the proposed western oil pipeline that is intended to transport Uganda's crude oil to the East African coast has seen an expression of interest from DRC for co-investment since both countries appear to have discovered commercial oil in fields adjacent to one another. Kenya too has undertaken to partake in the proposed pipeline noting that 'in line with the spirit of regional integration we committed to support each other in key infrastructure projects and we shall lend support to the Ugandan one. We shall take up a minimal 2.5 per cent stake in the refinery project' (Odhiambo 2015). Clearly, economic imperatives dictate that these countries continue to strengthen their economic cooperation, but broadly what these economic developments signal is that, in seeking to reconstitute the enabling conditions for economic integration, mutual interdependence and development, peaceful cooperation will take precedent as an overriding national interest, hence the evident thaw.

Conflicts can be contextual, in which case change of context can have far-reaching ramifications for the durability of a given conflict more than a change in the actions of the primary protagonists. In this case, the shifting regional dynamics have been crucial to realizing détente in as far as addressing the transnational threat the LRA and other subversive forces pose. For instance, we noted earlier that Sudan was a key and long-term supporter of the LRA in its effort to square things with Kampala due to the latter's acknowledged support for the South Sudan based Sudan People's Liberation Movement/Army (SPLM/A) (Prunier 2004). The cessation of hostilities accord (Comprehensive Peace Agreement) signed between the northern Government of Sudan and SPLM in January 2005 required Khartoum to cease and desist from funding LRA operations, which had formerly been aimed at destabilizing northern Uganda and weakening the SPLA (Prunier 2004: 359). This curtailing of logistical support saw restricting access to arms and refuged rebel families and in some cases active cooperation in combating the LRA by the SPLA and the Ugandan military. A slighted Kony in return directly threatened his previous benefactor warning 'I want to tell the Sudanese lords to keep away from us because if they attack us as they have done this month ... we will fight and set their villages on fire' (IRIN News 2004). The broader effect was a systematic weakening of the LRA. Equally, while Kampala, Kigali and/or Kinshasa were open and eager to support covertly or otherwise subversive forces against each other, the growing military and political cooperation through bi-lateral security frameworks where these forces are now apprehended and repatriated points to a change in regional relations and individual state attitude. The incarceration of General Nkunda (the M23 military head) in Rwanda and the political leadership enforced exile in Kampala are cases in point. Unprecedentedly, Kampala has been reported to be increasingly complicit in covertly apprehending and returning to Kigali wanted military and political fugitives. The various bilateral and multi-lateral security frameworks established concerning dialogue and mutual military and security interests have seen a fundamental transformation in behaviour and attitude establishing an environment conducive to cooperation and the resultant détente.

Third party actors have been theorized as important in conflict resolution but how has the UN played this role in the GLR? There is no doubt that the UN as an international agency has borne the greatest responsibility of mediation, peacekeeping and building in Africa (Keohane 1998; Ramsbotham, Woodhouse and Miall 2005; Wallensteen 2007: 9; Adebajo 2011). Increasingly though this responsibility has become not only more complex but equally demanding to meet high expectations. The most expensive UN Mission in the world now deployed in the DRC, the United Nations Mission in Congo (MONUC), and later trans-formed into the United Nations Stabilization Mission in the Democratic Republic of Congo (MONUSCO), has been central to peacekeeping and building in the DRC since 1998. However, 2 January 2015 marked for the first time a crucial turning point in the history of its operations. This was the deadline by which FDLR forces in the DRC had been given to voluntarily disarm or else face military action to neutralize their threat spearheaded by MONUSCO's Intervention Brigade alongside local FARDC forces. To quote its spokes-person Stephane Dujarric, 'The UN mission has pre-positioned its troops and enablers to support offensive operations against the FDLR in keeping with its mandate' (*The East African* 2015). That the threat of military action or credible threat exists and is poised for actual operationalization is a fundamental departure from the previously lethargic blue helmets and clearly signals a new approach to conflict resolution by the UN body. With the painful failure of 'responsibility to protect' during the Bosnia war and the Rwanda genocide still vivid, a change in its approach has become all the more apparent in the GLR deployment (Rams-botham, Woodhouse and Miall 2005: 137; Wallensteen 2007: 269). The Security Council chapter VII authorization for pro-active engagement and where necessary deadly use of force to protect civilians and maintain peace became a deployable tool kit in ensuring mission success and confronting 'spoilers'. With its strengthened mandate to keep the peace and where necessary create it, protect civilian populations and ensure the rule of law, the UN mission was directly put on a potential collision course with a multitude of local and regional militias operating in Eastern Congo, often systematically undermining state security in their struggle for territorial control and illicit mineral exploitation (Prunier 2009b). As a consequence, MONUSCO has been credited for forcefully enforcing peace in the problematic east, first through keeping the peace, but more proactively enforcing the peace through neutralizing and often disarming marauding rebels and militias, most notably the ADF, M23 and now the FDLR. The later outfit was actively defeated in 2013 with the active combat support of MONUSCO and the DRC national army. The 2 January 2015 deadline for the remnants of FDLR to disarm and potentially repatriate to Rwanda or else face military action supported by MONUSCO further evidences this proactive approach to peace-building. This has resulted in some remnants of the FDLR renouncing violence and offering to disarm with a number of them converging at disarmament camps provided by the UN. This changing role of the UN mission can therefore be claimed to be contributory to the recent thaw in violence and emergence of peace in the DRC region in particular and the GLR in general.

In addition, the US African Command (AFRICOM) authorized by George Bush in 2006 has seen a strategic albeit controversial overt military engagement in Africa and more specifically in the GLR (Englebert and Dunn 2013: 350). According to its mission statement, Africa Command protects and defends the national security interests of the USA by strengthening the defence capabilities of African states and regional organizations and when directed, by conducting military operations in order to deter and defeat transnational threats to provide a secure environment conducive to good governance and development (AFRICOM 2012: 1). As such, the US strategic military partnership with the African Union Regional Task Force to hunt down and bring to account the notorious LRA indicted leadership (Joseph Kony, Dominic Ongwen, Okot Odhiambo, Vincent Otti) from South Sudan and the Central African Republic was momentous. Justifying this intervention, the US noted that 'the LRA is one of the world's most notorious atrocity perpetrators … For nearly three decades, the LRA has displaced, maimed, and terrorized innocent people across four countries, including abducting tens of thousands of children and forcing them to become sex slaves or child soldiers and to commit unspeakable acts' (UPI 2014). Hence, President Obama's signing into law the Lord's Resistance Army (LRA) Disarmament and Northern Uganda Recovery Act of 2009, Public Law 111 172 in May 2010 was a reaffirmation of US commitment to supporting regional partners' efforts to end the atrocities of the LRA in the GLR and Central Africa (The White House 2011). This presidential initiative saw the deployment of Special Operations Forces with logistics, intelligence and advisory efforts to curtail LRA activities. For the first time, there were officially acknowledged 'boots on the ground', a unilateral initiative on the part of American military in an African conflict in general and the GLR in particular. In addition the US War Crimes Reward Program saw a US$ 5million bounty placed not only on the top LRA leadership but equally other notorious war criminals including the planners of the Rwanda genocide and can be seen as US determination to help in the efforts to pacify and bring to a closure one of Africa's longest insurgencies and ensure accountability for crimes against humanity in the broader sense (Kerry 2013). To that effort, pressure was brought to bear on the Khartoum government to stop its support of the LRA and consequently resulted in defections from rebel ranks, most notably of ICC indicted senior rebel commander Dominic Ogwen (Royce 2015). Between 2010 and 2014, it was estimated that the rate of abductions was down 50 per cent while that of civilian murders was down 75 per cent. This was a significant decline in the LRA threat in no simple measure precipitated in part by increased US military engagement and active support.

Finally, donor aid, development and good governance have increasingly become a critical part of the new security paradigm and by extension the broader conflict transformation agenda (Duffield 2001: 117; Ball 2002: 39; Schraeder 2006: 163; Williams 2011: 205). The terrorist attacks of 11 September 2001 and the subsequent American-led 'war on terror' have caused a fundamental shift in the way the broader security landscape especially in weak states is not only internalized but equally internationalized. While internal state dysfunctionality, poor governance, poverty and the like were originally seen as a prerogative of internal governance and at best a moral regional concern, today these have been squarely cast onto the international agenda. As Bush noted, 'September 11 taught us that weak states like Afghanistan can pose as great a danger to our national interest as strong states ... poverty, weak institutions and corruption can make weak states vulnerable to terrorists networks and drug cartels within their borders' (Bush quoted in Rice 2003). Obama echoed similar sentiments noting that 'extremely poor societies ... provide optimal breeding ground for disease, terrorism and conflict' (*The Economist* 2010). These American views broadly mirror the neoliberal thinking that seeks to frame unilateral and multilateral foreign policy specifically towards Africa in the context of security, development and state building. Within the current development aid discourse, donor support is now linked with internal coherence, good governance and security of recipient states. The conditionality serves not just the alleged interests of weak states but is in tandem with the national security interests of donor countries. To that extent a geopolitical approach to bi- and multi-lateral affairs is now in vogue, where development, security and political stability goals can be seen as mutually reinforcing (DFID 2005: 13). Like most African states, the GLR is heavily dependent on donor aid for budgetary support ranging from Rwanda's 40 per cent to Uganda's 25 per cent. This implies that many of these states will be susceptible to donor pressure. Inescapably, donor aid has strategically been used as conditionality to drive a broader regional agenda like good neighbourliness amongst GLR countries and good governance within. As such Uganda and Rwanda have been at the most recent receiving end of the squeezing of the fund tap to stimulate required behaviour. Following a very critical UN report about instability and violence in the eastern DRC that pointed direct fingers at Uganda and Rwandan alleged complicity and support of subversive forces in DRC (M23), the donor community withheld funds that in turn affected Rwanda's economic growth (UN Security Council 2012). With a forecast of 7.6 per cent annual growth rate at the height of the conflict in DRC 2013, aid cuts resulted in a financial squeeze to the Rwanda economy that saw its growth rate fall to 4.7 per cent. To quote US State Department spokeswoman Marie Harf, Rwanda's (*financial*) reprimand is for the 'support for the M23, a rebel group which continues to actively recruit and abduct children' and to threaten the stability of Congo (Heavey and Mohammed 2013). UK's International Development Secretary Justine Greening in a momentous change in UK aid policy noted that on the evidence of the Department for International Development, Rwanda's actions in the DRC 'constitute a breach of the partnership principles set out in the memorandum of understanding [between Britain and Rwanda], and as a result [we have] decided not to release the next payment (21 million GBP) of budget support to Rwanda ... We are committed to finding lasting solutions to the conflict in this region and will work with the governments of Rwanda and DRC to secure a peaceful resolution to the situation in eastern DRC' (*The Guardian* 2012; Smith 2012). Clearly, development aid and its attendant conditionality is part of the revamped tool kit to encourage acceptable and constructive behaviour and can be attributed to increasing reluctance for Great Lakes States to engage in conduct that is mutually destabilising. As if to reinforce this observation, Kagame, commenting on why he would not re-enter DRC to resolve the FDLR problem, noted 'we cannot have cross-border activities to create security on our territory ... We don't have authority, we don't have a say on the other side of the border, on other people's territory ... those who have the authority, the international community ... it has been in their hands for a long time and they will decide what to do' (Kagire 2015). This signals the generally expected behaviour from donor partners that is deemed conducive to cooperation, co-existence and mutual benefit. For the USA like other donor partners, through the Great Lakes Contact Group and the US Strategic Action Plan for Conflict Minerals in the Eastern DRC, 'committing to help regional governments both individually and in cooperation with one another resolve the domestic and cross border issues that challenge regional security and stability and continue to place millions of civilians at risk' serves both US and broader regional interests of peace and stability (Carson 2010). And this refocused US policy has greatly contributed to the détente.

Conclusion

Demonstrably, the GLR is a convergence of socio-political forces and environmental-social dynamics that have all interacted to facilitate a perpetual cycle of violence either within individual states or on a regional level. Inexorably, such complex causes have pointed to the need for an integrated and not least comprehensive approach to conflict de-escalation and resolution; an approach that considers not only the interests of relevant political actors, but also the economic, socio-cultural and environmental factors that have contributed to and sustained these hostilities (Salehyan 2009). If we are to follow the logic of some claims that there is some kind of contagion effect where countries contiguous to a conflict zone are more likely to experience conflict themselves, then there has been interesting evidence in respect to the GLR (Collier and Sambanis 2005; Salehyan and Gleditsch 2006). By implication therefore is it possible to postulate that where there is an emergence of an 'island of peace' then some knock-on effect is to be expected in prompting an end to conflict and the onset of peace in the region as a whole? The détente clearly evident in the GLR appears well placed to answer the above hypothesis in the affirmative. The core thrust of this effort was to account for the emergence of this thaw. While on the whole there are both common and distinct processes that have catalysed the onset of intrastate peace, it is also apparently evident that on a regional level this thaw is as much a result of a constellation of emergent opportunities as it is of a strategic contribution from external forces.

Further reading

Daley, P. (2006) 'Challenges to peace: conflict resolution in the Great Lakes Region of Africa', *Third World Quarterly*, 27 (2): 303–319.

Skrede, C. G., Salehyan, I. and Schultz, K. (2008) 'Fighting at home, fighting abroad: how civil wars lead to international disputes', *Journal of Conflict Resolution*, 52 (August): 479–506.

Strauss, S. (2012) 'Wars do end! Changing patterns of political violence in Africa', *African Affairs*, 111 (143): 179–201.

References

Acker, F. Van (2004) 'Uganda and the Lord's Resistance Army: The new order no one ordered', *African Affairs*, 103 (412): 335–357.

Adebajo, A. (2006) 'The United Nations' in K. M. Gilbert (ed.) *Security Dynamics in Africa's Great Lakes Region*, London: Lynne Reinner Publishers.

Adebajo, A. (2011) *UN Peacekeeping in Africa*, London: Lynne Reinner Publishers.

AFRICOM (2012) United States Military, Pentagon.

Akhavan, P. (2005) 'The Lord's Resistance Army Case: Uganda's Submission of the First State Referral to the International Criminal Court,' *The American Journal of International Law*, 99 (2): 403–421.

All Africa (2014) 'Uganda: Rwanda, Uganda and Kenya sign defense pact', 9 January; available at http://a llafrica.com/stories/201401120049.html (accessed 3 September 2015).

Allen, T. and Vlassenroot, K. (2010) *The Lord's Resistance Army: Myth and Reality*. London: Zed Books.

Ball, N. (2002) 'The reconstruction and transformation of war-torn societies and state institutions: How can external actors contribute' in T. Debiel and A. Kelin (eds) *Fragile Peace: State Failure, Violence and Development in Crisis Region*, London: Zed Books.

Ballentine, K. and Sherman, T. (2003) *The Political Economy of Armed Conflict: Beyond Greed and Grievance*. Boulder: Lynne Rienner Publishers.

Baregu, M. (2006) 'Congo in the great lakes conflict' in K. M. Gilbert (ed.) *Security Dynamics in Africa's Great Lakes Region*, London: Lynne Reinner Publishers, pp.59–80

Beardsley, K. (2011) 'Peacekeeping and the contagion of armed conflict', *Journal of Politics*, 73 (4): 1051–1064.

Bercovitch, J., Kremenyuk, V. and Zartman, W. I. (eds) (2009) *Conflict Resolution: The Sage Handbook*, London: Sage.

Berdal, M. (2003) 'How "new" are ,new wars? – Global economic change and the study of civil wars', *Global Governance*, 9 (4): 477–502.

Berdal, M. (2005) 'Beyond greed and grievance – and not too soon...' *Review of International Studies*, 31 (4): 687–698.

Berdal, M. and Malone, D. (2000) *Greed and Grievance: Economic Agendas in Civil Wars*, London: Lynne Reinner Publishers.

Borzello, A. (2001) 'Uganda declares Rwanda an enemy', 10 March; available at http://news.bbc.co.uk/2/ hi/africa/1213659.stm (accessed 5 October 2014).

Burton, J. (1990) *Conflict: Resolution and Prevention*, New York: St. Martin's Press.

Carson, J. (2010) 'The Great Lakes Region: current conditions and US policy', Bureau of African Affairs, Testimony before the House Foreign Affairs Committee subcommittee on Africa and Global Health, 25 March, Washington, DC.

Chazan, N., Lewis, P., Mortimer, R., Rothchild, D. and Stedman, S. J. (eds) (1999) *Politics and Society in Contemporary Africa*, Colorado: Lynne Rienner Publishers.

Chretien, J.-P. (2003) *The Great Lakes of Africa*, New York: Zone Books.

Cilliers, J., Gumedze, S. and Mbadlanyana, T. (2009) 'Africa and the 'Responsibility to Protect': What role for the ICC?' *Irish Studies in International Affairs*, 20: 55–67.

Clapham, C. (1998) *African Guerillas*, Oxford: James Currey.

Clark, J. F. (2000) 'Explaining Ugandan intervention in Congo', *Journal of Modern African Studies*, 39 (2): 261–287.

Clarke, M. K. (2012) 'Kony 2012, the ICC, and the problem with the Peace-and-Justice divide', Proceedings of the Annual Meeting (American Society of International Law), 106, pp.309–313.

Cohen, A. (1974) *Two Dimensional Man: An Essay on the Anthropology of Power and Symbolism in Complex Societies*, Berkeley: University of California Press.

Collier, P. (2000a) 'Rebellion as a quasi-criminal activity', *Journal of Conflict Resolution*, 44 (6): 839–853.

Collier, P. (2000b) 'Doing well out of war' in M. Berdal and D. M. Malone (eds) *Greed and Grievance: Economic Agendas in Civil Wars*, Boulder: Lynne Rienner Publishers, pp.91–111.

Collier, P. (2007) *The Bottom Billion*, Oxford: Oxford University Press.

Collier, P. and Hoeffler, A. (1998) 'On the incidence of civil war in Africa', *Journal of Conflict Resolution*, 46 (4): 563–573.

Collier, P. and Hoeffler, A. (2000) *Greed and Grievance in Civil War*, Policy Research Paper no. 2355, Washington, DC: The World Bank.

Collier, P. and Sambanis, N. (eds) (2005) *Understanding Civil Wars: Evidence and Analysis*, vol. 1 Africa. Washington DC: World Bank.

Collier, P. et al. (2003) *Breaking the Conflict Trap: Civil War and Development Policy*, Washington DC and New York: World Bank and Oxford University Press.

Daley, P. (2006a) 'Ethnicity and political violence in Africa: the challenge to the Burundian state', *Political Geography*, 25 (6): 657–679.

Daley, P. (2006b) 'Challenges to peace: conflict resolution in the Great Lakes Region of Africa', *Third World Quarterly*, 27 (2): 303–319.

DFID (2005) 'Reducing poverty by tackling social exclusion: A DFID Policy Paper', Department for International Development, London.

Dixon, J. (2009) 'What causes civil wars? Integrating quantitative research findings', *International Studies Review*, 11 (4): 707–735.

Doyle, W. M. and Sambanis, N. (2000) 'International peacebuilding: a theoretical and quantitative analysis', *The American Political Science Review*, 94 (4): 779–801.

Duffield, M. (2001) *Global Governance and the New Wars: The Merging of Development and Security*, London: Zed Books.

Englebert, P. and Dunn, K. C. (2013) *Inside African Politics*, London: Lynne Reinner Publishers.

Frontier Economics (2015) 'South Sudan: The Cost of War: an estimation of the economic and financial costs of on-going conflict', Juba.

Galtung, J. (1965) 'Institutionalized conflict resolution', *Journal of Peace Research*, 2 (4): 348–397.

Galtung, J. (1969) 'Violence, peace and peace research', *Journal of Peace Research*, 6 (3): 167–219.

Galtung, J. (1990) 'Cultural violence', *Journal of Peace Research*, 27 (3): 291–305.

Gartzke, E. (2007) 'The capitalist peace', *American Journal of Political Science*, 51 (1): 166–191.

Gleditsch, K. S. (2009) 'The spread of civil war' in J. Bercovitch, V. Kremenyuk and W. I. Zartman (eds) *Conflict Resolution: The Sage Handbook*, London: Sage, pp.595–612.

Gleditsch, K. S. and Salehyan, I. (2007) 'Civil wars and interstate disputes' in K. Strom and M. Oberg (eds) *Making Sense of Civil Wars*, London: Routledge.

Gleditsch, K. S., Salehyan, I. and Schultz, K. (2008) 'Fighting at home, fighting abroad: how civil wars lead to international disputes', *Journal of Conflict Resolution*, 52 (August): 479–506.

Goldstone, R. (1997) 'War crimes a question of will', *The World Today*, 53 (4): 106–108.

Gurr, T. R. (1970) *Why Men Rebel*, Princeton: Princeton University Press.

Hartung, D. W. and Moix, B. (2000) 'Deadly legacy: US Arms to Africa and the Congo War', World Policy Institute, available at http://www.worldpolicy.org/projects/arms/reports/congo.htm (accessed 3 January 2015).

Heavey, S. and Mohammed, A. (2013) 'US sanctions Rwanda, others over child soldiers', Reuters, 3 October 2013.

Henderson, E. and Singer, J. D. (2000) 'Civil war in the post-colonial world, 1946–1992', *Journal of Peace Research*, 37 (3): 275–299.

Herbst, J. (1990) 'War and the State in Africa', *International Security*, 14 (Spring): 117–139.

Holsti, K. (1983) *International Politics: A Framework for Analysis*, Englewood Cliffs: Prentice Hall.

Holtzman, S., Elwan, A. and Scott, C. (1998) *Post-Conflict Reconstruction: The Role of the World Bank*, Washington DC: The World Bank.

Homer-Dixon, T. F. (1994) 'Environmental scarcities and violent conflict: evidence from cases', *International Security*, 19 (1): 5–40.

House of Congress (2003) *Democratic Republic of Congo: Key to the Crisis in the Great Lakes Region Hearing*, Subcommittee on Africa of the Committee on International Relations, House of Representatives; One Hundred Eighth Congress, Washington DC, 3 April.

Howard, L. M. (2008) *UN Peacekeeping in Civil Wars*, New York: Cambridge University Press.

Hughes, E., Schabas, W. A. and Thakur, R. (2007) *Atrocities and International Accountability: Beyond Transitional Justice*, New York: United Nations University Press.

Huth, K. P. and Allee, T. L. (2002) *The Democratic Peace and Territorial Conflict in the Twentieth Century*, Cambridge: Cambridge University Press.

IRIN News (2004) 'Sudanese militia vow to fight LRA Rebels', UN Office for the Coordination of Humanitarian Affairs, 20 April.

Kagire, E. (2015) 'Kagame I will not pursue rebels in DRC', *The East African*, Nairobi, 17 January.

Kaldor, M. (1999) *New and Old Wars: Organized Violence in a Global Era*, Oxford: Polity.

Keohane, R. O. (1998) 'International institutions: can interdependence work'? *Foreign Policy*, 110: 82–96.

Kerry, J. (2013) 'More work to bring war criminal to justice', *The World Post*; available: http://www.huffingtonpost.com/johnkerry/war-crimes-rewards-program_b_3007049.html (accessed 10 December 2014).

Khadiagala, M. G. (2006) *Security Dynamics in Africa's Great Lakes Region*, London: Lynne Reinner Publishers.

Kiwuwa, D. E. (2012) *Ethnic Politics and Democratic Transition in Rwanda*, London: Routledge.

Lederach, J. P. (1997) *Building Peace: Sustainable Reconciliation in Divided Societies*, Washington DC: United States Institute of Peace Press.

Lederach, J. P. (2000) 'Conflict Transformation: A Working Definition' in C. Schrock-Shenk (ed.) *Mediation and Facilitation Training Manual*, Akron: Mennonite Conciliation Service.

Lemarchand, R. (1970) *Rwanda and Burundi*, London: Pall Mall.

Lemarchand, R. (1994) *Burundi: Ethnocide as Discourse and Practice*, Cambridge: Cambridge University Press.

Lemarchand, R. (1998) 'Genocide in the Great Lakes: Which genocide? Whose genocide?' *African Studies Review*, 41 (1): 3–16.

Lemarchand, R. (1999) 'The fire in the Great Lakes', *Current History*, 98 (628): 195–201.

Lemarchand, R. (2000) 'The crisis in the Great Lakes' in J. W. Harbeson and D. Rothchild (eds) *Africa in World Politics: The African State System in Flux*, Boulder: Westview Press, pp.324–352.

Lemarchand, R. (2009) *The Dynamics of Violence in Central Africa*, Philadelphia: University of Pennsylvania Press.

Levy, J. S. (1988) 'Domestic politics and war', *The Journal of Interdisciplinary History*, 18 (4): 653–673.

Levy, J. S. (1989) 'The causes of war: a review of theories and evidence' in P. Tetlock, J. L. Husbands, R. Jervis, P. C. Stern and C. Tilly (eds) *Behavior, Society, and Nuclear War*, vol. I. New York: Oxford University Press.

Mamdani, M. (2001) *When Victims Become Killers: Colonialism, Nativism and the Genocide in Rwanda*, Oxford: James Currey.

Melvern, R. L. (2000) *A People Betrayed: The Role of the West in Rwanda's Genocide*, London: Zed Books.

Mitchell, C. R. (1981) *Peacemaking and the Consultant's Role*, London: Dartmouth Publishing.

Molloy, I. (2001) *Rolling Back Revolution: The Emergence of Low Intensity Conflict*, London: Pluto Press.

Murdoch, J. C. and Sandler, T. (2004) 'Civil wars and economic growth: spatial dispersion', *American Journal of Political Science*, 48 (January): 138–151.

Museveni, K. (1999) 'Presidential Address', 30 August, Uganda Parliament: Kampala.

Nathan, L. (2008) 'The causes of civil war: The false logic of Collier and Hoeffler', *South African Review of Sociology*, 39 (2): 262–275.

Newman, E. (2004) 'The 'new wars' debate: a historical perspective is needed', *Security Dialogue*, 35 (2): 173–189.

Nzongola-Ntalaja, G. (2002) *The Congo: From Leopold to Kabila: A People's History*, London: Zed Books.

Odhiambo, A. (2015) 'Kenya acquires Sh5.6bn stake in Uganda refinery', *The Business Daily*, 19 January.

Olson, M. (2000) *Power and Prosperity*, New York: Basic Books.

Omeje, K. and Hepner, T. R. (2013) *Conflict and Peacebuilding in the African Great Lakes Region*, Bloomington: Indiana University Press.

Prunier, G. (1995) *The Rwanda Crisis: History of a Genocide*, London: Hurst.

Prunier, G. (2004) 'Rebel movements and proxy warfare: Uganda, Sudan and the Congo (1986–1999)', *African Affairs*, 103 (412): 359–383.

Prunier, G. (2009a) *From Genocide to Continental War: The Congolese Conflict and the Crisis of Contemporary Africa*, London: Hurst and Company.

Prunier, G. (2009b) *Africa's World War: Congo, The Rwandan Genocide, and the Making of a Continental Catastrophe*, Oxford: Oxford University Press.

Ramsbotham, O. and Woodhouse, T. (1996) *Humanitarian Intervention in Contemporary Conflicts*, Cambridge: Polity Press.

Ramsbotham, O., Woodhouse, T. and Miall, H. (2005) *Contemporary Conflict Resolution*, Cambridge: Polity Press.

Reno, W. (1998) *Warlord Politics and African States*, Boulder: Lynne Rienner Publishers.

Reno, W. (2007) 'Patronage politics and the behavior of armed groups', *Civil Wars*, 9 (4): 324–342.

Reyntjens, F. (2010) *The Great African War: Congo and Regional Geopolitics, 1996–2006*, Cambridge: Cambridge University Press.

Rice, S. E. (2003) 'The new national security strategy: focus on failed states'; available at http://www.brookings.edu/research/papers/2003/02/terrorism-rice (accessed 3 September 2015).

Roht-Ariazza, N. (1999) 'Institutions of international justice', *Journal of International Affairs*, Spring, 52 (2).

Royce, E. (2015) 'Chairman Royce statement on LRA leader reportedly being taken into custody', House Committee on Foreign Affairs, United States House of Congress; available at http://foreignaffairs.house.gov/press-release/chairman-royce-statement-lra-leader-reportedly-being-taken-custody (accessed 3 September 2015).

Salehyan, I. (2009) *Rebels without Borders: Transnational Insurgencies in World Politics*, Ithaca, NY: Cornell University Press.

Salehyan, I. and Gleditsch, K. S. (2006) 'Refugee flows and the spread of civil war', *International Organisation*, 60 (2): 335–366.

Samset, I. (2002) 'Conflict of interests or interests in conflict? Diamonds and war in the DRC', *Review of African Political Economy*, 29 (93/94): 463–480.

Sandole, J. D. (1993) 'Paradigms, theories, metaphors in conflict and conflict resolution: coherence or confusion?' in D. J. D. Sandole and H. van der Merwe (eds) *Conflict Resolution Theory and Practice: Integration and Application*, New York: Manchester University Press, pp.11–12.

Sarkees, M. R. and Wayman, F. W. (2010) *Resort to War: A Data Guide to Inter-State, Extra-State, Intra-state, and Non-State Wars, 1816–2007*, Washington DC: CQ Press.

Schneider, G. and Gleditsch, N. P. (eds) (2013) *Assessing the Capitalist Peace*, London: Routledge.

Schraeder, J. P. (2006) 'Belgium, France and the United States' in G. M. Khadiagala (ed.) *Security Dynamics in Africa's Great Lakes Region*, pp.163–186.

Smith, D. (2012) 'EU partially freezes aid to Rwanda', *The Guardian*, 27 September; available at http://www.theguardian.com/world/2012/sep/27/eu-partially-freezes-aid-to-rwanda (accessed 10 December 2014).

Ssenyonjo, M. (2005) 'Accountability of non-state actors in Uganda for war crimes and human rights violations: between amnesty and the International Criminal Court', *Journal of Conflict and Security Law*, 10 (3): 405–434.

Stearns, J. (2011) *Dancing in the Glory of Monsters: The Collapse of the Congo and the Great War of Africa*, New York: Public Affairs.

Stewart, F. (2002) 'Horizontal inequalities: a neglected dimension of development', QEG Working Paper Series, Working Paper Number 81, University of Oxford.

Strauss, S. (2004) 'How many perpetrators were there in the Rwanda genocide? An estimate', *Journal of Genocide Studies*, 6 (1): 85–98.

Strauss, S. (2012a) 'Wars do end! Changing patterns of political violence in Africa', *African Affairs*, 111 (143): 179–201.

Strauss, S. (2012b) 'Retreating from the brink: theorizing mass violence and the dynamics of restraint', *Perspectives on Politics*, 10 (2): 343–362.

Takeuchi, S. (2013) 'Twin countries with contrasting institutions: post conflict state building in Rwanda and Burundi' in Y. Mine, F. Stewart, S. Fukuda-Parr and T. Mkandawire (eds) *Preventing Violent Conflict in Africa*, New York: Palgrave Macmillan.

The East African (2015) 'UN troops prepare offensive against FDLR', *The East African*, 6 January; available at http://www.theeastafrican.co.ke/news/UN-troops-prepare-offensive-against-FDLR-rebels/-/2558/2580112/-/lkqpisz/-/index.html (accessed 6 January 2015).

The Economist (2010) 'Exploding misconceptions: alleviating poverty may not reduce terrorism but could make it less effective', 16 December; http://www.economist.com/node/17730424 (accessed 3 September 2015).

The Guardian (2012) 'UK withholds aid to Rwanda in light of Congo DRC allegations'; available at http://www.theguardian.com/global-development/2012/nov/30/uk-withholds-aid-rwanda-congo-drc (accessed 24 November 2014).

The White House (2011) 'Letter from the President to the Speaker of the House of Representatives and the President Pro Tempore of the Senate Regarding the Lord's Resistance Army', Office of the Press Secretary; available at http://www.whitehouse.gov/the-press-office/2011/10/14/letter-president-speaker-house-representatives-and-president-pro-tempore (accessed 4 November 2014).

United Nations Security Council (2012) 'Letter dated 12 November 2012 from the Chair of the Security Council Committee established pursuant to resolution 1533(2004) concerning the Democratic Republic of the Congo addressed to the President of the Security Council', 15 November 2012, S/2012/843.

UPI (2014) 'Obama orders additional special ops to hunt for Joseph Kony'; available at http://www.upi.com/Top_News/World-News/2014/03/24/Obama-orders-additional-Special-Ops-to-hunt-for-Joseph-Kony/4001395678959/ (accessed 3 September 2015).

Van der Vyver, J. J. D. (2010) 'Prosecutor v. Jean-Pierre Bemba Gombo (Decision Pursuant to Article 67 (1)(A) and (B) of the Rome Statute on the Charges of the Prosecutor Against Jean-Pierre Bemba Gombo)', *The American Journal of International Law*, 104 (2): 241–247.

Väyrynen, R. (1991) 'To settle or to transform? Perspectives on the resolution of national and international conflicts' in R. Väyrynen, (ed.) *New Directions in Conflict Theory: Conflict Resolution and Conflict Transformation*, London: Sage.

Wallensteen, P. (1991) 'The resolution and transformation of international conflicts: a structural perspective', in R. Väyrynen (ed.) *New Directions in Conflict Theory: Conflict Resolution and Conflict Transformation*, London: Sage.

Wallensteen, P. (2007) *Understanding Conflict Resolution*, London: Sage.

Walter, B. F. (2004) 'Does conflict beget conflict? explaining recurring civil war', *Journal of Peace Research*, 41 (May): 371–388.

Wilkins, T. B. (2001) 'Whose trial? Whose reconciliation?' in J. Aleksandar (ed.) *War Crimes and Collective Wrong Doing*, Malden: Blackwell Publishers, pp.85–96.

Williams, D. P. (2011) *War and Conflict in Africa*, Cambridge: Polity Press.

28

A GRADUALLY ESCALATING CONFLICT

Ukraine from the Euromaidan to the war with Russia

Tetyana Malyarenko

Introduction

In this chapter I identify and explain the critical junctures at which events in Ukraine could have taken a different turn depending on the choices (actions and reactions) of the main conflict parties. I argue that at the very beginning of the conflict escalation all sides made incorrect assumptions about one another's intentions, resources and potential. As a result, competition between Ukrainian elite groups has transformed into full-scale war. Due to the 'zero-sum' strategy to which every side adheres, the confrontation has evolved from peaceful protest through violent protest and low-intensity conflict to open warfare with the employment of tanks, heavy artillery, multiple rocket systems, and airpower. This chapter demonstrates that we have witnessed the employment by Russia of a novel form of warfare that combines destabilisation with 'creeping' indirect occupation (hard power) and effective propaganda (soft power). In the meantime, the crisis in Ukraine has been moving along a scenario of protracted conflict. Any delay in its settlement favours the continuation of tensions.

'Euromaidan'

In November 2013 the regime of President Viktor Yanukovych faced mass street protests in Kyiv (Kiev) (later tagged *the Euromaidan*), triggered by Yanukovych's sudden decision to postpone signing an Association Agreement with the European Union. The motivation of the government was rather pragmatic. Due to the high dependence of the Ukrainian economy on the Russian markets, the creation of a free trade zone with the EU leading to the free access of European goods to the Ukrainian market combined with establishment of customs duties for Ukrainian exports to Russia would, it was feared, bring the Ukrainian economy to immediate collapse. Yanukovych's government had to make a choice between two strategic, fatal and divisive decisions. On the one hand, the Association Agreement with the EU would lead to short-term euphoria among the most progressive pro-European part of civil society. However, in the mid-term it carried the risk of precipitating economic decline, unemployment, and poverty that, in turn, would cause wide-spread dissatisfaction and protests. On the other hand, a delay in signing, or rejection of, the Association Agreement would lead to immediate mass protests, but could have guaranteed a medium-term stable level of economic development. As both Russia and the EU insisted, the Ukraine's choice was defined in 'either–or' terms. The option of 'both', which for many years was the core of Ukraine's 'multi-vector' foreign policy of flirting both with the West and Russia, was unavailable in November 2013.

Thus, in November 2013 Yanukovych's decision to postpone the procedure of the signing of the Association Agreement at the Vilnius summit provoked student-led protests in Kyiv's main square *Maidan*. On 30 November 2013 the brutal use of violence against a relatively small number of students multiplied the number of protesters. The next day, about one million protesters demanded the resignation of Yanukovych's government. In the period between 1 December 2013 and 22 February 2014 both sides in the conflict (the street protesters and government) increased the level of violence. Despite reconciliatory declarations, both sides were interested in upping the ante. Since the protesters' main goal was the resignation of Yanukovych and his government, they did not believe that this could be achieved in a non-violent way. On the other side of the barricades, the hawks among Yanukovych's clan insisted on an uncompromising policy toward the protesters and the employment of intentional (instrumental) violence, the usage of which was designed to frighten society and prevent possible future protests. As had become evident by the end of February 2014, Yanukovych's choice was limited to two options: either to employ the armed forces against the rebels on Maidan or resign. At the same time, Ukrainian society itself was dramatically polarised and alarmed at the weakening support of Yanukovych's government in western Ukraine and in Kyiv and strong anti-Maidan and pro-Russian attitudes in Donbas and Crimea.

A compromise solution – an agreement on the settlement of crisis in Ukraine brokered by European Union mediators and foreign ministers Radoslaw Sikorski of Poland, Laurent Fabius of France and Frank-Walter Steinmeier of Germany – was signed on 21 February 2014 by Yanukovych and the leaders of the parliamentary opposition. Its terms included constitutional reform toward the creation of a parliamentary republic to be completed by September 2014 and the holding of early presidential elections in December 2014. There would also be an investigation into violence that had occurred in Maidan, amnesty for protesters and the evacuation of public buildings seized by the protestors. However, the agreement did not come into force because of the lack of trust between the conflict parties. The street protesters refused to accept the Agreement because they did not trust Yanukovych to adhere to its terms. On 22 February 2014 Yanukovych, his family and government fled from Ukraine to Russia.

The low-intensity phase of the conflict and the Russian annexation of Crimea

When one analyses the Russian operation to annex Crimea, two questions frequently appear. The first refers to the extent to which Russian tactics were planned or improvised. The second concerns the reaction of the new Ukrainian government to the annexation – was there any possibility of preventing the annexation either by effective diplomacy or by military means? Russian President Vladimir Putin answered the first question in the documentary film *Crimea: Journey to the Motherland*, when he acknowledged that the operation had in fact been planned in advance. As for the second question, there is no consensus, but it is doubtful that the Ukrainian Army could have done much to stem the Russian forces.

Opinion polls carried out in 2008 tell a very interesting story. According to data from the Razumkov Centre,[1] the share of the population in Crimea viewing themselves as patriots of

Ukraine was around 9 per cent, which is unsurprising given that 75 per cent consider themselves to have been subjected to forced 'Ukrainianisation'. Polls from the same organisation carried out between 18 October 2008 and 9 November 2008 also indicated that some 79 per cent of the population favoured the union of Ukraine with Russia and Belarus (Razumkov Centre 2008a). A different poll carried out between 8 and 18 February 2014, while allowing for a significant margin of error, found 41 per cent of Crimea's residents to be in favour of unification with Russia, compared with 33 per cent in the Donetsk and 24 per cent in the Lugansk provinces. The same poll put support for unification with Russia in the Odessa region at 24 per cent, at 6 per cent in Kyiv, with virtually no support for it in the western regions (Paniotto 2014). Data from 2011 also show that 51 per cent of Crimean residents viewed NATO as an important security threat to Ukraine, whereas the nationwide perception was much lower at 21 per cent (Razumkov Centre 2011). Interestingly the perception of Russia as a threat stood at 15 per cent of Ukrainians in general with 13 per cent of Crimean residents seeing Russia in this way. Finally, the question of whether or not the government in Kyiv (at the time run by Yanukovych) could be viewed as a threat showed a significant divergence of opinion: 33.4 per cent of Ukrainians in general saw the Yanukovych administration as a threat as opposed to 13 per cent of Crimean residents. In an alternative poll conducted by the Razumkov Centre between 17 October 2008 and 7 November 2008, 55.5 per cent of respondents stated that they associated themselves with the Russian 'cultural tradition', while 8.3 per cent associated themselves with the Ukrainian 'cultural tradition', 8.6 per cent with Crimean Tatar tradition, and 7.4 per cent with a pan-European cultural tradition (Razumkov Centre 2008b). Two interesting features emerge from this data. First, despite long-standing high support in Crimea for union with Russia, up until very recently this had not translated into a mass movement actively seeking Crimea's separation from Ukraine. Second, while triggered by the competition between the EU and Russia over influence in and on Ukraine, anti-Russian sentiment in Ukraine as a whole had not so far been a decisive political rallying cry. Rather protests in Maidan were initially primarily directed against the government of President Yanukovych and were as much about corruption and a lack of human rights and the rule of law as about his allegiance to Russia.

Three major factors accounted for stability in Crimea and in relations between Simferopol and Kyiv, and Moscow and Kyiv, respectively. The first was the status of Crimea's autonomy in Ukraine. The second concerned the status of the Russian language in Crimea (where it is common to all residents) and Ukraine; and finally the security of Russia's naval base in Sebastopol, which is strategically important to Russia, and seen as a 'guarantee' for the peninsula's status, as well as being a major economic factor. A threat to any, let alone all, of these factors could not but seriously destabilise the situation within Crimea, Ukraine, and between Russia and Ukraine. The Euromaidan revolution in 2013/14, similar to the Orange revolution almost a decade earlier, created a strong sense of insecurity in Crimea, in particular, regarding the status of autonomy and the Russian language. This was not unfounded as the new majority in the Ukrainian parliament annulled the 2012 law 'On foundations of the state language policy' that gave a number of privileges to the Russian language (as co-equal to Ukrainian) on 23 February 2014 and made statements to the effect that Crimea's status as an autonomous republic in Ukraine might be abolished. The pro-Russian Crimean political elites, in response to these events, took steps which they saw as logical for preserving the status quo and protecting the Republic's interests. The Crimean parliament passed a resolution announcing its intention to restore the 1992 constitution, previously abolished by the Ukrainian parliament, according to which Crimea and Ukraine formed a confederation, and announced its intention to hold a referendum on this issue in Crimea (Pro skasuvannya

Konstitucii i deyakih zakoniv AR Krym 1995). Russia, clearly fearful of being challenged by the new Ukrainian government over its naval base and feeling humiliated by the prospect of 'losing' Ukraine to the EU after all, took these threats as a welcome pretext to come to the 'rescue' of its co-ethnics and compatriots in Crimea. Moreover, the apparent weakness of the Ukrainian state created an opportunity for Russia to strengthen its position in the region relative to both the West and Ukraine.

Russia's operation to annex Crimea started when a group of armed camouflaged troops without military insignia occupied the buildings of the Crimean parliament and Cabinet of Ministers on 26–27 February 2014. Simultaneously, military and para-military troops set up check-points on the Pekerop isthmus and nearby Chongar village – two roads which connect 'continental' Ukraine with the Crimean peninsula. On 28 February 2014 the majority of Crimean parliamentarians voted to hold a referendum on Crimea's future status. The ballot was due to pose two questions. The first question proposed broad autonomy for Crimea within Ukraine. The second question recommended returning Crimea to the constitution of 1992.

The flight of Yanukovych and his inner circle, the collapse of state power, and post-Maidan euphoria caused confusion within the new administration in Kyiv. Over the next two weeks all parties increased the rhetoric of escalation, cutting all possible routes of negotiation. On 1 March 2014 the Russian Duma voted to authorise military action against Ukraine. On 6 March 2014 the date of the referendum was brought forward to 16 March. In addition the option to stay within Ukraine was deleted. After the referendum of 16 March, the parliament of Crimea declared the independence of Crimea whilst simultaneously appealing for unification with Russia. On 18 March, President Putin signed the Agreement on unification of Crimea with Russia.

The annexation of Crimea intensified discussions about low-intensity operations as a method of waging war by employing comparatively low levels of violence.

According to one definition,

> Low-intensity operation is a limited politico-military struggle to achieve political, social, economic or psychological objectives. It is often protracted and ranges from diplomatic, economic and psychological pressures through terrorism and insurgency. Low-intensity conflict is generally confined to a geographic area and is often characterized by constraints on the weaponry, tactics and level of violence.
>
> *(Molloy 2001: 16)*

The annexation of Crimea can be viewed as a classical low-intensity operation, primarily because it was carried out without any shots being fired. Demonstrations of violence and threats of military invasion by camouflaged Russian troops (defined in Russia as 'polite men' – 'vezhlivie lyudi') and exercises of the regular Russian army along the border with Ukraine were combined with strong psychological and informational components. The annexation of Crimea was the first in a chain of events in the framework of a "Russian Spring" informational campaign targeted at several audiences. The first was the population of Russia itself, ethnic Russians and Russian-speakers in the 'Near Abroad' for whom the annexation demonstrated new Russia's foreign policy of 'gathering of true Russian lands'. The West was the second audience. The annexation of Crimea manifested the re-appearance of Russia as a great power and demonstrated its geopolitical ambitions. Finally, Moscow sought to show to the new Ukrainian ruling elite that it could be curbed and forced to follow Russia's course. Obviously, Crimea was, is and will be the core of this complex and multi-layered conflict in Ukraine. No sustainable de-escalation and stabilisation will be possible without finding a way forward on the Crimean issue without addressing the different needs and demands of the parties involved.

Russia employed these low-intensity methods until mid-April 2014. Then Russian colonel Igor Girkin (aka Strelkov – 'The Shooter') and his team of mercenaries left the annexed Crimea and entered the city of Slavyansk in the Donbas. In turn, this action led to the intensification of protests in eastern Ukraine and brought about the conflict there.

The high-intensity phase of the conflict: war in eastern Ukraine

Officially, the beginning of the war in eastern Ukraine (or in the terminology of the Ukrainian legislation – anti-terrorist operation – ATO) began on 13 April 2014, when then acting president of Ukraine Oleksander Turchinov announced the start of a military campaign with the participation of the Ukrainian armed forces. This decision was a reaction to the seizure of Slavyansk – a city located in the north-eastern part of Donetsk administrative oblast of Ukraine – by a group of about 30 mercenaries led by Russian colonel Igor Girkin (aka Strelkov – 'The Shooter'). As soon as Strelkov entered Slavyansk, he dislodged both Ukrainian authorities and local pro-Russian protesters from the city. In fact, it was Strelkov who initiated real war in eastern Ukraine because he organised the defence of Slavyansk according to the rules of contemporary military art, and started to attack Ukrainian military units from there.

Since April 2014 with regard to conflict escalation, one can identify several stages of the armed conflict in eastern Ukraine. As a rule, parties of the conflict changed their strategies and employed greater violence when they entered new stages of direct confrontation. In Donbas the opposing parties moved from using small arms in the early clashes of April 2014 to using tanks, heavy artillery and multiple rocket systems, aircraft and anti-aircraft defence systems when the conflict reached its peak in August 2014.

The beginning of the first stage of conflict escalation in eastern Ukraine refers to the first (spontaneous or organised by the local pro-Russian eastern Ukrainian elites) mass protests in Odessa, Kharkiv, Dnipropetrovsk, Kherson and Luhansk in the framework of an 'anti-Maidan' campaign. The local eastern Ukrainian elites amplified the fears of ethnic Russians and Russian-speaking Ukrainians by blackmailing the new ruling elite in Kyiv with the possible separation of eastern Ukrainian provinces in order to get more resources and power. In different parts of Ukraine local clashes and conflicts between Kyiv and local elites were settled in various ways. In some cases, powerful local oligarchs immediately supported the new government and suppressed the mass protests (Dnipropetrovsk). In other cases, the local elites and Kyiv came to a local political agreement. Two eastern Ukrainian regions (Luhansk and Donetsk – the Donbas) were the exception to the rule. In both regions the flight of almost all representatives of the economic and political elites created a state of anarchy. In Donetsk, the wealthiest city of Ukraine after Kyiv, competition for the business heritage of Yanukovych's clan involved private armies of major Ukrainian oligarchs. Yanukovych and his clan mobilised their own private armies (battalions) to protect their property in Donetsk. Moreover, representatives of former anti-riot police 'Berkut', local militia, and special anti-terrorist forces (integrated into Yanukovych's business family) aided and stimulated the pro-Russian protesters. As soon as the anti-Maidan protests in Crimea started in late February 2014, Russian paramilitary troops ('Cossacks') crossed the Russia–Ukraine border and seized power in Luhansk.

Russia's formal involvement in the first stage of conflict escalation in Donbas was also evident in diplomatic efforts to pressure the new Ukrainian government to be part of an 'inclusive, transparent and accountable constitutional process in Ukraine [with the] immediate establishment of a broad national dialogue with outreach to all of Ukraine's regions and political constituencies' (*Washington Post* 2014). The Geneva statement released by diplomats meeting to discuss the Ukrainian crisis in April 2014 contained concrete steps aimed at de-escalating tensions and restoring security for all citizens. However, very little happened in terms of its actual implementation. Updates from the Organization for Security and Co-operation in Europe (OSCE) Special Monitoring Mission in Ukraine attested to the continuation of the status-quo – neither the Ukrainian government initiated the constitutional changes nor were the protesters disarmed; thus, two key points of the Geneva Agreement failed to be implemented.

The second stage of conflict escalation refers to the failure of the Geneva Agreement and the invasion by Russian mercenaries in Slavyansk. The abovementioned Russian mercenary Colonel Igor Girkin (aka Strelkov) admitted his crucial role in the escalation of the conflict:

'I was a trigger of war in Donbas. If my troops did not cross the Russia–Ukraine border, protest in Donbas would come to its end alike it was in Kharkov or Odessa…From the very beginning we have been fighting seriously…We were the first troops, who started killing Ukrainian diversion groups.'

(BBC 2014, 20 November)

The Colonel noticed that in April–June 2014 the Ukrainian troops did not want to fight: 'Ukrainians imitate assaults, but there is no strong wish of fighting' (Kotich 'Voennie svodki s Yugo-Zapadnogo Fronta'. Forum-antikvariat.ru. Posted on 13 May 2014).

He was surprised by the weakness of the Ukrainian army:

'An examination of the wreckage left by so-called unconquerable Ukrainian army was astonishing…Before, I candidly believed that the most possible imaginable mess and slovenliness is what that the Russian army demonstrates. But now I am confident: it is possible. If the state of affairs in all Ukrainian elements is the same, I do not understand … why we have stopped on the Crimean isthmus?'

(Kotich 'Voennie svodki s Yugo-Zapadnogo Fronta'. Forum-antikvariat.ru.
Posted on 13 March 2014)

The occupation of Donetsk by Strelkov's troops was the most crucial moment of conflict escalation. There is much evidence, including Strelkov's acknowledgement, that the local Donetsk elites and new ruling elites in Kyiv had come to an agreement by the end of June 2014. 'They have prepared to capitulate in Donetsk. Life in Donetsk was luxurious, everyone was drinking coffee in the café, swimming, sporting. Nobody wanted fighting' (Kotich 'Voennie svodki s Yugo-Zapadnogo Fronta'. Forum-antikvariat.ru.).

Before Igor Strelkov entered Donetsk, all institutions of the Ukrainian state functioned in their ordinary regime, including local councils, national bank, postage, railways and tax administrations.

'When we entered Donetsk, the Ukrainian side was completely embarrassed. They had already prescribed scenario of capitulation. When we entered Donetsk, everything was fine – there was a mayor of the city and other authorities subordinated to Kyiv. We were defending Donetsk for almost 40 days before the Russian *vacationers* came.'

(Kotich 'Voennie svodki s Yugo-Zapadnogo Fronta'. Forum-antikvariat.ru.
Posted on 6 July 2014)

Finally, the third stage started with Russia's invasion by '*vacationers*' in mid-August 2014.[2] The Russian *vacationers* crossed the Russia–Ukraine border and defeated the Ukrainian forces in several pockets, and sought to compel Kyiv to negotiate with representatives of Donetsk People's Republic and Luhansk People's Republic in Minsk.

Russia's strategy in Ukraine

In assessing the formal negotiation process between the parties to the conflict, concluded (and implemented) peace agreements and ceasefires would the main criteria for identifying the different 'periods of war' and 'periods of peace' in Donbas. Three stages of conflict, outlined above, were interrupted by meetings of the conflict parties: first, in Geneva on 17 April 2014, and second, in Minsk on 5 September 2014. However, if we use the different concepts of waging war on which the Russian strategy was built as an identification criterion, we can identify the existence of two periods of war. The first period is that of the low-intensity conflict Russia waged between 22 February 2014 and mid-August 2014. The second started in mid-August with the full-scale invasion by '*vacationers*' equipped with tanks and heavy artillery. This period started with the massive defeat experienced by the Ukrainian army at Ilovaysk (see below) and came to its (temporary) end with the Ukrainian withdrawal from Debaltsevo.

Russia and hybrid warfare

The concept of 'hybrid' war re-appeared on the academic and policy agendas after Russia's annexation of Crimea. According to one definition, hybrid warfare is:

> a conflict involving a combination of conventional military forces and irregulars (guerrillas, insurgents, and terrorists) which could include both state and non-state actors, aimed at achieving a common political purpose. Irregular forces need not be centrally directed, although in many cases they form part of a coherent strategy used to oppose an invader or occupation force. Hybrid warfare also plays out at all levels of war, from the tactical, to the operational, to the strategic.
>
> *(Murray and Mansoor 2012)*

In hybrid wars, actors use a variety of tactics, techniques and procedures to fit their goals and help to conclude a conflict successfully. In hybrid warfare, the distinction between large, regular wars and small, irregular wars becomes blurred. Most academic publications on Russia's role in the Ukrainian conflict are lacking in clarity regarding Russia's strategy, goals and methods. Two explanations are very popular. According to the first, Russia does not have any strategy at all (only tactics). The second antithetical explanation considers Russia's grand strategy as a combination of neo-Sun Tzu arts of waging war aimed at returning Russia to its previous position as a global superpower. In this chapter I argue that first, Russia does have a strategy and second, it is fighting not for global leadership, but for its Near Abroad. As a regionally focused power Russia is interested in a stable and friendly neighbourhood. Stability can be achieved either by 'soft' or 'hard' power or a combination of both. Like other post-Soviet countries, Ukraine is an important neighbour for Russia, and thus, Russia is interested in a predictable, secure and managed Ukraine. This goal can be supplemented through the export of a (friendly) political regime. Ukraine is a convenient subject for the export of a political regime because of a protracted and so far inconclusive transition process characterised by three mutually reinforcing dynamics: (a) systemic social and political conflicts; (b) economic stagnation and crisis; (c) incomplete state-building. In Ukraine, Russia's goal is to influence its domestic and foreign policy by establishing privileged relations with the Ukrainian elites either by supporting the current elites or appointing replacements. The aim of Russia's involvement in the current Ukrainian crisis is traditional – the export of a political regime via loyal political elites who can guarantee a predictable Ukraine. In Ukraine, Russia uses a set of different tools in order to destabilise the socio-economic and political situation within the country in order to weaken the current pro-Western government and exchange the current elite for a more pro-Russian counterpart.

As with all major wars in Russia's history, the war in Ukraine is a means through which Russia seeks confirmation and consolidation of its geopolitical identity. Russian geopolitical identity is built on ideas of neo-Eurasianism.[3] Neo-Eurasianism is a continuation of Slavophilism, the core of which is Orthodox Christianity, a particular system of values and traditions of the Russian people revitalised in 2014 as the concept of the Russian World and its practical implication – the Russian Spring. The intention to 're-unite' the Russian nation and to defend Russians living abroad, as well as to protect the core values and interests of Russia are the key factors that explain the rationale for the annexation of Crimea and war in Donbas. Secondly, eastern European states and their territory (named in the Russian geopolitical tradition as 'geopolitical channels'[4]) are significant with regard to the final design and scale of the Russian geopolitical footprint against the background of the blurred and fluid border of the Russian World. Third, one can find similarities in major wars which Russia has waged against neighbouring civilisations. Russia is either waging war in the geopolitical channels, or Russia is waging war on its core territory.

One of the innovative features of Russia's hybrid war in Donbas is the attempt to employ network structure for management of the processes of conflict escalation/de-escalation. Obviously, in comparison with traditional bureaucracies, a network structure is more adaptive, it stimulates innovation and creativity, and the line of command is shorter. There are four major organisations which coordinate Russia's policy toward its Near Abroad: (1) the Office of the Russian President Vladimir Putin; (2) the Ministry of Defence; (3) the Federal Security Service; (4) and various organisations of civil society under the umbrella of the government, for example, the Russian Orthodox Church, Russian patriotic and veterans associations and clubs, and the mass-media.

Each organisation acts almost independently in the framework of a 'corridor' allowed by the Kremlin, under its own strategy and budget. For an illustration of the style of leadership and decision making in the Kremlin see Gleb Pavlovsky (2014), a leading and very close advisor to Vladimir Putin. He speaks of a style of 'non-prohibition' leadership which causes an overlap in activities between the different bodies. Yet at the same time it is also the creation of a space for creativity. Putin's 'non-prohibition' involves many actors; it liberates their energy in order to create room for manoeuvre – a big advantage for every policy-maker. Vladimir Putin constructs the space for creativity independently, but formally, he is distant from their actions. What one can view as chaos and crudity is Putin's strategic and organisational innovation: he is creating new opportunities to which he is simultaneously connected and not connected, but only Putin can control and manage these opportunities. This style also applies to the above-mentioned organisations, participating in the conflict in Ukraine. There is real market competition between them. In the end, Putin chooses between several alternative competitive products (for example, politico-military scenarios) and maintains influence on his disconnected subordinates. For Russia's opponents, it is extremely difficult to figure out and therefore oppose Russia's strategy or rather a set of political, military, economic and informational strategies, realised by several actors on behalf of Russia at different levels (national, regional and global).

However, weak coordination and a "liberal style" of governance can backfire on the strategist when actions of excessively zealous subordinates change the course of war completely. This was the case in May–June 2014. Strelkov's successful campaign in Slavyansk resulted in dramatic conflict escalation in all parts of eastern Ukraine. Strelkov's freedom in the design and implementation of his tactics brought about an unexpected shift from low-intensity conflict to full-fledged war. First, as it is evident (and Strelkov himself has accepted it), he made an initial wrong assumption about the Kremlin's intentions regarding Donetsk and Luhansk. He assumed that Russia's intention was annexation of these territories and that his task was to maintain his power over them until the Russian army invaded:

> Novorossia is a part of Russian World. The territory from Donbas to Odessa is a part of Russia. It is not acceptable to talk about Novorossia as about separate from Russia entity...Donetsk and Luhansk cannot stand against the Ukrainian army alone...Initially, we assumed 'the Crimean scenario'. Nobody wanted fighting for Donetsk and Luhansk republics. We thought – the Russian administration would come...It would be one more republic in the Russian Federation. When it became clear that Russia would not take us, it was a shock for us.
>
> *(Kotich 'Voennie svodki s Yugo-Zapadnogo Fronta'. Forum-antikvariat.ru.*
> *Posted on 7 May 2014)*

Having based his activity on the assumption that Russia would intervene, Strelkov asked for more weapons and soldiers. On 13 May 2014 he complained: 'We don't have sufficient quantity of weapons for the conduct of long operations. The ratio between Ukrainian troops and rebels is 10 to 1. For weapons, the ratio is 50 to 1. We have at our disposal trophy armours and one cannon' (Kotich 'Voennie svodki s Yugo-Zapadnogo Fronta'. Forum-antikvariat.ru. Posted on 13 May 2014).

The Slavyansk campaign could have lasted a long time. However, Strelkov realised his importance as a decision-maker and decided to hasten the arrival of the Russian Empire in Donetsk. His ambitions were perfectly suited to the 'non-prohibition' mandate and Putin's leadership style: 'Now we are waging war for entire Ukraine. Casualties among civilians and pro-Russian soldiers will help us in the future fight for millions of citizens of Ukraine' (Kotich 'Voennie svodki s Yugo-Zapadnogo Fronta'. Forum-antikvariat.ru. Posted on 22 June 2014).

By June 2014 Strelkov was aware of growing rapprochement between the Donetsk elites and Kyiv. So, in order to prevent the return of Donetsk to Ukrainian rule he decided (unexpectedly for the Kremlin) to occupy the city, which was then under the dual control of the Ukrainian authorities and local paramilitary troops and refused to swear to new central government. Having occupied Donetsk, Strelkov intensified the conflict and provoked the full-scale invasion of '*vacationers*' in mid-August 2014.

'The Russian World' and 'the Russian Spring'

'The Russian World' is a logical continuation of *Eurasianism*. The traditional ideology of *Eurasianism* was born in the 1920s among Russian emigrants in contradistinction to the ideology of Bolshevism. In the 2000s 'the Russian World' was re-born as a political project aimed at the creation of an 'alternative reality' for Russians and Russian-speakers in the 'Near Abroad'. As a project aimed at persuasion and manipulation more than at the creation of new values, the contemporary concept of 'the Russian World' synthesises images, narratives, and historical memories about the victories and defeats of Russian people. 'The Russian World' combines in an eclectic manner nostalgia for the Soviet past, the values of Orthodox Christianity, contemporary technologies and patriarchal traditions. Since carnival and theatricality are the key characteristics of any post-modernist project, the Russian World and Russian Spring contain plenty of carnival elements in socio-political and military areas of strategy. Among examples of the carnival elements are: the employment of professional actors for participation in the street protests, thorough construction of major media images of Novorossia's heroes, military training along the Ukraine–Russia borders, Russian military aircraft flying near NATO countries, and escalating/de-escalating statements made by Russian politicians. A leading author of the contemporary concept P. Schedrovytsky (2000), proposed the following definition of the Russian World: 'The Russian World is a network structure of large and small societies who think in the Russian language'.

This wide definition of the Russian World (the main measure of which is creation and maintenance of the network structures) perfectly fits Putin's style of 'non-prohibition' and space for permanent competing creativities he supports. Putin is not claiming to have constructed a new ideology. He has exchanged his right of construction for the privilege of keeping control over mainstreaming messages, which the Kremlin brings to the public. Everyone who is looking in the same direction as him enjoys freedom of speech. As a result, the Russian World appears as a 'bricolage'.[5]

As long as the implementation of 'the Russian World' has domestic and foreign policy implications, the bricolage messages of the Russian World have both internal and external customers. In Russian foreign policy, 'the Russian World' appeared in Putin's Munich speech of 2007 as: (1) Russia's refusal to accept a unipolar world; (2) grievance and dissatisfaction with NATO enlargement; (3) the right of Russia to act independently and according to its national interests (Putin 2007).

Russia did not consider the processes of EU and NATO enlargement as a serious threat to its security while the enlargement involved countries of Eastern Europe ('geopolitical channels') which Russia has never considered part of its core territory – contrary to the countries of the so-called 'Near Abroad'. Russian foreign policy in the 'Near Abroad' ('the Russian Spring') includes the protection of ethnic Russians and Russian-speakers, embarking upon 'preventive measures' in the territory of foreign states and guaranteeing the right of Russians abroad to seek unification with the Motherland. The rapid change in the political regime in Kyiv in January–February 2014 supplemented by anti-Russian and anti-Putin rhetoric was (taken as) a signal of the West's invasion of the Russian World's core territory (at least as Russia understands it) and required immediate reaction. It is also worth remembering that establishing 'de-facto' states, for example, in Georgia and Moldova, was always a means to an end – to dictate the terms of 're-unification' and to gain permanent control over some former Soviet republics' foreign policy choices.

Russian tactics during the Donbas spring–summer 2014 campaign

The tactics of the spring–summer campaign of Russia's hybrid war in Ukraine had three main politica-military scenarios.

1   The optimistic scenario assumed that the annexation of Crimea and support of the pro-Russian protesters in eight administrative (primarily eastern) oblasts of Ukraine with money, weapons and mercenaries would counter-balance radical nationalistic pro-Ukrainian attitudes in Kyiv and Western Ukraine and possibly, through constitutional

changes, would bring to power a Ukrainian elite, loyal to Russia, which, in turn would recognise the annexation of Crimea or any other compromise solution.

2   The realistic scenario – mass protests and popular dissatisfaction in eastern Ukraine combined together with the threat of Russian invasion would convince Kyiv to compromise and would draw away the attention of Kyiv and the West from the annexation of Crimea. The Crimean question would be outside of any possible peace negotiations on the enduring settlement.

3   The pessimistic scenario – mass protests and civil unrest would lead to the creation of a de-facto state on the territory of eight administrative oblasts of south-eastern Ukraine (optimistic variant) or on the territory of Donetsk and Luhansk administrative oblasts (pessimistic variant). The new de-facto state 'Novorossia' created on the territory of the economically developed industrial part of Ukraine would be able to provide economic growth due to integration with the Eurasian Customs Union. At the same time, suffering the double impact of broken economic ties with Russia and the loss of the industrially developed parts of the country, the core 'right-bank' agricultural Ukraine would be forced to come to a compromise with Russia.

As is now evident, each of these scenarios was built on the following assumptions:

1   The war would not last for a long time (both Russia and Ukraine planned to win the war before September 2014).

2   The Ukrainian government would compromise/capitulate in the short-term period regarding the status of Crimea and federalisation of Ukraine.

3   There is a significant pro-Russian segment within Ukrainian society (ethnic Russians and Russian-speaking Ukrainians) which would support the protesters and rebellion in the eastern part of Ukraine. The eastern Ukrainian elites would support the rebellion.

4   Sanctions from the West, including economic ones, would be insignificant.

The optimistic scenario was taken as the base for actions. Having financed the protests in southern and eastern Ukraine (first of all, in Kharkiv and Odessa) in March 2014, the option of armed revolt or/and armed invasion was not considered seriously at that time. By the end of June 2014, the pro-Russian rebels were only equipped with small arms and a few howitzers. At the same time, Russia indirectly threatened Ukraine with possible military invasion and had been carrying out military exercises along the Ukrainian border. The key message of Russia's strategy is: 'We need ALL pro-Russian Ukraine. That is why we are fighting not for separate territories, but for the whole of Ukraine in Russia's orbit'.[6]

Russian tactics in the summer–autumn campaign of 2014

When it became evident that the main assumptions of Russia's strategy regarding conflict dynamics, and the attitudes of the population and elites in eastern Ukraine were incorrect, Russia changed its strategy toward more violent ways of exercising pressure. As Putin subsequently confirmed, in mid-August 2014 Russia invaded with troops – who officially were on vacation from their obligations in the Russian army (the so-called '*vacationers*'). However, the employment of regular troops and in particular, special forces ('*spetsnaz*') was limited to special operations and very decisive military engagements, for example, in Ilovaysk in August 2014, in the seizure of Donetsk airport in January 2015, and in Debaltsevo in late February and early March 2015.

Since mid-August 2014, the armies of the Donetsk People's Republic (DPR) and the Luhansk People's Republic (LPR) have been provided with weapons and supplies in convoys from Russia. The artillery of DPR and LPR shell the positions of the Ukrainian army, which provokes the Ukrainians into engaging in local clashes. As a result, there is a gradual 'creeping' occupation of the Ukrainian territories. Unfortunately, the Minsk II agreement of February 2015, which sought to shore up the ceasefire and restart dialogue between warring factions, did not change Russia's intentions. Low-intensity battles occur along the front line. As a result of this fighting, DPR and LPR are gaining territory.

The Ilovaysk 'pocket'

The battle for Ilovaysk (important for its railway hub located 45 km south-east from Donetsk) is regarded as the most bloody battle in the Russia–Ukraine war in Donbas. About 8,000 Ukrainian troops were surrounded in a 'pocket' near Ilovaysk in August 2014. According to official data from the Ukrainian government, 360 Ukrainian troops were killed (Report of Parliamentary Investigative Commission on Ilovaysk 2014). However, informal estimates by Ukrainian commanders, volunteers and pro-Russian rebels are different from official data. According to them, as many as 3,000 Ukrainian soldiers may have been killed in the pocket.[7]

At the beginning of August 2014 the Ukrainian military sought to cut Donetsk off both from Luhansk and from Russia. The first thrust of the Ukrainian army would come from north-east near Debaltsevo. The second thrust would come from south-east near Ilovaysk. If successful, Donetsk would be surrounded. Major railway communication lines and highways for supply of weapons, money and mercenaries from Russia would have been cut.

As became evident from the beginning of the military campaign for Ilovaysk, both the Ukrainian joint forces and the Russian Orthodox Army (pro-Russian troops subordinated to Donetsk People's Republic) failed to organise an all-round line of defence of their positions. The main armoured forces of the Ukrainian armed forces were located in the centre of the Ukrainian positions, whereas poorly equipped and weakly trained paramilitary battalions defended the flanks.

In August 2014, the Russian Orthodox Army attacked the flanks of the Ukrainian forces from the north (from Donetsk) and from the Russia–Ukraine border (Uspenka border control point), thus encircling Ukrainian armoured brigades. The pro-Russian forces cut the communications of the Ukrainian army and defeated its rear area forces. At the same time, Russian 'vacationers' passed throughout the Azov sea coast and stopped near Mariupol on the south of the front line and Volnovakha on the west of the front line. There was a real risk of occupation of Mariupol that would open a 'road' from Russian Rostov-on-Don to the annexed Crimea. All relief efforts of the Ukrainian army failed. The 92nd Ukrainian armoured brigade (about 2,000 troops) was confronted and pushed back pounded by Russian 'vacationers' on its way to Ilovaysk.

Nevertheless, the main tragedy still lay ahead. On 29 August 2014, Putin appealed to the Russian Orthodox Army via Russian mass-media to release the Ukrainian troops from the encirclement and indeed an agreement was reached, according to which the Ukrainian armoured brigades would leave the pocket unarmed. However, the surrounded Ukrainian forces broke the agreement. They attempted to break free from the encirclement taking with them with all their military equipment, including tanks and artillery. This provoked counter action by the separatists. The major column of the Ukrainian army was halted. About 1,000 troops were killed and about 700 were taken prisoner.

According to President Poroshenko's report, the Ukrainian army lost its most battle-hardened brigades and about 30 per cent of all tanks, 74 per cent of all troop carriers, 93 per cent of all howitzers, 60 per cent of all self-propelled artillery vehicles and 67 per cent of multiple rocket systems in the battle for Ilovaysk (Report of Parliamentary Investigative Commission on Ilovaysk 2014). This strengthened Russia's position at the negotiation table, caused a major re-think in Kyiv, and helped to bring about the first Minsk negotiations.

Novorossia or occupation?

By the start of the armed conflict in Donetsk and Luhansk, these two administrative *oblasts* were the most densely populated territories of Ukraine, with 4.825 million living in the Donetsk oblast and 2.5 million living in the Luhansk oblast. Donetsk city had a population of a million and 440,000 resided in Luhansk city (All-Ukrainian Census 2001). According to various estimates of the local authorities and international organisations, approximately 3.3 to 3.5 million still live in territory on which the Ukrainian state de-facto does not exercise its power. Ukraine's Ministry of Social Policy puts the number of registered internally displaced persons countrywide at 980,000. In addition since February 2014, some 600,000 Ukrainians have sought asylum or other forms of legal sojourn in neighbouring countries, particularly the Russian Federation, but also in Belarus and Moldova. This dramatic flight of the people of Donetsk and Luhansk tends itself to question the character and support of Novorossia.[8]

According to the census results of 2001 the ethnic structure in the Donetsk oblast was as follows: Ukrainians constituted about 56 per cent and Russians 38.2 per cent. Ukrainians formed 58 per cent of Luhansk oblast's population with Russians making up 39 per cent. The overwhelming majority of the population of both oblasts is Russian-speaking (All-Ukrainian Census 2001). This unique ethnic structure and common history led to the creation of a special regional (so-called 'Donetsk') identity in Donetsk whereas residents of Luhansk identified themselves either as ethnic Russians or as Russian-speaking Ukrainians.

Under the circumstances outlined earlier it is clear why a majority of the population in Donetsk and Luhansk considered *Euromaidan* as a threat to their safety and well-being (according to opinion polls, in April 2014, 70.5 per cent of respondent of Donbas assessed *Euromaidan* as a coup d'état). In February 2014, 25.8 per cent of the respondents of eastern Ukraine (Kharkov, Donetsk and Luhansk) claimed they would vote for the unification of Ukraine with Russia (Takoy Razniy Yugo-vostok 2015).

The creation of new 'states'

The brand 'Donetsk People's Republic' first came into the political life of Ukraine during the 'Orange Revolution' of 2004/5. The 'Donetsk Republic' was a typical 'pocket' party or, in the contemporary political lexicon, a 'technological project' funded and managed by the Party of the Regions. The 'Donetsk Republic' performed two tasks: (1) it brought to the Party of the Regions potential leftist voters, taking them away from the Communist Party of Ukraine; (2) it blackmailed Kyiv and the 'Orange' government with the threat of separatism in eastern Ukraine. In Yanukovych's time, the 'Donetsk Republic' did not appear in the political arena. It was simply unnecessary. As the president of Ukraine, Yanukovych concentrated on keeping Ukraine united through the reconciliation of western and eastern parts of the country, which traditionally support diametrically opposed directions of foreign policy. Under such conditions, support for the separatist 'Donetsk Republic' had little appeal to the ruling elite.

The re-appearance of the 'Donetsk Republic' occurred under similar circumstances to those of November 2004. In 2014, Yanukovych faced losing his power and influence on Ukraine's politics. The first 'Donetsk Republic' was rather a farce. The second 'Donetsk Republic' is more of a tragedy. There is a fatal set of inter-related factors that together brought this to a head in 2014. These include the flight of Yanukovych and his inner circle, external funding and organisation of the mass protests in Donbas, the entrance of Igor Strelkov and other Russian mercenaries, and finally, the open Russian invasion by the *'vacationers'*.

A *'white elephant'*

The technique of creation and support of de-facto states in the 'Near Abroad' is a well-known and well-developed strategy used by Russia as a means of creating internal instability and tensions through which Russia can impact the foreign policy of its post-Soviet neighbours. Transnistria, Abkhazia and South Ossetia are examples. In this chapter I argue that the establishment of the Donetsk People's Republic and Luhansk People's Republic was a complex combination of unplanned spontaneous actions by some actors (for example, Igor Strelkov), Russia's tactical steps, and mistakes by Moscow, Kyiv and local Ukrainian elites. All taken together they led to the birth of a 'white elephant' which both Russia and Ukraine are unable to rid themselves of and which neither can keep or integrate. Secondly, the processes within DPR and LPR and specific functions that local 'republican' elites deliver for their population allow me to argue that we are witnessing a process of military occupation as opposed to any attempt at state building.

The DPR declared its independence on 7 April 2014, with the LPR following suit on 12 May 2014 after simultaneous 'referendums' had taken place in both 'republics'. On 24 May the leadership of both 'republics' signed a confederation agreement on establishment of the state of 'Novorossia'. Nevertheless, the political regimes of DPR and LPR were different. After Yanukovych's flight, power in Donetsk was captured by the battalions (private armies) of local oligarchs, including former representatives of anti-riot police 'Berkut', police and special military troops, previously subordinated to Yanukovych's government. The ruling elite in Donetsk was a symbiosis of public officials still subordinated to Kyiv and organised criminal groups. At the same time, Russian paramilitary troops (Cossacks) entered Luhansk immediately after the flight of the local elite.

When Igor Strelkov entered Donetsk on 5 July 2014, he established a military dictatorship (so-called 'Orthodox sharia'), including the death penalty for looting, curfews, drum-head court martials, and severe thorough control of the population and vehicles in the city including an extensive network of check-points. In Luhansk, the disintegration of power and anarchy brought quasi-feudal rule. Since May 2014 local 'republican' authorities have failed to build state institutions and public governance in the areas of economy and social service as well as the financial and banking systems. The Donetsk railway and other strategic infrastructure on the occupied territories are managed by Kyiv. Most business on the territory of self-proclaimed states functions according to Ukrainian legislation and pays taxes to the Ukrainian budget. Local civil society delivers the most basic public services. As far as both Kyiv and Moscow refuse to fund the social infrastructure and pay social benefits for the residents of the uncontrolled territory of Donbas, socially vulnerable groups of the population are left to survive on their own.

All the above brings us to the conclusion that the first and foremost function of both 'republics' is to wage war against Ukraine formally, on their own behalf, but in fact, pursuing Russia's interests.

The failure of state-building initiatives in the Donetsk People's Republic and Luhansk People's Republic together with Russia's efforts to ban some local initiatives on state-building send a signal that we are dealing with leverage that is different to that previously employed by Russia. Russian tactics are not concerned with the creation of de-facto states, but about managed destabilisation through a combination of 'creeping' occupation with other methods, first of all, in the area of information, mass-media and propaganda.

At the same time, Kyiv also demonstrates a lack of clarity in legally defining the armed conflict in Donbas. Ukrainian legislation on this subject is rather confusing. At present, officials do not refer to Russia as a military occupier. On 14 April 2014 the acting president of Ukraine, Oleksandr Turchinov, signed a Decree authorising the commencement of anti-terror operations (ATO) in eastern Ukraine (which is still in force). According to Ukrainian law, the ATO are carried out by the Ministry of Internal Affairs and Security Service of Ukraine. The armed forces cannot be involved. After the conflict escalated in mid-August 2014 and after the failure of the first Minsk agreement, President Poroshenko isolated the territories defined as 'temporarily outside of the Ukrainian state's control' from other parts of Ukraine and banned any economic relation with them. Later on, the Ukrainian parliament appealed to the UN, European Parliament, Council of Europe, NATO, OSCE and all national parliaments demanding that they label Russia as a state that supports terrorism and terrorist organisations in Ukraine. Finally, on 17 March 2015, Ukraine issued a resolution on the 'temporarily occupied territories'. This resolution, nevertheless, does not identify any state as a military occupier and does not clarify relations between Kyiv and the 'occupied territories'. One of the main reason for this uncertainty lies in the problems of a legal definition of military occupation, in particular, when the occupying state has not announced or confirmed its military occupation directly. The international character of occupation and direct rule of the occupying country via military or civilian administrations are understood by all experts. Legal definitions of territories being occupied are problematic, for example, if the occupying state exercises its authority indirectly via proxies. It is even more difficult if the territory is captured by a non-state actor such as para-military troops or mercenaries.

There are several ways in which Russian mercenaries arrived in Donbas: patriotic organisations in Russia, associations of veterans of the militia, and Afghan and Chechen wars. The mercenaries are trained in special camps on the territory of Rostov-on-Don region of Russia or Donetsk oblast of Ukraine. As a rule, elite forces – veterans of the Russian special forces ('*spetsnaz*') – are sent to Donetsk whereas other mercenaries are sent to Luhansk. One of the Russian mercenaries describes his way to Donbas:

> There is high demand for qualified soldiers – gun layers, spotters, signallers. Others are sent to shooting subunits. There are consistent shaping of units and military trainings. The border between Russia and Ukraine looks like a sieve. You may go any direction – nobody asks. Everything is clear. The columns with the military equipment are crossing the border during all the day without any camouflage.
>
> *(Rosbalt 2015)*

Igor Strelkov writes about the motivation and ideology of the Russian 'irregulars': 'The irregular army gathers individuals of different opinions, united by common Russian language and hatred against Ukraine. It is injurious for our common deal to create any common ideology for them' (Kotich 'Voennie svodki s Yugo-Zapadnogo Fronta'. Forum-antikvariat. ru. Posted on 1 June 2014).

Igor Strelkov's statement brings us to the question about the key idea of the statehood for Novorossia and the main purpose of its creation. In fact, one can find three alternative projects of the Russian state in the narratives which leaders of Novorossia tell us. The first 'Russian state' is Ukraine. For many Russians and Vladimir Putin, Ukrainians are ethnically Russian people who have lost their Russian identity. As they believe, Ukraine is largely populated by Russian people, and as such the rationale for Ukraine's existence as a state has always been questioned by the majority of ethnic Russians. The second Russian State is the Russian Federation, the current political regime which is opposed by the majority of the Russian mercenaries in Donbas. Finally, Novorossia as a newly established 'true Russian' State could be a driving force for changes in both Russia and Ukraine and has a power to bring them to unification.

As confirmation of the role for Novorossia, Aleksandr Dugin in his speech to Donetsk said:

> Novorossia means New Russia. Your mission is not only to save yourselves. Your mission is to renovate Russia, which is currently a mix of compromises between anti-Russia and Russian World. The Russian State is not true Russia now. It is not Russia who will save you. You – Novorossia – will save Russia.
>
> *(Dugin 2014)*

The strategy of Ukraine in the ATO and the war against Russia

During the period between March and May 2014, the Ukrainian military command lacked a comprehensive strategy of how to oppose the separatist movements and/or to prevent Russia from supporting pro-Russian protests in eastern Ukraine. Russia's rapid annexation of Crimea yielded its fruits: Kyiv was completely shocked and demoralised. The newly appointed Ukrainian government preferred to avoid open military confrontation with Russia, instead appealing to international organisations and countries, which signed the Budapest Memorandum on Security Assurances in 1994, namely the United States of America and the United Kingdom, to influence Russia's return to the rules of international law and facilitate Russia's further respect of the territorial integrity of Ukraine. Later, Kyiv did accept the status quo. It evacuated a few Ukrainian battalions from the annexed Crimea to other parts of Ukraine. Second, the law of Ukraine 'On rights and freedoms of citizens and the legal regime on temporary occupied territories of Ukraine' was adopted on 15 April 2014. According to this law, the Ukrainian government established an economic blockade of the annexed Crimea. It also withdrew all public institutions and declared all economic activity illegal (*Zakon Ukraini* 2015).

The context of the post-Euromaidan atmosphere is important for understanding the frequently non-systemic, illogical and incomprehensive nature of Kyiv's strategic decisions, in particular during the first months of war until the invasion by Russian '*vacationers*' in mid-August 2014. Post-Euromaidan euphoria and wide-spread expectations for an easy and quick victory in Donbas created negative public attitude to any possible compromise with the rebels and/or Russia. Any compromise would have been seen as a national reproach or treason.

The Euromaidan revolution destroyed institutions of the repressive state. The Ukrainian society has considered this distraction as an action in favour of public interest and utility. That is why the new ruling democratic elite did worry about the legal quality of their politico-military decisions. Revolutionary expediency won over the rule of law. On the other hand, bureaucratic organisations of the Ministry of Defence and Military Headquarters requested the appropriate development of the legal framework for any operation/action, creating the way for obstacles for the conduct of war. Paramilitary troops, acting on the side of the

Ukrainian government did not have the official status of combatants. Confrontation between Headquarter and paramilitary battalions and the absence of the line of command led to a lack of centralised command, expertise, and, therefore, ultimately defeat.

During May–June 2014, when Strelkov's activity in Slavyansk required a reaction, Kyiv increased the mobilisation of paramilitary troops (still on a voluntary base). In May 2014, the Ukrainian forces acting together with local militia succeeded in recapturing Mariupol – the key industrial and seaport south of Donbas. At the same time, the Ukrainian army started re-organising its sub-units and employed the artillery and aircraft for attacks on the occupied cities in Donbas on a regular basis. As soon as the Ukrainian forces started to use aircraft the rebels received contemporary air-to-air defence systems. By mid-July 2014, the losses of the Ukrainian air forces had become significant. Since the MH17 crash near Donetsk in July 2014, the Ukrainian command had no aircraft operating in the conflict zone.

The Russian '*vacationers*' entered Ukraine in mid-August 2014. By way of reaction, Kyiv shifted gear. Ukraine's current political-military strategy is built on realistic assumptions about the impossibility of winning a war against regular Russian troops, but it also excludes any compromise on the status of occupied territories and federalisation of Ukraine (which was the core of demands Russia's). Kyiv intends to separate war-affected territories from the territories controlled by the Ukrainian state through economic and transport blockades and also by building fortifications along the Russia–Ukraine border and administrative borders of Donetsk and Luhansk. If the main message of Russia's strategy is: 'We need ALL pro-Russian Ukraine',[9] the main message of Ukraine's strategy is: 'Leave us alone'. Kyiv's main task is the minimisation of Russia's influence on all unoccupied parts of Ukraine.

Obviously, this combination of strategies brings us to a 'zero-sum' game in which neither conflict side wants to compromise. Under such conditions, the conflict will likely become protracted where the side with higher economic potential has the greater chance of winning.

All along, the foundations of Ukraine's strategy have rested upon three assumptions:

1   Russia would not intervene in conflict in eastern Ukraine with its regular armed forces. Kyiv would deal with pro-Russian separatists only.
2   The war, defined in terms of the Ukrainian legislation as an 'anti-terrorist operation', would not last for a long time; losses would be insignificant.
3   NATO or the USA would intervene and protect Ukraine from Russia's aggression. The threat of NATO involvement would keep Russia from a full-scale invasion.

Obviously, Ukraine's military strategy (or lack thereof) is a logical continuation of its political and socio-economic problems: Ukraine has not defined a new format of relations with Russia, taking into account both the war in eastern Ukraine and high dependence of the economy on Russian natural gas and Russian markets. Ukraine's informal consent to ceding territories to Russia is a consequence of such indecisiveness. Moreover, there is a lack of a common and comprehensive vision of the future Ukrainian statehood and national idea. Important reforms in the economy and public administration have not started yet. The country lacks any clear perspective for development. Institutional disintegration, corruption and extremism continue to corrode society.

Ceasefire and peace agreements

During the process of conflict escalation there were three major meetings of the warring parties together with international mediators aimed at conflict settlement. As a result of the

Geneva meeting on de-escalation of the situation in Ukraine between the European Union, the USA, Ukraine and Russia on 16 April 2014 the four parties issued a joint statement on concrete steps which all conflict sides should undertake in order to de-escalate tensions and restore security for Ukraine's citizens. 'All illegal armed groups must be disarmed. All illegally seized buildings must be returned to legitimate owners…Amnesty will be granted to protestors… The announced constitutional process will be inclusive, transparent and accountable' (*Washington Post* 2014).

Neither Russia nor Ukraine intended to compromise. Ukraine's position was that Russia should withdraw mercenaries and stop its support for pro-Russian rebels in eastern Ukraine. At the same time, Ukraine failed to implement its part of the Geneva agreement – to change the constitution toward granting autonomy for south-eastern Ukraine. For its part, Russia was waiting for the constitutional reform in Ukraine. Until then, the Kremlin would not de-escalate.

Given that peaceful conflict settlement was dead in the water, the warring parties continued a path of escalation for almost four months until Russian '*vacationers*' invaded Ukraine. Then, the Minsk agreement[10] drawn up on 5 September 2014 by the Trilateral Contact Group on Ukraine (Ukraine, Russia and the OSCE) ensured an immediate bilateral ceasefire, the decentralisation of power, permanent monitoring of the Russia–Ukraine border, and withdrawal of illegal armed groups and military equipment as well as mercenaries from Ukraine (Protocol on Results of Consultations of the Trilateral Contact Groups 2014).

In fact, the first Minsk agreement did not bring peace. The parties to the conflict continued fighting across the front line, in particular around Donetsk airport. After the pro-Russian rebels' victory at Donetsk airport, a new package of measures was agreed on 12 February 2015 (*The Telegraph* 2015[11]). Although major offensive operations have been banned since 12 February 2015 (except for the Debaltsevo 'pocket'), progress in other areas is limited and tactical fighting still goes on today.

Conclusion

In this chapter I argued that both Ukraine and Russia made initially flawed assumptions about intentions and the risks of escalation. These incorrect assumptions brought every side to a zero-sum strategy. When two opponents hold to a zero-sum strategy and neither side intends to compromise, conflict tends to be inevitable and protracted. In hindsight, Russia and Ukraine have realised the errors of their strategic thinking. However, it is unlikely that the understanding of mistakes will lead to conflict termination or settlement. The Minsk II Agreement proposes a plan of conflict settlement, but neither side demonstrates willingness to take concrete steps towards its implementation. Nor does it seem as if Ukraine, Russia or the West have a viable strategy to really change the situation any time soon.

Notes

1 The opinion poll was carried out between 18 October 2008 and 9 November 2008. For all data from Razumkov Centre opinion polls see http://www.razumkov.org.ua.
2 This new term 'Russian vacationers' (in Russian – 'otpuskniki') appeared after Vladimir Putin's explanation of Russian troops' presence in the territory of Ukraine as soldiers who spend their vacations there.
3 Neo-Eurasianism is a major contemporary Russian school of political-philosophical thought.
4 The theory which considers Eastern European countries as 'geopolitical channels' between Russia and Western Europe was proposed by leading Russian philosopher Vadym Tsymbursky in his article 'The Island Russia: The Cycles of Europe's Theft'. In this article the author compares Russia to an 'island at

the core of mainland'. According to Vadym Tsymbursky, as a geopolitical object Russia is an integral niche of the Russian ethnos, which lies at the East of the Western European civilisational platform; Russia is separated from liberal Western Europe by a belt of peoples and territories which border Western Europe, but do not form a true part of it. Due to their weak statehood, these countries periodically gravitate either toward Russian or toward Western civilizational platforms. http://old.russ. ru/antolog/inoe/cymbur.htm

5 In post-modernist literature, art and philosophy bricolage is a spontaneous and consistently changing process of creation of images and narratives from 'material at hand'.

6 Putinu nuzhna vsya Ukraina http://inosmi.ru/sngbaltia/20150410/227433743.html (accessed on 08/ 04/15).

7 Official Kyiv acknowledges losses of 360 combatants in the battle for Ilovaysk city. However, both commanders of Ukrainian paramilitary battalions, for example, the commander of 'Donbas' Semen Semenchenko and leaders of pro-Russian rebels, for example, Igor Girkin (aka Strelkov) gave similar estimations of losses of the Ukrainian armed forces as 2.5 thousand killed during the battle within the 'pocket' and 1 thousand killed during the attempt to leave it.

8 An opinion poll carried out between 8 and 18 February 2014 found 33 per cent of Donetsk's residents in favour of unification of Ukraine with Russia compared to 24 per cent in Lugansk (two major pro-Russian regions in Ukraine). The majority of respondents would support Russia and Ukraine as friendly, but independent states. With the start of the armed conflict a significant part of the pro-Ukrainian population left the occupied territories for Ukraine.

9 Putinu nuzhna vsya Ukraina http://inosmi.ru/sngbaltia/20150410/227433743.html (accessed on 08/ 04/15).

10 Commonly referred to as Minsk I.

11 Minsk II.

Further reading

Boyer, Y. and Lindley-French, J. (eds) (2012) *The Oxford Handbook of War*, Oxford University Press.
Molloy, I. (2001) *Rolling Back Revolution: The Emergence of Low Intensity Conflict*, Pluto Press.
Webel, C. and Galtung, J. (eds) (2007) *The Routledge Handbook on Peace and Conflict*, Routledge.

References

All-Ukrainian Census (2001) Available online at http://2001.ukrcensus.gov.ua/ (accessed 08/04/2015).

BBC (2014) Strelkov soobshil, chto eto on nachal voynu na Ukraine, 20 November. Available online at http://www.bbc.co.uk/russian/rolling_news/2014/11/141120_rn_strelkov_war_responsibility (accessed 08/04/2015).

Dugin, A. (2014) Novorossia – eto Novaya Rossia. *Den Svaroga*. Available online at http://www.svarogda y.com/dugin-aleksandr-novorossiya-eto-novaya-rossiya/ (accessed 08/04/2015).

Kotich 'Voennie svodki s Yugo-Zapadnogo Fronta'. Forum-antikvariat.ru. Various posts and various dates. Available online at http://forum-antikvariat.ru/topic/204348-voennye-svodki-s-yugo-zapadnogo-fronta/ (accessed 08/04/2015).

Molloy, I. (2001) *Rolling Back Revolution: The Emergence of Low Intensity Conflict*, Pluto Press.

Murray. W. and Mansoor, P. (eds) (2012) *Hybrid Warfare: Fighting Complex Opponents from the Ancient World to the Present*, Cambridge University Press.

Paniotto, V. (2014) Available online at https://www.facebook.com/volodymyr.paniotto/posts/ 647799925285310?stream_ref=10 (accessed 08/04/2015).

Pavlovsky, G. (2014) Interview, *New Left Review*, 88, July/August. Available online at http://newleftre view.org/II/88/gleb-pavlovsky-putin-s-world-outlook (accessed 08/04/2015).

Pro skasuvannya Konstitucii i deyakih zakoniv AR Krym (1995) Available online at http://zakon4.rada. gov.ua/laws/show/92/95-%D0%B2%D1%80 (accessed 08/04/2015).

Protocol on Results of Consultations of the Trilateral Contact Groups (2014) Available online at http://mfa. gov.ua/en/news-feeds/foreign-offices-news/27596-protocolon-the-results-of-consultations-of-the-trilateral-contact-group-minsk-05092014 (accessed 08/04/2015).

Putin, V. (2007) Vistuplenie Putina na Myunchenskoy Konferencii. Available online at https://www.you tube.com/watch?v=PkyjYKVYlWo (accessed 08/04/2015).

Razumkov Centre (2008a) Should Ukraine join the Russia-Byelorussia Union? Available online at http://www.uceps.org/eng/poll.php?poll_id=785 (accessed 08/04/2015).

Razumkov Centre (2008b) With which cultural tradition do you associate yourself? Available online at http://www.uceps.org/eng/poll.php?poll_id=394 (accessed 08/04/2015).

Razumkov Centre (2011) Public Opinion Polls, Crimea. Available online at http://www.razumkov.org.ua/eng/socpolls.php?cat_id=49 (accessed 08/04/2015).

Report of Parliamentary Investigative Commission on Ilovaysk (2014) Full text available online at http://glavcom.ua/articles/23466.html (accessed 08/04/2015).

Rosbalt (2015) Esli rodni net, mogut I na meste prikopat, 11 February. Available online at http://www.rosbalt.ru/piter/2015/02/11/1366640.html (accessed 08/04/2015).

Schedrovytsky, P. (2000) Russkiy Mir I Transnacionalnoe Russkoe, *Russkiy Zhurnal*. Available online at http://old.russ.ru/politics/meta/20000302_schedr.html (accessed 08/04/2015).

Takoy Razniy Yugo-vostok (2015) Zerkalo nedeli. Available online at http://opros2014.zn.ua/donbass (accessed 08/04/2015).

The Telegraph (2015) Minsk Agreement on Ukraine crisis: full text. Available online at http://www.telegraph.co.uk/news/worldnews/europe/ukraine/11408266/Minsk-agreement-on-Ukraine-crisis-text-in-full.html (accessed 08/04/2015).

Washington Post (2014) Joint Geneva Statement on Ukraine from April 17: the full text. Available online at http://www.washingtonpost.com/world/joint-geneva-statement-on-ukraine-from-april-17-the-full-text/2014/04/17/89bd0ac2-c654-11e3-9f37-7ce307c56815_story.html (accessed 08/04/2015).

Zakon Ukraini (2015) Pro zabezpechennya prav I svobod gromadyan I pravovoy regim na timchasovo okupovaniy teritorii Ukraini. Available online at http://zakon2.rada.gov.ua/laws/show/1207-18 (accessed 08/04/2015).

29

FAILING TO SECEDE

The dynamics of Kosovo's unsuccessful attempt
at secession in 1991

Argyro Kartsonaki

Introduction

This section explores the reasons why Kosovo's first attempt to secede in 1991 failed. This first attempt stands in sharp contrast to the subsequent unilateral secession of 2008 which led to the creation of a still contested, but gradually more and more consolidated state. Nevertheless, while much of the literature has focused on the 2008 declaration of independence and its possible global implications, little has been written on the first attempt for independence in 1991 and the reasons why it failed. In the 1990s both politicians and scholars had been absorbed by the Yugoslav wars and had put Kosovo aside as an issue of minor importance. Although Kosovo's demands were sometimes mentioned in short chapters in lengthy books studying the Yugoslav saga, these analyses focused predominantly on the nature of those demands and on their potentially explosive character, while a considerable amount of literature has also been written on the Kosovo war of 1999. This chapter seeks to fill this gap by focusing on explaining why Kosovo's first attempt to secede failed to create an independent state and examines possible reasons for this failure.

Although it is acknowledged that a seceding entity in addition to international recognition has to create an internally viable state for its secession to be successful, this chapter focuses only on the international dimension of Kosovo's failure. The reason for that is that Kosovo after the 1991 declaration of independence did not have the opportunity to demonstrate internal viability. Admittedly, the parallel Kosovar society showed a significant level of functionality; however, Kosovars were largely able to run their parallel system only because the Serbian apparatus allowed them to do so. The reason why Kosovo failed to establish a viable state is pretty straightforward then; it did not have the chance due to the overwhelming power of Serbia. On the contrary, the question of why Kosovo failed to receive international acceptance at a time when the former Yugoslavia was falling apart deserves closer scrutiny.

In order to address this issue the chapter is divided into two main sections. The first provides historical information on the Kosovo conflict, a long dispute between Albanians and Serbs that goes back to the years of Ottoman rule. Nevertheless, this study focuses mainly on the status of Kosovo and the Albanians in communist Yugoslavia as it seeks to lay the foundations for the better understanding of certain events that followed Kosovo's first declaration of independence. The clarification, for instance, of Kosovo's autonomous status within Serbia, as opposed to the status of the constituent republics of Yugoslavia, adds to the understanding of the opinions of the Badinter Commission that will be analysed later. Thereby, it is also clarified why Kosovo was regarded as an internal Serbian matter, this being one of the predominant reasons why Kosovo's first unsuccessful attempt to secede failed. Finally, this part offers some information regarding the interethnic relations between Albanians and Serbs, the two main ethnic groups in Kosovo. Although not directly connected with the failure of Kosovo's first attempt to secede, this background information places the conflict of Kosovo into a social context, demonstrating the longstanding grievances of both ethnic groups. Thus, this section seeks to shed light on how and why the situation in Kosovo escalated, deepening the understanding of the events that followed in subsequent decades.

The second part of the chapter continues with Kosovo's first declaration of independence and the actions the Kosovar society undertook after its demands were deliberately ignored by the international community. Various reasons are given for the explanation of this lack of attention to the Kosovo issue, including the opinions of the Badinter Commission, the geopolitical position of Yugoslavia in the aftermath of the Cold War and the role of an unprepared Europe as an international mediator. The chapter concludes that the main reason why Kosovo failed to attract international attention is the lack of armed conflict. It demonstrates how the absence of violence affected the decisions and priorities of the international community with the result that Kosovo was to remain a marginalised issue for the first half of the 1990s.

Historical background: an introduction to the Kosovo conflict

The origins of the contemporary conflict in Kosovo can be found in the beginning of the twentieth century and the Balkan wars. In the First Balkan War (1912–1913), Serbs, Montenegrins, Bulgarians and Greeks sought independence from the Ottoman Empire. The Albanians, although they declared independence from Ottoman rule, did not join the Balkan League in the war against the Ottoman Empire (Dragnich and Todorovich 1984). During the Balkan Wars, Serbia occupied Kosovo, a region populated by diverse ethnic groups with the majority of them Albanians and the second largest group Serbs (Ker-Lindsay 2009b).

The Albanians considered themselves as the rightful inhabitants of the area due to the belief that their nation has lived in the area since ancient times (Mertus 1999). On the other hand, for Serbs, Kosovo was a fundamental part of their civilisation and history. Kosovo was the heart of the great Serbian kingdom that flourished in the Byzantine period and it is believed to be the cradle of Serbian Orthodoxy. A number of monasteries dating back to those times are to be found in Kosovo, demonstrating until today the previous presence and glory of Serbs in the region. In addition the historic battle of 1389 against the Ottomans took place in Kosovo at the Field of Blackbirds, and the Serbs believe that they sacrificed their lives in this battle in order to save Europe from Ottoman invasion. The defeat of the Serbian army in this battle signalled the start of the fall of the Serbian Kingdom, eventually leading to its conquest by the Ottomans 70 years later. Thus, for Serbs, Kosovo represents both the connection with their glorious past and at the same time the place where the Serbian suffering began, it is where they lost their state and were subjugated in 500 years of Ottoman occupation. Therefore, the recapturing of Kosovo in the Balkan wars symbolised for Serbs the end of their suffering and the return to independence and freedom.

The Serb-Albanian conflict seems to stem from the firm conviction of both groups that 'the land has been theirs for all time' (Udovički 2000: 317), comparable to the Israeli-Palestinian conflict where 'two ethnic communities with distinct languages and religious traditions lay claim to the same territory with competing historical arguments as evidence' (Ramet 2001: 174).

Although Kosovo was an integral part of Yugoslavia, tensions between the two ethnic groups were deeply ingrained. Admittedly, open conflict in times of peace was rare. However, the two groups have largely lived throughout the twentieth century in a cycle of domination and suppression, where the position of the groups changed according to the shift of power dynamics. Beginning immediately with the inclusion of Kosovo into the Serbian state in 1912, the latter implemented several policies of both assimilation and exclusion against the Albanian population of the region (*inter alia*, Bieber and Daskalovski 2003; Dragnich and Todorovich 1984; Sörensen 2009).This relationship of dominance was reversed during the Second World War when a large part of Kosovo unified with Albania under Italian occupation with the Slavic population systematically expelled or exterminated and subsequently replaced by Albanians (Burg 1983; Ker-Lindsay 2009b).

In communist Yugoslavia, Kosovo was initially an autonomous region (ёбласт) of Serbia, elevated to autonomous province (пёкрајину) in 1963, reaching its highest position in the federation with the 1974 constitutional amendment (Constitution of the Federative People's Republic of Yugoslavia 1946; Constitution of the Socialist Federal Republic of Yugoslavia 1963; Constitution of the Socialist Federal Republic of Yugoslavia 1974). The 1974 Constitution guaranteed enhanced rights for two autonomous provinces: Kosovo and Vojvodina acquired extensive self-government, fully controlling internal matters such as education, judiciary, taxation and police in their respective provinces (ICJ 2009). Their full and equal participation was provided, as well as the right to approve or veto decisions concerning their provinces. Thus, they have often been referred to as virtual republics (*inter alia*, Dannreuther 2001; Mertus 1999), as they were republics 'in all but name' (Peci 2014).

Nevertheless, the Albanians of Yugoslavia had always been considered to be a nationality in the federal state never obtaining the status of nation. In Yugoslavia, the peoples or nations were those ethnic groups who had their nation-state inside the borders of the federation. Hence, for example the Croats and the Slovenians were nations because their country was located within the borders of Yugoslavia. The Albanians on the other hand were a nationality as Albania, their kin-state, was outside the boundaries of Yugoslavia. Nationalities also included Bulgarians in Eastern Serbia, Italians on the Adriatic Coast and Hungarians in Vojvodina (Detrez 2003).

Nationalities were not entitled to their own republics, and thus Kosovo never became an actual constituent republic of Yugoslavia. The reason why nationalities were not allowed to run their own republics was not adequately explained (Ramet 2002). A possible reason could be that nationalities having a nation-state outside the federal boundaries would be regarded to be more inclined to the idea to secede and join their fatherland (Detrez 2003).

The fact, however, that Albanians were not classed as a nation and Kosovo was not a republic also meant that Kosovo did not have the right to secession. Article 1 of the various Yugoslav constitutions stated that Yugoslavia was a federal state of peoples or nations (нарёда) who voluntarily associated and created a federation based on the principles of self-determination 'including the right to secession', 'укључујући правё на ётцепљење' (ФЕДЕРАТИВНЕ НАРОДНЕ РЕПУБЛИКЕ ЈУГОСЛАВИЈЕ 1946; Constitution of the Federative People's Republic of Yugoslavia 1946). Although it is unclear from the definition whether nations or republics had the right to secession, the fact that only nations were entitled to republics leads to the conclusion that only republics had the right to secession. This view was further strengthened by the concluding opinions of the Badinter Commission, arguing that only the constituent republics of Yugoslavia would be considered as its successor states, thus denying Kosovo this right.

Despite the enhanced rights Kosovars enjoyed in the former Yugoslavia after 1966,[1] it is alleged that Kosovo Albanians craved unification with Albania. As a non-Slavic population in a predominantly Slavic country they were regarded as 'second class citizens' in the rest of Yugoslavia (EU Diplomat 2014). They were considered to be more 'primitive', peasants or manual workers meant to do the toughest jobs (Udovički 2000: 319). Albanians themselves 'never felt part of this artificial construction of the state' and believed that 'Kosovo was mistakenly a part of Yugoslavia' (Civil Society Activist 2014).

This sentiment of not belonging in the country was further increased by the low living standards Kosovo suffered. Although the province had been allocated special treatment under the Federal Fund for Crediting Economically Underdeveloped Republics and Provinces between 1965 and 1990, and was receiving generous grants and low-interest loans from the Federal Development Fund, the levels of development and employment remained extremely low in comparison with other regions in Yugoslavia, with Kosovo being the poorest region in the country (IICK 2000).

Subsequently, tensions grew between Albanians and Slavs in general and Serbs in particular. The richer republics of Slovenia and Croatia complained that their revenues and labour supported the population in the underdeveloped South, while other less developed republics such as Bosnia and Macedonia claimed that Kosovo received more than its fair share of federal funds (Judah 2000). Kosovo Serbs in particular accused Kosovo Albanians of indolence maintaining that the younger generations of Albanians seemed to be reluctant to occupy themselves with traditional ways of production and agriculture and preferred studying instead of working (Guzina 2003; Poulton 1993). Kosovo Albanians on the other hand argued that Serbs and Montenegrins although comprising a significantly lower percentage of the population occupied almost one third of the state run enterprises (Mertus 1999).

Tensions increased further when the Serbs started to leave Kosovo and relocate to other regions of Yugoslavia. Albanians asserted that Serbs were leaving because of the severe economic situation in the region. The Serbs, however, talked about an 'Albanisation' of Kosovo (Arhsien and Howells 1981: 427) and claimed that they were leaving because of the constant harassment and discrimination against them (Malcolm 1999).

Eventually the situation escalated, and in 1981 Kosovo experienced one of the most violent demonstrations that ever occurred in the province during the existence of socialist Yugoslavia. The riots were triggered by a seemingly insignificant event in Prishtina University's cafeteria when a student furiously complained about the quality of the food (Binder 1981). Soon the event gained momentum and demonstrations erupted in Prishtina with students demanding better conditions in the University's facilities (Rogel 2003). The demonstrations rapidly grew into riots with protesters demanding the status of a republic for Kosovo, with a minority asking for unification with Albania (Malcolm 1999; Mertus 1999). The demonstrations were suppressed, but resumed some weeks later joined by people of all kinds of professions, mine workers, teachers, civil servants, turning the riots into a mass revolt demanding the status of a republic. The demonstrations were brutally crushed, a state of emergency was declared, and Kosovo's borders were sealed (IICK 2000).

The fierceness of the riots and the exaggerated way Serbia responded shed light onto some important concerns Belgrade had. First, it became apparent that Serbia still thought of

Kosovo as a weak link in the federation, whose demands could potentially cause destabilisation. Second, through this full-scale reaction, it was implied that if any other nationalist elements emerged elsewhere in the country, they would be likewise suppressed (Arhsien and Howells 1981).

The student protests of 1981, only 11 months after Tito's death, were the first sign that his structures had begun to collapse. Tito's ideal for Yugoslavia dictated that all citizens of the federal state were first and foremost Yugoslavs as defined by their citizenship and not their nationality. Thus, any expression of nationalism was rejected in favour of a creation of a common Yugoslav identity by virtue of the fact that all were citizens of Yugoslavia. The demonstration of 1981, however, revealed the long suppressed nationalistic sentiments to such an extent that in hindsight some claim that the disintegration of Yugoslavia started then in Kosovo (*inter alia*, EU Diplomat 2014; Civil Society Activist 2014). The 1981 riots were the first significant event of a turbulent decade that would ultimately end with the abolition of Kosovo's autonomy and the consequent open struggle for independence.

Kosovo declares independence for the first time

In 1989, Kosovo's Assembly voted for the revocation of its autonomous status. This bizarre decision was made under unusual conditions: federal forces had encircled the parliament, where its members under the threat of violence decided in favour of the abolition of the province's autonomy (Leon Malazogu 2014; Malcolm 1999; Perritt 2010). This annulment of Kosovo's autonomy constituted a milestone not only for Kosovo, but for the whole of Yugoslavia. This display of power was one of the first demonstrations of Milošević's intention to strengthen Serbia's position in the federal state (Ramet 1992). With the votes of Kosovo, Vojvodina and Montenegro, Serbia would have a comparative advantage against Croatia, Slovenia, and Bosnia and Herzegovina in the federal institutions. Should Milošević, President of the Republic of Serbia at the time, manage to take over one more of the republics, Serbia would gain firm control over the federal presidency (Malcolm 1999). Slovenia and Croatia regarded these events with suspicion and fear; and these sentiments, combined with economic grievances and rising nationalism, would soon escalate, playing a major role in the outbreak of the Yugoslav wars and the dissolution of Yugoslavia (BBC 1995).[2]

Following the change in Kosovo's status, new onerous laws regulating most aspects of everyday life had been introduced in the province. Albanians had been sacked from state institutions and enterprises and replaced by Serbian personnel (Malcolm 1999), while new property laws had been imposed, hindering Albanians from buying land or houses previously owned by Serbs (Judah 2000). These two measures effected demographic changes either by preventing Serbs from leaving Kosovo or providing incentives to migrate to Kosovo (O'Neill 2002). Furthermore, Albanian-language education was banned; Serbian curricula were introduced in schools, while Prishtina University was turned into an exclusively Serbian institution (Clark 2000; Kostovicova 2005). What is more, Albanian press, television and radio were closed down, as well as most if not all cultural institutions (IICK 2000; Judah 2000). Finally, Albanians were dismissed from the Kosovo security forces and replaced by Serbs, thus turning the Kosovo police into an exclusively Serbian unit. The police now, through harassment, arbitrary arrests, the use of violence and even murder, subdued Albanians in a physical and psychological state of continuous suppression and fear (Cohen 1994; Ramet 1996).

What the abolition of autonomy also meant was that the province was stripped of all its armed forces. Kosovo as an autonomous province had the right to have its own territorial defence forces in a similar way as the republics (Peci 2014). In Kosovo, however, the territorial defence forces were in a process of disarmament, which had been completed when Kosovo's autonomy was abolished. Kosovo, hence, was overwhelmed by Serbian power, not having the military capacity to oppose it (Miljanić 2014; Qehaja 2014).

Against this background, the Kosovar leaders gathered secretly in Kačanik in 1990 and declared the creation of the Republic of Kosovo: not a declaration of independence yet, but of a republic within the still existent Yugoslavia. It was only later in 1991, after the Slovenian and Croatian secessions were proclaimed that Kosovar deputies announced the independence of the Republic of Kosovo (IICK 2000; Judah 2000). In addition, a referendum was held, which clearly showed that the vast majority of the Kosovar population was in favour of independence (Abazi 2008; Guzina 2003; IICK 2000).

This referendum and declaration of independence, however, did not receive the same international acceptance as the declarations of independence of Slovenia and Croatia. The latter were recognised within a year by the majority of the international community and by May 1992 they were accepted into the United Nations, while Kosovo was recognised only by Albania (*inter alia*, Clark 2000; Phillips 1996; Vrieze 1995).

Kosovo's peaceful resistance

With the territorial defence forces being disarmed, armed guerrilla warfare for the pursuit of independence seemed to be out of the question for President Rugova and other Kosovar leaders. Thus, the Kosovars' reaction was to resist Serbian oppression peacefully and to establish a parallel society within Kosovo. Rugova's strategy for Kosovo was a threefold one, as Edita Tahiri, the Foreign Minister of the Democratic League of Kosovo (LDK) at the time said: 'first, we wanted to ensure cultural survival and prevent ethnic cleansing. Second, we wanted to create a parallel system and build an independent democratic state. Third, we wanted to win international support for independence' (Tahiri, cited in Stephan 2006: 72).

In order to ensure cultural survival and prevent ethnic cleansing Rugova knew that any violent revolt had to be prevented (Malcolm 1999). Seeing the events in other parts of Yugoslavia, and especially in Bosnia and Herzegovina, Rugova expected that the Serbs would engage in mass expulsions or extermination of the Albanian population when a pretext was given (Dannreuther 2001). Hence, any action that could provoke Serbian retaliation was to be avoided. Allegedly, 'whenever a violent episode involving Serbian police occurred, members of the Kosovar Youth Parliament and the Council for the Defence of Human Rights would go to the scene to document the incident and explain to fellow Albanians the rationale behind maintaining nonviolent discipline' (Stephan 2006: 73).

Rugova's government was largely successful with the implementation of their second goal and the establishment of a parallel society. Kosovo Albanians rejected every association with Serbian institutions, boycotted Serbian elections (Vrieze 1995) and certainly avoided in every way mandatory military service in the Yugoslav and subsequently Serbian army[3] (Civil Society Activist 2014). In order to fill the gap in services this boycott had produced, the LDK government created parallel structures extending to most aspects of everyday life, including education, health care, transportation, markets and the banking system (IICK 2000; Mertus 2009).

Arguably the greatest success of the parallel state was the education system (Kostovicova 1999). When, in 1990, the Serbian administration banned teaching in Albanian and demanded that schools introduce the Serbian curriculum, most Albanian teachers were removed and replaced by Serbs. Similarly, the University of Prishtina became fully Serbian and tutors were instructed to lecture in the Serbian language (Bellamy 2000). The Albanians rejected and opposed those measures by creating a parallel system of education in which the dismissed teachers delivered classes, even university classes, in private houses (Kosovo Press Personnel 2014).

What is worth mentioning, however, is that the Serbian authorities largely tolerated education in Albanian in primary schools (Mertus 2009). Even then though, Albanian and Serbian students were completely separated from each other. In some cases they used the same building but two different entrances and walls kept Albanian and Serbs students apart, or in some cases ethnic shifts had been established with students using the same rooms but at different times of the day (Kostovicova 1999).

Still secondary and higher education took place almost exclusively in private houses. Again what is interesting is that in fact the Serbian administration allowed this parallel system of education to continue. Serbian troops could have intervened and terminated by force this parallel structure. Everyday harassment certainly took place; however, Serbs did not actually commit to crushing this system. Thus, eventually Albanians and Serbian police got accustomed to co-existence, with the former allowed to continue their parallel society whilst the Serb police overlooked their activities (Pula 2004). Interestingly one interviewee remembers:

> You know...the Serb troops knew where our classrooms were it wasn't that they never intervened, they did intervene and [there] were cases that we had to run from the class, I speak for the University, they didn't touch the high schools, but Universities were scattered all around Prishtina. They knew where we were but they never touched us...
>
> *(Civil Society Activist 2014)*

Another aspect that the parallel society covered was the health care system. The Mother Teresa Society was founded, designed to provide humanitarian assistance and basic health care services for Albanians who were reluctant to visit Serb-dominated hospitals (Clark 2000; IICK 2000). Nonetheless, neither the Mother Teresa Society nor other clinics established at private houses were able to deal with complicated incidents where more sophisticated equipment was required. Thus, inevitably Albanians had to use state hospitals in those cases, and that is largely why Albanian doctors who kept their jobs in Serbian facilities were not rejected by wider society (Judah 2000).

Serbia, on the one hand, had allowed these parallel structures to continue, on the other hand, however, international reports publicised the deteriorating situation in Kosovo mentioning several incidents of violence against Albanians regardless of age or gender, while highlighting the lack of accountability and the impunity of the perpetrators (HRW 1994). Arbitrary raids by Serbian police in the middle of the night with the pretext of searching for weapons were also reported. Those raids, apart from being terrifying, were accompanied by the destruction of property and the excessive use of violence, often in front of the family (Amnesty International 1994).

Nonetheless, the Kosovo Albanians adhered to their non-violent resistance and out of fear and necessity two completely segregated, parallel societies were created (Ramet 1996). During the Yugoslav period, the population reportedly lived in ethnically mixed neighbourhoods, and memories of good neighbourly relations between the two ethnic groups are often mentioned today. However, in the early 1990s the population was divided according to ethnicity. In rural areas ethnically homogenous neighbourhoods were created, while in larger urban areas, where physical separation was more difficult, division took other forms. For instance the same street would not be used by both Albanians and Serbs or there were specific markets, cafés and bars for each ethnic group (Civil Society Activist 2014).

This commitment to non-violence brought the plaudits of the international community accomplishing, up to an extent, the third goal of the LDK government to win international support for independence. Rugova succeeded in placing Kosovo on the international agenda and in becoming recognised as the leader of Kosovo's Albanians. However, the endorsement of a peaceful approach was one thing, support for Kosovo's independence is quite another. Although, 'Rugova was very popular internationally, he wasn't taken as seriously [as other leaders] who were more successful in lobbying for their goals' and thus 'the Albanian cause was not as strongly understood or supported' (EU Diplomat 2014). Indeed, the international community had repeatedly affirmed its position that an independent Kosovo would not be supported (Caplan 1998).

Why Kosovo's demands were ignored

There is a variety of possible reasons that explain Kosovo's rejection by the international community. First, by the time Kosovo declared independence the war in the north of Yugoslavia had begun. This, instead of benefiting Kosovo's cause, proved to be a drawback for its success. The wars in Slovenia and Croatia, with their spill-over into Bosnia and Herzegovina pre-occupied the interest of the international community.[4] A war on the European continent in such proximity to European Community (EC) member states created waves of refugees, producing justified fears about the social and economic consequences for (Western) Europe.

Hence, the primary objective for Western European powers was the stabilisation of the region as soon as possible (Clark 2000). Serbia was a powerful Yugoslav republic, controlling a major part of the Yugoslav army forces. The presence of indigenous Serb populations in Croatia and Bosnia-Herzegovina escalated the already deteriorating situation even further. When the conflict eventually erupted, these were amongst the regions where the war raged most violently. The stabilisation of the northern front, therefore, seemed to be the key for the stabilisation of the region. This resulted in a policy of appeasement towards Serbia and Milošević, trying to get him to the negotiating table with peace as the ultimate goal.

Milošević, being then the most powerful man in Serbia and the main interlocutor in the negotiations, had insisted that Kosovo was an internal matter of Serbia (*inter alia*, Kursani 2014; Senior UN Personnel 2014). As such it was regarded as an issue that was completely under Serbia's authority to settle (EU Diplomat 2014). Thus, should any state have recognised the independence of Kosovo, it would have been considered as a direct interference in Serbian affairs. Such an involvement at a time when the 'right of the state was more important than human rights would be unthinkable' (EU Diplomat 2014). Besides, with Milošević being the principal Serbian representative such an action would possibly disengage him from the peace process, minimising the possibility of a solution to be found (Ker-Lindsay 2009a). Hence, the recognition of an independent Kosovo not only would not add anything to the efforts towards stabilisation, but on the contrary would lead to further destabilisation (Phillips 1996).

What is more, as Kosovo was still peaceful, it was not considered as an important and urgent factor of instability. Thus, its recognition would pose an additional potential risk to regional stability that the international community was not prepared to accept. The lack of violence and the Kosovars' stoic reaction to Serbian mistreatment made their demand for independence irrelevant for the international community whilst a terrible war was occurring in other republics (Qehaja 2014). Therefore, 'the international community was not really prepared to deal with the Kosovo Albanians, at that time they didn't consider it to be of particular importance' (Senior EULEX Personnel 2014). As a result, with the exception of the 'Christmas warning' in 1992 and its reiteration two months later, little effort had been made to restrain Serbia's oppression in Kosovo.[5]

Another sign of deliberate neglect by the international community and simultaneously one of the reasons why Kosovo's first declaration of independence failed, were the concluding opinions of the Badinter Commission. In 1991, the Arbitration Commission of the Conference on Yugoslavia, widely known as the Badinter Commission, was established with the aim of providing answers on major legal questions raised by the Yugoslav wars. The Badinter Commission resolved that Yugoslavia was in a process of dissolution and that its successor states would be its six republics, respecting the 'existing frontiers at the time of independence (uti possidetis juris)' (Conference on Yugoslavia 1992: 1498). When the Commission was asked to provide an opinion regarding whether the Serbs in Croatia and Bosnia-Herzegovina had the right to self-determination as one of the constituent peoples of Yugoslavia, the Commission repeated its adherence to the *uti possidetis* principle and the inviolability of first-order internal boundaries at the time of independence (Conference on Yugoslavia 1992: Opinion No 2). It added also that minorities inside the republics should be recognised and their rights should be respected according to the norms of international law.

The issue of Kosovo was not addressed at all, hence demonstrating its apparent insignificance at that time. Nonetheless, it can be derived from the Commission's opinion that Kosovo by not being a republic had no right to be regarded as one of the successor states of Yugoslavia (Hilpold 2009; Ker-Lindsay 2009a). In addition, by the time the Commission was founded, Milošević had already abolished the autonomous status of Kosovo, thus depriving Kosovo of its previously elevated status as a virtual republic. Hence, Kosovo could not even remotely be considered to be entitled to secession since it was neither a republic, and thus not regarded as a successor state (with a right to secede) by the Badinter Commission, nor were its inhabitants regarded as one of the constituent peoples of Yugoslavia with a right to secession under domestic constitutional law.

Still, Kosovo's previous peculiar status within the federation made Kosovo's claim different from the claim of Serbs in Croatia and Bosnia and Herzegovina. The Serbs in those regions had never had the status Kosovars enjoyed in the federal institutions of Yugoslavia (Caspersen 2008). What is more, however, is that the Badinter Commission requested recognition of the minorities' distinct identity within the Republics and respect of their rights, something that Serbia had already failed to honour. Hence, the Kosovo problem, although not addressed, was far from being that simple, and in light of subsequent events, far from being resolved.

On top of everything else, in 1991 the international system experienced a major transformation. The Cold War that had regulated the global state of affairs for almost half a century was over. The initial feelings of euphoria and relief that the end of the Cold War produced were followed by fears for the future (Evera 1991). Many questions concerning European security emerged; it was unclear whether the long peace in Europe would outlast the Cold War or whether the united Germany would be a threat once again. It was also uncertain whether the former communist states of Eastern Europe would achieve a successful transition to democracy, while the Soviet Union was dissolved into 15 successor states.

One of the most critical concerns the dissolution of the USSR caused for the West was the dispersal of its nuclear arsenal to some of its successor states. Suddenly states such as Belarus,

Ukraine and Kazakhstan that 'were in a complete state of political, economic, and military flux' found themselves possessing significant numbers of nuclear facilities and weaponry (Goodby 1993: 704) which redirected to ensure that nuclear and other weapons of mass destruction, materials and technology would be prevented from proliferating further either to non-state actors or other states (Doder 1993; Goodby 1993; Peci 2014).

Furthermore, with the end of the Cold War, Yugoslavia lost its strategic importance for the USA (Ahrens 2007; Doder 1993; Woodward 2000). The USA therefore turned its attention to settling open issues in the Middle East and Russia and left the European Community to deal with the crises in the Balkans. The EC responded willingly to this, sensing an opportunity to demonstrate its readiness for the imminent Maastricht Treaty and its plan to create a more integrated European Union (EU) (Guicherd 1993). In view of that, Luxembourg's Foreign Minister, Jacques Poos declared that Europe 'had a special responsibility to act in a crisis that threatened European stability' adding also that 'this is the hour of Europe [...] it is not the hour of the Americans' (Riding 1991).

However, despite grandiose statements, the EC proved to be wholly unprepared to deal with as complicated problems as the conflicts in the Balkans. To begin with, the EC lacked the experience to deal with a crisis of such scale as a coherent entity (Ahrens 2007). It was observed that Europe was largely divided, with each country acting according to its own interests as determined by domestic and geostrategic economic and political considerations (Glaurdić 2011). Notably, in essence Germany and Italy sided with the breakaway republics, while France, the United Kingdom, Spain and Greece were more eager to support the unity of Yugoslavia. A number of reasons had been offered to explain the reluctance of the latter to accept the independence of Slovenia and Croatia. Those included concerns of potential internal secessionist movements in the case of the United Kingdom and Spain, fears of potential conflict with an independent republic of Macedonia in the case of Greece, and historic ties with Serbia in the case of France (Steinberg 1992).

Europe's division became more evident with Germany's early recognition of Slovenia and Croatia, which its undermined the EC's uniform approach and weakened its trustworthiness as an objective mediator. The same can be also argued with regards to the decision not to recognise the Former Yugoslav Republic of Macedonia immediately along with Croatia and Slovenia because of Greek objections,[6] although it largely fulfilled the Badinter Commission's criteria. What further undermined the EC's coherence was the pro-Serbian inclination of France, the United Kingdom and Greece, which obstructed the timely and effective enforcement of measures against it. Another reason for the delayed and to some extent futile adoption of measures against Belgrade was that European countries were unwilling to alienate Russia, a traditional ally of Serbia. Finally, states in proximity or states which were significant recipients of refugees such as Italy, Greece and Germany dealt with the crisis accordingly, seeking to minimise the impact of the rapidly escalating conflict on their own countries (Guicherd 1993).

Moreover, the EC/EU lacked the necessary mechanisms to handle such crises. International concepts of preventive deployment of military force or responsibility to protect were not yet developed (Ahrens 2007). Various attempts had been made to stabilise the situation and create conditions for peace, including a series of peace conferences and deployments of unarmed missions to report on the human rights situation on the ground or to observe compliance with agreed measures. Yet the implementation of those actions had often been delayed and by the time they turned into reality, they often were no longer relevant (Guicherd 1993). Thus, all in all, the international reaction was only rarely preventive and most of the time it followed the developments on the ground (Ahrens 2007).

The issue of Kosovo could have been a successful example of preventive action. Some of the negotiators, realising that Kosovo was a part of the crisis and directly connected with the stability of the region, had insisted on Kosovo being included in the peace processes (Non-EU Diplomat 2014). Unfortunately, the EC was unable to deal with yet another conflict at the time. A lack of experience and consistency, combined with personnel and budget fatigue and the desire to settle or contain the problems as soon as possible, made the Kosovo issue one too many other to deal with (Ahrens 2007). Hence, with so many matters requiring urgent attention Kosovo was not a priority for the international community and it was excluded from the procedures until it exploded in the second half of the decade.

Conclusion

This chapter reviewed and assessed Kosovo's unsuccessful attempt to secede in 1991 and investigated the reasons explaining its failure. The section began with a historical analysis starting with the Balkan Wars and continuing to the late 1980s until the abolition of Kosovo's autonomy, illustrating the longstanding conflict between Serbs and Albanians for domination in Kosovo. The chapter proceeded with an evaluation of the approach of peaceful resistance the Kosovars adopted after the unsuccessful declaration of independence and demonstrated how this strategy failed to lead to the achievement of their goal. It is acknowledged that it certainly had some elements of success, for instance it won the endorsements of the international community and established Rugova as the leader of Kosovo Albanians. However, its success did not go so far as to secure international support for an independent Kosovo.

This chapter also revealed the negative role the Yugoslav wars had played for Kosovo's first attempt to secede. The Yugoslav wars had absorbed the time and energy of the European powers, with the chief priority of the latter being the stabilisation of the northern front in these wars as soon as possible. Kosovo, by neither being at war, nor geographically in similar proximity to European powers, was not on their priority list as it was not considered to be a major factor of instability. Considering also that Milošević had insisted that Kosovo was an internal matter for Serbia, recognition of Kosovo would possibly have disengaged Serbian leaders from the peace process. Hence, as Kosovo was both peaceful and, at the time, an internal matter for Serbia, its recognition not only would not have added to the European Community's efforts at stabilisation of the region, but would have further deteriorated the situation by reducing the possibilities for a settlement.

Moreover, in 1991 major changes were taking place in the international system. With the end of the Cold War Yugoslavia lost its strategic importance and the US focus redirected towards its renewed relations with Moscow and the developments in the Middle East. Therefore, Europe had been called upon to deal with the crises in the Balkans. Being internally divided with each member state supporting actions that promoted individual interests, and possessing neither the experience nor adequate conflict management mechanisms, the EC was overwhelmed by the complexity and magnitude of the Balkan wars. With the restoration of peace and stability in the region the main goal of the EC, Kosovo, by not being engaged in armed conflict, was not believed to be a cause of instability and hence not imperative to be addressed.

Finally, the argument that Kosovar demands were ignored because of lack of war is further strengthened in light of subsequent events. When the Kosovo Liberation Army emerged early in 1996, its actions provoked Serbian retaliation, escalating the level of violence, which in turn finally spurred the international community into action. Hence, 'it had to take the lives of people to become a successful case' of secession (Civil Society Activist 2014), demonstrating the critical role that violence played in Kosovo's quest for independence.

Notes

1 In the years 1953–1966 Alexander Ranković had been Minister of Internal Affairs of Yugoslavia and also head of the secret police. During his period in office the ethnic Albanians had been harshly treated, this having as a result the migration of a significant proportion of their population to Turkey. After Ranković was dismissed in 1966, a general change of attitude from the federal state towards Albanians followed. Albanians began gradually to enjoy more rights, the University of Prishtina was founded, as well as other institutes for Albanian language, cultural ties between Albania and Kosovo were permitted and the influx of Albanian books was possible (Daskalovski 2003; Mertus 1999; Nicolić 2003; Petrović and Stefanović 2010).
2 For detailed analyses for the break-up of Yugoslavia, see Glaurdić 2011; Lucarelli 2000; Magaš 1993; Ramet 2005; Rogel 1998; Woodward 1995.
3 Kosovo Albanians avoided joining the army out of fear that they would have been killed by Serbian soldiers before even going to war (Interview 18, Civil Society Activist). However, there is also the argument that this was a deliberate action against Serbia, strengthened by reports of Albanians defecting from the Serbian army to join the Croatian forces. See Judah 2000.
4 For the Yugoslav wars, see Denitch 1994; Misha 1996; Pavković 2000; Silber and Little 1995; Stokes et al. 1996.
5 George Bush warned Slobodan Milošević on 25 December 1992 that 'in the event of conflict in Kosovo caused by Serbian action, the United States will be prepared to employ military force against the Serbians in Kosovo and in Serbia proper'. In February 1993 Secretary of State of the newly elected Clinton administration Warren Christopher reaffirmed the US commitment by stating 'we remain prepared to respond against the Serbians in the event of a conflict in Kosovo caused by Serbian action' (*The New York Times* Archives 1999).
6 Greece refused to recognise the FYR Macedonia under its constitutional name – Republic of Macedonia – initiating a still ongoing name dispute. Greece considers the use of the term Macedonia without any geographical or other qualifier as usurpation of Greek history and historical symbols mostly referring to the Vergina Sun and Alexander the Great. In addition Macedonia as geographical region of the Balkans is divided among four states – Greece, Bulgaria, FYR Macedonia and Albania – and thus the use of the name Macedonia exclusively by one of those states is considered to entail expansionist claims over the other three countries. Finally, the dispute is exacerbated by the fact that approximately 2.5 million ethnic Greeks living in the Greek part of Macedonia identify themselves as Macedonians. Hence the use of the name Macedonia and the ethnic attribute Macedonians without any other qualifier, e.g. Slav Macedonians, is regarded by the Greek Macedonians as rejection of their cultural identity.

Further reading

Bieber, F. and Dasalkowski, Z. (eds) 2003. *Understanding the War in Kosovo*. London: Frank Cass.
Buckley, M. and Cummings, S. (eds) 2002. *Kosovo: Perceptions of War and its Aftermath*. New York: Continuum.
Judah, T. 2000. *Kosovo: War and Revenge*. New Haven and London: Yale University Press.
Malcolm, N. 1999. *A Short History of Kosovo*. New York: Harper Perennial.
Ramet, S.P. 2005. *Thinking about Yugoslavia: Scholarly Debates about the Yugoslav Breakup and the Wars in Bosnia and Kosovo*. New York: Cambridge University Press.
Udovicki, J. and Ridgeway, J. (eds) 2000. *Burn this House, the Making and Unmaking of Yugoslavia*. Durham and London: Duke University Press.

References

Abazi, E. 2008. Kosovo Independence: An Albanian Perspective. *SETA Policy Brief*, 11.
Ahrens, G.-H. 2007. *Diplomacy on the Edge*. Washington DC: Woodrow Wilson Center Press.

Amnesty International. 1994. *Yugoslavia: Police Violence Against Ethnic Albanians in Kosovo Province* [Online]. Amnesty International. Available: https://www.amnesty.org/en/documents/document/?indexNumber= EUR70%2F006%2F1994&language=en.

Arhsien, P.F.R. and Howells, R.A. 1981. Yugoslavia, Albania and the Kosovo Riots. *The World Today*, 37: 419–427.

BBC. 1995. *The Death of Yugoslavia: Enter Nationalism*. BBC Series, six parts.

Bellamy, A.J. 2000. Human Wrongs in Kosovo: 1974–1999. *The International Journal of Human Rights*, 4: 105–126.

Bieber, F. and Daskalovski, Z. (eds) 2003. *Understanding the War in Kosovo*. London: Frank Cass Publishers.

Binder, D. 1981. One Storm Has Passed but Others Are Gathering in Yugoslavia. *New York Times*.

Burg, L.S. 1983. *Conflict and Cohesion in Former Yugoslavia*. Princeton: Princeton University Press.

Caplan, R. 1998. International Diplomacy and the Crisis in Kosovo. *International Affairs*, 74: 745–761.

Caspersen, N. 2008. From Kosovo to Karabakh: International Responses to de Facto States. *Suedosteuropa*, 56(1): 58–83.

Clark, H. 2000. *Civil Resistance in Kosovo*. London: Pluto Press.

Cohen, P.J. 1994. Ending the War and Securing Peace in Former Yugoslavia. *Pace International Law Review*, 6: 19–40.

Conference on Yugoslavia. 1992. Conference on Yugoslavia. *Arbitration Committee International Legal Materials*, 31: 1494–1526.

Constitution of the Federative People's Republic of Yugoslavia. 1946. Belgrade: Official Gazette of the Federative People's Republic of Yugoslavia.

Constitution of the Socialist Federal Republic of Yugoslavia. 1963. Belgrade: Secretariat of Information of the Federal Executive Council.

Constitution of the Socialist Federal Republic of Yugoslavia. 1974. Kosovo's Status in Yugoslavia Before 1999. In: Krieger, H. (ed.) *The Kosovo Conflict and International Law: An Analytical Documentation 1974–1999*. Cambridge: Cambridge University Press.

Dannreuther, R. 2001. War in Kosovo: History, Development and Aftermath. In: Buckley, M. and Cummings, S. (eds) *Kosovo: Perceptions of War and its Aftermath*. New York: Continuum.

Daskalovski, Ž. 2003. Claims to Kosovo: Nationalism and Self-Determination. In: Bieber, F. and Daskalovski, Ž. (eds) *Understanding the War in Kosovo*. London: Frank Cass.

Denitch, B. 1994. *Ethnic Nationalism: The Tragic Death of Yugoslavia*. Minneapolis and London: University of Minnesota Press.

Detrez, R. 2003. The Right to Self-Determination and Secession in Yugoslavia: A Hornets' Nest of Inconsistencies. In: Coppieters, B. and Sakwa, R. (eds) *Contextualizing Secession*. New York: Oxford University Press.

Doder, D. 1993. Yugoslavia: New War, Old Hatreds. *Foreign Policy*, 91: 3–23.

Dragnich, A.N. and Todorovich, S. 1984. *The Saga of Kosovo*. New York: Columbia University Press.

Evera, S.V. 1991. Primed for Peace: Europe after the Cold War. *International Security*, 15: 7–57.

Glaurdić, J. 2011. *The Hour of Europe: Western Powers and the Break-up of Yugoslavia*. New Haven and London: Yale University Press.

Goodby, J.E. 1993. Averting Nuclear Chaos: The Tasks Before Us. *Department of State Dispatch*, 4: 704–707.

Guicherd, C. 1993. The Hour of Europe: Lessons from the Yugoslav Conflict. *The Fletcher Forum, World Affairs*, 17: 159–181.

Guzina, D. 2003. Kosovo or Kosova – Could it Be Both? The Case of Interlocking Serbian and Albanian Nationalisms. In: Bieber, F. and Daskalovski, Ž. (eds) *Understanding the War in Kosovo*. London: Frank Cass.

Hilpold, P. 2009. The Kosovo Case and International Law: Looking for Applicable Theories. *Chinese Journal of International Law*, 8: 47–61.

HRW. 1994. Human Rights Abuses of Non-Serbs in Kosovo, Sandžak and Vojvodina. *Human Rights Watch*, 6.

ICJ. 2009. Written Statement of the United States of America, Accordance with International Law of the Unilateral Declaration of Independence by the Provisional Institutions of Self-Government of Kosovo (Request for an Advisory Opinion). Washington DC and The Hague: United States Department of State.

IICK (Independent International Commission on Kosovo). 2000. *Kosovo Report*. Oxford: Oxford University Press.

Judah, T. 2000. *Kosovo: War and Revenge*. New Haven and London: Yale University Press.

Ker-Lindsay, J. 2009a. From Autonomy to Independence: the Evolution of International Thinking on Kosovo, 1998–2005. *Journal of Balkan and Near Eastern Studies*, 11: 141–156.

Ker-Lindsay, J. 2009b. *Kosovo: The Path to Contested Statehood in the Balkans*. London: I.B. Tauris.

Kostovicova, D. 1999. Albanian Schooling in Kosovo 1992–1998: 'Liberty Imprisoned'. In: Drezov, K., Gokay, B. and Kostovicova, D. (eds) *Kosovo: Myths, Conflict and War*. Keele: Keele European Research Centre.

Kostovicova, D. 2005. *Kosovo: The Politics of Identity and Space*. Oxon: Routledge.

Lucarelli, S. 2000. *Europe and the Breakup of Yugoslavia: A Political Failure in Search of a Scholarly Explanation*. The Hague: Kluwer Law International.

Magaš, B. 1993. *The Destruction of Yugoslavia: Tracking the Break-up 1980–92*. London: Verso.

Malcolm, N. 1999. *A Short History of Kosovo*. New York: Harper Perennial.

Mertus, J.A. 1999. *Kosovo: How Myths and Truths Started a War*. London: University of California Press.

Mertus, J.A. 2009. Operation Allied Force: Handmaiden of Independent Kosovo. *International Affairs*, 85(3): 461–476.

Misha, G. 1996. *The Fall of Yugoslavia: The Third Balkan War*. New York: Penguin Books.

Nicolić, L. 2003. Ethnic Prejudices and Discrimination. In: Bieber, F. and Daskalovski, Ž. (eds) *Understanding the War in Kosovo*. London: Frank Cass.

O'Neill, W.G. 2002. *Kosovo, an Unfinished Peace*. Boulder and London: Lynne Rienner Publishers.

Pavković, A. 2000. *The Fragmentation of Yugoslavia: Nationalism and War in the Balkans*. Basingstoke: Macmillan.

Perritt, H.H. 2010. *The Road to Independence for Kosovo: A Chronicle of the Ahtisaari Plan*. New York: Cambridge University Press.

Petrović, A. and Stefanović, Đ. 2010. Kosovo, 1944–1981: The Rise and the Fall of a Communist 'Nested Homeland'. *Europe-Asia Studies*, 62: 1073–1106.

Phillips, D.L. 1996. Comprehensive Peace in the Balkans: The Kosovo Question. *Human Rights Quarterly*, 18: 821–832.

Poulton, H. 1993. *The Balkans: Minorities and States in Conflicts*. London: Minority Rights Publications.

Pula, B. 2004. The Emergence of the Kosovo 'Parallel State,' 1988–1992. *Nationalities Papers: The Journal of Nationalism and Ethnicity*, 32: 797–826.

Ramet, S. 1992. *Nationalism and Federalism in Yugoslavia, 1962–1991*. Bloomington and Indianapolis: Indiana University Press.

Ramet, S. 1996. The Albanians of Kosovo: The Potential for Destabilization. *The Brown Journal of World Affairs*, 3: 353–372.

Ramet, S. 2001. The Kingdom of God or the Kingdom of Ends: Kosovo in Serbian Perception. In: Buckley, M. and Cummings, S. (eds) *Kosovo: Perceptions of War and its Aftermath*. New York: Continuum.

Ramet, S.P. 2002. *Balkan Babel*. Boulder: Westview Press.

Ramet, S.P. 2005. *Thinking about Yugoslavia: Scholarly Debates about the Yugoslav Breakup and the Wars in Bosnia and Kosovo*. New York: Cambridge University Press.

Riding, A. 1991. Conflict in Yugoslavia; Europeans Send High-Level Team [Online]. The *New York Times* Archive. Available: http://www.nytimes.com/1991/06/29/world/conflict-in-yugoslavia-europeans-send-high-level-team.html.

Rogel, C. 1998. *The Breakup of Yugoslavia and the War in Bosnia*. Westport: Greenwood Press.

Rogel, C. 2003. Kosovo: Where It All Began. *International Journal of Politics, Culture and Society*, 17: 167–182.

Silber, L. and Little, A. 1995. *The Death of Yugoslavia*. Harmondsworth: Penguin.

Sörensen, J.S. 2009. *State Collapse and Reconstruction in the Periphery*. New York: Berghahn Books.

Steinberg, J. 1992. *The Role of European Institutions in Security after the Cold War*. Santa Monica: RAND.

Stephan, M.J. 2006. Fighting for Statehood: The Role of Civilian-Based Resistance in the East Timorese, Palestinian, and Kosovo Albanian Self-Determination Movements. *The Fletcher Forum of World Affairs*, 30: 57–80.

Stokes, G., Lampe, J., Rusinow, D. and Mostov, J. 1996. Instant History: Understanding the Wars of Yugoslav Succession. *Slavic Review*, 136–160.

The *New York Times* Archives. 1999. Crisis in the Balkans; Statements of United States' Policy on Kosovo [Online]. *The New York Times*. Available: http://www.nytimes.com/1999/04/18/world/crisis-in-the-balkans-statements-of-united-states-policy-on-kosovo.html.

Udovički, J. 2000. Kosovo. In: Udovički, J. and Ridgeway, J. (eds) *Burn this House, the Making and Unmaking of Yugoslavia*. Durham and London: Duke University Press.

Vrieze, F.D. 1995. Kosovo: Stable and Explosive. *Helsinki Monitor*, 2.

Woodward, S.L. 1995. *Balkan Tragedy: Chaos and Dissolution after the Cold War*. Washington DC: Brookings Institution Press.

Woodward, S.L. 2000. International Aspects of the Wars. In: Udovički, J. and Ridgeway, J. (eds) *Burn this House, the Making and Unmaking of Yugoslavia*. Durham and London: Duke University Press.

ФЕДЕРАТИВНЕ НАРОДНЕ РЕПУБЛИКЕ ЈУГОСЛАВИЈЕ. 1946. Belgrade.

Interviews

Civil Society Activist. 2014. Interview, 12 June 2014

Civil Society Activist. 2014. Interview, 18 June 2014

EU Diplomat. 2014. Interview, 7 June 2014

EU Diplomat. 2014. Interview, 12 June 2014

EU Diplomat. 2014. Interview, 16 June 2014

EU Diplomat. 2014. Interview, 17 June 2014

Kosovo Press Personnel. 2014. Interview, 7 June 2014

Kursani, Shpend. 2014. Interview, 17 June 2014

Malazogu, Leon. 2014. Interview, 16 June 2014

Miljanić, Radovan. 2014. Ambassador of Montenegro to Kosovo. Interview, 5 June 2014

Non-EU Diplomat. 2014. Interview, 23 June 2014

Peci, Lulzim. 2014. Ambassador of the Republic of Kosovo to Sweden. Interview, 20 June 2014

Qehaja, Florian. 2014. Interview, 6 June 2014

Senior UN Personnel. 2014. Interview, 9 June 2014

Senior EULEX Personnel. 2014. Interview, 18 June 2014

INDEX

Note: page numbers in *italics* represent tables; page numbers followed by 'n' refer to notes

Dominican Republic 195
donor aid 165, 170, 199, 342
Dorn, W. 170
Downes, A. 116
Drummond, C.: and Bellamy, A. 172
Dugin, A. 364
Duguit, L. 59
Dujarrie, S. 340
Durham 20
dynasties 16

early warning technologies (EWTs) 176
East African Community (EAC) 339
East Timor 11, 183–5, 192, 201–2
Eastern Europe 111, 112, 276; communism
  collapse 102, 267, 276, 302
ecclesiastical feudatories 16
Economic Community of West African States
  (ECOWAS) 171, 176, 203; Early Response
  Network (ECOWARN) 171, 176–7; Protocol
  on the Mechanism for Conflict Prevention
  (1999) 171
economy 8, 32, 49, 62–3, 202, 208, 237;
  aggressive development policy 337–8;
  conflict prevention measures 174–5; free
  market 210–11; market 107; national 16, 19;
  Soviet Union 32
education 62
efficiency cult 33
Egypt 193; and Israel 193–5
Eichmann, A. 121–2
Eide, A. 303
El Salvador 145, 183, 191–2, 196–9; *Farabundo
  Martì* National Liberation Front (FMLN) 196
Elazar, D. 60
elections 104–5, 169–71, 174, 195, 201–2, 301;
  alternative vote (AV) 209, 282, 285; bargaining
  280–1; Borda count 282; cross-ethnic voting
  system 199, 278–86; distribution requirement
  281; incentives 280; parliamentary 281; PR
  system 244, 260, 275, 279–81, 286, 293–4,
  303; presidential 281–4; single transferable vote
  (STV) 282, 291, 294; vote-transfer system
  281–2
Eléments d'idéologie (Destutt de Tracy) 26
elites 8, 33, 130, 134; Sunni Arab 301; West
  Pakistan 148
empires 16
England 17, 71, 129; civic dichotomy 48–50
Engström-Baron, J. 6, 102–9
enoughism 37, 39n
equality: diversity reconciliation and unity
  229–30
Erdoğan, R.T. 323
Erdut Agreement (1995) 238
Eritrea 335
Ermolov, Gen A.P. 133

Escribà-Folch, A. 174
essentialism 114, 256
Estemirova, N. 34
Estonia 3, 61, 246–7, 261–2, 268–71, 282,
  304–5; Centre Party 199; Cultural Autonomy
  Law (1925) 246, 270–3; and German
  nationality 270–2; inter-war arrangements and
  corporate autonomy 246–8; National Front
  305; and Russia relationship 4; Russian
  population 270
ETA 258, 263
étatisme practice 29
Ethiopia 80, 156, 159, 253n, 335; Sudan model 162
ethnic cleansing 7, 111–17, 124, 139, 235–7;
  causes and consequences 110–17; definitions
  111–12; drivers 114–16; events listing 110–11;
  genocide 111–17; logic and tactics 113–14;
  policy implications 111–12; population
  transfers/exchanges 111–17
ethnic conflict 1–12; causes and consequences
  5–6, 296; definition 4, 91–3; history and
  ancient hatreds 91–3, 119; overview 93–4
ethnicity 6, 22–3; categorisation 80–4; and
  colour-blindness 50; as conflict generator 6,
  91–100; as cultural features 79; as group
  solidarity and political source 72–3; and
  nationalism 44–52; as non-violent conflict
  generator 94–6; and race 78–85; and religion
  67–74, 99; self-conceptions 73
ethno-politics 229–38; conflict and conflict
  settlement 235–7; and human rights 229–38;
  legal equality and standard setting 232–4;
  mobilisation and prevention 234–5, 238; and
  new democracies 305–7; reconstruction and
  reconciliation 237–8; and self-determination of
  peoples definition 230–2; unity, equality and
  diversity reconciliation 229–30
ethno-religious conflicts 67–74, 92–6; concepts
  69–72
ethno-symbolism 35, 46
eugenics 130
Eurasian Customs Union 359
Eurocentrics 50
European Charter for Regional and Minority
  Languages 233
European Community 378
European Convention on Human Rights
  (ECHR) 233, 236
European Council 173; Gothenburg (2001) 173;
  Treaty 234
European Jewry 7
European Nationalities Congress (ENC) 268–72
European Union (EU) 49, 56, 104, 198, 202–3,
  234, 252, 378; and conflict prevention 169–70,
  173–4, 177; and divisions 378; and Russia
  relations 174; and territorial pluralism 240, 244
Eurosceptics 44

political-institutional dimensions 8, 19
politics 20, 36; exclusionary 45, 48; and ideology relationship 26; multi-ethnic 280; and rights 104–5, *see also* ethno-politics
Politkovskaia, A. 34
Popov, G. 247
Popper, K. 141
population transfers/exchanges 110–17, 124, 133, 149; and death marches 124, 133; and expulsions 110–11, 114, 139–42, 149; German 112, 124; Greco-Turkish/Greco-Bulgarian 112, 124; Hungarian 112; Palestinians 124; and partition 139, 142, 148; and resettlement 147
Poroshenko, P. 363
Portugal 37, 123
Potsdam Agreement (1945) 124
poverty 192, 335–7
Power Sharing in South Africa (Lijphart) 290
power-sharing arrangements 60–1, 183, 209, 251, 301; complementarity 293–7; complex 295–7; consociational democracy 259–60, 286, 289–97
preference-swapping 282
presidential elections 281–4
Pretoria Protocol on Outstanding Issues (2003) 335
Pretoria Protocol on Political, Defence and Security Power Sharing (2003) 335
Prevention and Punishment of the Crime of Genocide (UN, 1948) 111
primordialism 18–22, 80, 92–3, 230, 235, 256
principalities 16
Prishtina University 372–3, 375
proceduralists 141
Production Sharing Contracts (PSCs) 319
propaganda 3, 34
proportional representation (PR) 244, 260, 275, 279–80, 286, 293–4, 303; and proportionality 186, 261
proselytism 68
Protazanov, S. 34
protectionism 149
Protestantism: Anglophone 69–73; Bohemian 71; majority/minority Catholic 71; political dominance 96
Protocol on the Mechanism for Conflict Prevention (ECOWAS, 1999) 171
Prunier, G. 127
Prussia 22
psycho-culturalism 6, 91
public law corporation 62
Puerto Rico 245
Putin, V. 3, 35, 95, 247, 250, 350–2, 356–7, 359–60, 364

Québécois 55–7, 60–1, 151, 248, 263–4
Quellette, A. 168
Qu'est-ce qu'une nation? (Renan) 48

Question of Nationalities and Social Democracy (Bauer) 61
Quinn, D. 3
Quiroga, A.: and Muro, D. 50

race 78–85; categorisation 80–4; as constructs 83–5; definitions and term usage 78–80; and ethnicity 78–85; geographical 80; historical context 82–3; as physical features 79; relations 84; spatial contexts 81–2; White supremacy 82–3
racism 6, 119, 130–2; institutional 95; new 80
Radcliffe Award 142; Commissions (1947) 145–8
radical leaders 119
Radio Prague 51
Radtke, F. 304
Ramet, S. 371
Ranger, T.: and Hobsbawm, E. 92–3
rape 113, 127, 132, 147, 235
rationalism 19
recognition 103
reconciliation 236, 237–8; diversity 229–30
reconstruction 8, 102, 202; and constructionist theory 210–12; economic 237; in ethnically-divided societies 206–12; federal structure introduction 209–11; and institutionalism 209; and liberal internationalism 210–12; neo-realist tradition 208; political 207; post-conflict 206–12; problem-solving approach 212; psychosocial 207–8; and reconciliation 237–8; and security dilemma 209; security-related 207; socioeconomic 208; standard operating procedure 206–8, 212
reductionism 33
referendums 56, 241
refugees 56, 82, 199, 319
Regional Organisations (ROs) 171; Asian 172
regionalism 281
rehabilitation 199, 236
Reilly, B. 9, 209, 278–88
reincorporation 161
reintegration 238
religion 2, 6, 27, 55; Christianity 27, 358; and ethnicity 67–74, 99; Greek Orthodox Church 246; as group solidarity and political resource 72–3, *see also* Catholicism; ethno-religious conflicts; Islam; Protestantism
Renan, E. 36, 48
Renner, K. 61–2, 246, 267–71, 274–6
representativeness 238
Repressive State Apparatus 30
Republic of Ireland: Constitution 82
Republik Srpska (RP) 113, 141, 251
research agendas 2, 70–1
resettlement 147
resolution 5–10
resolutions 5–10
resource exploitation 3

Sierra Leone 3, 11, 125, 171, 201, 208
Sikhs 69, 146, 162; Punjabi 143, 146, 242
Sikorski, R. 350
Sinai Peninsula 193
Singapore 172, 282
single transferable vote (STV) 282, 291, 294
Siniver, A. 8, 181–90
Sinn Féin 145, 293
Sinta people 130
Sisk, T. 251
slavery 48, 72
Sleeping Beauty thesis 18
Slovakia 49, 98, 236, 245, 307; Democratic
  Movement (MDS) 306; Slovak National Party
  307; Workers Association 306
Slovenia 99, 282, 371, 376
Smith, A.D. 16–18, 25–6, 31, 35, 45–6, 49,
  68–9, 72, 93
Smith, D.J. 9, 267–77
Smith, G. 257
Snyder, J. 102
Sobotka, E. 8, 191–205
social justice 38
social networks 100
social psychological approaches 98
Social-Democrat Party of Austria-Hungary
  61–2
socialism 6, 26, 34, 37, 69
Socialist-Communist 34
soft jurisprudence 233
solidarity 2, 67–9, 72–3; micro- 29
Solomon 145–6
Somalia 3, 11, 134, 159, 185, 191–3, 199–201,
  335; coup (1969) 160; irredenta against
  Ethiopia 156; US mission 186–7
Sontag, S. 27
Soresen, G. 105
Soto, A. de 196
South Africa 93, 183, 194, 261, 335; apartheid
  93–5, 261, 301; Office of the Status of
  Women 226
South Asian Association for Regional
  Cooperation (SAARC) 171–2
South Ossetia 3, 362
South Sudan 55–6, 292, 331, 341; and
  Comprehensive Peace Agreement (2005)
  340; Sudan People's Liberation Movement
  (SPLM/A) 340
South Tyrol 245, 260; Autonomy Statute (1948)
  292; People's Party (SVP) 305
Southeast Asia 3, 6, 110, 132, 171
sovereignty 16, 20, 33, 56–8, 229, 241–3,
  303; national 23, 168, 268, 271; territorial
  268–9
Soviet Union 6, 32, 33–4, 121, 251, 300–2;
  collapse 56, 92, 247, 264, 267, 273, 377; and
  kulak spiders 121, 130; New Economic Policy

(NEP) 32; as sham pluralist federation 250;
  strategic constraints removal 185; transfer of
  Poles 111, *see also* Russia
Spain 33, 61, 110, 240, 251, 257, 263, 305;
  Catalonia 50, 60, 164, 305
Special Adviser on the Prevention of
  Genocide 170
Spencer, P.: and Wollman, H. 49
Squire, V. 49
Sri Lanka 3–4, 69, 97–9, 151, 171–2, 249; and
  cross-voting 282–5; Federal party 156; and
  India 158–9, 162; military victory (2009) 3;
  Sinhala Only language policy 94; Tamils and
  separatist conflict 94, 98, 99, 158–62, 164n
Staat und Nation (Renner) 268
stability 20–2, 301, 343; political 20
Stalin, J. 30, 33, 116, 121; Great Terror 130; Year
  of the Great Turn 130
Stalinism 27, 149; extermination of kulaks 121, 133
State Language Law of Slovakia (1995) 20
State and Nation (Renner) 61
state-building 20, 31–3, 54, 71, 134
state-wide power-sharing 259–60
stateless nations 15, 54–64; minorities accommodations 63–4; and nation-states 54–6;
  recognition and autonomy 57–63
Stefanovic, D. 307
Steger, M.B. 38
Steinmeier, F.-W. 350
Stewart, F. 69
Stoel, M. van der 15, 230, 276
Strauss, S. 115–16
street gangs 94
Strelkov, I. (Col Girkin) 353–4, 357, 362–5
study conceptualisation 4–10
Sudan 55, 69, 94, 99, 145, 158, 197, 240, 330–1,
  335; Comprehensive Peace Agreement (2005)
  164n, 292; Darfur region 127, 134, 185, 331;
  and Ethiopian aid 159, 162; and Janjaweed
  militia 127; Liberal party 156
Sudetenland 22, 112
Suez crisis (1956) 193
Suhrke, A.: and Adelman, H. 167
Sunni/Shi'a conflict 91, 114
Sunstein, C. 222
Sweden 17, 231
Switzerland 22, 240, 249–51, 289–90
symbolism 71–2; and myth 72, 93, 96; politics
  theory 96–8
Syria 55, 67, 301, 323; Assad regime 324–5;
  Democratic Union Party (PYD) 323–6; Golan
  Heights 193; and Israel 193–5; Kurdish
  moment 323–6; Kurdish National Council
  (KNC) 324; and Kurdish town of Kobane
  316, 322–5; and Kurds 313–17, 319, 321;
  self-governing cantons 325; stalemate and civil
  war 169–70

World Wars: First (1914–18) 32, 61; Second (1939–45) 30, 83, 149, 371
Wusten, H. van der: and Knippenberg, H. 258

xenophobia 45

Yanukovych, V. 3, 349–51, 352, 361–2
Yemen 2, 195
Yudhoyono, S.B. 281
Yugoslavia 51, 69, 99, 119, 143, 193, 264, 271–2; civil wars 119, 126–7, 235–6, 247, 267; Constitution amendment (1974) 371; and ICTY 124–5; identity disappearance 92;

and Kosovo independence/secession 369–80; population expulsions 112; Socialist Federal Republic 231; Srebenica massacre (1995) 126, 131

Zakaria, F. 105
Zambia 330
Zartman, I.: and Touval, S. 187
Zeitgeist 27
zero-sum politics 211, 337, 349
Zimbabwe 335–6
Zimmer, O. 52
Zionists 140, 144

Taylor & Francis eBooks

Helping you to choose the right eBooks for your Library

Add Routledge titles to your library's digital collection today. Taylor and Francis ebooks contains over 50,000 titles in the Humanities, Social Sciences, Behavioural Sciences, Built Environment and Law.

Choose from a range of subject packages or create your own!

Benefits for you

» Free MARC records
» COUNTER-compliant usage statistics
» Flexible purchase and pricing options
» All titles DRM-free.

REQUEST YOUR **FREE** INSTITUTIONAL TRIAL TODAY

Free Trials Available
We offer free trials to qualifying academic, corporate and government customers.

Benefits for your user

» Off-site, anytime access via Athens or referring URL
» Print or copy pages or chapters
» Full content search
» Bookmark, highlight and annotate text
» Access to thousands of pages of quality research at the click of a button.

eCollections – Choose from over 30 subject eCollections, including:

Archaeology	Language Learning
Architecture	Law
Asian Studies	Literature
Business & Management	Media & Communication
Classical Studies	Middle East Studies
Construction	Music
Creative & Media Arts	Philosophy
Criminology & Criminal Justice	Planning
Economics	Politics
Education	Psychology & Mental Health
Energy	Religion
Engineering	Security
English Language & Linguistics	Social Work
Environment & Sustainability	Sociology
Geography	Sport
Health Studies	Theatre & Performance
History	Tourism, Hospitality & Events

For more information, pricing enquiries or to order a free trial, please contact your local sales team: www.tandfebooks.com/page/sales

Routledge
Taylor & Francis Group

The home of
Routledge books

www.tandfebooks.com